Social Issues Primary Sources Collection

Crime and Punishment

Essential Primary Sources

Social
Issues
Primary
Sources
Collection

Crime and Punishment

Essential Primary Sources

K. Lee Lerner and Brenda Wilmoth Lerner, Editors

THOMSON
—✦—
GALE

Detroit • New York • San Francisco • New Haven, Conn. • Waterville, Maine • London • Munich

Crime and Punishment: Essential Primary Sources

K. Lee Lerner and Brenda Wilmoth Lerner, Editors

Project Editors
Dwayne D. Hayes and John McCoy

Editorial
Luann Brennan, Grant Eldridge, Anne Marie Hacht, Joshua Kondek, Andy Malonis, Mark Milne, Rebecca Parks, Mark Springer, Jennifer Stock

Permissions
Susan J. Rudolph, Emma Hull, Andrew Specht

Imaging and Multimedia
Dean Dauphinais, Leitha Etheridge-Sims, Lezlie Light, Michael Logusz, Dan Newell, Christine O'Bryan, Kelly A. Quin, Denay Wilding, Robyn Young

Product Design
Pamela A. Galbreath

Composition and Electronic Capture
Evi Seoud

Manufacturing
Wendy Blurton

Product Manager
Carol Nagel

LIBRARY OF CONGRESS CATALOGING-IN-PUBLICATION DATA

Crime and punishment : essential primary sources / K. Lee and Brenda Wilmoth Lerner, editors.
      p. cm.
   Includes index.
   ISBN 1-4144-0324-0 (hardcover : alk. paper)
   1. Criminal justice, Administration of—History—Sources.   2. Crime—History—Sources.
I. Lerner, K. Lee.   II. Lerner, Brenda Wilmoth.
   HV7419.C743 2006
   364—dc22
                                           2006013092

This title is also available as an e-book.
ISBN 1414412606
Contact your Thomson Gale sales representative for ordering information.

Printed in the United States of America
10 9 8 7 6 5 4 3 2 1

Table of Contents

2   ECONOMIC AND NONVIOLENT CRIMES

3 CRIMES OF VIOLENCE

8   SOCIAL ISSUES AND FUTURE TRENDS

Advisors and Contributors

While compiling this volume, the editors relied upon the expertise and contributions of the following scholars, journalists, and researchers who served as advisors and/or contributors for *Crime and Punishment: Essential Primary Sources*:

Susan Aldridge, Ph.D.
London, United Kingdom

Steven Archambault (Ph.D. Candidate)
University of New Mexico
Albuquerque, New Mexico

James Anthony Charles Corbett
Journalist
London, United Kingdom

Bryan Davies, J.D.
Ontario, Canada

Sandra Galeotti, M.S.
S. Paulo, Brazil

Larry Gilman, Ph.D.
Sharon, Vermont

Amit Gupta, Ph.D.
Ahmedabad, India

Stacey N. Hannem
Journalist
Quebec, Canada

Brian D. Hoyle, Ph.D.
Microbiologist
Nova Scotia, Canada

Alexander Ioffe, Ph.D.
Russian Academy of Sciences
Moscow, Russia

Kenneth T. LaPensee, Ph.D., MPH
Epidemiologist and Medical Policy Specialist
Hampton, New Jersey

S. Layman, M.A.
Abingdon, MD

Adrienne Wilmoth Lerner (J.D. Candidate)
University of Tennessee College of Law
Knoxville, Tennessee

Pamela V. Michaels, M.A.
Forensic Psychologist
Santa Fe, New Mexico

Caryn Neumann, Ph.D.
Ohio State University
Columbus, Ohio

Nephele Tempest
Los Angeles, California

Melanie Barton Zoltán, M.S.
Amherst, Massachusetts

Crime and Punishment: Essential Primary Sources is the product of a global group of multi-lingual scholars, researchers, and writers. The editors are grateful to Ms. Christine Jeryan, Ms. Amy Loerch Strumolo, and Ms. Kate Kretschmann for their dedication and skill in copyediting both text and translations. Their efforts added significant accuracy and readability to this book. The editors also wish to acknowledge and thank Ms. Adrienne Wilmoth Lerner and Ms. Alicia Maria Cafferty for their tenacious research efforts.

We offer special thanks to Ms. Pamela V. Michaels and Mr. Bryan Davies for their special contributions to the chapter overviews and for their application of expert advice and experience regarding matters of forensics, forensic psychology, and law to many of the entries in this book.

The editors gratefully acknowledge and extend thanks to Mr. Peter Gareffa, Ms. Carol Nagel, and Ellen McGeagh at Thomson Gale for their faith in the project and for their sound content advice. Profound thanks go to the Thomson Gale copyright research and imaging teams for their patience, good advice, and skilled research into sometimes vexing copyright issues. The editors offer profound thanks to project managers Mr. Dwayne Hayes and Mr. John McCoy. Their clear thoughts and trusted editorial judgment added significantly to the quality of *Crime and Punishment: Essential Primary Sources.*

Acknowledgements

Copyrighted excerpts in *Crime and Punishment: Essential Primary Sources* were reproduced from the following periodicals:

American Prospect, July 14, 2000. Copyright 2000 The American Prospect, Inc. All rights reserved. Reproduced with permission from *The American Prospect*, 11 Beacon Street, Suite 1120, Boston, MA 02108.—*The Asian Pacific Post*, September 7, 2005. © 2004 *The Asian Pacific Post*. All rights reserved. Reproduced by permission.—*Casa Grande Valley Newspapers*, November 1, 2005. © Casa Grande Valley Newspapers Inc. 2005. Reproduced by permission.—*Computerworld*, June 17, 2005. Copyright 2005 International Data Group. All rights reserved. Reproduced by permission.—The Detroit News, March 9, 2004. Copyright 2004 *The Detroit News*. Reproduced with permission of *The Detroit News*.—*Economist Newspaper*, July 26, 2001. Copyright © 2001 The Economist Newspaper Ltd. All rights reserved. Further reproduction prohibited. www.economist.com—*Free New Mexican*, November 13, 2005. Copyright 2005 Santa Fe New Mexican. All rights reserved. Republished here with the permission of the New Mexican. No further republication or redistribution is permitted without written approval of the New Mexican.

The Globe and Mail, October 20, 2005; November 5, 2005. Copyright © 2005 Globe Interactive, a division of Bell Globemedia Publishing, Inc. Both reprinted with permission from *The Globe and Mail*./October 18, 2005 for "More than Saddam is on trial" by Michael R. Marrus. © Copyright 2005 Bell Globemedia Publishing Inc. Reproduced by permission of the author./June 3, 2005. Copyright © 2005 Globe Interactive, a division of Bell Globemedia Publishing, Inc. Reproduced by permission of the Canadian Press.—*The Guardian*, October 25, 2005. Copyright Guardian Newspapers Limited 2005. Reproduced by permission of Guardian News Service, Ltd.—*Guardian Unlimited*, October 8, 2005; October 19, 2005. Copyright Guardian Newspapers Limited 2005. Both reproduced by permission of Guardian News Service, Ltd./June 20, 2001 for "Special Report: The Bulger Case" by Diane Taylor. Reproduced by permission of the author.—*Houston Chronicle*, August 23, 2001. Copyright 2001 *Houston Chronicle*. *Reproduced by permission.—Insight Magazine*, November 21, 2002. Copyright 2002 News World Communications, Inc. All rights reserved. Reproduced with permission of *Insight*. —*Lethal Injection Machine Manual: State of Missouri*, November 15, 1988. Reproduced by permission of Fred A. Leuchter Associates, Inc.—*Los Angeles Times Magazine*, October 30, 2005 for "McMartin Preschooler: 'I lied'" by Kyle Zirpolo, as told to Debbie Nathan. Reproduced by permission of the authors.—*Markkula Center for Applied Ethics, Santa Clara University*, March 12, 2002, for "Racial Profiling in an Age of Terrorism" by Peter Siggins. Reproduced by permission of the author.—*Modular Electrocution System Manual: State of Tennessee*, November 27, 1989. Reproduced by permission of Fred A. Leuchter Associates, Inc.—*The Nation*, May 17, 1965. Copyright © 1965 by The Nation Magazine/The Nation Company, Inc. Reproduced by permission.

The New Abolitionist, February, 2000. Reproduced by permission of The Campaign To End The Death Penalty.—*New York Daily News*, November 4, 2005. © New York Daily News, L.P. Reprinted with permission.—*New York Times*, February 15, 2004; November 14, 2005. Copyright © 2004, 2005 by The New York Times Company. Both reproduced by permission.—

Psychiatric Times, v. XIX, April, 2002. Copyright 2002 by CMP Media LLC, 600 Community Drive, Manhasset, NY 11030, USA. Reproduced by permission.—*San Francisco Chronicle*, December 23, 2002; October 17, 2005. © 2002, 2005 *San Francisco Chronicle*. Both republished with permission of *San Francisco Chronicle*, conveyed through Copyright Clearance Center, Inc.— *The Village Voice*, March 28, 2003 for "The Mob was the City's Watchdog: During Giuliani Cleanup, a Mafia Associate Watched the Money" by Tom Robbins. Reproduced by permission of the author.—*The Washington Post*, September 13, 2005; October 14, 2005; October 17, 2005; November 2, 2005. Copyright © 2005, *The Washington Post*. All reprinted with permission.—*Washington Times*, April 3, 2004. Copyright © 2004 News World Communications, Inc. Reprinted with permission of *The Associated Press*.

Copyrighted excerpts in *Crime and Punishment: Essential Primary Sources* were reproduced from the following books:

From *Diagnostic and Statistical Manual of Mental Disorders*. Fourth Edition. American Psychiatric Association, 1994. Copyright © 2000 American Psychiatric Association. Reproduced by permission.— From *Sourcebook of Criminal Justice Statistics 2003*. Reproduced by permission.—From *United Nations Office on Drugs and Crime*, 2004. Reproduced by permission.— From *United States Institute of Peace*, January, 1995. Reproduced by permission.—Ainscough, Carolyn, and Kay Toon. From *Breaking Free*. Sheldon Press, 1993. Copyright © Carolyn Ainscough and Kay Toon 1993, 2000. All rights reserved. Reproduced by permission of The Society for Promoting Christian Knowledge. In the United States and Canada by permission of Da Capo Press, a member of Perseus Books LLC.—Dostoevsky, Fyodor M. From *Crime and Punishment*. Translated by Constance Garnett. William Heinemann, 1914. Reproduced by permission of A P Watt Ltd on behalf of The Executors of The Estate of Constance Garnett.—Johnson, Robert. From *Death Work: A Study of the Modern Execution Process*. 1st edition by Johnson, 1990. © 1990. All rights reserved. Reproduced by permission of Wadsworth, a division of Thomson Learning: www.thomsonlearning.com.— Lozoff, Bo. From *We're All Doing Time*. Human Kindness Foundation, 1998. Copyright 1985 by Bo Lozoff. All rights reserved. Reproduced by permission.— Nicholls, Andy. From *Scally*. Milo Books Ltd, 2002. Copyright © Andy Nicholls 2002. All rights reserved. Reproduced by permission.—Samenow, Stanton E. From *Inside the Criminal Mind*. Crown Business, 1984. Copyright © 1984, 2004 by Stanton E. Samenow. Used by permission of Crown Publishers, a division of Random House, Inc.

Photographs and illustrations appearing in *Crime and Punishment: Essential Primary Sources* were reproduced from the following sources:

Acehnese man is flogged, photograph. © Tarmizy Harva/Reuters/Corbis.—Adams, Dwight, FBI Lab Director, right, during a tour of the FBI's new state-of-the-art crime lab in Quantico, VA, April 24, 2003, photograph by Charles Dharapak. AP Images.— al-Rishawi, Sajida, shows how she strapped a device to her body, video image. © JTV/Via ReutersTV/ Reuters/Corbis.—All points bulletin (APB) from the Salt Lake City police announcing that Ted Bundy has escaped from their custody while in Aspen, Colorado. Page 4 from FBI files on Bundy, photograph.—All points bulletin (APB) from the Salt Lake City police announcing that Ted Bundy has escaped from their custody while in Aspen, Colorado. Page 5 from FBI files on Bundy, photograph.—Amber Alert sign displayed over I-80 near Omaha, NE, photograph by Nati Harnik. AP Images.—Amin, Rizgar Mohammed, back to camera, speaks to the defendants at the trial of Saddam Hussein, October 19, 2005, photograph. AP Images.—Andrade, Leandro, photograph. AP Images.—Anti-death penalty demonstrators march through the streets of Terre Haute, Indiana, June 10, 2001, photograph. © Reuters/Corbis.—Anti-war demonstrator throwing tear gas, Berkeley, CA, photograph. © Bettmann/Corbis.—Arnaout, Enaam, photograph by Chicago U. S. Attorney's Office. AP Images.—Assassination attempt on Queen Victoria by Roderick Maclean at Windson Railway Station. From *The Illustrated London News*. © Mary Evans Picture Library/Alamy.—Atkins, Daryl, third left, sits with his defense attorneys, Joseph Migliozzi, Jr., left, Mark Oliver, second left, Richard Burr, right, in a courtroom in Yorktown, Va., Aug. 5, 2005, photograph. AP Images.

Ballot Measure 2 proponents encourage voters to support the measure, November 2, 2004, Anchorage, Alaska, photograph. AP Images.—Bell, Ricky, the warden at Riverbend Maximum Security Institution gives a tour of the prison's execution chamber, Nashville, TN, October 13, 1999, photograph. AP Images.— Billboard warning of the dangers of on-line sexual solicitation and predators, photograph. © Andrew Holbrooke/Corbis.—Blackwell's Island Alms House for Females, photograph. © Bettmann/Corbis.— Blaine, Barbara, displays a picture of herself at the age of 12, April 11, 2005, photograph.—Bodies of Rwandan Tutsi decay after a massacre that killed 200 at Rukara Church, photograph. © Baci/Corbis.—Bogart,

Humphrey, in a scene from the film "The Maltese Falcon," photograph. © Springer/Corbis-Bettmann.—Boy selling magazines door-to-door in the 1950s, photograph. © Bettmann/Corbis.—Brady, Ian, left, and Myra Hindley, mug shots, photograph. © Bettmann/Corbis.—Brando, Marlon, in the film "The Godfather (Part I)" by Mario Puzo, photograph. The Kobal Collection. Reproduced by permission.—British soldier grabs a Catholic protestor from behind, Londonderry, Northern Ireland, January 30, 1972, photograph. THOPSON/AFP/Getty Images.—Brown, Eric, discusses his paintings for an art show, photograph. © Chip East/Reuters/Corbis.—Brown, James A., leaves the federal courthouse in Houston, TX, November 3, 2004, photograph. AP Images.—Buckey, Raymond, with Peggy McMartin, 1990, photograph. AP Images.—Bulger, Jamie, being led away by one of his abductors in Bootle Strand, Liverpool, England, photograph. © Mercury Press/Corbis Sygma.—Burns, Ellen, chants during a protest of the death penalty, Austin, Texas, photograph. AP Images.

Burns, Lucy, in jail, photograph. © Bettmann/Corbis.—Burns, Mitchell, April 11, 2001, photograph by Dave Martin. AP Images.—Buying bread on the Black Market in a Barcelona backstreet, late 1940s, Spain, photograph by Bert Hardy. © Hulton-Deutsch Collection/Corbis.—Canseco, Jose, raises his hand to be sworn in for testimony, photograph. © Jason Reed/Reuters/Corbis.—Capone, Al, photograph. AP Images.—CardSystems Solutions Inc. signage, Tucson, Arizona, photographed Friday, June 17, 2005. AP Images.—Carter, Rubin "Hurricane," photograph. © Bettmann/Corbis.—Cash, Johnny, singing for the inmates at the Cummins Prison Farm, photograph. © Bettmann/Corbis.—Certificate of Freedom No. 44 / 801 from the New South Wales State Records office, Australia, photograph.—Chicago White Sox team, 1919, photograph. National Baseball Library & Archive, Cooperstown, NY.—Child with Bloody Sunday commemorative cloth, photograph. © Christine Spengler/Sygma/Corbis.—Chintana, 16, a former prostitute, at a woman's rescue center in Bangkok, Thailand, Aug. 10, 2001. AP Images.—Client of an abortion doctor is being carried out of a raided apartment in 1944, photograph. © Bettmann/Corbis.—Clinton, Bill, photograph. © Reuters/Corbis.—"Code Civil des Francais," title page. Reunuion des Musees Nationaux/Art Resource, NY.—Compton, Chaplain Shirley, right, standing beside her, LeeAnn Lujan, center, holds a handmade rosary with sewn-in pictures of her four children, her mother, and herself inside a day room living area for inmates, photograph. AP Images.

Credle, Mitch, homicide detective, going over strategy with his Boys and Girls Club team before a game, photograph. © Marc Asnin/Corbis SABA.—Crime fighter board appealing for witnesses about a firearm incident, photograph. © Janine Wiedel Photolibrary/Alamy.—"Cybersitter," internet filter, photograph. © Andrew Holbrooke/Corbis.—Daniels, Mitch, Indiana Governor, right, surrounded by a group of inmates, July 26, 2005, photograph. AP Images.—Darrow, Clarence, at the Scopes Trial, 1925, photograph. © Bettmann/Corbis.—Dead members of the Dalton gang: from left are Bill Powers, Dick Brodwell, Grat Dalton, and Bob Dalton, photograph. © Bettmann/Corbis.—Defendants dock at Nuremberg trials, with military guards. Nuremberg, Germany, photograph. © Corbis.—Demonstration against drug laws, Austin, TX, photograph. © Daemmrich, Bob/Corbis SYGMA.—Demonstration against the execution of the murderer Percy Charles Anderson outside Wandsworth Prison in London, 1935, photograph. © Hulton-Deutsch Collection/Corbis.—Demonstrators march down Broadway to City Hall to protest the use of surveillance cameras in Washington Square Park and called for legalizing marijuana, May 2, 1998, New York City, NY, photograph by Suzanne Plunkett. AP Images.—Dillinger, John, his body on display in a Chicago morgue, photograph. © Bettmann/Corbis.—Dostoevsky, Fyodor, photograph on the exterior of the apartment building in Russia where he wrote many of his works, photograph. © Steve Raymer/Corbis.—Drawing by 10-year-old Jeremy from Texas reveal the link between the sexual act and a satanic ritual, photograph. © Sophie Elbaz/Sygma/Corbis.

E-mail message recovered by forensics lab, 2005, photograph by Kim Kulish. © Kim Kulish/Corbis.—Egyptian activists during a demonstration in Cairo, June 25, 2005, photograph. AP Images.—Eichmann, Adolf, identity card, photograph. © Bettmann/Corbis.—Elderly man passes a ripped poster reading "Vote-Don't let it happen again" and showing images of the 1999 NATO bombing, multi-zero banknotes, and leader of Serbian Radical Party Vojislav Seselj with a machine gun, Belgrade, June 23, 2004, photograph. AP Images.—Electric chair, Somers, Connecticut, photograph. UPI/Corbis-Bettmann.—Esserman, Dean, speaks next to poster illustrating child crime statistics, photograph. AP Images.—Execution chamber, Oregon State Penitentiary, photograph. AP Images.—FBI Agents and technicians from the New York City medical examiner's office equipped with backhoes dig in a deserted industrial lot on the border of Brooklyn and Queens in 2004, photograph. © Richard Cohen/Corbis.—FBI evidence response team exhumes the body of Emmett Till, photograph. © Frank Polich/Reuters/Corbis.—Female convicts at work in Brixton prison, 1860, illustration. From *The Criminal Prisons of London and Scenes of Prison Life* by Henry Mayhew and John Binny. Private Collection/ Bridgeman Art Library/The Stapleton Collection. Reproduced by permission.—Fishing schooner "Clinton" is shown at barge office. Behind the vessel is the rum chaser, "Reliance," New York, NY, November 4, 1930, photograph. © Bettmann/Corbis.—Fletcher, Deputy John, on horseback, 1887, photograph. © Bettmann/Corbis.—Football supporters flee the May 29, 1985 scene of the riots in the Heysel, Belgium football stadium, photograph. Getty Images.

Forensic scientist at George Washington University studies DNA evidence in a laboratory, photograph. © Richard T. Nowitz/Corbis.—Forensics experts unearth mass grave in the eastern village of Kamenica, close to the Bosnian border with Serbia, July 25, 2002, photograph. © Reuters/Corbis.— Frieze from the famous Elgin Marbles on display at the British Museum, London, June 5, photograph. © Reuters/Corbis.—Fugitive who fled from France's Devil's Island penal colony, Cayenne, French Guiana, January, 1938, photograph. AP Images.—Gang members harassing a woman in Los Angeles, photograph. © Creasource/Corbis.—Gang members in New York City fleeing the scene after a fight, 1962, photograph. © Bettmann/Corbis.—Giuliani, Rudolph, and FBI Director William Webster look at chart of "The Commission" of La Cosa Nostra during press conference, photograph. © Bettmann/Corbis.—Golstein, Helen, 20, and Mildred Luonce, 19, held by police, 1924, photograph. © Bettmann/Corbis.—Gonzales, Hector, hugs his mother, Gladys Gonzales, as he leaves the old Criminal Court House, New York, Wednesday, April 24, 2002, photograph. AP Images.—Group of men sing in Australia's Northern Territory, photograph. © Mission Australia/Handout/Reuters/Corbis.—Guard stands near the entrance to the prohibited area around the prison, town of Krasnokamensk, Siberia's Chita region, photograph. AP Images.—Guard talks with a death row prisoner at Ellis Unit, Huntsville, Texas, photograph. © Greg Smith/Corbis.—Hall, Anthony, stands in his room at the Supermax Prison in Boscobel, Wisconsin, photograph. AP Images.—Hallford, Tim, a contractor who installs ignition interlock devices, holds one that will be installed in the car of a DWI offender in Albuquerque, NM, December 23, 2002. AP Images.— Hanafiah, Nur Azizah bitni, age 22, receives a caning, Banda Aceh, Indonesia, January 27, 2006, photograph. © Nani Afrida/epa/Corbis.—Hands gripping the bars of a prison cell, photograph. © Royalty-Free/Corbis.

Handwritten evidence in the case against Bruno Hauptman, 1934, photograph. © Bettmann/Corbis.— Harrington, Terry, center, leaves the Clarinda Correctional Facility with his mother Josephine James, left, and daughter Nicole Brown, right, Clarinda, Iowa, April 17, 2003, photograph. AP Images.—Harris, Clara, cries during her attorney's closing remarks in the sentencing phase of her murder trial, Houston, TX, February 14, 2003, photograph by Pat Sullivan. AP Images.—Harris, Eric, left, and Dylan Klebold, carrying a TEC-9 semi-automatic pistol, Columbine High School, Littleton, Colorado, photograph. AP Images.—Hearst, Patricia, surveillance photo of her carrying a weapon, photograph. AP Images.—Hell's Angels Motorcycle Club member has oil gauge troubles, photograph. © Bettmann/Corbis.—Hoffman, Billy, poses with his campus debit card, July 3, 2003, photograph. AP Images.—Human rights activists sprawl on the main road to the parliament building, January 16, 2004, photograph. © Jamal Saidi/Reuters/ Corbis.—"J'Accuse!" ("I accuse you!"), the front page of *L'Aurore* newspaper, January 13, 1898, photograph. Snark/Art Resource, NY.—Jack the Ripper attacking a woman, illustration. © Bettmann/Corbis.—Jackson, Joseph "Shoeless Joe," photograph. AP Images.— Jackson, Michael, in booking shot, with police information on left, photograph. AP Images.—Jackson, Michael, leaving the Santa Barbara County Courthouse, March 21, 2005, photograph. © Carlo Allegri/Pool/Reuters/Corbis.

Jail inmates dig for bodies at a Gulf Coast beach, 1973, photograph. © Bettmann/Corbis.—Jenin refugee camp poster glorifies Palestinian suicide bomber Shadi Zakaria, photograph by Greg Baker. AP Images.—John Brown's Fort, photograph. © Corbis.—Kennedy, John F., slumps over after being hit by an assassin's bullet, Dallas, Texas, November 22, 1963, photograph. © Bettmann/Corbis.—Killen, Edgar Ray, is wheeled into the Neshoba County courthouse, Philadelphia, MS, June 14, 2005. © Kyle Carter/Reuters/Corbis.—Lafitte, Jean, illustration. © Bettmann/Corbis.—Liberatore, Ben, Connecticut State Trooper First Class, right, and Isam Saleh demonstrate a new Automated Fingerprint Identification System, Middletown, CT, October 15, 2003, photograph by Bob Child. AP Images.—Lindbergh baby kidnapping poster, photograph. © Bettmann/ Corbis.—Lively, Sara, 24, left, and Michelle Coler, 21, test their drinks for date rape drugs, San Jose, CA, September 19, 2002, photograph by John Todd. AP Images.—Loftus, Elizabeth, Dr., a psychology professor, discusses the study of memory and discrepancies found in testimony during a capital murder trial, photograph. © Siner Jeff/Corbis Sygma.—Looters make off with merchandise from several downtown businesses, New Orleans, LA, August 30, 2005, photograph. AP Images.—Male prisoner in solitary confinement, Sinop, Turkey, photograph. © Vehbi Koca/Alamy.—Malvo, Lee, photograph. © Brendan McDermid/Reuters/Corbis.—Man is tied ready for execution by guillotine in a still from a movie by Georges Melies. © Hulton-Deutsch Collection/Corbis.—Man stands in front of a cable company truck, arms crossed. The body of a cat, attached to the truck's bumper with rope, lies on the ground next to him, photograph. AP Images.—McCall, D. A., baptizes convicts on a prison farm near Parchman, August 18, 1946, photograph. © Black Star/Alamy.—Mediterranean pirate ship chasing a merchant ship, lithograph by Ferdinand Victor Perrot. Snark/Art Resource, NY.

Men handling pistols at National Rifle Association convention, Phoenix, AZ, May 1995, photograph. © Mark Peterson/Corbis.—Molina, Florencia, photograph. AP Images.—"Most Feared Internet Crimes" as of February 2001. Table by GGS Information Service, Gale. Reproduced by permission of Thomson Gale.—"Mugging and murder on a New York City street," illustration from Police Gazette, 1891. © Bettmann/Corbis.—Nation, Carry, photograph. The Library of Congress.—Nauman, Suzy, of Arlington, Massachusetts, leads the way as protesters demonstrate outside Cardinal Bernard Law's Sunday Mass at the Cathedral of the Holy Cross, Boston, MA, photograph. © Reuters/Corbis.—Note from Son of Sam killer, David Berkowitz, photograph. © Bettmann/Corbis.—Notorious Bowery and Five Points neighborhoods in Lower Manhattan, 1855, illustration. © Bettmann/Corbis.—Number of executions in the United States from 1930 through 2004, graph. U. S. Department of Justice; Office of Justice Programs; Bureau of Justice Statistics. Reproduced by permission of Thomson Gale.—Officials confiscate pirated DVDs during the raid of a local shop in Xian, in China's Shaanxi Province, May 29, 2005, photograph. AP Images.—Orphans work in the carpentry shop of the Five Points House of Industry, photograph. © Photo Collection Alexander Alland, Sr./Corbis.—Oswald, Lee Harvey, center, at the moment he was shot by Jack Ruby, right, 1963, Dallas, Texas, photograph. Popperfoto/Archive Photos. Reproduced by permission.—Palestine Liberation Organization member, top; bottom, member of International Olympic Committee, right, speaking with masked PLO terrorist, Munich Olympic Village, September 5, 1972, photograph. © Bettmann/Corbis.—Pankhurst, Emmeline, led away by police at Buckingham Palace, 1914, photograph. © Bettmann/Corbis.—Parents of Isaiah Eamon Shoels stand next to their son's grave marker, photograph. © Liss, Steve/Corbis Sygma.—Parker, Bonnie, and Clyde Barrow, photograph. AP Images.

Perugia, Vincenzo, mug shot and fingerprints, 1911, photograph. © Bettmann/Corbis.—Photographs of young Filipino women supposedly working overseas suspected as possible kidnap victims facing pressure to enter the sex industry, photograph. © Karen Kasmauski/Corbis.—Pirate heads hanging over the wall, Honam, China, c. 1900, stereoscopic photograph by Underwood and Underwood. © Corbis.—Police checking for drunk drivers, Sweden, photograph. © George Steinmetz/Corbis.—Police digging where the body of the murdered Lindbergh baby was found, photograph. © Bettmann/Corbis.—Police inspecting equipment in clandestine brewery during the prohibition era, Detroit, Michigan, photograph. National Archives and Records Administration.—Police officer holds a baby brought for treatment near the Superdome, New Orleans, Louisiana, September 1, 2005, photograph. © Rick Wilking/Reuters/Corbis.—Prejean, Sister Helen, played by Susan Sarandon in the 1995 film "Dead Man Walking" serves as a spiritual advisor to condemned murderer Matthew Poncelet, played by Sean Penn. Working Title/Havoc/The Kobal Collection/Todd, Demmie. Reproduced by permission.—Princip, Gavrilo, in police custody, June 28, 1914, photograph. © Bettmann/Corbis.—Prison buildings on Welfare Island, New York City, 1932, photograph. © Bettmann/Corbis.—Prison inmate crying as he talks with psychologist Lee Vallier, 1989, photograph. © Bettmann/Corbis.—Prison inmates marching in line at the Sumter County Florida Correctional Institution, 1989, photograph. © Bettmann/Corbis.—Prison official shows inmate group therapy room, April 27, 2005, photograph. © Adam Tanner/Reuters/Corbis.—"Prison Van Taking Up Prisoners at the House of Detention," ca. 1862, print. © Historical Picture Archive/Corbis.—Prisoner undergoes psychological testing with a primitive lie detector as a guard stands behind him with a pistol, photograph. © Bettmann/Corbis.—Prisoners on death row by race, 1968-2004, graph. U. S. Department of Justice; Office of Justice Programs; Bureau of Justice Statistics. Reproduced by permission of Thomson Gale.—Prisoners on death row, 1953-2004, graph. U. S. Department of Justice; Office of Justice Programs; Bureau of Justice Statistics. Reproduced by permission of Thomson Gale.

Protesters against the death penalty at the Federal Prison at Terre Haute, IN, June 19, 2001, photograph. © Reuters/Corbis.—Raznatovic, Zeljko "Arkan," and two other Serbian paramilitaries walk through the shattered remnants of the Croatian city of Vukovar, November, 1991, photograph. © Antoine Gyori/Corbis Sygma.—Riojas, Adam, right, in the office of Justin Brooks, left, director of the California Innocence Project, San Diego, CA, April 27, 2004, photograph. AP Images.—Roberts, John, U. S. Chief Justice, on the steps of the Supreme Court, October 3, 2005, photograph. © Brooks Kraft/Corbis.—Romanian military staff member stands in a doorway on the Mihail Kogalniceanu airbase, November 9, 2005, photograph. AP Images.—Rosenberg, Ethel and Julius, during their trial for espionage followed by part of an article entitled "Must They Die?" by William A. Reuben.—Rosenberg, Ethel and Julius, leaving New York City Federal court after their arraignment, August 23, 1950, photograph. © Bettmann/Corbis.—Ryan, George, photograph by Stephen J. Carrera. AP Images.—"Safe Area Gorazde," illustrations from the graphic novel. Illustrations © 2006 Joe Sacco. Reproduced by permission.—San Jose police officers, from left, Raul Martinez, Andrew Harsany and Eric Dragoo search through the residence motel room of a paroled sex offender, San Jose, CA, March 13, 2002, photograph. AP Images.—Scott, State Sen. Jack, D-Altadena, during a Capitol news conference in Sacramento, CA, December 10, 2002, photograph. AP Images.—Shanley, Paul, stands in the Middlesex Superior Court, Cambridge, MA, February 15, 2005, photograph. © Charles Krupa/Poll/Reuters/Corbis.—Simpson, O. J., as he tries on one of the leather gloves during his double-murder trial, Los Angeles, CA, June 15, 1995, photograph. AP Images.—SMART tracking system, ankle bracelet and cellular transmitter box, photograph by Jimmy May. AP Images.—Southern chain gang, photo taken between 1900 and 1906. The Library of Congress.—Speed camera positioned on the A3 road, 15 miles southwest of London, January 18, 2004, photograph by Adam Butler. AP Images.

"St. Valentine's Day Massacre," bodies of six men slain, February 14, 1929, photograph. AP Images.—Sweatshop in New York, engraving. © Bettmann/Corbis.—Teenage girl runaway on subway platform, New York City, 1999, photograph. © Robert Essel NYC/Corbis.—"The Bandits Bride," an illustration from the Herald, May 5, 1847. The Library of Congress.—Thomas, Rep. Samuel "Buzz," D-Detroit, center, addresses a news conference as the Rev. Wendell Anthony, NAACP president of the Detroit branch, left, and state Attorney General Jennifer Granholm, right, listen in, Detroit, Michigan, May 31, 2001, photograph. AP Images.—Towner, Carl, 14, by his father's side at a hearing, Cleveland, OH, photograph. © Bettmann/Corbis.—U. S. rape rate showing rate of rapes per 100,000 people from 1960 through 1998, graph. Federal Bureau of Investigations, Uniform Crime Reports. Reproduced by permission of Thomson Gale.—Venables, Jon, and Robert Thomson, courtroom sketch. © Polak, Matthew/Corbis Sygma.—Venables, Jon, February 20, 1993, police handout picture. AP Images.—Williams, W. C., his body hangs from an oak tree, 1938, photograph. © Bettmann/Corbis.—Women in bathing suits being arrested, July 12, 1922, photograph. © Bettmann/Corbis.—Women making counterfeit coins, ca. 1887, illustration from Police Gazette. © Bettmann/Corbis.—Women pray in Sarajevo as trucks pass carrying 610 victims of the Srebrenica massacre, July 9, 2005 photograph by Hidjet Delic. AP Images.—Yates, Andrea, at her murder trial in Houston, TX, February 18, 2002, photograph. © Reuters/Corbis.—Yates, Andrea, photograph. AP Images.

Copyrighted excerpts in Crime and Punishment: Essential Primary Sources were reproduced from the following websites or other sources:

"1,000 Boston Church Abuse Victims," CBS News, July 23, 2003. © MMIII, CBS Broadcasting Inc. All rights reserved. Reproduced by permission.—Cullen, Dave, "Let the Litigation Begin," Salon.com, May 28, 1999. Copyright © 2000 Salon.com. This article first appeared in Salon.com at http://www.salon.com. An online version remains in the Salon archives. Reprinted with permission.—Hayes, Kristen, "Former Merrill Execs Sentenced," washington.post.com, April 22, 2005. © 2005 The Washington Post Company. Reprinted with permission of The Associated Press.—Matthews, Bernie, "How maximum-security jails make the baddest of men even worse," On Line Opinion - Australia's e-journal of social and political debate, November 5, 2003. Reproduced by permission of Australia's National Forum.—Matthews, Bernie, "The John Tonge Centre, DNA evidence and miscarriages of justice - Part 3," On Line Opinion - Australia's e-journal of social and political debate, March 18, 2005. Reproduced by permission of Australia's National Forum.—Moenssens, Andre A., "Is Fingerprint Identification a 'Science?'" Forensic-Evidence.com, April 19, 2005. Reproduced by permission of the author.—Olin, Dirk, "Nuts to Whom? The insanity defense is crazy," Slate.com, November 18, 2003. © 2005 Washingtonpost.Newsweek Interactive Co. LLC. All Rights Reserved. Reproduced by permission of the author.—"Recent Firearms Research, 1/04-Present," Harvard Injury Control Research Center, April 6, 2005. Reproduced by permission.

"Rights of The Child," *United Nation Economic and Social Council: Commission on Human Rights (53rd Session)*, February 7, 1997. Reproduced by permission.—"Saudi Arabia: Execution of Nigerian Men and Women," *Amnesty International*, June 15, 2000. Copyright © 2000 Amnesty International Publications. 1 Easton Street, London WC1X 0DW, United Kingdom. Reproduced by permission. http://www.amnesty.org—"Sex Crimes Cover-Up By Vatican?" *CBS News*, August 6, 2003. © MMIII, CBS Broadcasting Inc. All rights reserved. Reproduced by permission.—"Sexual Assault Statistics," *Men Against Sexual Assault at the University of Rochester,* February 20, 2003. © 2003 Men Against Sexual Assault. Reproduced by permission.—"Special Protections Progress and Disparity," *UNICEF The Progress of Nations 1997.* Copyright © UNICEF. Reproduced by permission.—Stuntz, William J., "The Court and Law Enforcement," *The New Republic Online*, July 25, 2005. Copyright © 2005, The New Republic. Reproduced by permission of *The New Republic.*—Thomson, Iain, "Expert witness questions child porn jailings," *vnunet.com*, October 4, 2005. Reproduced by permission.

About the Set

Essential Primary Source titles are part of a ten-volume set of books in the Social Issues Primary Sources Collection designed to provide primary source documents on leading social issues of the nineteenth, twentieth, and twenty-first centuries. International in scope, each volume is devoted to one topic and contains approximately 150 to 175 documents that will include and discuss speeches, legislation, magazine and newspaper articles, memoirs, letters, interviews, novels, essays, songs, and works of art essential to understanding the complexity of the topic.

Each entry includes standard subheads: key facts about the author; an introduction placing the piece in context; the full or excerpted document; a discussion of the significance of the document and related event; and a listing of further resources (books, periodicals, Web sites, and audio and visual media).

Each volume contains a topic-specific introduction, topic-specific chronology of major events, an index especially prepared to coordinate with the volume topic, and approximately 150 images.

Volumes are intended to be sold individually or as a set.

THE ESSENTIAL PRIMARY SOURCE SERIES

- *Terrorism: Essential Primary Sources*
- *Medicine, Health, and Bioethics: Essential Primary Sources*
- *Environmental Issues: Essential Primary Sources*
- *Crime and Punishment: Essential Primary Sources*
- *Gender Issues and Sexuality: Essential Primary Sources*
- *Human and Civil Rights: Essential Primary Sources*
- *Government, Politics, and Protest: Essential Primary Sources*
- *Social Policy: Essential Primary Sources*
- *Immigration and Multiculturalism: Essential Primary Sources*
- *Family in Society: Essential Primary Sources*

Introduction

Crime, and the issues that relate to it, arouse compelling curiosity and fervent debate. In the human psyche, crimes and their underlying motives often capture equal measures of fascination and revulsion. In the media, criminals are both condemned and granted celebrity. Accordingly, the readings and resources offered in *Crime and Punishment: Essential Primary Sources* are designed to demonstrate the development, diversity, and duality of attitudes and arguments related to crime and punishment.

The selections in *Crime and Punishment: Essential Primary Sources* are intended to stimulate critical thought and debate about issues that generate social discourse and consume social resources. The selections attempt to reflect passionate debate about such issues as the death penalty, where impassioned pleas for mercy often contrast with the condemned's indifferent and brutal acts.

Crime and Punishment: Essential Primary Sources provides primary source documents related to leading social issues of the nineteenth, twentieth, and twenty-first centuries. The selection of primary sources draws from speeches, legislation, magazine and newspaper articles, memoirs, letters, interviews, novels, essays, songs, and works of art related to crime and punishment.

Because criminal intent and culpability can be critical components of debate, *Crime and Punishment: Essential Primary Sources* entries offer important insights into the criminal mind as they explore a range of crimes that range from economic and nonviolent crimes to crimes of violence, crimes against humanity,

war crimes, terrorism, and hate crimes. Moreover, because perceptions and impacts of crime also play key roles in framing social issues, the selection of entries attempts to portray the realities of systems of justice and punishment that change as social values evolve.

The articles presented in *Crime and Punishment: Essential Primary Sources* are designed to be readable and to instruct, challenge, and excite a range of student and reader interests while, at the same time, providing a solid foundation and reference for more advanced students and readers. In pursuit of that goal, *Crime and Punishment: Essential Primary Sources* draws on experts and resources from around the globe. Such pan-global perspective regarding issues related to crime is increasingly important as crime itself becomes increasingly globalized in an age of electronic commerce and connectivity.

While editing *Crime and Punishment: Essential Primary Sources* the editors attempted to focus on important aspects of the social issues surrounding crime, while minimizing descriptions of often horrific criminal acts and inhumanity. A book based upon primary sources, however, cannot—and should not—be sanitized of all coarse words and offensive thought. Accordingly, it was the editors' goal to balance sensitivity with their desire not to ennoble criminal thought, words, or behavior.

K. Lee Lerner & Brenda Wilmoth Lerner, editors
Siracusa, Sicily
April, 2006.

About the Entry

The primary source is the centerpiece and main focus of each entry in *Crime and Punishment: Essential Primary Sources*. In keeping with the philosophy that much of the benefit from using primary sources derives from the reader's own process of inquiry, the contextual material surrounding each entry provides access and ease of use, as well as giving the reader a springboard for delving into the primary source. Rubrics identify each section and enable the reader to navigate entries with ease.

ENTRY STRUCTURE

- Primary Source/Entry Title, Subtitle, Primary Source Type
- Key Facts—essential information about the primary source, including creator, date, source citation, and notes about the creator.
- Introduction—historical background and contributing factors for the primary source.
- Primary Source—in text, text facsimile, or image format; full or excerpted.
- Significance—importance and impact of the primary source related events.
- Further Resources—books, periodicals, websites, and audio and visual material.

NAVIGATING AN ENTRY

Entry elements are numbered and reproduced here, with an explanation of the data contained in these elements explained immediately thereafter according to the corresponding numeral.

Primary Source/Entry Title, Subtitle, Primary Source Type

---

[1] Saudi Arabia: Execution of Nigerian Men and Women

[2] Use of Beheading and Amputation in Saudi Penal System

---

[3] **Report excerpt**

[1] **Primary Source/Entry Title:** The entry title is usually the primary source title. In some cases where long titles must be shortened, or more generalized topic titles are needed for clarity, primary source titles are generally depicted as subtitles. Entry titles appear as catchwords at the top outer margin of each page.

[2] **Subtitle:** Some entries contain subtitles. Subtitle:

[3] **Primary Source Type:** The type of primary source is listed just below the title. When assigning source types, great weight was given to how the author of the primary source categorized the source.

Key Facts

[4] **By:** Amnesty International

[5] **Date:** June 15, 2000

[6] **Source:** Amnesty International. "Saudi Arabia: Execution of Nigerian Men and Women." London: Amnesty International, June 15, 2000. Available online at <http://web.amnesty.org/library/>. (accessed January 20, 2006).

[7] **About the Author:** Amnesty International (AI) is a human rights watchdog organization that engages in research and activities to prevent and end human rights abuses. AI operates as an organization independent from affiliation with government, political, or religious organizations.

[4] **Author, Artist, or Organization:** The name of the author, artist, or organization responsible for the creation of the primary source begins the Key Facts section.

[5] **Date of Origin:** The date of origin of the primary source appears in this field, and may differ from the date of publication in the source citation below it; for example, speeches are often delivered before they are published.

[6] **Source Citation:** The source citation is a full bibliographic citation, giving original publication data as well as reprint and/or online availability.

[7] **About the Author:** A brief bio of the author or originator of the primary source gives birth and death dates and a quick overview of the person's work. This rubric has been customized in some cases. If the primary source written document, the term "author" appears; however, if the primary source is a work of art, the term "artist" is used, showing the person's direct relationship to the primary source. For primary sources created by a group, "organization" may have been used instead of "author." Other terms may also be used to describe the creator or originator of the primary source. If an author is anonymous or unknown, a brief "About the Publication" sketch may appear.

Introduction Essay

[8] **INTRODUCTION**

During the beginning of the twentieth century, Abd al Aziz Al Saud (1880–1953) and the House of Saud forged Saudi Arabia into a unified kingdom. In a culture largely ruled by familial alliances, Abd al Aziz successfully created a state loyal to the House of Saud. In order to create this loyalty and stability, Abd al Aziz used a code of behavior and a security force to instill respect and obedience to the law. Abd al Aziz created the modern day penal system in Saudi Arabia based upon the Sharia, specifically the Hanbali, school of Sunni Islam. The Hanbali School is based on the teachings of Imam Ahmad ibn Hanbal (780–855), one of the founders of Sunni Islamic Law. Hanbal was a scholar on the traditions concerning the life of the Prophet Muhammad. The Hanbali judicial system is based on the traditions, sayings, and life of Muhammad. This system of law outlines three types of crimes: crimes explicitly defined by the Sharia, implicitly defined crimes found in the prohibitions of the Sharia,

and emerging more recently through governmental decrees, those crimes dealing with corporate law, taxation, immigration, and oil and gas.

For crimes that are explicitly defined by the Sharia—homicide, assault, adultery, theft, and robbery—a *hadd*, or penalty, is also outlined. Homicide, for example, is determined by Sharia as a crime against an individual rather than the western view of crime against society. As such, the victim's family has the right to enact punishment, which can range from granting clemency to demanding *diya*, or compensatory payment, or even the victim's next of kin enacting the same bodily injury. Those accused of a crime are not afforded the same basic rights as those in western societies. In certain situations, namely cases involving death and grievous injury, the court holds the accused without bail or communication with an attorney. Although lawyers can advise the accused, criminal trials in Saudi Arabia are often held without the benefit of council. The trials are closed and for trials involving foreign nationals, consular access is generally not allowed. A judge, considering the accounts of witnesses and the defendant's sworn testimony, determines the guilt or innocence of the accused, at which point a sentence is imposed. In the case of appeal, the Ministry of Justice examines a judge's decision, except for those sentences of death or amputation. In cases with a sentence of death or amputation, appeals are directed to a panel of five judges. The king automatically reviews the findings of this appellate court in all cases of capital punishment.

[8] **Introduction:** The introduction is a brief essay on the contributing factors and historical context of the primary source. Intended to promote understanding and equip the reader with essential facts to understand the context of the primary source.

To maintain ease of reference to the primary source, spellings of names and places are used in accord with their use in the primary source. According names and places may have different spellings in different articles. Whenever possible, alternative spellings are provided to provide clarity.

To the greatest extent possible we have attempted to use Arabic names instead of their Latinized versions. Where required for clarity we have included Latinized names in parentheses after the Arabic version. Alas, we could not retain some diacritical marks (e.g. bars over vowels, dots under consonants). Because there is no generally accepted rule or consensus regarding the format of translated Arabic names, we have adopted the straightforward, and we hope sensitive, policy of using names as they are used or cited in their region of origin.

Primary Source

[9] PRIMARY SOURCE

Saudi Arabia has one of the highest rates of capital punishment in the world. Of the 766 executions recorded by Amnesty International between 1990 and 1999, over half were of migrant workers and other foreign nationals. While a high proportion of those were Asian migrant workers mainly from Pakistan, Bangladesh, India, Indonesia, the Philippines and Nepal—who comprise between sixty and eighty per cent of Saudi Arabia's workforce—at least seventy-two were Nigerians, mostly convicted for drug smuggling or armed robbery. By mid-June 2000 Saudi Arabia had executed fifty-three people, twenty-five of them in May: nineteen were Saudi Arabian nationals and thirty were foreign nationals, including from Nigeria, India, Pakistan, Sudan, Eritrea, Yemen, the Philippines, Ethiopia, Egypt and Iraq. Migrant workers and other foreign nationals have faced discriminatory treatment under the criminal justice system in Saudi Arabia.

Saudi Arabia has expanded the scope of the death penalty to cover a wide range of offences, including offences without lethal consequences such as apostasy, drug dealing, sodomy and 'witchcraft'. The scores of people who are executed every year, many for non-violent crimes, are put to death after summary trials that offer them no opportunity to defend themselves and almost no protection against miscarriages of justice.

Execution is by public beheading for men and, according to reports, by firing squad or beheading for women, sometimes in public. Foreign nationals are sometimes not even aware that they have been sentenced to death and neither they nor their families are warned in advance of the date of execution. They are rarely if ever allowed to see their loved ones before they are executed.

For those in prison who fear they face execution, the psychological torment is extreme. A former prisoner released from a women's prison in 1999 described to Amnesty International the fear of a fellow woman prisoner accused of murder: 'Every time a guard opens her cell door she gets very scared [thinking] that they will come to take her out for execution.'

Relatives of those executed in many cases receive no formal notification that the execution has taken place. The governments of foreign nationals executed in Saudi Arabia are also not always informed.

Amnesty International is also concerned at the high levels of judicial amputation carried out in Saudi Arabia, which it considers to be a form of torture as defined under the United Nations Convention Against Torture and Other Cruel, Inhuman, and Degrading Treatment or Punishment, to which Saudi Arabia became a state party in 1997. So far this year twenty-three amputations have been recorded, compared with two in the whole of 1999. Seven of these were 'cross amputations' (amputation of the right hand and left foot). On 13 May 2000, cross amputations were carried out on Kindi Amoro Muhammad, Nurayn Aladi Amos, and Abdullah Abu-Bakr Muhammad, Nigerian nationals convicted of armed robbery and assault, with seven Nigerians executed on the same day (see above). In June, two Nigerian men had their right hands amputated following conviction for theft: on 1 June, Muhammad Othman Adam in Mecca, and on 4 June, Sanussi Sani Muhammad.

[9] **Primary Source:** The majority of primary sources are reproduced as plain text. The primary source may appear excerpted or in full, and may appear as text, text facsimile (photographic reproduction of the original text), image, or graphic display (such as a table, chart, or graph).

The font and leading of the primary sources are distinct from that of the context—to provide a visual clue to the change, as well as to facilitate ease of reading. As needed, the original formatting of the text is preserved in order to more accurately represent the original (screenplays, for example). In order to respect the integrity of the primary sources, content some readers may consider sensitive (for example, the use of slang, ethnic or racial slurs, etc.) is retained when deemed to be integral to understanding the source and the context of its creation.

Primary source images (whether photographs, text facsimiles, or graphic displays) are bordered with a distinctive double rule. Most images have brief captions.

The term "narrative break" appears where there is a significant amount of elided (omitted) material with the text provided (for example, excerpts from a work's first and fifth chapters, selections from a journal article abstract and summary, or dialogue from two acts of a play).

Significance Essay

[10] SIGNIFICANCE

A 1999 review by Human Rights Watch (HRW) determined that "The government of Saudi Arabia, an absolute monarchy, continued to violate a broad array of civil and political rights, allowing no criticism of the government, no political parties, nor any other potential challenges to its system of government. Arbitrary arrest, detention without trial, torture, and corporal and capital punishment remained the norm in both political and common criminal cases, with at least twenty-two executions and three judicial amputations of the hand carried out by mid-October. Human rights abuses were facilitated by the absence of an independent judiciary and the lack of public scrutiny by an elected representative body or a free press." The study also determined that women face discrimination within the penal code. For example, it takes the testimony of two women to equal the testimony of one man. HRW also cites that although the penal code is based on teachings of Imam Ahmad ibn Hanbal, few laws are published. The Saudi monarchy possesses the power to "appoint and dismiss judges and to create special courts, undermining judicial independence. In addition, judges [enjoy] broad discretion in defining criminal offences and setting punishments, which [includes] severe floggings, amputations and beheadings." The report also asserts that Saudi law allows for convictions based on uncorroborated confessions.

The crime rate in Saudi Arabia remains relatively low, and a recent increase in crime rates coincided with the increased presence of foreign workers. As a result, supporters of severe punishment, such as amputations and beheadings, attribute the prevailing system for the low crime.

[10] **Significance:** The significance discusses the importance and impact of the primary source and the event it describes.

Further Resources

[11] **FURTHER RESOURCES**

Books

Jerichow, A. *Saudi Arabia; Outside Global Law and Order.*New York: Routledge Curzon, 1997.

Web sites

Human Rights Watch. "Saudi Arabia." <http://www.hrw.org/worldreport99/mideast/saudi.html> (accessed January 6, 2005).

Global Security. "Hanbali Islam." <http://www.globalsecurity.org/military/intro/islam-hanbali.htm> (accessed January 6, 2005).

[11] **Further Resources:** A brief list of resources categorized as Books, Periodicals, Web sites, and Audio and Visual Media provides a stepping stone to further study.

SECONDARY SOURCE CITATION FORMATS (HOW TO CITE ARTICLES AND SOURCES)

Alternative forms of citations exist and examples of how to cite articles from this book are provided below:

APA Style

Books:

Klein, Malcolm W. (1997). *The American Street Gang: Its Nature, Prevalence, and Control.* New York: Oxford University Press. Excerpted in K. Lee Lerner and Brenda Wilmoth Lerner, eds. (2006) *Crime and Punishment: Essential Primary Sources,* Farmington Hills, Mich.: Thomson Gale.

Periodicals:

Hodson, Joel. (2003, October 1). A Case for American Studies: The Michael Fay Affair. *American Studies International.* Excerpted in K. Lee Lerner and Brenda Wilmoth Lerner, eds. (2006) *Crime and Punishment: Essential Primary Sources,* Farmington Hills, Mich.: Thomson Gale.

Web sites:

U.S. Department of Justice. Office of Justice Programs. Amber Alert. Retrieved February 2, 2006 from http://www.amberalert.gov. Excerpted in K. Lee Lerner and Brenda Wilmoth Lerner, eds. (2006) *Crime and Punishment: Essential Primary Sources,* Farmington Hills, Mich.: Thomson Gale.

Chicago Style

Books:

Klein, Malcolm W. *The American Street Gang: Its Nature, Prevalence, and Control.* New York: Oxford University Press, 1997. Excerpted in K. Lee Lerner and Brenda Wilmoth Lerner, eds. *Crime and Punishment: Essential Primary Sources.* Farmington Hills, Mich.: Thomson Gale, 2006.

Periodicals:

Hodson, Joel. "A Case for American Studies: The Michael Fay Affair." *American Studies International* (October 1, 2003). Excerpted in K. Lee Lerner and Brenda Wilmoth Lerner, eds. *Crime and Punishment: Essential Primary Sources.* Farmington Hills, Mich.: Thomson Gale, 2006.

Web sites:

U.S. Department of Justice. Office of Justice Programs. "Amber Alert." <http://www.amberalert.gov> (accessed February 2, 2006). Excerpted in K. Lee Lerner and Brenda Wilmoth Lerner, eds. *Crime and Punishment: Essential Primary Sources.* Farmington Hills, Mich.: Thomson Gale, 2006.

MLA Style

Books:

Klein, Malcolm W. *The American Street Gang: Its Nature, Prevalence, and Control,* New York: Oxford University Press, 1997. Excerpted in K. Lee Lerner and Brenda Wilmoth Lerner, eds. *Crime and Punishment: Essential Primary Sources,* Farmington Hills, Mich.: Thomson Gale, 2006.

Periodicals:

Hodson, Joel. "A Case for American Studies: The Michael Fay Affair." *American Studies International,* 1 October, 2003). Excerpted in K. Lee Lerner and Brenda Wilmoth Lerner, eds. *Crime and Punishment: Essential Primary Sources,* Farmington Hills, Mich.: Thomson Gale, 2006.

Web sites:

"Amber Alert." *U.S. Department of Justice. Office of Justice Programs.* 2 February, 2006 <http://www.amberalert.gov>. Excerpted in K. Lee Lerner and Brenda Wilmoth Lerner, eds. *Crime and Punishment: Essential Primary Sources,* Farmington Hills, Mich.: Thomson Gale, 2006.

Turabian Style

Books:

Klein, Malcolm W. *The American Street Gang: Its Nature, Prevalence, and Control.* (New York: Oxford University Press, 1997). Excerpted in K. Lee Lerner and Brenda Wilmoth Lerner, eds. *Crime and Punishment: Essential Primary Sources.* (Farmington Hills, Mich.: Thomson Gale, 2006).

Periodicals:

Hodson, Joel. "A Case for American Studies: The Michael Fay Affair." *American Studies International* 1 October, 2003. Excerpted in K. Lee Lerner and Brenda Wilmoth Lerner, eds. *Crime and Punishment: Essential Primary Sources.* (Farmington Hills, Mich.: Thomson Gale, 2006).

Web sites:

U.S. Department of Justice. Office of Justice Programs. "Amber Alert" available from http://www.amberalert.gov; (accessed February 2, 2006). Excerpted in K. Lee Lerner and Brenda Wilmoth Lerner, eds. *Crime and Punishment: Essential Primary Sources.* (Farmington Hills, Mich.: Thomson Gale, 2006).

Using Primary Sources

The definition of what constitutes a primary source is often the subject of scholarly debate and interpretation. Although primary sources come from a wide spectrum of resources, they are united by the fact that they individually provide insight into the historical *milieu* (context and environment) during which they were produced. Primary sources include materials such as newspaper articles, press dispatches, autobiographies, essays, letters, diaries, speeches, song lyrics, posters, works of art—and in the twenty-first century, web logs—that offer direct, first-hand insight or witness to events of their day.

Categories of primary sources include:

- Documents containing firsthand accounts of historic events by witnesses and participants. This category includes diary or journal entries, letters, email, newspaper articles, interviews, memoirs, and testimony in legal proceedings.
- Documents or works representing the official views of both government leaders and leaders of terrorist organizations. These include primary sources such as policy statements, speeches, interviews, press releases, government reports, and legislation.
- Works of art, including (but certainly not limited to) photographs, poems, and songs, including advertisements and reviews of those works that help establish an understanding of the cultural milieu (the cultural environment with regard to attitudes and perceptions of events).
- Secondary sources. In some cases, secondary sources or tertiary sources may be treated as primary sources. In some cases articles and sources are created many years after an event. Ordinarily,

a historical retrospective published after the initial event is not considered a primary source. If, however, a resource contains statements or recollections of participants or witnesses to the original event, the source may be considered primary with regard to those statements and recollections.

ANALYSIS OF PRIMARY SOURCES

The material collected in this volume is not intended to provide a comprehensive overview of a topic or event. Rather, the primary sources are intended to generate interest and lay a foundation for further inquiry and study.

In order to properly analyze a primary source, readers should remain skeptical and develop probing questions about the source. As in reading a chemistry or algebra textbook, historical documents require readers to analyze them carefully and extract specific information. However, readers must also read "beyond the text" to garner larger clues about the social impact of the primary source.

In addition to providing information about their topics, primary sources may also supply a wealth of insight into their creator's viewpoint. For example, when reading a news article about an outbreak of disease, consider whether the reporter's words also indicate something about his or her origin, bias (an irrational disposition in favor of someone or something), prejudices (an irrational disposition against someone or something), or intended audience.

Students should remember that primary sources often contain information later proven to be false, or contain viewpoints and terms unacceptable to future generations. It is important to view the primary source within the historical and social context existing at its creation. If for example, a newspaper article is written within hours or days of an event, later developments may reveal some assertions in the original article as false or misleading.

TEST NEW CONCLUSIONS AND IDEAS

Whatever opinion or working hypothesis the reader forms, it is critical that they then test that hypothesis against other facts and sources related to the incident. For example, it might be wrong to conclude that factual mistakes are deliberate unless evidence can be produced of a pattern and practice of such mistakes with an intent to promote a false idea.

The difference between sound reasoning and preposterous conspiracy theories (or the birth of urban legends) lies in the willingness to test new ideas against other sources, rather than rest on one piece of evidence such as a single primary source that may contain errors. Sound reasoning requires that arguments and assertions guard against argument fallacies that utilize the following:

- false dilemmas (only two choices are given when in fact there are three or more options)
- arguments from ignorance (*argumentum ad ignorantiam*; because something is not known to be true, it is assumed to be false)
- possibilist fallacies (a favorite among conspiracy theorists who attempt to demonstrate that a factual statement is true or false by establishing the possibility of its truth or falsity. An argument where "it could be" is usually followed by an unearned "therefore, it is.")
- slippery slope arguments or fallacies (a series of increasingly dramatic consequences is drawn from an initial fact or idea)
- begging the question (the truth of the conclusion is assumed by the premises)
- straw man arguments (the arguer mischaracterizes an argument or theory and then attacks the merits of their own false representations)
- appeals to pity or force (the argument attempts to persuade people to agree by sympathy or force)
- prejudicial language (values or moral judgments are attached to certain arguments or facts)
- personal attacks (*ad hominem*; an attack on a person's character or circumstances);
- anecdotal or testimonial evidence (stories that are unsupported by impartial information or data that is not reproducible);
- *post hoc* (after the fact) fallacies (because one thing follows another, it is held to cause the other)
- the fallacy of the appeal to authority (the argument rests upon the credentials of a person, not the evidence).

Despite the fact that some primary sources can contain false information or lead readers to false conclusions based on the "facts" presented, they remain an invaluable resource regarding past events. Primary sources allow readers and researchers to come as close as possible to understanding the perceptions and context of events and thus, to more fully appreciate how and why misconceptions occur.

Chronology

1600–1800

1679: The Habeas Corpus Act is formally passed by English Parliament.

1764: Italian Cesare Beccaria's publishes *Dei delitti e dlele*, when translated via French into English becomes the influential *Essay on Crimes and Punishment*.

1765: Englishman William Blackstone publishes his *Commentaries on the Laws of England*.

1789: Congress passes the Judiciary Act, which establishes the federal justice system and creates the Office of the Attorney General, as well as the U.S. Marshal Service.

1800–1849

1802: John Dalton introduces modern atomic theory into the science of chemistry.

1813: In France, Mathieu Orfila advances science of forensics as he uses a microscope for the analysis of blood and semen stains.

1817: German pharmacist Frederick Serturner announces the extraction of morphine from opium.

1818: Augustin Jean Fresnel (1788–1827), French physicist, publishes his *Mémoire sur la diffraction de la lumière* in which he demonstrates the ability of a transverse wave theory of light to account for such phenomena as reflection, refraction, polarization, interference, and diffraction patterns.

1828: Friedrich Wöhler synthesizes urea. This is generally regarded as the first organic chemical produced in the laboratory, and an important step in disproving the idea that only living organisms can produce organic compounds. Work by Wöhler and others establish the foundations of organic chemistry and biochemistry.

1828: Luigi Rolando (1773–1831), Italian anatomist, achieves the first synthetic electrical stimulation of the brain.

1830: Colt revolver introduced by gun maker Samuel Colt.

1833: Philadelphia establishes the first paid police force in United States.

1835: Henry Goddard at England's Scotland Yard uses comparison of flaws in bullets to catch a murderer.

1835: Texas Rangers formed.

1836: Toxicological evidence (related to arsenic poisoning) is first used in a trial (in UK).

1839: Semen and sperm characteristics defined by microscopic examination.

1843: Charles-Frédéric Gerhardt (1816–1856), French chemist, simplifies chemical formula-writing, so that water becomes H_2O instead of the previous H_4O_2.

1850–1899

1850: Pinkerton Detective Agency formed.

1857: New York Police Department (NYPD) establishes an investigative division that maintains criminal records.

1858: Rudolf Ludwig Carl Virchow publishes his landmark paper "Cellular Pathology" and establishes the field of cellular pathology. Virchow asserts that all cells arise from preexisting cells (*Omnis cellula e cellula*). He argues that the cell is the ultimate locus of all disease.

1861: 1861 Criminal Law Consolidation Act in UK limits use of the death penalty to murder, treason, mutiny and piracy.

1862: Dutch scientist J. Van Deen develops presumptive blood test.

1862: Department of Agriculture establishes the Bureau of Chemistry, the organizational forerunner of the Food and Drug Administration.

1864: First photographic plates made for the purpose of identification of criminals and questioned documents.

1865: United States Secret Service established to interdict counterfeit currency and its manufacturers.

1865: U.S. Secret Service formed primarily to combat currency counterfeiting.

1867: Secret Service responsibilities broadened to include "detecting persons perpetrating frauds against the government."

1868: England's last public hanging.

1870: Lambert Adolphe Jacques Quetelet shows the importance of statistical analysis for biologists and provides the foundations of biometry.

1870: U.S. Department of Justice formed.

1872: Ferdinand Julius Cohn publishes the first of four papers entitled "Research on Bacteria," which establishes the foundation of bacteriology as a distinct field. He systematically divides bacteria into genera and species.

1876: Robert Koch publishes a paper on anthrax that implicates a bacterium as the cause of the disease, validating the germ theory of disease.

1876: Italian Cesare Lombroso's publishes *L'uomo* (later translated into English as *Criminal Man*), a seminal text in criminology.

1877: Microscopic delineation of palm prints.

1877: Congress passes legislation prohibiting the counterfeiting of any coin, gold, or silver bar.

1878: Charles–Emanuel Sedillot introduces the term "microbe." The term becomes widely used as a term for a pathogenic bacterium.

1879: German pathologist Rudolph Virchow studies and characterizes hair.

1880: Louis Pasteur develops a method of weakening a microbial pathogen of chicken, and uses the term "attenuated" to describe the weakened microbe.

1880: Two Englishmen working abroad notice that fingerprints are unique to individuals. Sir William Herschel, a British Magistrate working in India, uses the impressions of fingers of local businessmen to validate contracts. As Herschel collects these fingerprints, he noticed that no two are alike. In Japan, British physician, Henry Faulds, studies fingerprints he finds on ancient pottery. He documents their individual patterns and develops a method for categorizing them. His work is published in the journal "Nature."

1882: Sir Francis Galton publishes a book titled "Fingerprints," that proves that fingerprints do not change during a person's lifetime. He also develops a set of characteristics, called minutia, that can be used to identify fingerprints. These characters, also called Galton's Details, are still used in modern forensics.

1882: The German bacteriologist Robert Koch (1843–1910) discovers the tubercle bacillus and enunciates "Koch's postulates," which define the classic method of preserving, documenting, and studying bacteria.

1883: French police worker Alphonse Bertillon links criminal behavior to body measurement (anthropometry).

1884: Herbert Spencer writes *The Principles of Sociology*.

1886: Thomas Byrnes writes *Professional Criminals of America*.

1887: Arthur Conan Doyle writes the first of a series of detective stories featuring the iconic fictional detective, Sherlock Holmes.

1888: Jack the Ripper commits serial murders in London's East End.

1889: In 1899 and 1900, Sir Edward Richard Henry improves on Galton's classification system, allowing forensics experts to handle larger numbers of fingerprints in their filing systems. Henry's system remains one of the most common systems used.

1892: Argentinean police worker Juan Vucetich advances fingerprint classification system. Vucetich identifies a woman who murdered her own sons by a bloody print on the doorpost.

1898: In Germany, Paul Jesrich compare bullets using photomicrographs.

1900–1949

1900: Friedrich Ernst Dorn (1848–1916), German physicist, demonstrates that the newly discovered radium gives off a gas as well as produces radioactive radiation. This proves to be the first demonstrable evidence that in the radioactive process, one element is actually transmuted into another.

1900: Karl Landsteiner discovers the blood-agglutination phenomenon and the four major blood types in humans.

1901: In England and Wales, fingerprints are incorporated into the criminal investigation system.

1903: The New York State Prison system begins systematically fingerprinting criminals.

1904: St. Louis Police department uses fingerprint identification during the World's Fair.

1904: Oskar and Rudolf Adler develop benzidine based presumptive test for blood.

1908: Formal beginning of the Bureau of Investigation (BOI) that became the FBI in 1935.

1910: In France, Edmond Locard establishes the first formal police laboratory.

1911: Fritz Pregl (1869–1930), Austrian chemist, first introduces organic microanalysis. He invents analytic methods that make it possible to determine the empirical formula of an organic compound from just a few milligrams of the substance.

1912: Joseph Thomson develops a forerunner of mass spectrometry and separation of isotopes.

1913: In Paris, Victor Balthazard identifies bullet marking classifications and techniques.

1915: International Association for Criminal Identification, a precursor of the International Association for Identification (IAI), is founded, with founder Harry H. Caldwell as its presiding officer.

1915: Germany uses poison gas at the Battle of Ypres.

1916: Vacuums used to collect trace evidence.

1919: October 28, 1919 Congress passes the National Motor Vehicle Theft Act, also known as the Dyer Act. This act authorizes the Bureau of Investigation to investigate auto thefts that cross state lines.

1920: In France, Edmond Locard publishes *L'enquete criminelle et les methodes scientifique* a seminal book for crime scene investigation and criminal forensics.

1921: William Marston develops first modern polygraph.

1921: Twenty-six year old J. Edgar Hoover named Assistant Director of BOI.

1922: White House police force created at request of President Warren G. Harding. Ultimately this will become the uniformed division of the United States Secret Service.

1923: The comparison microscope is used for bullet comparison.

1924: United States consolidates fingerprint files in the Identification Division of the Federal Bureau of Investigation and by 1946, there are more than 100 million fingerprint cards in their files. Eventually this collection of cards becomes the Automated Fingerprint Identification System, or AFIS. In 1999, the F.B.I. teamed with federal, state and local criminal investigation departments to establish IAFIS, the Integrated Automated Fingerprint Identification System. This facility electronically stores the fingerprints and criminal history information of more than 47 million individuals.

1924: Los Angeles Police Chief Vollmer, establishes the first U.S. police crime laboratory.

1924: BOI establishes an Identification Division after Congress authorized "the exchange of identification records with officers of the cities, counties, and states."

1924: J. Edgar Hoover is named director of the U.S. Bureau of Investigations (later the FBI).

1925: Johannes Hans Berger (1873–1941), German neurologist, records the first human electroencephalogram (EEG).

1925: Special Agent Edwin C. Shanahan becomes the first BOI agent killed in the line of duty.

1930: American Journal of Police Science begins publication.

1930: United States Food, Drug, and Insecticide Administration is renamed Food and Drug Administration (FDA).

1930: U.S. Treasury Department creates Bureau of Narcotics, which will remain the principal antidrug agency of the federal government until the late 1960s.

1930: Primitive anthrax vaccine developed.

1930: Uniform Crime Reports bulletins/reports established.

1932: Federal Bureau of Investigation (FBI) crime laboratory established.

1932: The Bureau of Investigation starts the international exchange of fingerprint data with friendly foreign governments. Halted as war approached, the program was not re-instituted until after World War II.

1932: In response to the Lindbergh kidnapping case and other high profile cases Federal Kidnapping Act is passed to authorize BOI to investigate kidnappings perpetrated across state borders.

1934: U.S. Congress passes National Firearms Act.

1935: Federal Bureau of Narcotics, forerunner of the modern Drug Enforcement Administration (DEA), began a campaign that portrayed marijuana as a drug that led users to drug addiction, violence, and insanity. The government produced films such as *Marihuana* (1935), *Reefer Madness* (1936), and *Assassin of Youth* (1937).

1935: U.S. Bureau of Investigations becomes the Federal Bureau of Investigations (FBI).

1941: Researchers publish studies of voiceprint identification.

1941: Arnold O. Beckman, American physicist and inventor, invents the spectrophotometer. This instrument measures light at the electron level and can be used for many kinds of chemical analysis.

1942: Formation of the American Society of Questioned Document Examiners.

1942: Alcohol Tax Unit (ATU) formed and given responsibility for enforcing the Firearms Act.

1946: R.R. Race advances Kell blood group system.

1950–1999

1950: Duffy blood group system advanced.

1950: American Academy of Forensic Science (AAFS) established.

1950: Puerto Rican nationalists attempt to assassinate President Harry S. Truman. As a result of this incident, in which a United States Secret Service (USSS) agent is killed, Congress greatly expands the duties of USSS.

1950: The FBI initiates the Ten Most Wanted Fugitives Program in May in order to draw national attention to dangerous criminals who have avoided capture.

1951: Kidd blood grouping system advanced.

1953: James D. Watson and Francis H. C. Crick publish two landmark papers in the journal *Nature*. The papers are entitled "Molecular structure of nucleic acids: a structure for deoxyribose nucleic acid" and "Genetic implications of the structure of deoxyribonucleic acid". Watson and Crick propose a double helical model for DNA and call attention to the genetic implications of their model. Their model is based, in part, on the x-ray crystallographic work of Rosalind Franklin and the biochemical work of Erwin Chargaff. Their model explains how the genetic material is transmitted.

1954: Indiana State Police Captain R. F. Borkenstein invents Breathalyzer.

1958: International Association for Identification establishes the John A. Dondero Memorial Award, first awarded to FBI Director J. Edgar Hoover.

1959: The microchip, forerunner of the microprocessor, is invented.

1960: Americans Richard Cloward and Lloyd Ohlin write *Delinquency and Opportunity: a Theory of Delinquent Gangs*.

1963: November 22, 1963 Lee Harvey Oswald assassinates President John F. Kennedy in Dallas, Texas.

1965: Federal Bureau of Investigations (FBI) establishes National Crime Information Center (NCIC).

1966: Naval Investigative Service, predecessor of the Naval Criminal Investigative Service, formed as an office within the Office of Naval Intelligence.

1966: In the United States, the Miranda Rights are established when The United States Supreme Court rules in Miranda vs. Arizona that an accused criminal has the right to remain silent; that prosecutors may not use statements unless the police have advise the accused of his or her rights and other rights.

1967: National Crime Information Center created by U.S. Federal Bureau of Investigation.

1968: U.S. anti-drug agencies in the Treasury and Health, Education, and Welfare departments merged to form the Bureau of Narcotics and Dangerous Drugs under the Justice Department.

1968: National Institute of Justice established under the authority of the Omnibus Crime Control and Safe Streets Act to provide independent, evidence-based tools to assist state and local law enforcement.

1968: James Earl Ray assassinates Dr. Martin Luther King, Jr. in Memphis, Tennessee on April 4. The FBI opened a special investigation based on the violation of Dr. King's civil rights so that federal jurisdiction in the matter could be established.

1968: As a result of Senator Robert F. Kennedy's assassination on June 5, Congress authorizes protection of major Presidential and Vice Presidential candidates and nominees.

1969: Microprocessor developed.

1969: Defense Department Advanced Research Projects Agency (ARPA) establish ARPANET, a forerunner to the Internet.

1970: Creation of the forensic odontology division of the American Academy of Forensic Sciences.

1970: United States Congress passes Controlled Substance Act (CSA).

1970: The Consolidated Federal Law Enforcement Training Center, a bureau of the Department of the Treasury, is established as an organization to provide training for all federal law-enforcement personnel. Today known as the Federal Law Enforcement Training Center, it is now part of the Department for Homeland Security.

1970: Congress approves the Organized Crime Control Act of 1970 in October. This law contained a section known as the Racketeer Influenced and Corrupt Organization Act or RICO. RICO becomes an effective tool in convicting members of organized criminal enterprises.

1971: Culliford publishes *The Examination and Typing of Bloodstains in the Crime Laboratory.*

1972: Recombinant technology emerges as one of the most powerful techniques of molecular biology. Scientists are able to splice together pieces of DNA to form recombinant genes. As the potential uses, therapeutic and industrial, became increasingly clear, scientists and venture capitalists establish biotechnology companies.

1972: The ATF Division of IRS becomes a separate Treasury bureau, the Bureau of Alcohol, Tobacco, and Firearms.

1974: Scanning electron microscopy with electron dispersive X-rays (SEMEDX) used to identify gunshot residue.

1975: The Federal Rules of Evidence enacted.

1975: Frenchman Michel Foucault publishes *Discipline and Punish: The Birth of the Prison* (Eng. Trans).

1977: Forensic scientists begin to use Fourier transform infrared spectrophotometer.

1977: FBI advances Automated Fingerprint Identification System (AFIS).

1981: First corpse donated for study received at the Body Farm.

1982: In January, federal law enforcement reorganization gives Drug Enforcement Administration (DEA) and Federal Bureau of Investigation (FBI) concurrent jurisdiction in drug-related criminal matters.

1982: The FDA issues regulations for tamper-resistant packaging after seven people died in Chicago from ingesting Tylenol capsules laced with cyanide. The following year, the federal Anti-Tampering Act was passed, making it a crime to tamper with packaged consumer products.

1984: Crime-fighting efforts bolstered by the Sentencing Reform Act, which stiffens prison sentences, requiring mandatory terms for certain crimes and abolishing federal parole; and by the Victims of Crime Act. Throughout the 1980s, numerous national and community-based organizations are formed to provide support to victims of rape, spousal abuse, drunk driving, and other crimes.

1984: Congress enacts legislation making the fraudulent use of credit and debit cards a federal violation.

1984: The United States Department of Energy (DOE), Office of Health and Environmental Research, U.S. Department of Energy (OHER, now Office of Biological and Environmental Research), and the International Commission for Protection Against Environmental Mutagens and Carcinogens (ICPEMC) cosponsor the Alta, Utah, conference highlighting the growing role of recombinant DNA technologies. OTA incorporates the proceedings of the meeting into a report acknowledging the value of deciphering the human genome.

1984: President Ronald Reagan issues a directive giving the NSA responsibility for maintaining security of government computers.

1985: Alec Jeffreys develops "genetic fingerprinting," a method of using DNA polymorphisms (unique sequences of DNA) to identify individuals. The method, which is subsequently used in paternity, immigration, and murder cases, is generally referred to as "DNA fingerprinting."

1985: Kary Mullis, who was working at Cetus Corporation, develops the polymerase chain reaction (PCR), a new method of amplifying DNA. This technique quickly becomes one of the most powerful tools of molecular biology. Cetus patents PCR and sells the patent to Hoffman-LaRoche, Inc. in 1991.

1985: The Global Positioning System becomes operational.

1986: First use of PCR-based forensic DNA analysis in the United State. Henry Erlich confirms that two autopsy samples came from the same person in the case *Pennsylvania v. Pestinikis.*

1986: First use of DNA to solve a crime as Alec Jeffreys uses DNA profiling evidence to identify Colin Pitchfork as a murderer.

1986: Computer Fraud and Abuse Act enacted, defining federal computer crimes.

1986: U.S. intelligence community establishes Intelligence Community Staff Committee on MASINT (measurement and signatures intelligence) to oversee all relevant activities.

1987: Based on RFLP analysis, DNA profiling is introduced into a U.S. criminal trial.

1987: Congress passes the Computer Security Act, which makes unclassified computing systems the responsibility of the National Institute of Standards and Technology (NIST) and not the NSA with regard to technology standards development.

1987: The idea to use patterns of the iris of the eye as an identification marker is patented, along with the algorithms necessary for iris identification.

1987: In England the first use of DNA typing.

1988: International Association for Identification establishes peer-reviewed publication: *Journal of Forensic Identification*.

1988: Pam Am Flight 103 is destroyed by a bomb over Lockerbie, Scotland.

1988: The Human Genome Organization (HUGO) is established by scientists in order to coordinate international efforts to sequence the human genome.

1988: The Federal Polygraph Protection Act prohibits employers from using polygraphs for employment screening.

1991: Forensic Science Service (U.K.) established as an executive agency of the Home Office of the U.K. government.

1992: National Crime Information Center consolidates with the FBI's Criminal Justice Information Services division.

1992: Naval Criminal Investigative Service formed as an entity separate from the Office of Naval Intelligence.

1993: A U.S. federal court relaxes Frye standard for admission of scientific evidence (*Daubert et al. v. Merrell Dow*).

1993: World Trade Center Bombing, February 26, 1993: The World Trade Center in New York City was badly damaged when a car bomb planted by Islamic terrorists explodes in an underground garage. The bomb left six people dead and 1,000 injured. The men carrying out the attack were followers of Umar Abd al-Rahman, an Egyptian cleric who preached in the New York City area.

1993: After a 51-day siege by the Bureau of Alcohol, Tobacco, and Firearms, federal teams assault a compound held by the Branch Davidians, a religious sect charged with hoarding illegal weapons. The Branch Davidians set the buildings on fire, killing 76 people, including cult leader David Koresh.

1994: DNA Identification Act of 1994 authorizes establishment of NDIS.

1994: The Genetic Privacy Act, the first United States Human Genome Project legislative product, proposed regulation of the collection, analysis, storage, and use of DNA samples and genetic information obtained from them. These rules were endorsed by the ELSI Working Group.

1995: Forensic Science Service (U.K.) established the world's first national criminal intelligence DNA database, the National DNA Database.

1995: Study by the Rand Corporation finds that every dollar spent in drug treatment saves society seven dollars in crime, policing, incarceration, and health services.

1995: A car bomb explodes outside the Alfred P. Murrah Federal office building in Oklahoma City, Oklahoma, on April 19, collapsing walls and floors. 169 persons were killed, including 19 children and one person who died in the rescue effort. Timothy McVeigh and Terry Nichols are later convicted in the anti-government plot to avenge the Branch Davidian standoff in Waco, Texas, exactly two years earlier.

1996: Forensic Science Service (U.K.) merges with the Metropolitan Police Laboratory, London, England.

1996: First computerized searches of the AFIS fingerprint database.

1996: First use of mitochondrial DNA typing evidence in a U.S. trial (*Tennessee v. Ware*).

1997: The National Center for Human Genome Research (NCHGR) at the National Institutes of Health becomes the National Human Genome Research Institute (NHGRI).

1997: The FBI announced its new National DNA Index System (NDIS) on December 8, allowing forensic science laboratories to link serial violent crimes to each other and to known sex offenders through the electronic exchange of DNA profiles.

1998: NDIS becomes operational.

1998: FBI and ATF agree to pursue joint development of one system, using only IBIS, and creates National Integrated Ballistics Information Network.

1998: DNA analyses of semen stains on a dress worn by Monica Lewinsky were found to match DNA from a blood sample taken from President Clinton.

1998: DNA fingerprinting used to identify remains of Russian Imperial Romanov family.

1999: The F.B.I. teams with federal, state and local criminal investigation departments to establish IAFIS, the Integrated Automated Fingerprint Identification System. This facility electronically stores the fingerprints and criminal history information of more than 47 million individuals.

1999: Osama bin Laden is added to the FBI's "Ten Most Wanted Fugitives" list in June, in connection with the U.S. Embassy bombings in East Africa.

1999: FBI personnel traveled to Kosovo on June 23 to assist in the collection of evidence and the examination of forensic materials in support of the prosecution of Slobodan Milosevic and others before the International Criminal Tribunal for the former Yugoslavia.

2000–

2000: Debut of the CBS television series CSI: Crime Scene Investigation.

2001: September 11, Islamist terrorists mount a coordinated terrorist attack on New York and Washington. The World Trade Center Towers are destroyed, killing nearly 3,000 people. In Washington, a plane slams into the Pentagon, but passengers aboard another hijacked airliner, aware of the other terrorist attacks, fight back. During the struggle for the aircraft, it crashes into a Pennsylvania field, thwarting the terrorist's plans to crash the plane into either the U.S. Capital or White House.

2001: The FBI dedicates 7,000 of its 11,000 Special Agents and thousands of FBI support personnel to the PENTTBOM investigation. "PENTTBOM" is short for Pentagon, Twin Towers Bombing.

2001: Letters containing a powdered form of *Bacillus anthracis*, the bacteria that causes anthrax, are mailed by an unknown terrorist or terrorist group (foreign or domestic) to government representatives, members of the news media, and others in the United States. More than 20 cases and five deaths are eventually attributed to the terrorist attack.

2001: In conjunction with the U. S. Post Office, the FBI on October 18 offered a reward of $1,000,000 for information leading to the arrest of the person who mailed letters contaminated with Anthrax in October to media organizations and congressional offices. A further anthrax contaminated letter was postmarked to a U.S. senator on October 8, resulting in closure of the Hart Senate building and other government offices and postal facilities.

2001: On October 26, 2001, President George W. Bush signs the Patriot Act into law, giving the FBI and CIA broader investigatory powers and allowing them to share confidential information about suspected terrorists with one another. Under the act, both agencies can conduct residential searches without a warrant and without the presence of the suspect and allows immediate seizure of personal records. The provisions are not limited to investigating suspected terrorists, but may be used in any criminal investigation related to terrorism. The Patriot Act also grants the FBI and CIA greater latitude in using computer tracking devices to gain access to Internet and phone records. Forensic science becomes more entwined with National Security interests.

2001: Enough closed-circuit television cameras (CCTV) are installed in public places in Britain that, on an average day in any large British city, security experts calculate that a person will have over 300 opportunities to be captured on CCTV during the course of normal daily activities.

2003: Office of Homeland Security becomes Department of Homeland Security on January 24.

2004: Total number of DNA profiles in the FBI NDIS database reaches 2,132,470; the total number of forensic profiles is 93,956; and the total number of convicted offender profiles is 2,038,470.

2006: In the United States, while deliberating a death sentence for French citizen Zacarias Moussaoui (as of early 2006 the only person to face criminal charges related to the September 11, 2001 terrorist attacks on the United States) jurors hear the first public playing from the cockpit voice recorder that contains sounds of struggle between passengers and hijackers aboard downed United Airlines Flight 93.

2006: In Afghanistan a man faces a possible death sentence for converting from Islam to Christianity.

2006: In England, robbers make off with currency with an estimated value of $40M to $80M in U.S. Dollars.

1 Criminals and the Criminal Mind

Criminals and the Criminal Mind

Psychologists argue that career criminals think differently than other people. The American correctional system calls it "criminal thinking."

There is an expansive body of research suggesting that people who will become criminals are often, but not always, behaviorally and temperamentally different than their peers (and, frequently, their siblings) from very early childhood. They are often characterized as exceptionally active, unable to entertain themselves or to "self-soothe" effectively, prone to rages and temper outbursts, likely to abuse or kill small or domestic animals. For example, the article "Cat dragged" show evidence of such abuse and describes some characteristics of those who hurt or kill animals, and explores parallels between those who abuse animals and those who perpetrate violent crime. These individuals are often characterized by psychologists as extraordinarily stubborn and strong-willed, insistent upon getting their way regardless of the cost (personally or financially), tremendously self-centered and unable to see the viewpoint of anyone else, and appearing to have been born with a strong desire to live "on the edge" craving adventure and seeking out risk-laden situations. Family make-up and social class are also correlated to how these traits are expressed.

As detailed in "Criminals' Self-Image: 'Decent People',", most of those incarcerated felons who admit to criminal behavior assert that they are good people who were in the wrong place at the wrong time, or who were pushed into a life of crime by friends or family who were already involved in "the life." They describe their wishes for a normal life "on the outside" (outside of prison), and sometimes wax poetic about their plans for fame and fortune.

In many crowded prison systems, inmates are given few educational or job training options, rendering their time in the correctional system more punitive than rehabilitative. For those who enter the prison system as juveniles, the opportunities for perfecting criminal behavior under the tutelage of older, more experienced and hardened inmates, are rife.

For those who are sentenced to the highest security facilities, hard time is exactly that. In a best case scenario, they will spend an average of twenty-three hours of each day locked into a solitary cell that averages eight by ten feet in size, with sparse furniture and few personal belongings. The other hour will be spent either showering and shaving, or locked into a recreation cage. When inmates are moved by escort officers, they wear shackles, cuffs, and belly chains. They have little interaction with other human beings. Recent class-action suits concur with the beliefs expressed in "How maximum-security jails make the baddest of men even worse," suggesting that solitary confinement may be most effective at inciting anger and antisocial behavior.

When the average person learns of the most heinous, or shocking, crimes, the first thought is that the perpetrator was mentally impaired or unbalanced. In fact, a plea of insanity is rarely employed, and even more rarely accepted as a legitimate defense. "Nuts to Whom? The Insanity Defense is Crazy" explores the use of the insanity plea.

This chapter offers sources depicting crimes and criminals and offering insights into their minds and character.

The Bowery and the Notorious Five Points Neighborhood

Illustration

By: Anonymous

Date: circa 1845

Source: The Bowery and the Notorious Five Points Neighborhood.

About the Illustrator: The author of the illustration is unknown.

INTRODUCTION

Five Points was an area of Manhattan built upon an infilled, pollution-plagued collect pond. Named for the intersection of Orange, Anthony, and Park streets, the land proved ill-suited for building, and soon gained a reputation as a haven for disease and vermin. As residents fled the once middle-class neighborhoods surrounding the pond, Five Points disintegrated into sordid, crime-ridden tenement slums.

The area began as a mixture of Irish, American, and African cultures, but the neighborhood's ethnic character shifted with subsequent waves of immigration. After 1820, Five Points residents were largely recent immigrants or free blacks. In the 1870s, Five Points and its environs had large Jewish, Eastern European, Chinese, and Italian populations. Though regarded today as one of America's first successful multiethnic neighborhoods, contemporary observers viewed the area's immigrant population as the root of its crime and social problems.

At its infamous height, Five Points rivaled the slums of London's East End as a notorious example of urban destitution, disease, unemployment, sweat-

PRIMARY SOURCE

The Bowery and the Notorious Five Points Neighborhood: Five Points in 1827 as depicted in *Valentine's Manual,* 1855.
© BETTMANN/CORBIS

shops, child mortality, and filth that was synonymous with crime and prostitution. The Bowery, on the eastern edge of Five Points, featured taverns, dance halls, oyster bars, and gambling establishments, and was known for its routine and brutal murders. Ethnic and neighborhood tensions were often played out in the violence of street gangs that controlled parts of Five Points, especially the Bowery area.

Given its poverty and violence, the area was a place of unrest. Riots in 1834, 1857, and 1862 originated there before spreading to other parts of New York. In addition, Five Points seated some of the most corrupt politicians of the nineteenth century, but also set trends for putting ethnic Americans in office at a time of high anti-immigrant, nativist sentiment.

PRIMARY SOURCE

THE BOWERY AND THE NOTORIOUS FIVE POINTS NEIGHBORHOOD

See primary source image.

SIGNIFICANCE

Certainly poverty, hard labor, disease, and a lack of sanitation were endemic to Five Points, which attracted the attention of prominent literary figures and social reformers of the era. In 1842, Charles Dickens fueled the area's reputation as place of violence and drunkenness: "[D]ebauchery has made the very houses prematurely old. See how the rotten beams are tumbling down, and how the patched and broken windows seem to scowl dimly, like eyes that have been hurt in drunken frays." Five Points was the subject of news articles and editorial cartoons, most of which focused on the neighborhood's penchant for vice. Illustrations, such as the one here, gave way to the camera. In 1890, Danish-born reformer Jacob Riis published *How the Other Half Lives*, a photographic essay of life in Five Points and other slum neighborhoods.

By the 1870s, Five Points had lost its reputation for hardened political corruption and gang activity, although it kept its reputation for crime, poverty, suffering, and squalor. New tenement laws in 1880 helped rid Five Points of some of its worst housing. Its limitations on renting sleeping space in cellars and attics largely went ignored, but new tenement housing required brick construction and at least minimal ventilation and light.

Five Points is no longer part of present-day New York, but perhaps in fitting tribute to the area's past, it is now home to several court buildings and one of New York's largest jails.

FURTHER RESOURCES
Books
Anbinder, Tyler. *Five Points: The 19th Century New York City Neighborhood That Invented Tap Dance, Stole Elections, and Became the World's Most Notorious Slum.* New York: Plume Books, 2002.

Web sites
The Five Points Site. " Archaeologists and Historians Rediscover a Famous Nineteenth-Century New York Neighborhood" <http://r2.gsa.gov/fivept/fphome.htm> (accessed March 9, 2006).

Crime and Punishment

Book excerpt

By: Fyodor M. Dostoevsky

Date: Reprinted in 2001; originally published in Russia in 1866.

Source: Dostoevsky, Fyodor M. *Crime and Punishment.* New York: Courier Dover, 2001.

About the Author: Fyodor M. Dostoevsky (1821–1881) was born in Moscow, but moved to St. Petersburg, Russia, with his family, where he graduated from military engineering school in 1841. The following year, Dostoevsky left the military to pursue literature. Dostoevsky created most of his famous works after 1860, including such novels as *Crime and Punishment*, *The Idiot*, and *The Brothers Karamazov*.

INTRODUCTION

Crime and Punishment recounts in feverish, compelling tones the story of Raskolnikov, an impoverished student tormented by his own nihilism (a philosophy which holds life and works as neither meaningful nor meaningless) and the struggle between good and evil. Believing that he is above the law, and convinced that humanitarian ends justify vile means, Raskolnikov brutally murders an old woman—a pawnbroker whom he regards as worthless. Overwhelmed afterwards by guilt and terror, Raskolnikov confesses to the crime and goes to prison. There he realizes that through suffering, he can achieve redemption and eventually, happiness.

PRIMARY SOURCE

On an exceptionally hot evening early in July, a young man came out of the garret in which he lodged in S. Place and walked slowly, as though in hesitation, towards K. Bridge.

He had successfully avoided meeting his landlady on the staircase. His garret was under the roof of a high, five-storied house, and was more like a cupboard than a room. The landlady, who provided him with garret, dinners, and attendance, lived on the floor below, and every time he went out he was obliged to pass her kitchen, the door of which invariably stood open. And each time he passed, the young man had a sick, frightened feeling, which made him scowl and feel ashamed. He was hopelessly in debt to his landlady, and was afraid of meeting her.

This was not because he was cowardly and abject, quite the contrary; but for some time past, he had been in an overstrained, irritable condition, verging on hypochondria. He had become so completely absorbed in himself, and isolated from his fellows that he dreaded meeting, not only his landlady, but any one at all. He was crushed by poverty, but the anxieties of his position had of late ceased to weigh upon him. He had given up attending to matters of practical importance; he had lost all desire to do so. Nothing that any landlady could do had a real terror for him. But to be stopped on the stairs, to be forced to listen to her trivial, irrelevant gossip, to pestering demands for payment, threats and complaints, and to rack his brains for excuses, to prevaricate, to lie; now, rather than that, he would creep down the stairs like a cat and slip out unseen.

This evening, however, on coming out into the street, he became acutely aware of his fears.

"I want to attempt a thing *like that* and am frightened by these trifles," he thought, with an odd smile. "Hm...yes, all is in a man's hands and he lets it all slip from cowardice, that's an axiom. It would be interesting to know what it is men are most afraid of. Taking a new step, uttering a new word is what they fear most...But I am talking too much. It's because I chatter that I do nothing. Or perhaps it is that I chatter because I do nothing. I've learned to chatter this last month; lying for days together in my den thinking...of Jack the Giant-killer. Why am I going there now? Am I capable of *that*? Is *that* serious? It is not serious at all. It's simply a fantasy to amuse myself; a plaything! Yes, maybe it is a plaything.

The heat in the street was terrible; and the airlessness, the bustle and the plaster, scaffolding, bricks, and dust all about him, and that special Petersburg stench, so familiar to all who are unable to get out of town in summer; all worked painfully upon the young man's already overwrought nerves. The insufferable stench from the pot-houses, which are particularly numerous in that part of town, and the drunken men whom he met continually, although it was a working day, completed the revolting misery of the picture. An expression of the profoundest disgust gleamed for a moment in the young man's refined face. He was, by the way, exceptionally handsome, above the average in height, slim, well-built with beautiful dark eyes and dark brown hair. Soon he sank into deep thought, or more accurately speaking into a complete blankness of mind; he walked along not observing what was about him and not caring to observe it. From time to time, he would mutter something, from the habit of talking to himself, to which he had just confessed. At these moments he would become conscious that his ideas were sometimes in a tangle and that he was very weak; for two days he had scarcely tasted food.

He was so badly dressed that even a man accustomed to shabbiness would have been ashamed to be seen in the street in such rags. In that quarter of the town, however, scarcely any shortcoming in dress would have created surprise. Owing to the proximity of the Hay Market, the number of establishments of bad character, the preponderance of the trading and working class population crowded in these streets and alleys in the heart of Petersburg, types so various were to be seen in the streets that no figure, however queer, would have caused surprise. But there was such accumulated bitterness and contempt in the young man's heart that, in spite of all the fastidiousness of youth, he minded his rags least of all in the street. It was a different matter when he met with acquaintances or with former fellow students, whom, indeed, he disliked meeting at any time. And yet when a drunken man who, for some unknown reason, was being taken somewhere in a huge wagon dragged by a heavy dray horse, suddenly shouted at him as he drove past: "Hey there, German hatter!" bawling at the top of his voice and pointing at him, the young man stopped suddenly and clutched tremulously at his hat. It was a tall round hat from Zimmerman's, but completely worn out, rusty with age, all torn and bespattered, brimless and bent on one side in a most unseemly fashion. Not shame, however, but quite another feeling akin to terror had overtaken him.

"I knew it," he muttered in confusion, "I thought so! That's the worst of all! Why, a stupid thing like this, the most trivial detail might spoil the whole plan. Yes, my hat is too noticeable....It looks absurd and that makes it noticeable.... With my rags I ought to wear a cap, any sort of old pancake, but not this grotesque thing. Nobody wears such a hat, it would be noticed a mile off, it would be remembered.... What matters is that people would remember it, and that would give them a clue. For this business one should be as little conspicuous as possible.... Trifles, trifles are what matter! Why, it's just such trifles that always ruin everything...."

He had not far to go; he knew indeed how many steps it was from the gate of his lodging house: exactly seven hundred and thirty. He had counted them once when he had been lost in dreams. At the time he had put no faith in those dreams and was only tantalizing himself by their hideous but daring recklessness. Now, a month later, he had begun to look upon them differently, and, in spite of the monologues in which he jeered at his own impotence and indecision, he had involuntarily come to regard this "hideous" dream as an exploit to be attempted, although he still did not realize this himself. He was positively going now for a "rehearsal" of his project, and at every step his excitement grew more and more violent.

SIGNIFICANCE

In one of his letters, Dostoevsky labeled *Crime and Punishment* as a psychological study of a crime. Featured in the book are several factors that many criminologists account for much of the crimes committed today: poverty, mental illness, and a dysfunctional family strucutre.

Crushed by poverty, Raskolnikov commits the murder thinking the end justified the means; that because he was more enlightened than his victim, he had the right to commit the crime for noble goals. After the murder, Raskolnikov is convinced to surrender to the police by his friend Sonya, who despite becoming a prostitute in order to provide for her mother and father, retains her faith in God and humanity. Raskolnikov is condemned to penal servitude in Siberia, and Sonya follows him there. As he serves his time, he rediscovers religious faith, and Sonya and Raskolnikov become convinced of their love for one another. Dostoevsky is quoted in his notebook as saying their "happiness is bought by suffering," a concept that resonated in many penal colonies and prisons around the world until the modern philosophy of rehabilitation through education and behavior modification took hold in the mid-nineteenth century.

The novel raises moral and religious issues, and gives a clear description of the way of life of Russia's poorest people. It should be noted that many ideas of that time discussed in the novel and condemned by the author, especially the idea that "ends justifying vile means," became popular later during turbulent times

A photograph of Fyodor Dostoevsky hangs on the exterior of the Dostoevsky Museum in St. Petersburg, Russia. The museum is housed in the apartment building where he wrote many of his works. © STEVE RAYMER/CORBIS

in Russian society. Russian revolutionaries headed by Lenin and who took power in Russia in 1917 followed similar principles, with revolution, forced labor camps, purges, and a socialist republic that gave its citizens few civil rights being the end result. Russia, however, was also industrialized by the enormity of collective work projects during this era. The Nihilist philosophy was a key element in both the book *Crime and Punishment* and in Russia's post-revolutionary, industrial, nuclear-armed society.

Paramount in Dostoevsky's *Crime and Punishment* is the idea that criminal action probably stems from desperate men, desperate times, and the need for desparate measures, and that the possibility for rehabilitation and redemption exists.

FURTHER RESOURCES

Books

Dostoevsky, Fyodor. *The Idiot.* New York: Oxford University Press, 1998.

——— *The Brothers Karamazov.* New York: Bantam Classics, 1984.

Hugo, Victor. *Les Miserables.* Seattle, Wash.: Signet, 1987.

Who are the Criminals?

The Legal Status of Abortion

Book excerpt

By: Edwin M. Hale

Date: 1867

Source: Edwin M. Hale. *The Great Crime of the Nineteenth Century.* Chicago: C. S. Halsey, 1867.

About the Author: Dr. Edwin M. Hale (1829–1899), a homeopathic physician, was born in Newport, New Hampshire. After qualifying, he worked in Jonesville, Michigan, before becoming professor of materia medica and therapeutics at Hahnemann Medical College in Chicago. His writings on women's health, reproduction, and marriage became popular in the second half of the nineteenth century. He wrote several books, including the anti-abortion treatise *The Great Crime of the Nineteenth Century*, which is excerpted below.

INTRODUCTION

Abortion, both legal and illegal, has long been controversial, balancing as it does the rights of the mother against those of her unborn child. Unwanted pregnancy has always been part of women's lives, even after the advent of reliable contraception in the 1960s in the form of the contraceptive pill. Therefore, abortion will always be an issue, where various interest groups seek to make changes to the legal framework surrounding it.

The legal status of abortion in the United States has changed dramatically over time. From the founding of the nation to the mid-nineteenth century, abortion was permitted until about the fourth month of pregnancy. That is, abortion was allowed until the fetus made perceptible movements, known as "quickening." Both the professional and popular medical lit-

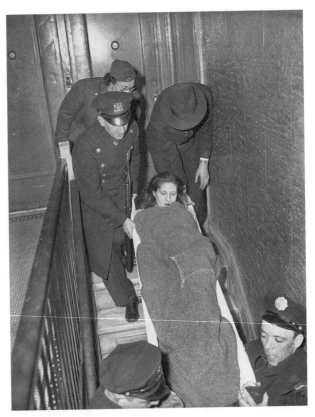

The client of an abortion doctor is carried out of a raided apartment in 1944, after detectives surprised the physician in the midst of an illegal operation being performed on a kitchen table. © BETTMANN/CORBIS

erature of the day contained frequent references to methods of abortion. The fetus was regarded, during this period, as part of the woman's body, with no independent life of its own. Therefore, destroying it was not murder, or even manslaughter.

Views on abortion began to change in the nineteenth century. The unborn child began to be perceived as having rights of its own, which had to be set against those of the mother. In the mid-nineteenth century, Massachusetts became the first state to make abortion at any stage of pregnancy a criminal offense. By the turn of the twentieth century, nearly all other states had adopted similar laws. Many in the medical profession had declared themselves against abortion and their views were no doubt influential in changing the law. Dr. Hale's views, outlined in the excerpt below, are clear and typical of the "hard line" prevalent at the time.

PRIMARY SOURCE

SECTION II.

WHO ARE THE CRIMINALS?

We deem it our duty, as a medical man and a citizen, to point out fearlessly and perspicuously those who are in any way connected, criminally, with this great evil.

Generally they consist of four classes, viz:

The PRINCIPALS.
Accessories BEFORE the fact.
Accessories TO the fact.
Accessories AFTER the fact.

THE PRINCIPALS.

There are generally but two persons in a case of criminal abortion, who are to be considered as *principals*. In rare cases there may be more. Usually they stand, relatively, as follows:

The Mother. That the mother, who carries in her womb her unborn child, should be the chief criminal, is a startling proposition. Many persons will be inclined to disbelieve that such is the case. Those, however, who have investigated the subject, or who have had opportunities for observation, will not dispute the assertion.

When it is known that the cases are very rare in which the crime is committed without the consent of the mother; when it is known that the cases are few in which the child is destroyed without her urgent desire; the proposition will not appear so improbable as at first sight.

Examine all the inducements to the crime, mentioned heretofore, and it will be found that the cases are few in which the mother herself does not originate the plea, or act willingly from influences brought to bear on her from other sources.

In either case, she must be considered as one of the *principals* in the crime.

Even in cases where the husband or other person persuades the mother to its commission, or to allow another person to destroy the foetus, she is still a principal; for in no case need she succumb to influences not extending to actual physical force. The woman is individually responsible for all her acts of immorality.

In the married state, the wife has the moral and legal right to become a mother as often as possible. No law, human or Divine, can compel her to destroy, or permit the destroying of the fruits of conception.

Why then, in this view of the matter, should not the woman be considered the chief criminal, in nearly all cases, except when the abortion was induced on her person, by violence and against her will?

The law in this respect, has not been strict enough to meet the demands of justice. It has recognized, in most instances, only the person who destroys the child by drugs, instruments, or some physical force.

In a few instances, it has named the mother, who, by either of the above means, has destroyed the child in her own womb.

In but one instance, (the law of California,) does the law make a *principal* of the woman on whom the abortion is induced. This should be done in nearly all instances. If the woman is innocent, and the crime was committed against her will, and she was powerless to prevent it, there are many ways in which her innocence could be made to appear.

Physicians are often informed against by one of the guilty parents, causing thereby, a malicious prosecution. Such a law would prevent such persecution.

In fact, she is often more guilty than the person inducing the abortion, for she may, by various improper means, as bribes, threats, and other inducements, influence the physician or other person to commit the crime, when his better judgment and principle would revolt against it.

I do not hesitate to assert that if the woman be made a principal in most cases of abortion, it would diminish the crime two-thirds, and perhaps to a greater extent, especially in large towns and cities.

2. *The Abortionist.* Among the most prominent are a class of creatures, of both sexes, known to the law as *Abortionists*. These people have their corresponding analogies in the Thugs of India, and murderers everywhere, and make it their chief business to destroy, for money, or worse inducements, the innocent and unborn child.

Not only does their loathsome presence poison the moral atmosphere of great cities, but they infest the smaller towns. They even leave their slimy track in the quiet country, and pollute the green fields, the flowery prairies, and the pure forests, where the homes of good men and women should be found.

In the great cities, however, these vampyres most abound. Certain streets and localities, *not* always low and abandoned in their moral surroundings, are selected by these creatures as their *habitat.* Sometimes their presence is known only by the bad location they occupy, for the simple "Doctor _____," on the sign would indicate no nefarious calling. At other times, the word "Accoucher," is prostituted from its legitimate significance, and means to the abandoned, and sinful, only an "Abortionist." More frequently, they sail under the name of "Astrologist;" the possessor of an "Anatomical Museum;" one who treats "secret diseases," or attends to "private matters."

Female Abortionists, assume the name of "Mid-wives," "Nurses," "Fortune-tellers," "Madam _____," "Female Physician," *et cetera*, and under these apparently harmless avocations, ply their murderous trade.

In the country, the business is managed differently. Hundreds of persons of both sexes, are constantly perambulating the country, stopping in the smaller towns villages, who have for their chief means of subsistence, no other means of support than the induction of criminal abortion.

Ostensibly they are "Professors," "Doctors," "Lecturers," etc., advertising to cure all the ills which flesh is heir to; perform wonderful surgical operations; lecture on anatomy, physiology, health, hygiene, phrenology, and various other topics of which they are perfectly ignorant.

In their advertisements, their harrangues to the public, their conversations with private visitors, or in their lectures, they are sure to let drop some hint, by which the unprincipled may imply of what their secret business consists.

Follow these miscreants to their private consultation rooms, and you shall see where the most disgraceful scenes are enacted, and where hands and souls are stained by the blood of unborn babes.

Sometimes the vocation of "nurse," which should be a noble and holy calling, is prostituted to the sole purpose of criminal abortion. Such instances have come to the knowledge of medical men, as occurring in this, and other cities. In the instances alluded to, the monthly nurse has intimated to the lying woman, that there is no need of passing through the perils and pains of childbirth again; that in the early months of pregnancy the menses can be safely brought back; that they will instruct them how to accomplish it. By this means the minds of how many woman hitherto pure, may have been poisoned by such false and sinful temptations?

Among those who figure in the list of chief criminals, are the unnatural father, be he husband, seducer, or unlawful companion. Instances are on record, where the father has administered the potion, used an instrument, or resorted to physical force to destroy his unborn offspring.

We have even heard from undoubted evidence, that there have been instances where the *mother* of the pregnant woman—both belonging to those circles of society considered as "respectable,"—has, with her own hands, given the drug to cause abortion, and most revolting of all, used upon the person of her daughter, an instrument which caused the death of the foetus.

In the name of humanity, religion, and civilization, is it not time that some serious and determined effort was made by men of the medical, legal, and religious professions, to extirpate these murderers?

Shall we allow the end of the Nineteenth Century to close upon a scene which will make the devils laugh, and the angels weep?

Can no law be framed, having for its object the prevention and punishment of the crime of abortion; a law so broad in its scope, so perfect in its details, that the principals above named, cannot escape detection, trial, and condign punishment?

It is a hopeful sign to see that the clergy are becoming aroused to a sense of their duty in this respect, and I cordially endorse the remarks of the author of a recent article on this subject, who says:

"Quack doctors, irregular practitioners, and the whole race of vagrant female hyenas who will take foetal life for fifty dollars, and gratuitously kill or ruin the credulous wife or "unfortunate," should be treated as pests to be "purified by fire," if necessary. The odor of such a burnt offering would be more grateful than their offences which smell to Heaven."

To recapitulate; The mother may be said to be *the* chief criminal (a) when the desire for, and the accomplishment of the crime originates within herself, i. e. when she destroys of her own will, by means of drugs or violence, the unborn child, or procures its destruction by others. She may be said to be *a* chief criminal when she is influenced by others, to the commission of the crime, and allows them to cause by any means the destruction of the child *in utero.*

Besides the mother, the person who administers, or causes to be administered, any drug, to a pregnant woman, or uses any instrument for the purpose of the destruction of the child, without the consent of the mother, becomes *the* chief criminal; but if the person giving the drug, or using the instrument, is employed or influenced in any way, by the mother or others, to the commission of the crime, he or she, becomes *a* chief criminal.

SIGNIFICANCE

Illegal abortion has always been risky. In 1930, an estimated 2,700 women in the United States died following an illegal abortion; by 1950, this figure had decreased to 300, no doubt following the introduction of antibiotics to treat dangerous infections caused by terminations carried out in non-sterile conditions. In the 1960s, opinion on abortion began to change. Only Pennsylvania continued to prohibit all abortions. In some states, however, abortion was allowed only if the mother's life would be endangered by continuing with the pregnancy. In others, an abortion could be obtained if the mother's mental or physical health would be endangered by the pregnancy—a requirement that could be liberally interpreted.

The situation in the 1960s was not one of "abortion on demand" and in practice, abortion was out of the question for many women without financial means. In 1967, Britain liberalized its abortion laws so that any woman was permitted an abortion with the written consent of two physicians. Many women traveled to the U.K. to take advantage of the change in the law—600 American women in the first three months of 1969 alone. Then, in 1970, abortion on request was introduced in four American states—Alaska, Hawaii, New York, and Washington.

The year 1973 was a milestone year in the history of U.S. abortion law. In the famous case of *Roe v. Wade*, the U.S. Supreme Court ruled that the Fourteenth Amendment of the Constitution provided a fundamental right for women to obtain abortions. The case had been brought by "Jane Roe" an unmarried woman wanting to overturn the Texas anti-abortion law. Also included were a married couple "John and Mary Doe" whose doctors had advised against pregnancy. In short, the Court said that although the state has an interest in protecting the life of the unborn fetus, the interest did not become compelling until fetal viability occurred during the third trimester of a pregnancy. That judgement invalidated all state abortion laws at a stroke.

Abortion-related deaths of women have fallen to an all time low since the *Roe v. Wade* judgment and late abortions—which carry the most risk—are far less common. However, many are still opposed to abortion on demand. Some religious groups, for example, argue that life begins at conception. Recent research showing that the fetus may feel pain earlier in its development than previously believed has created pressure to lower the time limit on legal abortion. At the same time, the vital role of sex education and contraception in reducing the demand for abortion should not be overlooked.

FURTHER RESOURCES
Web sites
Alan Guttmacher Institute. "Lessons From Before Roe: Will Past Be Prologue?" <http://www.agi-usa.org/pubs/ib_5-03.html> (accessed January 8, 2006).

AOL Abortion Law Homepage. "Overview." <http://members.aol.com/abtrbng/overview.htm> (accessed January 8, 2006).

Relation Between Occupation and Criminality of Women

Government report

By: Mary Katherine Conyngton

Date: 1911

Source: Mary Katherine Conyngton. "Report on Condition of Woman and Child Wage-Earners in the United States, vol. XV: Relation Between Occupation and Criminality of Women." Washington, D.C.: Government Printing Office, 1911.

About the Author: Mary Katherine Conyngton (1864–1942) was a turn-of-the-century suffragette and early feminist who wrote about the effect of workmen's compensation laws in diminishing the necessity of industrial employment of women and children, and on why women should have the ballot.

INTRODUCTION

In the late nineteenth and early twentieth century it was increasingly common for women to work in industry. Some criticized this trend, seeing industrial work as unsuitable for women and blaming it for social ills such as increasing crime among women. In an early twentieth century report commissioned by the U.S. Department of Labor, feminist and suffragette Mary Katherine Conyngton argued that the increased employment of women in the industrial sphere "can not be held responsible for a 'marked proportionate increase of criminality among women.'" To make her case, she first investigated the types of crimes for which women had been imprisoned and found that most female offenders were in jail for "the pursuits in which women have long been engaged," which had nothing to do with industrial employment. Her next line of argumentation questioned the very existence of the trend toward increased numbers of female offenders that critics of the employment of women in industry were decrying. In the primary source referenced in this section, Conyngton attempted to show that instead of a trend toward increased female criminality, there was instead a trend in the opposite direction.

The source article is a straightforward description of a falling trend in female criminality in the early twentieth century about which the authorities were genuinely puzzled. The article ends with three possible explanations for the trend: alternatives to prison in dealing with female crime may have emerged; laws had been less strictly enforced; or perhaps there was a

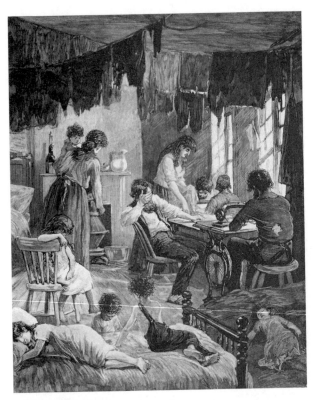

The terrible conditions of a New York sweatshop are depicted in this engraving, c. 1890. © BETTMANN/CORBIS

PRIMARY SOURCE

RELATION BETWEEN OCCUPATION AND CRIMINALITY OF WOMEN

Decreasing Number of Female Offenders in Confinement.

Now it is the general opinion among prison officials and prison workers that the number of female offenders is diminishing. "We don't get as many women as we did fifteen or twenty years ago" was a common statement. "We used to have as many as 50 women here at one time," said the warden of one institution, "but to-day we have 3, and I don't think we've had as many as 15 at once for five years past. Often we haven't enough to do the work of the institution." In one factory town where a decade or so ago a new house of correction was built with a large wing for women the number of female offenders has so diminished that it is not considered worth while to maintain a matron, and the women under sentence are boarded at the house of correction of a neighboring community. This arrangement was found in several places. Of course, in some States it is customary for several communities to unite in this way, but in this particular part of the country the device is not usual, and its adoption was directly due to the decreasing number of female offenders.

This tendency toward a decrease is most marked in States in which the laws are most exacting and most strictly enforced, and these are the States in which the largest numbers of women are committed. Naturally enough, it is more easily perceived in the serious offenses than in the misdemeanors. In New York the State prison for women has never been filled, and for years the number of inmates has either remained stationary or shown a slight tendency to decrease. The Massachusetts Reformatory Prison for Women was opened thirty years ago, and the year after its opening had 482 inmates. Of late years the number has shown a decided falling off. In 1906 the State commissioners thus commented on the decline:

> This place has had a very small number of prisoners throughout the year; it is a long time since the number has raised above 200...On September 30 there were 176 in prison. The reduction in number is not by a diversion of cases to other prisons, as sentences of one year or more, for felony or serious misdemeanor, to a house of correction, have for a time been exceedingly rare. The decrease indicates a general falling off in sentences.

The following year the number of inmates showed a still further decrease, getting down at one time to 127, the lowest number reached since the prison was opened. It rose a little after that, but on September 30, 1907, the

real decrease in female criminality. Conyngton did not hazard an interpretation in this passage. She let the facts of empty women prison wards speak for themselves.

The falling rate of female imprisonment had a quaint practical consequence: there were not enough female prisoners to clean the women's prisons, and male prisoners had to be sent in to do this work. Furthermore, the number of female prisoners had dropped so low that authorities questioned the need to "maintain a matron."

From a statistical perspective, Conyngton in her thoroughness encountered a dearth of potentially explanatory data. For example, records of crimes committed, as well as the use of probation and other alternatives to prison sentencing were mentioned as potentially explaining the drop in the female inmate population, but no hard data on these other trends appears to be available. Nevertheless, her basic argument that no proportionate increase in women offenders exists is well supported by simple statistics on the falling rate of female imprisonment as a proportion of an increasing population.

date of the annual report, it was only 142. The same diminution shows itself all over the State, and for all kinds of offenses. "In some of the county prisons," says the latest report of the Board of Prison Commissioners, "there are no women at all. In others the number has become so small that there are not enough to do the domestic work, and male prisoners have taken their places. In all prisons the number of women has fallen far below any condition which has existed for a long time." In 1895 the whole number of women sentenced in Massachusetts for offenses of all kinds was 3,061; in 1905, when the population had increased by something over 500,000, it was 3,010. Two years later, in 1907, it was 2,513. The number of convictions not only failed to keep pace with the increase of population, but showed an actual falling off.

It is not possible to get equally conclusive data for the country as a whole, but all the figures accessible seem to point to the same result. In 1904 the United States Census Bureau made a study of prisoners and of juvenile delinquents in confinement. The figures obtained show that for the United States, as a whole, and for each main division of it, there had been a falling off in the number of female prisoners between June 1, 1890, and June 30, 1904, the date at which the later census was taken.

Possible Explanations of Decrease in Number of Prisoners

There are three possible explanations for this falling off. First, it is conceivable that public standards might be growing laxer, the laws might be less strictly enforced, and as a consequence the decreasing number of commitments might really accompany an increase of criminality among women. Second, other methods of treatment, such as fines, probation, or commitment to private reformatory institutions might be growing in favor, and hence the diminished number of women in prison might bear no relation whatever to their criminality. And as a last explanation, it may be that the prison statistics reflect the real state of affairs and that criminality among women is actually diminishing.

SIGNIFICANCE

In her Labor Department report, Conyngton maintains that there is little statistical basis for determining whether society is experiencing a trend toward more strict or more lax enforcement of laws. Every statistic on female imprisonment available at the time pointed toward decreasing crime rates among women. Although one might interpret this trend to be indicative of greater laxity in law enforcement, Conyngton does not attempt to refute this explanation. She observes that when fewer arrests are made within various crime categories over time, the case can be made

that "the standard of public morals is rising, not falling." She concludes that "if there is a progressive decrease in the number of arrests and convictions within a certain class…the criminality of that class is at least not increasing."

Conyngton urges the liberalization of public attitudes toward working women and of employer policies toward the hiring of women, and defuses one of the more emotive arguments against liberalization: that employment leads to the deterioration of women's morality. Subsequent research on female offenders appears to leave intact her conclusion that employment does not increase female criminality. However, other social influences, including unemployment, might indeed increase the numbers of female offenders.

The situation regarding the numbers of female offenders in Massachusetts at the turn of the twentieth century appears to be the mirror image of the situation one hundred years later in our own time. Information posted on the Florida Department of Corrections (DOC) describes a disturbing trend in the incarceration of women. According to the National Bureau of Justice Statistics, 90,668 women were incarcerated in U.S. jails, 6.6 percent of the total jailed population. While this number is still only a small fraction of the total population, the growth rate of female adult offenders has exceeded that of males every year since 1981.

The number of women entering the nation's state and federal prisons between 1980 and 1994 increased nearly fourfold, while the number of men only doubled. In 1990 the American Correctional Association published a profile of contemporary female offenders based on a survey of 2,094 female offenders in four hundred state and local prisons. This profile of surveyed offenders showed that most are between the ages of 25 to 29, economically disadvantaged minorities with children, not married or single parents and former runaways from home as teenagers. About twenty-five percent had attempted suicide and many had drug addictions. Over half of the offenders were physical abuse victims and most of these victims had been sexually abused. A high proportion of the offenders had not graduated from high school and more than twenty-five percent had been unemployed in the three years before incarceration. The latter statistic points to unemployment as being a potential cause and at least a consequence of female criminality, which lends support to Conyngton's perspective of a century ago.

According to the survey, the most common crimes leading to female imprisonment are larceny, theft, or drug crimes. Drug crimes are highly correlated with

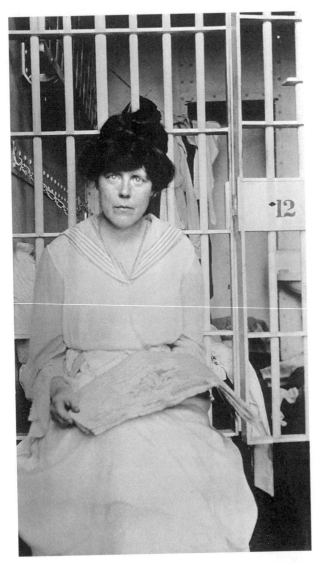

Lucy Burns was jailed following a suffragette picket in Washington, D.C., in December 1917. © BETTMANN/CORBIS

committing higher rates of crimes of types not traditionally committed by females.

This "tougher punishment" interpretation of statistics appears to be at best only half of the correct explanation. The profile of female offenders relates to a more racially diverse female prison population than a hundred years ago, with more problems of drug addiction, which in turn have contributed to rates of theft and larceny. Yet the Department's statement that most of the women inmates were first-time offenders and that many of the most serious crimes were against men who had assaulted them still seems to indicate that the U.S. has not seen a fundamental shift in women's tendency toward criminal activity. While the employment of women in industry has exploded, the types of female crime have remained basically the same.

On the other hand, the present time has been described as harsh and censorious, and many a politician has made his or her political fortune by taking a "tougher" stand on crime (even as crime rates have recently fallen in many large U.S. cities). While circumstances such as the drug epidemic, social disintegration and family breakdown over the past half-century may have increased the female crime rate, the Florida DOC's suggestion that society has been prosecuting offenses more aggressively is plausible.

Employment may have a beneficial effect on crime rates among contemporary women, who are subject to social stressors not widely experienced in Conyngton's time. It is possible to view employment as a type of social "glue" that reinforces social responsibility and self-management in today's society, while traditional morality and female roles are considerably weakened as forces that prevent women from committing the types of crimes that they have done in the past.

FURTHER RESOURCES

Books

Young, Cathy. *Ceasefire!: Why Women and Men Must Join Forces to Achieve True Equality.* New York: Free Press, 1999.

Web sites

Young, Cathy. *Reason Online.* "License to Kill: Men and Women, Crime and Punishment." <http://reason.com/0207/co.cy.license.shtml> (accessed February 26, 2006).

Florida Department of Corrections. "National Profile of the Female Offender." <http://www.dc.state.fl.us/pub/Females/status102001/national.html> (accessed February 26, 2006).

prostitution, one of the "pursuits" that Conyngton found accounted for rates of female imprisonment. When the survey was taken, the offenders were serving time for drug crimes, murder, larceny, theft, or robbery. A high proportion of women convicted of manslaughter or murder had killed a boyfriend or husband who abused them. Half of the women committed for homicide were first time offenders.

Based on their own review of literature, the DOC observes that "Crimes committed by women have not gotten more serious; instead, the system is now 'tougher' on all offenses, including those traditionally committed by females." Nowhere is there any mention of an indication in the statistics that women are

Gangster Al Capone Charged on Income Tax Violations

Photograph

By: Anonymous

Date: October 14, 1931

Source: Corbis.

About the Photographer: This image is part of the stock collection at Corbis photo agency. The photographer is not known.

INTRODUCTION

Alphonse "Al" Capone, one of the most notorious gangsters of the Prohibition era, escaped prosecution for violent crimes but went to prison for tax evasion in 1931.

Capone was born in Brooklyn, New York on January 17, 1899 to immigrants from Naples, Italy. Upon dropping out of school in the sixth grade, he joined a gang of young thugs in lower Manhattan. A razor slash across the left cheek gave Capone the nickname of "Scarface." At twenty, he killed his first man.

In 1922, Capone followed his mentor in crime, Johnny Torrio, to Chicago. Torrio specialized in gambling, prostitution, and bootlegged liquor. When a murder attempt in 1925 left him seriously wounded, Torrio retired and left his business to Capone.

Although he listed his occupation on business cards as "secondhand furniture dealer," Capone became the top gangster in Chicago and one of the best-known gangsters in the world. The crime boss of Chicago, he divided the city into districts that were controlled by different gangs. He enforced his will with baseball bats and Thompson submachine guns. By the mid-1920s, two hundred murders a year were linked to Capone. However, since he only targeted fellow gangsters and not the general public, Capone became a folk hero to many Americans.

By the late 1920s, Capone grossed about $70 million annually from liquor, prostitution, loan sharking, extortion, slot machines, and gambling. Unfortunately, he failed to report his earnings. While he could intimidate and bribe the Chicago police, Capone could not control the U.S. Treasury Department. Indicted for federal income tax evasion in June 1931, he was convicted in October. Capone received a sentence of eleven years in prison, first served in Atlanta and then at Alcatraz, the notorious prison in San Fran-

PRIMARY SOURCE

Gangster Al Capone Charged on Income Tax Violations: The infamous mobster Al Capone, attending a football game in 1931. AP IMAGES

cisco Bay. Suffering from advanced syphilis, he was released from prison in 1939 and died in bed in Florida on January 25, 1947.

PRIMARY SOURCE

GANGSTER AL CAPONE CHARGED ON INCOME TAX VIOLATIONS

See primary source image.

SIGNIFICANCE

Capone is significant both for his criminal activities and his place in popular culture. The best-known gangster of the Prohibition era, Capone's wealth and fame underscored the failure of the anti-liquor law. Despite spending great amounts of money and making a tremendous effort, the federal government could not halt the demand for liquor that made Capone into an exceptionally wealthy man. Although Capone was never convicted for his bootlegging crimes, his prison sentence for income tax violation resonated through subsequent decades as evidence that no one was exempt from paying their taxes.

Capone showed as much skill in public relations as he did with criminal enterprises. Always eager to talk to reporters and a colorful man, Capone became the first media star gangster. Americans were infatuated by the gangster as represented by Capone, whose stylish dress and fancy cars demonstrated victory over humble beginnings.

Capone helped turn the figure of the gangster into an American folk hero. He became a model of the American man of the 1920s. Capone forged a style that emphasized self-made success, businesslike demeanor, lavish consumerism, fierce independence, violent pursuit of self-interest, and an unabashed flouting of the nation's social, economic, and legal systems. For thumbing his nose at society and government, Americans loved this antihero.

FURTHER RESOURCES

Books

Irey, Elmer L. *The Tax Dodgers: The Inside Story of the T-Men's War with America's Political and Underworld Hoodlums.* New York: Greenberg, 1948.

Kobler, John. *Capone: The Life and World of Al Capone.* New York: Putnam's, 1971.

Schoenberg, Robert J. *Mr. Capone.* New York: William Morrow, 1992.

Patty Hearst With Rifle Inside Bank

Photograph

By: Anonymous

Date: April 15, 1974

Source: "Patty Hearst with Rifle Inside Bank." AP Images, 1974.

About the Photographer: This photograph was taken by a security camera at the Hibernia Bank branch in San Francisco, California, on April 15, 1974.

INTRODUCTION

On February 4, 1974, Patricia Campbell (Patty) Hearst was kidnapped from her Berkley apartment by members of the urban guerrilla group known as the Symbionese Liberation Army (SLA). Hearst was the twenty-year-old granddaughter of the newspaper magnate and millionaire William Randolph Hearst, a scion of the American establishment.

The SLA grandly called themselves an Army, but were in reality never more than a ragtag brigade whose membership never exceeded twenty-five and whose crimes had until then barely registered a flicker of media attention. The most notorious of the pre-Hearst crimes came in November 1973, when the SLA murdered the Oakland Superintendent of Schools, Dr. Marcus Foster, and seriously injured his deputy, Robert Blackburn, as they left an Oakland school board meeting. Their premise was that Foster's plan to introduce identification cards into Oakland schools was "fascist." Yet in kidnapping Hearst and apparently converting her to their cause, they captured global attention in a story that dominated the American news media for more than two years.

While the SLA had a knack of obtaining publicity that went far in excess of its small membership base, its aims were confused. They claimed to propagate Maoism, although Maoism when described by even its most articulate backers was well known to be merely an incoherent form of revolutionary socialism. (The fixation with Maoism has been attributed to the fact that several SLA members came from the defunct Maoist group Venceremos). Indeed the SLA's very name hinted at its confused outlook: "Symbionese" was taken from the word symbiosis, which they defined as the merger of dissimilar parts within a body harmonizing in its best interests. In practice, they extolled a mishmash of contrary ideas, including black power, sexual freedom, collectivist economics, and anarchism.

Initially, the SLA made demands that the Hearst family distribute millions of dollars of food relief amongst the poor of San Francisco in exchange for Patty's release. These efforts were abandoned when her freedom was not forthcoming and riots broke out at food distribution points.

Rather than tapping into the Hearst family wealth, the SLA's reasons for targeting Patty Hearst were largely publicity orientated. As her family owned many of America's largest newspapers and her father was himself a San Francisco newspaper editor, the SLA were guaranteed thousands of column inches from which the rest of the American news media would take its lead.

Two months after Hearst's capture, however, the SLA had an even bigger publicity coup in store. Days after the abandonment of the food distribution program, Patty Hearst made a statement in which she announced that she had renounced her family, joined her abductors, and adopted the name Tania [after the mistress of the South American revolutionary, Che Guevara].

Whether this statement was made under coercion was initially the subject of some debate, but the SLA were soon to put this beyond doubt. On April 15, a black man and four white women walked into the Hibernia Bank branch in San Francisco's Sunset district before producing semiautomatic guns from their long black coats. They ordered staff and customers onto the floor while two of the women raiders rushed to the cash drawers and began emptying them of cash. Another woman proclaimed "We're from the SLA", and gestured over to another and shouted: "This is Tania Hearst! "

■ PRIMARY SOURCE

PATTY HEARST WITH RIFLE INSIDE BANK

See primary source image.

■■■

SIGNIFICANCE

Despite the apparent incontrovertibility of the photographic evidence against Patty Hearst (more than 1,200 security pictures were taken during the five-minute raid), there was initially furious debate about whether she had willingly participated in the robbery. The FBI only issued a warrant for her arrest as a "material witness" but at the same time charged her four companions with bank robbery. The FBI believed the raid was a macabre stunt designed to demonstrate that the SLA had tightened its grip on the millionaire. Her father, Randolph A. Hearst, appeared on television as an anguished figure proclaiming: "It's terrible! Sixty days ago, she was a lovely child. Now there's a picture of her in a bank with a gun in her hand."

Invariably, a number of speculative theories abounded about Patty Hearst's involvement in the robbery. These included the notions that she had been killed and the bank robber was an imposter; that she was an SLA member all along; that fearing she might be killed she had "pretended" to convert to the SLA; or that after two months of intense psychological pres-

■ PRIMARY SOURCE

Patty Hearst With Rifle Inside Bank: This surveillance camera photo from the Hibernia Bank in San Francisco shows Patty Hearst holding a gun and apparently taking part in the bank robbery staged by the Symbionese Liberation Army (SLA) on April 15, 1974. The SLA had kidnapped Hearst that February. AP IMAGES

sure she had been brainwashed into joining her captors.

The FBI's search for Hearst came to assume the complexion of an odyssey and was one of the most widely publicized manhunts in history. Over the following seventeen months, they would arrest or shoot most of the members of the SLA before finally catching up with Patty Hearst in September 1975.

When the case came to trial in January 1976, Hearst renounced her willing involvement with the SLA and her defense claimed that she had been physically and sexually coerced into membership and that she had been intimidated into her part in the bank robbery. It was widely debated whether Hearst suffered from "Stockholm Syndrome," a term given to victims who become psychologically dependent and attached to their abusers (this is most often applied to battered wives). However, by common consent, Hearst's defense gave a poor showing and she was convicted of bank robbery. President Jimmy Carter later commuted her sentence, and she was freed from prison in February 1979. President Bill Clinton granted her a full pardon in January 2001.

Hearst's case and particularly the issue about her culpability in the bank robbery has retained resonance since her release. Her memoir, *Every Secret Thing*, maintained her court argument that she was a victim of the SLA, but she also included a critique of the American social structure that gave rise to the organization and offered views on class and race which could be construed as sympathetic to the SLA. Her then fiancé, Steven Weed, was just another individual involved in the case who put his memories into print: one of a score of books published on the case. In 1988 *Every Secret Thing* was made into a film called *Patty Hearst*. A documentary of the case, *Guerilla: The Taking of Patty Hearst*, premiered in 2004.

The wider significance of the Hearst case was that it showed how a well-thought-out and publicity-conscious act of extremism could bring minority political views—no matter how incoherent or repugnant—into the mainstream. By degrees, the acts of individuals like Ted Kaczynski, the Unabomber, and Timothy McVeigh, the Oklahoma bomber, continued the tradition set by the SLA when it targeted Hearst. Both of these men held marginalized political views that gained worldwide publicity through acts of violence.

FURTHER RESOURCES

Books

Hearst, Patty, with Alvin Moscow. *Every Secret Thing*. London: Methuen, 1982.

Periodicals

"The Hearst Nightmare." *Time* (April 29, 1974). <http://www.time.com/time/archive/preview/0,10987,911211,00.html> (accessed March 5, 2006).

Web sites

Mental Health Matters. "Stockholm Syndrome." <http://www.mental—health—matters.com/articles/article.php?artID=469> (accessed March 5, 2006).

Note from Son of Sam: Serial Killers

Note

By: David Berkowitz

Date: 1977

Source: Corbis

About the Author: This is a photograph of a note left by David Berkowitz. Berkowitz is a serial killer who terrorized the city of New York with his shooting sprees in 1976 and 1977. He killed six people, five of them women, and wounded several others. He was sentenced on June 12, 1978, to 365 years in prison.

INTRODUCTION

Berkowitz's first victim was eighteen-year-old Donna Lauria; initially, this was assumed to be a gangland killing but police became seriously concerned after two more murders and several attacks. All the crimes appeared to involve a 0.44 caliber revolver, suggesting a serial killer was on the loose. On April 17, 1977, a young couple—Alexander Esau and Valentina Suriani—were shot to death. The killer left a note—part of which is seen in the image below—in a nearby street. He claimed he had been ordered to carry out the murders by his father, Sam, a vampire. The notes were kept secret, but the killer sent a letter to a journalist for the *New York Daily News* who published it and gave him the name "Son of Sam." Another attack took place in Queens in June—but neither of the intended young victims was seriously hurt. On July 31, 1977, Son of Sam claimed his sixth and final victim, 20-year-old Stacy Moskowitz, who was attacked with her boyfriend Bobby Violante, who survived his injuries.

Witnesses to the last murder saw Berkowitz flee in a car with a parking ticket on it. This provided police with the final clue they needed to identify Berkowitz as the Son of Sam killer. Police in Yonkers had already begun monitoring him because of odd behavior reported by his neighbors. When taken into custody, he admitted all six murders and the other shootings. He claimed that he had been ordered to kill by his neighbor Sam Carr, who passed messages through his "demon" dog. Psychiatrists disagreed as to whether or not he was a paranoid schizophreniac. In the end, he was judged fit to stand trial and sentenced to six life sentences.

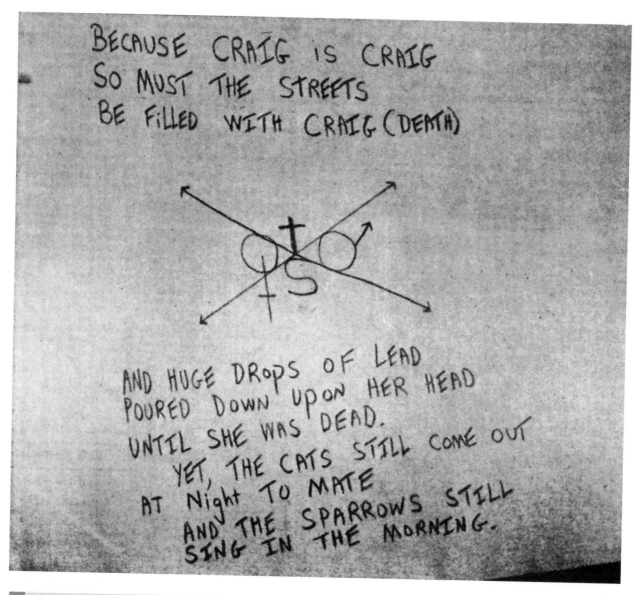

PRIMARY SOURCE

Note from Son of Sam: Serial Killers: A note from Son of Sam Killer David Berkowitz. © BETTMANN/CORBIS

PRIMARY SOURCE

NOTE FROM SON OF SAM: SERIAL KILLERS

See primary source image

SIGNIFICANCE

Berkowitz's note, from its content, suggests insanity. After his conviction, he claimed that the letters and tales of demonic voices were hoaxes. Sexual frustration and a hatred of women had driven him to kill. There is another theory, supported by the mother of his last victim, that Berkowitz, along with Sam Carr's two sons, was involved in a cult called the Disciples of Hell and the killings were part of an occult ritual. Thus far Berkowitz has neither confirmed nor denied this theory. His two supposed accomplices both died under mysterious circumstances.

The motives of a serial killer are usually much less obvious than those of a person who commits a single homicide. Victims are often picked on at random and are not usually known to the attacker. As the homicides mount, the pressure on the police to catch the perpetrator becomes intense. Often they call upon a psychological profiler to tell them what kind of man they are looking for. This knowledge, combined with the increasing likelihood that the killer will make a mistake as the killing spree escalates, often results in capture. In addition, many serial killers—including Berkowitz—like to generate their own publicity, typically in the form of notes left at the scene or sent to police.

Serial killers are psychopaths. They are often sentenced to the maximum because they either cannot or will not express any remorse for their crimes. They are manipulative too, so any guilt they may express could be a ploy to obtain parole. When Berkowitz first appeared before the parole board, in 2002, the two members judged him to have only limited insight and understanding of the motivation for his crimes. It would have been a relief to the families of his victims to learn that Berkowitz does not want parole and says he will appear before the board only to apologize publicly for his crimes. He has also written to Governor George Pataki expressing remorse.

Berkowitz remains something of an enigma—he has become a born-again Christian with his own website which he uses to spread his faith. He has also released two evangelical videos which have been distributed to prison chaplains and youth conselors. There has even been a film about him—Spike Lee's *Summer of Sam* which was released in 1999.

FURTHER RESOURCES

Books

Douglas, Lyle. *Forensics for Dummies*. Hoboken, N.J.: 2004, Wiley

Web sites

USA *Today*. "Son of Sam Killer Denied Parole." <http://www.usatoday.com/news/world/2002/07/09/son-of-sam.htm> (accessed February 4, 2006).

BBC. "Crime Case Closed: Infamous Criminals—David Berkowitz, Son of Sam" <http://www.bbc.co.uk/crime/caseclosed/berkowitz1.shtml> (accessed February 4, 2006).

Criminals' Self-Image: Decent People

Book excerpt

By: Stanton E. Samenow

Date: 1984

Source: Samenow, Stanton E. *Inside the Criminal Mind*. New York: Crown Business, 1984.

About the Author: Stanton E. Samenow is a clinical psychologist whose private practice specialties are assessment, evaluation, and treatment of youthful and adult criminal offenders. During the 1970s, he was a clinical research psychologist at St. Elizabeth's Hospital in Washington, D.C., where he collaborated with Samuel Yochelson to collect data on the personality dynamics of convicted felons. He has published several books on criminal offenders and their underlying personality structures.

INTRODUCTION

Rarely, if ever, do individuals (male convicted felons, as the demographic profile of female convicted felons is somewhat different) who have been convicted of, and incarcerated for, felony offenses readily admit to guilt and offer a straightforward motive for criminal behavior. If there is an admission of guilt, it is generally accompanied by explanations of extenuating circumstances, stories of an abusive or deprivation-filled childhood, or discussion of peer pressure and of "being in the wrong place at the wrong time."

In order for a criminal trail to result in a conviction, there must be proof "beyond a reasonable doubt" that the defendant acted willfully and volitionally (also called *actus reus*) and with intent to commit the crime (*mens rea*, or criminal mind). The premise of the insanity defense is that a defendant who was seriously mentally ill at the time of the commission of the crime, to such an extent as not to be able to behave volitionally (as in the case of a severely psychotic individual who is existing in a state of altered reality, under the influence of delusions or hallucinations at the moment of the criminal behavior) might not be held criminally responsible for the act. In such a situation, the defendant would be remanded to a forensic psychiatric institution. This is extremely rare. One notable example of this was John Hinckley, Jr., whose attorneys successfully utilized the insanity defense at his 1982 trial for his attempted assassination of the late American President Ronald Reagan.

Defrocked priest Paul Shanley stands in handcuffs in Cambridge, MA, with baliffs on either side, following his sentencing of 12 to 15 years in prison for the rape of a child more than twenty years earlier. © CHARLES KRUPA/POLL/REUTERS/CORBIS

In the 1960s, the noted psychologist and personality theorist Hans Eysenck posited that there was a constellation of traits, characteristics, and inherited tendencies that could combine, under certain types of circumstances, to result in the formation of what has been termed a criminal personality. Eysenck quantified personality along several scalar dimensions, having to do with several sets of traits: introversion, extroversion, emotional stability, neuroticism, and psychoticism. The normative personality would be emotionally stable and neither excessively introverted nor extroverted. Eysenck believed that those who were very neurotic, extremely extroverted, and with a high degree of psychoticism (per his personality scales) would be predisposed toward criminality. At the extreme end of the continuum would be what he—and Samenow—termed the psychopathic or sociopathic personality. Individuals with criminal personalities were likely, in Eysenck's theoretical system, to be thrill seekers, to act impulsively, to be predis-

posed toward violence, to be emotionally unstable, to abuse drugs and alcohol, and to have a difficult time learning and capitulating to societal rules. Sociopaths and psychopaths are incapable of learning or following cultural and societal rules, they are extremely aggressive and impulsive, they are unable to form emotional bonds with other human beings, they do not function well within normal society, and they are incapable of experiencing guilt or remorse. They are at the extreme end of the diagnostic spectrum for antisocial personality, and of antisocial personality disorder.

■ **PRIMARY SOURCE**

The place is the Oregon State Hospital, a meeting of a therapy group where dangerous sex offenders are receiving psychiatric treatment. Among them is a man who raped babies, a fellow who sodomized a six-year-old boy, another who raped a fourteen-year-old girl at gunpoint, and ten others who have committed almost every other imaginable sex offense as well as other types of crimes. The therapist has just asked the men why society has rules. One man replies, *We have rules to protect society and so people won't hurt others.* Another speaks up, *Society would fall apart without rules. There's be mass confusion.* A third says, *Rules are designed to teach people their responsibilities.*

All these responses are rational and to the point. They come from the lips of men who, without question, know that rape, kidnapping, child molestation, and other forms of sexual abuse are wrong and why they are wrong. These men will acknowledge that, from society's point of view, they are criminals. But not one really regards *himself* that way. Every member of that group believes that he is basically a decent human being. How is it possible for a criminal to believe that he is a good guy when he has left behind him a trail of destruction?

The criminal knows right from wrong. He may be more knowledgeable about the laws than many responsible citizens. When it suits him, he is law-abiding and even takes pride in being meticulous about it. One ruthless teenage gang member, for example, would never spit on a sidewalk or break the speed limit when he motorcycled through a school zone. Despite his knowledge of what is legal and what is illegal, the criminal decides that he can make exceptions for himself just because it suits him at a particular time. The fact the *he* wants to do it makes it right. *I was born with the idea that I'd do what I wanted. I always felt that the rules and regulations were not for me,* asserted one fourteen-year-old who then added, "Others may think I'll burn in hell, but at least I'll have a nice time doing what I want while I'm here."

If a criminal regards something as wrong for him personally, he will not do it. An act is wrong if it is too risky. An act is also considered wrong by a criminal if he thinks it is too petty. A big-time operator may consider shoplifting wrong only because it is not worth bothering with. If a criminal makes an error in judgment and is caught, he will say what he did was wrong, but only because he was caught.

The semantics of this last point are interesting. One teenager said that lately he'd been "messing up" and he needed to stop doing that. My probing into what he meant revealed a totally different message than his words conveyed. To the untrained ear, it might have sounded as though this youth wanted to reform, but that was not so. By "messing up" he meant getting caught. If he hadn't been caught for a crime, he would not have called it "messing up" What was wrong was getting caught, not his commission of the offense.

The criminal not only knows right from wrong, but he also believes that wrongdoers must be apprehended. Criminals are portrayed as hating the cops, but this is not so. As children, they admire policemen and imagine themselves in badge and uniform brandishing a nightstick and revolver and driving a speeding cruiser. Fascination with the police continues into the criminal's adult years, and he is an avid viewer of police shows and detective thrillers. He regards police as absolutely necessary to lock up lawbreakers, and, on occasions, he may help them out. After assisting officers in the arrest of a burglar, one criminal wrote to a law enforcement agent, "You have impressed me as a very efficient, no-nonsense guy who won't tolerate inefficient police work, and I really hope that you will match any criminal power thrust with an overwhelming display of power on the side of law and order." The criminal has contempt for law enforcement officials mainly when they pose an immediate threat to him.

Although the criminal may not accept what others consider moral standards, he claims to have his own set of morals. Other people are liars, perverts, scoundrels, and criminals, but not he. Sociologist Joseph Rogers points out that even in prison an inmate "is not likely to see himself as a 'real' criminal." It is the other inmates, "whom he views as the 'real' ones." He looks down on them as depraved because they do things that he would not. Specific crimes are wrong and thus off-limits for him simply because he personally finds them offensive. Criminals differ as to what they find most revolting. One says that a child molester should be killed while another advocates that a rapist be castrated. But each considers whatever he does as beyond reproach. One tough guy of the streets said that sneaking up on an adult male and mugging him is all in a day's work, but if he were to see anyone do the same to a child or elderly lady, he would rip the attacker to shreds. To his way of thinking, the two situations are completely different.

If there is something that the criminal wants, he knocks down every barrier until he gets it. If this requires maiming or killing, so be it. There is no need to justify a crime to himself either before or at the time he commits it. In cold-blooded fashion, he does whatever suits him; he is the only one who matters. A twenty-five-year-old man who served a sentence for two counts of assault and battery commented, "A realistic person will have to admit that this is a dog-eat-dog world and basically every man is for himself first, others second. Only the fit will survive. Take what you want out of life, without any qualms or doubts, ruthlessly if necessary. But above all be true to yourself." He went on to say, "The question of being right or wrong is not a major one for when you are dead and gone some will say, 'He was a good son of a bitch' and some will say 'He was a dirty son of a bitch.'

Either way, you're a dead son of a bitch, and there won't be any dispute over that."

The criminal does not think he has hurt anyone unless he draws blood. He does not see himself as harming his victims when he vandalizes their property, forges their checks, cons them out of savings, or breaks into their homes. Yet, if someone did any of these things to him or to his family, he would assist the police or personally seek revenge. One fifteen-year-old had recurrent thoughts of sneaking up on old people and robbing them, but he said about the prospect of someone's doing this to his grandmother, "If I found the person, I'd kill him."

An exchange that took place in juvenile court reveals a characteristic attitude. Sixteen-year-old Stu was asked by the judge, "Why did you forge the checks?" Blandly, Stu replied, "It was an opportunity. I didn't need the money." Incredulously, the judge retorted, "It was an opportunity to be a thief!" Stu stared at the judge and said adamantly, "No, I'm not a thief." It might appear that Stu could not add two and two. Knowing that he had broken the law, he had admitted his guilt in court without excuses. Yet he declared that he was not a thief, a conclusion totally different from that of the judge or the victim. From his standpoint, Stu did what he wanted to; it was as simple as that. Thieves hurt people by causing them loss, anxiety, and inconvenience. Had Stu even imagined he was doing that, he would not have stolen the checks and forged them. When a criminal is confronted with tangible evidence that he has harmed someone, he blames the victim or minimizes the damage. At most he passes it off perhaps as poor judgment on his part but certainly not as reflecting anything basic about his character.

Psychiatrist Willard Gaylin calls guilt "the guardian of our goodness." He says that feeling guilt is so painful because "it is like tearing apart our inner structure." Most of us seek to avoid such pain and are usually deterred from serious wrongdoing. How does a criminal who experiences little guilt live with himself? He can maintain a view of himself as a decent person because psychologically he can do what most of us can't. Criminals isolate unpleasant emotions such as fear, guilt, and self-doubt so that they do not interfere with their objectives. Psychologist Hans Eysenck's explanation is a biological one. He maintains, "Criminality can be understood in terms of conditioning principles." He goes on to observe, "Criminals fail to condition adequately the socially adequate responses which society requires them to integrate into some form of 'conscience.'" Freudians would explain lack of conscience in terms of a *superego deficit* due to disturbed *object relations* in the early years.

As I see it, criminals do experience guilt and remorse. They have a conscience, but it is not fully operational. When they commit a crime, they can shut off considerations of conscience as quickly and totally as they can shut off an electric light. Just the fact that the criminal can *feel* guilt, no matter how ineffective it is as a deterrent, helps him to maintain the belief that he is decent.

Some criminals are religious, and this figures prominently in their good opinion of themselves. Schooled in religion as youngsters, they took what they learned very much to heart. In the primary grades, they were not defiant or hell-raisers. Rather, they were super good, regularly attending church and Sunday school, helping in the home, and looking out for kids who were the underdogs. Believing that God was watching them all the time, they tried to merit His approval. One criminal reported that as an eight year old he pictured God dwelling in a tower like a church steeple, looking down upon him, and judging everything he did to determine whether he'd rest in heaven or burn in hell. Another, at eight, was convinced that if he were bad the devil would snatch him and he'd die before his ninth birthday. One boy crossed himself each time the word "damn" slipped out of his mouth. As children, these criminals were ready to condemn adults and other children for the slightest impropriety. As for themselves, they believed that to remain in God's good graces, they had to be better than good, purer than pure. But their determination, though sincere, did not last. In a manner typical of criminals, they shifted from one extreme to another. As the youngster's world expanded beyond his family circle, there was both greater temptation and an ever more active mind that dwelled increasingly on the forbidden. The slow but steady erosion of his purity was almost impossible to observe. Those who thought they knew him were astounded when this model child exploded into antisocial activity. Yet religion was not abandoned forever. Criminals keep returning to it, some out of nostalgia for their childhood, others in a personal crisis when they long for the serenity of a church with its soothing music and familiar ritual. As with everything else, the criminal exploits religion to serve his own purposes. He not only presents God with his list of wants, but he also asks God to be an accessory to his crimes. He prays for success in his ventures and later, when he gets himself into a jam, implores God to bail him out. After the police apprehended one man for assault with a deadly weapon, he silently beseeched the Lord from the patrol car, "God, if you'd only help me now, I won't do any more things." The criminal bargains with God for salvation after he is confined and resolves to mend his ways.

Fifteen-year-old Vic was shocked when a judge finally ordered him locked up after he had repeatedly violated probation. His first stint in confinement was sobering. There he began reading the Bible and a small book written by a minister. He devoted considerable thought to the nature of sin and resolved to sin no more. Vic found the smaller volume so absorbing that he considered swiping it to take home. Then he was jolted by his parents' reminder that it was a sin to steal a book that he thought might keep him from sinning.

Leaving the book where it belonged, he reflected more on the nature of sin and told his parents with tears in his eyes that he wanted them to help him reform. Vic's sincerity was temporary. Nearly as soon as he was released from detention, he returned to crime.

Religion has little to do with how the criminal lives. As a child he may serve as an altar boy at a ten o'clock service and two hours later go on a shoplifting spree. As an adult, he may pray in church in the morning and that very evening stick a gun to someone's head. (A Time feature on the Mafia reported, "A Mafioso cultivates the image of a solid, church-going, charity-supporting citizen.") For criminals, religion and evil exist side by side, one compartmentalized from the other. A striking example of this is thirty-year-old Bill, who had murdered his girlfriend. Bill had always considered himself a religious man. In his adult years, he still went to church, although not regularly. At the conclusion of one service, he went to the pulpit to talk with the minister and showed him a book on Christian ethics. Ethics book in hand, he lied to the minister by telling him that he had been released from confinement and was starting a new life. Actually, Bill was a fugitive from a federal institution, sought by the authorities.

The lament of most clergymen is that their congregants fail to live by the teachings of their religious faith. They emerge from church brimming with righteousness and feeling virtuous just because they managed to get out of bed and sit through a service. Then they curse their fellow congregants as they scramble to get out of the parking lot. But the fact remains that, despite their human frailties, unlike the criminal, they retain a sense of social boundaries, obey laws, and fulfill obligations. The criminal, on the other hand, has a remarkable capacity to shut off considerations of responsibility or morality from his thinking so totally that he can freely commit murder, rape, arson, extortion, and a myriad of other crimes. He perceives no contradiction between prayer and crime. Both are right for him, depending on what he wants at a particular time.

Ironically, the criminal's religiosity fosters crime for, when it is genuine, it bolsters his opinion of himself as an upstanding citizen. It is as though by having felt remorse, prayed, and confessed his sins to God, the criminal empties his cup of whatever evil it might have contained so that he has even more latitude to do as he pleases.

As the criminal sees it, he is a good person, making his way as he sees fit in a world that is his to conquer. But the world does not cater to him, and many times every day his unrealistic view of life is threatened. The slightest disappointment can trigger a total collapse of his inflated self-concept. Small daily frustrations that most people cope with routinely are calamities for him—having to wait in line when time is short, receiving criticism from his boss, having his wife disagree with him. These things are not supposed to happen. He assumes that he should give the orders, make the decisions, and not have to put up with the idiosyncrasies of others. His self-concept is easily shattered because he defines failure as being anything short of an immediate resounding success. If a kid wants to be known as a champion ballplayer, he shows up for regular practice. Not the criminal. If he isn't recognized right away as a top-flight athlete, that to him is the same as others regarding him as a spastic, and he'll refuse to play at all. If he fails to be the most popular in a group, he'll believe that he is looked at as a social misfit. So he'll tell others to go to hell or will plot to get even. If a woman doesn't jump into bed with him, he'll consider it a threat to his manhood rather than recognizing that she has a right to make her choice. The threat of being less than top dog, the possibility that he won't achieve unusual distinction, the chance that things will not go as he wants constitute a major threat to the criminal, almost as though his life were at stake. From his standpoint it is, because the puncturing of his inflated self-concept is psychological homicide. It is like pricking a balloon with a pin so that the entire thing blows apart. The result is a desperate and sometimes violent reaction to gain control of a situation and assert his worth.

Criminals, then, are almost always angry, even though they often conceal it. Only a slight jolt to the self-image sets them off, and anyone or any object in the vicinity may be a target. A derogatory name, a snide remark, a criticism may have an explosive effect similar to pouring lighter fluid onto a smoldering bed of coals.

Responsible people also get angry when things don't work out as they hope. But one frustration of disappointment does not threaten them with total psychological annihilation. They don't expect to be number one in everything or to be right on every occasion. Having learned to be self-critical, they realize that perhaps they did make a mistake, not the other guy. Consequently, instead of automatically thinking about retaliation, they are inclined to consider how to make amends or do better the next time. The criminal simply does not operate this way. He takes stock of himself only to try to ensure that he will come out on top the next time. What matters to him is not self-improvement but making a conquest.

Regarding himself as decent, the criminal approaches the responsible world with scorn. An ordinary life is a living death, clearly not for him. Said one youthful housebreaker and lock-picking expert, "I'd rather be dead than be a clerk." Yet, the criminal occasionally envies the responsible person. He eyes the trappings of success—a comfortable home, a car, a family, a high-paying job—and believes that the holder of these is on easy street. A seventeen-year-old delinquent said, "Sometimes I wish I was like regular kids." He saw his friends ready to graduate and driving cars which they bought with job earnings. He mused, "I could have had all that. Sometimes I feel like a fool." But this youth quit school, would have no part of working, and turned his back on a devoted family.

SIGNIFICANCE

Criminal thinking, as conceptualized by Samenow and Yochelson, is an aspect of the criminal personality, which incorporates a constellation of thinking patterns, rational choice-making, and free will. Essentially, Samenow and Yochelson argue that criminals' faulty thinking patterns cause them to make choices to break the law, to hurt, abuse, or kill others, to violate personal and property rights. They assert that criminals behave impulsively, do not envision future consequences for their actions, are irresponsible and self-centered, and tend to have a great deal of difficulty with abstract thought. As a result, they tend to reside on a foreshortened emotional continuum, and experience primarily anger and fear—which drive their actions. Although their theory appears to make sweeping generalizations about the criminal population, it appears to be more accurate for career criminals who have been in trouble since childhood or early adolescence than for those who commit a crime during a moment of extreme fear, rage, or passion or who plot and plan to kill an abusive spouse or partner after many years of being victimized. Yochelson and Samenow drew their theoretical assumptions from the criminal population with which they worked: a group of hard core incarcerated male adolescent and adult felons on a forensic psychiatric unit at St. Elizabeth's Hospital in urban Washington, D.C. They found these men to be resistant to change, to be entrenched in their thinking styles and behavior patterns, and to be unresponsive to traditional rehabilitation efforts. As a result of their research and clinical work with this group, they developed both the notion of criminal thinking and that of corrective thinking as a means of breaking the counterproductive (not necessarily from the viewpoint of the incarcerated felon) behavior patterns.

Corrective thinking is a learning paradigm, based on Samenow's theories, in which incarcerated felons (who meet certain criteria, as defined by the particular prison system's education and classification departments) are put through a specially designed curriculum in which they are repeatedly confronted with evidence of their faulty reasoning processes as well as with the need to take responsibility for past criminal behaviors. One of the primary objectives of the process is to break down and deconstruct ineffective, criminal thinking and behavior patterns and replace them with new, healthy ways of thinking and moving in the world. In the confrontation and responsibility process, Samenow and those who espouse his theory believe that it is possible to teach hard-core criminals to feel empathy (for their victims and for society as a whole), guilt, remorse, and some degree of self-loathing for their criminal behavior and criminal thinking patterns. By so doing, these cognitive behavioral theorists believe that criminals will reject old thinking patterns or replace them with non-criminal thoughts and behaviors. If the process is successful, those individuals who fully participated in the Corrective Thinking program will complete it as transformed individuals who are capable of refraining from committing criminal acts and of contributing positively to society.

Although the data is still being collected in the states and facilities that employ the Corrective Thinking programming, preliminary results strongly suggest that, for those individuals who fully and honestly engage in the coursework and report taking it seriously, rather than using it as a means of attempting to ensure a quicker trip to the parole board, the recidivism (return to prison) rates have declined considerably.

FURTHER RESOURCES
Books

Department of Justice, Federal Bureau of Investigation. *The School Shooter: A Threat Assessment Perspective*. Quantico, Virginia: National Center for the Analysis of Violent Crime, 2000.

Eysenck, Hans J. *Crime and Personality*. Boston, Massachusetts: Houghton Mifflin Company, 1964.

Lanier, Mark M., and Stuart Henry. *Essential Criminology*. Boulder, Colorado: Westview Press, 1998.

Samenow, Stanton E. *Inside the Criminal Mind*. New York, New York: Crown Business, 1984.

Periodicals

Lynam, Donald R. "Early identification of chronic offenders: Who is the fledgling psychopath?." *Psychological Bulletin*. 120(2) (1996): 209–234.

Web sites

WashingtonTimes.com. "Psyching out crime excuses." <http://www.washingtontimes.com/commentary/> (accessed March 07, 2006).

302.84 Sexual Sadism

Book excerpt

By: American Psychiatric Association

Date: 1994

Source: American Psychiatric Association. *Diagnostic and Statistical Manual of Mental Disorders*, 4th ed. Washington, D.C.: American Psychiatric Association, 1994.

About the Author: The fourth edition of the Diagnostic and Statistical Manual of Mental Disorders was researched and written by the members of a series of Work Groups under the auspices of the DSM-IV Task Force, with clinical and administrative oversight provided by the American Psychiatric Association.

INTRODUCTION

Sexual sadism belongs to a class of psychopathology called the *paraphilias*, which refers to any of three different categories of pathological sexual activity: it can either include nonconsensual behavior with children or other unwilling individuals (not a willing partner), or it may involve non-human objects such as animals (bestiality) or objects such as shoes or umbrellas (fetishism), or it may entail the infliction of pain, suffering, or degradation/humiliation for either participant (masochism or sadism). The sexual activity can involve intense and arousing fantasies, sexual thoughts and desires, or actual sexual behaviors, and must occur over a period of at least six months (the activity can be recurrent or continuous) in order to meet diagnostic criteria. The objects or activity involved would not be considered sexually arousing to the general public. Another diagnostic component of the paraphilias is that they must significantly interfere with the individual's life in some manner, either in terms of personal relationships, occupational functioning, or in some other central way.

There are nine categories of paraphilia in the DSM-IV (as well as in the most current, DSM-IV-TR edition). They are: exhibitionism, fetishism, frotteurism, pedophilia, transvestic fetishism, voyeurism, sexual masochism, and sexual sadism, as well as paraphilia not other wise specified. In exhibitionism, the individual exposes his/her genitals to non-consenting strangers; persons with fetishism find inanimate objects such as specific articles of clothing (for example, shoes, women's undergarments, leather clothing) or specific body parts (for example, buttocks or feet) sexually stimulating. Pedophiles engage in sexual behavior with children who have not yet reached sexual maturity. Diagnostically, the pedophile must be at least five years older than the child; many incarcerated pedophiles report being attracted to a specific gender, age range, appearance, or body type. Persons with frotteurism make physical contact with non-consenting persons by either rubbing against them or touching them in some other intrusive or intimate manner with the hands or genitals. Frotteurism is often reported to occur in crowded public places such as buses, subways, escalators, or other locations in which rapid exit (from the area) and anonymity are the norm. Persons with transvestic fetishism are virtually always heterosexual males; they cross-dress in order to act out sexual fantasies. This generally involves arousal and masturbation.

In sexual masochism, the individual engages in sexual activity that involves being humiliated, degraded, or caused physical pain, by either being bound, hit or beaten, or injured in some other way (binding, whipping, cutting, burning, etc.). In sexual sadism, the individual inflicts the types of pain just described to others in order to become sexually aroused. In all of the paraphilias, the behavior must interfere with social, educational, or occupational functioning in order to meet diagnostic criteria. By definition, some of the paraphiliac behaviors are illegal (for example, pedophilia).

■ PRIMARY SOURCE

302.84 SEXUAL SADISM

The paraphiliac focus of Sexual Sadism involves acts (real, not simulated) in which the individual derives sexual excitement from the psychological or physical suffering (including humiliation) of the victim. Some individuals with this Paraphilia are bothered by their sadistic fantasies, which may be involved during sexual activity but not otherwise acted on; in such cases the sadistic fantasies usually involve having complete control over the victim, who is terrified by anticipation of the impending sadistic act. Others act on the sadistic sexual urges with a consenting partner (who may have Sexual Masochism) who willingly suffers pain or humiliation. Still others with Sexual Sadism act on their sadistic sexual urges with nonconsenting victims. In all of these cases, it is the suffering of the victim that is sexually arousing. Sadistic fantasies or acts may involve activities that indicate the dominance of the person over the victim (e.g., forcing the victim to crawl or keeping the victim in a cage). They may also involve restraint, blindfolding, paddling, spanking, whipping, pinching, beating, burning, electrical shocks, rape, cutting, stabbing, strangulation, torture, mutilation, or killing. Sadistic sexual fantasies are likely to have been present in childhood. The age at onset of sadistic activities is variable, but is commonly by early adulthood. Sexual Sadism is usually chronic. When Sexual Sadism is practiced with nonconsenting partners, the activity is likely to be repeated until the person with Sexual Sadism is apprehended. Some individuals with Sexual Sadism

may engage in sadistic acts for many years without a need to increase the potential for inflicting serious physical damage. Usually, however, the severity of the sadistic acts increases over time. When Sexual Sadism is severe, and especially when it is associated with Antisocial Personality Disorder, individuals with Sexual Sadism may seriously injure or kill their victims.

Diagnostic criteria for 302.84 Sexual Sadism

A. Over a period of at least 6 months, recurrent, intense sexually arousing fantasies, sexual urges, or behaviors involving acts (real, not simulated) in which the psychological or physical suffering (including humiliation) of the victim is sexually exciting to the person.

B. The fantasies, sexual urges, or behavior cause clinically significant distress or impairment in social, occupational, or other important areas of functioning.

SIGNIFICANCE

People who exhibit criminal sexually sadistic behavior as adults typically have a lengthy history of

Jail inmates dig for bodies at a Gulf Coast beach in 1973 where they discovered two of the 23 bodies of young boys murdered in a three-year spree of sex and sadism. © BETTMANN/CORBIS

cruel, aggressive, humiliating, or degrading behavior toward others, often beginning in childhood. Early research on sadism referred to a constellation of behaviors called "the three D's": dread, dependency, and degradation. In essence, this means that the sexual sadist causes the sexual partner to feel terror or to fear for personal safety (possibly feeling as though death may be at the end point of the encounter), renders the sexual partner unable to defend him/herself, and then humiliates and causes him or her significant pain (typically of a sexual nature, sometimes involving various acts of torture). For a sexually sadistic individual, the act of inflicting significant pain (whether they involve fantasy alone, or actual physical behavior) is sexually arousing.

From a forensic standpoint, the weapon use, wound patterns, and timeline of the crime are analyzed in an effort to determine sexual sadism. In most sexually sadistic crimes, particularly those resulting in death (murder), there are indications—either at the scene, on the victim, or discernible at autopsy—that the physical suffering or torture of the victim occurred over a prolonged period of time (hours, days, or sometimes longer—weeks or months). Sexual sadists tend to have specific sets of behaviors in which they engage, often in particular sequences. They may use tools (either standard ones like saws, razors, fishing line, wire, and screwdrivers, or burning devices such as soldering tools, jeweler's torches, etc.) to cut, brand, shock (electrical shock), burn, mutilate, whip, hang, impale, or otherwise torture their victims, or to bind or restrain them (ligatures, tape, various types of cages, cuffs, masks, and the like). There is often a specific scenario involved in the act—from capture and abduction of the victim (either by coercion or by force), through restraint and torture, through release, escape, or eventual death. In a subcategory of paraphilia, some sexual sadists continue to mutilate the body after death (a variant of necrophilia).

As in most sexually related crimes, the motivations for the sexual sadist revolve around acting out issues around power, control, and rage. The release of sexual tension comes from the experience of causing another person to feel pain, to be humiliated, or to feel unrelenting fear.

The concept of sexual sadism was well documented in forensic and psychological literature by the late nineteenth century Krafft-Ebing; the concept of sadism is named for an eighteenth century French author called the Marquis de Sade, whose works combined eroticism, punishment, torture, and murder.

In the present day, sexual sadism falls on a continuum of behavior from fantasy that is not acted upon (extremely mild) to role play (very mild) to non-harmful consensual behavior in the BDSM (bondage-domination-sadism-masochism) subculture (mild) to damaging, dangerous, harmful but still consensual behavior (moderate) to non-consensual behavior, possibly ending in murder (severe and criminal). Statistically, criminal sexual sadism is predominantly practiced by males. The behaviors are generally first exhibited in late adolescence or early adulthood, and generally progress over time in degree, intensity, and frequency.

FURTHER RESOURCES
Books

The Clinical and Forensic Assessment of Psychopathy: A Practitioner's Guide, edited by Carl B. Gacono. Mahwah, N.J.: Lawrence Erlbaum Associates, 2000.

Stephen J. Giannangelo. The Psychopathology of Serial Murder: A Theory of Violence. Westport, Conn.: Praeger Publishers, 1996.

Louis B. Schlesinger. Sexual Murder—Catathymic and Compulsive Homicides. Boca Raton, Fla.: CRC Press, 2004.

Periodicals

Web sites

NARTH. "Should These Conditions Be Normalized? American Psychiatric Association Symposium Debates Whether Pedophilia, Gender-Identity Disorder, Sexual Sadism Should Remain Mental Illnesses." <http://www.narth.com/docs/symposium.html> (accessed February 17, 2006).

Park Dietz and Associates. "Areas of Expertise." <http://www.parkdietzassociates.com/index3.htm> (accessed February 17, 2006).

University of Iowa Hospitals and Clinics. "Sadism." <http://www.uihealthcare.com/topics/mentalemotional-health/ment3168.html> (accessed February 17, 2006).

Solitary Confinement

Photograph

By: Vehbi Koca

Date: c. 1990s

Source: Alamy Images. " Prisoner in His Solitary Confinement, Sinop, Turkey" <http://editorial.acionline.biz/search.pp> (accessed March 6, 2006).

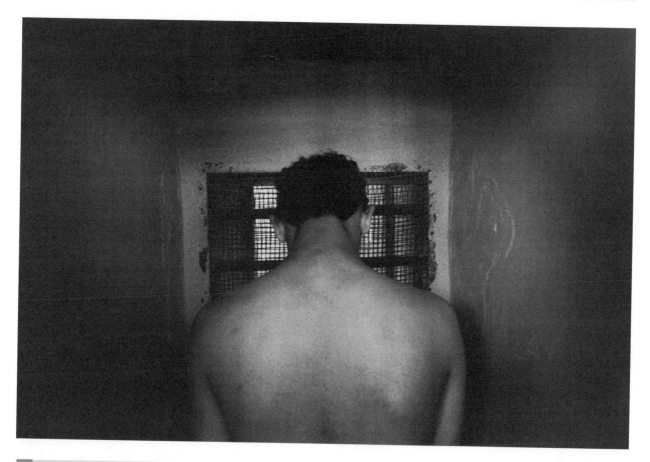

PRIMARY SOURCE

Solitary Confinement: A male prisoner is shown held in solitary confinement in Sinop, Turkey. © VEHBI KOCA / ALAMY

About the Photographer: Vehbi Koca is a photographer who lives in Great Britain. He works in a variety of photographic styles, including fine art and photojournalism. Many of his photos were taken in Turkey and he has dedicated numerous photo essays to Turkish subjects. He holds degrees in photography and visual design from the University of Westminster, Southwark College, and the London College of Printing.

INTRODUCTION

Throughout history, different forms of discipline and imprisonment have been used to enforce laws and support government rule. Prisons are typically divided by degrees of security, depending upon the severity of the crime committed and the perceived threat that prisoners present. Solitary confinement is often used for the most unruly inmates or for those that authorities want to discipline even more harshly. Inmates can be transferred between the various sections of the prison in response to their behavior.

Solitary confinement, in which an inmate is separated from the general prison population, is one of the most difficult conditions to which prisoners can be subjected. They may be allowed out of their cells for as little as one hour a day—or never. As a result of human rights and prisoner advocacy groups' efforts, the strictness of solitary confinement, particularly in Western countries, has lessened considerably. Solitary cells can range from comfortable cells with beds and sunlight to tiny dark enclosures that are designed to inflict mental torture.

The primary criticism of solitary confinement is the psychological damage that it can cause. Inmates subjected to solitary confinement can experience memory loss, hallucinations, and even insanity. These prisoners may also be less likely to acclimate back into society when they are released.

Correctional facilities that use solitary confinement believe that its use as a punishment is necessary to deter bad behavior.

PRIMARY SOURCE

SOLITARY CONFINEMENT

See primary source image.

SIGNIFICANCE

This undated photo was taken in Turkey, a solid trade partner with Europe and the Western world—a regime not known for cruel judicial practices. Yet this picture reveals that this type of treatment is used in Turkey, illustrating that in less progressive parts of the world, the inhumane torture and mistreatment of prisoners goes on, even as other countries pass laws to ban such mistreatment.

Extreme solitary confinement combines physical and emotional discomfort. The inmate is deprived of human contact, a factor that psychologists argue is a major factor in driving people to insanity. Turkish authorities, because of their use of prison cells like this one, have been criticized by human rights organizations for using cruel practices that should not be part of any criminal justice system. Proponents say that while solitary confinement as seen in this photo is uncomfortable and demeaning, it is an effective and necessary form of discipline central to preserving the safety of guards and other inmates. Prison officials also note that placing prisoners in solitary confinement may prevent them from harming themselves.

While solitary confinement is used in prison systems throughout the world, this photo does not necessarily indicate the types of cells used in other systems. While the prisoner here appears to be suffering from physical restraint because of the size of his cell, solitary confinement in other prisons and countries could only indicate that a prisoner is housed separated from the general population, but in more humane and hospitable conditions.

FURTHER RESOURCES

Web sites

Amnesty International. "Amnesty International Urges Turkish Authorities to End Ocalan Solitary Confinement." <http://web.amnesty.org/library/Index/> (accessed February 15, 2006).

American Kurdish Information Network.M "Torture and Prisons in Turkey" <http://kurdistan.org/Prisons/watson.html> (accessed February 15, 2006).

Does the Insanity Defense Have a Legitimate Role?

Magazine article

By: James F. Hooper and Alix M. McLearen

Date: April 2002

Source: Hooper, James F., and Alix M. McLearen. "Does the Insanity Defense Have a Legitimate Role?" *Psychiatric Times* 39 (April 2002). Available online at: <http://www.psychiatrictimes.com>.

About the Author: Dr. James Hooper is a forensic psychiatrist. He is the medical director of the Taylor Hardin Secure Medical Facility and a professor at the University of Alabama. Ms. McLearen was a doctoral candidate in the clinical psychology-law program at University of Alabama when this article was written.

INTRODUCTION

Mental illness can lead to involvement in crime and many individuals in prison have a mental health problem for which they may not be receiving appropriate treatment. The forensic psychiatrist, working within the justice system, has an important role in ensuring that "insanity" on the part of the defendant is correctly identified and assessed. Once judgement has been handed down, consideration must be given to whether prison or a hospital is the most appropriate destination for the accused (if guilty) and what treatment should be given. Only then can the mentally ill individual be properly helped and society protected from further crimes.

Isaac Ray was the founding father of forensic psychiatry in the United States and his book *Treatise on the Medical Jurisprudence of Insanity*, published in 1838, helped to shape the profession. Ray's opinions influenced many judges and he developed treatments for the criminally insane at his hospital in Rhode Island. The use of psychiatry within the criminal justice system increased during the 1960s and 1970s. In the article below, a leading forensic psychiatrist discusses the modern view of the insanity defense and how it arose.

PRIMARY SOURCE

Public perceptions are that the insanity defense occurs far more commonly than records indicate. In fact, the insanity defense is used in less than 1% of criminal proceedings and is successful in approximately one-quarter

Andrea Pia Yates, the Texas mother who confessed to the 2001 bathtub drowning of her five children while she was deeply depressed, listens to opening arguments at her first murder trial in 2002. Convicted of murder and sentenced to life in prison, a new trial was ordered in 2006 based on mistaken testimony given by a psychiatrist in her original trial.
© REUTERS/CORBIS

of those cases. Furthermore, defendants who are found insane spend as much, or more, time in state custody than their criminally convicted counterparts. The media may foster the notion that criminals get away with feigning mental defect, only to be released and recidivate. However, the insanity plea is actually based on a long-standing legal tradition and is rarely successfully completed. In fact, approximately 70% of insanity acquittals result from agreements between opposing attorneys, in which the prosecution agrees that society would be better served by placing the defendant in treatment, rather than in prison (Blum, 1992; Bogenberger et al., 1987; Cirincione, 1996; Rogers et al., 1984; Smith and Hall, 1982).

Outside of assisting in sentencing, there are two places for mental disease in the legal system. The first is a defendant's ability to understand the trial process. Peo-

ple who do not understand the nature of the charges or the functioning of the legal system are considered unfit for trial. More germane to this article, if mental illness had a direct effect on a given criminal act, an individual can be found legally insane.

Harvard Law School professor Sheldon Glueck stated in 1927, "Perhaps in no other field of American law is there so much disagreement as to fundamentals and so many contradictory decisions in the same jurisdictions." The concept of insanity has changed over time and locale, but the basic notion of this defense is that some individuals, by reason of mental condition, are not capable of controlling or understanding their own unlawful behavior. However, the presence of a mental illness or other condition does not automatically predict a successful insanity finding.

A great historical pendulum swings between protective and punitive laws. In the normal course of events, laws slowly evolve to allow more and more efforts to treat those mentally ill offenders who can be safely removed from the prison population. Eventually, a psychotic individual commits a highly publicized crime, usually an assassination, and the lawmakers throw up their hands over "doctors dictating the law" and "getting criminals off the hook."

This happened in England in 1841, when the Prime Minister's secretary was killed by a delusional woodturner from Scotland named Daniel M'Naughten. In this landmark mental health case, the defendant was found not guilty by reason of insanity (NGRI), and the Queen demanded an appellate ruling, resulting in the very strict "M'Naughten Rules" in 1843. These essentially said a person could be found insane if, at the specific time of a crime, they were unable to know the difference between right and wrong. This is known as a "knowledge-only" based test, with no room for uncontrollable impulses.

In the United States, this definition was considered by the courts but was seen as too restrictive. Instead, the American judiciary took a slightly different tack. For example, in *Parsons v Alabama* (1886), the State Supreme Court opined that a person was NGRI if they had lost "free agency" as a result of mental disease. This would allow an insanity defense if a person knew an act was illegal, but could not control their behavior.

Later, the American Law Institute (ALI) promulgated a Model Penal Code that included a two-pronged provision for insanity. Specifically, an individual is "not responsible for criminal conduct if, at the time of such conduct as a result of mental disease or defect he lacks substantial capacity either to appreciate the criminality [wrongfulness] of his conduct or to conform his conduct to the requirements of the law." It is important to note the *or*, allowing either knowledge or impulse to be a basis for insanity. By the 1970s, most states had adopted these rules.

In 1981, President Ronald Reagan was shot by John Hinckley. Hinckley had incorporated scenes from a popular movie (*Taxi Driver*) into his delusional system and was attempting to gain the love of a famous actress (Jodie Foster). He was found NGRI under the impulse control part of the ALI law, which led to hospitalization rather than imprisonment. Immediately, the federal government, and many states, tightened the insanity laws back to those of 1843 England.

CURRENT LEGAL REQUIREMENTS

Currently, the requirements for insanity vary by state. The typical standards require that a person be unable to differentiate between right and wrong at the time of the crime. The inability to appreciate the wrongfulness of conduct must be the direct result of a mental disease or defect. Such defects typically include psychotic disorders, mood disorders and organic conditions such as mental retardation. Virtually no state allows sociopathy to be grounds for an NGRI defense, and voluntary intoxication cannot by itself end culpability. Only a few states still contain the volitional question.

At the federal level, the Supreme Court, in USC Title 18, Chap 1, Sec 17, stated:

> It is an affirmative defense to a prosecution under any Federal statute that, at the time of the commission of the acts constituting the offense, the defendant, as a result of a severe mental disease or defect, was unable to appreciate the nature and quality or the wrongfulness of his acts. Mental disease or defect does not otherwise constitute a defense.

Some states have another legal option aside from insanity: guilty but mentally ill (GBMI). On its face, this seems to be a good idea, as jurors have several options. However, there are two inherent problems. First, juries have two choices that find a person guilty, but only one that finds them innocent, leading away from giving the benefit of doubt to the defendant. Additionally, the GBMI finding assumes that prisons will engage in the same level of treatment as a hospital, so that a defendant can be equally well-served in either setting. A GBMI finding also yields a set sentence, which the person will serve even if completely psychiatrically stabilized. Alternatively, the defendant may have to be released even if they are still ill.

LOOPHOLES AND PITFALLS

The existence of an insanity defense has always been controversial. There have been several attempts to "eliminate the loophole" and thereby force mentally ill individuals into prison. Several state decisions have noted that criminal intent is an absolutely necessary part of any crime. In recent years, some states have redefined their laws to focus more tightly on the mens rea, or guilty mind. Under those laws, a person must, as a result of a mental illness, lack the ability to willingly or knowingly commit an act. This looks at criminal intent, rather than psychiatric diagnoses, therefore claiming an end to criminals getting off free.

Of course, as previously noted, the truth is that there is no evidence to suggest that this defense has ever been widely misused. A minority of states (Montana, Idaho, Utah, Kansas and Nevada) have omitted the insanity defense per se entirely, instead allowing mental state to be raised only as a mitigating factor.

Some people favor the abolition of the insanity defense for reasons unrelated to political gain. They argue that far too often (certainly in our experience) a person who is chronically mentally ill is automatically found NGRI, even when the evidence would not convict them of a crime (Halpern, 1992). In addition, some critics see it as a simple plea bargain that saves time for the lawyers and judges and locks up a possibly innocent person for many years.

We would argue that in the absence of laws to force hospitalization of mentally ill offenders, many would go to prison and be victimized. This goes against all historical and humane thinking that some people truly cannot be held to general standards of conduct because of mental conditions over which they have no control.

BURDEN OF PROOF

Defining the burden of proof presents another issue in the insanity defense. Who has to prove what and how do they prove it? Since the average citizen is presumed to be sane, if they claim insanity, who decides? Does the prosecution have to prove defendants are not insane, or do the people who ask the court to find them not guilty by reason of insanity have to justify themselves? Most states have gone with the latter, but it certainly has not always been that way. In the aftermath of the Hinckley case, many states shifted the burden of proof to the defendant.

There has also been discussion on the amount of proof required. Should insanity be proved only by 51% (e.g., a preponderance of evidence), or does it need a standard of "beyond a reasonable doubt"? Generally, laws give the benefit to the accused and logically would not require more than the preponderance standard. This issue was addressed when, in *State v Coffman* (1864), California was the first jurisdiction to review M'Naughten officially. Soon after, in 1879, the Alabama Supreme Court, in *Boswell v State*, rendered an opinion that we see as holding to the spirit of the original insanity laws and which, in our opinion, reads well:

> Since an unsound mind cannot form a criminal intent, insanity, when proved, is a complete defense, but no defense is more easily simulated, and the evidence must therefore be carefully and considerably scanned. The workings of a diseased mind are so variant that it is difficult to lay down an absolute rule for the government of all cases. Each case must depend, more or less, on its own particular facts. It ought to be proved that at the time he committed the act, he did not consider it a crime against the laws of God and nature. If there is any reasonable doubt as to sanity, the jury should acquit him.

CONCLUDING THOUGHTS

Currently, insanity is a well-established defense in this country. Although efforts to eliminate this way of escaping punishment will continue to generate attention, it is unlikely that our laws will eliminate the essential difference between those who choose to break the law and those who cannot choose.

SIGNIFICANCE

A number of mental conditions can lead to involvement in crime and, in these cases, the perpetrators genuinely may not appreciate that their actions are wrong. People with schizophrenia—especially paranoid schizophrenia—may hear voices that tell them to commit a crime. This was the defense mounted by the Yorkshire Ripper, serial killer Peter Sutcliffe, who murdered thirteen women (several of them prostitutes) in the north of England in the late 1970s. At his trial in 1981, he claimed that the voice of God had told him to cleanse the streets of prostitutes. However, the prosecution argued that Sutcliffe was not mentally ill—but had learned to mimic schizophrenia from his wife, Sonia, who was. A skilled forensic psychiatrist should be able to tell when someone is feigning mental illness in this way, but, of course, the expert witnesses for prosecution and defense may disagree on the diagnosis.

There have been several well-publicized cases in which people with schizophrenia have been released from jail and have committed additional violent crimes. This is especially likely when they stop taking medication or escape regular medical supervision. Although a schizophrenic in the grip of delusions can kill and be judged legally insane, the vast majority of people with this mental illness are harmless. They are far more likely to hurt themselves than anyone else. There are also effective treatment programs, mainly medication-based, for schizophrenics.

More rarely, an individual with a dissociative identity disorder will commit a crime they are genuinely unaware of. A number of different personalities can co-exist within the mind of a single person and one can "act out" without there being any awareness of his or her behavior on the part of the other personalities. These are difficult cases, but treatment can, eventually, integrate the personalities and restore the individual to mental health.

Perhaps the most difficult dilemma is posed by the perpetrator with anti-social personality disorder (ASP, also known as psychopathy). A significant proportion of all crime is committed by individuals with ASP because one of the hallmarks of this condition is an inability to feel guilt or remorse. Brain imaging and physiological studies have shown that ASP is also linked to a lower than usual level of arousal, so individuals may be able to commit crimes of violence without the feelings of revulsion that most people would feel. However, there is still debate over whether the person with ASP is "mad" or "bad"; there also is no successful treatment for the condition at the present time. Therefore, many people with ASP end up in prison and, once released, go on to commit more crimes.

Another increasingly important issue is the role of drugs and alcohol in crime. Both prescription and illegal drugs can affect memory and behavior. Some claim that fluoxetine—the antidepressant Prozac—can trigger violent behavior, and the role of alcohol in releasing aggression is well known. Many suspects who were "high" on cocaine claim to have no memory of committing a crime. The forensic psychiatrist must assess whether substance or alcohol abuse rendered the person legally "insane" at the time of the crime.

The psychiatric examination consists of formal questioning, medical tests such as magnetic resonance imaging, blood tests and X-rays to assess any brain damage, neuropsychology tests, and the assessment of medical records. The psychiatrist will judge the defendant's state of mind at the time of the crime and at the time of the trial to see if he or she is competent to understand the proceedings. Mentally ill offenders are not usually detained for life and, perhaps, the most difficult role of the psychiatrist is to assess if and when they are no longer a danger to the public. Premature release, especially without supervision, can put innocent people at risk. Excessive detention, however, is an affront to the liberty of the individual, if he or she has served his or her sentence.

FURTHER RESOURCES

Books

James, Stuart H., and Jon J. Nordy, eds. *Forensic Science: An Introduction to Scientific and Investigative Techniques.* Boca Raton, Fla.: CRC Press, 2003.

Web sites

Hooper, James F. "Landmark Cases." <http://smith.soehd.csufresno.edu/landmark.html> (accessed January 19, 2005).

Nuts to Whom?

The Insanity Defense Is Crazy

Internet article

By: Dirk Olin

Date: November 18, 2003

Source: Olin, Dirk. "Nuts to Whom? The Insanity Defense Is Crazy." *Slate*, November 18, 2003. <http://www.slate.com/id/2091364/> (accessed January 7, 2006).

About the Author: Dirk Olin is the national editor of *National Lawyer* magazine. He contributed this piece to *Slate*, an online news and entertainment magazine owned by the Washington Post Co. *Slate* receives over one million visitors each month.

INTRODUCTION

Over a three-week period in October 2002, the population of Washington, D.C., Maryland, and Virginia was terrorized by a spate of random shootings that claimed the lives of ten individuals and wounded three more. The killer, known as the Washington Sniper, shot, apparently at random, through a hole in the trunk of an ordinary family sedan using a telescopic rifle. At one of the crime scenes, a Tarot card was found, bearing the legend "Dear Mr. Policeman, I am God," and at another crime scene a letter was found stating "Your children are not safe anywhere at any time." The Washington Sniper also demanded ten million dollars from the U.S. government to stop the killings.

After many false leads, the Washington sniper was identified as a team of two people—forty-two-year-old John Allen Muhammad and seventeen-year-old Lee Boyd Malvo. At his trial, Malvo's lawyers claimed that their client was "not guilty by reason of insanity." The article below presents the weaknesses of such a defense and explains how it does a disservice to all concerned, not least the defendant.

■ PRIMARY SOURCE

Does Malvo's defense make sense? The jury in the trial of accused D.C.-area sniper John A. Muhammad has returned multiple guilty verdicts. The trial of his alleged accomplice, teenager Lee Malvo, is now under way. The prosecution of the first case is essentially the defense in the second: that Malvo was merely following the demented orders of his father figure, Muhammad. To get that defense before the jury, Malvo is pleading not guilty by reason of insanity.

The very notion of a teenager crouched in the trunk of a car assassinating people willy-nilly does seem crazed on its face. But Malvo's courtroom tack has provoked the predictable outrage engendered by every attempt at the insanity plea (with Dennis Miller's adolescent blather leading the pack.)

Invocations of the insanity defense often pique the public because of a widespread misperception that the plea offers an opportunity to get away with murder. Such fears are almost completely groundless. Yet they've already led to the intellectually dishonest construct of "guilty but insane" pleas passed by legislatures in a number of states. These hybrid pleas promote a beguiling oversimplification of how society should apportion blame. Bright lines are often unavoidable in the law, but the precision of modern psychiatry demands that we stop asking juries to make medical determinations of insanity once and for all.

Malvo's plea is closer to that of Patty Hearst, the heiress kidnapped in the 1970s who took up bank robbery with her captors, than that of Jeffrey Dahmer, the cannibalistic mass murderer, or that of Andrea Yates, the postpartum depressive who drowned her five kids. Like Hearst, Malvo claims he was brainwashed, in his case by the older Muhammad. Juries typically put more stock in the concept of brainwashing than do members of the psychiatric field. Still, the jurors might prove tough to persuade in this case, if only because polls have shown that verdicts are more conditioned by jurors' visceral fear of the defendant than by their understanding of insanity's legal contours. And there's no question that Malvo's said some chilling stuff when interrogated about his part in the killing spree. So, Malvo now faces a two-part challenge: First, prove he was programmed into this serial monstrosity; second, evoke the jury's pity, or at least neutralize its terror of him.

The woolly-headed denunciations of the insanity defense are actually far more common than their invocation by criminal defendants. A reputable study funded by the National Institute of Mental Health in the early 1990s found this defense used in less than 1 percent of a representative sampling, with only one-quarter of those pleas argued successfully. (Hearst, Dahmer, Yates, and even the Unabomber all failed with their insanity pleas, for example.) And even when such pleas do work, they almost never amount to a "get out of jail free" card. Studies show that an insanity pleader's average stay in a mental institution exceeds the average sentence served by those criminally convicted.

Prior to the 19th century, guilt was more frequently judged according to causation than intent. If your cart ran over my foot, it didn't matter whether you meant to do it or not. You were adjudged blameworthy. As an appreciation of criminal motivation took hold, however, a door was opened to a greater variety of defenses. In 1843, the modern insanity defense was born after a Scottish psycho named Daniel M'Naughton tried to shoot British Prime Minister Sir Robert Peel, killing his secretary instead. A jury was persuaded by the testimony of various psychiatrists who said M'Naughton was delusional. The next year, a panel of judges created the standard that's been largely used in America ever since—that a defendant is not guilty if he or she didn't know what they were doing or didn't know it was wrong. (Competence to stand trial is weighed separately, because the defendant's mental state may have changed one way or the other since commission of the offense.)

Seems fair. But after John Hinckley was acquitted by reason of insanity in 1982—because he had shot President Reagan in an effort to impress actress Jodie Foster (a motivation that Dennis Miller would no doubt find squarely within the bounds of sanity), various lawmakers started twitching. Reactionaries essentially equated insanity pleas with Twinkie defenses, and they wanted their constituents to know they weren't going to stand for any mollycoddling of criminals. So, many states passed statutes that created pleas of "guilty but mentally ill." Under such systems the deranged, if deemed guilty, are incarcerated in prisons with "sane" inmates (though they may be accorded special pharmaceutical arrangements). Failing to differentiate these populations is like treating all illnesses with a blanket quarantine. Whether any cures are possible is still an open question, of course, but one we're much less likely to answer via unvariegated warehousing.

It was society's previous failure to think through this issue that made the system susceptible to such ineffectual changes. The "guilty but mentally ill" plea represents an ill-advised lurch toward a standard that feels both righteous and firm. But out of an understandable desire to heighten accountability came a logical absurdity: You're guilty—but you're not. You are sick and thus not wholly accountable, yet you are treated exactly the same as the guilty. The mutual contradiction inherent in such a construct takes the "oxy" out of oxymoronic.

Do the semantics of all this really matter for purposes of our criminal justice system? If the goal is to protect us against violent perps, does it make a difference whether we call them nuts or no-good? It might. A recent study by Human Rights Watch concluded that as many as one in five of the 2.1 million Americans in jail and prison are seriously mentally ill. That's roughly five times the number of people in mental hospitals. The far-ranging lack of appropriate therapy can hardly be reducing recidivism, and it certainly carries no deterrence for mentally ill criminals. It also fails to meet the retributive goal of reserving punishment for the guilty.

One modest solution? The system should separate medical diagnoses from legal judgments. We should employ disinterested experts—appointed by the court, rather than hired by otherwise appropriately adversarial players—to address such questions empirically, as opposed to strategically. Insanity has historically been a legal, not medical, term. Junk it. If a defendant claims mental illness, better to let a panel of psychiatric professionals parse the severity of any condition than leave it to the vicissitudes of a jury. (Defendants need not waive right to trial: If they are determined to be sane, the fact-finding would go forward; if not, they could reach a plea deal based on the medical panel's finding.)

Sniper suspect Lee Malvo, center, being escorted by Fairfax County Sheriffs out of Fairfax County juvenile court in Virginia, on November 15, 2002. In December 2003 Malvo was sentenced to life in prison for his part in the random killings that terrorized the Washington, D.C. area in the autumn of 2002. © BRENDAN MCDERMID/REUTERS/CORBIS

Juries are impaneled to try facts. Judges are responsible for interpreting the law. A jury shouldn't diagnose Lee Malvo's maladies (or lack thereof), any more than it should rule on evidentiary admissibility or perform tonsillectomies. If we lock up violent offenders without understanding why they did what they did, we vitiate the meaning of retribution, which society demands. We also mitigate the possibility of rehabilitation, which basic humanism requires. We can, of course, choose to continue ignoring this problem, locking up more and more insane defendants while treating them less and less. But that way madness lies.

SIGNIFICANCE

John Allen Muhammad was sentenced to death for his part in the Washington Sniper murders; Lee Malvo was sentenced to life in prison without parole. In Malvo's case, the use of the insanity defense was novel, since Malvo was not suffering from any obvious mental illness, such as schizophrenia. But this defense allowed the presentation of otherwise inadmissible evidence concerning Malvo's childhood and his relationship with Muhammad with the aim, many legal experts believe, of stirring the sympathy of the jury. Malvo was born in Jamaica and his early years were dominated by poverty and uncertainty. His parents, who never married, separated and from that time Malvo rarely saw his father. He met Muhammad in Antigua, having moved there with his mother when he was fourteen and the two became very close. According to Malvo's mother, Una James, speaking publicly for the first time in 2003, her son saw Muhammad as the father figure he had sought all his life.

Malvo's lawyers argued that the boy was so much under Muhammad's influence that he was, in effect, indoctrinated, which counted as a form of insanity. Malvo was, they said, unable to distinguish right from wrong—a crucial point—and so was not fully responsible for his part in the killings. Punishment would not, therefore, be reasonable or appropriate. However, as the prosecutor argued, indoctrination is not listed by the American Psychiatric Association Manual as a mental illness.

In jail, prior to the trial, Malvo met with psychiatrists several times. They looked at drawings and writings containing allusions to the Muslim faith, references to the 1999 science fiction movie *The Matrix* (where the hero shoots his way out of a virtual, computer-generated world), and lyrics from the songs of Jamaican musician Bob Marley. Whether these were truly signs of mental illness or just the aggressive imagery of a confused adolescent was open to debate.

In the end, the jury was more convinced by the prosecutor's argument that Malvo should share responsibility for the killings with Muhammad. Malvo's prints were on the gun used in the crimes and he had bragged of his role in the attacks, even claiming it was he—not Muhammad—who had carried out all the shootings. He also said to a detective "I intended to kill them all," and bragged that he and Muhammad could have continued killing, despite the massive manhunt mounted by the police and the FBI.

Under the law of the state of Virginia (where the case was tried), Malvo also could have been sentenced to death for the Washington-area murders, even though he was a juvenile at the time he committed the crimes. His age was probably a factor in his receiving, instead, a sentence of life imprisonment. It was his age, too, which the defense used to support the "not guilty by reason of insanity" defense—younger people, presumably, are more prone to indoctrination. However, the jury chose to use the age factor to spare Malvo's life rather than absolve him from guilt for his crimes.

FURTHER RESOURCES

Books

Sutherland, John, and Diane Canwell. *True Crime*. London: Flame Tree, 2003.

Web sites

BBC News. "Profile: Lee Boyd Malvo." <http://news.bbc.co.uk/1/hi/world/americas/3178504.stm> (accessed January 7, 2006).

How Maximum Security Jails Make the Baddest of Men Even Worse

Internet article

By: Bernie Mathews

Date: November 05, 2003

Source: *ON LINE opinion: Australia's e-journal of social and political debate*. "How maximum-security jails make the baddest of men even worse." <http://www.onlineopinion.com.au/view.asp?article=842> (March 02, 2006).

About the Author: Prior to his current work as a journalist, Bernie Mathews served time in correctional facilities in Australia, for the crimes of burglary and absconding from a jail.

INTRODUCTION

The correctional classification system, by which prisoners are placed into security and housing levels, is based on a number of factors such as nature and severity of offense, assessed level of dangerousness, length of sentence to be served, number and status of previous convictions, substance abuse and treatment history, mental health history, security threat group status (gang membership), ability to co-exist with other inmates in a particular housing unit, protective custody status, nature of crime as perceived by other inmates (persons convicted of certain types of crimes, such as child abuse, rape, and domestic violence are often subjected to harsh treatment in general population settings), gender issues such as obvious femininity in a man or transgender issues for either sex, and other individual considerations. Each inmate, in most settings, is assigned a specific number of points based on their offender status, which determines their basic security classification status. This, coupled with the other listed issues, will determine placement within the security level system of the facility.

Although each state and federal facility has its own particular classification scheme, most fall between four and six levels. In a four-level classification system, inmates can be placed according to security risk: minimum security (Level I), medium security (Level III), close security (Level IV), or maximum security (Level V). A six level system adds minimum restrict (Level II) between minimum and medium, and super maximum (Level VI) or administrative segregation beyond maximum security.

Minimum security inmates can exist in a general population setting. They are considered low risk for violence or for absconding (escape). They often are taken in groups to work sites, and have the ability to walk about the facility freely during the day. There is generally a fairly high inmate to staff ratio. Level II conditions are similar, and the primary distinction is that these inmates typically do not leave the facility for school or work assignments as individuals. They move in groups, with a low inmate to security staff ratio, and are employed in settings such as road crews, highway maintenance, etc. where they wear brightly colored uniforms and work with armed guards nearby. Medium security inmates do not leave the facility for work assignments. These three security levels all exist in general population settings, with dormitory style housing, and communal showers, toilets, and sinks. They are allowed to participate in communal activities for work, education, meals, and socialization. The facility is contained and locked, with armed patrols at the perimeter, as well as central and local security stations. Dormitories are locked at night. They have access to the telephone and to visits. Visits may be contact or non-contact type visits.

Close security inmates have individual cells, in which they are locked at night. They may participate in congregate education, work, and some activities. Meals may be taken in their cells, or in small groups. They have individual sinks and toilets in their cells. They use individual showers on their cell blocks. They generally do not engage in communal activities, and do not have contact with the general prison population. They are likely to spend most of their time in the cell block, and to recreate in very small groups, segregated from other prisoners.

Maximum and super-maximum security inmates are confined to their individual cells for twenty-three hours per day. They may engage in group activities through the use of individual locked cages placed in close proximity, or by being shackled to stationary rings in the floor. They eat their meals within their cells, and food is given to them by means of a tray passed through a food port. Educational programming is accomplished by means of individual study. Visits and telephone calls are restricted, no contact is allowed. They are taken individually to recreation cages. When moved from their cells, they are manacled and shackled, and wear wrist and ankle cuffs, as well as chains around their abdomen. They are strip-searched and put through a scanning procedure similar to full-body X ray each time they exit their cells, in order to make certain that they do not pose a security threat. Maximum security inmates may earn privileges concerning work outside their cells, small group meals, and small group educational programming, depending on the regulations of the particular facility.

PRIMARY SOURCE

I heard voices from the Gatehouse. The clicking of handcuff ratchets. The noise heralded the arrival of the transfer escort. I looked around my cell for the last time. Two coir mats stood at attention against the back wall. My bed since the summer of '71 after I was transferred to Grafton as an intractable prisoner.

Plastic containers for jam and salt nestled in their allocated positions on the timber log I used for a table. Spartan conditions made every item special. Each had

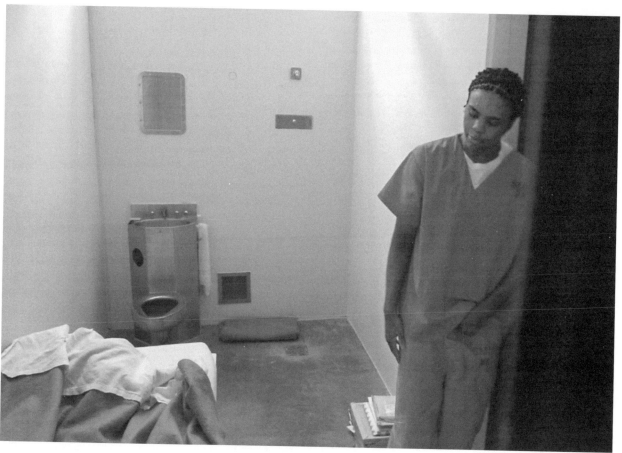

Prisoner Anthony Hall stands inside of his cell at the Supermax security prison in Boscobel, Wisconsin, September 25, 2001. Like other supermax prisoners, Hall is confined to his room for 23 hours a day and has little or no contact with other prisoners. AP IMAGES

their very own place in the regimented confines of the cell. Even the toilet paper and library books had significant places. I tried to remember how many times I copped a serve for having one item out of the designated place before I learned the routine—countless times. Grafton floggings were routine and didn't require a reason. Everything at Grafton was routine. A mindless never-ending routine of isolation and solitary confinement that was punctuated by a screw's baton, boot or a fist. The prison system called it "rehabilitation."

My thoughts drifted back to '72 when Apps forgot about the two cigarette butts he left in his shirt pocket. Contraband. The Breed, Footballer and Brown "rehabilitated" him by baton-whipping him unconscious before dragging his bloodied body into the solitary-confinement cell to recuperate. Not to be left out, The White Alsatian "rehabilitated" Mitchell for having a button undone.

It seemed strange that on the eve of my departure from Grafton the memory of previous floggings were rekindled. The two things synonymous with HM Grafton Jail were solitary confinement and institutionalised brutality. If any benefit can be derived from solitary confinement it is the fact that memories never fade.

Memories of solitary confinement inside a brutalising prison system never faded for James Richard Finch or John Andrew Stuart. Both men endured the rehabilitation concept that was Grafton Jail during the 1960s. Queensland suffered the consequences of that incarceration concept when Brisbane's Whisky Au-Go-Go nightclub was firebombed in March 1973. Stuart and Finch were convicted of the firebombing and the subsequent deaths of 15 people. It is simplistic to suggest that Grafton propelled Stuart and Finch into a life of crime that culminated with the deaths of 15 people but an incarceration process that moulds destinies steeped in violence and solitary confinement must share proportionate blame if the following case histories are indicative of what isolation and solitary confinement does produce.

Stan Taylor was a product of H Division inside Pentridge during the 1970s where solitary confinement was a blissful respite from the mindless and institutionalised brutality meted out by prison guards. Taylor was eventually released from prison only to end his criminal career with the 1986 car-bomb attack on Russell Street Police Headquarters in Melbourne where a young police constable was blown to pieces. Taylor was convicted with two other men for the Russell Street bombing and is currently serving a life sentence.

While Taylor was incarcerated in H Division another young prisoner was introduced to the rehabilitative qualities of isolation by solitary confinement. After ten years, Christopher Dale Flannery was released from prison to earn a reputation as Australia's first contract killer with over a dozen murders to his credit. Flannery disappeared during the 1985 Sydney underworld gang wars. He is presumed dead.

Solitary confinement and the Grafton rehabilitation concept were significant factors in the life of Kevin Crump who teamed up with Alan Baker after his release from prison in 1973. The pair kidnapped a pregnant Colarenabri grazier's wife and took her into Queensland where they raped and butchered her at Goondiwindi. After they were captured at Maitland the pair were charged with conspiracy to murder under NSW law. Details of the atrocities committed on the victim before her death, although never made public, prompted Mr. Justice Taylor to recommend the pair never be released from prison after he sentenced them to life imprisonment.

Archie McCafferty was a non-violent offender who traveled the well-worn paths of the NSW juvenile/justice system during the 1960s before he was sent to Grafton for "rehabilitation" during 1970. McCafferty was released from prison in 1971 and barely one year later he became Australia's answer to Charlie Manson with a spate of thrill killings throughout NSW. McCafferty was sentenced to three consecutive terms of life imprisonment and served twenty-three years before he was deported to Scotland in May 1997.

Peter Schneidas was another non-violent offender prior to the Grafton rehabilitation process. Originally imprisoned for fraud, Schneidas was transferred to Grafton in 1975. Four years later he attacked Long Bay prison guard, John Mewburn, and pulverised his head with hammer. Mewburn died from his injuries and Schneidas was sentenced to life imprisonment. Schneidas was isolated in solitary confinement within the NSW prison system for the next ten years and died eight months after his 1997 release from a heroin overdose after becoming addicted in prison.

Although the incarceration concepts of H Division and Grafton have been dismantled and roundly condemned during Royal Commissions and public inquiries the products of those places are still being convicted for what some consider to be the worst violent crimes ever committed in this country.

The NSW and Victorian prison systems have already travelled the retributive road to the community's detriment. Will history continue to repeat itself in Queensland? If the October 27, 2003 edition of Australian Story on ABC television is any gauge then Queensland is already destined to suffer the consequences of an incarceration process that makes bad men badder and mad men madder.

Australian Story depicted the isolation, solitary confinement and sensory deprivation of Postcard Bandit, Brenden James Abbott, inside Queensland's Maximum Security Units. The incarceration process of solitary confinement in a jail within a jail is indicative of the hate factories created by places like Grafton, H Division, Katingal Special Security Unit and Jika Jika. Punishment blocks that became counter productive to the society they were supposed to serve until they were dismantled by the NSW and Victorian governments.

Queensland legislators have ignored those failings and opted to adopt hard-line incarceration policies similar to the ones imposed upon Brenden Abbott after he escaped the Sir David Longland Correctional Centre in November 1997 but are those policies beneficial to the general community and future generations of Queenslanders?

The observations of a 20th century troglodyte who lived life as a successful failure on the prison yards of NSW and Queensland would suggest not. I idly ponder who will be the Stuart, Finch, Taylor, Flannery, Crump, McCafferty or Schneidas of Queensland's tomorrow if the current Queensland incarceration process of solitary confinement by sensory deprivation persists.

SIGNIFICANCE

The realities of solitary confinement vary according to the circumstances under which it occurs, as well as the location of the correctional facility (there are considerable differences from state to state, as well as between security levels). When it is used as a disciplinary measure, the inmate who committed some sort of major infraction is generally searched, and either put into a single confinement cell, or returned to his cell. Inmates who are on disciplinary segregation generally have no television privileges, are allowed no reading materials, do not go to recreation outside their cells, and are not given a mattress and bedding except for a specified period during the night. The period of disciplinary segregation is determined by the nature and severity of the offense or infraction, but is designed to be time-limited.

Inmates who are in administrative segregation housing (Levels V and VI) can sometimes work their way back to lower security levels, depending on their behavior and progress through educational and institutional programming. Some inmates, particularly those who are in protective custody, will serve their entire sentences within the same level (usually maximum or super-maximum). Prisoners in administrative segregation housing live in cells that are typically from seven to ten feet by ten to twelve feet in size. The bed is a bunk welded to the floor. The table and chair are similarly fastened. The toilet is usually steel, as is the sink. The mirror is usually polished metal. The lights in the room are typically covered by fine wire mesh. The inmate generally cannot operate the lights from within the room. The cell is closed and locked electronically. There may be a narrow window in the door and the wall, with mesh-covered glass. The window will be narrow enough that the slenderest human could not get through it.

In some facilities, the inmates are allowed a specific number of certain types of books, minimal amounts of writing paper, envelopes, and safety pens (pens that are not easily turned into weapons), and controlled access to television (generally located within the cell), with restricted hours of viewing, and access to limited stations. Many facilities use television as a means of delivering educational programming. Inmates are allotted toilet paper in limited quantities, and safety razors are kept outside of the cells (to be utilized only in the shower). Sometimes inmates can purchase other writing or drawing materials. They are generally allowed to purchase some personal hygiene items (lotions, shampoo, etc.) and a small range of snacks from the commissary. They have a restricted number of clothing items that can be purchased and kept in the cell (sweats, different types of socks or additional underwear, sometimes they may be permitted to purchase watch caps, and they may be able to purchase specific types of sneakers, depending upon the rules of the facility). They see other inmates only when they are outside in recreation cages. They generally have access to mental health professionals, and can be brought from their cells for individual therapy sessions (with a guard posted outside the office door).

There is considerable social isolation inherent in this type of confinement; inmates readily admit that it is difficult for them to function in society after spending significant time without human contact. Reports of increased mental health issues as well as lasting effects from prolonged periods of social isolation and limited sensory stimulation have led to several class action lawsuits, some of which have been settled or adjudicated in favor of the inmates. Inmates who develop psychiatric or psychological difficulties, or those with pre-existing conditions that have worsened, and are unable to function within the conditions of confinement are generally moved to special housing units and given wider access to a therapeutic environment.

Although there are rules and laws protecting against abuse of prisoners, the conditions are unequivocally harsh in maximum and super-maximum facilities. Inmates are subjected to unexpected cell searches, their mail is read and censored before it is given to them (with the exception of legal mail), they are searched every time they exit and enter their cells, they move about in heavy shackles and chains that are said to be both uncomfortable and highly restrictive, they have extremely limited contact with the outside world, and minimal sensory or intellectual stimulation. Some sociologists argue that this level of confinement is far more punitive than rehabilitative in intent, although it is widely regarded within the judicial system and the correctional community as a strong incentive for inmates to improve and control their behavior, leading them to work their way to a less restrictive setting. It is also considered a relatively cost-effective way to house multiple high-risk (for violence, for flight, for gang activity, and the like) offenders within the same facility.

There is ongoing research concerned with the short- and long-term effects of solitary confinement. Because there is an institutional culture among prisoners that discourages interaction with mental health staff, it is not always easy to determine the extent to which inmates are actually experiencing symptoms as a result of the conditions of their confinement. There is data suggesting that high security inmates are more likely to report symptoms consistent with anxiety, depression, agitation, and other mood disorders than are lower security inmates. It is difficult, however, to determine whether the inmates who exhibit conduct that leads to high security placements might already have had behavioral health issues (perhaps contributing to the negative behaviors), or whether the symptoms are elicited by the environment and an innate predisposition to develop them. To a significant extent, the ability of an individual inmate to tolerate long term administrative segregation depends upon personal characteristics, coping style, social support system, beliefs about the nature and intent of the individual's level of confinement, previous exposure to similar conditions, mental health status, and physical condition/physical health, as well as length of confinement.

FURTHER RESOURCES

Books

Kupers, Terry. *Prison Madness: The Mental Health Crisis Behind Bars and What We Must Do About It*. San Francisco, California: Jossey-Bass, 1999.

Lozoff, Bo. *We're All Doing Time*. Durham, North Carolina: Human Kindness Foundation, 1998.

Rhodes, Lorna. *Total Confinement: Madness and Reason in the Maximum Security Prison*. Berkeley, California: University of California Press, 2004.

Web sites

CNN.com. "Trend toward solitary confinement worries experts." <http://www.cnn.com/US/9801/09/solitary.confinement/> (accessed March 12, 2006).

Third World Traveler. "Supermax prisons: high-tech dungeons and modern-day torture." <http://www.thirdworldtraveler.com/Prison_System/Supermax_Prisons.html> (accessed March 12, 2006).

1,000 Boston Church Abuse Victims

Internet article

By: Anonymous

Date: July 23, 2003

Source: *CBS News/Associated Press*. "1,000 Boston Church Abuse Victims." <http://www.cbsnews.com/stories/2003/07/21/national/main564121.shtml> (accessed: March 2, 2006).

About the Author: This article was written by an Associated Press writer and published on the CBS News Web site. The Columbia Broadcasting System (CBS) was founded in 1927 as a radio network. It later came to incorporate television channels, magazines, and publishing divisions under its name. Like most broadcast organizations, CBS set up an Internet service in the 1990s. The source is syndicated from the Associated Press, the world's largest newsgathering agency.

INTRODUCTION

The latter years of Pope John Paul II's papacy (1978–2005) were consumed by global allegations of institutional child abuse within the Catholic Church. Most high-profile in Canada, the Republic of Ireland, and the United States, the well-publicized charges took on a similar complexion wherever they were made: that Catholic clergy (and in some cases laymen) had sexually and physically abused children in their care; and in some instances Bishops and other senior clergy had been aware of abuse and deliberately covered up the crimes, or given primacy to Canon law over the secular criminal justice system. Throughout the late 1990s and early twenty-first century, hundreds of lawsuits were filed against Catholic dioceses worldwide. Although not all stood up before a court of law, the political and financial implications for the Catholic Church were devastating, with a number of bishops forced to resign and several dioceses left facing bankruptcy.

In the United States, where the scandal would have its most devastating impact, more than two hundred of its 46,000 priests were forced to resign or removed from their ministries within six months of the revelations of sexual misconduct emerging in the press in 2002. In May of that year, Pope John Paul II summoned America's twelve Cardinals to the Vatican to discuss the matter. The meeting was unprecedented but seemed to produce no new policy, despite Pope John Paul deploring sexual abuse.

It was the revelations from the diocese of Boston that were most damaging, however. Cardinal Bernard Law's way of resolving the issue of disgraced priests had essentially been to merely move them to other parishes (although he later claimed that he sought the advice of psychiatrists, clinicians, and therapists before deciding whether a priest accused of sexually abusing a child should be returned to the pulpit). Like many of his contemporaries, he viewed such behavior as an internal disciplinary matter and not one for the secular authorities. Law was found to have systematically failed to alert civil authorities or parishioners. As a result, many of the priests guilty of sexual abuse simply reoffended.

Revelations about Cardinal Law's inaction resulted in his resignation as Boston's Archbishop in December 2002. For many victims, however, this was not enough and there was a widespread belief that he should be prosecuted for criminal negligence. Although he was subpoenaed in the subsequent investigation by the Massachusetts Attorney General, criminal charges were not made against him because of a lack of evidence. Law was later appointed to an administrative role within the Vatican and remains one of the Catholic church's most senior Cardinals.

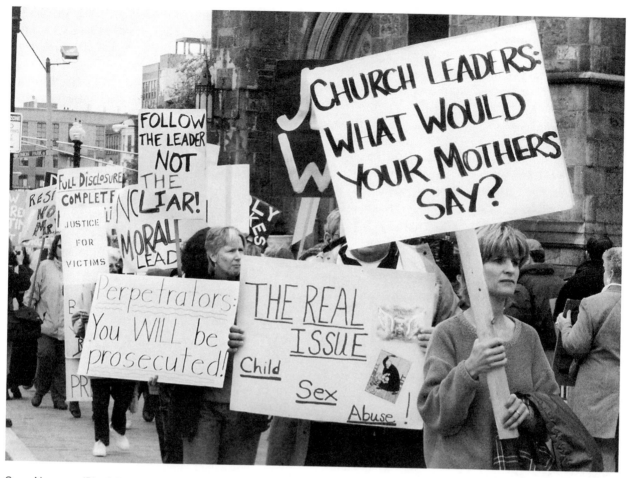

Suzy Nauman (R) of Arlington, Massachusetts, leads protesters demonstrating against child sex abuse in the Boston Archdiocese outside Cardinal Bernard Law's Sunday Mass at the Cathedral of the Holy Cross in Boston, on Mother's Day, 2002. © REUTERS/CORBIS

PRIMARY SOURCE

(CBS/AP)—Clergy members and others in the Boston Archdiocese likely sexually abused more than 1,000 people over a period of six decades, Massachusetts' attorney general said Wednesday, calling the scandal so massive it "borders on the unbelievable."

The report, the result of a grand jury investigation that explored whether church hierarchy should be charged criminally for turning a blind eye to allegations of abuse, said the archdiocese received complaints from 789 alleged victims, involving more than 250 clergy and other workers.

However, when other sources are considered, the attorney general said, the abuse likely affected more than 1,000 victims from 1940 until today.

Cardinal Bernard Law, who resigned as archbishop last December, "bears the ultimate responsibility for the tragic treatment of children that occurred during his tenure," Attorney General Tom Reilly said in the 91-page report.

"But by no means does he bear sole responsibility. With rare exception, none of his senior managers advised him to take any of the steps that might have ended the systemic abuse of children."

The sheer number of abuse allegations documented by investigators in Boston appears unprecedented, even amid a scandal that has touched dioceses in virtually every state and has prompted about 1,000 people to come forward with new allegations nationwide in the last year.

"The mistreatment of children was so massive and so prolonged that it borders on the unbelievable," Reilly said in his cover letter to the report.

Despite the attorney general's scathing remarks about what he called an "institutional acceptance of abuse," no charges are to be filed because child-protection laws in place while abuses were taking place were too weak.

Word had leaked out earlier in the week that church officials were unlikely to be charged, prompting a protest by alleged victims at Reilly's Boston office on Tuesday.

"How dare there be no indictments," said Kathleen Dwyer, 58, who said she was sexually abused by a priest at her church in Braintree in the early 1950s, when she was 7 years old. She was among two dozen protesters who demonstrated outside the attorney general's office.

One protester carried a sign that read, "They let children be raped. Their punishment: NOTHING."

The investigation did not uncover any evidence of recent or ongoing sexual abuse of children. But Reilly said the investigation didn't find any information that would explain the drop-off in recent complaints.

"Given the magnitude of mistreatment and the fact that the archdiocese's response over the past 18 months remains inadequate, it is far too soon to conclude that the abuse has, in fact, stopped or could not reoccur in the future."

The report is the culmination of a 16-month investigation into how church leaders handled the scandal.

"They chose to protect the image and reputation of their institution rather than the safety and well-being of the children entrusted to their care. They acted with a misguided devotion to secrecy," the report says in its conclusion. "And they failed to break their code of silence even when the magnitude of what had occurred would have alerted any reasonable, responsible manager that help was needed."

Law resigned in December after nearly a year of criticism over his role in allowing abusive priests to remain in parish work.

In addition to Law, at least eight other top officials in the Boston Archdiocese were subpoenaed to answer questions about their handling of complaints against priests, including the Rev. Thomas V. Daily, now a bishop in New York City; the Rev. Robert J. Banks, now bishop in Green Bay, Wis.; and the Rev. John B. McCormack, now bishop in Manchester, N.H.

Public outrage over the scandal prompted the state to enact a law making reckless endangerment of children a crime. Under the law, someone who fails to take steps to alleviate a substantial risk of injury or sexual abuse of a child can face criminal charges.

But during the time period when much of the abuse took place—from the 1950s through the 1990s—no such laws were on the books, and Reilly has said that prevented him from prosecuting church supervisors.

Attorney Roderick MacLeish Jr., who represents more than 200 alleged abuse victims in lawsuits against the archdiocese, said he understands why Reilly concluded his hands were tied.

"The attorney general has to act within the law, and as disappointed as I am, I truly believe he has tried to do his best. The worst thing for victims would be for him to prosecute someone and have that prosecution fail," he said.

The archdiocese is facing about 500 civil suits from alleged victims of clergy sex abuse. Church officials have repeatedly said they remain committed to working toward an out-of-court settlement.

A state law passed last year adds members of the clergy to a list of professionals required to inform state officials of suspected child abuse.

SIGNIFICANCE

At the root of the global child abuse scandal was a conflict between canonical and civil law. Bishops and cardinals aware of sexual abuse occurring within the Catholic church had repeatedly used their own authority within the church's infrastructure to apply justice, rather than referring the matter to the police. Worse still, their own brand of justice was proven time and again to be ineffective and culprits repeatedly reoffended. At the same time there was a lack of clear guidance from the Vatican, meaning that bishops dealt with miscreant priests in an ad hoc and inconsistent manner. All this combined to give the impression of an institutional cover-up.

The number of offenders, as the Catholic Church frequently pointed out, was relatively small. But they still had an enormous effect. The contrast between the crimes and the sacred calling of the Church made the abuse seem even more heinous. The individual and isolated cases of abuse developed into an institutional scandal due to the perception that senior clergy often acted more out of a desire to hush up the abuse than to end it, for instance by using internal Church discipline rather than involving the secular authorities.

A report by the Catholic League for Religious and Civil Rights in February 2004 attempted to place the sexual abuse into context. By its own admission it did not seek to "exculpate anyone," but it wished to provide "baseline data" so that "meaningful conversation" could take place on the issue. It quoted research by the *Washington Post* and the *New York Times* that found (respectively) that only 1.5 percent and 1.8 percent of priests ordained between 1950 and 2001 had been *accused* of sexual abuse. It suggested that this compared favorably with Protestant clergy, where the figure ranged between two and three percent, and other professions, such as teaching.

The revelations were nevertheless serious and widespread enough to warrant a number of multi-million dollar lawsuits. The Catholic Church in Boston alone paid out some $85 million to settle the claims of 552 litigants in September 2003. Although the claim was partly paid by insurers, the diocese was still responsible for a large portion of the liabilities. In order to pay these claims, the diocese closed churches and sold parcels of land, arousing widespread protests from congregations across Boston's large Catholic community.

By comparison to other dioceses in the United States, however, Boston got off comparatively light. In 2004, the dioceses of Spokane, Portland, and Tucson all declared bankruptcy. In January 2005, the diocese of Orange, south of Los Angeles, paid $100 million to ninety litigants, but was still to settle a further 544 claims by alleged victims of sexual abuse. That brought the total paid out by the U.S. Roman Catholic Church to $900 million. Yet this was without the release of documents showing the church to be negligent in the wider sense. If such papers existed, it was feared that the Roman Catholic Church in the U.S. would be financially ruined.

Part of the problem and the cause of public anger was the purported secrecy of the Catholic church and its slowness to address events. At the height of the allegations in 2002, the Catholic Church's Ad Hoc Committee on Sexual Abuse made a number of recommendations toward a "zero tolerance" policy on sexual abuse. This included the removal from ministry of any priest found to have abused more than one child in the past (although it stopped short of recommending their defrocking), and that bishops turn over any new allegation of child abuse to the police or relevant district attorney. These recommendations, however, needed the approval of the Vatican to be universally implemented, and Rome was unwilling— as a position of principle—to cede such autonomy. To do so, it was argued, would be to relinquish eight centuries of centralized Roman Catholic rule.

Perhaps this was the most shocking element of the case: that the Catholic church was not systematically implementing new procedures that addressed complaints dealing with sexual impropriety. Nor was this the first time they had failed to do so. In 1985, the Reverend Gilbert Gauthe was sentenced to twenty years imprisonment for molesting dozens of children, who were awarded a combined $18 million in damages. His trial gave way to more big cases and large

financial settlements, totaling up to $1 billion, but resulted in no fundamental change to complaint procedures.

The ongoing litigation also brought to the surface other scandals lurking within the U.S. Roman Catholic Church. In May 2002, Archbishop Rembert Weakland of Milwaukee was forced to resign after it was revealed he had an "inappropriate relationship" and had paid $450,000 to cover it up. This had nothing to do with the child abuse scandals that were dominating America's front pages of the time, but was a consenting homosexual relationship—inappropriate only in the eyes of the Catholic church—for which Weakland was later blackmailed. His resignation showed how the wider pressures facing the Catholic church in America brought other hidden revelations to the surface and contributed to the perception of a faith in crisis.

FURTHER RESOURCES

Web sites

Boston Globe. "Cardinal Law and the Laity." <http://www.boston.com/globe/spotlight/abuse/law_laity> (accessed March 2, 2006).

Catholic League. "Sexual Abuse in Social Context: Catholic Clergy and Other Professionals." <http://www.catholicleague.org/research/abuse_in_social_context.htm> (accessed March 2, 2006).

Time. "Can the Church Be Saved?" <http://www.time.com/time/archive/preview/0,10987,1002114,00.html> (accessed March 2, 2006).

Cat Dragged

Photograph

By: Atlantic City (New Jersey) Police Department

Date: January 7, 2004

Source: Associated Press. *Cat Dragged.* Associated Press Archives, Number 7090005, 2004.

About the Photographer: The Atlantic City, New Jersey, Police Department is headed by Chief Arthur Snellbaker, and is reported to have some four hundred sworn officers and about one hundred fifty support personnel.

INTRODUCTION

Every state in America has some form of legal statute criminalizing the abuse of animals. In most states, animal abuse or animal cruelty is a misdemeanor, but more than half of the states (thirty) have specific categories of animal abuse or animal cruelty legislation that are at the felony level. In general, animal abuse or neglect is any avoidable behavior, whether willful or unintentional, that causes an animal to experience distress, physical discomfort, harm, or death. Animal abuse and cruelty includes a wide range of actions. Neglectful behavior such as confining an animal in too small a shelter for comfort or for too long a period of time, leaving an animal with an inadequate supply of food or water, or failing to take adequate medical (veterinary) care of an animal, constitutes animal abuse. Examples of outright animal cruelty include intentional physical punishment that is greatly in excess of "correction of undesired behaviors," intentional starvation or water deprivation, abandonment, physical and emotional torture, maiming, burning, mutilating, or killing an animal — whether wild or domestic. The American Society for Prevention of Cruelty to Animals and the Humane Society of the United States both state that the majority of abuses reported fall under the category of unintentional, and easily remedied, neglect. Cruelty and abuse to animals are socially and culturally, as well as legally, defined. Legal hunting, and the sanctioned use of animals in laboratory settings with appropriate oversight, are not legally considered to be animal abuse, although many animal activists would disagree.

In contrast to cases of domestic violence in which there is police involvement, cases of animal abuse and cruelty do not appear to be systematically tracked or categorized by local law enforcement agencies; rather, it is local humane societies that often respond, track, enforce statutes and laws, and seek prosecution of those who perpetrate violence against animals. That may be due, in part, to preoccupation by many law enforcement agencies with human-related crime, or it may be due to a lack of training, knowledge, and expertise concerning animal abuse issues.

Of increasing concern to animal protection and humane societies, to law enforcement professions, and to the behavioral health professional communities is the link between animal cruelty and violent crime against humans. Beginning with data reported by the Federal Bureau of Investigation more than a quarter of a century ago, there has been a strong connection drawn between adult perpetrators of violent (often lethal) crime and childhood or adolescent histories of repeated animal abuse, cruelty, and torture. A similar link has been drawn between those who intentionally commit acts of animal cruelty and those who commit abuse to their children, their spouses, or their elders.

PRIMARY SOURCE

CAT DRAGGED

See primary source image.

SIGNIFICANCE

The American Psychiatric Association, in the fourth edition of the Diagnostic and Statistical Manual of Psychiatric Disorders lists cruelty to animals among the diagnostic criteria for Conduct Disorder appearing in either childhood or adolescence. In terms of motivation for animal abuse, there is a distinction drawn between those who harm their own animals and those who abuse those of others. Often, people who abuse animals belonging to other people do so as an act of revenge or as a means of threatening or intimidating someone they wish to affront, terrorize, or punish.

In the 1990s, there was a spate of lethal violence committed by extremely youthful offenders, such as Eric Harris and Dylan Klebold (seventeen and eighteen year olds who perpetrated Columbine high school killings), Kip Kinkel (fifteen year old who killed his parents and two classmates, and shot others at Thurston high school in Oregon), Andrew Golden and Mitchell Johnson (eleven and thirteen year olds who killed five people and wounded ten others in Arkansas), and Luke Woodham (seventeen year old who killed two classmates and wounded seven others at Pearl High School in Mississippi). All of them reported engaging in acts of animal abuse and cruelty as younger children.

Many of those who go on to become violent offenders, whether they perpetrate against animals of humans, have an early history of experiencing child abuse (physical, emotional, or sexual) or neglect, or witnessing domestic violence. A significant number of incarcerated felons, when asked about childhood histories, report coming from backgrounds in which there was significant physical punishment for alleged misdeeds, even if it did not meet threshold criteria for child abuse or domestic violence. In addition, many adults who engage in domestic violence, elder abuse or neglect, or animal cruelty or abuse grew up in households in which those events also occurred: that is, there is often a multigenerational history of violent and aggressive behavior.

■ **PRIMARY SOURCE**

Cat Dragged: A defiant cable company employee stands with arms crossed while the body of a dead cat attached to his truck's bumper by a rope lies on the ground next to him. This man and another cable employee were charged with felony animal cruelty for allegedly dragging the cat behind their vehicle in 2003. AP IMAGES

Much of the research on the relationship between an early history of animal abuse or cruelty and the later development of criminally violent behavior has been retrospective. The apprehended or incarcerated offenders, when questioned about their past behavior, voluntarily report experiences of youthful aggression against animals. However, this is anecdotal data rather than rigorous scientific research. It is often, although certainly not always, difficult to substantiate the nature and extent of the reported animal abuse behavior. There are well-substantiated links between the types of personality characteristics that encourage some convicted felons to discuss episodes of violent and aggressive behavior (such as the offenses for which they are incarcerated) and a propensity to divulge other shocking, aberrant, or heinous behavior. That is, not all of the behavior reported may have occurred, or it may be significantly exaggerated in order to achieve a desired audience effect. In other instances past behavior may be understated, or the inmate may refuse to discuss his history at all.

When looking at aggression against animals on a developmental continuum, it is not abnormal for young children to enthusiastically kill insects, and to inflict harm on small animals such as lizards, birds, and small rodents. Most children do not move on to causing harm to larger animals, nor do they go on to become perpetrator of violent crimes. Perhaps the dividing lines between those who stop this behavior in childhood and those who continue and escalate center around experiences of violence, either as observer or victim, in the home, or differences in perceptions around the acts themselves. When most children come to understand that they are injuring another creature, they halt the behavior and feel remorse. It may well be that those who derive enjoyment or excitement from causing pain and suffering to other creatures (human or lower animal) are those most likely to escalate the behavior across the lifespan.

FURTHER RESOURCES

Books

Kistler, John. *People Promoting and People Opposing Animal Rights: In Their Own Words.* Westport, Connecticut: Greenwood Press, 2002.

Nussbaum, Martha C., and Cass R. Sunstein. *Animal Rights: Current Debates and New Directions.* New York, New York: Oxford University Press, 2004.

Periodicals

Tannenbaum, Jerrold. "Animals and the Law: Property, Cruelty, Rights." *Social Research.* 62(3) (1995): 539-607.

Web sites

Atlantic City Police Department. "Mission Statement." <http://www.acpolice.org/Home.htm> (accessed February 18, 2006).

The Humane Society of the United States. "Legislation and Laws." <http://www.hsus.org/legislation_laws/> (accessed March 04, 2006).

Animal Legal Defense Fund. "Zero tolerance for cruelty!." <http://cats.about.com/gi/dynamic/offsite.htm> (accessed March 04, 2006).

Strip Clubs, Gambling & His Own TV Show!

Newspaper article

By: Bill Hutchinson

Date: November 4, 2005

Source: Hutchinson,Bill. "Strip Clubs, Gambling & His Own TV Show! That's House Arrest for Mob Boss' Son." *New York Daily News* (November 4, 2005): 4.

About the Author: Bill Hutchinson is a regularly contributing journalist working for the *New York Daily News.* With a daily circulation of more than 700,000, the *New York Daily News* is one of the most widely circulated newspapers in the United States. Well known for its tabloid layout and hard-hitting New York style, the *New York Daily News* has been in operation since 1919.

INTRODUCTION

The Italian Mafia, popularly referred to as the mob, has become a favorite subject of American popular culture. The film *The Godfather,* based on the mob-themed novel by Mario Puzo, is regularly cited as a favorite of movie lovers. The television series *The Sopranos* has received similar popular acclaim. Despite the association that the Mafia has with organized crime, society in general seems to find the mob's dedication to family and honesty coupled with violence and crime an ideal combination for entertainment.

While family-oriented organized crime groups exist among many ethnicities, the Italian Mafia, which originated in nineteenth century Sicily, is, undoubtedly, the best known. When large numbers of Italian immigrants began to arrive in the United States, the Mafia made its presence felt in the Italian neighborhoods of the major cities. Although the major mob operations originated in Chicago, by the latter half of the twentieth century the five leading Mafia families were based in New York.

The Mafia structure is based on an adherence to strict loyalty to the family; traitors typically are punished by death. At the head of the family is the Don, who served as the figurehead, with the operations and daily activities falling upon his soldiers, or made men as they are called. The Mafia's income derives from ownership and management of businesses. Stereotypically, certain industries, like sanitation, restaurants, and construction, have been associated with the Italian Mafia and have been highlighted in popular culture's portrayal of the mob.

In recent decades, the activities and scope of the Mafia have been sharply curtailed through the efforts of federal law enforcement authorities to clamp down on organized crime. Many of the key figures have been prosecuted and imprisoned as a result of these investigations. With the gradual assimilation of the Italian community into the broader society of the United States, and as the older generation of Mafia figures has begun to die off, the mob's influence has dwindled. At the same time, its operations continue in the major American urban centers, and its influence has expanded around the world. The Italian mafia still remains the largest operator of organized crime in the United States.

PRIMARY SOURCE

The son of murdered mob boss Joe Colombo is putting a new twist on house arrest—one where strip clubs, fancy restaurants and card games are part of his "confinement."

Chris Colombo, 44, isn't just sitting around his Orange County home polishing his ankle bracelet. He's

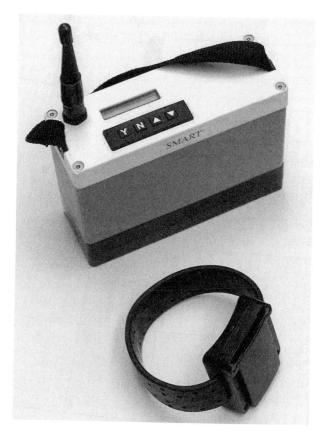

An electronic ankle bracelet and cellular transmitter box used to monitor and control the movements of convicts living at home. AP IMAGES

pushing his legal limits for an upcoming TV show that he hopes will be a hit without violating his bail restrictions.

"How do I feel? I've got a guy filming the top of my head ... and I'm about to go to the Blue Moon [topless club] that's known for the ugliest girls in the world," Colombo says in a snippet from his HBO program, aptly titled "House Arrest."

The show is scheduled to debut Thanksgiving night, well in advance of Colombo's federal trial next year on charges of loansharking, extortion and gambling.

"I always try to look for the good side of things, the funny side," Colombo told Ganglandnews.com reporter Jerry Capeci. "I'm like a human anti-depressant, always have been."

Colombo's attorney, Jeremy Schneider, said yesterday that his client knows his critics will likely include FBI agents looking for missteps to nail him.

"He does know that he can't do anything to violate his parole. He knows that," Schneider told the Daily News. "Is a strip club against the law? As far as I know, it's not."

Under conditions of his bail, Colombo is free to leave his luxurious Blooming Grove home at 7 a.m. daily. But he must be back at his 9-acre estate by 9 p.m.

He must have his electronic monitoring device attached to his left ankle at all times, and make sure he doesn't break the law.

"This could be a violation of my bail restriction," Colombo says in a scene from the show in which a pal uses a credit card to try to open the locked door of a church so Colombo can confess his sins.

Colombo hopes the show, which HBO calls a "docu-comedy based on reality," will lead to bigger on-screen gigs.

"I always wanted to host 'Saturday Night Live,'" he told Ganglandnews.com, "and play my father in a movie about his life."

HIS DAD DIDN'T SHY AWAY FROM SPOTLIGHT

Many old-time mobsters tended to shy away from publicity, but Joe Colombo embraced it—and that's likely what got him whacked.

The late Godfather of the Colombo crime family—and dad of soon-to-be HBO TV star Chris Colombo—took the pledge of *omertà*, but fashioned himself as an outspoken civic leader.

He became a made man in the late 1950s in the Profaci crime family and graduated to capo in the 1960s. At age 48, Colombo ascended to boss of the crime family that would take his name.

Colombo, who was raised in Brooklyn, was the founder of the Italian-American Civil Rights League.

As a self-styled civic leader, the charismatic Colombo got the words "Mafia" and "Cosa Nostra" banned from Justice Department reports and from "The Godfather" movie.

But while leading a rally in Columbus Circle in 1971, Colombo was shot three times in the back of the head by a gunman who then also was gunned down.

Colombo lingered in a vegetative state until his death in 1978 at age 64.

SIGNIFICANCE

The Mafia in the United States has always enjoyed a relationship with law enforcement of elusiveness and antagonism. This article, in highlighting one mobster's effort to stretch the law to its limits, directly addresses this phenomenon. The choice of this subject—chronicling the day-to-day activities of a member of the Mafia while awaiting his trial—for a television show points to the overwhelming interest that the American public has in characters associated with the Mafia.

This article also attempts to promote the image of the mobster as a carefree character who enjoys frequenting strip clubs and gambling joints, with little concern for whether the authorities will catch him or what might be the broader repercussions of his actions. Programs of this type and Hollywood's image of the Mafia portray these characters as people who, if it were not for their criminal activities, would be highly likable. The mobster's dual personality, which is discussed in detail in this article, has always been an aspect of these figures that the general public finds appealing.

Unlike many other criminals, Mafia leaders are often well integrated into their surroundings and are involved in civic and community affairs. They have a strong appreciation for their Italian heritage and work to advance causes that improve the image of Italians in American society. Many believe that although the Mafia is involved in violent crimes and murder, its members aren't a threat to individuals unless the mob's trust is violated. For this reason, the mob is rarely portrayed as an evil entity by popular culture, but rather as an entertaining one, with a unique set of values. As this article indicates, Joe Colombo, who served as the head of the Colombo crime family until his death, was actively involved in efforts to erase the gangster conception of Italian Americans and worked to promote the more positive aspects of Italian Americans to the larger American society.

By becoming involved with a television program that highlights the lighter side of the Mafia, Chris Colombo is helping to fuel the public's fascination with all things related to the mob.

FURTHER RESOURCES

Books

Raab, Selwyn. *Five Families: The Rise, Decline, and Resurgence of America's Most Powerful Mafia Empires*. New York: Thomas Dunne Books, 2005.

Reppetto, Thomas. *American Mafia: A History of Its Rise to Power*. New York: Henry Holt, 2004.

Periodicals

Hibbs, Thomas. "The Mafia, Misunderstood: Hollywood Fails to Capture the Complexity of the Real Thing." *National Review Online*, September 29, 2004, <http://www.nationalreview.com/hibbs/hibbs20040929 0835.asp> (accessed February 28, 2006).

Economic and Nonviolent Crimes

Economic and Nonviolent Crimes

Economic and nonviolent crimes cover a broad range of illegal activities that do not involve perpetration of violence directly against another person. Often termed "white collar" crime, such activities can still be devastating.

Such crime sometimes victimizes through usually trusted channels as discussed in an entry on a computer hacking scandal—"Security Breach that may Have Exposed Forty Million Credit Cards,"—or by illegal transactions that put investor money at risk, as discussed in the entry "Former Merrill Execs Sentenced." As the internet has progressively broadened the purchasing arena for the global population, there have been increasing concerns expressed about the safety of personal financial information. The legitimacy of the public's fears concerning the safety of their debit and credit cards are detailed in "Debit Card Fraud More Widespread Than Banks Believe."

Historically, nonviolent crimes have always been the most prevalent forms of illegal activity. Gambling and confidence games have a long history. Sports betting, for example can be legitimate, so long as it is practiced honestly and without attempt to influence the outcome of a contest or sporting event. However, a history of corruption and illegality in sports betting is also ancient (often openly discussed in ancient Greek and Roman texts). In the United States such betting came under intense public scrutiny during the early 1920s, when there were accusations made concerning the "throwing" of the World Series of 1919 for the purposes of illegal gambling. "Shoeless" Joe Jackson and seven of his colleagues were tried for the alleged criminal activity, as detailed in the "Black Sox Trial Indictment" and "This is the Truth! Shoeless Joe Jackson Tells His Story."

There are worldwide concerns surrounding issues of illicit drug regulation and control, ranging from safety and health hazards inherent in the highly combustible "meth labs," to human trafficking concerns in international drug smuggling organizations. Women and children are often exploited by large, and sometimes brutal, organizations, as a means of moving drugs across borders in an effort to avoid arousing undue suspicion.

However, in the present day, few illegal activities are more contentious than those involving the growing, manufacture, transport, procurement, trafficking, or usage of illegal so called recreational drugs. There has been recent court action aimed at legalizing the use of marijuana in medical settings, and for personal medicinal consumption for those suffering from cancer or intractable and chronic pain. Public perceptions toward some of these issues are discussed in "Attitudes Towards the Legalization of the Use of Marijuana" and other aspects of drug related issues are detailed in "A former U.S. Police Chief Stirs the Pot on Drug Laws".

This chapter will explore aspects of economic and nonviolent crimes, ranging from the counterfeiters of the late nineteenth and early twentieth centuries to "Prohibition Rum Runners" and further still to twenty-first century cybercriminals.

They Were Money-Makers

Illustration

By: Anonymous

Date: May 21, 1887

Source: Corbis.

About the Illustrator: This illustration is part of the stock collection at Corbis photo agency, headquartered in Seattle and provider of images for magazine, films, television, and advertisements. The artist is not known.

INTRODUCTION

The practice of creating and producing counterfeit money probably began shortly after the very first money was produced. It was especially prevalent at times and in places where money was created by more than one source, or when multiple types of currency were popularly used. In the United States, counterfeiting was particularly common during a period of time in the nineteenth century, when banks were responsible for production of their own legal tender and their own checks. According to the United States Secret Service, during the Civil War between one third and one half of all United States currency then in circulation was counterfeit, posing an enormous threat to the stability of the nation's economy.

The United States Secret Service has reported that there were more than 1,500 state banks, each producing their own currency, by the middle of the nineteenth century. The result was more than 7,000 unique types of bank notes being used by the general public. In addition to that vast quantity of legitimate currency, the Secret Service estimated that there were at least an additional 4,000 forms of counterfeit money in use at the same time. It was nearly impossible to distinguish genuine from counterfeit money, and the economy was quite fragile as a result. Due in part to the proliferation of counterfeiting, and in part to the lack of a national financial infrastructure, banks often failed, leaving people with legal tender that was worthless. In an effort to stabilize the economy by standardizing the monetary system, a national system of currency was adopted by the United States in 1863. It was hoped that the new currency would also discourage the practice of counterfeiting, but the desired result was not achieved. In fact, the rate at which counterfeit money was introduced into circulation continued to rise.

The United States Secret Service was created in July of 1865 as a branch of the United States Treasury Department, in an effort to investigate and ameliorate the problem of counterfeiting in America. The proliferation of counterfeit money, because it created an artificially large amount of circulating currency, made the economy of the country potentially unstable.

Shortly after the passage of the National Currency Act of 1863 (the act that created a single monetary system across the United States), President Lincoln ratified the National Bank Act, laying the foundation for a nationwide financial infrastructure. The goal of the legislation was to create a unified banking system that was organized under the federal jurisdiction of the Comptroller of the Currency.

The new banking system, involving the use of currency, United States government securities, and national bank notes, was quite effective. The economy stabilized, and the prevalence of counterfeit money in financial circulation dropped substantially.

PRIMARY SOURCE

THEY WERE MONEY-MAKERS

See primary source image.

SIGNIFICANCE

Between the end of the banking crisis and the ensuing Great Depression in the 1920s and 1930s, and the rise of technological sophistication near the end of the twentieth century, it was relatively difficult to produce successful counterfeit paper money in America for local use. It required considerable printing and engraving equipment, large printing plates, and significant artistic skill—as the renderings had to be hand-copied and etched into the production plates. The equipment was large and cumbersome, not portable, and difficult to hide or to disguise.

However, because the American currency design had been created and produced early in the twentieth century, and had remained unchanged for many decades, it became progressively simpler to successfully counterfeit American money for use internationally. Because many businesses outside of the United States accepted American money, yet were not as intimately familiar with its texture and appearance as American merchants would be, it was easier to pass counterfeit money abroad than within the United States. When the money was eventually returned to the American banking system, and reached the advanced scanning equipment utilized by the United yearly, and the amount increased to nearly $40 million per year during the first decade of the twenty-first century.

Interestingly, many of the new "casual counterfeiters" are teenagers and young adults—high school and college students who are well educated and very bright, if somewhat lacking in worldliness and sophistication. Casual counterfeiters are those that do not develop a detailed plan and system in advance of attempting to fabricate money. They tend to stumble upon the idea when, in exploring the limits of their computer and peripheral equipment, they first attempt to scan and copy a piece of American paper money. If this is met with relative success, they may try to rapidly refine and perfect the copy, and then try to produce a two-sided copy. If the paper has the appropriate feel and the copy appears to be sufficiently clear and detailed, it is very tempting to try to pass the fraudulent tender. Rarely is the effort successful.

In an effort to stave off the flood of casual counterfeiters, the United States Treasury began producing redesigned paper currency in 1996. More recently, redesigned twenty-dollar bills were introduced in 2003, fifty-dollar bills in 2004, and ten- and one-hundred-dollar bills in 2006. Because of their greater value, the larger (larger than one or five dollars) bills are expected to be redesigned once or twice per decade.

Counterfeiting is a federal offense, carrying graduated penalties. An adult who is charged with simply making exact-sized color copies of United States currency can receive a fifteen-year sentence. If the money is passed into circulation, whether or not the attempt is successful, there is an additional potential fifteen-year sentence added to the one for manufacturing counterfeit currency. Each counterfeit bill that is tendered can carry a separate criminal sentence, as well as a fine of up to $250,000 in addition to replacement of the original costs (the amount of counterfeit money exchanged for goods or services). The Secret Service, as well as the District Attorneys in the jurisdictions in which juveniles have been arrested for casual counterfeiting, struggle with individual decisions on the legal consequences given to the youth. Most of the time, the counterfeiting is done in very limited amounts, with no forethought or appreciation for the severity of the offense. The general consensus seems to be that the newest currency has surpassed the capabilities of even the most sophisticated home computer, printer, and scanner systems, and will thwart youthful counterfeiters. In the interim, many juvenile counterfeiters will have earned criminal records and probation histories, and some will have faced jail or prison terms.

PRIMARY SOURCE

They Were Money-Makers: *Police Gazette* illustration depicting women making counterfeit coins c. 1887. © BETTMANN/CORBIS

States Bureau of Engraving and Printing, the fraud would almost certainly be detected.

With the advent of high-resolution printers and scanners, as well as sophisticated art and design computer software, the production of counterfeit money has experienced a renaissance and has taken on an air of near artistry. Since 1985, the degree of computer, software, and printer refinement has been such that it has been possible to create convincing-looking counterfeit money using relatively simple technology. In the late 1980s, the United States government stepped up its level of research on making American paper currency more difficult to counterfeit and successfully use. By the early 1990s, nearly $10 million worth of counterfeit money produced on easily obtained commercial and home office equipment was confiscated

FURTHER RESOURCES

Books

Paradise, Paul R. *Trademark Counterfeiting, Product Piracy, and the Billion Dollar Threat to the U.S. Economy*. Westport, Conn.: Quorum Books, 1999.

Periodicals

De Jager, Peter. "The New Money Laundering?" *ABA Banking Journal* 95, 12 (2003): 8.

Hamilton-Wright, Kimberly J. "Funny Money: Counterfeit Money Scams Persist." *Black Enterprise* 34, 3 (October 2003): 135.

Web sites

PBS.org. "Secrets of Making Money." <http://www.pbs.org/wgbh/nova/transcripts/2314secr.html> (accessed March 6, 2006).

United States Treasury Bureau of Engraving and Printing. "Anti-Counterfeiting Security Features." <http://www.moneyfactory.gov/section.cfm/7/35> (February 26, 2006).

United States Treasury Bureau of Engraving and Printing. "The New Color of Money. Safer. Smarter. More Secure." <http://www.moneyfactory.gov/newmoney> (accessed March 6, 2006).

Vincenzo Perugia, Thief of the *Mona Lisa*

Photograph

By: Anonymous

Date: c. 1900

Source: Corbis.

About the Photographer: This image is the Italian police photograph and fingerprint record for the Italian Vincenzo Perugia. The photographer is unknown.

INTRODUCTION

This image is the police photograph and fingerprint record from the arrest of Vincenzo Perugia (born 1881), one of the most famous art thieves in history. In 1911, Perugia walked into the room in the Louvre Museum, Paris, which housed the *Mona Lisa*, the famous portrait of a smiling woman painted in 1503–1507 by the Italian painter Leonard da Vinci (1452–1519). Perugia had worked briefly as a carpenter for the museum in 1908 and was familiar with its layout. Security measures were minimal at the time: Perugia simply took the painting off its hook, hid it under his smock (a loose overgarment worn to protect the clothes while working), and walked out. In a nearby service stairwell, he paused to cut the painting from its bulky frame, then left the building with the piece hidden under his clothing. (The *Mona Lisa* is painted on a wooden panel, not on canvas, and is only seventy by fifty-three centimeters (thirty by twenty-one inches).

Perugia took the painting back to Italy hidden in the bottom of a trunk and kept it in his bedroom for two years. During this period, there was tremendous national grief in France, and many thousands of visitors came to view the empty spot on the wall where the *Mona Lisa* had hung. Speculation about its fate was rampant: Pablo Picasso was questioned as a suspect in the theft. Eventually, becoming impatient with the accomplice who had promised to pay him for the painting, Perugia tried to sell the painting to an art dealer in Florence, Italy. He asked for five hundred thousand lire and assurances that the painting would never be returned to France. The art dealer, suspicious of fraud, called the director of a Florence art gallery and asked him to come with him to the stranger's room to see the supposed treasure. The two art experts were amazed to see Perugia produce the *Mona Lisa* from the bottom of a trunk full of "wretched belongings." Telling Perugia that they would have to take the painting to the museum to have its authenticity verified before paying him, they carried it away with them and hastily compared it to photographs from the Louvre. Its authenticity was confirmed, and the police were sent to arrest Perugia.

For two months, the *Mona Lisa* toured Italy and was viewed by tens of thousands. Perugia was put on trial in Florence. He claimed that his motivation for stealing the painting had been patriotic, that he had fallen in love with its beauty and could not rest until it was restored to its native land. Perugia was apparently unaware that the reason the *Mona Lisa* was in France to begin with was that Leonardo da Vinci himself had sold it to King Francois I of France for three thousand gold coins. Perugia rose at once to hero status and received love letters, cakes, and bottles of wine in jail. A sympathetic jury sentenced him to seven months in jail: since he had already been held for almost eight, he was released immediately.

PRIMARY SOURCE

VINCENZO PERUGIA, THIEF OF THE *MONA LISA*
See primary source image.

Vincenzo Perugia, Thief of the *Mona Lisa*: Mug shot and fingerprints of Vincenzo Perugia, the Italian man who stole the Mona Lisa out of the Louvre Museum in Paris in 1911. Perugia claimed he completed the act out of patriotism, insisting the painting belonged in Leonardo da Vinci's home country, Italy, and not France. © BETTMANN/CORBIS

SIGNIFICANCE

Although Perugia alleged patriotism as a motive for his theft of the *Mona Lisa*, the motive for most art theft is the motive for most other theft: money. Estimates of how much art is stolen around the world every year range from five billion dollars to ten billion dollars. According to the European police agency Interpol, the black market in art is the fourth largest

A tourist views a marble frieze from the famous "Elgin Marbles" on display at the British Museum in London. Greece has long maintained that the marbles, taken from the Parthenon in Athens in 1806, should be returned. © REUTERS NEWMEDIA INC./CORBIS

criminal enterprise globally after illegal drugs, money laundering, and weapons. Approximately five percent of all art has been stolen at some point in its history; most stolen art is never recovered by its rightful owners.

Far more common than art theft by patriotic individuals is theft by institutions and governments for nationalistic self-aggrandizement. The Roman Empire took fine statuary from Greece for the adornment of Rome, and during the centuries of modern imperial and colonial European expansion, the theft of art objects from conquered countries was routine. Perugia's belief that France had stolen the *Mona Lisa* was incorrect, but not ridiculous: the French emperor Napoleon, who ruled France from 1802 to 1815 and conquered most of continental Europe, systematically stripped other countries' art museums and had their treasures sent to France. The only reason *Mona Lisa* was not stolen by Napoleon was that it happened to be a French possession already. Indeed, Perugia was only the second man to keep the *Mona Lisa* in his bedroom: for two years, Napoleon had it hung in his own bedchamber.

Exceeding even Napoleon as regards art theft was the Nazi regime, which conquered most of Europe in the early years of World War II (1939–1945). The Nazis stole tens of thousands of art objects, many from Jews whom it killed. Many of these stolen art objects have since passed into museum and private collections.

An ongoing controversy over possibly stolen art with patriotic or nationalistic overtones concerns the Elgin Marbles displayed in the British Museum in London. The marbles are a large set of illustrative carvings in marble that originally adorned the Parthenon in Athens, Greece (built in the fifth century B.C.). Thomas Bruce, 7th Earl of Elgin, was British ambassador to the Turkish Ottoman Empire from 1799 to 1803. At that time, the Turks occupied Greece. Accounts vary as to whether Elgin simply took the marbles or obtained legal permission: if he did obtain permission to remove the marbles, he obtained it from the Turks, not the Greeks. In any case, over fifty blocks of magnificent ancient carvings were removed to England. In 1816, the British Museum bought the marbles from Elgin for £35,000.

Today, Greece views the Elgin Marbles as stolen property, and pressure from the Greek government and others to return the marbles to Greece has been strong. President Bill Clinton was among those saying that the marbles should be returned. The British Government refuses. In 2005, Egypt also demanded the return of a number of art objects now held by American and British museums which it says were stolen from it during the nineteenth and twentieth centuries and has threatened to end work in Egypt by archaeologists from those countries if the works are not returned. Also, a 1970 Convention of the United Nations Educational, Scientific and Cultural Organization (UNESCO) established a legal framework in which nations may request the return of stolen cultural property.

FURTHER RESOURCES

Web sites

British Broadcasting System (BBC). "Elgin Marbles: The story so far …" <http://news.bbc.co.uk/1/hi/uk/543362.stm> Nov. 30, 1999 (accessed March 5, 2006).

Public Broadcasting System (PBS). "Finding that Mona was missing." <http://www.pbs.org/treasuresoftheworld/a_nav/mona_nav/mnav_level_1/missing_monafrm.html> (accessed March 5, 2006).

Orphans Working in Carpentry Shop

Photograph

By: Robert L. Blacklow

Date: c. 1900

Source: Photo Collection Alexander Alland, Sr./COR-BIS.

About the Photographer: This photograph was supplied by a nondenominational Christian missionary organization, Mission Australia, that organizes volunteer patrols to pick up people intoxicated in public and take them to alternative accommodations.

INTRODUCTION

Although the boys in this photograph are orphans, not criminals, and the institution housing them is an orphanage, not a prison, their status is linked to the history of crime. They are being trained in carpentry skills so that they will have a better chance of not being exploited as unskilled child labor or becoming criminals themselves when they leave the orphanage. In 1900, as throughout all of the preceding century, it was taken for granted that children could and would work in factories and other commercial enterprises from a very young age. Those who had special skills, like these boys, were less likely to end up in the most dirty and dangerous jobs.

The boys shown here are wards of the Five Points House of Industry, a charity orphanage founded in the notorious Five Points slum of New York City (since replaced by part of Chinatown) by Methodist minister Lewis M. Pease. Pease was originally the minister appointed to the Five Points area by the First Union Mission, a Protestant organization seeking to convert Catholics. Pease found that trying to talk Catholics out of their Catholicism was usually futile and decided that he should provide job training instead to help raise people out of poverty, crime, and prostitution. Although this picture shows only boys, the House of Industry housed and job-trained women, boys, and girls and offered occasional public meals which were attended by hundreds. The orphan children were eventually placed with adoptive parents, usually in the American West. The products of the carpentry shop shown here were almost certainly sold to provide income for the orphanage. Girls and women were employed in separate shops at tasks considered feminine, such as dressmaking.

ORPHANS WORKING IN CARPENTRY SHOP
See primary source image.

SIGNIFICANCE

Despite its name, the Five Points House of Industry was not an industrial institution but a charity for destitute women and children. It was highly regarded during its period of operation, which lasted for well over half a century. However, the boys in this photograph are not practicing carpentry for the sake of general skill development, like most children in a modern "shop" class, but are preparing for actual skilled work, as opposed to the unskilled labor that would otherwise be their lot outside the orphanage. Throughout the Industrial Revolution, starting in the late 1700s, child labor was standard in both Britain and America. In the 1830s, about a third of the New England workforce consisted of children under the age of sixteen: the lower limit on age was set only by a child's ability to walk, talk, and work. Not only did full-time labor by a child preclude their further education, but the labor was often brutally difficult, children were exposed to exploitation and abuse by adult supervisors and others in the workplace, and injuries were common. In the culture of the time, the use of children even for dangerous labor was not necessarily seen as a bad thing; as late as the American Civil War (1860s), boys called "powdermonkeys" were employed on warships to fetch powder for the guns, their small size enabling them to access to the cramped powder storage areas. When a ship went down, these boys went down with it.

In 1842, Connecticut and Massachusetts passed laws requiring that children not be made to labor more than ten hours a day. In 1848, Pennsylvania made twelve the minimum age for child laborers. Legal efforts to abolish child labor were not successful, however, until well into the twentieth century: In 1900, about the time this photograph was taken, a quarter of the workers in cotton mills in the American South were children under the age of fifteen. In 1916 and 1918, Federal laws were passed controlling child labor, but these were overturned by the Supreme Court as unconstitutional in 1918. A constitutional amendment to ban child labor was passed by Congress in 1924, but was never ratified. Not until 1938, with passage of the Fair Labor Standards Act, was the employment of children under sixteen in mining and manufacturing prohibited. Today, child labor is relatively rare in the United States.

PRIMARY SOURCE

Orphans Working in Carpentry Shop: Orphans c. 1890 at work in the carpentry shop of the Five Points House of Industry, an orphanage set in the worst slum in nineteenth-century Manhattan. Founded by Christian missionaries, the object was to prevent children from turning to a life of crime by providing them with a marketable skill. © PHOTO COLLECTION ALEXANDER ALLAND, SR./CORBIS

However, child labor remains a problem globally. About 250 million children between five and fourteen years of age are working in developing countries, according to the International Labor Organization, over 120 million of them full-time: sixty-one percent in Asia, thirty-two percent in Africa, seven percent in Latin America. Millions of children are forcibly recruited into soldiering and prostitution. Five percent of child workers are employed in export industries, that is, in the manufacture of goods for export to Europe, the U.S., and other wealthier countries.

Sometimes the use of in-house child labor is used to raise funds for an institution, as the labor of the boys and girls at the Five Points House of Industry probably was. For example, as of 1996 approximately 71,000 Chinese primary and high schools had set up cottage industries to raise money. Some of these children must work against their will, according to some news accounts. The fact that school businesses are exempt from taxation has probably encouraged the use of student labor.

Importation of products made using child labor is illegal in the United States. Further, article thirty-two of the Convention on the Rights of the Child (1990), an international treaty signed by most of the world's nations, states that children shall be "protected from economic exploitation and from performing any work that is likely to be hazardous or to interfere with the child's education, or to be harmful to the child's health or physical, mental, spiritual, moral or social development." As of 2006, the United States had not ratified the Convention.

FURTHER RESOURCES
Web sites

Human Rights Watch. "Promises Broken: An Assessment of Children's Rights on the 10th Anniversary of the Convention on the Rights of the Child." <http://www.hrw.org/campaigns/crp/promises/labor.html> 2000 (accessed March 5, 2006).

Black Sox Trial Indictment

Indictment & Bill of Particulars in People of Illinois v Cicotte

Legal decision

By: Robert E. Crowe

Date: July 5, 1921

Source: "Indictment & Bill of Particulars in People of Illinois v Cicotte." <http://www.law.umkc.edu/faculty/projects/ftrials/blacksox/indictpartic.html> (accessed March 12, 2006).

About the Author: Robert E. Crowe was the State's Attorney for Cook County, Illinois in 1921.

INTRODUCTION

In December 1856, the *New York Mercury* first referred to baseball as America's "national pastime." By 1869, the first professional team, the Cincinnati Red Stockings, began to play. Two years later, the National Association of Professional Base Ball Players emerged and baseball's infancy as an amateur sport ended. By 1876, the conflict between labor and capital took the form of players versus the owners as the National League of Professional Base Ball Clubs began to regulate the game. Ty Cobb's stellar career propelled the game through the next decade. However, by 1919, the legacy of the game became mired in a scandal known as the 1919 World Series.

During the 1919 season, the Chicago White Sox performed extremely well and earned a position in the World Series against the Cincinnati Reds. However, many of the players on the White Sox were unhappy with the team's owner, Charles Comisky. One of the players, right-handed pitcher Eddie Cicotte, bore a special grudge against Comisky after the owner promised a bonus of $10,000 for winning thirty games. Comisky then benched Cicotte after his 29th win. In addition, Comisky was known for not paying for the team's uniforms to be laundered. The ill-will felt between the ownership and the players of the 1919 White Sox proved fertile ground for a plot to fix the World Series.

Chicago White Sox First Baseman Chick Gandil served as the ringleader for the conspiracy. Gandil assembled seven other players before the Series began and solicited their participation in a plot financed by Arnold Rothstein, a notorious New York gambler. Those seven players included pitchers Eddie Cicotte and Lefty Williams, third baseman Buck Weaver, shortstop Swede Risberg, utility infielder Fred McMullin, and outfielders Oscar "Happy" Felsch and Shoeless Joe Jackson. Gandil promised the group $20,000 for each game lost.

The White Sox had been three-to-one favorites to win the series before the odds changed in favor of the Cincinnati Reds at eight to one. The first game, pitched by Eddie Cicotte, was lost to Cincinnati 9–1. However, the players did not receive payment for their loss. They continued with the agreement and lost the second game, pitched by Lefty Williams, 4–2. Dickie Kerr, who did not participate in the fix, pitched the third game, which was won by Chicago 3–0. The Sox then lost the fourth game by 2–0 and the fifth game by 5–0. However, the money agreed to from the gamblers did not materialize. As a result, the players abandoned their plot in an effort to win the series and be awarded a bonus by Comisky. However, the series ended in the eighth game with a loss for Chicago.

By 1920, allegations of the fix led to a grand jury investigation of the events. According to reports, Eddie Cicotte and Joe Jackson were the first to admit involvement in the tampering. However, the initial testimonies that led to indictments disappeared before the trial and the men were acquitted due to a lack of evidence. Prior to the indictments, Comisky suspended the eight players indefinitely. The men would never play professional baseball again.

PRIMARY SOURCE

INDICTMENT & BILL OF PARTICULARS IN PEOPLE OF ILLINOIS V CICOTTE (THE BLACK SOX TRIAL)

BILL OF PARTICULARS

STATE OF ILLINOIS

SS:

COUNTY OF COOK

IN THE CRIMINAL COURT OF COOK COUNTY:

A group shot of the 1919 Chicago White Sox team, including the players involved in the "Black Sox Scandal." NATIONAL BASEBALL LIBRARY AND ARCHIVE, COOPERSTOWN, NY.

THE PEOPLE OF THE STATE OF ILLINOIS vs EDWARD v. CICOTTE et al.

Bill of Particulars as to Count 1, Count 2, and Count 3, of Indictment No. 23912, filed in conformity to rule entered July 5th, 1921, by his Honor Judge Hugo Friend, one of the Judges of the Criminal Court of Cook County.

The defendants in the above entitled cause, and each of them, are hereby notified that the State will offer evidence tending to show that the defendants, Edward Vs Cicotte, Claude Williams, Joe Jackson,, Fred McMullin, Arnold Gandil, George Weaver, Oscar Felsch and Charles Risberg in September and October of 1919 were engaged as base ball players and were members of a base ball club known as the American League Base Ball Club of Chicago, a corporation;

That said American League Base Ball Club of Chicago was engaged to play in competition with a certain other base ball club known as the National League Base Ball Club of Cincinnati, Ohio, a certain series of games of base ball; some of the games of said series to be played In Chicago and other games of said series to be played in Cincinnati, Ohio;

That the defendants, William Burns and Hal Chase were at various times connected with base ball as professional base ball players but were not participants in any of the games of the above mentioned series;

That the defendants, Joseph J. Sullivan, Rachael Brown Abe Attel, Carl Zork, Ben Franklin, Ben Levi, Louis Levi, and David Zelzer were not connected with base ball as players, but were reputed to be gamblers or prize fighters and interested in the promotion of gambling enterprises and sporting events of questionable character;

That considerable public interest was manifested in the outcome of said series of games and each game of said series;

That each of said games was publicly regarded as an important sporting event and that the spectators of said games and each of them was required to pay an admission fee to the field where said games were played;

That the defendants participating in said games as players conspired confederated and agreed together with the defendants not participating therein to so conduct themselves throughout the said games and each of said games and so manipulate their playing in each of said games as to make certain in advance of the playing of said games the outcome thereof and the winner thereof, and so as to make certain in advance of the playing of all of the games of said series the outcome of the majority of the games of said series and the winner of the majority of said series of games;

And the defendants not participating in said games as base ball players, conspired, confederated and agreed together and with the defendants participating in said games to operate among the spectators of said games and others and the general public to procure divers large sums of money by means of and by use of the confidence game.

That one Charles C. Nims a resident Of Chicago, Illinois, was unlawfully, fraudulently and feloniously swindled out of the sum of $250.00 by the defendant, Joseph J. Sullivan, who was then and there engaged in carrying out the conspiracy aforesaid and who did then and there obtain from the said Charles C. Rime the sum of $250.00 by means and by use of the confidence game contrary to the Statute In such cases made and provided, And for further particulars, the defendants are respectfully referred to the first, second, and third counts of said indictment.

SIGNIFICANCE

F. Scott Fitzgerald described Arnold Rothstein as the man who "tampered with the faith of fifty million people." In an effort to redeem baseball's tarnished image, the owners acted to mitigate the impact the scandal had on the disillusioned public. The owners replaced the three-man National Commission with an independent commissioner. The owners picked federal judge Kenesaw Mountain Landis to serve as the first commissioner. Prior to this appointment, Landis had been best known for handing down a $29 million fine to Standard Oil in a 1907 anti-trust case. Landis stated, "Baseball is something more than a game to an American boy. It is his training field for life work. Destroy his faith in its squareness and honesty and you have destroyed something more; you have planted suspicion of all things in his heart." Immediately following the 1921 acquittal of the eight players, Landis

placed the men on baseball's ineligible list—barring them from baseball for life.

Although the most notorious sports-related crime, the 1919 World Series is not the only scene of notoriety within sports. In recent years, the use of drugs for recreation or for enhanced development has been on the rise in society as well as the sports community. In 1985, Keith Hernandez and Dave Parker testified to widespread cocaine usage within baseball. Before a congressional committee in 2005, Rafael Palmeiro denied the use of steroids. However, he was suspended months later after a failing a drug test. Whether drug usage or game fixing, issues such as these put a blight on the sporting community. Dave Kindred of the *Sporting News* asserts that these activities are "a breach of the contract with fans who pony up good money to see games contested on a level playing field."

FURTHER RESOURCES
Periodicals
Kindred, Dave. "A Shot in the Arm Baseball Didn't Need." *Sporting News* (November 24, 2003).

Skretta, David. "Baseball Has a Long History of Notoriety." *USA Today* (August 2, 2005).

Ward, Geoffrey C., and Ken Burns. "Game Time." *US News and World Report* (August 29, 1994).

Web sites
Chicago Historical Society. "History Files: Chicago Black Sox." <http://www.chicagohs.org/history/blacksox.html> (accessed March 12, 2006).

This is the truth! Shoeless Joe Jackson Tells His Story

Magazine article

By: Joe Jackson

Date: 1949

Source: Sports Magazine

About the Author: Joe Jackson began his career in the major leagues in 1908. In 1915, he was traded from the Cleveland Indians to the Chicago White Sox. Jackson's career batting average was .356, an average which has only been surpassed by two other players. In 1920, following the scandal of the 1919 World Series,

Jackson was placed on the ineligible list, where he has remained.

INTRODUCTION

In 1920, the world of baseball was perilously close to demise due to the scandal of the 1919 World Series. The scandal involved eight players from the Chicago White Sox. In the early years of professional baseball, players were often at the mercy of the ownership. The Chicago White Sox owner, Charles Comiskey, was known for his thrift when managing the team. The term Black Sox actually originated from the 1918 season when Comiskey refused to pay to launder the team's uniforms. However, the phrase became synonymous with the eight players accused of fixing the 1919 World Series.

The accused ringleader of the fix was first baseman Chick Gandil. Gandil recruited pitchers Lefty Williams and Eddie Ciocotte. Ciocotte exemplified the financial conflict between players and owners. Comiskey had agreed to pay Cicotte a $10,000 bonus after winning 30 games. However, after Cicotte won the 29th game, Comiskey benched the pitcher. In addition to Williams and Cicotte, the remaining players involved were third baseman, Buck Weaver, shortstop Swede Risberg, center fielder Happy Felsch, utility infielder Fred McMullin, and Shoeless Joe Jackson. The men were promised $20,000 for each game lost, with the money financed from a group of gamblers led by the notorious New York gambler, Arnold Rothstein.

The first game, pitched by Eddie Cicotte, was lost to Cincinnati 9-1. However, the players did not receive $20,000 promised to them by Rothstein. In spite of that, the second game, pitched by Williams, was lost 4-2. At this point, the players were given only $10,000. Dickie Kerr, a rookie member of the White Sox who was not part of the scandal, pitched the third game to a 3-0 win. The gamblers then paid $20,000 to Gandil, who reportedly split the proceeds between Risberg, Felsch, Williams and Jackson. This led to the losses in the fourth game by 2-0 and the fifth game by 5-0. However, the gamblers once again failed to pay the players. As a result, the players, feeling betrayed, sought to end the deal in favor of winning the series—which would earn them a bonus from Comiskey. The series came to an end in the eighth game as the Sox lost 10-5.

Even before the series ended, there was talk of a fix. By 1920, the Cook County Court in Illinois convened to investigate allegations of corruption in baseball. Before the grand jury handed down any

"Shoeless Joe" Jackson of the Chicago White Sox. © BETTMANN/CORBIS

indictments, Comiskey suspended the eight players in question indefinitely. Cicotte was the first to admit to the grand jury involvement in the scandal. However, before the 1921 trial, Cicotte's and Jackson's testimony before the grand jury disappeared. As a result, the players were acquitted as the result of a lack of evidence. Four months before the trial began, the newly appointed baseball Commissioner placed the players on baseball's ineligible list. Prior to the acquittal, Commissioner Landis stated, "Regardless of the verdicts of the juries, no player who entertains proposals or promises to throw a game, no player who sits in conference with a bunch of crooked players and gamblers where the ways and means of throwing games are discussed and does not promptly tell the club about it, will ever play professional baseball."

PRIMARY SOURCE

THIS IS THE TRUTH!

Just 30 years ago this month, the infamous World Series between the Chicago White Sox and the Cincinnati Reds took place. The leading figure in the great scandal that followed, the famous White Sox slugger of 1919, tells in his own words his side of the story.

By SHOELESS JOE JACKSON AS TOLD TO FURMAN BISHER

EDITOR'S NOTE: Almost any day of the week, if you drive down East Wilborn Street on the South side of Greenville, South Carolina, you'll find an aging man with sparse white hair sitting in the shade of a sapling oak at No. 119. He will be Joe Jackson—Shoeless Joe Jackson, sometimes known as the greatest natural hitter in baseball history. But you'll never find Joe's name in the record books, because he was black-listed for life after the great baseball scandal broke in 1920. Jackson has never raised his voice in protest, though he has stoutly maintained his innocence. In his South Carolina textile country, where he lives comfortably, he is revered as an idol and as a persecuted man. They will always believe Joe innocent. Here, for the first time in national print, is Joe Jackson's own story, just as he tells it himself. Jackson, one of the game's most brillant batters, hit over .400 during the 1911 season.

"When I walked out of Judge Dever's courtroom in Chicago in 1921, I turned my back completely on the World Series of 1919, the Chicago White Sox, and the major leagues. I had been acquitted by a twelve-man jury in a civil court of all charges and I was an innocent man in the records. I have never made any request to be reinstated in baseball, and I have never made any campaign to have my name cleared in the baseball records. This is not a plea of any kind. This is just my story. I'm telling it simply because it seems that 30 years after that World Series, the world may want to hear what I have to say.

If I had been the kind of fellow who brooded when things went wrong, I probably would have gone out of my mind when Judge Landis ruled me out of baseball. I would have lived in regret. I would have been bitter and resentful because I felt I had been wronged.

But I haven't been resentful at all. I thought when my trial was over that Judge Landis might have restored me to good standing. But he never did. And until he died I had never gone before him, sent a representative before him, or placed before him any written matter pleading my case. I gave baseball my best and if the game didn't care enough to see me get a square deal, then I wouldn't go out of my way to get back in it.

Baseball failed to keep faith with me. When I got notice of my suspension three days before the 1920 season ended—it came on a rained-out day—it read that if found innocent of any wrongdoing, I would be reinstated. If found guilty, I would be banned for life. I was found innocent, and I was still banned for life.

It was never explained to me officially, but I was told that Judge Landis had said I was banned because of the company I kept. I roomed with Claude Williams, the pitcher, one of the ringleaders, they told me, and one of the eight White Sox players banned. But I had to take whoever they assigned to room with me on the road. I had no power over that.

Sure I'd heard talk that there was something going on. I even had a fellow come to me one day and proposition me. It was on the 16th floor of a hotel and there were four other people there, two men and their wives. I told him: "Why you cheap so-and-so! Either me or you—one of us is going out that window."

I started for him, but he ran out the door and I never saw him again. Those four people offered their testimony at my trial. Oh, there was so much talk those days, but I didn't know anything was going on.

When the talk got so bad just before the World Series with Cincinnati, I went to Mr. Charles Comiskey's room the night before the Series started and asked him to keep me out of the line-up. Mr Comiskey was the owner of the White Sox. He refused, and I begged him: "Tell the newspapers you just suspended me for being drunk, or anything, but leave me out of the Series and then there can be no question."

Hugh Fullerton, the oldtime New York sportswriter who's dead now, was in the room and heard the whole thing. He offered to testify for me at my trial later, and he came all the way out to Chicago to do it.

I went out and played my heart out against Cincinnati. I set a record that stills stands for the most hits in a Series, though it has been tied, I think. I made 13 hits, but after all the trouble came out they took one away from me. Maurice Rath went over in the hole and knocked down a hot grounder, but he couldn't make a throw on it. They scored it a hit then, but changed it later.

I led both teams in hitting with .375. I hit the only home run of the Series, off Hod Eller in the last game. I came all the way home from first on a single and scored the winning run in that 5-4 game. I handled 30 balls in the outfield and never made an error or allowed a man to take an extra base. I threw out five men at home and could have had three others, if bad cutoffs hadn't been made. One of them was in the second game Eddie Cicotte lost, when he made two errors in one inning. One of the errors was on a throw I made trying to cut off a run. He deflected the ball to the grandstand and the run came in.

That's my record in the Series, and I was responsible only for Joe Jackson. I positively can't say that I recall anything out of the way in the Series. I mean, anything that might have turned the tide. There was just one thing that doesn't seem quite right, now that I think back over it. Cicotte seemed to let up on a pitch to Pat Duncan, and Pat hit it over my head. Duncan didn't have enough power to hit the ball that far, particularly if Cicotte had been bearing down.

Williams was a great control pitcher and they made a lot of fuss over him walking a few men. Swede Risberg missed the bag on a double-play ball at second and they made a lot out of that. But those are things that might happen to anybody. You just can't say out and out that that was shady baseball.

There were supposed to have been a lot of big gamblers and boxers and shady characters mixed up in it. Well, I wouldn't have recognized Abe Attell if he'd been sitting next to me. Or Arnold Rothstein, either. Rothstein told them on the witness stand that he might know me if he saw me in a baseball uniform, but not in street clothes.

I guess the biggest joke of all was that story that got out about "Say it ain't so, Joe." Charley Owens of the Chicago Daily News was responsible for that, but there wasn't a bit of truth in it. It was supposed to have happened the day I was arrested in September of 1920, when I came out of the courtroom.

There weren't any words passed between anybody except me and a deputy sheriff. When I came out of the building this deputy asked me where I was going, and I told him to the Southside. He asked me for a ride and we got in the car together and left. There was a big crowd hanging around the front of the building, but nobody else said anything to me. It just didn't happen, that's all. Charley Owens just made up a good story and wrote it. Oh, I would have said it ain't so, all right, just like I'm saying it now....

They write a lot about what a great team the White Sox had that year. It was a good team. I won't take that away from them. But it wasn't the same kind of team Mr. Connie Mack had at Philadelphia from 1910 to 1914. I think that was the greatest team of all time. Our team didn't have but two hitters high in the .300's, Mr Eddie Collins, as fine a man as there ever was in baseball, and me. It wasn't a hard-hitting team, not the kind they make out it was.

It was sort of a strange ball club, split up into two gangs, Collins and Chick Gandil were the two leaders. They played side by side at second and first, but they hadn't spoken to each other off the field in two seasons. Bill Gleason was the manager, but Collins ran the team out on the field. Cicotte was the best pitcher in the league, next to Walter Johnson, I guess.

They called Williams the biggest and the littlest man in baseball. He had a great big neck and shoulders, but a small body. He had only been up two or three years when he was kicked out. Looked like he would have been a real fine pitcher. They hadn't thought much about Dickie Kerr in the World Series, at least not for the sort of pitching he did. Red Faber was the relief man mostly. We had Swede Risberg at short and Buck Weaver at third, me and Hap Felsch and Nemo Liebold in the outfield, and one of the smartest catchers ever, Ray Schalk. It was a good ball club, but not like Mr. Mack's.

I'll tell you the story behind the whole thing. The trouble was in the front office. Ban Johnson, the president of the American League, had sworn he'd get even with Mr. Comiskey a few years before, and that was how he did it. It was all over some fish Mr. Comiskey had sent to Mr. Johnson from his Wisconsin hunting lodge back about 1917. Mr. Comiskey had caught two big trout and they were such beauties he sent them to Johnson. He packed the fish in ice and expressed them, but by the time they got to Chicago the ice had melted and the fish had spoiled. They smelled awful and Mr. Johnson always thought Mr. Comiskey had deliberately pulled a joke on him. He never would believe it any other way.

That fish incident was the cause of it all. When Mr. Johnson got a chance to get even with Mr. Comiskey, he did it. He was the man who ruled us ineligible. He was the man who caused the thing to go into the courts. He did everything he could against Mr. Comiskey.

I'll show you how much he had it in for him. I sued Mr. Comiskey for the salary I had coming to me under the five year contract I had with the White Sox. When I won the verdict—I got only a little out of it—the first one I heard from was Mr. Johnson. He wired me congratulations on beating Mr. Comiskey and his son, Louis.

I have heard the story that Mr. Comiskey went to Mr. Johnson on his deathbed, held out his hand and asked that they let bygones be bygones. They say Mr. Johnson turned his head away and refused to speak to him.

I doubt if I'd have gone back into baseball, anyway, even if Judge Landis had reinstated me after the trial. I had a good valet business in Savannah, Georgia with 22 people working for me, and I had to look after it. I was away from it about a year waiting for the trial. They served papers on me which ordered me not to leave Illinois. I finally opened up a little place of business at 55th and Woodlawn, across from the University of Chicago. It was a sort of pool room and sports center and I got a lot of business from the University students.

I made my home in Chicago, but I didn't follow orders completely. I sneaked out of Illinois now and then to play with semi-pro teams in Indiana and Wisconsin. I always asked my lawyer, Mr. Benedictine Short, first and he told me to go if I could get that kind of money.

They kept delaying the trial until I personally went to the State Supreme Court judge, after which he ordered that the case be heard. They tried me and Buck Weaver together, and it took seven weeks. They used three weeks trying to get a jury, and I was on the witness stand one day and a half. After it was all over, Katie, my wife, and I went on back to Savannah, settled down there, and lived there until we came back to Greenville to bury my mother in 1935.

I have read now and then that I am one of the most tragic figures in baseball. Well, maybe that's the way some people look at it, but I don't quite see it that way myself. I guess one of the reasons I never fought my suspension any harder than I did was that I thought I had spent a pretty full life in the big leagues. I was 32 years old at the time, and I had been in the majors 13 years; I had a life time batting average of .356; I held the all-time throwing record for distance; and I had made pretty good salaries for those days. There wasn't much left for me in the big leagues.

All the big sportswriters seemed to enjoy writing about me as an ignorant cotton-mill boy with nothing but lint where my brains ought to be. That was all right with me. I was able to fool a lot of pitchers and managers and club owners I wouldn't have been able to fool if they'd thought I was smarter....

I guess right here is a good place for me to get the record straight on how I got to be "Shoeless Joe." I've read and heard every kind of yarn imaginable about how I got the name, but this is how it really happened: When I was with Greenville back in 1908, we only had 12 men on the roster. I was first off a pitcher, but when I wasn't pitching I played the outfield. I played in a new pair of shoes one day and they wore big blisters on my feet. The next day we came up short of players, a couple of men hurt and one missing. Tommy Stouch—he was a sportswriter in Lancaster, Pennsylvania, the last I heard of him—was the manager, and he told me I'd just have to play, blisters or not.

I tried it with my old shoes on and just couldn't make it. He told me I'd have to play anyway, so I threw away the shoes and went to the outfield in my stockinged feet. I hadn't put out much until along about the seventh inning I hit a long triple and I turned it on. That was in Anderson, and the bleachers were close to the baselines there. As I

pulled into third, some big guy stood up and hollered: "You shoeless sonofagun, you!"

They picked it up and started calling me Shoeless Joe all around the league, and it stuck. I never played the outfield barefoot, and that was the only day I ever played in my stockinged feet, but it stuck with me.

When I started out in the majors a fellow named Hyder Barr and me reported to the Athletics in the middle of the season. We got in right close to game time one day, so we checked our bags at the station and went straight to the park. They were playing the Yankees, and I hit the first pitch Jack Warhop threw me for a double. I got a single later and had two for three.

But I didn't stick around Philadelphia long then. I went back to the station to get my bag that night, and while I was waiting for it I heard the station announcer call out: "Baltimore, Washington, Richmond, Danville, Greensboro, Charlotte, Spartanburg, Greenville, Anderson" and so on. I couldn't stand it. I went up to the window and bought a ticket to Greenville and caught that train.

Sam Kennedy came after me on the next train. He found out I'd gone from Barr. I was supposed to get Barr's bag, too. He was quite a ladies man and he'd taken up with some girl while I went for the bags. When I didn't come back, he came after me and found out I'd gone. That was just the first time. I went back with Sam Kennedy, after he offered me more money. But I came home three other times before the season was over. It wasn't anything I had against Mr. Mack or the ball club. Mr Mack was a mighty fine man, and he taught me more baseball than any other manager I had. I just didn't like Philadelphia. I was traded to Cleveland later on and I liked it there. Charley Somers, who owned the Indians, was the most generous club owner I have ever seen. We couldn't play Sunday ball in Washington then, and when we were playing the Senators over a weekend, we'd make a jump back to Cleveland for a Sunday game, then back to Washington Sunday night. There never was a time we made that jump that Charley Somers didn't come down the aisle of the train and give all the players $20 gold pieces.

He was a generous man when it came to contracts, too. The first year I came up to Cleveland, in 1910, I led the league unofficially in hitting. When I went to talk contract with him for 1911, I told him I wanted $10,000. He wasn't figuring on giving me more than $6,000, and he wouldn't listen to me.

"I'll make a deal with you," I told him. "If I hit .400 you give me $10,000. If I don't, you don't give me a cent."

It was a deal, I signed the contract, and I hit .408. But I still didn't win the American League batting title. That was the year Ty Cobb hit .420. I was hitting .420 about three weeks before the season was over and Mr. Somers called me in to pay off, told me I could sit it out the rest of the season. I told him to wait until the season was ended and I wasn't quitting. I wrote my own contract the rest of the time I was in Cleveland.

Babe Ruth used to say that he copied my batting stance, and I felt right complimented. I was a left-handed hitter, and I did have an unusual stance. I used to draw a line three inches out from the plate every time I went to bat. I drew a right-angle line at the end next to the catcher and put my left foot on it exactly three inches from the plate. I kept both feet together, then took a long stride into the ball.

They say I was the greatest natural hitter of all time. Well that's saying a lot with hitters like Wagner, Cobb, Speaker and Ruth around. I had good eyes and I guess that was the reason I hit as well as I did. I still don't use glasses today.

I have been pretty lucky since I left the big leagues. No man who has done the things they accuse me of doing could have been as successful. Everything I touched seemed to turn to money, and I've made my share down through the years. I've been blessed with a good banker, too—my wife. Handing the money to her was just like putting it in the bank. We were married in 1908 when I was just 19 and she was 15, and she has stood by me through everything. We never had any children of our own, but we raised one of my brother's boys from babyhood.

He never was interested in baseball, but they used to tell me he would have been a fine football player. He didn't get to go to college. The war came along and he went into the Navy as a flier. He was killed accidentally a couple of years ago when a gun he was cleaning went off. Katie and me felt like we'd lost our own boy....

I hadn't been able to do much work for a year until last Summer because of liver trouble. A good doctor in Greenville took my case when I thought my time was about here, and he brought me back to good health. I went back to my liquor store last July and I'm running the business now myself, I had leased it out while I was sick. I've been doing about $50,000 to $100,000 a year business.

Some people might think it's odd, but I still have a connection in baseball, sort of a judicial connection, I guess you'd call it. I am chairman of the protest board of the Western Carolina Semi-Pro League. I think that is an indication of how I stand with my own people. They have

stood by me all these years, the folks from my mill country, and I love them for their loyalty.

None of the other banned White Sox have had it quite as good as I have, I understand, unless it is Williams. He is a big Christian Science Church worker out on the West Coast. Last I heard Cicotte was working in the automobile industry in Detroit. Felsch was a bartender in Milwaukee. Risberg was working in the fruit business out in California. Buck Weaver was still in Chicago, tinkering with softball, I think. Gandil is down in Louisiana and Fred McMullin is out on the West Coast. I don't know what they're doing....

I'm 61 years old now, living quietly and happily out on my little street close to Brandon Mill. I weighed 186 and stood six feet, one inch tall in my playing days. I'm still about the same size.

There never were any other ballplayers in my family that went to the big leagues. I had five brothers, but only one, Jerry, played pro ball long. He was a pretty good minor-league pitcher, they tell me. Jerry's 48 years old now and he's one of my umpires in the Western Carolina League.

Well, that's my story. I repeat what I said when I started out—that I have no axe to grind, that I'm not asking anybody for anything. It's all water over the dam as far as I am concerned. I can say that my conscience is clear and that I'll stand on my record in that World Series. I'm not what you call a good Christian, but I believe in the Good Book, particularly where it says "what you sow, so shall you reap." I have asked the Lord for guidance before, and I am sure He gave it to me. I'm willing to let the Lord be my judge."

SIGNIFICANCE

The scandal of the 1919 World Series ended the promising career of Shoeless Joe Jackson. Jackson's career batting average of .356 is only surpassed by Ty Cobb at .367 and Rogers Hornsby's average of .358. The son of a mill worker from Brandon Mills, South Carolina, Jackson quit school by twelve years old and was illiterate when he started the major league in 1908. Jackson began playing for Chicago in 1915 and his performance in the series has led many to believe that he was not part of the fix. Jackson batted .375 and played errorless on the field. In addition, Jackson hit a home run during the series, a feat that was rare in Jackson's time.

Commissioner Landis's comment exemplifies the legacy of the 1919 World Series and the importance of avoiding the impression of impropriety. Landis stated, "Baseball is something more than a game to an American boy. It is his training field for life work. Destroy his faith in its squareness and honesty and you have destroyed something more; you have planted suspicion of all things in his heart." This no gambling edict was revisited years later in 1989 when Pete Rose was banned from baseball after a federal prosecutor revealed evidence that Rose had bet on baseball. Rose initially admitted to only betting on college and pro basketball, as well as NFL games. However, in 2004 Rose admitted to also betting on baseball. Supporters of Jackson, like baseball legend Ted Williams who sought to have Jackson reinstated, asserted that Jackson should only be judged on his on field performance. However, those who support Rose and Jackson's lifetime ineligibility suggest that baseball cannot endure without the faith of the fans.

FURTHER RESOURCES

Periodicals

Ward, Geoffrey C. & Ken Burns. "Game Time". *US News and World Report* (August 29, 1994).

Skretta, David. "Baseball has a long history of notoriety". *USA Today* (August 2, 2005).

Kindred, Dave. "A shot in the arm baseball didn't need". *Sporting News* (November 24, 2003).

Police Seize an Illegal Brewery in Detroit

Photograph

By: Anonymous

Date: circa 1925

Source: "Police Seize an Illegal Brewery in Detroit." National Archives and Records Administration.

About the Photographer: This image comes from the National Archives and Records Administration's American Cities Collection. The photographer is unknown.

INTRODUCTION

The January 1919 ratification of the Eighteenth Amendment to the Constitution banned the manufacture, sale, and transportation of intoxicating beverages. In the wake of the ratification, Congress adopted the Volstead enforcement act to define an intoxicating beverage as any drink containing more than .05 percent alcohol, including beer and wine as well as distilled spirits.

Most Americans obeyed Prohibition. Alcohol consumption dropped by nearly two-thirds. Yet the public perceived Prohibition as a failure because of the difficulties in enforcing the law. Corruption, inefficiency, and lack of cooperation with other law enforcement agencies hampered the efforts of the Prohibition Bureau and its predecessors.

Prohibition enforcement underwent frequent reorganizations in an effort to make the law workable. The Volstead Act assigned responsibility for Prohibition enforcement to the Commissioner of Internal Revenue in the Treasury Department rather than to the Department of Justice because Treasury agents had earlier collected liquor taxes. Tax collectors were not especially efficient or skilled at catching lawbreakers. Corruption was also widespread with many of the agents chosen for political reasons rather than competence. In 1927, Congress tried to remedy the problem by establishing the Prohibition Bureau within the Treasury Department and placing the agents under civil service regulations. The Bureau moved to the Justice Department in 1930.

Turnover was high among the Prohibition Bureau agents. Between 1920 and 1930, the Prohibition Bureau and its predecessors appointed nearly 18,000 agents for field positions that never numbered more than 2,300. The average turnover in the enforcement branch was nearly forty percent. By 1931, the federal government had dismissed 1,604 agents for cause, commonly drunkenness or bribery.

A lack of cooperation among law enforcement agencies further hampered enforcement of Prohibition. At the federal level, the Coast Guard and the Customs Service had shared responsibility for enforcing the ban on the importation of intoxicating beverages but no coordinated enforcement program was established. The states made few efforts to enforce Prohibition, despite bearing concurrent responsibility for enforcement.

Lured by the promise of high profits and little risk, moonshiners made homemade liquor. Home distillers commonly used a pot still. This device consisted of a closed copper kettle placed above a source of heat. A copper pipe at the top of the pot led to a coiled pipe, or worm, contained within a water-cooled chamber. The "wash," initially grain or potatoes, was placed in the kettle and heated. The alcohol rose into the worm and cooled back to a liquid. Spirits then dripped through the end of the pipe at the bottom of the con-

Police Seize an Illegal Brewery in Detroit: Uniformed and plainclothes police inspect the equipment found at an illegal brewery in Prohibition-era Detroit, Michigan. NATIONAL ARCHIVES AND RECORDS ADMINISTRATION

denser to be collected. The product was generally of poor quality. Repeating the procedure removed impurities and increased the alcohol content.

PRIMARY SOURCE

POLICE SEIZE AN ILLEGAL BREWERY IN DETROIT

See primary source image.

SIGNIFICANCE

By 1930, the federal government had spent $15 million to enforce Prohibition. The enforcement effort generally succeeded in stopping the consump-

tion of intoxicating drinks. Between 1921 and 1929, Prohibition agents made 539,759 arrests and seized 45,177 vehicles. The number of Prohibition cases in federal courts increased from 29,114 in 1921 to 65,960 in 1932. For the period of 1921 to 1933, Prohibition cases constituted 64.6 percent of all cases in federal district court.

Enforcement of the law helped to bring about its demise. To catch criminals, Prohibition agents searched automobiles without warrants, wiretapped telephones, and engaged in gun battles that sometimes sent bullets flying into terrified bystanders. The excesses caused a backlash from an angry public that increasingly sensed a breakdown of respect for law and order.

The lawlessness created by Prohibition sparked a public outcry for changes in policing. In response, President Herbert Hoover commissioned an unprecedented study of law enforcement. The resulting Wickersham Commission report, issued beginning in 1931, summed up the prevailing wisdom about crime and criminality, police, prosecutions, prison, and parole. In response to Wickersham, the Federal Bureau of Investigation began something that chiefs of police had been requesting for years: the collection of Uniform Crime Reports based on the number of incidents reported to police departments across the country.

The Great Depression that began in 1929 focused attention on the economic effects of Prohibition, particularly the enforcement costs. Arresting violators of the law consumed police time, jammed federal and state courts, and dramatically increased the prison population. By 1930, two-thirds of those found guilty received only fines but federal prisons bulged with twice the number of inmates for which they were designed. The overflow of federal inmates filled state and local jails.

The liquor trade had once been the seventh-largest industry in the United States. When the Twenty-first Amendment in 1933 repealed the Eighteenth Amendment, brewers and bottle-makers returned to legal work.

FURTHER RESOURCES
Books

Pegram, Thomas R. *Battling Demon Rum: The Struggle for a Dry America, 1800–1933*. Chicago: Ivan R. Dee, 1998.

Sinclair, Andrew. *Prohibition: The Era of Excess*. New York: Harper & Row, 1962.

Unintended Consequences of Constitutional Amendments, edited by David Kyvig. Athens Ga.: University of Georgia Press, 2000.

Prohibition Rum Runner

Photograph

By: Anonymous

Date: November 4, 1930

Source: Corbis

About the Photographer: This image, by an unknown photographer, is owned by Corbis, a photo agency headquartered in Seattle, Washington. Corbis licenses images for use in magazines, films, television, and advertisements.

INTRODUCTION

Prohibition was part of a century-long effort by Americans to solve the problems caused by alcohol abuse. Since attempts to persuade individuals to stop drinking often failed, reformers wanted coercive measures placed into law. In 1917, Congress approved a Constitutional amendment that banned the manufacture, sale, or transportation of intoxicating beverages. In 1919, the states ratified the Eighteenth Amendment and Prohibition became law.

Prohibition had widespread support among the public and consumption of alcoholic beverages dropped dramatically during the years that it remained in effect. But many Americans viewed Prohibition as an improper curtailment of their personal liberty. Opposition centered in the cities, where many immigrant groups regarded Prohibition as an attack on their cultural norms and religious practices. The Germans and the Irish, in particular, did not see the dangers in having a beer with dinner. Thus demand for alcoholic beverages remained high.

The chief problem for law enforcement during Prohibition was that while the United States had banned the sale of alcohol, Mexico, Cuba, and Canada had not. The governments of these neighboring countries were more than happy to see their citizens make a profit by selling alcohol to Americans. Boats and ships, known as "rum runners" easily ran liquor across the border into the U.S. In addition, a fleet of ships sat in international waters, just outside the three-mile limit, catering to Americans who sailed out to indulge in wine and liquor. Liquor and wine imported for "medicinal purposes" found its way into the stomachs of healthy citizens, while the sale of grape vines jumped dramatically. Home-brewed beer and cider appeared on dining room tables alongside "bathtub" gin. Millions of gallons of industrial alcohol were converted into bootleg liquor and bottled under counterfeit labels. Such bottles sometimes included poisonous wood alcohol that killed or blinded many unsuspecting drinkers.

Prohibition also encouraged the growth of organized crime, particularly the Mafia. Many of the gangsters who had operated gambling and prostitution rings entered the lucrative market of illegal liquor

Prohibition Rum Runner: Seized off Fire Island in 1930, the fishing schooner *Clinton* held 800 cases of rum. Behind the vessel is its captor, the rum chaser, *Reliance.*
© BETTMANN/CORBIS

PROHIBITION RUM RUNNER

See primary source image.

SIGNIFICANCE

By the end of the 1920s, it had become apparent to many Americans that Prohibition had failed. As the many rum runners demonstrated, Prohibition had not succeeded in stopping the manufacture, sale, or transportation of liquor. The law simply proved ineffective against high demand.

While Prohibition was successful in virtually eliminating the working class saloons, it encouraged the growth of new drinking establishments, such as speakeasies, that catered to the middle and upper classes. For the first time, respectable middle-class women were patronizing bars because it was now the fashionable thing to do. Raids on restaurants, bars, and nightclubs that served liquor only had temporary success. The owners soon reopened, often after bribing the police. In the cities, nearly every neighborhood had a bootlegger. Law enforcement was ineffective since it simply was not possible to close the long Mexican and Canadian borders or to establish a naval blockade of the entire American coastline. The inability of law enforcement agencies to halt the distribution of liquor contributed to contempt for the law.

In 1933, Prohibition was repealed, partly in an effort to create jobs and tax revenue during the Great Depression. Opponents of the law argued that it had retarded the cause of temperance by inciting crime, hypocrisy, and corruption. In the decades that followed, few people remembered the successes of Prohibition because its failures were so very obvious.

FURTHER RESOURCES
Books

Hallwas, John E. *The Bootlegger: A Story of Small-Town America.* Chicago: University of Illinois Press, 1998.

Pegram, Thomas R. *Battling Demon Rum: The Struggle for a Dry America, 1800–1933.* Chicago: Ivan R. Dee, 1998.

Sinclair, Andrew. *Prohibition: The Era of Excess.* New York: Harper & Row, 1962.

trafficking. The funds generated by bootlegging were so much greater than those created by other illegal activity that organized crime and the corruption of officials flourished on an unprecedented scale. Chicago's Al Capone (1899–1847), perhaps the most notorious gangster of the Prohibition era, reaped huge profits from selling bootlegged liquor. The crime business often included violence as rival gangs confronted each other to protect their respective turfs. In Chicago, over 200 gang-related killings occurred during the first four years of Prohibition.

Attitudes Towards the Legalization of the Use of Marijuana

Chart

By: The Gallup Organization

Date: 2005

Source: *Sourcebook of Criminal Justice Statistics 2003.* Reprinted by permission.

About the Author: This chart was created for the U.S. Department of Justice by the Gallup Organization. The Gallup Organization is an American firm that provides market research, health care, and consulting services on a global scale. It routinely conducts polls to gauge public opinion on various issues. Since its establishment in 1958 by American statistician George Gallup (1901–1984), it has become a respected indicator of public opinion.

INTRODUCTION

Also called cannabis, ganja, hash, and spliff, marijuana is the common name of the dried leaves of the hemp plant *Cannabis sativa*, consumed in a variety of ways for recreational or medicinal purposes. Marijuana makes users feel overjoyed, dreamy, and sometimes hallucinated. Overdose or long-term consumption can lead to nausea, anxiety, distress, and severe behavioral problems.

Until well into the twentieth century, the possession and use of marijuana was legal, and it was a frequent ingredient in patent medicines. In 1925, however, trade in marijuana and its more potent, concentrated cousin, hashish, were restricted under the International Opium Convention of 1925. The Marijuana Tax Act of 1937 imposed fines and severe penalties on anyone dealing in the drug, effectively criminalizing its use, and it was removed from the U.S. pharmacopoeia as an accepted medicine in 1942. Finally, the Controlled Substances Act of 1970 listed it as a schedule I drug—grouping it with the most tightly regulated substances, including heroin, LSD, and PCP.

The current federal penalty for marijuana trafficking in the United States can be at the most five years for possession of less than 50 kilograms of marijuana and up to ten years for possession of 1,000 kilos or more. The same penalty applies for possession of the same number of marijuana plants in lieu of weight.

Demonstrators in Austin, Texas, urge then-Governor George W. Bush in 2000 to soften the laws on drugs in Texas as well as in the whole country. © DAEMMRICH, BOB/CORBIS SYGMA

Sentences are harsher for repeat offenders, for whom the penalty extends to at most ten years for possession of less than 50 kilograms of marijuana and at least twenty years to life imprisonment for possession of 1,000 kilos or more.

Marijuana has a long history of therapeutic and sedative use, and many recent studies cite it as beneficial in the treatment of glaucoma and multiple sclerosis, while others indicate substantial relief from the side effects of chemotherapy. Some states have passed laws to encourage scientific study for medicinal use. The problem is that federal and state law conflict on this issue. Since Federal law supercedes state law, federal agents have made arrests in states that have legalized the medical use of marijuana and warned doctors that they risk arrest if they prescribe marijuana.

Attitudes toward legalization of the use of marijuana

UNITED STATES, SELECTED YEARS 1969–2003

Question: "Do you think the use of marijuana should be made legal, or not?"

	Yes, legal	No, illegal	Don't know/ refused
1969	12%	84%	4%
1972	15%	81%	4%
1973	16%	78%	6%
1977	28%	66%	6%
1979	25%	70%	5%
1980	25%	70%	5%
1985	23%	73%	4%
1995	25%	73%	2%
2000[a]	31%	64%	5%
2001	34%	62%	4%
2003[a]	34%	64%	2%

Note: Sample sizes vary from year to year; the data for 2003 are based on telephone interviews with a randomly selected national sample of 1,004 adults, 18 years of age and older, conducted November 10–12, 2003.

[a]Asked of a half sample.

SOURCE: The Gallup Organization, Inc., *The Gallup Poll* [online]. Available: http://www.gallup.com/poll/[June 28,2004]. Table adapted by Sourcebook staff. Reprinted by permission.

■ PRIMARY SOURCE

Attitudes Towards the Legalization of the Use of Marijuana: Years of polling by the Gallup Organization show that support for legalization of marijuana grew in the 1970s, declined slightly in the 1980s, and then rose to new heights in 2000s. *SOURCEBOOK OF CRIMINAL JUSTICE STATISTICS 2003.* REPRINTED BY PERMISSION.

The possession and use of marijuana remains illegal in most other countries as well, although some, like the Netherlands, have adopted a nonenforcement policy that tolerates small amounts in personal possession and consumption in "coffee houses." That said, marijuana supporters in the various countries including the United States, Canada, Australia, and Britain have campaigned for the legalization of marijuana use.

"Attitudes toward Legalization of the Use of Marijuana. United Sates. Selected Years, 1969–2003." based on a Gallup poll, was published in July 2004.

■ PRIMARY SOURCE

ATTITUDES TOWARDS THE LEGALIZATION OF THE USE OF MARIJUANA

See primary source image.

SIGNIFICANCE

Marijuana is the most widely used prohibited substance in the United States. Typically, it's brewed into a tea, smoked in pipes, mixed with food, or taken in combination with other drugs. Other ways of consuming marijuana include vaporizing and burning it to inhale its fumes.

The U.S. Drug Enforcement Administration (DEA) estimates the number of marijuana users at around 11.5 million and says that at least a third of the American population has experimented with the drug at some point, because despite enforcement of drug laws, it is relatively easy to obtain and consume. There were close to a million new users of this drug in 2002 alone.

Although considered relatively harmless by many people, detailed studies by the National Institute of Drug Abuse (NIDA) to assess the effects of marijuana noted an increased risk of addiction and possible damage to the brain, heart, throat, and lungs. Studies conducted on pregnant women indicate increased risk to the well-being of mother and the child. Children born to such mothers may exhibit behavioral irregularities and may also have poorer memory and lower levels of attentiveness. Children who use marijuana often lose interest in school and are more likely to drop out.

Despite such potentially serious effects, the Gallup poll above showed that by 2003 the number of respondents who thought that marijuana should be legalized had nearly tripled from the 12 percent who thought so in 1969. Not surprisingly, respondents who wanted to keep marijuana illegal dropped from 84 percent in 1969 to 64 percent in 2003.

Many of those who support marijuana's legalization claim its active ingredient, THC, is an effective therapy for the pain and nausea of AIDS, cancer, glaucoma, and other diseases. Critics, including the DEA, however, do not agree and maintain marijuana has no proven medical benefits.

FURTHER RESOURCES

Web sites

Alliance for Cannabis Therapeutics. "Information about Medical Uses of Marijuana."<http://marijuana-as-medicine.org/alliance.htm> (accessed January 14, 2006).

DEA: U.S. Drug Enforcement Administration. "Drug Trafficking in the United States."<http://www.dea.gov/concern/drug_trafficking.html> (accessed January 14, 2006).

——— "Exposing the Myth of Smoked Medical Marijuana."<http://www.dea.gov/ongoing/marijuana.html> (accessed January 14, 2006).

NIDA: National Institute on Drug Abuse. "NIDA Infofacts: Marijuana."<http://www.nida.nih.gov/Infofacts/marijuana.html> (accessed January 14, 2006).

USA Today. "Attitudes Ease toward Medical Marijuana."<http://www.usatoday.com/news/nation/2003-05-22-marijuana-usat_x.htm> (accessed January 14, 2006).

Asia Hunts Sex Tourists

Internet article

By: The Asian Pacific Post

Date: September 7, 2005

Source: "Asia Hunts Sex Tourists." *The Asian Pacific Post,* September 7, 2005, <http://www.asianpacific-post.com/portal2/pageView.html?id=402881910674ebab010674f5aaf11ef9> (accessed February 22, 2006).

About the Author: *The Asia Pacific Post* is an English-language Asian newspaper published in Vancouver, British Columbia. Established in 1993, its aim is to provide Asian news and views with a Canadian perspective. It is issued biweekly and reaches 160,000 readers.

INTRODUCTION

In a testimony before the U.S. Congress, Professor Mohamed Mattar of The Protection Project identified a significant rise in sex tourism in the developing countries of Cambodia, Vietnam, the Philippines, Sri Lanka, the Dominican Republic, Costa Rica, Thailand, and Cuba. He defined sex tourism as the travel to a county with the purpose of illicit sexual encounters, many with under-age girls and boys. The countries that Professor Mattar identified have all experienced a surge in tourism due to the availability of cheap airfares and hotel rooms. Emerging from the oppression of the Khmer Rouge and Pol Pot, Cambodia's yearly foreign visitors have grown since 1988 from 280,000 to more than a million. The main attraction for these visitors is the temples of Angkor Wat. However, as the result of the rapidly developing tourist economies, many in these countries also have discovered that money can be made from tourists willing to pay for sex.

Pierre Legros, the director of AFESIP (Acting for Women in Distressing Situations), a refuge and rehabilitation center for rescued sex workers in Cambodia, asserts that approximately 6,000 child sex offences are committed daily in Asia. Activists working toward better prosecution of sex tourism estimate that Cambodia, alone, employs 20,000 child prostitutes, some as young as ten years old. Rescued sex workers estimate that as many as half of these workers are sold into the business, some by their families. Local activists believe that one of the impediments to deterring sex tourism is tolerance of the trade based on the local attitude that children are a commodity to pull a family from poverty. Therefore, buying children for sex is acceptable. Education programs intended to change this view are seen by some locals as anti-family, since the child prostitute is often alleviating a family's poverty.

In addition to the societal view of children as a commodity, the police system often places a different value on child prostitution and sex tourism. According to Christian Guth, a retired French policeman participating in an education program for law enforcement in Thailand, the Thai police system does not share western views of decency toward minors. He explains in a *Time International* article, "When I said under 16 was rape, they laughed because 14 to 16 is considered the best age in brothels." The rise in HIV/AIDS cases in Asia has compelled sex tourists to seek out younger, inexperienced girls. These entrenched attitudes are not the only reason pedophilia offenses are not prosecuted in Asia. Rescued sex workers identify the police and uniformed military as a big part of their clientele. Corrupt police and judges can also be bribed to obtain the release of foreign sex offenders.

PRIMARY SOURCE

When police arrived at the ramshackle computer shop at the Baligbago village in Philippines' Angeles City, the Canadian had vanished. Huddled inside were six Filipinas who were cybersex models.

As police swept through the building, they found James Paul Kelly, 66, from America.

Members of the raiding team rescued the six women and confiscated several units of computer sets from the suspect's house.

Kelly, police say was the alleged operator of the cybersex den along with a Canadian identified as Dave Fischer.

Chintana, 16, a former prostitute, poses in profile at a woman's rescue center in Bangkok, Thailand, in 2001. Chintana was one of twenty prostitutes imprisoned in a brothel near Bangkok's port, forced to service two or three customers a night, mostly construction, factory, and port workers. AP IMAGES

Fischer is now being hunted in the Philippines.

Just a few weeks earlier in the same area, police busted another sex den. This one was was allegedly run by an American couple, Tom and Virginia Deassy.

The couple, who are said to be the owners of cybersex dens operating in different tourist areas in the Philippines, are on the run.

The police raids on the sex dens in the Philippines, which cater to everyone from Western expatriates to rich businessmen from Japan and Korea, are not being done in isolation.

They are part of a regional crackdown on the multi-million dollar sex-tourism industry that victimizes thousands of children and women every year, say government officials.

At a recent Singapore conference on child sex tourism and trafficking attended by about 130 delegates from 14 countries, participants pledged greater recognition that they must cooperate to prevent the trafficking of women and children and the movement of known sex offenders across borders.

While there is no definitive data on the size of the child sex trade in the region, non-governmental organizations estimate there are over a million child prostitutes in Asia.

A study conducted by Johns Hopkins University in the United States and presented at the conference, revealed that Cambodia, the Philippines and Thailand are hot spots for those seeking sex with minors and teenaged girls.

Vietnam and Myanmar are emerging hot spots. In the Philippines, lawmaker Joseph Santiago is pushing for local governments to reinforce their supervision of Internet and computer shops that could possibly be fronting for illicit cybersex operations.

He said that over 200,000 Filipinos—women, men and children—have been lured by cybersex operators, according to the registry of adultfriendfinder.com, a popular web site peddling sexual activities on the Internet.

Angeles City alone, Santiago said, has been classified a cybersex and sex-tourism hotspot by the Philippines National Police since at least 10 dens have been busted there this year.

Canadian companies are also beginning to keep an eye on their employees who travel to Asia frequently says a Singapore-based professional child sex tourist buster.

Veteran private investigator P Kalastree, 58, is the managing director of Mainguard International Pte Ltd. He has been in the private eye business for almost 30 years. His wife, Dora Woo, 54, is a director in the firm.

In the last five years, they have handled 25 child sex cases. And, they reckon, they'll probably see more in future, according to Singapore's *New Paper*.

Kalastree said the companies include those from Canada, US, UK, Germany and Switzerland.

He said they didn't want their employees to violate the laws of that respective country which might embarrass the company.

"The 25 cases I've handled involved mostly Caucasian men," said Kalastree.

"Southeast Asia is a haven for them. Most of them went for young girls and only two went for boys." He said more and more countries are coming down hard on their citizens suspected of child exploitation.

Kalastree said some of these child sex tourists set up businesses in Asian countries so they have an excuse to travel there often.

"They may be from the IT or the garment trade. Most of the men are professionals such as engineers."

Last year, he and his wife travelled to Thailand to observe an Irish accountant in his 40s who was married with a 10-year-old daughter and an 8-year-old son.

"His employers suspected him of buying sex from children. He liked teenage girls around 14 to 16 years old and would frequent lounges where these girls would dance naked in front of him on bar tops."

"Some of these lounges or nightclubs are connected to apartments and he would then take one or two of the girls to his room later."

He said they monitored the man for about six months before submitting reports to the man's employers, who then told the wife.

The woman sued her husband for compensation then divorced him.

Then there was the case of the British oil and gas executive in his 50s who was married and travelled often to Thailand to stay with young teenage boys in his room.

In Vietnam, anyone caught buying sex will have their name published in local newspapers.

Lawyer Tan Heng Thye in Hanoi told *The New Paper* : "Men, either locals or foreigners, who are caught patronising prostitutes will be shamed by having their details published in newspapers."

"Both the tourists and the operators can be fined or punished."

"Women who are caught will be sent to 're-education camps,' where they are given vocational training and attend lectures aimed to reform their ways." The sentence can range between three and 18 months.

Vietnam aside, Thailand, the Philippines, Cambodia, Laos, Indonesia and Sri Lanka are among the top destinations sex tour operators hawk to their customers.

Most of these organised sex tours come from Australia, Germany, the US, Japan and South Korea. The industry is said to be worth billions annually.

A 1998 report by the International Labour Organisation estimates that 2 to 14 percent of the gross domestic product of Indonesia, Malaysia, the Philippines and Thailand is derived from sex tourism.

In the case of Indonesia, revenue from sex tourism can go as high as C$5 billion.

Braema Mathi, president of women's rights group Aware, said that harsher and clearer laws have to be implemented to stop the proliferation of sex tours, as they often involve the exploitation of women and children who have been forced into the trade.

"There should be punitive action taken against those who continue to make the trade flourish—be it the brothel owners, tour operators or sex tourists."

Meanwhile, the 10-member Association of Southeast Asian Nations (ASEAN) is embarking on a campaign against child sex tourism.

ASEAN officials are now working on the appropriate language for the "Asean Travelers' Code," the association's secretary-general, Ong Keng Yong, told *The Straits Times*.

Warning messages intended to resonate strongly with travelers—in the same way that the region is now known for its zero-tolerance policy on drug trafficking—could be carried on immigration forms, visas, and publicity materials at immigration checkpoints.

The Australian government is now funding a program called Child Wise Tourism which aims to build child-safe tourism destinations.

Child Wise Tourism is a training and network development program that promotes ethical and sustainable tourism practices.

With the support of the Australian Government, Child Wise is planning to conduct 50 community-based training sessions in seven ASEAN countries over the next year in Thailand, Indonesia, Cambodia, Philippines, Laos, Vietnam and Myanmar.

Meanwhile, the Canadian-based Cybertip.ca said this month its online child sexual exploitation service has shown another big jump in reports by the public.

Of the 4,541 reports of child pornography filed since Cybertip.ca started as a pilot project in Manitoba in September 2002, 55% have been filed since the tipline was launched as a national service on January 24, 2005 and an intensive public awareness campaign was implemented.

In the six months between its official launch on Jan 24 and July 30, 2005, Cybertip.ca received 2,297 reports of child sexual exploitation on the Internet. This is up from 743 reports for the six months prior to launch, representing a 200% increase.

Over the same period, reports of child pornography have increased more than 300%, from 516 to 2,132.

About 50 of the cases involved child sex-tourism.

The public is urged to report child sexual exploitation they encounter to www.cybertip.ca or by calling toll free 1 866 658 9022.

SIGNIFICANCE

The United Nations Convention on the Rights of a Child states that children under the age of eighteen should be protected against sexual exploitation. As a result, many countries have initiated policies to curb sex tourism and target pedophiles entering countries with the intent to elicit sex from a child. In Cambodia, the government has launched the "Sex Tourism—NO" campaign and is creating a database of foreigners who have engaged in sex tourism. As a result, the number of police arrests for sexual offenses has risen from zero in 1998 to 200 in 2004.

On April 13, 2003, the U.S. Congress passed the Prosecutorial Remedies and Other Tools to End the Exploitation of Children Today Act (PROTECT Act), which provides penalties for those who engage in sex tourism. As a result, at least four arrests have been made. The act provides for prosecution within the U.S. for those traveling to foreign countries to engage in illicit sexual conduct. The first two charges were drawn against Michael Lewis Clark, who traveled to Cambodia and allegedly paid two homeless boys, aged ten and thirteen, two dollars to have sex with him. In addition to the PROTECT Act, the Reauthorization Act provides for education and dissemination of the information that sex tourism is illegal and will be prosecuted.

UNICEF spearheads education programs aimed at eradicating sex tourism and the group asserts that information campaigns dissuade those interested in traveling to developing nations to have sex with children. UNICEF suggests that the travel industry also could aid in deterring sex tourism by informing travelers of the punishment for such activities, notifying the authorities of suspected activities, discouraging tourism companies from hosting prostitutes, developing a code of conduct for the travel industry, and working with local tourism partners to keep them from referring tourists to sex establishments.

FURTHER RESOURCES

Periodicals

Penh, Kay Johnson Phnom. "Asia: Pedophile Playground. Cambodia Says It Wants to Crack Down on Child-Sex Offenders. A British Teacher's Trial Will Test Its Resolve." *Time International* (November 13, 2005).

Tuke, Frances. "Holidays with Lolita." *Travel Weekly* (May 3, 2004).

"A Walk on the Depraved Side." *The Economist* (March 30, 2000).

Web sites

The Protection Project. "Statement of Mohamed Y. Mattar. Hearing before the Senate Committee on the Judiciary, Subcommittee on the Constitution, Civil Rights and Property Rights. Examining U.S. Efforts to Combat Human Trafficking and Slavery. July 7, 2004." <http://www.protectionproject.org/re3.htm> (accessed February 22, 2006).

A Former U.S. Police Chief Stirs the Pot on Drug Laws

Newspaper article

By: Gary Mason

Date: October 20, 2005

Source: Mason, Gary. "A Former U.S. Police Chief Stirs the Pot on Drug Laws." *Globe and Mail* (October 20, 2005): A14.

About the Author: Gary Mason began his career as a journalist in British Columbia. He worked for the *Vancouver Sun*, for nineteen years, as a legislative bureau chief, city editor, and deputy managing editor. Mason started with the *Globe and Mail* in 2005, as a national columnist covering British Columbia issues. He received British Columbia's highest journalism honor, the Jack Webster Award, twice. He has won other awards and is the author of several best-selling books.

INTRODUCTION

Drug abuse is generally believed to be one of the most significant social and health problems facing the United States. Studies by the National Institute of Health (NIH) estimate that the costs of substance abuse exceed the costs of any other disease, when taking into account health care expenditures, earnings lost, and the costs associated with crime and accidents. U.S. drug policy considers drug use, trade, and cultivation to be criminal activities. However, there is an ongoing debate as to whether or not drug use should be legalized in the U.S.

The mainstream viewpoint in the U.S. is that the legalization of drugs would, in fact, exacerbate existing drug addiction and crime rates. However, critics say current U.S. drug policy is ineffective, leading to a lack of control of the inevitable drug use and the overcrowding of prisons with non-violent drug users. It is also said that the U.S. spends too much money trying to enforce an unenforceable policy. Some estimates are that only five to fifteen percent of illegal drugs arriving in the U.S. are intercepted by authorities, at costs as high as $40 billion. It is thought that the illegal drug trade is a $200 billion industry, with nearly thirteen million Americans using illegal drugs in any given month. Another argument against U.S. drug policy is that it is unjust to punish individuals for using drugs when they do so at their own discretion and do little harm to anyone else.

Former police officer Norm Stamper spent the last six years of his thirty-four-year career as the Seattle Chief of Police. He draws upon his experience with drug law enforcement to take a position strongly in favor of the legalization of all types of illegal drugs. Stamper speaks of neighborhoods where illegal drug markets put children and other innocent citizens at risk. He describes U.S. anti-drug foreign policies as causing instability and creating problems for subsistence farmers in developing countries like Colombia and Afghanistan. Police forces have had to confront the problem of police officers giving in to the temptation of doing such things as planting drugs on suspects, stealing money from drug dealers, and using drugs themselves. Stamper, and others, believe many of these difficulties could be reduced or eliminated with legalization of drugs.

▮ PRIMARY SOURCE

One of the most e-mailed stories from the *Los Angeles Times* website this week was an opinion piece written by Norm Stamper, former chief of the Seattle Police Department, entitled: "Let those dopers be." "Sometimes people in law enforcement will hear it whispered that I'm a former cop who favors decriminalization of marijuana laws and they'll approach me the way they might a traitor or a snitch," Mr. Stamper begins the piece. "So let me set the record straight…. I don't favor decriminalization. I favor legalization and not just of pot but of all drugs, including heroin, cocaine, meth, psychotropics, mushrooms and LSD."

If this sounds familiar, it should. On Tuesday, the Health Officers' Council of British Columbia released a groundbreaking report calling for exactly the same action. It's one thing, however, for a group of physicians and academics to make such a suggestion in a relatively liberal-minded country like Canada. It's quite another for a former cop of Mr. Stamper's pedigree to make a similar call in George W. Bush's America. Which is why the piece has created such a stir.

Mr. Stamper's thoughts on the United States's failed "war on drugs" are also contained in his new book called *Breaking Rank: A Top Cop's Exposé of the Dark Side of American Policing.* And while there is all sorts of juicy stuff about the level of corruption, sexism, racism and homophobia that still exists in the modern police force, it's Mr. Stamper's radical views on drugs that are the most thought-provoking.

In his piece for the *Los Angeles Times,* Mr. Stamper says he has never understood why adults shouldn't enjoy illicit drugs in the same way they do their pack of Marlboros or bottle of scotch. "Prohibition of alcohol fell flat on its face," he writes. "The prohibition of other drugs rests on an equally wobbly foundation. Not until we choose to frame responsible drug use—not an oxymoron in my dictionary—as a civil liberty, will we be able to recognize the abuse of drugs, including alcohol, for what it is: a medical, not a criminal, matter."

Mr. Stamper contends that the U.S.'s Draconian approach to drug use may be the most "injurious" domestic policy since slavery. "Want to cut back on prison overcrowding and save a bundle on the construction of new facilities?" he asks in the newspaper article. "Open the doors. Let the nonviolent drug offenders go." The huge increases in federal and state prison populations during the 1980s and 90s (from 139 per 100,000 residents in 1980 to 482 per 100,000 in 2003) were mainly for drug convictions.

"In 1980, 580,900 Americans were arrested on drug charges. By 2003, that figure had ballooned to 1,678,200. We're making more arrests for drug offences than for murder, manslaughter, forcible rape and aggravated assault combined. Feel safer?"

Supporters of a ballot measure to legalize the use and sale marijuana encourage voters to support the proposal on election day 2004 in Anchorage, Alaska. The proposition was rejected, but proponents said it would not be the end of their efforts to change the law. AP IMAGES

Mr. Stamper even recommends a plan for how "regulated legalization" might work. This includes: a) permitting private companies to compete for licences to cultivate, harvest, manufacture, package and peddle drugs; b) creating a new federal regulatory agency; c) setting and enforcing standards of sanitation, potency and purity; d) banning advertising. He believes legalizing all drugs would eventually dry up most stockpiles of currently illicit drugs. Combined with treatment, education and other public-health programs, Mr. Stamper feels U.S. cities and towns would be far healthier and safer places to live. And various levels of government would see dramatic savings on the estimated $69-billion (U.S.) being spent annually to stamp out illegal drug use.

Reached at his home on Orcas Island, Wash., Mr. Stamper said he began formulating his thoughts on legalizing drugs as a young beat cop in San Diego. When he arrested hippies for smoking pot, he'd listen to them in the back of his car talking about getting their hands on some chips or chocolate bars and it occurred to him what

a waste of taxpayers' money it was throwing these people in jail. "I just kept saying to myself, 'What the hell are we doing?'" he said.

Mr. Stamper often receives a hostile reaction when he is asked to speak at conferences about his views on drugs. At one recent conference, however, he was heartened by a conversation he had with the chief of police of one of the biggest cities in the United States. The chief told Mr. Stamper he had read his book and agreed entirely with his views on drugs. Momentarily stunned, Mr. Stamper asked the chief if he could quote him on that. The chief looked at him like he was crazy. "What the heck have you been smoking, man?" he laughed.

SIGNIFICANCE

The U.S. Drug Enforcement Administration (DEA) has a campaign to promote current drug policy, in response to lobbying for the legalization of drugs. The DEA says that enforcement of current laws has been successful in bringing down the overall use of drugs and that legalization would diminish this success. The DEA justifies money spent on the fight against drugs, saying that high social costs of drug abuse and addiction would outweigh the rise of preventative costs if drug use was legalized. The DEA plays down the argument of overcrowded prisons, saying that only five percent of federal prisoners are in jail because of drug possession. They go on to say that most drug criminals, including those in jail for the possession of drugs, have plea-bargained down from more serious charges. The DEA feels that most non-violent drug users get treatment, not jail time.

The highest elected official to speak on behalf of the legalization of drugs is the former Republican Governor of New Mexico, Gary Johnson. Johnson's claim is that all drugs should be allowed, as long as they are controlled, regulated, and taxed. Johnson claims to be against drug use but thinks society would be healthier with the legalized use of drugs. Other leaders have called Johnson's remarks irresponsible, saying most health care professionals advocate for drugs to remain illegal.

Stamper and other analysts say that part of the reluctance to rethink U.S. drug policy is due to the fact that drug users have been demonized and portrayed as people that society should fear. It is said to create a political and social climate that resists finding answers to society's drug problem. Stamper says this is exemplified by President George W. Bush's resistance to the legalization of the medical uses of marijuana. President Bush has said that doing to do so would 'coddle' the enemy. Some U.S. states have passed laws allowing marijuana to be used for medical treatment.

FURTHER RESOURCES
Books
Belenko, Steven R., editor. *Drugs and Drug Policy in America: A Documentary History*. Westport, Conn.: Greenwood Press, 2000.

Husak, Douglas N. *Legalize This! The Case for Decriminalizing Drugs*. New York: Verso, 2002.

Periodicals
Stamper, N. "Let Those Dopers Be." *Los Angeles Times*, October 16, 2005, <http://www.latimes.com/news/opinion/commentary/la-op-legalize16oct16,0,4914395.story?coll=la-news-comment-opinions> (accessed January 8, 2006).

Web sites
CNN. "New Mexico Governor Calls for Legalizing Drugs." <http://edition.cnn.com/US/9910/06/legalizing.drugs.01/> (accessed January 8, 2006).

National Institute on Drug Abuse. <http://www.nida.nih.gov> (accessed January 8, 2006).

U.S. Department of Justice Drug Enforcement Administration. "Speaking Out Against Drug Legalization." <http://www.dea.gov/demand/speakout/speaking_out-may03.pdf > (accessed January 8, 2006).

Debit Card Fraud More Widespread Than Banks Believe

Newspaper article

By: Sandra Cordon

Date: June 3, 2005

Source: *The Globe and Mail* (http://www.globeandmail.com).

About the Author: Sandra Cordon is a contributor to *The Globe and Mail*, a leading Canadian daily newspaper with a circulation of over one million.

INTRODUCTION

They may look very similar, but credit and debit cards are quite different. Both are plastic cards with a magnetic strip encoding details of the owner's account and they are generally used with a PIN (Personal Identification Number). But a credit card is linked to money lent to its owner by a bank, while debit card money comes directly from his or her account. Both can be used either at an ATM machine, which dispenses cash (although a charge will be made if a credit card is used) in a shop, restaurant or other retail outlet, over the phone, for mail order, and on the Internet.

Credit and debit cards have been available for over thirty years now, but it is only relatively recently that there has been so many outlets for their use. Their convenience has made them increasingly popular—some people carry ten or more plastic bank cards and the use of paper checks is becoming almost a rarity. Banks like cards too, because they can charge customers for using them and merchants for accepting them. But there is a downside because it is all too easy for criminals to steal money from a credit or debit card, however careful the owner is. Credit and debit card fraud may seem like victimless crimes—compared to robbing someone for their cash—because it is commonly assumed that the bank always pays for any losses. This is not so, particularly where debit card fraud is concerned, as the article below points out.

■ PRIMARY SOURCE

An unexpectedly large percentage of Canadians say they've been victims of debit card fraud and many complain their bank hasn't been much help, according to a poll done for the federal government.

About four percent of people surveyed by Environics Research for the Industry Department last fall said they had been a victim of fraud through their debit card in the pervious years.

That figure is a great deal larger than the official fraud statistic of 1/10 of one percent publicized by the banking sector and the debit card association.

With 19 million regular card users identified by the debit card industry association, four percent would represent about 760,000 Canadians. One-third of respondents told Environics their bank refused to reimburse them for their losses.

That suggests the public might not fully understand the risks around debit cards, which directly debit a consumer's bank account for the amount of a purchase, and how little support they may find if they become a fraud victim, says a public interest watchdog.

The typical debit card agreement between client and bank isn't very clear on who gets tagged with losses, said John Lawford, lawyer for the non-profit Public Interest Advocacy Centre in Ottawa.

"It doesn't say: 'You are responsible,' but its says basically that 'We are not responsible for any loss … in using the system.' And people don't know that—they think if something goes wrong, of course the bank will cover it."

The Environics survey was commissioned by the federal government as part of a broader review of consumer protection in the new world of electronic banking.

It also confirmed just how much Canadians love using their debit cards, either to withdraw cash and pay bills at an automated banking machine, or to buy all kinds of goods and services.

Eighty-six per cent of the 2,027 people surveyed by Environics said they use a debit card, a figure that cuts evenly across regions of the country, income and education levels.

Senior citizens were the least likely to use the cards, with sixty-seven percent of respondents over sixty saying they do so.

The poll, with a margin of error of 2.2 percentage points nineteen times out of twenty, also suggests the incidence of fraud may be underreported and not well-known.

The 1/10 of one percent is widely used by the Interac Association, representing the industry, and the Canadian Bankers Association.

But that actually represents just the most common type of debit-card fraud known as skimming, said Caroline Hubbersety, director of media relations for the bankers association.

There, thieves use tiny, hidden cameras to record the victim's personal bank access number at a machine while also making a clandestine copy of the card. The thieves then have all they need to get into the victim's bank account and clean it out.

About 49,000 cards were reimbursed for fraud cases involving skimming last year, said Sara Feldman of the Interac Association.

"We are trying to raise awareness, letting people know that they're covered by the debit code of practice, that anyone who is proven victim of a confirmed fraud, theft or intimidation will be reimbursed," Ms. Feldman said.

But that voluntary code places a high and unfair burden of proof on the victim, said Mr. Lawford of the advocacy centre. "You're often not covered, there's no safety net at the end of the day."

If a fraud victim has let a spouse or family member use their card, they won't likely be able to press a fraud claim. Or, if a person has carelessly picked a personal identification number—such as one's date of birth of phone number—or even written it down, that can invalidate any fraud claim, he added.

Canada's embrace of debit cards is one of the highest in the globe, according to the Interac Association.

In 2003, we used our debit cards an average of fourty-three times each, compared with an average user rate of forty times per capita in Britain and thirty-seven in the United States and Sweden, according to the Interac Association.

■

SIGNIFICANCE

The U.S. Electronic Funds Transfer Act, which controls electronic payments, says that personal liability for debit card fraud could be as much as five hundred dollars if the problem is not reported to the bank within forty-eight hours. Within this time, liability is limited to fifty dollars. However, the victim of debit card fraud may end up with their account being

Georgia Tech student and computer hacker Billy Hoffman poses in 2003 with his campus debit card. Hoffman got into trouble when he hacked into the system using a knife and a laptop. The debit card system is used at Tech and 223 other colleges. AP IMAGES

drained of funds—even to their overdraft limit—if they delay reporting any loss or fraud. The problem is that some methods of fraud are not simple loss or theft. The skimming technique mentioned in the article is only one of the ways in which a card criminal works. Some unscrupulous merchants will make extra copies of debit card slips and send these off to the bank to extract extra payments which will be charged to the owner. Criminals may hunt for discarded slips and sell details to counterfeiters or use them to order goods which are then shipped to another address. The card owner would not be aware of these operations until their bank statement arrived, which could be some days or weeks later. Credit card owners enjoy better protection—usually their liability is limited to fifty dollars.

New technologies are trying to beat the creation and circulation of counterfeit cards, however. For example, a holograph—which is a three-dimensional, laser produced optical device that changes its color and image as the card is tilted—is used on most major credit cards. Ultra-violet ink, which is visible only under ultra-violet light, can be used to display the bank's logo. Retinal eye scanners, which links a card to its owner at an ATM, are also being gradually introduced. Perhaps the biggest development, however, is the use of the Chip and PIN system, which eliminates the need for a signature when a card is used. The use of Chip and PIN has already led to a decrease of thirteen percent in total card fraud losses in Britain between 2004 and 2005.

However, internet fraud—including debit card fraud—continues to grow around the world. Secure shopping sites help but it is always safer to use a credit, rather than debit, card when purchasing online. Not only are losses limited to fifty dollars, but credit card owners are also protected against faulty purchases and goods that do not arrive. Until the law is amended to give debit card owners the same rights as those of credit card owners, then the former need to exercise their plastic with caution. Part of this, as the article above implies, involves banks moving into line with courts—and assuming the victim of fraud is innocent, rather than guilty, while the matter is being investigated.

FURTHER RESOURCES
Web sites

U.S. Public Interest Research Group. "PIRG Consumer Fact Sheet." <http://www.pirg.org/consumer/banks/debit/debitcards1.htm> (accessed March 27, 2006).

Card Watch. "Card Watch Raises Awareness of All Types of Plastic Card Fraud" <http://www.cardwatch.org.uk/> (accessed March 27, 2006).

Federal Reserve Bank of San Francisco. "Plastic Fraud." <http://www.frbsf.org/publications/consumer/plastic.html> (accessed March 27, 2006).

Former Merrill Lynch Execs Sentenced

Newspaper article

By: Kristen Hays

Date: April 22, 2005

Source: Hays, Kristen. "Former Merrill Lynch Execs Sentenced." *Washington Post*, April 22, 2005, <http://www.washingtonpost.com/ac2/wp-dyn/> (accessed February 10, 2006).

About the Author: Kristen Hays is a writer with the Associated Press. The Associated Press, founded in New York in 1848 to facilitate the collection of international news for publication by a consortium of several New York newspapers, is today a global news gathering and reporting organization.

Former Merrill Lynch banker James A. Brown leaves the federal courthouse in Houston after being found guilty, along with four others, of conspiracy and fraud in the first criminal trial to emerge from Enron's collapse. AP IMAGES

INTRODUCTION

As the United States entered the twenty-first century, the American public witnessed first hand the boom and bust cycle of what was now called "the new economy." Traditional industrial and commercial giants, such as General Motors, were giving way to a different, more responsive, and internationally focused type of enterprise. No company better reflected this nimble, entrepreneurial face of American business than did Enron.

Based in Houston, Texas, Enron had grown from its traditional and prosperous roots in the southwestern U.S. energy sector to become a worldwide commodities trading giant, notably with respect to energy futures. Through the late 1990s, Enron boomed in what seemed to be a limitless growth curve. By January 2001, Enron stock value exceeded $82 per share. Enron employees were collectively the largest owners

of available company stock, and, for most Enron personnel, their Enron shares represented the essence of their individual retirement savings plans. In support of the dramatic surge in Enron stock value, the company had published a series of corporate valuations, which by early 2001 proclaimed Enron to be worth over $70 billion.

Enron, the glamorous, seemingly solid gold Colossus of American business, was in fact constructed from paper. A trail of falsified earnings reports, bogus filings made with the Securities Exchange Commission (SEC), and sham transactions—often made with the complicity of Enron's Big Five accounting firm, Arthur Anderson, or through powerful bankers Merrill Lynch—had created a false Enron. Enron declared bankruptcy in December 2001, the largest such filing in American history. This triggered a series of criminal investigations, SEC reviews, and class action civil suits directed at the Enron executives who had personally profited by many millions of dollars from these transactions.

The purported sale of Nigerian power barges to Merrill Lynch in 1999, for which James Brown and Daniel Bayly were prosecuted, was a classic Enron scheme. Brown and Bayly did not orchestrate the phony sale, which created a book value profit of $50 million for Enron. Their sin was willful blindness, as both men knew how the Enron executives would characterize the barge transaction on the Enron books. Brown and Bayly agreed to treat what they knew was a Merrill Lynch loan to Enron as a sale and corresponding fraud. These sophisticated bankers also knew that Enron would ultimately use these false barge profits to assist in boosting the publicly stated value of Enron. In a real sense, Brown and Bayly were stooges to Enron's scheming; by permitting a sham deal to proceed, they signed off and made a powerful client happy.

Prior to the sentencing of Brown and Bayly in May, 2005, Merrill Lynch paid the SEC $80 million in civil penalties arising from the Nigerian barge transactions.

■ PRIMARY SOURCE

Two former Merrill Lynch & Co. executives convicted in Enron's bogus sale of power barges to the brokerage were sentenced Thursday to prison terms far shorter than the punishment sought by the government.

James A. Brown, former head of the brokerage's asset lease group, was sentenced to three years and 10 months in prison and a year's probation. Daniel H. Bayly, former head of investment banking for Merrill Lynch, was sentenced to 2 1/2 years incarceration and six months probation. Each was ordered to pay $840,000 in fines and restitution. Both men live in Darien, Conn.

Federal probation officers had recommended up to 15 years for Bayly and up to 33 for Brown. Their case illustrated Wall Street participation in Enron crimes through the brokerage's choice to take part in a sham deal to make a client happy.

U.S. District Judge Ewing Werlein, who sentenced the men, criticized the pursuit of sentences longer than the maximum 10-year sentence that awaits former Enron finance chief Andrew S. Fastow, who ran bogus schemes that rotted Enron.

"The defendant is correct to observe that this would be a harsh and irrational result," Werlein said of the recommended term for Brown.

Both men made statements before their separate sentencings.

"Since I was indicted, I have been branded a liar and a criminal; I could no longer make a living in my chosen profession," Brown said.

"This whole experience has been devastating to me," Bayly said.

Fastow had faced 98 counts including fraud, conspiracy, insider trading and money laundering. Last year, he pleaded guilty to two counts of conspiracy for hiding Enron debt and inflating profits while pocketing millions for himself.

Werlein said the term awaiting Fastow and the five years former Enron treasurer Ben F. Glisan Jr. is serving "established some benchmarks" for the defendants in the barge case. The judge said the Merrill defendants faced "unjustified disparate sentences" in comparison.

Bayly and Brown were convicted of one count of conspiracy and two counts of fraud. Brown also was convicted of perjury and obstruction for lying to a grand jury about whether he knew Enron had promised to resell or buy back the barges within six months of the late 1999 deal, which meant the purported sale was really a loan. Fastow confirmed that promise.

The judge said the barge deal was "rather small and relatively benign in the constellation of the Enron frauds."

"Our position is there is no benign fraud when it comes to playing God with the reported earnings of publicly traded companies," prosecutor Matt Friedrich said.

"That a person who served as a leader in the investment banking world goes to prison at all serves a deterrent effect," Werlein said.

SIGNIFICANCE

No prosecution, however far reaching, could ever rebuild Enron. The jailing of every Enron executive who was complicit in any one of the hundreds of multi-million-dollar manipulations so blithely executed by the company prior to its spectacular collapse in late 2001 would not adequately compensate the thousands of Enron employees whose life savings were significantly diminished or lost forever.

High profile corporate prosecutions are conducted for a number of broadly stated public goals. The sentencing of those involved, especially those on the secondary corporate tier, such as Merrill Lynch bankers James Brown and Daniel Bayly, engages the application of a number of powerful, and often contradictory legal principles.

"Let the punishment fit the crime," proclaimed Gilbert and Sullivan's *Mikado* in 1885. For many citizens, this credo is at the heart of how the criminal sentencing process should be conducted. While Merrill Lynch itself did not profit from the willful complicity of its executives, Brown and Bayly became its public face for the role played by a powerful bank in a massive public stock fraud.

Another relevant legal principle maintains that one cannot do indirectly what one cannot do directly. Brown and Bayly, through their positions at Merrill Lynch, were clearly secondary prosecutorial targets; a key Enron player, Andrew Fastow, the financial guru who directed most of the manipulations of Enron data that were at the very heart of the frauds, could not receive a sentence greater than ten years in prison. Where a reasonably informed member of the public might take serious exception to that limitation, given the scope of the criminal conduct of Enron executives, Judge Werlein's ruling regarding the concept of a legal "benchmark" reflects a modest triumph of judicial fair play over the understandable desire on the part of the prosecution to make an example of anyone involved in this landmark case.

Both of the Merrill Lynch defendants was demonstrably humiliated and disgraced through the criminal process. Both lost their employment and are unlikely to return to employment in the financial sector. Both paid $840,000 in personal financial penalties and were held up to exposure and shame for their wrongdoing by the world media. Are these extra-legal consequences more important than the imposition of the traditional prison sentences of the criminal courts?

This issue has been examined, albeit obliquely, in a number of well publicized American trials involving the actions of private citizens who manipulated corporate organizations for spectacular personal gain. In

2005, the founder of media giant Adelphia Communications, eighty-year-old John Rigas, received a sentence of fifteen years in prison for a lengthy series of fraudulent transactions that effectively looted the communications giant. The prospect of Rigas dying in prison did not trouble his sentencing judge.

Traditional Anglo-American legal theory concerning sentencing is rooted in the proposition that every offender must be assessed on their own merits. It is plain that the Merrill Lynch cases and the larger Enron web are an indication from the American courts that the creation of a public example through denunciatory sentences is the primary sentencing objective.

FURTHER RESOURCES

Books
Sterling, Theodore F. *The Enron Scandal.* New York: Nova Science Publishing, 2002.

Periodicals
Schorr, Daniel. "The Real Enron Scandal." *Christian Science Monitor* (January 18, 2002).

Web sites
Time. "Behind the Enron Scandal." <http://www.time.com/time/2002/enron/#> (accessed March 8, 2006).

The security division of MasterCard International Inc. detected multiple instances of fraud that tracked back to CardSystems Solutions Inc., exposing up to 40 million cardholders to a breach of customer information. AP IMAGES

Security Breach May Have Exposed 40M Credit Cards

Magazine article

By: Tom Krazit

Date: June 17, 2005

Source: ComputerWorld. "Security Breach May Have Exposed 40M Credit Cards." June 17, 2005. < http://www.computerworld.com/securitytopics/security/story/0,10801,102631,00.html> (accessed January 14, 2006).

About the Author: The Information Data Group (IDG) is a leading global information technology organization. Besides hosting international IT events, the group publishes as many as 300 journals and magazines worldwide, including *PC World, Computer World, GamePro,* and *Macworld.* Tom Krazit, the group's U.S. correspondent for news and events in personal computing, peripherals, and handheld devices, has several articles to his credit on various information technology topics.

INTRODUCTION

Every credit card is issued by an authorized financial institution and given a unique identifying number. Credit card data also contains personal details and other confidential information such as social security numbers. Credit card transactions use electronic methods of transmitting, storing, and retrieving account numbers, which are stored in electronically accessible databases. Data security is key to preventing identity theft and other financial frauds. Despite electronic safeguards and data security measures, such as secure online transmission between commercial nodes such as banks, credit card processors, and business establishments, the data is potentially vulnerable to abuse.

In mid-2005, network security at CardSystems Solutions Inc., a MasterCard processing company, was compromised by a hacker, exposing as many as 40 million credit card numbers to potential theft and abuse. Although MasterCard's fraud-detection system detected the breach in May 2005 and informed issuing banks about the incident, the sheer size of the breach—the largest to date—raised concerns worldwide.

"Security Breach May Have Exposed 40M Credit Cards" is a news report from the *Computer World* website.

PRIMARY SOURCE

Security Breach May Have Exposed 40M Credit Cards

News Story by Tom Krazit

A hacker was able to access potentially 40 million credit card numbers by infiltrating the network of a company that processed payment data for MasterCard International Inc. and other companies, MasterCard said Friday.

MasterCard has notified banks that issue its credit cards about the security breach, which victimized CardSystems Solutions Inc., a Tucson, Ariz. back-office processing company, said Jessica Antle, a MasterCard spokeswoman. Those banks will then take steps to notify their customers as they see fit, she said.

The network at CardSystems had certain vulnerabilities that allowed an outsider to access the card numbers, 13.9 million of which were connected to MasterCard cards, Antle said. MasterCard's fraud detection system first became aware of the infiltration in May, and the company promptly launched an investigation into the breach.

However, the complicated investigation was not completed until earlier this week, when MasterCard was able to determine which credit card numbers were exposed and notify the banks that issued those cards, Antle said. Ubizen NV handled the initial investigation, and the case has also been turned over to the FBI. As far as MasterCard is aware, the person who infiltrated the CardSystems network has not yet been identified.

Companies such as CardSystems process payment data for multiple credit card companies, which is why MasterCard numbers only accounted for 13.9 million of the numbers, Antle said. No other types of personal information, such as Social Security numbers, were compromised in the breach, she said.

Cardholders can dispute purchases that were not made by them with the bank that issued their card, and card holders will not be held liable for any purchases determined to have been made fraudulently, Antle said.

Security breaches don't always happen through hacking into a company's network. Citigroup Inc. recently notified customers that the credit information of 3.9 million customers was inside a package that disappeared while in transit from New Jersey to Texas in the care of United Parcel Service Inc.

SIGNIFICANCE

Electronic crime, especially unauthorized access to data in electronic information systems, has risen with the with the number of transactions conducted on the internet. American corporations lose around one billion dollars each year to credit card fraud. As a result, credit card security has become an increasing concern.

The credit card transaction system originally considered only the logistics of business transaction involving physical goods and services traded by real buyers and sellers. However, the advent of online shopping, auctions, and e-services such as online bill payment have made the system vulnerable to determined hackers.

To quell customer fears about the security and privacy of personal data, most financial institutions and credit card processing services adopt high-tech encryption and antihacking software to ensure highest level of security. As security systems become more advanced, however, hackers become more determined to crack them.

Despite the introduction of new technologies like Secure Socket Layer (SSL), a type of encryption that ensures maximum security, authentication, and address verification, credit card fraud continues to occur frequently. Various processing companies, merchant establishments, and financial institutions combat these threats with ever more sophisticated technology and advanced security measures. As of 2005, Visa and MasterCard announced various initiatives, safety measures, and multidimensional plans that look at risk perception from various angles to combat possible losses and credit card frauds.

FURTHER RESOURCES

Web sites

BBC News. "The growing threat of Internet fraud" <http://news.bbc.co.uk/2/hi/business/526709.stm> (accessed January 14, 2006).

CNNMoney.com. "Info on 3.9M Citigroup Customers Lost" <http://money.cnn.com/2005/06/06/news/fortune500/security_citigroup/> (accessed January 14, 2006).

Federal Bureau of Investigation. "Internet Fraud" <http://www.fbi.gov/majcases/fraud/internetschemes.htm> (accessed January 14, 2006).

Washington Post. "40 Million Credit Card Numbers Hacked" <http://www.washingtonpost.com/wp-dyn/content/article/2005/06/17/AR2005061701031.html> (accessed January 14, 2006).

Officials Confiscate Pirated DVDs

Photograph

By: Associated Press

Date: April 29, 2005

Source: Associated Press

About the Photographer: The Associated Press, founded in 1848, is the world's largest and oldest news gathering organization. Functioning as a non-profit cooperative, it is the single largest source of news, photographs, and graphics that are distributed to thousands of print and media organizations around the world. Its staff includes more than 3,700 people in 240 offices worldwide. The Associated Press partners with CHINATOPIX for news and photographs from China.

INTRODUCTION

Since the early 1990s, many companies based in the United States have shifted production and other corporate activities to China to take advantage of cheaper labor and manufacturing costs. However, the globalization of American trade and industry has not come without its share of problems especially for American music, film, and software companies. The greatest threat the American industry faces, especially in the Chinese market, is piracy, counterfeiting, and the theft of intellectual property.

The rapid growth of the Internet and cheaper computer technology has given rise to rampant production of counterfeit and pirated DVDs in China. The scale of piracy has concerned U.S.-based companies for a number of years. Soon after software or a movie is released in the United States, Chinese entrepreneurs obtain master copies, subtitle them in Chinese, and mass produce them for the Chinese market. These end up in almost every video shop and street market in China.

Movie admission in China costs about $6 per ticket, whereas a pirated DVD costs $1–$3. Pirated versions of Microsoft software are available for $1–$4. Piracy is not limited to just software or movies alone. Published reports state that although China has become the production site for authentic American goods, it has also become a center for producing counterfeited American goods like branded footwear, clothing, and designer luggage.

The photograph reproduced here shows officials inspecting and seizing counterfeit DVDs from a video store in Xian, located in Shaanxi Province of China.

PRIMARY SOURCE

OFFICIALS CONFISCATE PIRATED DVDS

See primary source image.

SIGNIFICANCE

China became a signatory to the World Trade Organization (WTO) in December 2001. Since then China has been required to obey international trade laws and rules, including strict observance of intellectual property rights (in simple terms, anti-piracy laws). However, the United States continues to be concerned about the growing menace of counterfeiting in the Chinese market. According to various sources, piracy in China is costing the American film industry around $168 million annually. On a global scale, the music industry loses about $5 billion per year to piracy alone, and the U.S. recording industries claim to lose about $1 million a day.

Most counterfeit DVDs made in China are created using technologies developed in the United States. This fact adds insult to the injuries already inflicted by Chinese piracy, since the efficiency of those technologies makes it very difficult for officials to distinguish pirated DVDs from original ones. Chinese entrepreneurs distribute pirated DVDs through a wide variety of traditional and nontraditional channels—corner stores, street peddlers, Internet sites—making this activity even more difficult to police.

U.S. anti-piracy officials claim that the scale of counterfeiting has grown to such an extent that it has become integrated into the fabric of the local Chinese economy. The Chinese counterfeiting industry employs a substantial number of people and provides them with employment during a time of growing unemployment in China. As a result, Chinese authorities are concerned that tackling piracy will lead to job losses and, potentially, social instability. Nevertheless, since the early 2000s, the United States and other governments have increased pressure on the Chinese government to eliminate the counterfeit DVD industry. The Chinese government does routinely conduct raids (as can be seen in the accompanying image), yet the United States claims that these efforts are inadequate and have not done much to stop these illegal practices.

PRIMARY SOURCE

Officials Confiscate Pirated DVDs: Officials confiscate pirated DVDs during the raid of a local shop in Xi'an, in China's Shaanxi Province in 2005. AP IMAGES

Discussions with the Chinese government concerning the protection of intellectual property rights and related issues have failed on several occasions in the past. Chinese officials maintain that a number of barriers make it difficult to curb piracy. China has the largest population in the world, and, with a low per capita Gross Domestic Product (per capita Gross Domestic Product can be thought of as how much an average citizen produces, or earns, in a year), poverty is a major issue in China. Because of the gradual opening of the Chinese market, many Chinese are anxious to try new cultural experiences, especially those related to the previously forbidden western cultures. When they want to watch a Hollywood film, most of them would rather purchase a cheaply priced, pirated DVD with Chinese subtitles, rather than going to an expensive movie theater. Many experts believe that this is a primary reason for the growing DVD piracy market in China.

However, to prevent DVD piracy and protect intellectual property rights, Chinese officials do routinely conduct inspections and make arrests to deter the practice. In June 2004, two U.S. nationals were arrested for DVD piracy in Shanghai, China, as a result of a joint operation between U.S. and Chinese authorities. There have been many more reported arrests as well. These measures have been effective, but limited. Anti-piracy officials state that only tougher implementation of trade rules and growing awareness about counterfeited goods will lead to an appreciable decrease in the scale of piracy and intellectual property theft in China.

FURTHER RESOURCES

Web sites

Fighting Piracy News Desk. "Fight Against Piracy." <http://www.dvd-intelligence.com/news_desk/piracy_newsdesk.htm> (accessed February 14, 2006).

Huilin, Zou. "US Nationals Arrested for DVD Piracy," *China Daily*, July 30, 2004, <http://www2.chinadaily.com.cn/english/doc/2004-07/30/content_353431.htm> (accessed February 14, 2006).

RIAA (Recording Industry Association of America). "Anti-Piracy." <http://www.riaa.com/issues/piracy/default.asp> (accessed February 14, 2006).

U.S. Department of State. International Information Programs. "Trade Official Urges China To Punish IPR Violators Forcefully." <http://usinfo.state.gov/ei/Archive/2005/Apr/15-94765.html> (accessed February 14, 2006).

Welcome to Penal Colony YaG 14/10

Billionaire Gets Six Years in Siberian Border Region

Newspaper article

By: Tom Parfitt

Date: October 25, 2005

Source: Parfitt, Tom. "Welcome to Penal Colony YaG 14/10." *The Guardian* (October 25, 2005).

About the Author: Tom Parfitt is Moscow correspondent for *The Guardian* . He previously worked for the *Sunday Telegraph*.

INTRODUCTION

The history of post-Soviet Russia has been characterized by the emergence of an enormous economic gap between the country's haves and have nots. As large parts of the country sank into economic and social turmoil following the collapse of the Communist state in 1991, a tiny elite—known as "oligarchs"—emerged. They amassed immense fortunes at a faster rate, according to the *Economist*, than any men at any other time in history. When *Forbes* published a survey of wealthy Russians in 2004, it claimed that the country boasted 36 billionaires—not bad for a country where personal wealth was a virtually unheard of concept barely a decade earlier.

Topping that list with a fortune of $15.2 billion was Mikhail Khodorkovsky, a thirty-nine-year-old oil magnate who faced charged of fraud, embezzlement, and tax evasion. Like many of his fellow oligarchs, Khodorkovsky had gathered his enormous fortune through a mixture of ingenuity, exploitation, luck, and fraud.

Khodorkovsky had been an official in the Communist youth league in the 1980s, giving him important friends when President Mikhail Gorbachev initiated his program of *glasnost* (change) reforms in the late 1980s. In 1988, ensuring he held a considerable stake, Khodorkovsky started what would become the Menatep bank, which began managing government money. When the USSR collapsed a few years later, Menatep began acquiring former government-run enterprises at prices far below their market valuation. Khodorkovsky also began buying up companies that had been privatized through the distribution of "vouchers" to their employees. Often this literally meant going to each company employee and paying each employee cash for the voucher. In 1995, Khodorkovsky bought Yukos, a vast oil conglomerate, at a state auction for just $350 million.

In the chaos of the immediate post-Soviet years, it was sometimes difficult to say which of Khodorkovsky's methods—and those of fellow oligarchs, which were usually the same—were actually illegal. The buying up of vastly undervalued state interests—known as "loans for shares"—was as much a symptom of the corruption of Russian President Boris Yeltsin's government as a reflection on the business practices of those who bought them. Yeltsin needed funds to remain in power and stave off Communist political challengers as his country teetered towards economic disaster. Naivety played a part also. Yeltsin's economic reformers were desperate to get rid of Russia's state assets so that economic reform could be properly initiated, even if it meant selling those assets far below their market value.

The buying up of vouchers by men like Khodorkovsky was arguably the biggest tragedy for the Russian people. This voucher scheme—which placed the ownership of industries into workers' hands through the distribution of shares—was intended in the late 1980s and early 1990s to be the state's mechanism to distribute the wealth it had held during the Communist era. However, the majority of the people who received the vouchers had no understanding of what they meant, what they were worth, or of concepts like entrepreneurship. When Russia went into economic meltdown in the early 1990s and many workers were left unpaid for months on end, it was only through selling these vouchers—at prices far below their actual value—that they could survive. Once in control of these new companies, the oligarchs rendered existing vouchers worthless by offering vast share issues.

Khodorkovsky was also an astute businessman. He modernized Yukos and attracted western invest-

A view of the Russian penal colony YaG 14/10. Two years after oil tycoon Mikhail Khodorkovsky's dramatic dawn arrest by heavily armed special forces, Russia's once-richest man was back in the hinterlands of Siberia in 2005, settling into prison life six time zones away from Moscow. AP IMAGES

ment. By the end of the 1990s, Yukos was responsible for two percent of the world's oil output.

However, as Russia woke up to what Khodorkovsky and the other oligarchs had done, their unpopularity grew. When President Vladimir Putin came to power in 2000 an uneasy pact was sealed with the oligarchs in which they agreed to stay out of politics and the state's sphere in order to be allowed to continue their business activities. Khodorkovsky, however, continued to fund political parties across the spectrum. He also publicly clashed with Putin over government corruption in February 2003. There were also talks about a merger between Yukos and Sibneft, an oil company owned by fellow oligarch, Roman Abramovich. When these discussions collapsed, there were rumors of a deal with a big U.S. oil company. Either deal would have moved control of Russian energy policy farther away from the Kremlin.

In mid-2003, there was talk of a Khodorkovsky run for the presidency. This, however, appeared to be the final straw for Putin. In October that year, armed policemen stormed Khodorkovsky's private jet at an airfield in Siberia and arrested the tycoon on charges of embezzlement, fraud, and tax evasion. When the case came to trial in 2005 the charges focused on Khodorkovsky's partial privatization of Apatit, a fertilizer company. The accusations leveled against Khodorkovsky included the embezzlement of Apatit's profits and leadership of an "organized criminal group." Khodorkovsky defended himself by maintaining that he was not personally responsible for the alleged crimes and that, in any event, the actions were not illegal. The court disagreed and found Khodorkovsky guilty, sentencing him to nine years imprisonment. This sentence was reduced to eight years when the case was appealed, and Khodorkovsky also was given credit for the two years he served in prison while awaiting trial.

■ PRIMARY SOURCE

Three thousand one hundred miles from Moscow, the rough stone track crests a rise and all is revealed. Hunched on the open steppe stands a group of tatty grey buildings, swept by plumes of dust. Welcome to Krasnokamensk, a town at the edge of civilisation.

Nearly two centuries have passed since Tsar Nikolai I banished the rebellious aristocrats known as the Decembrists to remote corners of eastern Siberia. In Soviet times, enemies of the people were dispatched to similar benighted spots in the network of labour camps called the gulag.

Today, in Vladimir Putin's Russia, the price of dissent comes no cheaper. For Mikhail Khodorkovsky—former billionaire, oil tycoon and convicted criminal—the road to internal exile ended here in Krasnokamensk. After speculation about where he would serve his term, prison officials confirmed last week that Khodorkovsky had been delivered to this outpost to complete his term on charges of fraud and tax evasion. On the edge of this wind-blasted company town near the Chinese border—it was built to serve a giant uranium mine nearby—stands penal colony YaG 14/10, the place that will be his home for up to six years.

BITTER WINDS

In winter, temperatures drop to -40C (-40F) and bitter winds sweep across the steppe. Visitors are rare and the tycoon's arrival has sent a ripple of disruption through the town of 60,000, once off limits to all outsiders. "He's the biggest bird that ever flew in here," admits a guard at the camp.

Once Russia's richest man with a personal fortune of $15bn, Khodorkovsky ran afoul of the Kremlin when he lobbied for private oil pipelines and dripped cash into parties opposed to Mr Putin. He was arrested two years ago and convicted in May after proceedings widely condemned as a farce.

This morning the 42-year-old father of three, who previously lived in a villa in Moscow and was driven to work in an armoured saloon, wakes up in barracks No 8 of YaG 14/10. Dressed in blue fatigues, he will shuffle off with his fellow zeks (slang for inmates) to a breakfast of porridge and black tea.

Yuri Yakushevksy, Siberia spokesman for the federal penitentiary service, told Interfax the colony spent 65.44 roubles daily (£1.29) on each prisoner, of which 35 were spent on food. "All the prisoners eat in the same canteen," he said. "They prepare the food themselves and they do the washing up. The bread is baked by the prisoners. On the menu today is porridge, bread, meat. Soon they will get a wagon of seafood and fish."

He said inmates rose at 6am, and those on duty worked for two hours, while all could watch TV for two hours a day. "Khodorkovsky is no exception and works like all the others," he said, adding that he had brought in two cases of books and was studying for an unspecified doctorate. He would sleep on a bunkbed in a dormitory 40 metres by 15 metres, in a two-floor building holding an estimated 160 prisoners.

Old habits die hard in these parts, and even approaching the prison—known to locals as "the zone"—prompts a warning to retreat quickly. A ramshackle collection of huts behind a wall held up by slumped concrete pillars, about a mile outside the town, is all one can glimpse before guards bear down. An observation post provides a clear field of fire over the road and surrounding wasteland.

JUMPY

Guards are already jumpy: three local reporters were arrested and their cameras confiscated for getting too close at the weekend. Outside yesterday, men in camouflage erected a checkpoint to stop prying eyes. But details of life inside soon leak out.

"There's only a few old hands left over from the days when it was a harsh regime camp," says one prison source. "Khodorkovsky's got nothing to worry about—they're mostly fraudsters and thieves, just like him."

Work offers one desirable perk: a salary of up to 23.23 roubles (46p) a day. Inmates are largely in their mid–20s and are keen for a job to alleviate boredom and earn money for cigarettes and chocolate, bought in the prison shop.

"There's a kind of sewing workshop where they make uniforms for policemen and some of them get to look after cows and pigs," says Valery Dereshov, a local reporter who went inside two years ago. Natalia Terekhova, a local lawyer who visited Khodorkovsky on Friday, says he was calm but disoriented. "Mikhail Borisovich had a lot of questions about the conditions, his rights, his access to newspapers and television," she says. "Imagine an intellectual person finding himself for the first time in such a place. He does not want to lose touch with the outside world."

ISOLATION

Khodorkovsky's legal team in Moscow is less restrained. Anton Drel, his defence lawyer, accuses the Kremlin of isolating the tycoon from his family. "This is the pursuit of a certain goal: it's vengeance," he says, adding that he is preparing a complaint to the European court of human rights on grounds that prisoners are habitually allowed to serve their sentences close to home. Khodorkovsky's mother, Marina, has said she and his wife, Inna, may take turns living nearby.

In Krasnokamensk, sympathy for Khodorkovsky is thin on the ground. "We survive here and so will he," says Gennady, 58, a geologist fixing his car in nearby Oktyabrsky village, where tests a decade ago found radon levels at 190 times their recommended maximum.

Irina, a chemist at the uranium plant, says: "He's an oligarch after all. If his relatives want to come and visit they can use his private jet."

SIGNIFICANCE

Human rights groups and supporters of Mikhail Khodorkovsky immediately condemned the trial and sentence as politically motivated, stating that it was merely the latest and most infamous example of political persecution in modern Russia. Within a month of his sentencing, in July 2005, even the British Foreign and Commonwealth Office, a keen ally of Putin's Russia, had expressed its concerns about the nature of the trial.

Within Russia, however, there was broad public ambivalence about the fate of the so-called robber baron. The sense that someone who had taken from the masses had got his comeuppance was palpable, and few inside Russia mourned the break up of Yukos. The Russian government's vast claims and penalties for unpaid taxes—eventually amounting to more than $28 billion—were also broadly supported by the Russian public.

Outside Russia, however, these vast government claims and penalties heightened the sense that the case was merely a state-led asset-grab. In one year, for example, Yukos was said to owe more in taxes than it made in revenues. Unsurprisingly, the company, and with it the bulk of Mr Khodorkovsky's wealth, returned to the control of the state.

The greatest significance of the Khodorkovsky case was the clear signal it sent to other oligarchs—that they should stop using their money and influence in the political sphere and accept Putin's hold on Russia. Roman Abramovich, for example, resigned his governorship of the Chukotka province in Siberia, and also protected himself by investing heavily in Chelsea Football Club. Practically overnight, he created the world's richest and most expensive soccer team, and he became a global celebrity, presumably more difficult to prosecute than Khodorkovsky.

Khodorkovsky maintains his innocence. He has used his time in prison to denounce the inequities of the reforms that made him rich and what he calls the "tyranny of wealth." Still a relatively young man, it has even been rumored that he may run for President upon his release from prison.

FURTHER RESOURCES
Books

Hoffman, David. *The Oligarchs: Wealth and Power in Modern Russia.* New York: Public Affairs, 2004.

Hosking, Geoffrey. *Russia and the Russians.* London: Allen Lane, 2000.

Periodicals

Levy, Adrian, and Cathy Scott-Clark. "He Won, Russia Lost." *The Guardian* (May 8, 2004).

"Mikhail Khodorkovsky's Downfall." *The Economist* (May 19, 2005).

3

Crimes of Violence

Crimes of Violence

Violent crimes, according to the Bureau of Justice Statistics, include rape and sexual assault, robbery, aggravated and simple assault, and homicide. The Federal Bureau of Investigation's Uniform Crime Report categorizes violent crime as murder or non-negligent manslaughter, forcible rape, robbery, and aggravated assault. Violent crimes involve either the actual or the threatened use of aggressive force against a victim. A crime of violence can be perpetrated either with or without the use of a weapon. It can also be an end in and of itself, as in a murder, rape, or sexual assault intentionally committed upon an individual, or a part of another crime, such as aggravated assault and homicide committed during a robbery.

Under United States laws, assault is a violent crime that need not necessarily involve physical contact: in some cases of simple assault, it is sufficient for one person to make a menacing gesture, or to use threatening words, against another. In some jurisdictions, a simple assault can occur when one person either intends or threatens to injure someone, or when he actually does physical harm to another human being, either with or without employing a weapon that can potentially cause serious or fatal injury. Aggravated assault occurs when there is serious or fatal injury attempted or inflicted upon another, with "callous or reckless disregard" for the value of human life.

People are simultaneously intrigued and horrified by violent crime. They are drawn to an image of "Bonnie Parker and Clyde Barrow" and horrified by the baffling murder of five children by their mother as detailed in "NOW Will Raise Funds for Yates' Legal Defense".

There is often an intense desire to seek to understand the motives and characteristics of those responsible for carnage, which are rarely satisfactorily explained, either by the alleged criminals or by the justice system. As evidenced by the "Assassination of President John F. Kennedy" and "Ruby Shoots Oswald; Photographic Evidence of the Moment of Crime" violence often leaves unanswered questions as to motive.

This chapter will explore various aspects of crimes of violence, from an "Illustration Depicting Jack the Ripper Attacking a Woman" to consideration of modern serial killers such as Ted Bundy ("Theodore Robert Bundy, AKA Ted Bundy—Fugitive"). The chapter also depicts the inanity of violence as expressed in the phenomena of football (soccer) hooliganism depicted in "County Road Cutters"

Roderick Maclean Attempts to Assassinate Queen Victoria at Windsor Railway Station, 1882

Photograph

By: Mary Evans Picture Library

Date: 1882

Source: *Alamy Images.* <http://www.alamy.com> (accessed February 9, 2006).

About the Photographer: The Mary Evans Picture Library, founded in 1964, specializes in historical images from books, magazines, and advertisements. The photograph shown below appeared originally on the cover of the *Illustrated London News*, a popular magazine in Victorian times.

INTRODUCTION

Queen Victoria (1819–1901) ascended to the throne in 1837 and ruled until her death in 1901, making her the longest serving monarch in British history. The Victorian era was a time of great social and economic change, marked by huge scientific and technological advance. Queen Victoria married Prince Albert of Saxe-Coburg in 1840. She was pregnant with their first child when a young man named Edward Oxford tried to assassinate her. He fired a gun at her twice while she was traveling in her carriage with Prince Albert. Both bullets missed and Oxford was acquitted on grounds of insanity. The case was controversial— for many felt that a political conspiracy of some kind lay behind the assassination attempt.

In 1842, there were three more attempts on the Queen's life; Parliament passed the Treason Act under which threatening the monarch in any way was punishable by seven years imprisonment with flogging (although the latter part of the sentence was never carried out). Then, in 1849, an unemployed Irishman named William Hamilton fired a pistol at the Queen and two years later an ex-Army officer, Robert Pate, struck her with a cane. This time she was bruised and her bonnet was crushed. Pate failed to prove insanity at his trial and received the maximum sentence of imprisonment. Roderick Maclean's attempt on Victoria's life in 1882 was to be the last and the scene is depicted in the photograph below.

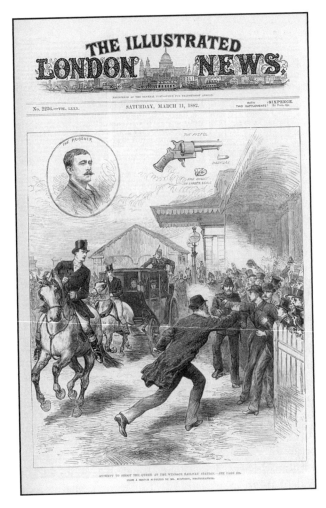

PRIMARY SOURCE

RODERICK MACLEAN ATTEMPTS TO ASSASSINATE QUEEN VICTORIA AT WINDSOR RAILWAY STATION, 1882

See primary source image.

SIGNIFICANCE

Maclean, a Scot, fired a bullet towards the Queen when she was sitting in her carriage at Windsor railway station. He had sent her some of his poetry and was, apparently, angry at her less than enthusiastic response. While the Queen's other would-be assassins had been tried under the 1842 Act, Maclean was tried for high treason, which carried the death penalty rather than a prison term. He was, however, acquitted on grounds of insanity and ended his days in an asylum. Annoyed at his acquittal, Victoria pressed Parliament to introduce a change in the law to allow for a guilty but insane verdict.

All monarchs, politicians, and other figures in the public eye have to live with the threat of assassination. Contract killings, done for financial gain or to eliminate a rival, may also be considered a form of assassination. The victims of assassination are usually prominent or important individuals in their sphere. President John F. Kennedy, his brother Robert, Mahatma Ghandi, and Martin Luther King, Jr. are among those political figures whose lives were claimed by an assassin. The motivation for an assassination attempt is often political. A high profile assassination often prompts controversy and speculation about conspiracy—the Kennedy assassination is a prime example of this. In addition, there are many who still believe that the death of Diana, Princess of Wales, in 1997 was no accident.

Some assassins do not kill for financial gain or political reasons. They murder to get attention and are often mentally unstable. For instance, John Hinckley who tried to kill President Ronald Reagan stated that his motive was to impress the actress Jodie Foster. Mark Chapman, who shot John Lennon in 1980, also falls into this category.

Sometimes governments are behind assassinations. During World War II, M16, Britain's secret service, trained a group of operatives to kill a top Nazi general in an attempt to change the course of the conflict. There were also many attempts by British, Soviet, and U.S. government agencies to assassinate Adolf Hitler. Some may argue that the assassination of Osama bin Laden or Saddam Hussein would be of great benefit to society. Although such assassinations may save many lives through settling or cutting short a war, their moral and ethical basis is somewhat suspect. It is, say opponents, the death penalty without the safeguard of the judicial process. Moreover, as a political tool, assassination does not always have the desired effect. The victim may be seen as a martyr and this may promote more instability in the shape of popular uprisings. Assassinations of leading political figures can change the course of history. World War I was triggered by the assassination of Archduke Franz Ferdinand. And the assassinations of no fewer than four American Presidents—Abraham Lincoln, James Garfield, William McKinley, and John F. Kennedy—and five Russian emperors have had a profound and lasting impact on those countries.

FURTHER RESOURCES

Books

Weintraub, Stanley. *Victoria: An Intimate Biography*. New York, Dutton, 1996.

Web sites

The Official Website of the British Monarchy. "Victoria." <http://www.royal.gov.uk/output/Page118.asp> (accessed February 9, 2006).

Illustration Depicting Jack the Ripper Attacking a Woman

Illustration

By: Anonymous

Date: circa 1888

Source: "Illustration Depicting Jack the Ripper Attacking a Woman." Corbis, ca. 1888.

About the Illustrator: This image is part of the stock collection at the Corbis photo agency. It originally appeared in an 1888 edition of *Police Gazette*, an official newsletter issued by the London police. The name of the illustrator is unknown.

INTRODUCTION

Jack the Ripper is a popular name given to a serial killer who murdered a number of prostitutes in London's East End over the course of several weeks in the latter half of 1888. The killer was never caught, despite the investigations of two police forces and extensive publicity.

As so often with serial killers, especially in the absence of an arrest and a trial, there is dispute over how many victims Jack the Ripper actually claimed. Some say as many as nine. However, it is widely accepted that Mary Ann Nichols, Annie Chapman, Elizabeth Stride, Catherine Eddowes and Mary Kelly were killed by the Ripper, with Stride and Eddowes both being dispatched on the same night, September 30, 1888. After the death of Kelly on November 9, the killings suddenly stopped.

PRIMARY SOURCE

Illustration Depicting Jack the Ripper Attacking a Woman: This illustration from an 1888 edition of the London Police publication *Police Gazette* depicts Jack the Ripper attacking one of his victims. © BETTMANN/CORBIS

of the killings probably occurred out of doors. Then he would mutilate the woman, usually carrying off some part of her anatomy, such as the kidney or uterus. The butchery was so precise that police officers believed the Ripper must have had special anatomical knowledge and might have been a doctor—or a butcher.

PRIMARY SOURCE

ILLUSTRATION DEPICTING JACK THE RIPPER ATTACKING A WOMAN

See primary source image.

SIGNIFICANCE

Jack the Ripper remains a figure of fascination even in the 21st century. In London, tours around the murder sites are a popular tourist attraction, while researchers continue to argue the killer's identity. He was not the first serial killer the world has ever known but his crimes were perhaps the first to occur in a big and densely populated city. His actions, and those of the investigating police force, were widely publicized in the newspapers, both in England and abroad.

The murders took place in the overcrowded and poverty-stricken districts of Whitechapel, Spitalfields, Aldgate, and the City of London. The first three came under the jurisdiction of the Metropolitan Police, but the latter (where Catherine Eddowes was killed) had its own police force. The public and the newspapers were critical of the police investigation and the supposed lack of cooperation between the forces. But it is always hard to investigate serial killings, even with modern technology. This was in the days before the development of forensic science where police had to either rely on witnesses or catch someone in the act. The streets of the East End were a crowded maze which made any kind of criminal investigation especially difficult.

The Ripper left little by way of evidence but the police made many drawings and took photographs of the crime scenes—just as they would today. On the night of the double murder, a chalked message implying that Jews were responsible was found on a door near the crime scene. The Commissioner of the Metropolitan Police, Sir Charles Warren, ordered a cover-up of the message for fear it might incite riots against the Jewish population in the area, for there were already rumors that an immigrant Jew might be responsible for the murders and feelings were running high.

On September 27, the Central News Agency received a letter signed by "Jack the Ripper"—one of many received by police and reporters during the course of the investigation. It is generally believed that all of the letters were hoaxes, wasting valuable police time, for each one had to be followed up and investigated. Since the true name of the killer was never revealed, the title "Jack the Ripper" lives on in popular mythology.

The drawing below shows Jack the Ripper attacking a woman. He attacked from the front, first strangling his victim and then cutting her throat to silence her. This meant there was not much blood shed which attracted less attention—an important point as some

Police officers investigating the killings had their own views about who was responsible, but there was never a consensus. In 1903 Frederick Abberline, who had been in charge of the investigation on the ground, said he thought the Ripper was the multiple wife-poisoner Severin Klosowski, a theory that modern criminal profiling has rejected. Another suspect was a Polish Jew called Aaron Kosminski who went mad and was confined to a lunatic asylum shortly after the murders, dying soon afterwards. Other evidence, however, suggests that Kosminski was harmless and did not die till 1919. He may have been confused with another, more dangerous, Polish Jew who had a similar name. The latest suspect in the frame for the Ripper murders is a Dr. Francis Tumblety, who apparently fled to America after the crimes; this emerged in 1993 from investigation of a collection of letters belonging to a crime journalist which dates back nearly a century. There are many other theories as to the identity of Jack the Ripper. If the case can help understand modern serial killers, then the ongoing investigations clearly have some value.

FURTHER RESOURCES

Books

Sugden, Philip. *The Complete History of Jack the Ripper*. New York: Carroll and Graf, 1994.

Web sites

Casebook. "Jack the Ripper." <http://www.casebook.org> (accessed February 17, 2006).

London Walks. "Jack the Ripper Information." <http://www.london-walks.co.uk/28/index.shtml> (accessed February 17, 2006).

Mugging and Murder on a New York City Street, 1891

Illustration

By: Anonymous

Date: 1891

Source: Corbis.

About the Illustrator: This illustration appeared in the *National Police Gazette*, a nineteenth century periodical devoted to lurid coverage of crime and criminals.

INTRODUCTION

The *National Police Gazette* capitalized on the American fascination with blood and gore to become the most popular men's publication of the late nineteenth century. Printed on pink paper, the Police Gazette horrified Victorian society and New York City's elite press but delighted ordinary folk with lavish illustrations of violent events.

The *Police Gazette*, as it was commonly called, began in 1845 chronicling crimes of the day. After the Civil War, George Matsell, a former New York City chief of police, took over the newspaper and began sensationalizing crime coverage. However, circulation dwindled and the newspaper nearly died. Richard Kyle Fox, an Irish immigrant journalist, purchased it in 1876 and made significant changes—including adding pictures to the crime stories. New York City had an enormously high percentage of immigrants, many of whom could not read English. Fox guaranteed the survival of his newspaper by including plenty of graphic depictions of murders, seductions, and horrible accidents.

Such regular features as "Noose Notes" and "Crimes of the Clergy" particularly appealed to the magazine's almost entirely young male working-class readership. They also scandalized the New York City Society for the Suppression of Vice. The newspaper was taken to court several times for its shocking articles. Promising atrocities of a number to satisfy any man, the column "Homicidal Horrors" covered the hanging of a Texas wife murderer, a fatal love affair in Cleveland, and a murder trial in San Antonio in a personal, chatty tone. "Vice's Varieties" offered brief descriptions of wrongdoing contributed by readers from every state. The newspaper typically featured headlines that were often gruesome and frequently sexual in nature.

The *National Police Gazette* made Fox a multimillionaire and became so well-known a publication that the James Boys, notorious bank and train robbers, sent their autographed pictures to its New York City headquarters. While it saw itself as a national institution, most of its material came from New York City.

PRIMARY SOURCE

MUGGING AND MURDER ON A NEW YORK CITY STREET, 1891
See primary source image.

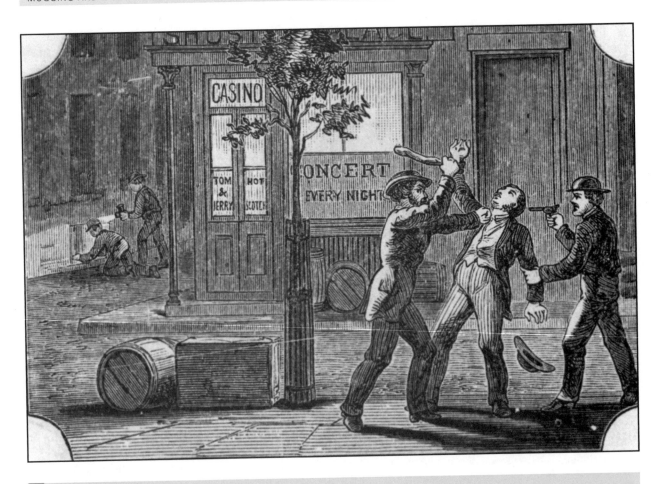

PRIMARY SOURCE

Mugging and Murder on a New York City Street, 1891: An illustration from the *Police Gazette,* in 1891 depicts mugging and murder on a New York City street. © BETTMANN/CORBIS

SIGNIFICANCE

The *National Police Gazette* became one of the top American periodicals of the late nineteenth century. By 1886, the newspaper had subscribers in twenty-six countries and a weekly circulation of 150,000. Many of these readers were part of a new audience developed by Fox—men who were at the bottom of the social ladder and who had little interest in upholding the traditions of Victorian society. Fox allowed them to escape the repression of the times.

The *Gazette* offered a new type of entertainment for the dawning age of consumerism. The success of the newspaper showed other publishers the value of brightening solid pages of newsprint with attractive pictures. In devoting lavish illustrations to bloody and violent events, the *Gazette* was visionary. Covering human interest stories such as crimes set an example

for daily papers and revolutionized newspaper standards, shifting the focus from an emphasis on moral purity to an emphasis on spectacle.

By the 1890s, the "new journalism" as practiced by the dailies packaged the news as series of heavily illustrated melodramas and atrocities. The *National Police Gazette* pioneered the techniques that gave rise to the famed "yellow press" of William Randolph Hearst and Joseph Pulitzer.

FURTHER RESOURCES
Books

Lamay, Craig L., and Everette E. Dennis, eds. *The Culture of Crime.* New Brunswick, NJ: Transaction, 1995.

Van Every, Edward. *Sins of New York: As "Exposed" by the Police Gazette.* New York: Frederick A. Stokes, 1930.

Dead Members of the Dalton Gang

Citizen Justice in the Old West

Photograph

By: Anonymous

Date: October 5, 1892

Source: Corbis.

About the Photographer: The photographer is unknown.

INTRODUCTION

The Dalton Gang attempted to rob two banks simultaneously in Coffeyville, Kansas, on October 5, 1892. The townspeople, warned in advance, armed themselves and shot four of the five bank robbers to death in one of the most celebrated episodes of violence in the Old West.

Sons of poor sharecroppers, the Dalton brothers were born around the time of the Civil War to Lewis Dalton and Adeline Lee Younger. The Younger brothers of the James–Younger gang notoriety and the Dalton boys shared the same grandfather, Charles Lee Younger. The family lived in western Missouri, an area plagued before, during, and after the Civil War by border conflicts and rampant outlawry. About 1882 the family moved to Coffeyville and shortly thereafter into Indian Territory near present-day Vinita, Oklahoma.

The Daltons were initially law-abiding. Robert (Bob) and Gratton (Grat) Dalton served as deputy U.S. marshals in Indian Territory in the late 1880s. The first recorded incidence of lawbreaking by any of the Dalton boys occurred on Christmas Day 1889, when Bob and youngest brother, Emmett, sold whiskey to Indians. In August 1890, Bob, Emmett, and Grat were charged with the capital offense of horse stealing. Grat was jailed for a time, but eventually the charges were dropped. In 1891, while visiting brother Bill in California, all four Dalton brothers were charged with robbing a Southern Pacific train

PRIMARY SOURCE

Dead Members of the Dalton Gang: Dead members of the Dalton gang in 1892. From left are Bill Powers, Dick Brodwell, Grat Dalton, and Bob Dalton. After attempting to rob two banks at once in their hometown, four of the members of the Dalton Gang were shot and killed by the locals of Coffeyville, Kansas. © BETTMANN/CORBIS

and attempting to murder the conductor. Bob and Emmett fled back to Indian Territory, while Bill was acquitted and Grat was convicted. He soon escaped from jail and joined his brothers.

The Dalton gang, led by Bob and often including such outlaws as George "Bitter Creek" Newcomb, Charlie "Black Face" Bryant, and Bill Doolin, robbed several express trains in Oklahoma and California. Eager to top the exploits of the James–Younger gang, Bob planned a double bank robbery that would make the Daltons famous.

On October 5, 1892, Bob, Grat, Emmett, Bill Powers, and Dick Broadwell attacked the Condon and First National Banks in Coffeyville. The town, a trading center for a wide section of Kansas, was known to be wealthy. Unfortunately for the Daltons, the town's citizens had been alerted and they confronted the gang as the robbers emerged from the banks. A fierce gunfight erupted that led to the deaths of four citizens, including the town marshal, and all the gang's members except Emmett. Badly wounded when he attempted to pull Bob into a saddle and escape, Emmett received a life sentence for murder in March 1893.

PRIMARY SOURCE

DEAD MEMBERS OF THE DALTON GANG

See primary source image.

SIGNIFICANCE

Bob Dalton succeeded in making the Dalton gang famous. The double bank robbery attempt at Coffeyville ensured them a place in the national memory as one of the most daring outlaw gangs of the West. They are now mentioned in the same breath with Jesse and Frank James.

Emmett Dalton took advantage of his fame. Pardoned by the governor of Kansas in 1907, he left Kansas State Penitentiary for a life in California as a respected Los Angeles businessman. Emmett wrote two books recounting the experiences of the Daltons. In his books and in speeches, he pointed out that every famous outlaw wound up in an early grave and that every outlaw could count on such a fate. Emmett died in 1937.

In 1907, Oklahoma entered the Union as the forty-sixth state, an event that the Daltons had done their best to delay. The Dalton record cost the Oklahoma Territory many votes in Washington during the

years while the bill for its admission went to Congressional committees. Oklahoma attained statehood only after Oklahoma's nonvoting delegate, Bird Segle McGuire, convinced members of Congress that outlaws like the Dalton gang had disappeared.

FURTHER RESOURCES

Books

Barndollar, Lue Diver. *What Really Happened on October 5, 1892: An Attempt at an Accurate Account of the Dalton Gang and Coffeyville.* Coffeyville, Kansas: Coffeyville Historical Society, 2001.

Preece, Harold. *The Dalton Gang: End of an Outlaw Era.* New York: Hastings House, 1963.

Assassin Arrested

Photograph

By: Corbis

Date: June 28, 1914

Source: Anonymous

About the Photographer: The photographer is unknown.

INTRODUCTION

Gavrilo Princip (1894–1918) assassinated Austrian Archduke Franz Ferdinand, heir to the throne of Austria–Hungary, and his wife Sophie on June 28, 1914, in Sarajevo, Bosnia. These murders set off World War I.

Pricip, born to a Serbian family in Bosnia, became an ardent Serbian nationalist following Austria–Hungary's annexation of Bosnia and Herzegovina in 1908. The annexation was in direct conflict with the interests of Serbia and threatened a possible future Serbian-led pan-Slav state. In 1911, Princip joined Young Bosnia, a secret society that hoped to detach Bosnia from Austria and link it to a larger Serb state. During the First Balkan War of 1912, Princip attempted to join the Serbian army's irregular forces, but was rejected for being too small and weak. A humiliated Princip then determined to do something great for his people.

On June 28, 1914, Franz Ferdinand arrived in Sarajevo on an official visit designed to showcase the power of Austria–Hungary rule in Bosnia. The day

PRIMARY SOURCE

Assassin Arrested: Police officers drag Gavrilo Princip away from an angry crowd and into police headquarters in Sarajevo, Bosnia, on June 28, 1914. Princip had just assassinated Archduke Franz Ferdinand, heir to the throne of the Austro-Hungarian Empire, an act that led to the First World War. © CORBIS

chosen for his visit, Saint Veit's Day, was a national holiday in Serbia. Austrian officials knew that Serbian nationalists would view the visit as a provocation but they failed to take adequate precautions. Security preparations were careless.

Princip had obtained weapons and training from the Central Committee of Unity or Death (popularly known as the Black Hand), a secret terrorist organization that opposed Austria. While seven men conspired to assassinate Franz Ferdinand, Princip is the only one who actually fired a weapon. He used a pistol to shoot the archduke in the neck and his wife in the abdomen. Both died that day. Princip attempted to turn the gun on himself but he was mobbed by the crowd and immediately arrested.

Tried at Sarajevo on October 28, 1914, he was convicted but spared the death penalty because he was a minor. Instead, Princip received a sentence of twenty years in prison, the maximum permissible. He died in prison, probably of tuberculosis, on April 28, 1918. The events he set in motion would cost the lives of thousands of Serbs and millions of other Europeans in World War I.

PRIMARY SOURCE

ASSASSIN ARRESTED

See primary source image.

SIGNIFICANCE

The government of Austria–Hungary held Serbia responsible for the nationalist murders that Princip committed. It gave Serbia an ultimatum to stop all subversion in Austria and all anti-Austrian propaganda in Serbia. It also demanded that a thorough investigation of all aspects of the assassination be undertaken in Serbia by a joint commission of Serbian and Austrian officials—which was essentially an attempt to control Serbia. When Serbia replied moderately but evasively, Austria declared war on July 28, 1914. This act led directly to the start of World War I.

Germany unconditionally supported Austria–Hungary although it knew that Russia would not stand idly by and watch fellow Slavs be crushed. Russian pan-Slavs saw Russia as the protector and eventual liberator of the southern Slavs of Serbia. On July 29, 1914, Russia began mobilizing to fight Germany and Austria. Germany responded by launching an attack on Russia's ally, France, by marching through neutral Belgium. It planned to knock France out then turn on Russia. In defense of Belgium, Great Britain joined France in declaring war on Germany in August 1914. World War I had begun.

When the war ended in 1918, at least 10 million people lay dead and 20 million suffered from wounds. Of the 300,000 Serbs who fought in the war, only 109,000 survived. The 1917 Pact of Corfu united Croats, Slovenes, and Serbs into Yugoslavia. This new country would last until another rise of nationalism in the 1990s. Austria–Hungary did not survive the war. The casualty rate among that nation's soldiers was 87 percent, the highest among the major powers. By the time that Austria–Hungary sued for peace in October 1918, crowds were rioting for bread. In November 1918, the government dissolved itself and the empire ceased to exist.

FURTHER RESOURCES

Books

Cassels, Lavender. *The Archduke and the Assassin: Sarajevo, June 28th 1914*. New York: Stein and Day, 1985.

Dedijier, Vladimir. *The Road to Sarajevo*. New York: Simon and Schuster, 1966.

Joyce, C. Patrick. *Sarajevo Shots: A Study in the Immediate Origins of the First World War*. New York: Revisionist Press, 1978.

St. Valentine's Day Massacre

Photograph

By: Anonymous

Date: February 15, 1929

Source: AP Images

About the Photographer: The St. Valentine's Day Massacre is widely believed to have been carried out by Al Capone and his gang, although this was never proven in court. The photographer is unknown.

INTRODUCTION

The St. Valentine's Day Massacre, celebrated in films, television, and books, was a sequence of murders that gave Al Capone total control of Chicago's underworld. Capone's gang and the rival Northside Gang, organized by Dion O'Banion, had clashed violently over control of the city's bootlegging and vice businesses. O'Banion's 1924 murder in the flower shop that he ran began the brutal gangland wars that ended on February 14, 1929.

George "Bugs" Moran took charge of the Northside gang after O'Banion's death and plotted to take over Capone's empire. Capone, in turn, was determined to dominate the north and eliminate Moran. Their struggle was a bloody one: In the years following O'Banion's death, more than 215 unsolved murders were attributed to mob hits.

On Valentine's Day in 1929, seven men waited in the garage of the SMC Cartage Company for Moran, who was due to arrive at 10:30 A.M. The men were waiting for what they thought was a truckload of stolen liquor that was due to arrive. Such business deals were common—but this was a trick designed to gather Moran's gang in one place for easy killing.

The men who waited were Adam Heyer, owner of the garage and a man with many aliases; Frank and Peter Gusenberg, brothers and veteran gunmen; James Clark, Moran's brother-in-law; Albert Weinshank, owner of a speakeasy called the Alcazar Club; John May, a former safe blower and father of seven who served as the gang's mechanic; and Dr. Reinhart H. Schwimmer, an ophthalmologist who had left medicine for the more glamorous work of bootlegging.

At 10:30, when Moran was expected, a Cadillac touring car of the kind typically used by Chicago police detectives pulled up at the garage. Two men in police uniforms entered the garage followed by two

PRIMARY SOURCE

St. Valentine's Day Massacre: The aftermath of the Valentine's Day Massacre of February 14, 1929. The bodies of six members of the O'Banion-Moran gang can be seen on the floor. They were murdered after surrendering to rival mobsters disguised as police officers. AP IMAGES

men, presumably detectives, in civilian clothes. The neighbors who observed their arrival assumed that it was just another police raid. The gangsters in the garage apparently came to the same conclusion.

The Moran gangsters prepared to be arrested. They lined up, facing the rear wall of the garage, and let themselves be disarmed. Then the two men in

civilian clothing stepped forward, produced a submachine gun and a sawed-off shotgun from beneath their overcoats, and opened fire. The men in police uniforms fired their revolvers. Six victims fell backward where they stood. May turned and leaped at the assassins. A shotgun blast stopped him. When the real police arrived, the garage was filled with smoke and brick dust. More than 100 empty shells lay on the floor.

PRIMARY SOURCE

ST. VALENTINE'S DAY MASSACRE

See primary source image.

SIGNIFICANCE

The St. Valentine's Day Massacre, the climax of Chicago's gangster era, cemented Al Capone's control of the city's bootlegging and vice operations. No one doubted that Capone had ordered the executions. Moran, who turned the corner just as the false policemen were stepping out of their car, fled the scene rather than be arrested. He went into hiding, and, his power gone, was reduced to robbing banks. He died in federal prison in 1957.

Many Chicagoans initially thought that the "officers" involved in the shootings were real Chicago police. Their corruption was well known, and the massacre seemed like yet another black eye for the force. However, a ballistics expert brought in from New York City found that the bullets did not come from police-issued guns but could be traced to the Capone gang. The getaway car, discovered just as gangsters were hacking it apart with acetylene torches, had originally been owned by Cook County Commissioner Frank J. Wilson, who had just traded it to a car dealer.

The St. Valentine's Day massacre shocked and revolted Chicagoans, whose admiration for the powerful gangsters had lead to a tolerant and easygoing attitude toward organized crime. Most citizens believed that gangsters killed only one another and that gangland problems were not especially important. This time, however, the number of victims, the fact that they had been butchered while they stood with hands up, and that the killers had dressed as police officers, were seen as insults to law and order.

Police Commissioner William F. Russell declared the massacre to be the last straw. A newly appointed reformer, he issued an order requiring all poolrooms, restaurants, clubs, stores, soft-drink establishments, and similar businesses to remove all barriers to free public access and view. The order shut down most of Chicago's speakeasies, which badly hurt the bootlegging trade. Many of Chicago's gangsters left town, though gangland activity did not stop.

Despite widespread knowledge of his guilt, Capone never went to jail for the killings. Tried and convicted of tax evasion, he was sent to federal prison for cheating the U.S. Treasury. Only Jack McGurn, the Capone gunman who had hired the killers, was tried for massacre. His case was dropped for lack of evidence. He died in Chicago on the seventh anniversary of the massacre when three never-identified men shot him.

FURTHER RESOURCES

Books

Kobler, John. *Capone: The Life and World of Al Capone.* New York: Putnam's, 1971.

Schoenberg, Robert J. *Mr. Capone.* New York: William Morrow, 1992.

Bonnie Parker and Clyde Barrow

Photograph

By: Anonymous

Date: 1930s

Source: AP Images

About the Photographer: The photographer is not known.

INTRODUCTION

When it comes to America's most famous and notorious criminals, no legend has been larger than real life than that of the robber duo Bonnie and Clyde. Immortalized in the 1967 film that took their names and starred Warren Beatty and Faye Dunaway, they were portrayed as a latter-day Romeo and Juliet against a background of bank robbing and spectacular getaways. The film won two Oscars and is regarded a classic.

Yet because of the weight of movie legend, the real story of Bonnie Parker and Clyde Barrow has been almost wholly obscured. The two were both born in Texas in 1910 (some sources put Barrow's date of birth as March 1909) to poor families, although neither knew each other until adulthood. Bonnie Parker married Roy Thornton, a drifter and petty criminal, at the age of 15, but the marriage was never happy and the two were separated for most of its duration.

PRIMARY SOURCE

Bonnie Parker and Clyde Barrow: Notorious bank robbers Bonnie Parker and Clyde Barrow. Their romance and violent exploits made them celebrities. AP IMAGES

Clyde Barrow was also a petty thief from adolescence, robbing drugstores and stealing cars, though at the same time apparently holding down a series of manual jobs. In January 1930 he met Bonnie Parker and the two began seeing each other regularly. However, Barrow and his gang's larceny had attracted police attention and after police staked out the home of Parker's mother, he was arrested for burglary and car theft in February 1930 and sentenced to two years imprisonment.

As with his contemporary John Dillinger, Barrow's spell behind bars—where he lived hand-in-hand with fellow offenders—was believed to have transformed him from small-time larcenist into a hardened criminal. Following his release in 1932, he repaired to Massachusetts to make a clean break, but lasted there just weeks before returning to Texas apparently with the intention of gaining the release of one of his former co-felons.

Barrow soon returned to the old pattern of crime, but this now took on a brutality that soon assumed murderous proportions. In April 1932, Barrow and an associate attempted to break into a Texas hardware store. They were spotted by a night watchman, exchanged fire, and fled at high speed in their car. Though no one was murdered this time, it set the pattern for further crimes: the relatively small scale of the theft (Barrow would never get away with more than $3,500 in a single raid); the willingness to engage in violence at the slightest provocation; the use of a high-speed getaway car. Later that month, Barrow shot dead a grocer whose safe he was raiding. The grocer's widow identified him via photos shown to her by police as the killer and Barrow was again a wanted man and on the run.

At this stage he took his sweetheart, Bonnie Parker, on the run with him and his gang. Over the following two years the gang was credited with scores of thefts and robberies, all small-scale and mostly of remote and therefore vulnerable rural outposts: drugstores, filling stations, and private citizens. They shot at anyone who got in their way, sometimes without provocation, and were guilty of at least twelve murders, including four police officers. Newspapermen magnified Barrow into one of the "worst killers of the Southwest," and as was common at the time, he sometimes gave interviews to journalists ingenious enough to catch up with him.

The romance between Barrow and Parker, combined with the gang's ubiquity, captured the wider public's imagination, even if they were feared and reviled throughout the communities and towns they haunted in the Midwest and Southwest. And despite the glamorous image they gained, their trail across America was mostly a desperate one, constantly tinged with fear of the law and recognition by the public, always on the move to avoid detection. They were ambushed by police on a number of occasions and several members of the gang died, including Buck Barrow, Clyde's brother.

Finally, on May 23, 1934, police caught up with the pair after tracking them down to their hideout, near Bienville Parish, Louisiana, following a tip-off. After setting up a roadside ambush to stop Barrow's car, police hidden behind bushes opened fire on his vehicle, emptying 150 rounds of ammunition into the pair and killing them instantly.

PRIMARY SOURCE

BONNIE PARKER AND CLYDE BARROW

See primary source image.

SIGNIFICANCE

Behind the romantic edifice perpetuated by some contemporary newspaper coverage and later by the duo's immortalization on film, Clyde Barrow and Bonnie Parker were part of a gang of hardened and brutal criminals, who would stop at nothing to retain their freedom. Though the romanticized view was not universally held—not least in the areas they terrorized—there was more to them than the sympathetic portrayal painted by many journalists and filmmakers.

Had such a widely known and brutal crime spree been carried out even just fifteen years earlier, it is unlikely that the duo would have gained such a benevolent reaction. However, America had gone through seismic cultural changes during the 1920s, an era when crime became normalized due to the proliferation of an underworld that sated America's thirst for booze, outlawed since 1919 by a constitutional amendment. Prohibition saw previously respectable and law-abiding citizens seek their daily drink in illegal drinking dens, run and frequented by criminals, or from smugglers and bootleggers. Crime became a way of life as Americans sought to maintain the habits they had always held. Lawbreakers became accepted as at no time in modern history.

Moreover, the huge wealth gained by bootlegger-barons was often accompanied by huge acts of largesse and generosity that saw them feted and even adored by polite society. The most notable example was Al Capone, who became one of the most famous men in the world, and the trend continued on into the 1930s. Bonnie and Clyde were just one of a succession of lawbreakers idealized and lionized, an outcome they shared with other criminals, including John Dillinger and the Ma Barker Boys, who found public favor in 1930s.

As with many famous criminals, controversy and myth surrounds their ending. Police shot at them without warning and without returning fire, although as they later pointed out when criticized for doing so, they were merely treating Barrow in the same way he had acted towards their colleagues. More contentious still was the fate of Bonnie Parker. Although part of the gang, she had not been implicated in any of the murders they had carried out and had apparently never fired a gun in her life.

The police who carried out their killings were further discredited after allowing members of the public to raid Bonnie and Clyde's corpses and battered vehicle in search of souvenirs. The bullet-ridden Ford V-8 was later sold by the state of Louisiana and is now on display at a Nevada casino.

FURTHER RESOURCES

Books

Sinclair, Andrew. *Prohibition: The Era of Excess.* New York: Little Brown, 1962.

Treherne, John. *The Strange Life of Bonnie and Clyde.* Lanham, Md.: Cooper Square Press, 2000.

Web sites

Federal Bureau of Investigation. "Famous Cases: Bonnie and Clyde." <http://www.fbi.gov/libref/historic/famcases/clyde/clyde.htm> (accessed February 25, 2006).

Assassination of John F. Kennedy

Photograph

By: Anonymous

Date: November 22, 1963

Source: Bettman/Corbis

About the Photographer: This photograph, originally from the Bettmann Archive, is currently owned by Corbis, a photo agency headquartered in Seattle, Washington. Corbis licenses images for use in magazines, films, television, and advertisements.

INTRODUCTION

At 12:30 p.m. on November 22, 1963, while driving through downtown Dallas, Texas, in a motorcade, John F. Kennedy, the thirty-fifth President of the United States, was shot by a lone gunman firing from the window of a nearby building. He was hit four times and declared dead at Parklands Hospital one hour later. Texas Governor, John Connolly, who was riding in the front of the Kennedy car, was also shot and seriously wounded, but survived.

Kennedy was the fourth American president to be assassinated and the eighth to die in office. Vice President Lyndon B. Johnson, who had been driving in the same motorcade but a different car, was sworn in

Assassination of John F. Kennedy: First Lady Jacqueline Kennedy leans over to assist her husband, U.S. President John F. Kennedy, seconds after he is shot as the Presidential motorcade passes through Dealey Plaza on Elm Street in Dallas, Texas, on November 22, 1963. Kennedy was pronounced dead at Parkland Hospital later the same day. © BETTMANN/CORBIS

as president at 2:38 p.m. on Air Force One as it flew back to Washington, D.C., with President Kennedy's body.

ASSASSINATION OF JOHN F. KENNEDY

See primary source image.

SIGNIFICANCE

The assassination of John F. Kennedy sent the western world into a period of collective mourning. It was not only the most notorious murder in twentieth century American history, but also the most investigated. The notion of a "JFK moment"—i.e. where an individual was when he or she heard the astonishing news—became engrained in popular culture. When Kennedy's assassin, Lee Harvey Oswald, was himself murdered less than forty-eight hours after his arrest, a multitude of conspiracy theories arose, which still abound four decades later.

Oswald, a twenty-four-year-old former Marine who had spent time in the USSR, was arrested hours after Kennedy's assassination after shooting and killing a police officer. The ten-month-long investigation into Kennedy's murder by the Warren Commission concluded in 1964 that Oswald—and Oswald alone—carried out the shooting. Evidence given to the Commission painted a portrait of a wife-beating tyrant with delusions of grandeur. He had failed at everything he had attempted in life—a military career, a professional life, a flirtation with Marxism—except, it seemed, the murder of the President of the United States.

Oswald's reasons for carrying out the killing went with him to his grave. Oswald was himself shot dead on November 24, 1964, by Jack Ruby, a minor figure in the Dallas underworld, who had lunged from a crowd of journalists and police at the police department building where Oswald was being held. Unable to elicit Oswald's testimony, the Warren Commission concluded that it could not "ascribe to him any one motive or group of motives." However, it went on to state that "Oswald was moved by an overriding hostility to his environment."

A quotation from an October 2, 1964, *Time* magazine article sums up Oswald in these terms:

> He does not appear to have been able to establish meaningful relationships with other people. He was perpetually discontented with the world around him. Long before the assassination he expressed his hatred for American society and acted in protest against it. Oswald's search for what he conceived to be the perfect society was doomed from the start. He sought for himself a place in history—a role as the 'great man' who would be recognized as having been in advance of his times. His commitment to Marxism and communism appears to have been another important factor in his motivation. He also had demonstrated [through the attempt to kill General Walker] a capacity to act decisively and without regard to the consequences when such action would further his aims of the moment. Out of these and the many other factors which may have molded the character of Lee Harvey Oswald there emerged a man capable of assassinating President Kennedy.

Yet Oswald's death before he could stand trial and his murder by a shady figure like Ruby gave rise to a multitude of conspiracy theories, many of which were originally dealt with and dismissed by the Warren Commission. Nevertheless, these theories continued to re-emerge over subsequent decades. The idea that

Kennedy was murdered on the instructions of some greater force was given credence in 1979 by a House Select Committee on Assassinations, which directly contradicted the Warren Commission. Using acoustic evidence it concluded that Oswald "probably did not act on his own" and that a second gunman was operating from a grassy knoll. It claimed that Kennedy was probably killed as the result of a conspiracy. In addition, it said it did not know who might have conspired with Oswald in the shooting, but it specifically excluded many of the usual scapegoats, including the FBI, the CIA, the Secret Service, the Soviet government, the Cuban government, anti-Castro Cuban groups, and the Mafia.

The 1991 Oliver Stone movie *JFK* engendered a renewed interest in the case. The movie, which its critics claimed was replete with historical inaccuracies and half truths, followed the story of New Orleans district attorney Jim Garrison, who in the late 1960s prosecuted the only Kennedy case that ever went to trial. Garrison had claimed a vast plot involving homosexual intrigue, the U.S. military-industrial complex, and Fidel Castro, but after thirty-four days of evidence, the jury threw the case out after less than a day of deliberations, finding the defendant, businessman Clay Shaw, not guilty. Following the release of the film, the U.S. government took the unprecedented step of declassifying thousands of documents pertaining to the case. None of these documents pointed to anything other than what the Warren Commission had found thirty years earlier—that Lee Harvey Oswald alone killed President Kennedy.

More than 1,000 books have been published about the Kennedy assassination, many of which also question the findings of the Warren Commission that Oswald acted alone. Unlike the 1979 House Select Committee on Assassinations many draw their own conclusions as to who was behind Kennedy's assassination.

The two principal conspiracy theories center on America's Mafia. The first variation was that Oswald was operating under the instructions of Fidel Castro and killed Kennedy as revenge for an abortive CIA plot—in conjunction with Chicago mobster Sam Giancana—to kill the Cuban leader. The second revolved around the American Mafia's sense of betrayal by the Kennedy administration. President Kennedy's father, Joseph Kennedy, had longstanding connections with the Mob that dated back to his time as a Prohibition-era bootlegger. During his son's run for president in 1960 he had called in numerous favors, not least in Illinois where widespread ballot stuffing and other electoral fraud carried out by local Mafiosi had helped secure a narrow and crucial

Democratic victory. Mobsters who had hopes for an easy time under the Kennedy presidency soon were disappointed with the appointment of the president's brother, Robert, as Attorney General. Under his leadership, the U.S. Justice Department waged a war against organized crime, indicting 116 members of the Mob. According to those who perpetuate this theory, the president's assassination was carried out by the Mafia as retribution for promises of immunity—made in return for favors in voting rigging key states—that were betrayed once he became president. Jack Ruby then murdered Oswald to silence him.

Yet, despite the glut of conspiracy theories and accompanying literature, firm evidence linking some wider plot to the murder of President Kennedy has never been forthcoming. Nevertheless, America remains unconvinced. Even forty years after President Kennedy's death, opinion polls still regularly find that only between one in five and one in three Americans believe Oswald acted alone. As long as books continue to be written about this case, such speculation and uncertainty will almost certainly continue.

FURTHER RESOURCES

Books

Dallek, Robert. *John F Kennedy: An Unfinished Life*. London: Penguin, 2004.

Hersh, Seymour. *The Dark Side of Camelot*. London: Harper Collins, 1998.

Posner, Gerald. *Case Closed*. New York: Random House, 1993.

Russo, Gus. *The Outfit: The Role of Chicago's Underworld in the Shaping of Modern America*. London: Bloomsbury, 2003.

Periodicals

Rosenbaum, Ron. "Taking a Darker View." *Time* (January 13, 2004).

Ruby Shoots Oswald

Photographic Evidence of the Moment of Crime

Photograph

By: Robert H. Jackson

Date: November 24, 1963

Source: Robert H. Jackson. "Ruby Shoots Oswald." November 24, 1963.

About the Photographer: At the time surrounding the events of the John F. Kennedy assassination, Dallas native Robert H. Jackson was a 29-year-old staff photographer for the *Dallas Times Herald*. His photograph of Lee Harvey Oswald's subsequent murder won Jackson the Pulitzer Prize in 1964.

INTRODUCTION

When President John F. Kennedy was shot dead in downtown Dallas on November 22, 1963, it took officers just hours to arrest his murderer, Lee Harvey Oswald, a violent and delusional left-wing activist. Oswald was found hiding in a Dallas cinema having earlier shot dead a police officer who had tried to arrest him. He was taken to the Dallas police department where he was detained and questioned.

Inevitably, the assassination of Kennedy sent the western world into mourning. Millions were deeply affected by the death of the glamorous young president, turning to fledgling round-the-clock news broadcasts to follow the unfolding story. One such man, Jack Ruby, a small-time Dallas mobster, was deeply upset by Kennedy's murder, "unable, " he told the Warren Commission, which investigated the assassination, "to stop crying."

The day after the Kennedy murder and amidst lax security, Ruby hung around the Dallas Police Department and also the *Dallas Times* newsroom, claiming to be a translator for the Israeli press. The Warren Commission was unable to clarify whether his presence around the epicenter of the world's biggest news story tipped him towards his act of violent vigilantism, but the following day Jack Ruby was to enter history with an act almost as notorious as that carried out by Oswald himself.

On Sunday, November 24, after only a few hours sleep, Ruby arose in a nervous state, mumbling to himself and pacing the floor. He would later tell the Commission that he had seen in the paper a "heartbreaking letter" to President Kennedy's six-year-old daughter Caroline, and that "alongside that letter on the same sheet of paper was a small comment in the newspaper that, I don't know how it was stated, that Mrs. Kennedy may have to come back for the trial of Lee Harvey Oswald."

At approximately 11 A.M. he left his apartment armed with a revolver. First he drove to the point where Kennedy had been shot and looked at wreaths scattered along the street before driving to the Western Union office. Here he paid for a telegram (his receipt was stamped 11:17 A.M.) before walking in the direction of the police department building where

PRIMARY SOURCE

Ruby Shoots Oswald: Jack Ruby shoots Lee Harvey Oswald, accused assassin of President John F. Kennedy, as Oswald was being transferred through the underground garage of Dallas police headquarters on November 24, 1963.
POPPERFOTO/ARCHIVE PHOTOS

Oswald was being held. At 11:21 A.M., as police officers were preparing to take Oswald to the county jail, Ruby emerged from a crowd of police and journalists and shot and fatally wounded Lee Harvey Oswald.

PRIMARY SOURCE

RUBY SHOOTS OSWALD

See primary source image.

SIGNIFICANCE

The murder of Lee Harvey Oswald was captured live on American television and seen by millions both at the time and over subsequent days. Jack Ruby, who was arrested immediately in the full glare of the cameras, claimed that his action served as proof that "Jews have guts" and was vindication for the city of Dallas. At his trial in spring 1964, at which he was found guilty and sentenced to death by electric chair (the death sentence was later struck down on appeal), he pleaded insanity. However, he testified before the Warren Commission later on that year and claimed that he shot Oswald because he didn't want Kennedy's widow to have to go through with the ordeal of a trial.

In late 1966, while on his deathbed, Ruby gave another recorded testimony. This time he ascribed the murder to destiny, saying: "The ironic part of this is I had made an illegal turn behind a bus to the parking lot. Had I gone the way I was supposed to go—straight down Main Street—I would've never met this fate, because the difference in meeting this fate was thirty seconds one way or the other." Ruby died of a pulmonary embolism on January 4, 1967.

Inevitably, Ruby's dramatic intervention in the Kennedy assassination has seen his role and life investigated in minute detail. He has also been cast in an entire gamut of conspiracy theories. Of principle interest was Ruby's role in the American underworld. He had started out as an enforcer of Al Capone in prohibition-era Chicago and at the time of the Kennedy assassination was running a Dallas strip club. This invariably led to the conclusion that Ruby had somehow been involved in a mafia plot to kill Kennedy and had been deployed to kill Oswald, lest he reveal who had put him up to the killing when it came to trial.

The Warren Commission, which ruled out the involvement of a third party in the Kennedy killing, found no evidence to support this claim. Likewise it rejected claims that the Dallas Police Department had been complicit in Oswald's death by allowing Ruby into its building. Nor did it find any evidence that Ruby had been involved in either left wing or right wing plots to kill the president. It also ruled out that Ruby and Oswald had had a homosexual affair and this had somehow served as motivation. Instead, it concluded that "Ruby was regarded by most persons who knew him as moody and unstable—hardly one to have encouraged the confidence of persons involved in a sensitive political conspiracy."

In fact the truth about Jack Ruby is probably no more complicated than that: like the man he killed, he was violent and delusional and somehow saw his actions as righteous. According to his attorney he genuinely believed he would spend no more than a night in jail and after his arrest he had told the Assistant District Attorney, Bill Alexander, "Well, you guys couldn't do it. Someone had to do it. That son of a bitch killed my President." Thirty years later, Alexander told author Gerald Posner: "Jack actually thought he might come out of this as a hero of sorts. He thought he had erased any stigma the city had by knocking off Oswald."

FURTHER RESOURCES
Books

Dallek, Robert. *John F. Kennedy: An Unfinished Life*. London: Penguin, 2004.

Posner, Gerald. *Case Closed*. New York: Random House, 1993.

Periodicals

"The Man Who Killed Oswald." *Time* (December 6, 1963).

Ted Bundy

Government document

By: Federal Bureau of Investigation

Date: June 9, 1977

Source: *Federal Bureau of Investigation.* "Freedom of Information and Privacy Acts. Subject. Ted Bundy." <http://foia.fbi.gov/bundy/bundy1a.pdf> (accessed February 2, 2006).

About the Author: The Federal Bureau of Investigation (FBI), founded in 1908, is the investigative branch of the U.S. Department of Justice. Its mission is to protect the country from terrorist and other foreign threats, investigate major domestic crimes, and provide criminal justice services to agencies and partners at federal, state, municipal and international levels.

INTRODUCTION

Ted Bundy is one of the most notorious serial killers the United States has ever seen. He was responsible for a number of brutal murders in the Pacific Northwest, Utah, Colorado, and Florida between 1969 and 1978. Bundy's early years had been unsettled and he had a history of petty theft; but he fooled many people because he was a charming and handsome young man, a law school graduate who did charity work and campaigned for the Republican Party.

Bundy procured his victims by pretending to be injured, then asking women for help so he could drag them into his car. He had already killed several women in Seattle when, on November 8, 1974, he approached Carol DaRonch in Salt Lake City. This was to be his downfall—at least temporarily. He got her into his car, then tried to handcuff her and pulled out a gun. But DaRonch escaped. Bundy went on to kill seventeen-year-old Debbie Kent that same night.

Caught in August 1975, he was identified by DaRonch in a police lineup, convicted of her kidnapping, and sentenced to fifteen years. In April 1977 Colorado indicted him for the January 1975 murder of twenty-three-year-old Caryn Campbell and transferred him to Garfield County jail to await trial. Because he acted as his own attorney, Bundy was allowed to use the courthouse library to prepare his defense. He jumped from a window in June 1977 during one such visit, an escape that is the subject of the police memo below. Bundy was recaptured eight days later.

FD-36 (Rev. 7-27-76)

FBI

TRANSMIT VIA:
[X] Teletype
[ ] Facsimile
[ ] Airtel

PRECEDENCE:
[ ] Immediate
[ ] Priority
[X] Routine

CLASSIFICATION:
[ ] TOP SECRET
[ ] SECRET
[ ] CONFIDENTIAL
[ ] E F T O
[X] CLEAR

Date _____ 6/9/77 _____

FM SALT LAKE CITY (88-6895) (P)

TO DENVER   ROUTINE

SEATTLE   ROUTINE

BT

CLEAR

THEODORE ROBERT BUNDY, AKA TED BUNDY - FUGITIVE.   UFAC -

ESCAPE.   OO:SALT LAKE CITY.

ON JUNE 9, 1977, SALT LAKE COUNTY ATTORNEY'S OFFICE

ISSUED ESCAPE WARRANT FOR SUBJECT, REQUESTED UNLAWFUL FLIGHT

WARRANT BE ISSUED.   SAME DATE AUSA JAMES W. MC CONKIE II,

SALT LAKE CITY, AUTHORIZED FILING OF COMPLAINT CHARGING SUBJECT

WITH VIOLATION TITLE 18, U. S. CODE, SECTION 1073.   COMPLAINT

FILED BEFORE U. S. MAGISTRATE DANIEL A. ALSUP BY SA▮▮▮▮▮▮▮

▮▮▮▮▮▮▮ WARRANT ISSUED.   BOND RECOMMENDED $100,000 CASH.

SUBJECT DESCRIBED AS: WMA, DOB NOVEMBER 24, 1946 AT

BURLINGTON, VERMONT, 6',175 LBS., BLUE EYES, BROWN HAIR,

SSAN 533-44-4655.

SEARCHED
SERIALIZED
INDEXED
FILED

Approved: _____   Transmitted _____   Per _____
                          (Number)   (Time)
                                                    GPO : 1977 O - 225-539

PRIMARY SOURCE

Ted Bundy: This all-points bulletin (APB) from the Salt Lake City police announces that Ted Bundy has escaped from their custody while in Aspen, Colorado. PUBLIC DOMAIN

FD-36 (Rev. 7-27-76)

FBI

TRANSMIT VIA:
- ☐ Teletype
- ☐ Facsimile
- ☐ Airtel

PRECEDENCE:
- ☐ Immediate
- ☐ Priority
- ☐ Routine

CLASSIFICATION:
- ☐ TOP SECRET
- ☐ SECRET
- ☐ CONFIDENTIAL
- ☐ E F T O-
- ☐ CLEAR

Date _____

SU 88-6895   PAGE TWO

DENVER AT ASPEN, COLORADO. CONDUCT APPROPRIATE INVESTI-

GATION TO LOCATE SUBJECT.

SEATTLE. ██

██

bk

bTP

██

██

████████████

SALT LAKE CITY AT SALT LAKE CITY, UTAH. OBTAIN ADDRESS

FOR ████████████████████████████████ AND SET OUT LEADS

bk

TO ████████████████ ALSO MAINTAIN CONTACT WITH SALT LAKE

COUNTY SO FOR ADDITIONAL BACKGROUND AND SET OUT ADDITIONAL

LEADS.

"IN VIEW OF TYPE OF CRIME SUBJECT HAS BEEN CONVICTED OF

HE SHOULD BE CONSIDERED ARMED AND DANGEROUS - ESCAPE RISK."

BT

Approved: _____   Transmitted _____   Per _____

(Number)   (Time)

GPO : 1977 O - 225-539

PRIMARY SOURCE

Ted Bundy: This all-points bulletin (APB) from the Salt Lake City police announces that Ted Bundy has escaped from their custody while in Aspen, Colorado. PUBLIC DOMAIN

PRIMARY SOURCE

TED BUNDY

See primary source image.

SIGNIFICANCE

Bundy escaped again in December 1977 by cutting a hole in the ceiling of his cell with a hacksaw blade. He remained at large much longer this time, adopting a false name and living by theft. On January 15, 1978, he broke into the Chi Omega sorority house at Florida State University, where he attacked four students. Lisa Levy was raped and beaten to death; Margaret Brown was strangled. The other two were beaten with a wooden club but survived.

A month later, Bundy sexually assaulted and strangled twelve-year-old Kim Leach, who was to be his final victim. By the time he was caught, driving a stolen car, he was wanted for murder in several states. In June 1979 he went on trial for the Chi Omega murders and again insisted on conducting his own defense. No fingerprint evidence was found at the scene. But the case was significant from a forensic point of view: Lisa Levy had bite marks on her breast and her buttock—a common finding in violent rape. He was forced to give a dental impression, which matched the marks—major evidence for the prosecution.

Bundy was found guilty of the two Chi Omega murders and sentenced to death. After ten years on death row, he finally admitted to the murders of thirty women; some believe he may have killed as many 100. His known victims comprised eight young women in Seattle, four in Salt Lake City, and Caryn Campbell in Aspen, as well as Lisa Levy, Margaret Bowman, and Kim Leach. As his execution date approached, he confessed to still more murders, hoping for a reprieve. He claimed an entity inside him drove him to murder, referring to himself in the third person.

While psychiatrists judged him neither psychotic nor sexually deviant, he was obsessed with hard-core sadomasochistic pornography and had a huge fear of being humiliated by women; he enjoyed the power he wielded over his victims. Rape, he said, was his prime motive. The murder was then carried out to silence his victim.

Bundy was executed in the electric chair on January 24, 1989. While some executions attract demonstrators who protest capital punishment, in this case they were few. People instead set off fireworks and cheered when his death was announced.

FURTHER RESOURCES

Books

Lyle, Douglas P. *Forensics for Dummies.* Hoboken, NJ: Wiley, 2004.

Jackson, Andrew R.W., and Julie M. Jackson. *Forensic Science.* Harlow, UK: Pearson Education, 2004.

Web sites

British Broadcasting Corporation. "Crime. Case Closed. Infamous Criminals. "Ted Bundy." <http://www.bbc.co.uk/crime/caseclosed/tedbundy1.shtml> (accessed February 2, 2006).

Columbine High School Security Video Shows Klebold and Harris in Cafeteria

Video still

By: Anonymous

Date: December 13, 1999

Source: AP Images.

About the Author: This image was taken by a security video camera in the cafeteria of Columbine High School.

INTRODUCTION

On April 20, 1999, students Eric Harris and Dylan Klebold, entered Columbine High School in Littleton, Colorado, armed with propane and pipe bombs, semiautomatic weapons, and sawed-off shotguns. In just under an hour they shot and killed twelve students, one teacher and injured twenty-four other students. They then killed themselves inside the school.

The worst school shooting in United States history, the incident horrified America and the world, and triggered a series of copycat shootings at schools in the United States and Canada. Because Harris and Klebold had amassed such a formidable cache of weapons, ammunition, and explosives, the incident also spurred an intense debate about gun laws in America.

Columbine High School Security Video Shows Klebold and Harris in Cafeteria: A still photograph from a digital security camera shows Eric Harris (left) and Dylan Klebold (right) in the cafeteria of Columbine High School during their April 20, 1999, shooting rampage. © REUTERS/CORBIS

COLUMBINE HIGH SCHOOL SECURITY VIDEO SHOWS KLEBOLD AND HARRIS IN CAFETERIA

See primary source image.

SIGNIFICANCE

Experts point to several factors that influence school violence. These incidents are caused by deep and complex problems that affect contemporary American society.

A CNN survey conducted in August 1999 discovered that four out of five middle school students behave like bullies at least once in a month, indulging in name-calling, teasing, beating, and threatening other students. Bullies single out others who don't fit in and subject them to torment. If bullying is left uncontrolled, its victims often develop severe hostility and may even resort to serious acts of violence.

Often victims bear the brunt silently; over a period of time, however, they drift away into a world of emptiness and delusion. Such children often become extremely isolated and may resort to violence.

Bullying behavior is often reinforced by media, movies, television programs, and video games targeted at adolescents and teenagers that depict extensive violence. Easy access to guns is also a factor.

America is one of the few countries in the world where possessing a weapon is a fundamental right. Nearly 49 percent of American households own a firearm. Although federal and state laws prohibit juveniles from owning or possessing a weapon, in many instances they are able to get one.

Klebold and Harris were loners and outcasts who didn't fit into the culture at Columbine High. Other students picked on them for their different behavior. They were part of a group of students called the trench-coat mafia, a gang who wore black trench coats and were known for rebellious behavior.

Though juveniles at the time of the killings, Klebold and Harris still managed to acquire weapons illegally and assemble bombs from easily available materials. They also maintained a website (since taken down) about the violent computer games Doom and Wolfenstein 3D, and posted online diaries and blogs full of hateful comments about other students.

As of 2006, a ban on semiautomatic weapons (which was in place at the time of the Columbine High School massacre) has been lifted. A debate still rages on standards of public education, bullying, gun laws, and other cultural issues especially affecting teens and adolescents in the United States.

FURTHER RESOURCES
Web sites

BBC News. "Americans Split on Gun Ban's end" <http://news.bbc.co.uk/2/hi/americas/3654012.stm> (accessed February 14, 2006).

BBC News. "Timeline: U.S. School Shootings" <http://news.bbc.co.uk/2/hi/americas/4371403.stm> (accessed February 14, 2006).

CNN "Are U.S. Schools Safe?" <http://edition.cnn.com/SPECIALS/1998/schools> (accessed February 14, 2006).

Just Facts "Gun Control" <http://justfacts.com/gun_control.htm> (accessed February 14, 2006).

Time.com "Guns and Violence" <http://www.time.com/time/daily/special/denvershooting> (accessed February 14, 2006).

World Socialist Website "School shooting in Canada: Wave of "Copycat" Threats in U.S. follow Columbine tragedy" <http://www.wsws.org/articles/1999/may1999/schm04.shtml> (accessed February 14, 2006).

The Bulger Case

Newspaper article

By: Diane Taylor

Date: June 20, 2001

Source: *Guardian Unlimited*. "Special Report: The Bulger Case." Interviews by Diane Taylor. <http://www.guardian.co.uk/bulger/article/0,,509699,00.html#article_continue> (accessed January 22, 2006).

About the Author: Diane Taylor is a contributor to *Guardian Unlimited*, the online presence of the British daily newspaper *The Guardian*, which was founded in 1821. Together with its Sunday paper *The Observer*, *The Guardian* and *Guardian Unlimited* reach an audience of over 4.5 million adults in the United Kingdom each week.

INTRODUCTION

On February 12, 1993, two-year-old James Bulger became separated from his mother Denise while out shopping in a mall in Liverpool, England. Shortly afterwards, a security camera showed him being led outside by two young boys. What then happened shocked the nation and drew comment and controversy from around the world. The boys, Jon Venables and Robert Thompson, were only ten years old, yet they beat and battered James to death, perhaps also subjecting him to a sexual assault. They finally abandoned his body on a railway line to be run over by the next train. His remains were discovered by a group of children the following morning.

A trail of evidence led the police to pick up Venables and Thompson for questioning on February 18, 1993. Thirty-eight witnesses had seen James in their company on their journey to the railway and, indeed, the child had almost been rescued on several occasions. The boys' age made their interrogation by detectives difficult. They lied, contradicted themselves, blamed one another, and became extremely distressed. But Venables soon broke down and admitted his guilt. Thompson did not admit his part in the crime for several more years. As the age of criminal responsibility is set at ten in England, the police were able to charge them with James's murder and they had to stand trial. The article reproduced below discusses the issues surrounding criminal responsibility and was written around the time of the boys' release in 2001.

PRIMARY SOURCE

The question: The age of criminal responsibility in England is 10, which allowed James Bulger's killers to be prosecuted. Should it be altered?

Dr. Ann Hagell
Co-director, Policy Research Bureau

There is no other legal or social arena where we give children complete responsibility at 10, mostly for good reason. The important thing is the consequence of being over the age of criminal responsibility, not the age per se. Other countries with a very low age (10 or less) usually have a period where responsibility is not absolute until mid-to late teens, or where the response to breaking the law is welfare-oriented rather than retributive. For example, the age in Scotland is eight but the consequences are almost all framed within the welfare system.
Verdict: Age isn't the issue

Frances Crook
Director, Howard League for Penal Reform

Our age of criminal responsibility is one of the lowest in Europe. Other European countries have set the age at 14, 15, 16 or, in some cases, at 18. If children do something wrong they should be dealt with through the care system not the criminal justice system. Children know if they have done something wrong, but they don't know the difference between various levels of wrongdoing. What all children know is that the world of adults is capricious and that parents don't always respond to things in the same way. The age should be raised to 14 and then 16.
Verdict: Yes, to 14

Laurence Lee
Solicitor for Jon Venables at his trial

I think that Thompson and Venables did know the difference between right and wrong at the age of 10, but they were treated like circus animals at the trial. When the case went to the European court, it ruled that proceedings in future cases of this kind should be more informal.

If the age of criminal responsibility at the time of the Bulger killing had been 12, the boys wouldn't have been prosecuted and there would have been outrage. It could be argued that their sentence starts the day they are released. With their new identities they will have to live a lie.
Verdict: No

Carolyn Hamilton
Director, Children's Legal Centre

I would say about 14. I think that at that age children are better able to understand the consequences of what they are doing. A child of 10 who has committed an offence is more appropriately dealt with in the care system than in the criminal justice system. The European court says that a child must be able to participate in their own defence and I think a child of 14 is able to do that. The Committee on the Rights of the Child has said that 10 is too young for criminal responsibility. If our aim is rehabilitation, it is best done under the civil system, not the criminal justice system.
Verdict: Yes, to 14

Lyn Costello
Mothers Against Murder and Aggression

Children of 10 know the difference between right and wrong. They know you don't hurt small children. The killing of James Bulger was a planned and covered-up crime. Any parent will tell you there are cases where children play rough and get hurt, but they know it's wrong to kill a child and Thompson and Venables knew that, otherwise they wouldn't have covered it up and lied about it. We have children as young as eight, or even six, terrorising people on estates such as the one I live on. I also think parents should be held responsible for their children's behaviour.
Verdict: Yes, to 8

Beate Raedergard
Mother whose child was killed by young boys

My five-year-old daughter, Silje, was killed by two boys near our home in Trondheim, Norway. It was a year after the killing of James Bulger, and the two incidents were compared in the press. In Norway, where the age of criminality is 15, the boys were treated differently. Silje was stripped, stoned and beaten, and left for dead. I do not understand why and I will never recover, but I don't hate the boys. I think they understood what they had done, but not the consequences. The boys went back to school, were helped by psychologists and have had to learn how to treat others to fit back into society.
Verdict: Yes, to 15

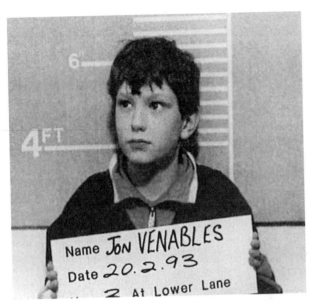

This is a 1993, police handout picture made available in June 2001, of Jon Venables. Venables and Robert Thompson, who were 10 when they tortured and killed 2-year-old James Bulger in Bootle, northern England, were released despite a long campaign by the toddler's mother to keep them behind bars. Both young men were given new identities, which a judge barred the British media from disclosing. AP IMAGES

SIGNIFICANCE

The trial of Jon Venables and Robert Thompson took place in November 1993 amidst huge publicity. Prior to this, they had been housed in special secure units, separate from one another, under false identities. They appeared at Liverpool Crown Court where they entered not guilty pleas; on this occasion Venables began to hyperventilate. A psychiatrist judged him fit to stand trial, however, and established that he understood the severity of the crime of which he was accused. Another psychiatrist used dolls to get Thompson to re-enact some of the details of the crime. She reported that he, too, was fit to stand trial and that although, like his friend, he had a poor school record, was of above average intelligence.

Both boys were small for their age and had to stand on a specially raised platform during the trial, so that they could view the proceedings. The judge referred to the defendants as Child A and Child B but, of course, they were still on view to all court observers, including the Bulger family. The defense argued that a fair trial would be impossible because of the intense publicity the case had generated, but the judge dismissed these objections. Because the defendants were under the age of fourteen, it was necessary for the prosecution to establish that they knew their actions were severely wrong. Their teachers and psychiatrists claimed that they were so aware and knew the difference between right and wrong. The defense argued, however, that although both boys came from a disturbed background, they had no record of violent crime, only of shoplifting and truancy. The murder of James was, they said, a prank that had gone horribly wrong.

The jury began its deliberations on November 24, three weeks after the trial began. It did not take many hours before the guilty verdict was returned. Venables and Thompson were sentenced to detention for as long as it took for them to be fully rehabilitated. The judge also allowed the media to publish the boys' names.

The case did not rest there. It was referred to the European Commission on Human Rights. In 1999, the European Court ruled that Venables and Thompson had not had a fair trial. They were too young, it was ruled, to have been tried in an adult court. The raised platform proved to be a particular issue—it was inappropriate and degrading, the court said. Furthermore, the boys could not be expected to understand the complexities and formalities of the British legal system to which they had been exposed. The European Court ruling upset both the Bulger family and Albert Kirby, the detective who led the investigation. The issue over how long the two boys should remain in custody and who had the legal right to free them remained. It has always been clear that their release would be problematic—they would need to be provided with new identities and would need protection indefinitely. Too many people have threatened the boys and their families for them to walk free without appropriate provisions being made for their safety. Venables and Thompson were released from custody in 2001 and their current whereabouts are unknown.

FURTHER RESOURCES

Books

Morrison, Blake. *As If.* London: Granta Books, 1998.

Web sites

Crime Library. "Young Killers—The Death of James Bulger." <http://www.crimelibrary.com/classics3/bulger/> (accessed January 22, 2006).

NOW Will Raise Funds for Yates' Legal Defense

Spotlight Placed on Depression Issue

Newspaper article

By: Lisa Teachey

Date: August 24, 2001

Source: Teachey, Lisa. "NOW Will Raise Funds for Yates' Legal Defense; Spotlight Placed on Depression Issue." *Houston Chronicle* (August 24, 2001).

About the Author: Lisa Teachey is a newspaper reporter for the *Houston Chronicle*. She covered the Andrea Yates case in a series of newspaper articles throughout 2001 and 2002.

INTRODUCTION

On June 20, 2001, Andrea Yates called the Houston, Texas 911 hotline to report a problem with her children. When police arrived, they found seven-year-old Noah, five-year-old John, three-year-old Paul, two-year-old Luke, and seven-month-old Mary dead in the house, all five children having been drowned by their mother. Yates, a former nurse, was a stay-at-home mother who home schooled her older children. She and her husband, Russell "Rusty" Yates, a NASA engineer, were devout Christians, and Andrea believed that she had destroyed her children by being a bad mother; the only way to save their souls, she believed, was to kill them. She told police that she had been thinking about harming her children for more than two years, because, in her words, they were "not developing correctly." She did not elaborate on what she meant.

The case quickly made national headlines. When psychiatrists revealed that Andrea Yates was suffering from post-partum psychosis, a rare condition in which a mother experiences psychotic episodes within the first year after giving birth, some women's groups, such as the National Organization for Women, began to frame Andrea Yates's crime as one that stemmed from severe mental illness. Media analyses examined infanticide laws, which pose lighter penalties in countries such as England, and which also carry heavy mental health services as part of the sentence. The drowning of the Yates children polarized public sentiment in the United States; while many viewed Andrea Yates as a cold-blooded killer who told police that she chased down her seven-year-old son, Noah, after he saw his siblings' bodies and realized what was happening, others portrayed Yates as an over-stressed, highly controlled, submissive wife of a religious-fundamentalist husband who ignored her post-partum depression after her fourth child.

As new details from the Yates's life emerged, feminist groups and critics began to portray Rusty Yates as a responsible party to the crimes—not for his actions, but for his inaction. Andrea Yates struggled with post-partum depression after giving birth to her fourth child, Luke; pundits questioned why the couple went on to have a fifth child when doctors warned them not to have more children. Andrea Yates was hospitalized for mental health problems and attempted suicide twice in 1999 and twice in 2001, before the drownings. She stopped taking her psychiatric medications—with Rusty's knowledge. Rusty Yates revealed that on the day of the murders he left for work knowing that Andrea was unstable; Rusty's mother was on her way to help Andrea, but Rusty left a two-hour window between his departure and his mother's arrival. It was during that two-hour window that Andrea drowned her five children.

■ PRIMARY SOURCE

The Houston Area National Organization for Women is rallying support for Andrea Pia Yates, the Clear Lake mother who has admitted to drowning her five children.

In addition to forming the Andrea Pia Yates Support Coalition, the local chapter of NOW plans to help raise money for Yates' defense fund, the organization's state president said Thursday.

The women's rights group also said it will offer support to Yates' husband, Russell.

Meanwhile, Harris County District Attorney Chuck Rosenthal has received correspondence critical of Russell Yates.

Of the 72 e-mails and letters Rosenthal received regarding whether Andrea Yates should be punished by death, some said Russell Yates should be held accountable, too. Seventeen blasted him for leaving the children with his wife because, they said, he knew she was mentally unstable.

Andrea Yates, 37, faces capital murder charges in the deaths of three of her children - sons Noah, 7, John, 5, and Mary, 6 months. She is not charged with the other children's deaths, but prosecutors plan to present evidence about the deaths of Paul, 3, and Luke, 2, during trial.

The mother, who relatives said suffered severe depression, has pleaded not guilty by reason of insanity.

So far, the support coalition has not taken in any money for Yates, but the president of Texas NOW said fund-raisers could be in the works.

"Right now we're just giving out information about the defense fund," said Deborah Bell of Houston. "We're trying to bring attention to this issue and attention to the fund."

The fund was established at Horizon Bank by Yates' hired lawyers after Rosenthal announced he would seek the death penalty. Rosenthal said the decision was made to give a jury a full range of punishment options.

Yates called Houston police to her home in the 900 block of Beachcomber on June 20 and admitted drowning the children in the bathtub. Russell Yates told police his wife was depressed and had been medically treated for her condition. She is under suicide watch in the psychiatric unit of the Harris County Jail.

Shortly after Andrea Yates was arrested, NOW adopted a resolution regarding postpartum depression during a national conference, Bell said. The resolution urges the judiciary to "consider tragedies of this sort in the full context of the nature of postpartum depression," and calls for more research into the illness.

The coalition also plans to hold a candlelight vigil the night before a competency hearing on whether Yates is fit to stand trial. The hearing is set for Sept. 12. Other support efforts are in the works, including a court watch, a march and an educational forum.

Bell said despite the criticism of Russell Yates, the local coalition is in place to support all of the Yates family.

"As long as he is standing by her, we are standing by him," Bell said.

Some of Rosenthal's mail regarding Russell Yates questioned why the husband was not being criminally prosecuted.

Her lawyers have said she suffered a prolonged history of mental disease and defect, including two prior hospitalizations, at least two attempts of suicide and prior diagnosis of major depression and postpartum depression with psychosis.

"It was evident she was not well for some time and her husband was fully aware of it," wrote one person, who was against the death penalty in this case. "He needs to be arrested as an accomplice."

"He is just as guilty," wrote another, who thinks the mother should be put to death. "He did not protect his children against a very dangerous woman...He should be charged and sent to prison."

A lawyer not involved with the case said Russell Yates committed no crime.

Under Texas law, an accomplice is defined as someone who intentionally aided, solicited or encouraged a crime to be committed, Brian Wice said.

A neglect charge against the husband would not be feasible either because there is no evidence the mother abused, starved or neglected the children, Wice said.

"Should he have been able to look into the future and seen that she was going to snap? No. Mental illness isn't a justification that someone is going to violate the law with impunity, particularly when it concerns your own flesh and blood."

"He may be condemned, and rightfully so, in the court of public opinion, but there is no legal basis for him to stand trial in a court of law."

Former District Attorney John B. Holmes Jr., who was regarded nationally for his tough stance on seeking death penalties, also weighed in on the subject.

"It's (seeking death) the right call," Holmes wrote in an e-mail. "That is why I had a reputation of going for it so much. It is part of the range. Amazingly the public went for it most of the times that we included it in the range. I suspect your experience will be the same."

Rosenthal could not comment on the e-mails because state District Judge Belinda Hill has imposed a gag order on all parties involved in the case. Under an open records request, the Chronicle received Rosenthal's correspondence because they are public record.

Not all of Rosenthal's responses were included. But of the ones that were, he typically answered that his decision was based on evidence and applicable law.

"I do all of this after seeking wisdom from God," Rosenthal wrote one person. "My oath of office requires me follow the law without consideration of public opinion."

The correspondence was sent unsolicited and is not a scientific sampling of how the community feels.

Twenty were for death by lethal injection. Twenty-nine were against. An e-mail from Vote.com, an Internet voting site, said its poll showed 729 were for seeking death in this case, while 495 were against it.

SIGNIFICANCE

In the weeks and months that followed Andrea Yates's arrest, Rusty Yates emerged as a controversial character. Rusty and Andrea followed a charismatic Christian leader named Michael Woroniecki. Woroniecki claimed to be a prophet and preached in public; over time, Rusty and Andrea moved into a converted bus, where they lived until after having their fourth child. According to newspaper and court

Andrea Pia Yates sits in a Houston courtroom on September 22, 2001, awaiting the verdict in her competency hearing. Yates was eventually found guilty of drowning her five children and sentenced to life in prison. AP IMAGES.

accounts, the family moved into a house in Houston where Andrea took care of the children, home schooled the older ones, cared for her ailing mother and father, and appeared to be under a great deal of stress from her lifestyle and from Rusty's expectations.

When Rusty revealed that he had known that Andrea should not be left alone with the children, and yet chose to leave for work the morning of June 20, 2001, before his mother arrived to help Andrea, much public sympathy turned to public outrage. NOW organized fundraisers for Andrea Yates's legal expenses, but, in the weeks and months that followed this article, feminist groups, including NOW, called for some responsibility for the murders of the children to be placed on Rusty Yates.

Andrea Yates's diagnosis of post-partum psychosis triggered intense discussion of the little-known disorder. While seventy-five percent of all women experience "baby blues"—a temporary hormonal shift that makes women weepy and slightly depressed for no longer than ten days post-partum—and ten percent of

post-partum women experience post-partum depression, only 0.5 percent, or 1 in 500, women experience post-partum psychosis in the twelve months after giving birth. Andrea Yates's break with reality, her hallucinations, thoughts of harming her children, and difficulties coping with daily life were all components of her disease. As defense lawyers submitted an insanity defense on her behalf for the killings, post-partum psychosis was in the media spotlight.

Texas law and the insanity defense created problems in the trial. Under Texas law, an insanity defense is possible only if the defendant is insane at the time of the killings. The fact that Yates waited until she was alone with the children, had thought about hurting her children for over two years, chased her seven year old and forced him into the bathtub, and then calmly called 911 and then Rusty's workplace indicated intent and careful calculation. A public debate over the definition of insanity ensued.

On March 12, 2002, a Texas jury found Andrea Yates guilty in the murder of three of her children (she was not tried for two of the murders for technical reasons). Because she murdered more than one person, and because some of the murders involved children younger than the age of six, Andrea was eligible for the death penalty. In the end, she was sentenced to life in prison, and was eligible for parole in 2041.

During and after the trial, Harris County District Attorney Chuck Rosenthal received a large volume of e-mail, regular mail, and telephone calls requesting that Rusty Yates be held responsible for failing to protect his children. The District Attorney investigated the legalities of charging Rusty, but could find no law under which the father could be tried.

On January 6, 2005, an appeals court overturned Andrea Yates's conviction on the grounds that one of the psychiatrists testifying during the trial had given false testimony. Dr. Park Dietz stated that shortly before Yates murdered her children, an episode of the television series *Law and Order* had centered around a woman who drowned her children. This testimony was proven to be false; no such episode existed. Andrea Yates would receive a new trial.

NOW stands behind their support of Andrea Yates and their commitment to widespread education and understanding of post-partum mental health issues. In 2004 Rusty Yates filed for divorce from Andrea Yates.

FURTHER RESOURCES
Books
Spencer, Suzy. *Breaking Point*. New York: St. Martin's, 2002.

Web sites

National Public Radio. "One Mother's Story." <http://www.npr.org/programs/morning/features/2002/feb/postpartum/020218.postpartum.html> (accessed January 18, 2006).

Time. "Andrea Yates: More to the Story." <http://www.time.com/time/nation/article/0,8599,218445,00.html> (accessed January 18, 2006).-//Gale Research//DTD Document V2.0//EN">

County Road Cutters

An Eye For an Eye

Book excerpt

By: Andy Nicholls

Date: October 2002

Source: Nicholls, Andy. *Scally: The Story of a Category C Football Hooligan.* Ramsbottom, UK: Milo Books, 2002.

About the Author: Andy Nicholls was born in 1962 and has followed the Everton Football Club since childhood. He edited the football fanzine *Get into Them*, whose publication was banned after only two editions. A "Category C" football hooligan—the British police's most notorious classification—Nicholls has been banned from many football stadia and claims to have lost interest in the sport.

INTRODUCTION

Hooliganism—riotous and destructive behavior by spectators at sporting events—once seemed synonymous with British football. Although the game was given a codified set of rules with the formation of the Football Association in 1863, this did little to dampen the passions of those who loved and watched the sport, and off-the-field violence soon tarnished the game's image.

This was largely intermittent and spontaneous until the 1950s, when mass transportation brought large numbers of "away" fans (supporters of visiting clubs) to the matches. Such excursions were often synonymous with heavy drinking, brawling, vandalism, occasionally within the stadium itself. These acts were usually carried out by a small minority of spectators,

but as the clashes were very visible and sometimes even spectacular, the problem became exaggerated and the game as a whole began to suffer.

Hooliganism escalated during the 1960s and 1970s, and English clubs in European competition regularly had their visits marred by the violent actions of their supporters. Even worse, fans of continental rivals sometimes tried to outdo the so-called "Hooligan Kings of Europe."

In Britain, hooliganism plunged the sport into crisis: attendance spiraled and clubs left with huge debts and rotting stadia. Throughout the 1980s, although individual acts of hooliganism actually declined, football-related violence became a national crisis, and was alternatively seen as a symptom of national decay, inner-city deprivation, lack of education, poverty, or simple moral bankruptcy.

Things went from bad to worse with the Heysel Stadium disaster of May 1985, when a riot by Liverpool fans caused a wall to collapse and kill 39 rival supporters. Prime Minister Margaret Thatcher declared war on the violence and worked with Parliament to pass legislation to curb the hooligan blight.

Most clubs had their own hooligan fringe. Usually they were loosely affiliated but like-minded men who regarded a brawl with rival fans as part of their match day experience. Some took on names—the Chelsea Headhunters, the West Ham Inter City Crew, the Leeds Service Crew.

The County Road Cutters were a notorious faction of hooligans—probably numbering no more than a dozen members—associated with Everton, a Liverpool-based team and one of the country's preeminent clubs. County Road is the main thoroughfare running to the west of Goodison; "cutters" refers to their weapon of choice—a Stanley knife or box cutter. They lurked in alleyways and side streets surrounding Goodison Park, the club grounds, plotting ambushes against rival hooligans.

The following incident took place in January 1989 at an FA Cup replay with West Bromwich Albion at Goodison. After a draw the previous Saturday, an Everton supporter—not involved with hooliganism—lost an eye after being attacked and beaten in a deliberate ambush by West Bromwich Albion fans. The incident received much local press coverage and aroused much anger. This is the tale of how one County Road Cutter exacted his revenge.

Football (soccer) fans flee the May 29, 1985, riots in the Heysel, Belgium, stadium. Thirty-nine fans of the Turin, Italy, team died during the rioting at the European Cup Final between England's Liverpool and Turin. The city of Brussels marked the anniversary in 2005 for the first time in twenty years. DOMINIQUE FAGET/AFP/GETTY IMAGES

PRIMARY SOURCE

AN EYE FOR AN EYE

The chase was over and he was finished. The dimly lit cobbled streets had become his prison and were soon to become his graveyard. The cocky [expletive deleted] was cocky no more.

As he stood penned in the cul de sac, his annoying Brummie drawl was making me madder: "'Ere mate, give me a break, leave it out."

I don't know why I wasted my breath, but I didn't. "Shut the [expletive deleted] up. You're not me mate and very soon you're going to get it, and no amount of cry-arsing is gonna get you off the hook, [expletive deleted]."

That was all he was worth. His fate had already been decided three days earlier when his little crew had attacked a group of Everton supporters, yes, supporters, not hooligans like me, just lads who went to watch the match, and that is out of order. They blinded one bloke; lost his eye, he did, when they smashed a brick in his face as he tried to fight back when his cheery FA Cup trip to West Brom turned sour. I read about it in the *Echo* on the Monday and was made up, we only got a draw at The Hawthorns, as I wouldn't have to wait long to get even.

West [expletive deleted] Brom. I stood there with a fresh new blade in my hand and still couldn't get me head 'round the fact that I was tooled up for West Brom. But I had to be, 'cos as the Good Lord says in the Bible, an eye for an eye.

He didn't look as hard now as he had in the ground [at the stadium], safe behind the fences and 100 bizzies [police]. He was the one with the big mouth singing:

He's only a poor little Scouser [person from Liverpool]

His face is all tattered and torn

He made me feel sick

So I hit him with a brick

And no he won't see any more.

Bum bum. Dead funny. That was his mistake, well his second one: His first was coming to Everton and marching around County Road, chest out in a big and brace and silver baseball cap. His sort have no hiding place at Everton.

I loved the Upper Park End Stand, I did. Get in the front row and clock the mouthy [expletive deleted] below. After the game we would come out the same gate as them and were soon in with them, and then they were not so hard. The chase never lasted long.

Goodison was ace, it was, loads of little alleyways, no street lights, none that the kids hadn't smashed, anyway. And when the first punch was thrown and the roar went up, not many stood to fight.

This [expletive deleted] was no different and he was gonna soon regret coming to Everton.

I ran at him in a frenzy and slashed him and just, well, carried on slashing him. Slash after slash after slash, through his clothing. But I couldn't get my target—I wanted his eye. He was on the deck now screaming, pleading for me to stop. [expletive deleted] off.

I tried to prize his fingers back from his face but he was a strong lad and he wasn't giving an eye up that easy. I cut his fingers to the bone but in the end his screams made me do one as the curtains began to twitch and the bizzies must have been on their way.

I had failed, but had given it a good shot. He was in a bad way but, unlike the Everton fan on Saturday, this mouthy West Brom [expletive deleted] would be able to see his scars through both eyes. That [expletive deleted] me off. Still, he would remember this night for the rest of his life.

So what? Welcome to Everton, you have just met the County Road Cutters.

SIGNIFICANCE

The attack on the West Bromwich Albion fan was just one of thousands of acts of football hooliganism committed during the 1980s. It followed an FA Cup Third Round replay, of which Everton had won 4—starting a run that would take them to the final that May against local rival Liverpool.

By then, however, the city of Liverpool was reeling from the worst disaster in British football history. On Saturday, April 16, 1989, at an FA Cup semifinal between Liverpool and Nottingham Forest at Hillsborough Stadium, Sheffield, ninety-six Liverpool supporters were crushed to death against a fence when massive crowds outside flooded into already crowded tunnels leading to popular seating areas. The disaster had had nothing to do with hooliganism—but the fencing had been put up to keep hooligans away from the pitch [field].

The report into the tragedy by Lord Justice Taylor concluded that the game as a whole was suffering a "general malaise or blight," the result of which were decaying stadia and a self-perpetuating spiral of decline. The Taylor reports made a number of recommendations, but the most significant was a call for the transformation of antiquated football venues into all-seater stadia, a huge public investment in the game's infrastructure.

Results were dramatic: Football's missing millions began to return. During the 1990s a huge influx of TV money helped further football's renaissance. Since all-seater stadia were easier to police than the old terraces, the hooligans of previous decades were all but forced out. Though they never quite went away—rioting British fans have made international headlines on a number of occasions—and organized skirmishes between sets of rival gangs still occur, football hooliganism has ceased to be a national preoccupation.

The County Road Cutters have disbanded, although recollections such as the one above and others who were hooligans or claimed to be part of such groups appear from time to time in fanzines like *When Skies Are Grey*. These accounts are replete with exaggerations and misty-eyed nostalgia for the good old days when football was as much about the fighting off the pitch as the game on it.

Everton fans, unlike many of their counterparts, never had a serious reputation for hooliganism, although small-scale violence often accompanied games with local rivals Liverpool and Manchester United. In February 2005, after an FA Cup tie with United, thirty-three men were arrested from both sets of fans. Far from being the norm, however, such incidents are now the exception.

FURTHER RESOURCES

Books

Corbett, James. *Everton: The School of Science*. London: Macmillan, 2003.

Williams, John, Eric Dunning, and Patrick Murphy. *Hooligans Abroad*. 2nd ed. London: Routledge, 1985.

—— *Football on Trial: Spectator Violence and Development in the Football World.*. London: Routledge, 1990.

Periodicals

Web sites

Rivals.net. "When Skies Are Grey. The Everton Fanzine." <http://everton.rivals.net> (accessed March 2, 2006).

Crime Fighter Board Appealing for Witnesses about a Firearm Incident

Photograph

By: Jenine Wiedel

Date: May 2005

Source: Janine Wiedel Photolibrary

About the Photographer: Jenine Wiedel is a freelance photographer based in London. She runs the Janine Wiedel photograph library, which stocks a thirty-year collection of over 100,000 documentary pictures on various subjects such as education, leisure, entertainment, medicine, society, and women's issues.

INTRODUCTION

Occasionally, investigators are required to appeal for witnesses, some of whom may be afraid to come forward. In the United Kingdom police post placards containing the name and contact details of the investigating police force, a short description of the incident, and a telephone number witnesses can contact anonymously.

A photograph of one such placard is featured here. It was posted in Brixton about a firearms incident that took place on May 2, 2005, in which shots were fired at a queue of people standing outside a bar.

In this case, the police unit investigating the case was the Brixton metropolitan police, and the appeal for witnesses was made by Crime Stoppers, an international crime fighting board. Since its inception in 1988, calls to Crime Stoppers have resulted in the recovery of over 65 million pounds ($112 million) and more than 84 million pounds of drugs. Calls to the agency result in the arrest of over 20 people each year.

Such methods give people who are reluctant, apathetic, or afraid of retaliation a chance to help solve crimes.

PRIMARY SOURCE

CRIME FIGHTER BOARD APPEALING FOR WITNESSES ABOUT A FIREARM INCIDENT

See primary source image.

PRIMARY SOURCE

Crime Fighter Board Appealing for Witnesses about a Firearm Incident: A crime fighter board appeals for witnesses about a firearm incident. © JANINE WIEDEL PHOTOLIBRARY / ALAMY

SIGNIFICANCE

Witness to a crime can play a vital role in identifying and prosecuting those responsible. Many witnesses fear that if they come forward and provide information on a crime their identity will become known to dangerous criminals, and they or their friends will seek revenge against the witness. To help people overcome this fear, several agencies offer a service that lets people remain anonymous yet divulge crime-related details.

Investigating agencies use a variety of methods to appeal for witnesses. They may reenact a crime and broadcast it on television, publish appeals in the local newspapers, distribute pamphlets, put up notices at prominent locations in towns and cities, or post a placard at the scene of the crime.

In 1976, when Michael Carmen, a university student working at a gas station in Albuquerque, New Mexico, was stabbed to death, police appealed for witnesses unsuccessfully for six weeks before reenacting the scene and broadcasting it on local television. They promised anonymity and a cash reward for anyone who came forward with information. A caller responded immediately, and the police were able to find the killer within seventy-two hours. This breakthrough led to the formation of Crime Stoppers in the United States. The agency has since worked in conjunction with police forces throughout the United States.

In the United Kingdom, Crime Stoppers and other similar agencies use placards to appeal for witnesses, assuring anonymity in every case. Crime Stoppers now operates in 1,000 locations worldwide, including the United States, Britain, Australia, Bahamas, British West Indies, South Africa, and other countries. In most of these countries it uses similar strategies to find witnesses for various crimes.

FURTHER RESOURCES

Web sites

CrimeStoppers. "Solving Crimes" <http://www.crimestoppers-uk.org/solving> (accessed February 14, 2006).

CrimeStoppers. "Success Stories" <http://www.crimestoppers-uk.org/solving/successstories> (accessed February 14, 2006).

Durham Crime Stoppers. "What Is Crime Stoppers?" <http://durhamcrimestoppers.tripod.com/what_is_it.htm> (accessed February 14, 2006).

Crimes Against Humanity

This section deals with crimes against humanity, crimes of war, genocide, terrorism, and hate crimes. Although the scale of such crimes varies from the massacre of whole populations to the murder of an individual because of their race or sexual preference, the concepts are linked by intolerance and a fundamental indifference to the evolved concepts of humanity and civilization. In many ways, the leap from lynch mob to terrorism is short.

The 1945 London Agreement specified the definition of crimes against humanity to include "murder, extermination, enslavement, deportation, and other inhumane acts committed against any civilian population, before or during the war; or persecutions on political, racial, or religious grounds in execution or in conjunction with any crime. . . " Crimes against humanity are considered, by legal scholars, so serious as to constitute an assault against all people everywhere; they are carried out in order to advance political or philosophical objectives. The extermination of Jews during World War II, for example, was deemed a crime against humanity. It was also a war crime. War crimes are defined similarly to crimes against humanity, with the proviso that they are committed during a time of declared war. (See, for example, "Punishment of Nazi War Criminals" and "Adolf Eichmann's Identity Card.")

The trial of those accused of crimes against humanity and war crimes is often criticized as being "too little too late" especially when it is argued that more vigorous international action might have averted catastrophe. Trials and tribunals themselves can be controversial and deemed ineffective as discussed in

"Rwanda: Accountability for War Crimes and Genocide".

In 1951, the United Nations (U.N.), developed a treaty concerning genocide. As defined by the U.N., genocide is the eradication of "a national, ethnic, racial, or religious group;" it may occur either in peace or in wartime. The entry "Srebrenica Massacre" discusses genocide as now designated by the International Criminal Tribunal for the Former Yugoslavia (ICTY).

The definition of terrorism found in the United States Code is "premeditated, politically motivated violence perpetrated against noncombatant targets by subnational groups or clandestine agents, usually intended to influence an audience." Although the intricacies and controversies associated with terrorism are treated in detail in volume one of this series, no chapter concerning crimes of hatred and intolerance could exclude some discussion and depiction of terrorists and terrorist acts (see, for example "Terrorists at Summer Olympics").

Although the concept of a "hate crime" is very old, the definition and legal ramifications thereof have been specified only quite recently. Hate crimes are motivated either entirely or in part by the belief that a victim is substantially different from the perpetrator. Although a hate crime would be illegal simply because of its occurrence, it is further described by who it is perpetrated against, and the fact that the motivation for the behavior stems from some identified difference between victim and offender. Accordingly several articles detailing hate crimes and various aspects of hate crimes are also included in this section (see, for example: "A Hate Crime and a Courageous Love").

Lynching Victim Hangs Above White Crowd

Photograph

By: Anonymous

Date: October 15, 1938.

Source: "Lynching Victim Hangs Above White Crowd." Corbis, 1938.

About the Photographer: This photograph is part of the stock collection at Corbis photo agency, headquartered in Seattle and provider of images for magazine, films, television, and advertisements. The photographer is not known.

INTRODUCTION

"Lynching" is a term given to vigilante justice handed out by a mob that is beyond the jurisdiction of normal legal process. It usually concludes in death or at the very least serious physical assault. The term derives from "Lynch Law," which originates with the American Revolution when Colonel Charles Lynch responded to criminal and pro-British elements by handing out a brutal form of summary justice according to his own rules. In reality, the practice of vigilante or mob justice has existed since the start of human civilization, although the term "lynching" is largely synonymous with the United States, and particularly its southern states.

As America spread westward in the years after independence, vigilante law and lynching was often the only form of justice available and was applied frequently and—one can assume—haphazardly. The actual term "lynching," however, only moved into popular parlance after the Civil War.

The practice of lynching was carried out most commonly in the four decades following the Civil War's end, and although incidence of lynching decreased in the twentieth century, such attacks were still carried out in significant numbers (e.g., eighty-three in 1919; thirty in 1930) until the Second World War, and did not die out until the late 1950s. Between 1882 (when reliable statistics were first collated) and 1968, 4,743 people died as a result of lynching, 3,446 of whom were black men and women.

What was most shocking about this form of justice was the racial motivation often underlying the attack and the ritualistic complexion lynching sometimes assumed. Hundreds of seemingly respectable citizens could and did attend lynchings, and on one occasion, 15,000 were estimated to have turned up to one southern lynching. Authorities frequently looked the other way as the people carried out their own form of justice. Mark Twain, one of lynching's most vehement opponents, characterized a typical mob as consisting of "5,000 Christian American men, women, and children, youths and maidens." Desecration of a victim's body for "souvenirs" or prior disembowelment were not uncommon. In the primary source photograph below, an apron covers the victim's waist, probably because his genitalia had been removed. Note also what appears to be a young boy at the scene.

The practice of lynching in the United States unofficially ceased after 1955, when the case of Emmett Till provoked national and global outrage. Till was an African-American teenager from Chicago visiting relatives in Money, Mississippi. At a local grocery store, Till was alleged to have wolf-whistled or flirted with the proprietor's wife, Carolyn Bryant, and word spread around the small town. When Bryant's husband, Roy Bryant, returned from a business trip, he plotted revenge with his half-brother J.W. Milam. The two brutally beat Till and gouged out an eye before finally shooting him several hours later. They then dumped his body in a river. Yet when the case came to trial a month later, Bryant and Milam were acquitted by an all-white jury after just sixty-seven minutes of deliberations. A year later the duo admitted the crime to *Look* magazine, but were unable to be prosecuted because of their rights under double jeopardy.

PRIMARY SOURCE

LYNCHING VICTIM HANGS ABOVE WHITE CROWD

See primary source image.

SIGNIFICANCE

Nothing was more synonymous with white man's unchecked persecution of blacks in America's south than the activities of lynch mobs. Although by the mid-twentieth century the perception about their prevalence was usually worse than the reality, the number of notorious cases that periodically emerged, often combined with the failure of the authorities to prosecute those who had carried out such acts, was seen as incontrovertible evidence of discrimination against the south's black communities. Lynching was an appalling example of the absolute power, outside any process of law, justice, or rationality that could be

PRIMARY SOURCE

Lynching Victim Hangs Above White Crowd: The bullet-riddled body of W. C. Williams hangs from an oak tree in 1938, less than 150 yards from the spot in Louisiana where the murder and assault for which he was lynched were committed. A mob of 300 took Williams from the posse that had captured him, strung him up to this tree, then riddled his body with bullets after Williams admitted that he clubbed a mill worker to death and assaulted his female companion. © BETTMANN/CORBIS

imposed in order to maintain white power. With blacks often disenfranchised in southern states, local officials usually felt no obligation to respect their interests, and worse still could sometimes be seen leading or partaking in a lynching.

Lynchings and the other injustices suffered by Southern African Americans were one of the reasons behind their mass migration from the rural south to the urban northeast and Midwest. This "Great Migration" started during World War I and continued until the 1960s, and fundamentally altered the racial complexion of the north's urban conurbations. Although northern cities were usually more tolerant than the

rural south and often without officially sanctioned segregation or political disenfranchisement, black southern migrants were still amongst the poorest sections of their populations and were economically marginalized. Their communities often became ghettoized and cut off from mainstream society, leading to deep-seated racial tensions and periodic urban violence. Riots in Chicago in 1919, Detroit in 1943 and 1967, and Los Angeles in 1965 and 1992 were periodic if not extreme reminders that the schism between black and white communities had never been fully healed.

Following the end of slavery, lynching became a cause célèbre for liberals both in and outside the

United States. In Britain, where liberals stood at the forefront of the global anti-slavery movement and a stance against lynching was seen as an extension of their work, the incidence of lynching was watched closely. Streams of protests would periodically wind their way to the U.S. Ambassador or any American politician or public individual seen to be supporting or sympathizing with lynching. Frances Willard, President of the Woman's Christian Temperance Union, was one such individual harangued by British anti-slavery activists after making comments construed as being sympathetic to lynching.

The most famous opponent to lynching, however, was Mark Twain, who gave numerous lectures and wrote several essays opposed to the practice. His 1869 essay *Only a Nigger*, which originally appeared anonymously in the *Buffalo Express*, clearly illustrated the depth of his opposition:

"Mistakes will happen, even in the conduct of the best regulated and most high-toned mobs, and surely there is no good reason why Southern gentlemen should worry themselves with useless regrets, so long as only an innocent "nigger" is hanged, or roasted or knouted to death, now and then… Keep the lash knotted; keep the brand and the faggots in waiting, for prompt work with the next "nigger" who may be suspected of any damnable crime! Wreak a swift vengeance upon him, for the satisfaction of the noble impulses that animate knightly hearts, and then leave time and accident to discover, if they will, whether he was guilty or no."

Twain's involvement in the anti-lynching movement is just one example of the issue being brought into popular culture. Other famous references include Billie Holiday's *Strange Fruit* (1937), the Bob Dylan song *The Death of Emmett Till* (1962), the Toni Morrison play *Dreaming Emmett* (1986), and Richard Powers' novel *The Time of Our Singing* (2001).

Perhaps more than any other event, it was the 1955 murder of Till that mobilized the American civil rights movement. Within three months of his body being recovered, the Montgomery Bus boycott had begun, kick-starting one of America's largest and most significant protest movements. Within a decade, the so-called Jim Crow laws and segregation had become a thing of the past in principle if not practice. Racially motivated lynching in the U.S. was effectively banished to the past.

Beyond the United States, however, lynching continues to rear its head. This tends to be in areas of the world where there is little faith in criminal justice systems or in times of conflict, particularly when collaboration is suspected. In Apartheid-era South African townships, where there was no faith in white-administered justice, lynch mobs would periodically try and impose their own form of justice—this effort was publicly supported by Winnie Mandela, then-wife of the imprisoned Nelson Mandela. More recently, in Israel's occupied territories, Palestinians have been known to lynch and desecrate the bodies of Israeli collaborators and, in one well-publicized attack in Ramallah in October 2000, Israeli soldiers. Far-right Israeli extremists have also been known to carry out unprovoked lynchings of Palestinian Arabs.

FURTHER RESOURCES

Books

Powers, Ron. *Mark Twain: A Life.*. New York: Free Press, 2005.

Wells, Ida B. *On Lynchings.*. New York: Humanity Press, 2002.

Web sites

PBS.org. "American Experience: The Murder of Emmett Till." <http://www.pbs.org/wgbh/amex/till> (accessed March 5, 2006).

Punishment of War Criminals

Legal decision

By: International Military Tribunal for the Trial of Nazi War Criminals

Date: October 1, 1946

Source: "Two Hundred and Eighteenth Day—Judgment of the International Military Tribunal for the Trial of Nazi War Criminals, Defendant Hermann Goering." *Nuremberg Trial Proceedings Volume 22: Two Hundred and Twelfth Day–Two Hundred and Eighteenth Day.* Washington, D.C.: U.S. Government Printing Office, 1949. pp. 523–526.

About the Author: The International Military Tribunal was established on August 8, 1945, by the governments of the United States, Great Britain, France, and the Soviet Union. The Tribunal adjudicated cases against Nazi war criminals and other perpetrators of the Holocaust.

Nazi leaders accused of wartime atrocities and crimes against humanity sit under guard in the defendants dock at the Nuremberg Trials in 1946. Among them (front row, l to r) are the head of the Gestapo, Hermann Wilhelm Goering, Rudolph Hess, Joachim von Ribbentrop, Wilheim Keitel and Ernst Kaltenbrunner with (second row) Koenitz, Raeder, Schirach and Sauckel seated behind them. © CORBIS

INTRODUCTION

As Allied troops moved across Europe in the final months of World War II, the world began to see the full scope of the Holocaust and other Nazi war crimes. Representatives of the Allied victors convened in London to draft a proposal to bring the perpetrators of Nazi atrocities to justice. The London Charter of August 8, 1945, established an international tribunal to adjudicate Nazi war criminals. The charter defined new crimes under international law. Infringing on the sovereignty or borders of another nation or peoples was defined as crimes against peace. Crimes against humanity encompassed grave and despicable acts on a large scale, such as genocide. Torture, abuse, and extermination of prisoners of war were some of the enumerated war crimes in the charter. Despite the military origin of the tribunal, mere obedience to authority was discounted as a viable defense.

Though the London Charter only applied to crimes committed by members of the European Axis, the principles set forth in the document laid the foundation for present-day international human rights law. The success of the Nuremberg Trials, in which two hundred Nazi war crimes defendants were tried, was pivotal to post-War efforts to heal and rebuild Europe.

In all, some 2,100 Nazi war criminals were brought to justice through international, national, and military courts.

PRIMARY SOURCE

Defendant, Hermann Goering

Goering is indicted on all four counts. The evidence shows that after Hitler he was the most prominent man in the Nazi Regime. He was Commander-in-Chief of the Luftwaffe, Plenipotentiary for the Four Year Plan, and had tremendous influence with Hitler, at least until 1943 when their relationship deteriorated, ending in his arrest in 1945. He testified that Hitler kept him informed of all important military and political problems.

Crimes against Peace

From the moment he joined the Party in 1922 and took command of the street-fighting organisation, the SA, Goering was the adviser, the active agent of Hitler and one of the prime leaders of the Nazi movement. As Hitler's political deputy he was largely instrumental in bringing the National Socialists to power in 1933, and was charged with consolidating this power and expanding German armed might. He developed the Gestapo, and created the first concentration camps, relinquishing them to Himmler in 1934, conducted the Roehm purge in that year, and engineered the sordid proceedings which resulted in the removal of von Blomberg and von Fritsch from the Army. In 1936 he became Plenipotentiary for the Four Year Plan, and in theory and in practice was the economic dictator of the Reich. Shortly after the Pact of Munich, he announced that he would embark on a five-fold expansion of the Luftwaffe and speed rearmament with emphasis on offensive weapons.

Goering was one of the five important leaders present at the Hoszbach Conference of 5th November, 1937, and he attended the other important conferences already discussed in this Judgment. In the Austrian Anschluss, he was indeed the central figure, the ringleader. He said in Court: "I must take 100 per cent responsibility.... I even overruled objections by the Fuehrer and brought everything to its final development." In the seizure of the Sudetenland, he played his role as Luftwaffe chief by planning an air offensive which proved unnecessary and his role as a politician by lulling the Czechs with false promises of friendship. The night before the invasion of Czechoslovakia and the absorption of Bohemia and Moravia, at a conference with Hitler and President Hacha he threatened to bomb Prague if Hacha did not submit. This threat he admitted in his testimony.

Goering attended the Reich Chancellery meeting of 23rd May, 1939, when Hitler told his military leaders "there is, therefore, no question of sparing Poland," and was present at the Obersalzburg briefing of 22nd August, 1939. And the evidence shows he was active in the diplomatic manoeuvres which followed. With Hitler's connivance, he used the Swedish businessman, Dahlerus, as a go-between to the British, as described by Dahlerus to this Tribunal, to try to prevent the British Government from keeping its guarantee to the Poles.

He commanded the Luftwaffe in the attack on Poland and throughout the aggressive wars which followed.

Even if he opposed Hitler's plans against Norway and the Soviet Union, as he alleged, it is clear that he did so only for strategic reasons; once Hitler had decided the issue, he followed him without hesitation. He made it clear in his testimony that these differences were never ideological or legal. He was "in a rage" about the invasion of Norway, but only because he had not received sufficient warning to prepare the Luftwaffe offensive. He admitted he approved of the attack: "My attitude was perfectly positive." He was active in preparing and executing the Yugoslavian and Greek campaigns, and testified that "Plan Marita," the attack on Greece, had been prepared long beforehand. The Soviet Union he regarded as the "most threatening menace to Germany," but said there was no immediate military necessity for the attack. Indeed, his only objection to the war of aggression against the U.S.S.R. was its timing; he wished for strategic reasons to delay until Britain was conquered. He testified: "My point of view was decided by political and military reasons only."

After his own admissions to this Tribunal, from the positions which he held, the conferences he attended, and the public words he uttered, there can remain no doubt that Goering was the moving force for aggressive war second only to Hitler. He was the planner and prime mover in the military and diplomatic preparation for war which Germany pursued.

War Crimes and Crimes against Humanity

The record is filled with Goering's admissions of his complicity in the use of slave labour. "We did use this labour for security reasons so that they would not be active in their own country and would not work against us. On the other hand, they served to help in the economic war." And again: "Workers were forced to come to the Reich. That is something I have not denied." The man who spoke these words was Plenipotentiary for the Four Year Plan charged with the recruitment and allocation of manpower. As Luftwaffe Commander-in-Chief he demanded from Himmler more slave labourers for his underground aircraft factories: "That I requested inmates of concentration camps for the armament of the Luftwaffe is correct and it is to be taken as a matter of course."

As Plenipotentiary, Goering signed a directive concerning the treatment of Polish workers in Germany and implemented it by regulations of the SD, including "special treatment." He issued directives to use Soviet and French prisoners of war in the armament industry; he spoke of seizing Poles and Dutch and making them prisoners of war if necessary, and using them for work. He agrees Russian prisoners of war were used to man anti-aircraft batteries.

As Plenipotentiary, Goering was the active authority in the spoliation. of conquered territory. He made plans for the spoliation of Soviet territory long before the war on the Soviet Union. Two months prior to the invasion of the Soviet Union, Hitler gave Goering the over-all direction for the economic administration in the territory. Goering set up an economic staff for this function. As Reichsmarshal of the Greater German Reich "the orders of the Reichmarshal cover all economic fields, including nutrition and agriculture." His so-called "Green" folder, printed by the Wehrmacht, set up an "Economic Executive Staff, East." This directive contemplated plundering and abandonment of all industry in the food deficit regions and from the food surplus regions, a diversion of food to German needs. Goering claims its purposes have been misunderstood but admits "that as a matter of course and a matter of duty we would have used Russia for our purposes," when conquered.

And he participated in the conference of 16th July, 1941, when Hitler said the National Socialists had no intention of ever leaving the occupied countries, and that "all necessary measures—shooting, desettling, etc." should be taken.

Goering persecuted the Jews, particularly after the November, 1938 riots, and not only in Germany where he raised the billion mark fine as; stated elsewhere, but in the conquered territories as well. His own utterances then and his testimony now show this interest was primarily economic— how to get their property and how to force them out of the economic life of Europe. As these countries fell before the German army he extended the Reich's anti-Jewish laws to them; the Reichsgesetzblatt for 1939, 1940, and 1941 contains several anti-Jewish decrees signed by Goering. Although their extermination was in Himmler's hands, Goering was far from disinterested or inactive, despite his protestations in the witness box. By decree of 31st July, 1941, he directed Himmler and Heydrich to bring "about a complete solution of the Jewish question in the German sphere of influence in Europe."

There is nothing to be said in mitigation. For Goering was often, indeed almost always, the moving force, second only to his leader. He was the leading war aggressor, both as political and as military leader; he was the director of the slave labour programme and the creator of the oppressive programme against the Jews and other races, at home and abroad. All of these crimes he has frankly

admitted. On some specific cases there may be conflict of testimony, but in terms of the broad outline his own admissions are more than sufficiently wide to be conclusive of his guilt. His guilt is unique in its enormity. The record discloses no excuses for this man.

Conclusion

The Tribunal finds the defendant Goering guilty on all four counts of the Indictment.

SIGNIFICANCE

From November 20, 1945, to October 1, 1946, the Tribunal tried twenty-four of the most infamous Nazi criminals and six of the highest-ranking Nazi organizations. The defendants were indicted and tried on counts of crimes against humanity, war crimes, and crimes against peace. Most all of the charges at Nuremberg directly linked to the defendants roles as perpetrators of the Holocaust.

Over the course of the year, the tribunal heard testimony from forensic experts, Holocaust survivors, Nazi officials, rank-and-file members of the German military and Nazi government, and witness testimony. The primary source included here is the Tribunal's final judgment against Herman Goering—perhaps the most notorious of the Nuremberg Trial's defendants. Goering was a Reichsmarshall and Luftwaffe (Air Force) chief who was responsible for the plunder of Jewish owned properties and businesses. He was instrumental in the development of the Final Solution, the Nazi plan to exterminate European Jews. Goering was sentenced to death by hanging for his role in the Holocaust. However, before he could reach the gallows, Goering was found dead in his jail cell. He committed suicide the night before his execution.

The international community continued to routinely locate and prosecute Nazi war criminals for over two decades. American, British, and Israeli intelligence forces sought suspected war criminals who had gone into hiding after the war. Israeli agents located Nazi war criminal Adolf Eichmann living in Argentina under an assumed name. In 1961, he was kidnapped and brought to Israel to stand trial for crimes against humanity. Other notorious perpetrators Holocaust atrocities eluded capture and trial. Nazi doctor Joseph Mengle, who performed gruesome medical experiments on prisoners at Auschwitz, successfully evaded intelligence forces for 35 years, hiding in South America until his death in 1979.

The Nuremberg Trials and other international trials of Nazi war criminals forged present-day international laws defining and prohibiting war crimes. In recent years, the now permanent International Criminal Court has heard cases against perpetrators of genocide and "ethnic cleansing" in the Former Yugoslav Republics, as well as heard evidence against perpetrators of crimes against humanity in Africa and South America.

FURTHER RESOURCES

Books

Baumslag, Naomi. *Murderous Medicine: Nazi Doctors, Human Experimentation, and Typhus* . Westport, Conn.: Praeger, 2005.

Periodicals

Kious, B. M. "The Nuremberg Code: Its History and Implications." *Princeton Journal of Bioethics*. vol. 4 (2001): 7–19.

Web sites

United States Holocaust Memorial Museum. "Online Exhibitions: War Crimes Trials" <http://www.ushmm.org/wlc/article/> (January 28, 2006).

Identity Card of Adolf Eichmann

Photograph

By: Anonymous

Date: 1950

Source: Bettmann/Corbis

About the Photographer: The Argentinean government issued identity cards to all citizens and resident foreigners. Eichmann obtained his identity card under an assumed name. The card was photographed after World War II (1938–1945) by an anonymous photographer.

INTRODUCTION

Born in Solingen, Germany, in 1909, Adolf Eichmann rose quickly through the ranks of the Austrian and then German *Schutzstaffel*, or SS. Eichmann was one of the main architects of the "Final Solution," the Nazi plan to exterminate Europe's Jews. He supervised the capture and transportation of Jews from newly conquered territories, ghettos, and concentration camps to extermination centers such as Auschwitz. The "Chief Executioner of the Third Reich" supervised genocide in Poland and Hungary, reportedly boasting that his transportation network enabled the efficient slaughter of millions of Jews.

After World War II, the Allies established a series of international courts to bring perpetrators of the Holocaust to justice. The most famous of these International Military Tribunals sat in Nürenburg, Germany. From November 20, 1945, to October 1, 1946, the court tried twenty-four of the most famous Nazi war criminals. Adolf Eichmann, the transportation master of the Holocaust, however, was not among them.

PRIMARY SOURCE

IDENTITY CARD OF ADOLF EICHMANN

See primary source image.

SIGNIFICANCE

In the final days of World War II, Eichmann fled Hungary, where he had assumed a regular army commission. He returned to Austria and was captured by Allied forces in 1945. Going by the name Otto Eckmann, however, Eichmann managed to conceal his identity and escape in 1946.

Eichmann spent several years on the run, hiding in Germany, Austria, and Italy. A friend helped him obtain immigration papers to Argentina and a humanitarian passport from the Red Cross. Under the assumed name Ricardo Klement, Eichmann moved his family to Argentina in July 1950.

Although Eichmann remained at large, he was hunted by Allied and Israeli intelligence agents who tracked and captured Nazi war criminals. After receiving tips from Holocaust survivors who had emigrated to Argentina, the Israeli intelligence Mossad service found Eichmann in 1960. After observing him for several months and confirming his idenity, Mossad agents kidnapped him from outside his home on May 11, 1960. He was flown to Israel to stand trial for war crimes.

Indicted on fifteen separate criminal charges, including "crimes against humanity" as established at Nürenburg, Eichmann's trial began in April of 1961. The trial was open to the press and broadcast around the world. Like his fellow Nazi officers, Eichmann asserted that his involvement in the Holocaust had not been a conscious decision but that he had merely followed orders from superiors. Eichmann challenged the jurisdiction of the Israeli court and much of the

PRIMARY SOURCE

Identity Card of Adolf Eichmann: Photo of an identity card issued to Adolf Eichmann, Nazi war criminal, born in Solingen, Germany. Captured by U.S. forces in 1945, he escaped from prison some months later, having kept his true identity hidden, and in 1950 reached Argentina. Eichmann was traced by Israeli agents, taken to Israel in 1960, condemned, and executed. © BETTMANN/CORBIS

testimony of survivors presented against him. He was convicted on all counts. After exhausting all appeals, he was executed by hanging on June 1, 1962.

FURTHER RESOURCES

Books

Arendt, Hannah. *Eichmann in Jerusalem: A Report on the Banality of Evil.* New edition. New York: Penguin, 1994.

Cesarani, David. *Eichmann: His Life and Crimes.* New York: Vintage Books, 2005.

Web sites

United States Holocaust Memorial Museum. <www.ushmm. org> (accessed March 12, 2006).

Terrorists at the Summer Olympics

Photograph

By: Anonymous

Date: September 5, 1972

Source: Bettman/Corbis

About the Photographer: This photograph was taken in Munich, Germany, during the 1972 Olympics hostage crisis by an unidentified photographer.

INTRODUCTION

The Summer Olympics of 1972 were held in Munich, West Germany. On September 4, eight members of a sub-group of the Fatah organization, a Palestinian group using terrorist methods to resist the Israeli occupation of the West Bank and Gaza, entered the Olympic Village compound and sought out the apartments of the Israeli Olympic team. In the process of taking hostages, two Israelis were killed and several escaped. Nine were taken alive.

The terrorists demanded the release of hundreds of Palestinian and other prisoners being held in Israel. Israel refused to negotiate. The German government sent in police untrained in counter-terror operations, who bungled the operation: it also offered the terrorists the substitution of high-ranking Germans as hostages and the payment of an amount of money to be named by the terrorists. However, the terrorists refused these offers.

After some hours, the terrorists changed their demand: now they wished safe passage to Egypt. The German authorities had two helicopters transport the kidnappers and their hostages to a nearby military airbase, telling the terrorists that they were being taken to an international airport. The terrorists discovered the ruse and the ambush turned into a chaotic gun battle. In the resulting shooting, explosions, and fires, all the hostages were killed and one German police officer was killed. Three terrorists were captured alive.

The Olympic Games, with the endorsement of the Israeli government, continued after a brief pause.

On October 29, other terrorists hijacked a Lufthansa (German state airline) passenger jet and demanded the release of the three surviving Munich kidnappers. Germany complied.

<hr>

PRIMARY SOURCE

TERRORISTS AT THE SUMMER OLYMPICS

See primary source image.

<hr>

SIGNIFICANCE

The Israeli government's response to the kidnappings was a series of extrajudicial international killings known officially as Operation Wrath of God. Israeli Prime Minister Golda Meir authorized the operation, which was in fact a cluster of operations. Within a few weeks of the disaster, agents of Mossad (the Israeli secret service) tracked their first target, a Palestinian man named Wael Zwaiter, to Rome. Two Mossad agents shot Zwaiter sixteen times in the lobby of the

apartment building where he lived. Whether Zwaiter was actually involved with the Munich kidnappings has been disputed. The next to die was Mahmoud Hamshire, spokesman in France for the Palestine Liberation Organization. Mossad agents removed the marble top of the table on which Hamshire's telephone sat, replaced it with an explosive-filled copy, and blew up the table when Hamshire answered the phone, taking care to do so while his wife and daughter were out. Further killings occurred in Paris, Cyprus, and, in 1973, in Lebanon. In contrast to the highly selective killing of Hamshire, the Lebanon operation killed at least nine bystanders: a neighbor, seven Lebanese police, and the wife of one of the targeted Palestinians.

The assassination campaign against the Munich terrorists broadened into a campaign against other high-level Palestinian militants. In 1973, Mossad assassinated three more Palestinians using hidden bombs. Also in 1973, Mossad agents flew to the Norwegian city of Lillehammer—site of the 1994 Winter Olympics—and gunned down a man they assumed was one of the Munich terror planners, but who was in fact an innocent Moroccan waiter who had been living in Norway for five years. Five Mossad agents were arrested, tried, and convicted for the murder. They were only briefly imprisoned, however, and went back to Israel in 1975.

All of Mossad's operations took place without the permission of the countries in which they occurred and were illegal according to local and international laws, but only in Norway were the criminals apprehended and tried. The bystander death toll of Operation Wrath of God was almost as high as the number of hostage deaths. The Mossad agents taking direct part in the Lebanon operation, which killed more bystanders than targets, were never prosecuted. One, Ehud Barak (1942–), later became prime minister of Israel (1999–2001). Not all Israelis were sympathetic with the methods used by their government: the widow of the Israeli Olympic fencing coach taken hostage and killed at Munich said, "It should have happened in a different way, taking out these people, not by shooting them but by bringing them to justice, to trial."

Mossad's methods have been employed by the intelligence agencies and secret police of many major military powers. Operations on the soil of other states have been carried out, for example, by the United States and France. In 1985, French secret agents exploded the Greenpeace sailboat *Rainbow Warrior* while it was docked in New Zealand, killing a photog-

PRIMARY SOURCE

Terrorists at the Summer Olympics: Two scenes from the hostage-taking at the Munich Olympic Village in 1972. In the top photo a masked Palestinian Liberation Organization (PLO) terrorist stands on the balcony of the building where the Israeli hostages were kept. The bottom photo shows a member of the International Olympic Committee (right) as he negotiates with one of the terrorists. © BETTMANN/CORBIS

rapher, and in 2005 in Italy, Europe-wide arrest warrants were issued for the arrest of 22 American agents of the Central Intelligence Agency (CIA) who allegedly kidnapped a Muslim cleric from Rome for "special rendition" to Egypt for torture.

FURTHER RESOURCES

Periodicals

Meyer, Josh. "CIA Expands Use of Drones in Terror War." *Los Angeles Times.* Jan. 29, 2006. Available at <http://www.truthout.org/docs_2006/012906G.shtml> (accessed March 20, 2006).

Web sites

Calahan, Alexander B. "Countering Terrorism: The Israeli Response to the 1972 Munich Olympic Massacre and the Development of Independent Covert Action Teams." Thesis submitted to the Faculty of the Marine Corps Command and Staff College in partial fulfillment of the requirements for the degree of Master of Military Studies. April, 1995. Available through the Federation of American Scientists, <http://www.fas.org/irp/eprint/calahan.htm> (accessed March 20, 2006).

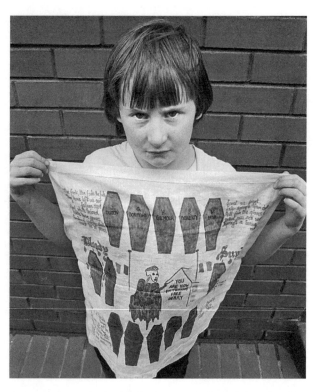

A young boy somberly displays a cloth dedicated to the fourteen civilians killed on January 30, 1972, known as "Bloody Sunday," when British soldiers opened fire on unarmed and peaceful demonstrators in Londonderry, Northern Ireland. © CHRISTINE SPENGLER/SYGMA/CORBIS

A British Soldier Drags a Catholic Protester during Bloody Sunday

Photograph

By: Anonymous

Date: January 30, 1972

Source: Getty Images

About the Photographer: The primary source photograph was taken by an unknown photographer for AFP, a worldwide, multilingual news agency based in Paris.

INTRODUCTION

The conflict between Protestants and Catholics in Northern Ireland date back centuries to the Anglo-Norman invasion of Ireland. However, the root of the most recent "Troubles"—as the conflict is known in Britain—is found in 1921 with the partition of the island of Eire into Ireland, a sovereign nation, and Northern Ireland, a part of Great Britain. The population of the agricultural southern region that would become Ireland was mainly Catholic. In contrast to this, Protestants, many of whom descended from British settlers in Ireland, sought union with England. The conflict between Protestants and Catholics was, instead, a conflict of home rule versus union with England. The new state of Northern Ireland consisted of a protestant majority. With this majority, protestant unionists began a campaign of discrimination against Catholics, beginning with housing and employment.

In 1965, the Northern Ireland Civil Rights Association (NICRA) emerged in with the expressed goals of ending discrimination against Catholics. The movement sought free and fair elections, with one representative to vote in council elections and the end of gerrymandering electoral boundaries; a repeal of the Special Powers Act that gave police liberal arrest and detention powers; fairness in public housing; and the disbanding of the largely Protestant auxiliary police force. Members of the NIRCA witnessed the civil rights movements in the United States and sought to mobilize Northern Ireland toward the same end. They marched in Londonderry on October 5, 1968, even though the demonstration had been banned by the Minister for Home Affairs William Craig. Craig assumed that the civil rights movement operated as a political front for the Irish Republic Army (IRA) terrorists. Camera crews from the Irish nationalist television station, RTE, took images of the protesters being beaten by police.

As the civil rights movement grew, so did the armed conflict between the Irish Republic Army and the unionists. The police began the widespread use of interment as a tool to gather intelligence as well as hamper the activities of the IRA. Many of the detainees were badly beaten and subjected to sleep

PRIMARY SOURCE

A British Soldier Drags a Catholic Protester during Bloody Sunday: A British soldier grabs a Catholic protestor from behind in Londonderry, Northern Ireland, on Bloody Sunday, January 30, 1972. THOPSON/AFP/GETTY IMAGES

deprivation and other forms of torture. On January 30, 1972, the NICRA organized a demonstration in Londonderry in protest of the policy of interment without trial. Although demonstrations such as these had been banned by the parliament, approximately ten thousand people gathered in Creggan Estate and proceeded toward Guildhall Square. British paratroopers sealed off the square and led the marchers away from the organizers who were already in the square. Groups of demonstrators lagged behind to confront the soldiers at the barricades by throwing stones. The paratroopers responded with CS gas and water cannons. Shortly after 4:00 PM, the paratroopers requested per-

mission to make arrests and less than thirty minutes later, thirteen of the protesters had been shot dead.

PRIMARY SOURCE

A BRITISH SOLDIER DRAGS A CATHOLIC PROTESTER DURING BLOODY SUNDAY

See primary source image.

SIGNIFICANCE

The Lord Chief Justice of England, Lord Widgery, was commissioned by the Prime Minister to conduct an official inquiry of the indicent. In April 1972, Widgery released his findings that although the paratroopers shots had "bordered on the reckless" the soldiers had been fired upon by the protesters first. These findings were controversial and in conflict with the Londonderry coroner who believed that the events were, "sheer unadulterated murder."

The events of January 30, 1972 became known as Bloody Sunday and served to revitalize the violent opposition to British presence in Northern Ireland. In response to the events of Bloody Sunday, the IRA began a new wave of bombings including the "Bloody Friday" string of 22 bombs detonated in Belfast in July of 1972. In the anniversary of Bloody Sunday in 1998, Prime Minister Tony Blair declared that a new inquiry of the events would take place. Blair appointed Lord Saville to direct the inquiry, which ended in November 2004. The final report and conclusions by Lord Saville were expected in 2005. However, due to the volume of testimony and evidence, the publication has been delayed.

FURTHER RESOURCES

Periodicals

"Leaders: The truth, however unpalatable; Bloody Sunday." *Economist.* (January 26, 2002).

Web sites

BBC News. "War and Conflict: The Troubles." <http://www.bbc.co.uk/history/war/troubles/origins/bloody-sun.shtml> (accessed January 6, 2005).

PBS. "The IRA and Sinn Fein." <http://www.pbs.org/wgbh/pages/frontline/shows/ira/etc/cron.html> (accessed January 6, 2005).

HIV-Related Crime

Human Whole Blood, Human Whole Blood Derivatives, and Other Biologics: Enforcement

Law

By: California Legislature

Date: 1988

Source: California Codes. Health and Safety Code. Section 1621.5. <http://www.leginfo.ca.gov/cgi-bin/displaycode?section=hsc&group=01001-02000&file=1617-1621.5> (accessed April 26, 2006).

Unlawful Carrying and Possession of Weapons

Law

By: California Legislature

Date: 1988

Source: California Codes. Penal Code. Section 12022.85. <http://www.leginfo.ca.gov/cgi-bin/displaycode?section=pen&group=12001-13000&file=12020-12040> (accessed April 26, 2006).

About the Author: The bicameral California legislature writes and approves California's laws and penal code. The lower house, or Assembly, has eighty members; the upper house, or Senate, has forty.

INTRODUCTION

The first cases of HIV/AIDS were identified in 1978 among gay men. By 1982, HIV transmission was linked to blood and other body fluids, which meant that the disease could be spread through sexual intercourse, intravenous drug use, and transfusion of infected blood and blood products. Several states, including California, have since passed laws making it a crime to knowingly expose others to HIV infection.

All states have generic criminal laws that can be used to prosecute people with HIV/AIDS who intentionally expose others to the disease. These include laws concerning the transmission of communicable disease, including sexually transmitted diseases and sodomy, which is still technically illegal in some states. During the 1980s, lawmakers passed legislation aimed specifically at those who knowingly exposed their partners or victims to the risk of HIV/AIDS, adding extra penalties to violent crimes like rape or assault when the perpetrator is HIV positive. The extracts from California law given below, passed in 1988, are examples of such legislation.

■ PRIMARY SOURCE

Health and Safety Code.

Division 2. Licensing Provisions

Chapter 4. Human Whole Blood, Human Whole Blood Derivatives, and Other Biologics

Article 6. Enforcement

1621.5. (a) It is a felony punishable by imprisonment in the state prison for two, four, or six years, for any person to donate blood, body organs, or other tissue, semen to any medical center or semen bank that receives semen for purposes of artificial insemination, or breast milk to any medical center or breast milk bank that receives breast milk for purposes of distribution, whether he or she is a paid or a volunteer donor, who knows that he or she has acquired immune deficiency syndrome, as diagnosed by a physician and surgeon, or who knows that he or she has tested reactive to the etiologic agent of AIDS or to the antibodies to that agent. This section shall not apply to any person who is mentally incompetent or who self-defers his or her blood at a blood bank or plasma center pursuant to subdivision (b) of Section 1603.3 or who donates his or her blood for purposes of an autologous donation.

(b) In a criminal investigation for a violation of this section, no person shall disclose the results of a blood test to detect the etiologic agent of AIDS or antibodies to that agent to any officer, employee, or agent of a state or local agency or department unless the test results are disclosed as otherwise required by law pursuant to any one of the following:

(1) A search warrant issued pursuant to Section 1524 of the Penal Code.

(2) A judicial subpoena or subpoena duces tecum issued and served in compliance with Chapter 2 (commencing with Section 1985) of Title 3 of Part 4 of the Code of Civil Procedure.

(3) An order of a court.

(c) For purposes of this section, "blood" means "human whole blood" and "human whole blood derivatives," as defined for purposes of this chapter and includes "blood components," as defined in subdivision (k) of Section 1603.1.

PRIMARY SOURCE

Penal Code.

Part 4. Prevention of Crime and Apprehension of Criminals.

Title 2. Control of Deadly Weapons.

12022.85. (a) Any person who violates one or more of the offenses listed in subdivision (b) with knowledge that he or she has acquired immune deficiency syndrome (AIDS) or with the knowledge that he or she carries antibodies of the human immunodeficiency virus at the time of the commission of those offenses, shall receive a three-year enhancement for each violation in addition to the sentence provided under those sections.

(b) Subdivision (a) applies to the following crimes:

(1) Rape in violation of Section 261.

(2) Unlawful intercourse with a person under 18 years of age in violation of Section 261.5.

(3) Rape of a spouse in violation of Section 262.

(4) Sodomy in violation of Section 286.

(5) Oral copulation in violation of Section 288a.

(c) For purposes of proving the knowledge requirement of this section, the prosecuting attorney may use test results received under subdivision (c) of Section 1202.1 or subdivision (g) of Section 1202.6.

SIGNIFICANCE

Although there are no federal laws on HIV exposure, Congress encouraged individual states to develop such legislation. In 1990, two years after the above law was passed, the Ryan White CARE Act, which funds AIDS treatment and care, required states, in return, to ensure that their laws could prosecute an HIV-positive person who knowingly infected another. By 2000, when all states met these stipulations, the requirement was removed,

As of mid-2005, twenty-four states had HIV-specific laws like California's, although they varied considerably. Many concern sexual activity, needle sharing, and blood donation. More rarely, they address acts of biting or spitting, which are less likely to spread HIV. Penalties range from a year to life in prison. Twelve states also have sentence-enhancement laws, in which additional penalties are added for HIV-positive sexual assault. Three other states have enhancement laws, but no HIV-specific laws. Six continue to rely on existing STD laws to control HIV exposure, and seventeen use general criminal law and have neither HIV-specific nor STD laws.

The HIV Criminal Law and Policy Project claims that there have been 316 prosecutions of people for HIV exposure or transmission between 1986 and 2001. Most cases involved sexual activity without disclosure of HIV status, and a minority involved selling infected blood. Of these, 164 people were convicted, although it was not always possible to determine under which kind of law they had been prosecuted. Cases in which sentence enhancement was applied peaked in 1993 and between 1998 to 1999. Twelve states and Puerto Rico reported no prosecutions and only California, Florida, Illinois, Missouri, Ohio and Pennsylvania had more than fifteen prosecutions each in all.

Significantly, there is little evidence to suggest that legislation against HIV exposure has had any impact on the transmission of the disease. Some individuals have received long prison terms even though the victim escaped infection. It is important that awareness of HIV law is raised among those who are HIV positive and by those agencies that support them, but criminalizing someone for not disclosing their HIV status does not promote greater condom use or safer sexual practices.

FURTHER RESOURCES

Books

Web sites

HIV Criminal Law and Policy Project. "HIV-specific Criminal Transmission Laws." <http://www.hivcriminallaw.org/laws/hivspec.cfm> (accessed January 15, 2006).

University of California San Francisco. Center for AIDS Prevention Studies—AIDS Research Institute. "Is There a Role for Criminal Law in HIV Prevention?" <http://www.caps.ucsf.edu/publications/criminalization.html> | |accessed January 15, 2006).

Yugoslavian Federal Army Destroys Croatian City of Vukovar

Photograph

By: Antoine Gyori

Date: November 21, 1991

Source: Corbis Corporation

About the Photographer: Antoine Gyori is a photographer for the Sygma photo agency, and has also contributed photogrpahs to the Corbis and Contrasto collections. Gyorgi specializes in photographing events in Eastern Europe and the Middle East.

INTRODUCTION

The former Yugoslavia—a federation of six republics—Slovenia, Croatia, Bosnia, Serbia, Montenegro, and Macedonia plus two autonomous regions within Serbia: Vojvodina and Kosovo—was founded after the Second World War by Josip Broz (better known as Tito.). Tito ruled by a policy of "brotherhood and unity" that in reality only suppressed longstanding ethnic identities and hatreds.

Not surprisingly, when Tito died in 1980, Yugoslavia started to disintegrate. The key figure in the breakup and the hostilities that followed was the communist Serbian politician, Slobodan Milošević who exploited Serb nationalism within Serbia and among Serb minorities in other republics to extend his political influence. In 1988 he became president of Serbia, and arguably the most powerful politician within the Yugoslav federation. Seeking to extend his influence further still, he stripped the semiautonomous provinces of Kosovo and Vojvodina of their freedoms within the federation, and took control of their votes in the rotating presidency that had replaced Tito's rule.

His actions aroused deep concerns in Yugoslavia's other republics, many of which had large Serb minorities. Slovenia and Croatia seceded from the federation in 1991; Bosnia followed a year later.

Although Slovenia left the federation after only the briefest of independence wars, both Croatia and Bosnia became embroiled in bitter conflicts with Serb-led Yugoslav forces. These were supplemented by Serb militias, usually operating in parts of Croatia and Bosnia with large Serb populations. Purporting to protect Serbs in these areas, they actually engaged in brutal ethnic cleansing—including rape and mass murder—to rid Serb areas of their Croatian and Bosnian Muslims. Nominally independent of Milošević's government, they actually received arms and funding from Belgrade and were involved in massive violence against non-Serb populations.

The most notorious of these groups was the Serb Volunteer Guard or "Tigers," led by Željko Ražnatović—better known as Arkan—a Slovenian-born Serb and career criminal. Born into a military family, by the 1970s Arkan had become an international bank robber and political assassin for Tito. He returned to Belgrade in the mid-1980s both rich and, through his patronage of brigades of football hooligans, powerful.

When war broke out in 1991 he turned his thugs into an irregular armed force called the Tigers. They carried out acts of extreme violence and ethnic cleansing in Croatia and Bosnia for the Milošević government, but were detached enough to afford Milošević a vestige of deniability.

The men like Arkan who ran these militias became almost messianic figures for ethnic Serbs, because they were thought to bring nationalistic dreams of a Greater Serbia—a homeland that extended beyond the country's borders into other former Yugoslav republics—closer to reality. Even after the war ended in 1995 and the full extent of their crimes became known, they were largely untouchable

PRIMARY SOURCE

Yugoslavian Federal Army Destroys Croatian City of Vukovar: Serbian paramilitaries, including the notorious "Arkan", walk through the shattered remnants of the Croatian city of Vukovar, a city they helped destroy, November 1991.
© ANTOINE GYORI/CORBIS SYGMA

figures within the former Yugoslav republics of Serbia and Montenegro.

PRIMARY SOURCE

YUGOSLAVIAN FEDERAL ARMY DESTROYS CROATIAN CITY OF VUKOVAR

See primary source image.

SIGNIFICANCE

Although Arkan was implicated in the November 1991 Vukavor massacre in Croatia, when three hundred civilians taking sanctuary in a hospital were massacred by his men, he was not indicted for this crime for a further six years. In Bosnia he was accused of leading horrific attacks against civilians in Bielijina in

April 1992 and of throwing mutilated Bosnian Muslim bodies in the Drina at the town of Visegrad. But in a conflict where excess and disregard for humanity were daily occurrences on every side, where atrocities were perpetrated by both militias and regular armed forces, and with propaganda and misinformation dominant, it was sometimes difficult to get an accurate picture of the reality.

Certainly though, Arkan's reputation preceded him. A mere rumor of his force's arrival was usually enough to empty a Bosnian Muslim or a Croatian village, so appalling were crimes of which he had been accused.

In the West a more complicated view emerged. Journalists documented a string of crimes against humanity and linked them directly to Arkan and the Tigers. Despite this, Arkan, who spoke fluent English, courted Western journalists and even allowed an

A ripped poster in Belgrade reads "Vote-Don't let it happen again" and is highlighted by a photo of ultra-nationalist leader of Serbian Radical Party Vojislav Seselj with a machine gun. The poster was displayed during the Serbian presidential campaign of 2004. AP IMAGES

American photographer, Ron Haviv, to follow him and the Tigers.

When the Bosnian war ended in 1995, the Tigers were officially disbanded. In reality, however, they remained a sleeper force, ready to be called up in case of "national emergency." When war erupted in Kosovo in 1998, although Arkan publicly urged his men to join the army, they still operated under his orders and carried out appalling attacks against the province's Muslims. His continued presence in Pristina's main hotel (which he also owned) throughout the conflict pointed to a man once more directing militia operations.

In 1997 he was indicted by the UN for war crimes, although this was not made public for two years. It did not matter. In Milošević's gangster state

the law could not touch him. His business interests were many and the legal ones ranged from hotels to a football club. He entered Serbian politics, and in 1995 became half of the country's most famous couple when he had married the pop star Ceca. On top of all that he had his own private army.

On January 15, 2000, he was assassinated in the lobby of Belgrade's Intercontinental Hotel. It was initially assumed that his death had been ordered by foreign agents or rival gangsters, but more likely his killing was carried out on Milošević's instructions to protect him from the testimony of his allies in the event of a UN trial.

Although democratic elections have taken place in Serbia and Montenegro, many warlords still live freely, their interests spanning legitimate business and the underworld. Several became politicians or transferred the wealth they accrued during the civil war into business concerns, while at the same time maintaining underworld interests such as gunrunning, drug smuggling, and human trafficking.

FURTHER RESOURCES
Books

Glenny, Misha. *The Balkans: Nationalism, War and the Great Powers 1804–1999.* London: Granta, 2000.

Judah, Tim. *The Serbs: History, Myth and the Destruction of Yugoslavia.* New Haven, CT: Yale University Press, 2000.

Sacco, Joe, and Christopher Hitchens. *Safe Area Gorazde: The War in Eastern Bosnia 1992–1995.* London: Random House, 1997.

Rwanda

Accountability for War Crimes and Genocide

Government report

By: United States Institute of Peace

Date: January 1995

Source: United States Institute of Peace. "Rwanda: Accountability for War Crimes and Genocide." Special Issue 13. Available at <http://www.usip.org/pubs/specialreports/early/rwanda1.html> (accessed January 8, 2006).

About the Author: The United States Institute of Peace is an independent organization created by the U.S. Congress to promote the prevention and resolution of international conflicts. The Institute achieves its goals through research, professional training, and educational programs.

INTRODUCTION

One million people, primarily of the Tutsi ethnic minority, were killed by the majority Hutus during the Rwanda genocide between April and August of 1994. A power struggle between the Tutsis and Hutus has existed as far back as 1300, when the Tutsis first arrived in central East Africa. The Tutsis, making up fourteen percent of the population, eventually established power in present-day Rwanda and Burundi. The genocide was a culmination of nearly thirty-five years of violence, following the Rwandan independ-

The bodies of Rwandan Tutsi decay after a massacre that killed 200 people during the 1994 genocide. More than 800,000 people perished in the three-month killing spree. © BACI/CORBIS

ence from Belgium in the early 1960s, when the Hutus gained control of the country. To end the cycles of violence in the region, there have been attempts by the international community, the Rwandan government, and local communities in Rwanda to seek justice and reconciliation for the crimes committed during the genocide.

Nearly 140,000 people were imprisoned as suspected instigators and participants the Rwandan genocide. In addition to Tutsi men, women, and children, those Hutus who were sympathetic to the Tutsi cause, or refused orders to carry out killings, were also killed. In many cases, those who carried out the killings had been living side-by-side with their victims, in the same villages.

Because of the overcrowding of Rwandan prisons, and the inability of the local Rwandan judicial system to handle so many cases, the Rwandan government developed plans for alternative ways of dealing with the prisoners. In 2003, the government declared that those prisoners who had pleaded guilty, were elderly or seriously ill, or were minors would be released from prison. Those who were suspected ringleaders of genocide killings were not released. The government also began using a traditional justice system, called Gacaca, which allows local communities to try and judge the suspects.

The United Nations (UN) Security Council responded to what it called crimes against humanity and serious violations of humanitarian law by establishing the International Criminal Tribunal for Rwanda (ICTR) in September 1994. The court, which is located in Arusha, Tanzania, was mandated to prosecute those individuals responsible for inciting and leading the genocide in Rwanda. The tribunal's deadline to complete prosecutions was set for the end of 2008, with appeals continuing until 2010. The former Prime Minister of Rwanda, Jean Kambanda, was one of the first suspects convicted and given a life sentence by the ICTR for his role in the genocide. In addition to government officials, the court has also convicted militia leaders, businessmen, doctors, religious leaders, and journalists. Many of those convicted are serving life prison terms in international prisons located in several West African countries.

PRIMARY SOURCE

This report, commissioned by the United States Institute of Peace, a bipartisan organization created by Congress, contains information about the genocide movement in Rwanda and the Hutu-Tutsi conflict.

INTRODUCTION

Within a matter of weeks this past spring, the name "Rwanda" became synonymous with carnage and violence on a massive scale. Images of executions and massacres flooded the media, shocking the international community. An organized campaign of violence was carried out, during which the Tutsi were referred to as "cockroaches" and "the enemy," and Rwandan radio broadcasters exhorted every Hutu to kill Tutsi, complaining that "graves are still only half full." In less than four months, between 500,000 and a million people were killed. Before 1994, Rwanda was the most densely populated country in continental Africa. Between April and August 1994, that statistic shifted radically, as Rwanda lost 20 percent to 40 percent of its population to slaughter or exile.

As one participant in the Institute conference stated, "Genocide has worked in Rwanda." Precise figures are difficult to obtain. Over the past thirty years, however, the cycle of violence and counter-violence in Rwanda and neighboring Burundi has resulted in the killing of between 300,000 and 600,000 people—and that was before the carnage in 1994. Elites maneuvering for power have, for decades, been able to manipulate ethnic rivalries for political ends without any fear of being called to account for their actions. Rejection of this culture of impunity will be crucial to ending the cycle of violence and achieving authentic national reconciliation. To this end, the Rwandan government and the international community must provide a clear and public demonstration that those who organize or engage in such genocidal activity will be held accountable.

The United Nations Security Council has taken the first important step toward the goal of accountability by establishing the "International Tribunal for the Prosecution of Persons Responsible for Genocide and Other Serious Violations of International Humanitarian Law Committed in the Territory of Rwanda and Rwandan citizens responsible for genocide and other such violations committed in the territory of neighboring States, between 1 January 1994 and 31 December 1994." The approach adopted by the Security Council largely affirms the conclusions reached at the Institute's conference, at which a variety of options and approaches for establishing an international tribunal were analyzed and debated by senior officials and policymakers from Rwanda, the United States, and the UN, and by several academic experts. This report discusses the choices made by the UN Security Council on key features of the International Tribunal for Rwanda and recommends several further steps to be taken.

BACKGROUND

The population of Rwanda is composed primarily of two ethnic groups, the Hutu (85 percent) and the Tutsi (14 percent). In 1959, Rwanda's Hutu majority rebelled against their former Tutsi overlords. By 1960, the Hutu-dominated party, Parmehutu, had gained political control of Rwanda, which it retained after the country achieved independence in 1962. Ethnic violence erupted in December 1963, with the killing of more than 20,000 Tutsi and the exodus of 100,000. Tutsi refugees tried unsuccessfully to invade Rwanda from neighboring countries a number of times. After each failed invasion, the Tutsi in Rwanda faced severe reprisals; one attack in late 1963 for instance, resulted in the killing of 10,000 Tutsi. After a few years of relative calm, tensions between Hutu and Tutsi again escalated in the early 1970s. In 1973, Juvenal Habyarimana seized power in a coup d'etat, citing the need to establish order, and continued as president for the next twenty-one years.

Over the next two decades, although President Habyarimana claimed to have instituted a program to ease ethnic tensions and create a balance between the two ethnic groups, most observers saw the initiative as perpetuating discrimination against the Tutsi. Worsening economic conditions in the late 1980s also increased opposition to Habyarimana. Responding to both international and domestic pressures, Habyarimana had recently announced a new program of political reform when the Rwandan Patriotic Front (RPF) invaded Rwanda from bases in Uganda on October 1, 1990. The government responded by arresting and imprisoning 8,000–10,000 people around the country, primarily Tutsi and suspected opponents of Habyarimana, and holding many of them without charge for several months. The conflict continued through 1991 and 1992, resulting in the deaths of thousands and the displacement of an estimated 100,000 persons.

Early in 1992, political organizations affiliated with President Habyarimana formed two militias—the Interahamwe ("Those Who Attack Together") and the Impuzamugambi ("Those Who Have the Same Goal"). Trained and supplied by the Rwandan army, the militias were involved in the killing of more than 2,000 civilians, mostly Tutsi. They would play a central role in the atrocities that commanded the world's attention in 1994.

During late 1992 and 1993, the Rwandan government and the RPF negotiated a series of agreements in Arusha, Tanzania, culminating in the signing of a comprehensive accord in August 1993 that provided for a programmed demobilization, the creation of an integrated army, a new transitional government with a prime minister acceptable to both sides, and multiparty general elections with the full participation of the RPF. Hutu extremists, including many close to Habyarimana, were vehemently opposed to the accords and the consequent reduction of their own power.

Unfortunately, the tentative peace resulting from the Arusha Accords was short-lived. Massive ethnic massacres in Burundi in October 1993 fueled tensions in Rwanda. Political assassinations and a reign of terror by the militias increased. On April 6, 1994, a plane carrying Habyarimana and Burundian President Cyprien Ntaryamira crashed near Kigali airport, killing both men and igniting an explosion of violence and brutality.

Hutu extremists immediately accused the RPF of assassinating President Habyarimana. Almost instantly, Hutu soldiers, the presidential guard, and the militias began to hunt down and kill Tutsi civilians. Sufficient evidence exists to confirm that the slaughter that ensued was not chaotic, uncontrolled violence, but rather a planned and organized campaign of genocide. Hutus suspected of opposing extremist policies were also targeted for slaughter, including moderate members of Habyarimana's cabinet who were searched out and killed within hours of the plane crash.

In many countries that have suffered a campaign of massive violations of human rights, the violence has been perpetrated mainly by military and political organizations associated with the regime, leaving the rest of society to go about its business with relatively clean hands. In striking contrast, the Rwandan atrocities were characterized by the deliberate attempt to force public participation on as broad a basis as possible, co-opting everyone into the carnage against Tutsis and moderate Hutus. The militias were tightly organized throughout the country, inciting civilians to participate in the massacres. Many Hutu were forced to choose between killing or being killed. If Tutsi deaths were not of sufficient number in a region, experienced killers were brought in from other areas to intensify the massacres.

Fighting between the Rwandan army and the RPF resumed on April 7, the day after the plane crash. On July 18, 1994, with the Hutu-dominated Rwandan government in flight, the RPF declared victory and established a new government of national unity. After three months of fighting, between 500,000 and a million Tutsi had been exterminated. Up to two million refugees, overwhelmingly Hutu and constituting 25 to 30 percent of the pre-April population of Rwanda, are estimated to have fled the country for refugee camps in Zaire and Tanzania. The capital city, Kigali, was left in ruin. Of the 350,000 inhabitants before the war, only 40,000 to 50,000 remained. There was no running water, no electricity, no government infrastructure, and nearly every building was damaged.

On July 1, 1994, the UN Security Council called for the appointment of a Commission of Experts to investigate and make recommendations concerning "grave violations of international humanitarian law" and "evidence of possible acts of genocide" in Rwanda. On September 29, 1994, the Commission of Experts submitted a preliminary report to the Security Council in which it recommended the establishment of an international tribunal to prosecute war crimes and genocide committed in the country since April 6 of this year. Rather than awaiting the commission's final report and recommendations, the Security Council voted on November 8 to create the tribunal. In accordance with its mandate, the Commission of Experts submitted its final report at the end of November.

In the absence of a formal judicial process, it has been difficult to contain a surge of counter-violence and revenge killings of returning refugees suspected of participation in the April-July massacres, as RPF soldiers and civilians dispense a more brutal form of "justice." These violent incidents of collective vengeance not only threaten the international assistance that the new government desperately needs to rebuild the country, but also impede the return of the refugees and risk plunging Rwanda into a new round of widespread violence. The prompt beginning of a visible prosecution process is required to demonstrate that people need not take the law into their hands.

SIGNIFICANCE

Some observers, and current leaders in Rwanda, have criticized the ICTR, saying it is an inefficient method for trying perpetrators of the genocide, since the proceedings in an international court move slowly. The pace at which the court is said to be operating is blamed in part on the complexity of the cases and on the fact that lawyers and judges brought in from around the world often approach court proceedings differently. Also, English and French were deemed the official languages of the ICTR, with many of the witnesses speaking only Kinyarwandan, the official language in Rwanda. A series of translators have been required for the hearings.

The Secretary-General of the UN, Kofi Annan, pointed out the importance of the ICTR, the first international court to pass judgment on the crimes of genocide. He said that the ICTR will assist in the long-term process of national reconciliation in Rwanda and crimes against humanity elsewhere, by demonstrating to leaders that ethnic killing is not tolerated by the international community.

Another concern is that many organizers of the Rwanda genocide have escaped punishment by moving to other countries. Several cases involving the genocide were carried out in Belgium, which passed laws in 1994 to allow the country to hear cases regarding human rights abuses, even if the abuses did not occur in Belgium. Some human-rights groups hope that by holding these genocide trials in Belgium, it will become more difficult for war criminals to seek sanctuary in other countries.

Critics in Rwanda, and observers elsewhere, say the post-genocide government of Rwanda did not act quickly enough to ensure that suspects held in prisons go to trial. Some experts also maintain that, in order for community court hearings to be successful, it is necessary to ensure that the communities trying the cases are not seeking vengeance. It is unclear if such neutrality had been established for the Gacaca process. Families of victims in Rwanda also have criticized the process, since suspects released from prison are brought back to be tried and to live in the villages where the crimes were committed.

The post-genocide government in Rwanda promoted unity among Tutsis and Hutus, saying a single Rwandan identity is key to erasing ethnic labels. The extent to which the government has been successful in this endeavor has been debated. Analysts say that the success of reconciliation in Rwanda will dictate the country's future stability.

FURTHER RESOURCES

Books

Moghalu, Kingsley. *Rwanda's Genocide: The Policies of Global Injustice.* New York: Palgrave Macmillan, 2005.

Web sites

BBC News. "Rwanda Genocide: Ten Years On." <http://news.bbc.co.uk/1/hi/in_depth/africa/2004/rwanda/default.stm> (accessed January 8, 2006).

Frontline (PBS). "The Triumph of Evil." <http://www.pbs.org/wgbh/pages/frontline/shows/evil/> (accessed January 8, 2006).

Global Policy Forum. "International Criminal Tribunal for Rwanda." <http://www.globalpolicy.org/intljustice/rwandaindx.htm> (accessed January 8, 2006).

United Nations. "International Criminal Tribunal for Rwanda." <http://65.18.216.88/default.htm> (accessed January 8, 2006).

Srebrenica Massacre

Cartoon

By: Joe Sacco

Date: June 2005

Source: Joe Sacco, *Safe Area Gorazde: The War in Eastern Bosnia* 1992–1995. Seattle, Fantagraphics, 2005

About the Artist: Joe Sacco is a Maltese-born cartoonist and journalist who combines eyewitness reportage with comic strip storytelling. He has spent time in Israel and the occupied territories from which his award-winning book *Palestine* emerged in 1993. Sacco was one of few journalists to cover the Bosnian War from Gorazde—which, although designated a safe area, was in fact extremely dangerous. *Safe Area Gorazde* is the book resulting from this stay and the cartoon below is extracted from it. Sacco was invited to cover the Bosnian War Crimes Trials for *Details* magazine in 1998 and his next project was a book about the south Gaza Strip.

INTRODUCTION

Srebrenica was a small town in the east of Bosnia which had been declared a United Nations Safe Area in 1993. But in 1995, it was to become the scene of the worst massacre of the Bosnian War. In fact, conditions had been deteriorating in the area for many months while thousands of civilians took refuge against earlier Serb attacks in north-eastern Bosnia. By early July 1995, food and fuel were running out and the population was under the protection of just six hundred lightly armed Dutch soldiers. When Serb forces began to shell the town, Bosnian Muslims requested the return of their weapons but the peacekeepers refused and called for support from United Nations Headquarters in Sarajevo, but help was delayed.

On July 11, Dutch fighter planes dropped bombs on Serb positions; the Serbs responded with a threat to kill Dutch hostages and bomb the Bosnian refugees. Bosnian Serb commander Ratko Mladic entered the town later that day and met with the Dutch commander, demanding the Bosnian Muslims hand over any weapons. The next day, buses took women and children away while the Serbs separated out the men, supposedly for interrogation about war crimes.

The next few days saw a wave of killings of unarmed Bosnian Muslims in various locations in the area. Meanwhile, the peacekeepers handed over five thousand Muslims who had been sheltering nearby in return for the release of Dutch hostages. The first reports of the massacre came from survivors who had fled through the mountains to safety in Muslim-held territories. Evidence that emerged in years to follow suggested that more than seven thousand Muslim men had been killed at the hands of Serb forces in Srebrenica. Depicting such a grim event in a cartoon is a

A funeral cortege of trucks carry the remains of 610 victims of the 1995 Srebrenica massacre from an identification center in Sarajevo on July 9, 2005. Europe's worst massacre since World War II, the slaughter by Bosnian Serb soldiers claimed the lives of 8,000 Muslims, mostly men and boys, in a one-month period. AP IMAGES

PRIMARY SOURCE

Srebrenica Massacre: Illustrations from the graphic novel *Safe Area Gorazde,* by Joe Sacco, depict a massacre of Muslim Bosnians by Serbs. ILLUSTRATIONS © 2006 JOE SACCO; FROM THE GRAPHIC NOVEL SAFE AREA GORAZDE.

particularly effective way of creating impact—and builds on the long tradition of using this form of expression to make a political point.

SREBRENICA MASSACRE

See primary source image.

SIGNIFICANCE

The Srebrenica Massacre is the worst event of its kind in Europe since the Holocaust of World War II. It was certainly the most dire event of the Bosnian War and has been designated as genocide by the International Criminal Tribunal for the Former Yugoslavia (ICTY), which was set up by the United Nations Security Council to investigate war crimes arising from the conflict that devastated the region during the 1990s.

The war crime concept is relatively new. Before World War II, the atrocities of war were generally accepted as being part of the nature of conflict. But the Holocaust and the mistreatment of prisoners of war and civilians by the Japanese made the Allies determined that someone should be held to account for the suffering they had caused. The Nuremberg Trials of 1945 and 1946 led to the execution of twelve Nazi leaders for war crimes. Article 147 of the Fourth Geneva Convention gives a broad definition of a war crime which includes wilful killing, torture, unlawful deportation, hostage taking and deliberate destruction of property. In fact the definition of a war crime is continually evolving; rape was a particularly common occurrence in the Yugoslav conflict and was declared a war crime by the ICTY in 2001.

Rape in a war context is an example of a crime against humanity, defined as a crime committed in armed conflict but directed towards a civilian population. Genocide is the most serious example of a crime against humanity and is defined as acts (usually murder) targeted toward the destruction of a national, ethnic, racial or religious group. This applies in the case of the Srebrenica Massacre as most of the victims were Muslims.

The ICTY was the first war crimes trial to bring a Head of State, the former Serb leader Slobodan Milosevic, to account. However, Milosevic died before his trial could be completed. Mladic and the former Bosnian Serb leader Radovan Karadzˆic have been indicted for their part in the Srebrenica Massacre and the Tribunal wants them handed over as soon as possible. Both are thought to be alive and in hiding in remote areas of Bosnia or Serbia and Montenegro, protected by dedicated followers. The EU has warned Serbia that they will block their entry to EU membership unless Mladic, at least, is handed over soon.

FURTHER RESOURCES

Web sites

Bosnian Institute. "Report on the Events in Srebrenica." <http://www.bosnia.org.uk/news/> (accessed March 28. 2006).

BBC Online. "Srebrenica Timeline." <http://news.bbc.co.uk/ 1/hi/world/europe/> (accessed March 28, 2006).

Suspected Ku Klux Klansman Tried

June 1964 Murders of Three Civil Rights Workers

Photograph

By: Kyle Carter

Date: June 14, 2005

Source: Corbis.

About the Photographer: Kyle Carter is a freelance photographer based in Meridian, Mississippi.

INTRODUCTION

The early 1960s were a time of many changes in America, particularly in the area of African-American Civil Rights. Although African-Americans had been given the Constitutional right to vote previously (the Fifteenth Amendment was ratified in 1870), many were barred from registering or voting in the Southern regions of the country. Many areas required that African-Americans pass prohibitively stringent "literacy" tests, mandated that they pay exorbitant poll taxes, or actively prevented them from gaining access to voting registration areas by changing hours, physically moving to different locations, and employing fear-based or violent techniques such as threats, lynchings, burnings (homes, vehicles, stores, etc.).

Mississippi had an extremely low percentage of registered African-American voters, and civil rights activists sought to change that by assisting citizens to secure their voting privileges. In 1964, there was a large-scale movement coordinated by the National Association for the Advancement of Colored People

(NAACP), the Mississippi Council of Federated Organizations, Student Nonviolent Coordinating Committee (SNCC), and the Congress of Racial Equality (CORE) to end voting discrimination in the South, called "Freedom Summer." Several hundred (predominantly Caucasian) college students, primarily from the Northeast, traveled to Mississippi to engage in a multidimensional program involving education, health care, transportation and accompaniment through the registration process, among other things. There was a great deal of media coverage of the program, and it garnered considerable public support. The young people involved in the "Freedom Summer" programs received many threats, and were threatened, harangued, and accosted, not just by white supremacists and extremist group members, but by the general population and by public servants such as police officers as well. Homes and businesses associated with the movement were vandalized, firebombed, or burned, many of the program volunteers were arrested or harassed by local law enforcement officers, others were threatened or physically beaten, and still others were subject to violence by large groups of local citizens.

The most significant acts of violence (from a social change perspective), and those that had the greatest, longest-lasting impact on the African-American civil rights movement concerned the abduction and murders of three young activists named Andy (Andrew) Goodman, Michael Schwerner, and James Chaney. They had gone to investigate the firebombing of a church near Philadelphia, Mississippi, and had been arrested for an alleged traffic violation while en route. Subsequent to their arrests, they were jailed for several hours, and then released. They were not seen alive again after that. Their bodies were recovered about six weeks later, buried under a clay dam on a farm. Schwerner and Goodman, who were both Caucasian, had been shot once, at close range, in the chest. Chaney had been beaten as well as shot (some reports state that he was beaten to death, and was not shot). There was a great deal of nationwide media coverage concerning the murders, and much public sentiment suggested that this was primarily because two of the victims were Caucasian; this was supported by the fact that hundreds of crimes against African-Americans, including murders, remained uninvestigated and unsolved. It was believed that the Ku Klux Klan had ordered the trio murdered; nineteen men stood trial for the killings, and seven were convicted as a result, the first time that a case had successfully been prosecuted in Mississippi for the killing of civil rights activists.

There is a plaque affixed to the rebuilt Mt. Zion Methodist church, the firebombing of which Schw-

erner, Chaney, and Goodman had been on their way to investigate on the day they were killed. It reads, in part: "Victims of a Klan conspiracy, their deaths provoked national outrage and led to the first successful prosecution of a civil rights case in Mississippi."

■ PRIMARY SOURCE

SUSPECTED KU KLUX KLANSMAN TRIED FOR THE JUNE 1964 MURDERS OF THREE CIVIL RIGHTS WORKERS
See primary source image.

SIGNIFICANCE

In addition to the lynching deaths of Goodman, Chaney, and Schwerner, during the summer months of 1964, there were more than thirty churches burnt or firebombed, more than one thousand civil rights activists or "Freedom Summer" volunteers arrested, and several thousand beatings were reported in Mississippi.

The three young men were reported missing within hours of their failure to complete a required safety check-in. They were reported kidnapped, and the Federal Bureau of Investigation quickly became involved in a massive search for them. The high profile case was codenamed "Mississippi burning, or MIBURN" by the FBI. The car that the men had been using was found within a couple of days of their disappearance. It had been burned out. Several days after the disappearance of the three men, the FBI established their first permanent office in Mississippi. After a reward was offered for information leading to the resolution of the case, informants came forward and the bodies were recovered (six weeks after the men were abducted). Ultimately, several Klan members became FBI informants, and one, James Jordan, decided to testify on behalf of the prosecution, in return for a financial reward and governmental assistance with relocation for himself and his family. The first nineteen arrests in the case were made in December of 1964. The charges were dismissed six days later. One month later, federal grand jury indictments were returned against the nineteen. One month later (February of 1965), a federal judge dismissed the indictments against seventeen of those charged, leaving only Sheriff Rainey and Deputy Sheriff Price to stand trial. The case was heard by the United States Supreme Court in March of 1966, and indictments against eighteen men were reinstated (some of these were different than the first group of nineteen). The case went to trial in October of 1967, with three Klan informants

PRIMARY SOURCE

Suspected Ku Klux Klansman Tried: Eighty-year-old Edgar Ray Killen is wheeled into the Neshoba County courthouse in Philadelphia, Mississppi, June 14, 2005, during his trial for the 1964 murders of civil rights workers James Chaney, Michael Schwerner, and Andrew Goodman. Ironically, the conviction of the ordained Baptist minister on three counts of manslaughter, each carrying a twenty-year sentence, came on the forty-first anniversary of the killings. © KYLE CARTER/REUTERS/CORBIS

providing significant testimony for the prosecution, one of whom was a witness to the murders (James Jordan). The jury was initially deadlocked, but eventually returned convictions on seven of the defendants, acquitted eight of the others, and was unable to reach a verdict in the case of three men (one of whom was Edgar Ray Killen). The felony convictions represented a landmark for civil rights in Mississippi, as this was the first time that there had been a successful prosecution in that state for the murder of civil rights workers. It also served to focus nationwide, and global, attention to the lack of civil rights for African-Americans in the American South. Thirty-five years later (1999), the

state of Mississippi reopened the case, which had been tried on a federal, but not a state, level. In addition to a strong belief in seeing that justice is served a part of the reason for re-examining the case would be to exorcise some of the lingering negative perceptions concerning racism in the American South.

On June 23, 2005, Edgar Ray Killen, the eighty year old preacher who was not convicted in 1967, was found guilty of manslaughter in connection with the murders of James Chaney, Andrew Goodman, and Andrew Schwerner, and sentenced to three twenty year terms of imprisonment (two decades for each victim). For many, there was a significant degree of satisfaction in the public demonstration that justice had eventually been served, and that the concept of racism.

FURTHER RESOURCES

Books

Ball, Howard. *Murder in Mississippi: United States v. Price and the Struggle for Civil Rights.* Lawrence, Kansas: University Press of Kansas, 2004.

Krane, Dale, and Stephen D. Shaffer. *Mississippi Government & Politics: Modernizers Versus Traditionalists.* Lincoln, Nebraska: University of Nebraska Press, 1992.

Levy, Peter B. *The Civil Rights Movement.* Westport, Connecticut: Greenwood Press, 1998.

Web sites

BBC News. "Mississippi Murders Revisited." <http://news.bbc.co.uk/1/hi/world/americas/4167913.stm> (accessed March 7, 2006).

core-online.org. "Freedom Summer." <http://www.core-online.org/history/freedom_summer.htm> (accessed March 7, 2006).

Knight Ayton Management. "Justin Webb." <http://www.knightayton.co.uk/frameset.html?http://www.knightayton.co.uk/justin_webb.html> (accessed March 7, 2006).

Trafficking of Filipino Women to Malaysia

Examining the Experiences and Perspectives of Victims, Governmental and NGO Experts

Government report

By: Diana Wong

Date: 2004

Source: Diana Wong. "Trafficking of Filipino Women to Malaysia: Examining the Experiences and Perspectives of Victims, Governmental and NGO Experts." United Nations Office on Drugs and Crime, 2004.

About the Author: Dr. Diana Wong earned a degree in sociology from the University of Singapore and earned a PhD from the University of Bielefeld. Since 1999, she has held the position of Senior Fellow at the Institute of Malaysian and International Studies at Universiti Kebangsaan Malaysia.

INTRODUCTION

The International Organization for Migration has stated that 2.5 percent of the world's population is international migrants. Of those migrants, the United Nations' High Commission for Refugees (UNHCR) approximates that close to 120,000 women and children become victims of human trafficking, with a final destination of the European Union, and seventy-five percent of those trafficked are under the age of twenty-five. The United Nations Office on Drugs and Crime (UNODC), in its Protocol to Prevent, Suppress and Punish Trafficking in Persons identifies trafficked persons as victims, stating, "Trafficking in persons shall mean the recruitment, transportation, transfer, harboring or receipt of persons, by means of threat or use of force or other forms of coercion, of abduction, of fraud, of deception, of the abuse of power or of a position of vulnerability or of the giving or receiving of payments or benefits to achieve the consent or a person having control over another person, for the purpose of exploitation. Exploitation shall include, at a minimum, the exploitation of the prostitution of others or other forms of sexual exploitation, forced labor or services."

Although the UNODC concentrates on the criminal cartels that operate in human trafficking, trafficking is not an activity exclusive to organized crime. Trafficking of humans is becoming a highly lucrative and widely expanding operation. In her research for the UNHCR, Jenna Shearer Demir identifies human trafficking as the third most lucrative international criminal activity, following only the trafficking of arms and drugs. Because of weak domestic laws and poor coordination between states of origin and destination for trafficking, punishment for human trafficking is relatively weak compared to sentences for those of drug and arms trafficking.

Economic opportunities entice migrants and provide the lure by which traffickers attract victims. The UN estimates that by 2025, sixty percent of the world's population will be living in cities. Much of this migration has begun as internal migration from rural regions to urban centers. However, the lack of employment opportunities provides the motivation for international migration. The European Commission asserts that the factors leading to international migration, particularly for women, include unemployment, extreme poverty, and marginalization.

Many of those who fall victim to human trafficking are recruited by fake ads, mail order bride catalogues, and casual acquaintances. The phony job opportunities range from domestic servants, nannies, and caregivers to the elderly to waitresses, or factory

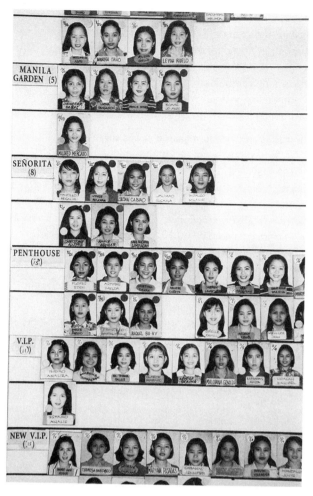

Photographs of young Filipino women hired as overseas workers. Though trained as entertainers, many face pressures to enter the sex industry. © KAREN KASMAUSKI/CORBIS

and supermarket workers. Often the victims are provided transportation for migration, which includes the cost of passports, visas and other official travel documents. This becomes one of the controls by which the traffickers elicit cooperation on the part of their victims—debt bondage. The victims are forced to repay their traffickers for these expenses and any other expenses, such as food and lodging, which their captors determine. The victims generally enter the country by a social, tourist, or student visa, which are confiscated, along with other official documents like personal identifications and passports, by the traffickers and become an additional form of control and coercion. After allowing the visa to expire, the traffickers advise the victims that they are immigration offenders and risk criminal proceedings in the new country. As such, the victims remain under the control

of their captors in order to pay for proper documentation. Traffickers also threaten the lives of the victims' family members in order to elicit cooperation.

The Filipino experience of human trafficking varies little from others around the world. However, there are other factors in migration motivation and recruitment of Filipino women. In 1974, the Philippine Labor Act created the mechanisms for the export of labor. The government created licensing agents, to include the Philippines Overseas Employment Agency, whose goal is to promote and regulate labor contracts. In the late 1970s, the majority of exported labor was skilled or semi-skilled men contracted to the Middle East, which was experiencing a construction boom. By 1997, however, the Philippines was the largest exporter of female labor and officials deemed the Filipina migrant as the "heroine of the Philippines economy" due to the remittances back to their families in the Philippines.

As a government-sanctioned institution, labor migration is entered into by both the educated and uneducated Filipino women. According to Mary Rose Fernandez, an estimated forty-two percent of Filipina who emigrate have some college education, while only seven percent have less than a high school education. The lure to migrate is based on the ability to return to the Philippines with additional skills, in addition to providing income relief to families remaining in the Philippines. Women seeking similar successes to those of other migrants fall prey to the human traffickers and are often recruited by other Filipinos.

PRIMARY SOURCE

TRAFFICKING OF FILIPINO WOMEN TO MALAYSIA: EXAMINING THE EXPERIENCES AND PERSPECTIVES OF VICTIMS, GOVERNMENTAL AND NGO EXPERTS

Coercion

Victim respondents did not indicate threats against their families or physical or sexual violence against the women themselves. While violence against women has been known to occur, in the victim survey, physical violence by the club owner as means to control or punish the women does not appear to occur. One woman who declined to work even after two weeks in the quarters, reported that she was given an ultimatum, to either go to work immediately or be sold to another syndicate. She also reported that when the women went against the instructions of the syndicate/company, the threat of violence, or real violence, was used, however, this was not confirmed by the other women interviewed in the entertainment centre. While none of the respondents in the study reported being victims of rape, cases of rape against trafficked victims have been recorded by the NGO Tenaganita in a research study and subsequent publication on trafficking in women in Malaysia.

Despite the lack of physical or sexual violence as a means to coerce or control victims, the 26 women working for the entertainment company were all "forced" to work as sex workers. The vulnerability of the women was due to their debt to the company, as well as the fact that their passport was held by the company. The seizure of the travel documents—reported by the 26 respondents trafficked to work in the entertainment center—was the main means of control over the women. As long as they were still indebted to the company, they were kept under strict surveillance at the entertainment centre by the manager and at their quarters by the security guard. Even after their debt had been paid off, their freedom of mobility was restricted by the fact that they were immigration offenders and hence it was safer to remain indoors in order to evade detection. If the women were arrested by immigration officials, it was almost certain that the entertainment centres would not give their passport back.

Seizure of documents and what was done to "buy" them back

In the case of the 26 women working in the entertainment centre, the passport was seized by the employer, to be redeemed only when the loan was repaid, or if someone else was prepared to "buy" the woman. After one month the social visit pass would have expired, as the syndicate/company failed to renew the social visit pass. This posed two kinds of problems: upon returning to the Philippines, the women would have to pay RM 1,000 ($265) to the same syndicate/company which would arrange for their passage through the immigration gate at Sandakan Port. Alternatively, if they were caught by immigration officials, they would be charged with remaining in Malaysia without a valid pass and get six (6) months prison.

Rotation between groups and cities

According to one expert from an NGO there is evidence of trafficked victims being rotated between cities in West Malaysia. From West Malaysia, there is also further trafficking to Japan, Singapore and Thailand, Hong Kong, Taiwan, and Europe. In Sabah, according to a law enforcement officer, there is also evidence that trafficked victims are sold from club to club. In the victim survey, however, no instance of such rotation was reported, although there was a report by one victim that when she had still refused to take a "booking" after two weeks, she was threatened with being sold to another club.

Despite the fact that women interviewed were not rotated among clubs or cities, according to key informants as well as victims interviewed, this practice occurs frequently. There is a high level of rotation of women within the clubs due to the fact that the women sometimes run away, return voluntarily to the Philippines after working off their debt, are "bought" by someone else, or have been detained and deported. Thus the market demand for women remains constantly high and new women are constantly entering the clubs.

Organised crime group: organisation and scope

According to an expert interviewed at an NGO in West Malaysia, there are eleven (11) criminal groups in West Malaysia involved in the smuggling/trafficking of human beings from the Philippines. Groups vary in size but are relatively small. The most prevalent groups vary in size from between 6 and 10 members, followed by fewer groups of less than 5 members. Less common are larger groups comprising between 11 and 20 members. The structure of these organised criminal groups comprise four levels:

- Level 1 includes persons of which very little is known (not even their true identities), except that they are 'well known powerful' persons;
- Level 2 includes those individuals who receive orders, pass on information and give directives to the third level;
- Level 3 carries out the actual work of organising activities on the ground. They work closely with the fourth level. These persons may be pimps, madams, or small brothel owners. They have 'close ties' with government officials in the police and immigration departments;
- Level 4 consists of 'errand boys' who arrange transportation, buy food for the women and pass on information. They also look for potential new clients and areas for expansion. This group identifies potential trafficking victims, generally young women who they befriend, or to whom they promise work (or in some cases kidnap). They inform level three of these women for overseas markets. The level four group is also known to the sex workers (locally). They may also deal with illicit pharmaceutical and hard drugs.

During an interview, a senior law enforcement officer in Sabah, attested to the existence of such syndicates in Sabah, although no number was mentioned. According to this expert, the approximate size of the groups in terms of membership varies between six to ten members, while other groups have less than five. According to this expert, the structure of these organised criminal groups comprise three levels:

- Level 1, the "penganjur", are the entertainment companies in Sabah, Malaysia. These "penganjur" or organisers receive the trafficked women and force them into prostitution;

- Level 2, the "agents", are the groups of persons, almost always employment agencies, who recruit and sell or hand over the women to the "penganjur" in Malaysia or to the agents in the Philippines. In the Philippines, the agents are almost always Filipinos;
- Level 3, the "recruiters", are persons hired by the agents to recruit the girls in the Philippines. Their target groups are broad and include young girls from poor families, as well as university or college students and graduates, school leavers and girls who are already in employment but are looking for better opportunities abroad.

The information supplied by the senior law enforcement officer concerning the nature of the criminal groups in Sabah tallies with the picture that emerges through the victim survey, the key informants and other experts interviewed.

Conclusions and Recommendations

The study has found clear evidence of trafficking of Filipino women by organised syndicates into the vice industry in Sabah/Malaysia based on deception and debt bondage. There were reports by victims of specific incidences of collusion and corruption on the part of individual law enforcement officers with the syndicates. The geographical scope of these syndicates in Sabah/Malaysia remains limited. Close collaboration is found between the Malaysian syndicates and Filipino partners, usually employment agencies. Women are also found to be further trafficked to West Malaysia from Sabah, but the radius of circulation appears to be restricted to the region. The study found that the vulnerability of the trafficked women was heightened by the fact that in Sabah, there is an absence of a Philippine consular office, or local NGOs, to which the women can turn to for help and assistance.

As this study has proven the existence of trafficking of Filipinas into the entertainment clubs in Sabah, law enforcement agencies in Malaysia must exercise tighter inspections and control over the conditions under which the women are employed in these clubs. Malaysian law enforcement agencies should be more closely monitored for corruption. A bilateral task force should be established to co-ordinate enforcement of existing laws against trafficking-related offences in both countries. The Philippine Government should consider establishing a consular office in Sabah with an officer responsible for the protection of its workers there. As deception appears to be facilitated by the employment agencies in the Philippines, employment agencies should be more closely monitored.

SIGNIFICANCE

In March 1999, the United Nations Interregional Crime and Justice Research Institute and the UNODC designed the Global Programme against Trafficking in Human Beings (GPAT). The GPAT was created to research, address, and combat human trafficking. A protocol was created to promote an effective criminal justice response within signatory states. At the international level, the goal of GPAT is to assist states in designing effective responses to trafficking. At the national level, GPAT aims to educate potential victims as well as governments, to train legal entities to effectively respond and to create a strong system of victim and witness support.

FURTHER RESOURCES

Periodicals

Demir, Jenna Shearer. "The Trafficking of Women for Sexual Exploitation." *United Nations High Commission for Refugees* (March 2003).

Fernandez, Mary Rose. "Commodified Women." *Peace Review* (September 1997).

Web sites

HumanTrafficking.com. <http://www.humantrafficking.com> (accessed March 5, 2005).

Interpol. "Trafficking in Human Beings." <http://www.interpol.int/Public/THB/default.asp> (accessed March 5, 2005).

A Hate Crime and a Courageous Love

Film review

By: Neely Tucker

Date: October 14, 2005

Source: Neely Tucker. "A Hate Crime and a Courageous Love: 'Untold Story of Emmett Louis Till' Offers Powerful Images, but Few New Details." *Washington Post* (October 14, 2005): C05.

About the Author: Neely Tucker is a staff writer for the *Washington Post*, a position he has held since 2000. Prior to joining the staff at the *Washington Post*, Tucker was a foreign correspondent for the *Detroit Free Press*.

INTRODUCTION

Emmett Louis Till was fourteen years old when he left his home in Chicago for a vacation visit with relatives who were cotton sharecroppers in Mississippi. The young man was described by his friends and relatives as bright, cocky, funny, and confident. Although he lived in a segregated area of Chicago, his experience with racism was limited, and he had never experienced anything akin to the strong racial divide that existed in the rural south in the 1950s. His mother, Mamie Till Mobley, was born in Mississippi. She was wary of allowing her son to travel to the area and warned him of potential dangers, admonishing him to steer clear of white people.

Till and his cousins spent their mornings picking cotton, and the rest of their time enjoying one another's company. It was not uncommon for the group of African-American (then referred to as Negro) youngsters to go to a local store owned by Carolyn and Roy Bryant, play checkers at the outside tables, and purchase some small treats in the evenings. The store, operated by the Bryants, catered to the local sharecroppers, nearly all of whom were African-American.

On August 24, 1955, Emmett Louis Till was one of a dozen or so adolescents who went to Bryant's Grocery and Meat Market in Money, Mississippi. Till had been boasting to his peers of his alleged relationships with white girls; they dared him to flirt with the Caucasian woman running the store (21-year-old Carolyn Bryant). According to published reports of the ensuing events, Till went into the store, made some flirtatious remarks to Ms. Bryant, and then wolf-whistled at her. At that point, the other youngsters reported becoming fearful of the consequences of such forward behavior, and pulling Till back out to the truck in which they had arrived. Three nights later, Bryant's husband Roy, who had just returned from out-of-town business, and his brother-in-law J.W. Milam, kidnapped Emmett Louis Till. He was pistol-whipped, beaten severely, stripped naked, cut with an axe, had one of his eyes gouged out, shot through the head, fastened to a large cotton gin fan, and thrown into the Tallahatchie River. A few days later, his body was found, significantly disfigured and decomposed. He was identified based on a signet ring that he had been known to be wearing.

His mother, Mamie Till Mobley, insisted that his body be shipped back to Chicago. She pried open his casket and had his body publicly displayed, so that as many people as possible could see what the consequences of racial hatred were to her only child. *Jet* magazine published photographs of the mangled corpse. Although it was widely believed that consider- ably more than two people were involved in the kidnapping and subsequent murder of Emmett Till, only Bryant and Milam were arrested and charged in the crime. Their trial was held in the middle of September and lasted for only four days. The jury was composed of twelve Caucasian males. Deliberations took slightly more than an hour, and both men were acquitted of the crime. Several months later, both men granted a (paid) interview with *Look* magazine, in which they confessed to the crime. Because of the double jeopardy law, they could not be tried again for the crimes of kidnapping and murder. The nation was rocked by the brutality of the slaying, as well as the acquittal of the (later confessed) murderers. The death of Emmett Louis Till served to catalyze the early Civil Rights Movement in the United States. For more than half a century, it has stood as a centerpiece of the fight against racism.

PRIMARY SOURCE

In "The Untold Story of Emmett Louis Till," the latest documentary film about the notorious lynching in Mississippi half a century ago, we see how a grieving mother created a landmark moment in American history.

The sheriff in the Delta county where Till was murdered in August 1955 ordered the boy's mutilated corpse to be buried almost immediately after it was dredged from the Tallahatchie River, relatives recount in this fast-paced retelling. The funeral had taken place and they were about to bury the body when the call came from Chicago—Mamie Till Mobley, the 14-year-old's mother, was having none of it.

She ordered the pine box containing her son to be sent home. She then had it pried open and displayed what was inside to all and sundry.

It was a genuinely shocking moment—the disfigured face, an eye out of the socket, the facial skin almost detached from the bone. He had been shot through the head. Then he had been tied by the neck with barbed wire to a 70-pound fan and dumped in the river.

This, for supposedly whistling at a woman at a country store in a two-bit town called Money.

The decision to display that rotting corpse was an act of grief and courage and outrage and, in the end, sheer brilliance. Till's mutilated face exposed Mississippi racism for what it was—a sadistic mixture of bloodlust, sexual hysteria and a level of violence worthy of a psychopath. Till's murder became myth and history personified. All the age-old word-of-mouth horror stories of what white Southern men would do to black men who dared approach white women were put on display in a Chicago church, and, famously, in photographs in Jet magazine.

The outrage Mobley created with that open-casket funeral set the stage for the most racially charged trial in the Deep South since the Scottsboro Boys. Of course, the two killers, Roy Bryant, the offended woman's husband, and his half-brother, J.W. Milam, were acquitted by an all-white jury in nothing flat. This raised the nation's fear and loathing of the white South, and the moral impetus for the civil rights movement was crystallized.

This is a familiar story, told in other documentaries, books and lengthy magazine stories, most notably in a Look magazine story in which the accused acknowledged their guilt after being acquitted, and thus were protected from double jeopardy. Director Kevin Beauchamp therefore faces a heavy burden in telling us what's new, or, as the title has it, "untold."

He sets out the story in straight chronological order, with current interviews with Till's now-elderly friends and family to recount the days before and after the killing. There is no narration, only placards to move us along to each chapter.

The best moments, by far, are the black-and-white archival footage. There is the all-white courtroom, people fanning themselves, the unusual close-ups of faces, Mobley's remarkable composure at the time. We see Medgar Evers there, eight years before his assassination. When Bryant gives his wife a long, open-mouth kiss on camera just after acquittal—they look like they're at the twin bill at the drive-in—it makes the flesh crawl.

The archival interviews with Moses Wright, the dead boy's grandfather, belong in a museum.

Old even then, unadorned, plain-spoken, country, he gave the trial its most electrifying moment. On the witness stand, he was asked if he saw the killer in the courtroom. He stood and pointed at the men—this iconic image is in the film—and uttered the immortal two-syllable indictment: "Thar he."

That is what is known as poetry, and it is frustrating the documentary doesn't have more of it. For a movie that bills itself as "untold," there's no "gee-whiz" moment of revelation. There are many fine interviews, apparently some of them new, but there is no narration to tell us which ones. There is a predictable soundtrack of tinkling piano and a gospel choir. There is a disjointed series of events at the end of the film, including what appears to be a New York City Council meeting where the killing was discussed, but I wasn't sure why it was included.

Further, there are no significant modern-day interviews with any of the white participants in the trial, the killer's families, or even local political figures discussing the case. (Both killers are now deceased. They were shunned by the white community in Mississippi after their magazine tell-all and did not lead happy lives thereafter. There's no mention of that sort of interesting postscript.) If those people refused to be interviewed, it would have been helpful to know, and a subtle buttressing of the argument that perhaps people still living know more than they are saying.

The Till murder case has been reopened—the film tells us it's because of the film itself, an odd bit of self-reference—but I left the theater not knowing exactly what the new evidence was. Does it tell us that other people might have been involved? Yes, but that's always been known. Are some named here? Well, sort of, but as I understood it, these were black men who may have been coerced into helping subdue Till that night.

The movie rolls to an end, the lights come up, and you leave the theater feeling moved by a mother's courage, sickened by the crime and a little frustrated, wondering if this unquiet moment in our history will ever rest easy.

SIGNIFICANCE

Emmett Louis Till was the victim of lynching, and his death has been classified as a racially motivated hate crime. After the end of the Civil War in the United States, racial tensions were extremely high. Between 1880 and 1940, the criminal practice of lynching was used as a fear-based bias crime against disliked or feared racial, ethnic, or cultural groups. Historically, the largest numbers of lynchings were perpetrated against African-Americans. The majority of the lynchings took place between 1880 and 1920; their prevalence dwindled considerably thereafter. Very few lynchings were recorded after 1968.

The practice of lynching, widely written about by the media (primarily in local and regional newspapers) and in the popular press, involved the murder, either spontaneous or planned, by a group of people (often times a large crowd, or mob), of a member of a socially undesirable group, usually by some combination of hanging or shooting. At times, torture, in the form of cutting, mutilation, dismemberment, or burning, was employed as well. The victim of the lynching is usually accused of a crime. The bodies were generally left in conspicuous public places. Although lynchings occurred throughout the country, significantly more were reported in southern areas than in northern regions.

All categories of lynchings were more likely to take place in rural than in urban areas and far more

Friends and family watch as members of the FBI evidence response team exhume the body of Emmett Till at Burr Oak Cemetery in Alsip, Illinois, in 2005. A crane is lifting Till's coffin onto a truck. © FRANK POLICH/REUTERS/CORBIS

prevalent among the people of lower socioeconomic status than among the middle or upper classes. Those who participated in lynchings were seldom arrested or prosecuted for their crimes.

As legally defined, hate crimes (also called bias crimes) are based on an underlying assumption that the victim is fundamentally different, and somehow inferior to, the perpetrator. What is legally novel about this definition is that it qualifies or characterizes already existent types of crime and provides particular penalties based on their occurrence. That is, it increases the penalty for certain types of behavior or activity that have already been deemed criminal. It also specifies that the rationale for the criminal act has to do with an underlying belief system; the perpetrator must target the victim based on convictions regarding the race, gender, age, ethnicity, religion, disability status, sexual orientation, sexual minority group membership, or cultural group to which the victim is believed to belong.

The term "hate crime" originated during the 1980s in response to an incident in New York City in which a group of white adolescents who were heard to

be shouting racist remarks killed an African-American man who was running from them. The term "bias crime" may be a more accurate descriptor for this type of event, it the crimes typically arise from prejudice or bias against a group or type of individual, and may be motivated more by a belief system than by underlying emotions or feelings of hatred (although the two often occur simultaneously).

The perpetrators of hate crimes are often adjudicated differently than those whose crimes are believed to be of a random nature. Many are given enhanced sentences in which they receive a higher or more stringent penalty for the commission of this type of activity. In large part, this is due to the underlying philosophy in which bias is likened to terrorist or extremist behavior: it targets an entire class or type of person based on a belief system, and therefore it consists of symbolic behavior as much as it does of actual behavior. The perpetrator may view the target group as subhuman and therefore believe that it is acceptable to seriously harm or kill its members. The crime itself is meant to communicate a message to the entire group: when a synagogue is burned down in a bias crime, it is meant to cause symbolic harm to all persons who are Jewish. The same is true of the lynching of an African-American, the murder of a homeless person, or the beating of an openly gay male.

FURTHER RESOURCES

Books

Crime and Justice: A Review of Research, edited by Michael Tonry. Chicago: University of Chicago Press, 1997.

Jenness, Valerie, and Kendal Broad. *Hate Crimes: New Social Movements and the Politics of Violence*. New York: Aldine De Gruyter, 1997.

Nelson, Marilyn, and Philippe Lardy. *A Wreath for Emmett Till*. New York: Houghton Mifflin Company, 2005.

Herbert Shapiro. *White Violence and Black Response: From Reconstruction to Montgomery*. Amherst, Mass.: University of Massachusetts Press, 1988.

Thompson, Julius E. *The Black Press in Mississippi*. Gainesville, Fla.: University Press of Florida, 1993.

Till-Mobley, Mamie, and Christopher Benson. *Death of Innocence: The Story of the Hate Crime that Changed America*. New York: Random House, 2003.

Wakefield, Dan. *Revolt in the South*. New York: Grove Press, 1960.

Web sites

The American Experience: The Murder of Emmett Till. "Killers' Confession: The Shocking Story of Approved Killing in Mississippi." <http://www.pbs.org/wgbh/amex/till/sfeature/sf_look_confession.html> (accessed March 10, 2006).

Southern Poverty Law Center. "Intelligence Report: Recognizing and Responding to Hate Crimes." <http://www.splcenter.org/intel/law.jsp> (accessed March 10, 2006).

Yale-New Haven Teachers Institute. "The Negro Holocaust: Lynching and Race Riots in the United States, 1880–1950." <http://www.yale.edu/ynhti/curriculum/units/1979/2/79.02.04.x.html#b> (accessed March 10, 2006).

More Than Saddam Is On Trial

Newspaper article

By: Michael R. Marrus

Date: October 18, 2005

Source: Marrus, Michael R. "More Than Saddam Is On Trial." *The Globe and Mail* (October 18, 2005): A25.

About the Author: Michael Marrus is the dean of the University of Toronto's School of Graduate Studies. He holds graduate degrees from the University of California at Berkeley and has served as a fellow of the Royal Historical Society and the Royal Society of Canada. He is an internationally recognized historian for his work on the holocaust and has written five books on the subject. He also serves as a Vatican advisor.

INTRODUCTION

In December 2004, following the U.S. led invasion of Iraq, American forces captured Saddam Hussein near his hometown of Tikrit. His incarceration marked the end to his rule of Iraq, which began in 1979 when he seized the presidency of the country. During his twenty-four-year rule, at least 280,000 Iraqis were allegedly killed under his orders, including the use of mustard and nerve gas to kill over 5,000 civilians on a single day in the town of Halabja. As a result, the government that replaced Saddam Hussein's regime plans to charge the former leader with a series of crimes, many deemed as crimes against humanity that carry the death penalty.

On July 1, 2004, the Supreme Iraqi Criminal Tribunal (originally known as the Iraqi Special Tribunal) brought seven preliminary charges against Saddam Hussein, advising that more precise charges would follow. The preliminary charges cover the duration of Hussein's rule and range from the killing of religions leaders to the gassing of civilians and the invasion of Kuwait.

Since his rise to the presidency, many allegations of crimes against humanity have been raised against Saddam Hussein. The preliminary charges initially brought against him span the years of his rule and include retaliation for uprisings and assassination attempts. According to the BBC, the United Nations High Commission for Refugees denounced Hussein's regime for "widespread, systematic torture and the maintaining of decrees prescribing cruel and inhuman punishment as a penalty for offenses." Many of the offenses relate to religious or ethnically motivated activities. Spanning thirty years, the initial charges include the July 1974 arrest and execution of Shia religious leaders. In addition, thousands of Shia Muslims who were arrested on suspicion of supporting the 1979 Iranian revolution have never been seen again. With evidence emerging of at least 270 mass graves throughout Iraq, many believe that these graves hold the remains of these religious dissidents. The Kurds

Presiding Judge Rizgar Mohammed Amin, back to camera, speaks to the defendents at the trial of Saddam Hussein, charged with crimes against humanity, begins in a heavily fortified courthouse in Baghdad's Green Zone in October 2005. Hussein's co-defendants are: second row, right to left, Abdullah Kazim Ruwayyid, Mizhar Abdullah Ruwayyid, and Taha Yassin Ramadan. In the third row, right to left, are Barzan Ibrahim, Ali Dayim Ali, and Mohammed Azawi. AP IMAGES

also were targets for oppression under the Hussein regime. One of these operations, which appears in the preliminary charges against Saddam Hussein, occurred in 1983. Under Hussein's orders, Iraqi security forces entered the northern province of Arbil and arrested approximately 8,000 male members of the Brazani clan. The men were taken to southern Iraq and have yet to be accounted for.

Additional charges brought against Saddam Hussein relate to an organized effort to eradicate Kurds from Iraq in 1988. Between February and September 1988, Hussein initiated the Anfal campaign of ethnic cleansing against the Kurdish population of northern Iraq. Documentation secured following the 1991 Gulf War and eyewitness accounts gathered by international human rights organizations suggest that almost 182,000 Kurds were killed during the campaign. In August 1988, approximately 5,000 civilians, including women, children, and babies, were gassed in a single day. Under the orders of General Ali Hassan

al-Majid, Saddam Hussein's cousin and the commander of the Anfal campaign, Iraqi forces bombarded the Kurdish town of Halabja with bombs made of mustard and nerve gases.

Other charges of crimes against humanity brought against Saddam Hussein relate to the events preceding to and following the Iraqi invasion of Kuwait in August 1990. In addition to the alleged torture and execution of Kuwaiti citizens after the invasion, Iraqi soldiers are said to have looted Kuwait City and kidnapped Kuwaiti citizens under the orders of Saddam Hussein. Also under orders, Iraqi soldiers set fire to more than 700 oil wells and opened pipelines so that the oil would pour into the Persian Gulf. Following the war, northern Kurds and southern Shia Muslims rebelled against the Hussein regime. Hussein took revenge for the uprisings by using massive military force and destroying southern marshlands and habitat, depopulating many indigenous Arabs.

PRIMARY SOURCE

The trial of Saddam Hussein for crimes against humanity begins tomorrow in Baghdad. Will this be, as some predict, "the trial of the century"? Will it advance global human rights? And will it, as some supporters of the Bush administration hope, lend legitimacy to the U.S.-promoted Iraqi regime and the American cause in Iraq, for which the humanitarian objective is perhaps the last credible justification for the original U.S. policy?

Proponents of the trial rightly advance the justice-seeking context of the proceedings against the former Iraqi dictator, who will be charged, to start, with the murder of more than 140 Shia Muslim inhabitants of the village of Dujail in 1982 in retaliation for a failed assassination attempt. Tomorrow's proceedings will initiate a series of made-in-Iraq trials of Mr. Hussein and senior members of his Baath Party. Champions of international law and the cause of human rights hope that the trial will focus on more than a dozen separate instances of grotesque atrocities as well as Mr. Hussein's naked aggression against Kuwait in 1990. They also hope Zimbabwe's Robert Mugabe, among others, will take note.

Unfortunately, a positive outcome in advancing global human rights is very much in doubt. The reason has to do with the nature of high-profile war crimes trials and the messages that emanate from them. "The purpose of a trial is to render justice, and nothing else," Hannah Arendt wrote in criticism of the Israeli prosecution of Adolf Eichmann in 1961, arguing that such trials should be narrowly confined to specific charges against the accused. Others maintain that successful prosecutions of those who have committed grave human-rights violations should serve wider purposes—to assert the international community's principled rejection of impunity for gross wrongdoing, and to set standards by which all powerful leaders must stand ready to be judged.

Robert Jackson, chief U.S. prosecutor at Nuremberg, put it famously at the International Military Tribunal in 1945: "We must never forget that the record on which we judge these defendants today is the record on which history will judge us tomorrow. To pass these defendants a poisoned chalice is to put it to our own lips as well. We must summon such detachment and intellectual integrity to our task that this trial will commend itself to posterity as fulfilling humanity's aspirations to do justice."

How will the trial of Saddam Hussein commend itself to posterity? Much will depend on the procedures followed, including fairness to the accused—and on this we need to wait and see. But, as for the trial's wider pedagogic purposes, there are both worrying signs and serious structural defects.

The three-judge Iraqi panel that will decide Mr. Hussein's fate will certainly have difficulty establishing its credibility as an independent tribunal. According to The Associated Press this week, the Iraqi judges "received special training from American, British and Australian experts" (that is, from the leading countries in the invasion coalition). And although the Iraqi Special Tribunal's statute says costs will be borne by the Iraqis, AP notes that "the court and the training were financed by a $75-million U.S. budget allocation" in 2004. Quite unlike Nuremberg, then, where there was no doubt about the independence of those sitting in judgment, legitimate questions have been raised about whether the Iraqi panel meets international standards in this respect.

The Hussein trial also will face one of the gravest defects of Nuremberg—the complicity of one party to the trial, sitting in judgment, namely the Soviet Union, with Nazi Germany's criminal rampage against Europe in 1939. Charged with the massacre of Iraqis in 1982, the Iraqi dictator will surely point to how closely associated he was, immediately afterward, with the United States, now the leading voice, after the Iraqi government, in identifying Mr. Hussein's crimes against the Iraqi people. In the early 1980s, the Reagan administration reached out to Mr. Hussein, renewed ties broken off in 1967 and backed him in his fight against Iran—and this notwithstanding Mr. Hussein's notorious criminality at the time.

You can find photographs on the Internet showing Donald Rumsfeld, then a presidential envoy and now Secretary of Defence, shaking hands with the Iraqi dictator just when the latter was using chemical weapons against Iraqi Kurdish insurgents. If permitted, Mr. Hussein will give his side of this seemingly compromising relationship; if not, he will be seen to have been unfairly silenced. In either case, the intended didactic message will be severely qualified.

Critics of the Iraqi Special Tribunal—including Amnesty International and Human Rights Watch—also have pointed to the scope of the charges, which seem to have been narrowly cast in order to avoid another of Nuremberg's embarrassments: tu quoque arguments alleging that accusers share guilt with the accused for the kinds of crimes committed by those in the dock. According to the Special Tribunal's statute, its jurisdiction extends only to crimes committed up to May 1, 2003—the day when President George W. Bush announced the end of "major combat operations" associated with the invasion of Iraq. As with Nuremberg, when the accused denounced the Allies for their own criminality, Mr. Hussein's lawyers will almost certainly accuse coalition forces of war crimes and crimes against humanity. Undeserving though these arguments may be when compared with the scale of Mr. Hussein's atrocities, their exclusion via the tribunal's statute is likely to leave a very bad taste.

No one expects the Iraqi Special Tribunal to be perfect, and the history of international humanitarian law, including that defined at Nuremberg 60 years ago, shows that justice-seeking can rise above the imperfections in pioneering efforts. For all its flaws, the Nuremberg prosecution represented a historic effort to overcome its deficiencies. "That four great nations, flushed with victory and stung with injury, stay the hand of vengeance and voluntarily submit their captive enemies to the judgment of the law," Robert Jackson said, "is one of the most significant tributes that power has ever paid to reason." Saddam Hussein's trial will have difficulty meeting that standard.

SIGNIFICANCE

The first trial date for Saddam Hussein was set for October 19, 2005. The charges against Hussein and seven other defendants relate to the 1982 execution of approximately 150 men and boys from the town of Dujail. These events are pursued as the first trial because the events are well documented, including video recordings of the massacre. The charges involve retaliation for an assassination attempt on Saddam Hussein by members of the Dawa religious party on July 8, 1982.

The Supreme Iraqi Criminal Tribunal is the court that will try Saddam Hussein. The court was created during the Coalition Provisional Authority and funded by the American Justice Department unit called Regime Crimes Liaison Office. The U.S. has provided $75 million for the court's formation. Unlike the U.S. court system, the defendants will appear before a lead judge who will possess complete knowledge of the findings of the investigative tribunal that referred the case. Defendants are allowed at least one counsel in the court and have access to an appellate system, if convicted. Also, unlike U.S. courts, if the defendant chooses to remain silent, this may be taken as a sign of guilt and the court holds no requirement to prove guilt beyond a reasonable doubt. Once the convicted defendant has exhausted the appeals, sentences are to be carried out within 30 days. Raid Juhi, the chief investigative judge for the Iraqi Special Tribunal, asserts that the "mass of evidence is consistent with the civilized international standards that have been set for the tribunal." Although many in the international community sought a trial similar to that of Slobodan Milosevic at the Hague, the Iraqi court has sought to establish itself with Iraqi judges trained in international criminal law by the U.S., the United Kingdom, the Netherlands, Italy, nongovernmental organizations, academics, and other legal experts. In addition to the training, the court has convened mock trials in the United Kingdom.

Legal custody of Saddam Hussein was transferred to the Iraqis on July 1, 2005, shortly after the interim government took office. The Iraqi government then reinstated the death penalty, which the U.S. had abolished. The Iraqi government has opted to try Saddam Hussein on twelve to fourteen individual charges, most of which carry the death penalty.

FURTHER RESOURCES

Periodicals

Burns, John F. "First Case Against Hussein, Involving killings in 1982 is Sent to a Trial Court." *New York Times* (July 18, 2005).

Burns, John F., and Neil A. Lewis Washington. "First Court Case of Saddam Stems from "2 Deaths." *New York Times* (June 6, 2005).

Web sites

BBC News. "Charges Facing Saddam." <http://news.bbc.co.uk/2/hi/middle_east/3320293.stm> (accessed January 10, 2005).

Human Rights Watch. "Saddam's Day in Court: Fair Trial at Risk." <http://www.hrw.org/english/docs/2005/10/16/iraq11883.htm> (accessed January 10, 2005).

Bicycling While Black

Federal Appeals Court Revives Michigan Lawsuit

Legal decision

By: Boyce F. Martin, Jr.

Date: June 8, 2005

Source: *Bennett v. City of Eastpointe,* 410 F.3d 810 (6th Cir. 2005).

About the Author: Boyce F. Martin, Jr. was appointed by President Jimmy Carter as Circuit Judge to the United States Court of Appeals for the Sixth Circuit in 1979. He served as Chief Judge from 2000 to 2003.

INTRODUCTION

Police in the northeastern Detroit suburb of Eastpointe regularly stopped young black males who were riding bicycles in the predominantly white city. While

Eastpointe police denied that they used race as the sole reason to stop the bicyclers, a federal appeals court ruled that the city had engaged in racial profiling and unreasonable searches.

The Fourth Amendment declares that the people have a right to be free from "unreasonable searches and seizures." The Supreme Court has interpreted this protection, as well as the words "search" and "seizure," in different ways at different times. In the years after 1969, an unreasonable search has been defined as almost any search carried out without a warrant.

Eastpointe had experienced a series of bicycle thefts by young black men. The police received instructions from their chief to investigate any black youths riding through Eastpointe subdivisions. While such an admission by the police appeared to reveal that they had engaged in illegal conduct, police also looked for suspicious behavior in deciding whether to stop young men.

The ACLU argued that racial profiling was especially dangerous to apply to children because it held the potential of stigmatizing them for life. The ACLU sought $21 million in damages—$1 million for each person suing Eastpointe. The organization also asked the U.S. District Court to appoint someone to monitor the city's police practices. Eastpoint police were also accused of singling out black motorists for traffic stops.

▮ PRIMARY SOURCE

I.

Eastpointe, formerly East Detroit, is a suburb adjacent to Detroit. The 2000 census figures indicate that Eastpointe is 92.1 percent white and 4.7 percent African-American. Detroit was found to be 12.3 percent white and 81.6 percent African-American. Eight Mile Road, made famous by the popular movie "8 Mile" divides the two cities and is commonly known as a racial dividing line. The plaintiffs claim that they were subjected to racial discrimination when they crossed Eight Mile Road into Eastpointe. Against the backdrop of each individual Fourteenth Amendment claim is reference to the "DeWeese Memorandum." This memorandum was drafted by Eastpointe's current Chief of Police, Fred DeWeese, following a meeting he had with Charles King, Sr., the plaintiff and next friend to his minor-son-plaintiffs in King. In that memo, distributed only to the city manager, DeWeese wrote that when he was a Lieutenant, "[f]rom May of 1995 to August of 95…I was assigned as a Shift Commander on the Afternoon Shift…. My instructions to the

officers were to investigate any black youths riding through our subdivisions…. I would expect that our officers would investigate younger black males riding bicycles."…

Here, the plaintiffs rely on the DeWeese Memorandum as the policy that wrought the constitutional violations upon them. For the plaintiffs to prevail, therefore, they must demonstrate that DeWeese had policymaking authority. The plaintiffs have failed, however, to account for the fact that at the time of the instructions, now-Chief of Police DeWeese was simply a lieutenant, and not a policy-making official. [citation omitted] ("DeWeese was not Chief of Police during the time these earlier bike stops occurred, so his action or inaction could not result in ratification of a policy behind those incidents."). The plaintiffs argue that when DeWeese became Chief of Police, he did not rescind his earlier instructions, and therefore the Memorandum became city policy. We decline to adopt such a broad reading of the Memorandum without any evidence to support the assertion. The Memorandum, though arguably discriminatory, was only memorializing prior and limited instructions, made to four or five officers under his command on an afternoon shift. There is no evidence whatsoever, that after becoming Chief of Police, DeWeese renewed these instructions or that they motivated the conduct of the officers, who were not on the afternoon shift, years later. In sum, we hold that the DeWeese Memorandum did not constitute official city policy and therefore affirm the district court's grant of summary judgment in favor of the City of Eastpointe.…

C. INCIDENT # 5, APRIL 18, 1996

Incident # 5 occurred on April 18, 1996, involved plaintiff Wilson and his two friends, non-plaintiffs Johnson and Traylor, and defendant-Officer Lulko. The plaintiff alleges that he and his friends, all on their own bikes, were riding along the sidewalk at a normal pace, not doing tricks or interfering with traffic, but once they crossed Eight Mile Road, Officer Lulko pulled his patrol car into an intersection in front of the youths and blocked their path. Wilson alleges that Lulko then interrogated them about what they were doing and where they were headed, that Lulko patted Wilson down, and asked who owned the bikes and if they went to school around there.

Officer Lulko asserts that he observed three bike riders riding between parked vehicles, jumping the curb in front of businesses, and allegedly interfering with traffic in violation of state law. Because this allegedly observed activity raised safety and theft concerns, Lulko stopped the youths. According to Lulko, he never left his vehicle, which contradicts Wilson's claim that Lulko patted him down. Lulko states the encounter lasted five minutes during which he explained the safety concerns and provided the youths with directions.

1. § 1983 Racial Discrimination Claim

[W]e reverse the district court's grant of summary judgment in favor of the defendant-officers.

2. § 1983 Fourth Amendment Search and Seizure Claim

...[T]here are genuine issues of material fact in dispute as to both whether Officer Lulko had reasonable suspicion to stop the plaintiffs and whether Officer Lulko frisked Wilson. When viewing the facts in the light most favorable to Wilson, it is clear that summary judgment for the defendants was inappropriate.

...[W]e affirm the district court's grant of summary judgment in favor of Chiefs DeWeese and Danbert, as well as the City of Eastpointe to the extent the plaintiffs have alleged a Fourth Amendment claim against those parties....

E. INCIDENT # 8, APRIL 29, 1997

Incident # 8 occurred on April 29, 1997, and involved plaintiff-brothers James and Jermaine Shaffer, non-plaintiffs McCree and Loker, and defendant-Officer Lulko. The youths rode to Arbor Drugs to buy a carton of milk for the Shaffers' mother and were on their way back to the Shaffers' house, riding down Brock Street in Eastpointe, a few blocks from the Detroit border, when Officer Lulko turned his car in front of the youths and blocked their paths. Officer Lulko exited the car and ordered the boys to get off their bikes and put their hands on the car. Three of them submitted, while James Shaffer did not stop and instead dismounted his bike and walked two blocks toward Eight Mile Road. As he was about to cross back into Detroit, another Eastpointe officer pulled his patrol car in front of James, threw him against the car, handcuffed him, and forcibly detained him in the patrol car. During this time, Lulko ordered the youths to place their hands on the hood of the police car and conducted patdown searches of the other three youths and told them they should have receipts for their bikes when they come over "Eight Mile" into Eastpointe. Eventually, the boys were released, but as they walked back toward Eight Mile Road, the officers followed behind in the police car until they crossed back into Detroit.

Officer Lulko claims to have encountered four bicyclists riding double, which is in contrast to the youths' claims that they were all riding their own bikes, and would conflict with the fact that James got off of his own bike and continued toward Eight Mile disregarding Lulko's order to stop. The defendants also note that James admits to riding "four abreast" through side streets, which would be a violation of state-law.

1. § 1983 Racial Discrimination Claim

...[W]e reverse the district court's grant of summary judgment in favor of the defendant-officers. Moreover, in this instance, summary judgment was particularly inappropriate because of the alleged racial tones to the officers's conduct—specifically, Officer Lulko's statement that the youths should have receipts for their bike when coming into Eastpointe and the officers' conduct in driving their police cruisers behind the youths until they crossed over Eight Mile back into Detroit. These allegations at the very least raise a genuine issue of material fact as to whether the stop was more burdensome or intrusive than it otherwise would have been because of race. We hold that a genuine issue of material fact does exist as to whether race contributed to the stop and intrusions during the stop, and therefore reverse the grant of summary judgment in favor of Officer Lulko.

2. § 1983 Fourth Amendment Search and Seizure Claim

While it may be disputed whether the youths were riding double or whether they were riding four abreast down the street, either version amounts to a violation of state law, see Mich. Comp. Laws §§ 257.658, 257.660, and therefore provides reasonable suspicion for the initial stop. Furthermore, James failed to obey a lawful order of a police officer, a violation of Eastpointe Ordinance § 658.03, and that justified stopping him. The parties do not dispute that a stop within the Fourth Amendment occurred. Because Officer Lulko had reasonable suspicion for the initial stop, the only remaining issue is whether his actions during the stop were justified. For the reasons discussed above in each of the other incidents, we reverse the district court's grant of summary judgment in favor of the defendants with regard to Jermaine Shaffer. The officers point to no facts that would justify a pat-down search of Jermaine....

F. INCIDENT # 10, JUNE 27, 1998

Incident # 10 occurred on June 27, 1998, and involved plaintiff Bush and his two friends, non-plaintiffs Thrasher and Ware, and defendant-Officer Magrita. All three youths allege that they were riding on separate bikes home from the Eastland Mall. While riding one block north of Eight Mile Road into Eastpointe, the youths were pulled over by Officer Magrita, who pulled behind them and flashed his overhead lights. The defendants allege that two of the youths were riding double. Magrita states that he observed the youths riding bikes behind closed businesses. After driving by and making eye contact with the youths, he continued on his way. Five minutes later he returned to see the youths still riding in the same place.

Bush alleged that Magrita asked whether the youths knew "anything about people coming across Eight Mile and stealing bikes on this side of Eight Mile." Bush also alleged that Magrita made a joke about a "monkey" and ordered the youths to get off their bikes and walk "back across Eight Mile," and waited to observe that they do so.

1. § 1983 Racial Discrimination Claim

...[W]e reverse the district court's grant of summary judgment in favor of the defendant-officers....

It goes without saying that we both recognize the risks and appreciate the sacrifices that law enforcement officers make on a daily basis. We are compelled to comment here, however, that we are both frustrated and concerned with what appears to be consistent disregard for basic Fourth Amendment principles by the Eastpointe Police Department and its officers, and an apparent misunderstanding by counsel as to the legal requirements for Terry stops. Counsel may shout "officer safety" until blue-in-the-face, but the Fourth Amendment does not tolerate, nor has the Supreme Court or this Court ever con-

doned, pat-down searches without some specific and articulable facts to warrant a reasonable officer in the belief that the person detained was armed and dangerous. The Supreme Court has, in interpreting the Fourth Amendment, struck a balance between the justifiable concern for officer safety when confronting an individual and the substantial individual interest in being free from unreasonable intrusion. The Framers' concerns and clear intent to protect individuals from arbitrary government intrusion was enshrined in the Fourth Amendment to prevent situations such as those alleged here—officers, having no reason to fear for their safety, may not require citizens, whom they have not arrested, to stand up against gates or place their hands on police cars, and submit to searches. This has long been the law.

For the reasons given above, we AFFIRM the district court in part, REVERSE in part, and REMAND for further proceedings consistent with this opinion....Furthermore,

Rep. Samuel "Buzz" Thomas, D-Detroit, center, addresses a news conference as the Rev. Wendell Anthony, NAACP president of the Detroit branch, left, and state Attorney General Jennifer Granholm, right, listen in Detroit, Michigan, May 31, 2001. A coalition of lawmakers and community leaders unveiled legislation designed to end racial profiling by Michigan police, saying they hoped that other states and the federal government would follow their example. AP IMAGES

we REVERSE and REMAND for further proceedings the following additional claims: ... Incident # 5: The Fourth Amendment claim for the allegedly unconstitutional stop and unconstitutional pat-down searches by Officer Lulko; ... Incident # 8: The Fourth Amendment claim for the allegedly unconstitutional stop and pat-down searches by Officer Lulko with regard to Jermaine Shaffer; Incident # 10: The Fourth Amendment claim for the allegedly unconstitutional seizure of Bush; ... On all other claims and with respect to all other defendants, we AFFIRM the district court's grant of summary judgment.

SIGNIFICANCE

Racial profiling of African American and Latino men is assumed to be widespread, but the tactic is difficult to prove. The federal government and the states only began studying the problem after the millennium, following numerous complaints by blacks who believed that they had been targeted for "driving while black." The issue has become an increasingly volatile political issue.

According to a U.S. Department of Justice study conducted in 2002 with 77,000 Americans over age 16, black, Hispanic, and white motorists are equally likely to be pulled over by the police. Theses reports give support to the argument by police officers that they stopped minorities for legitimate reasons. However, blacks and Latinos are much more likely to be searched, handcuffed, arrested, and subjected to force or the threat of it. Blacks were more likely to be arrested than whites, while Hispanics were more likely to be ticketed than blacks or whites.

Several states have investigated possible racial profiling within their borders. New Jersey discovered in 2005 that black drivers were more likely to be stopped than white drivers on the New Jersey Turnpike. In 1999, the New Jersey police had admitted to targeting minority motorists for traffic stops and agreed to federal monitoring aimed at ending the practice. A 2005 study of two million traffic stops in Illinois discovered that black and Hispanic drivers in large cities were pulled over by police at a rate that far exceeded their share of the local population. State lawmakers in Illinois, at the urging of minority groups complaining about profiling, required every police department to record details of all 2004 traffic stops. In 2005, Missouri statistics showed that for the fifth year in a row, black motorists were stopped proportionately more often than whites.

The events of 2001 made many Americans support racial profiling in some instances, as only Arab men were involved in the terrorism of September 11.

A similar fear of attack has led many Americans to approve of racial profiling of minorities. Since more minority members than whites fill the prisons, some people believe that minorities are more likely to be criminals. This point is hotly challenged by minorities and by civil libertarians such as the American Civil Liberties Union (ACLU). Kary Moss, ACLU of Michigan Executive Director stated that the Sixth Circuit ruling "is a clear sign that the court will not tolerate race-based discrimination and reinforces the constitutional principle that people cannot be searched by police in the absence of evidence of criminal activity."

FURTHER RESOURCES

Books

Bumgarner, Jeffrey B. *Profiling and Criminal Justice in America: A Reference Handbook.* Santa Barbara, Calif: ABC-CLIO, 2004.

Heumann, Milton. *Good Cop, Bad Cop: Racial Profiling and Competing Views of Justice.* New York: P. Lang, 2003.

Pampel, Fred C. *Racial Profiling.* New York: Facts on File, 2004.

Jordan Arrests Iraqi Woman in Hotel Blasts

Newspaper article

By: Hassan M. Fattah

Date: November 14, 2005

Source: Fattah, Hassan M. "Jordan Arrests Iraqi Woman in Hotel Blasts." *The New York Times* (November 14, 2005).

About the Author: Hassan Fattah serves as a Middle East correspondent for *The New York Times*. Based in Baghdad, he is also the editor of an English language newspaper *Iraq Today*. He has contributed to publications like *The New Republic* and is a sought-after commentator on issues relating to the war in Iraq and subjects relating to the Arab world.

INTRODUCTION

In late 2005 with the United-States-led war against insurgents continuing in Iraq, the Al Qaeda

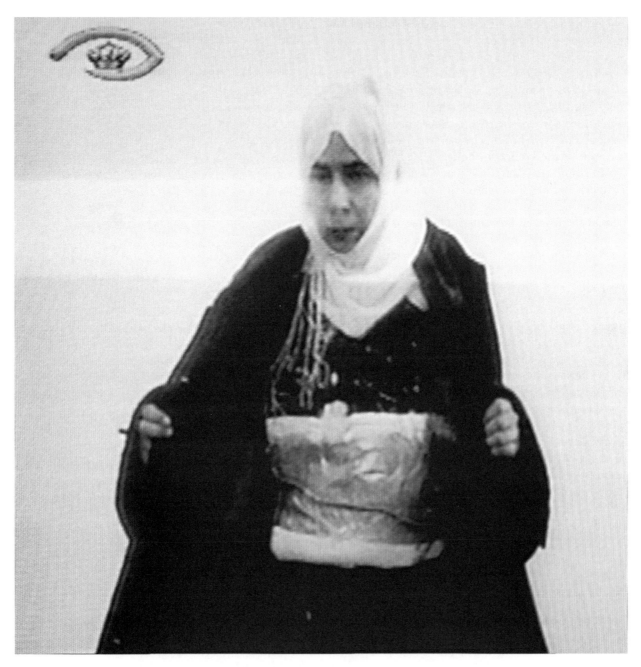

A video image shows Sajida al-Rishawi, confessing on Jordanian TV to trying to blow herself up at a hotel in Amman, showing how she strapped a device to her body, November 13, 2005. © JTV/VIA REUTERSTV/REUTERS/CORBIS

international terrorist group, which was leading the insurgency aimed against the occupation, began to seek other targets for their attacks in other parts of the world. On November 9, 2005, in an attack master-minded by Jordanian-born Abu Musab al- Zarqawi, fifty-seven people were killed in three separate attacks in the Jordanian capital of Amman. The three bomb-ings were coordinated to take place simultaneously, and all occurred in large hotels. They resulted in one of the highest one-day death tolls from terrorism in Jordanian history. The deadliest attack took place at the Radisson Hotel where a Jordanian wedding was taking place, leading to the deaths of many members of the wedding party.

A fourth attack—alleged to have been planned for an adjoining area at one of the three sites—was averted when the female suicide bomber was unable to detonate the explosives strapped to her waist. Within a day of the bombings, Jordanian security officials announced her arrest and brought her before television cameras where she admitted that she intended to serve as a fourth bomber. The woman, whose husband was one of the bombers who succeeded in detonating his explosives, was a sister of a senior aide to al-Zarqawi, and her involvement served to confirm that the Iraqi-based Al Qaeda terrorist organization was behind the Amman bombings. This was of particular significance to the Jordanian people, since al-Zarqawi was born in Jordan and it was especially shocking that a man born in Jordan would order an attack against Jordanians.

The attacks served to demonstrate al-Zarqawi's intent to make his insurgency international, extending beyond the borders of Iraq into Jordan. Even though the attacks took place at hotels primarily frequented by Westerners, the vast majority of the casualties were Jordanians. In the statement claiming responsibility for the attacks, Al Qaeda admitted that those sites were chosen because they largely cater to Westerners. In the wake of the attacks, demonstrations in support of the Jordanian monarchy and against the terrorist policies of al-Zarqawi were seen as evidence that his hopes of influencing Jordanian public opinion away from an alliance with the West and toward support of the insurgency had largely failed.

▮ PRIMARY SOURCE

AMMAN, Jordan, Nov. 13—Jordanian security officials on Sunday announced the arrest of an Iraqi woman they said was closely linked to the terrorist leader Abu Musab al-Zarqawi as a fourth bomber in the Amman hotel attacks. They also broadcast a taped confession showing her wearing a translucent explosive belt packed with ball bearings, in which she described how she had tried unsuccessfully to blow herself up.

Looking tired and nervous in a head scarf and long black coat partly concealing the bomb belt, the woman, who identified herself as Sajida Mubarak al-Rishawi, 35, was shown recounting the moments when she and her Iraqi husband, whom she described as another member of the suicide squad and who killed himself in the bombing, entered a ballroom in the Radisson Hotel last Wednesday.

"He took one end and I took another," she said. "The hotel had a wedding in it and there were women and children. My husband executed the attack. I tried to detonate but it failed. People began to run, and I ran out with them."

Fifty-seven people died at the Radisson, Days Inn and Grand Hyatt hotels in one of the worst terrorist attacks in Jordan.

Marwan Muashar, Jordan's deputy prime minister, said Ms. Rishawi is the sister of Mubarak Atrous al-Rishawi, a senior aide to Mr. Zarqawi who was killed last year by American forces in the restive Iraqi city of Falluja.

Her confession included some details of how the plot was organized and was seen here as likely to yield significant intelligence into the methods and plans of Mr. Zarqawi's group, Al Qaeda in Mesopotamia, which took responsibility for the Amman blasts.

The case has raised the possibility that Mr. Zarqawi, a Jordanian fugitive who has become the most wanted terrorist leader in Iraq, is adjusting his tactics in Jordan, where he has tried—and failed, according to Jordan security officials—to orchestrate more than 150 attacks against government targets in the past few years.

Now, these officials say, he appears out of frustration to be shifting to more vulnerable civilian targets here like hotels, where security has been less stringent.

While the videotaped confession of Ms. Rishawi appeared to represent a breakthrough and was greeted enthusiastically by many Jordanians, much about the confession remained undisclosed.

Jordanian officials would not say when or where she was arrested, when the tape was made, and whether she was told to wear the bomb belt by her interrogators.

It is unclear how much of the tape, which runs less than five minutes, was edited. It is also unclear to what extent, or indeed whether, Ms. Rishawi had been coerced into making the confession.

Jordanian officials would not say where they had detained Ms. Rishawi or explain the precise charges against her.

News of the arrest and broadcast, which were clearly aimed at showing progress in the investigation, also appeared to reflect the Jordanian government's efforts to reinforce its image of security following the bombings. Up until now, Jordan had been considered one of the Middle East's most stable and safe countries.

On Sunday, King Abdullah, speaking to CNN, stressed that he believed the ultimate targets of the bombers were Jordanians, even though the three hotel chains are Western and some of the victims were foreigners.

"Those that know Jordan, the hotels, especially the Days Inn, is a favorite place for Jordanians and Iraqis," Abdullah said. "These suicide bombers actually went and aimed at Jordanian targets. The Radisson Hotel was a Jordanian wedding with Jordanians and Palestinians, where innocent people were killed. So this was nothing to do with the West. This targeted Jordanian citizens, innocent men, women and children."

The other two bombers, also Iraqis, were identified as Rawad Jassem Muhammad Abed, 23, and Safaa Muhammad Ali, 23. The three men set off their belts almost simultaneously at the Radisson Hotel, the Grand Hyatt Hotel and the Days Inn on Wednesday night.

On the confession tape, Ms. Rishawi said she and her husband, Ali Hussein al-Shumari, 35, left Ramadi, Iraq, for Jordan on Nov. 5 with explosives belts specifically to bomb hotels in Amman. They rented an apartment in an Amman neighborhood earlier in the week, rented a car and set out for the Radisson last Wednesday evening.

An official with Jordan's intelligence services, who spoke on condition that he not be identified by name because he was not authorized to do so, said Sunday that Ms. Rishawi had been spotted on a hotel security camera and police had been searching for her for several days.

The presence of a female bomber was announced in an Internet posting claiming responsibility for the attacks by Mr. Zarqawi's group, but the posting said that she had died in the bombings.

Security men reconstructed the bodies of the suicide bombers and said they had made positive identifications using DNA analysis.

The arrest of Ms. Rishawi brought a sense of relief—even car-honking celebrations—on Amman streets, as demonstrations against the attacks continued for the fourth day. Security officials said Sunday that they were still on the lookout for 10 rental cars and several cars with Iraqi plates believed to be tied to the attacks.

Jordanian security officials said Sunday that they had found no evidence that the bombers had been assisted by Jordanians here. The officials also said they had found no evidence of contact between the bombers and Mr. Zarqawi after they had crossed into Jordan.

SIGNIFICANCE

The attacks launched against three Jordanian hotels on the November 9, 2005, forced the people of Jordan to realize that the insurgency taking place in neighboring Iraq affected their nation as well. The bombings demonstrated the growing internationalization of Al-Qaeda terrorism, showing that adherents to the group were willing to attack sites in any country that would allow them to demonstrate their opposition to the West. This article suggests that Al Qaeda had been active for some time in trying to attack targets in Jordan. After attacks on high-profile, secured targets were circumvented, al-Zarqawi adjusted his strategy and went after "softer" civilian targets. The attack, thus, demonstrates that the insurgency had entered a new phase.

In describing the arrest of Sajida Mubarak al-Rishawi, this article suggests that the Jordanian authorities used her confession as a tool to further incite public opinion against Al Qaeda. Her confession was made as public as possible—in front of television cameras—with her explosive belt still attached to her waist (details that some believed were staged by the police). In raising the possibility that the authorities "dramatized" the confession, the article sheds light on their desire to use the arrest as a means to shift public opinion further away from the terrorists.

In light of the Jordanian public's vehement reaction against the attacks, it is clear that the bombings largely failed to meet Al Qaeda's (and al-Zarqawi's) goal—winning over the hearts and minds of the Muslim world against the West. While suicide bombings in Israel have enjoyed some degree of support in the Arab world, the Jordanian attacks—resulting in mostly Muslim casualties—were met largely with outrage. Jordan's King Abdullah, who studied in the West and has established strong diplomatic ties with Western governments, made a concerted effort to emphasize that Jordanian Muslims were the targets. With this characterization of the attacks, the Jordanian leader aimed to publicly proclaim the failure of the attacks to terrorize his society and change its support of the West. The impact of these responses—both from the governments and the public at large—will best be gauged by the location and type of international targets selected by the Al Qaeda terrorist network in the future.

FURTHER RESOURCES

Books

Gunaratna, Rohan. *Inside Al Qaeda: Global Network of Terror.* New York: Berkley Trade, 2003.

Netanyahu, Benjamin. *Fighting Terrorism: How Democracies Can Defeat Domestic and International Terrorists.* New York: Farrar, Straus and Giroux, 2001.

Human Trafficking Goes On in the U.S., Too

Newspaper article

By: David Crary

Date: November 1, 2005

Source: Crary, David. "Human Trafficking Goes On in the U.S., Too." *Associated Press* (November 1, 2005).

About the Author: David Crary is a national writer with the Associated Press. He covers a variety of topics of national interest.

INTRODUCTION

The illegal trafficking in human workers to provide a source of cheap forced labor continues to exist in the twenty-first century, long after the nineteenth century banning of slavery. People from Africa, Asia, and Latin America are recruited with the promise of worthwhile employment, or are kidnapped, and then forced to work for little or no pay at menial, strenuous, or sexually exploitative jobs in locations throughout the world. There are estimates that 10,000–15,000 people are trafficked into the U.S. each year, many used as forced laborers.

Forced laborers often sign an agreement that indentures them for a certain amount of work at very low wages. They may be coerced into a contract that gives a middle man a certain percentage of the laborer's earnings. In some cases, workers may be provided by a family or village to another family or individual to pay off debts. Forced laborers are often closely monitored by their employers, required to work long hours, not allowed to go out in public alone, and often abused. In many cases, the laborers have little knowledge of their legal rights, and often may not speak the local language. These deficiencies, along with threats from the employer that they will be beaten or jailed, often make laborers reluctant to attempt to remedy their situations.

Research by the Human Rights Center at the University of California, Berkeley, has shown that forced laborers in the U.S. come from many different racial groups. Chinese make up the largest percentage, followed by Mexicans and Vietnamese. Sometimes these forced workers do not come from abroad, but are forced into labor from within the U.S. Forced labor operations have been found in at least ninety U.S. cities, typically in large states such as California, Florida, New York, and Texas, which have large immigrant populations. There are five main sectors in which forced laborers are generally found—prostitution and sex services, domestic and household services, agriculture, sweatshops or factories, and restaurant and hotel work.

PRIMARY SOURCE

LOS ANGELES—Florencia Molina's personal hellhole was a dressmaking shop on the outskirts of Los Angeles. She worked there up to 17 hours a day, seven days a week, and lived there, too, without the option of showering or washing her clothes.

Other victims of American-style human trafficking have had very different venues for ordeals just as bad or worse—brothels in San Francisco, bars in New Jersey, slave-labor farm camps in Florida, a small-town tree-cutting business owned by a New Hampshire couple.

Trafficking is a stubborn problem and a staggering one worldwide, affecting an estimated 600,000 to 800,000 victims a year. Federal officials say 14,500 to 17,500 of them are trafficked to the United States, where the myriad forms of modern-day slavery present an elusive target for those trying to eradicate it.

Victims have come from at least 50 countries in almost every part of the world and are trafficked to virtually every state—to clandestine factories, restaurants, farms, massage parlors, even private homes where women and girls are kept in servitude.

"Human trafficking is so hidden you don't know who you're fighting—the victims are so scared, they're not going to tell you what's happening to them," said Given Kachepa, himself a former victim of a scam which exploited Zambian orphans touring the United States in a boys' choir.

Aligned against the traffickers is an array of federal, state and local government agencies, teamed up with an odd coalition of private groups that include Christian conservatives and left-of-center immigrant-rights advocates. The result is perhaps the most far-reaching anti-trafficking campaign of any nation, yet some victim support groups are questioning its effectiveness.

They contend that federal criteria offering assistance to victims only if they help prosecute their traffickers deters some from seeking help. Others say the government has placed too much emphasis on sex trafficking and too little on workplace abuses at sweatshops, farms and elsewhere.

"We see sex cases being prioritized (by federal prosecutors), but other cases we're having a hard time getting looked at," said Elissa Steglich, an attorney for the Chicago-based Midwest Immigrant and Human Rights Center. "Whatever type of slavery you're dealing with, they're horrors all the same."

Molina was the beneficiary of one case in which the anti-trafficking campaign worked as intended. Her helpers—as she escaped from the dress shop, learned English and gained legal U.S. residence—included the FBI and the Los Angeles-based Coalition to Abolish Slavery and Trafficking, which provides victims with shelter, legal aid, self-help workshops and other services.

Now a cashier at a discount store and an anti-trafficking advocate, Molina was enticed to California by a woman back home in Mexico's Puebla state, who promised a job and free accommodations.

"I came to the United States with lots of dreams, but when I got here, my dreams were stolen," said Molina, 33, who left three children behind in Mexico.

On Jan. 1, 2002, she worked her first shift at the dressmaker's, sewing roughly 200 party dresses over 12 hours.

Later, the shifts often stretched to 17 hours a day. Molina was locked into the shop at night—sleeping with a co-worker in a small storage room. The shop manager paid Molina roughly $100 a week, confiscated her identity documents, and told her she would be arrested if she went to the authorities.

"For me, it was completely dark, without money, without English, no papers, nothing," Molina said in an interview. "The owner told me, 'You can try to do whatever you want. Dogs in this country have more rights than you.'"

After working 40 days, Molina summoned up the nerve to flee, and soon encountered FBI agents who were investigating the dress shop. They sought her cooperation in prosecuting the owner, and Molina—after difficult deliberations—agreed to help.

"It was really a hard decision," she said. "The owner had always told me I would pay the consequences—or my family in Mexico would suffer—if I went to the authorities. But I thought to myself, 'I don't want one more person to be in the situation I was in.'"

In exchange for her cooperation, Molina received a T-visa—a special status created by Congress in 2000 that allows trafficking victims who assist prosecutors to remain in the United States for three years and then apply for permanent residence. Under the visa provisions, Molina's three children—14, 12 and 9—have received permission to join her in California.

Though Congress authorized up to 5,000 T-visas per year, fewer than 700 had been issued overall as of Sep-

tember. Some victim-support experts say the relatively low numbers result from overly strict criteria, notably the requirement that victims assist prosecutors.

"It can be a very difficult decision to come forward and begin a criminal complaint when a victim has every reason to believe a trafficker can make good on a threat against family members," said Steglich, the Chicago immigrant rights attorney.

"There are concerns we're not able to do all we can for those victims who don't want to come forward. We'd like to see more flexibility."

Federal officials defend the rules as necessary to separate fraudulent claims from genuine trafficking cases and to put traffickers out of business.

"The cooperation requirement is essential," said Bradley Schlozman, the Justice Department's acting assistant attorney general for civil rights. "These traffickers are extraordinarily evil—if a victim doesn't come forward, that trafficker is going to turn around and exploit other individuals."

Wade Horn, assistant secretary for children and families with the Department of Health and Human Services, said reaching victims and getting them to speak up is a key goal of a new federal program. A national hot line has been set up, fielding more than 2,500 calls to date; the hot line is being advertised in ethnic newspapers and printed on matchbooks distributed in places where victims might find them, such as ladies' rooms in bars and fast-food restaurants.

"The problem is the traffickers are very good at controlling their victims," Horn said. "They don't have access to TV, their ability to learn English is restricted, so getting the message directly to the victims is difficult."

Anti-trafficking task forces have been established in 22 areas nationwide, and training sessions are being held for social workers, health care workers and police officers to educate them about trafficking.

"A cop arrests some street prostitutes, puts them in jail and tries to get someone to deport them—that's exactly what traffickers say to their victims," Horn said. "The cops think they're just doing what they're supposed to do. ... We're training them to know what to look for, what to ask."

Some victims are forcibly abducted to the United States by criminal gangs, but many come willingly, swayed by promises of good jobs or marriage that turn out to be false. Their documents are confiscated by their traffickers, and they are forced into slave labor or prostitution.

Maria Suarez, for example, came from Mexico to Los Angeles legally in 1976, a naive 16-year-old with sixth-grade education and no English, hoping to find work. She was offered a housecleaning job at the home of a 68-year-old man who instead converted her into a virtual slave—threatening her and her family if she told anyone of the rapes and beatings that ensued over the next five years.

In 1981, the man was killed by a neighbor; Suarez agreed to hide the weapon, was convicted of conspiracy to commit murder and sentenced to 25 years to life. Officials later confirmed Suarez's claim of being a battered woman; she was paroled in 2003 and subsequently certified as a trafficking victim eligible for a T-visa. She can stay in the United States at least though next year.

Now 45, Suarez attends Pasadena City College, hoping to gain U.S. citizenship and become a social worker. She urges authorities to be understanding of sex-trafficking victims who are reluctant to speak out.

"It was a disgrace," she said. "How was I going to confront my family and tell them what was happening to me?"

Had the neighbor not killed her abuser, "I would have died there," Suarez said. "I was too scared to tell anyone what was happening. You're overwhelmed by threats of harm to you or your family."

Prior to the Trafficking Victims Protection Act of 2000, no comprehensive federal law existed to prosecute traffickers. Since 2001, the Justice Department says it has prosecuted 277 traffickers—a threefold increase over the previous four years—and has obtained convictions in every case.

Schlozman said the Justice Department is intent on combating all types of trafficking, but estimated that about 75 percent of the prosecutions involved sex trafficking.

Some victims' advocates say the government stresses the sex cases because they generate more news coverage or because they are the priority of conservative Christian groups that form an important part of the Bush administration's political base.

"Christian evangelicals see this as an important mission—rescuing women from sex trafficking," said New York University law professor Michael Wishnie, a specialist in immigrant labor issues. "There's a risk of distracting attention from much more common situations (in sweatshops) that many more people find themselves in."

Wing Lam, head of the Chinese Staff and Workers Association in New York City's Chinatown, tries to assist low-paid workers who are abused by their employers but may not qualify as trafficking victims.

Many pay to be smuggled into the United States, then take grueling jobs paying under minimum wage. Because of their illegal status, they hesitate to complain to authorities; the employers are rarely punished.

"The authorities think the workers are colluding with the bosses—that they're not victims because they don't complain," Lam said.

Laura Germino, who combats slave labor on farms as a leader of the Florida-based Coalition of Immokalee Workers, said federal agencies could undermine trafficking by cracking down on all types of workplace exploitation.

"You can't view trafficking in a vacuum," she said. "It takes root in industries that already have a range of labor violations—subpoverty wages, no benefits, no labor relations."

Traditionally, law enforcement agencies were unsympathetic to undocumented immigrants, regardless of their situation. However, the recent anti-trafficking initiatives have changed the equation, both for the authorities and the private groups they now rely on to win the confidence of victims.

"Federal prosecutors are not used to dealing with immigrant victims of crime from a positive perspective, so there's been a very difficult, steep learning curve," said immigration law expert Gail Pendleton. "It takes time to build trust with immigrant communities. You can't just put up a sign saying 'We help trafficking victims' and expect people to come."

An estimated 40 percent of trafficking victims are under 18, most of them girls. Susan Krehbiel of the Lutheran Immigration and Refugee Service said many of these children are sexually exploited in the United States after traveling here with the consent of relatives who were told genuine opportunities awaited.

Krehbiel conducts workshops with child welfare workers who are unfamiliar with trafficking. "A lot of people thought we were going to talk about the problem overseas—they didn't realize it's a problem in their own backyard," she said.

Given Kachepa was one such young victim; as an 11-year-old orphan in his homeland of Zambia he was recruited into a boys choir that toured the United States for 18 months. Promises of education, free clothes and money for his family proved false, and the boys—constantly threatened by their handlers—were forced through an arduous concert schedule until authorities finally intervened.

Kachepa was taken in by a Colleyville, Texas, couple who became his guardians. Now 19, he obtained a T-visa and entered college in August; he also has become a spokesman on behalf of trafficking victims.

"The most important thing is constant educating of people," he said in a telephone interview. "There's help out there—but victims don't know it."

SIGNIFICANCE

The U.S. passed the Victims of Trafficking and Violence Protection Act (Trafficking Act) in 2000, as a means of addressing the issue of forced laborers, and allocated budgets over $80 million annually for related activities. The money is used to enforce U.S. anti-trafficking laws, raise public awareness of the issue, and assist and protect victims. There are also efforts to reduce the vulnerability of individuals who may be coerced into forced labor by providing educational and alternative economic opportunities. The U.S. says working directly with other countries, and with the United Nations (U.N.), is key to combating the problem.

The U.N. International Labor Organization (ILO) is an important international body for discussing the issues of forced labor. The ILO formulates international agreements and recommendations for international labor standards. One such agreement, the Convention Concerning Forced Labor, came into force in 1930. The Convention has amended and changed over the years to address modern modes of forced labor. The ILO's Convention on the Elimination of the Worst Forms of Child Labor deals specifically with the sale and trafficking of children, debt bondage, forced labor, child prostitution, and the use of children for drug trafficking. Such conventions give countries a starting point for creating laws and procedures to deal with trafficking issues.

The U.S. provides immigration privileges, in the form of T-visas and U-visas, to victims of severe trafficking and various types of crimes, including forced labor. Severe trafficking includes the trafficking of people under 18 years of age for sexual exploitation and the recruiting of people for labor or service by use of force or coercion. The visas expire after three years, at which time the recipient can adjust to the longer term status of Lawful Permanent Resident (LPR). The number of these visas that can be issued annually is limited to 5,000 T-visas and 10,000 U-visas. Holders of either of these visas are typically eligible for all governmentally funded programs, and are often eligible for refugee-specific programs.

Despite efforts made to combat forced labor, analysts suggest that more could be done to raise public awareness, particularly in immigrant communities. Also, it is thought that law enforcement should be better prepared to deal with crimes related to forced

Illegal immigrant Florencia Molina, a victim of human trafficking, became virtually enslaved at a dressmaking shop on the outskirts of Los Angeles. AP IMAGES

labor. Monitoring the sectors known to use forced labor, such as agriculture and food services, is suggested by the Human Rights Center at the University of California, Berkeley, to ensure legal protection of workers. It is also reported that certain migration policies, such as not allowing immigrants to work for more than one employer, give incentives for using forced labor. Some analysts believe more could be done in the U.S. to provide incentives for victims of forced labor to come forward and report crimes against them.

FURTHER RESOURCES
Books

Kempado, K., Sanghera, J., and B. Pattanaik, editors. *Trafficking and Prostitution Reconsidered: New Perspectives on Migration, Sex Work, and Human Rights.* Boulder, Colo.: Paradigm Publishers, 2005.

Periodicals

Roche, W. F., Jr. "Trapped in Servitude Far From Their Homes." *Orlando Sentinel* (September 15, 2002).

Sun, L. H. "U.S. has 10,000 Forced Laborers, Researchers Say." *Washington Post* (September 23, 2004).

Web sites

Human Rights Center. University of California, Berkeley. "Hidden Slaves: Forced Labor in the United States."

<http://www.hrcberkeley.org/download/hiddenslaves_report.pdf> (accessed January 10, 2006).

International Labor Organization. "Campaign Against Trafficking in Persons." <http://www.ilo.org/public/english/protection/migrant/projects/traffick/index.htm> (accessed January 10, 2006).

U.S. State Department. "Trafficking in Person's Report, June 2005." <http://www.state.gov/documents/organization/47255.pdf> (accessed January 10, 2006).

5 Social Perceptions and Impacts of Crimes

Social Perceptions and Impacts of Crimes

Crime, in all of its myriad forms, impacts society and, in turn, how crime is viewed can be a perception shaped by culture and time. The definition of crime and criminal can change and the reaches of criminality into society can be varied, and tenuous.

This section explores the various ways crime is characterized and depicted.

As discussed in "Certificate of Freedom" the impacts of crime, justice and punishment systems can reshape whole societies. In Australia former convicts of the British penal system and their descendents became founders of the modern Australian nation and led Australia from penal colony, to colony, to modern democratic state. As a consequence of this positive social transformation, however, indigenous Aboriginal peoples suffered. The rise of one society came at a cost to another.

Social perceptions of crime sometime simply reflect a morbid fascination with the causes, manner, and circumstances of celebrity death (see "Public Viewing of John Dillinger's Body"). But social percep-

tions about the relationship of social inequities to crime or in the unfairness of what is argued to be racially-based prosecution can turn killers into symbols of inequity, even to the point of exerting pressure to exonerate or release those deemed unfairly convicted (see "Hurricane.")

In one era the teaching of the scientific theory of evolution can be branded criminal (see "Darrow's Eloquent Appeal"), while in the modern era the teaching is accepted by all scientists as fundamental to sound education in science.

What can be technically branded a crime in one era (see "Anti-War Demonstrator Throwing Tear Gas") can also be more understandable and, to many, more excusable, as history unfolds. What was once scandle (see "Women in Bathing Suits Being Arrested") can become heroic.

Society also harbors fascination with fringe culture or subgroups, who in effect define their own society as depicted in "The Motor Cycle Gangs: Losers and Outsiders".

Mediterranean Pirate Ship Chasing a Merchant Ship

Illustration

By: Ferdinand Victor Perrot

Date: early 1800s

Source: Snark/Art Resource, NY

About the Artist: This undated lithograph by French artist Ferdinand Victor Perrot (1808–1841) from the first half of the nineteenth century depicts pirates chasing a merchant ship in the Mediterranean.

INTRODUCTION

This lithograph from the early nineteenth century depicts a pirate ship in pursuit of a merchant vessel in the Mediterranean. The incident shown is probably representative rather than a record of a particular attack. As shown here, pirate ships were typically smaller than the vessels they attacked: the pirates wanted not to sink the target, but to overtake and board it, a feat that required a small, fast craft. Also, pirate ships typically had to ride high so they could hide in shallow coves and inlets.

The pirate ship shown here may well have been a vessel of the Barbary Pirates (or Corsairs), who were a Mediterranean power from the sixteenth to the early nineteenth century. The Corsairs were Muslim pirates operating from the North African coast (Algiers, Morocco, and elsewhere) and were authorized by their host countries to attack ships from Christian countries; similarly, Christian Corsairs operated out of Malta and Spain, and were authorized to attack Muslim shipping. The Barbary Corsairs remained a threat in the Mediterranean longer than the Malta Corsairs. They used long, narrow sailing ships that could also be rowed (faster than sailing under typical conditions): each oar was typically manned by six slaves chained to a bench. Their goal was to overtake, and ram the tar-

PRIMARY SOURCE

Mediterranean Pirate Ship Chasing a Merchant Ship: This undated lithograph from the first half of the nineteenth century depicts pirates chasing a merchant ship in the Mediterranean. Piracy no longer affects European waters, but is common in parts of South Asia and off the coast of Somalia. SNARK/ART RESOURCE, NY

Jean Lafitte led a community of pirates and smugglers on the U.S. Gulf Coast during the early 19th century. Lafitte was famously charming, and well-mannered, and claimed to be a privateer who only attacked America's enemies, never U.S. shipping. © BETTMANN/CORBIS

get vessel. Pirates could then use ropes and planks to move onto the target ship and overpower or kill its crew. Galleys of this type were suitable only for use in the relatively calm waters of the Mediterranean, as opposed to the open Atlantic.

PRIMARY SOURCE

MEDITERRANEAN PIRATE SHIP CHASING A MERCHANT SHIP
See primary source image.

SIGNIFICANCE

Although pirates have become romanticized icons, they have throughout history been a real threat on the seas. Pirates are seagoing robbers who prey on other ships (as distinct from coastal raiders, who prey on land dwellers). They overtake target vessels, board, and capture cash, cargo, people, or even the ship itself. Such actions have occurred ever since the use of ocean

vessels for trade developed in the Mediterranean and Far East well over 2,000 years ago. The Barbary and Malta Corsairs made seagoing trade in the Mediterranean a risky business for centuries. Large pirate communities also developed along the coasts of South Asia; some numbered in the tens of thousands and acted, in effect, as rogue microstates extorting stiff taxes from merchant vessels plying nearby trade routes. Piracy was also rife in the Caribbean from the mid 1500s to the early 1700s; Atlantic pirates often sold slaves in the markets there, and about a third of Caribbean pirates were escaped slaves.

Piracy decreased sharply in the nineteenth century, after British and Dutch bombardment of the port of Algiers in 1816 destroyed most of the Barbary Corsairs fleet. Those navies also systematically hunted pirates in the seas of China and Southeast Asia. Privateers, however—pirates authorized by governments to prey on the shipping of other countries—continued to flourish until most nations with significant fleets signed the Declaration of Paris in 1856, outlawing the practice.

In the late twentieth century and beyond piracy again became a serious. According to the International Maritime Organization (IMO, the United Nations organization devoted to improving maritime safety and reducing pollution from ships), pirate attacks on shipping, especially in Indonesian and other South Asian waters as well as off the East African coast near Somalia, tripled from 1993 to 2003, with over 200 attacks in the first half of 2003 alone. Modern pirates are heavily armed gangs that issue from coastal hiding places in fast-moving motor launches when large vessels, often slowed to navigate straits or canals, approach. The pirates' target is often the cash stored in the master's safe aboard the target vessel, but they may also take personal belongings from the crew, capture them as hostages, or (more rarely) steal the ship itself.

Modern heavily mechanized cargo vessels carry small crews, making them more vulnerable to boarding. To increase shipboard security, the IMO recommends including the establishment of secure areas, radio alarm procedures, routing away from known piracy areas, increased security watches, the use of alarm sirens and distress flares, and the like. Bright lights and fire hoses may be used to repel attackers, but the IMO does not recommend pitched gun battles with pirates.

FURTHER RESOURCES
Web sites

Royal Naval Museum. "Information Sheet 80: Piracy." Undated. <http://www.royalnavalmuseum.org/info_ sheets_piracy.htm> (accessed March 8, 2006).

International Maritime Organization. "Piracy and Armed Robbery against Ships." <http://www.imo.org/Safety/> (accessed March 8, 2006).

Certificate of Freedom No. 44/801

Government document

By: Anonymous

Date: May 21, 1844

Source: The New South Wales Government's Archives and Records Management Authority

About the Author: This is a facsimile of a document placed online in image format by the New South Wales Government's Archives and Records Management Authority, Australia.

INTRODUCTION

This document certifies that a woman, "Catherine Maguire alias Murphy," had finished serving her sentence as a convict in the penal colonies in Australia as of May 21, 1844. The document shows that Maguire was convicted in the Irish county of Fermanagh in 1837 of an offence not, for some reason, specified here, and sentenced to seven years of penal servitude in Australia. Maguire was thirty-six when tried and sentenced, forty-three when freed. The document describes her as a house servant by "Trade or Calling" and, besides a general description of her by height and coloring, describes identifying marks by which she could be definitely known: "Lost a front tooth in lower Jaw and canine tooth in the upper Jaw[,] Mole on right side of neck."

Thousands of such documents have been preserved by the government of Australia. This is a typical Certificate of Freedom, but the convict's offence was not always omitted: another exemplary Certificate, for a male convict, specifies that he was convicted of "extorting money" when twenty years old and also sentenced to seven years of penal servitude. Sentences of seven, ten, and fourteen years were commonplace. Other forms of partial or complete termination of penal servitude were recorded by Tickets of Leave and Pardons. Tickets of Leave allowed individual convicts to work for themselves for pay provided that they stayed in a specified area, reported themselves period-

CERTIFICATE OF FREEDOM.

No. 44/801
Date, 21 May 1844
Prisoner's No. 37/458
Name.......... Catherine Maguire alias Murphy
Ship .... Sir Charles False
Master .... Leslie
Year 1837
Native Place ...... Fermanagh
Trade or Calling ... Houseservant
Offence ....
Place of Trial...... Fermanagh
Date of Trial....... 10 March 1837
Sentence......... Seven yrs
Year of Birth..... 1801
Height.......... 4 feet 9 1/2 Inches
Complexion...... Dark
Hair............ Brown
Eyes .... Chestnut
General Remarks. , Lost a front tooth in lower

, Jaw and canine tooth in the upper Jaw

Mole on right side of neck.

PRIMARY SOURCE

Certificate of Freedom No. 44/801: Certificate of Freedom Number 44/801 from the New South Wales State Records office, Australia. The certificate describes the history of Catherine Maguire, a convict recently transported to Australia from the British Isles. NEW SOUTH WALES STATE RECORDS

ically to the authorities, and went to church every Sunday if possible. Pardons were occasionally issued to convicts who had received life sentences and might be either conditional or absolute; conditional pardons required the convict to remain in Australia, and absolute pardons (much rarer) allowed the convict to return to Britain if they so desired and could pay for their own passage. Recipients of Certificates of Freedom were also free to return to Britain.

Since the convict in this case, Catherine Maguire, had an Irish name and was sentenced in Ireland, she was probably Irish. About a third of convicts transported—as transfer to a penal colony was called—

were Irish; about a fifth were women. The noting of an alias on this Certificate of Freedom may indicate that Maguire had been sentenced under the name of Maguire and since been married. Convicts who wished to marry while still serving their sentences could do so only with permission from the Governor of the colony where they were imprisoned.

CERTIFICATE OF FREEDOM NO. 44/801

See primary source image.

SIGNIFICANCE

Before the American Revolution, about fifty thousand convicts were transported from Britain to the colonies in North America. After the United States achieved independence, this was no longer feasible. However, in 1770 the English explorer James Cook had discovered what seemed an ideal substitute: New Holland, now known as Australia. (The term "Australia" did not come into use until about 1800.) The first expedition to transport prisoners and guards to Australia was sent in 1787, a fleet of eleven ships carrying a total of 775 convicts and several hundred other persons, including crew, soldiers, officials, and families of the non-convict members of the party. This expedition established the first permanent European colony on the continent in the area of what is now Sydney, the capital. Several other penal colonies were also established in Australia, and a large prison, Port Arthur, was constructed on the island now known as Tasmania. Convicts who were deemed worthy of additional punishment (e.g., those that committed new crimes in Australia) were sent to Port Arthur for closer confinement. The colonies were self-supporting, rather than supplied from abroad, making them penal "colonies" rather than remotely-located jails. By the time the last convicts arrived in Australia in 1868, about 160,000 had been sent. Voluntary emigration to Australia began in the 1790s and proceeded in parallel with convict settlement. Moreover, former convicts such as Catherine Maguire mostly stayed in Australia and constituted a growing local population. As decades passed, the character of non-indigenous Australian society gradually shifted from penal colony to simply a colony. Australia was federated as a democratic, independent Commonwealth state in 1901. Indigenous Australians did not have the vote until the early 1960s.

The consequences of British penal and voluntary settlement for the indigenous population of Australia, at first numbering about half a million, were catastrophic. The Aborigines were driven from their land to make way for settlements and perished in large numbers—much like the natives of North America—from infectious diseases inadvertently imported by the Europeans. By 1900, the indigenous population of Australia was down to about a tenth of its original size.

Penal servitude has been used by various governments that have access to remote, less-desirable territories and who wish to dispose of some persons without executing them. (Most convicts deported to Australia were not violent criminals: the latter were usually hung in Britain.) France used Devil's Island, near South America, as a comparatively small penal colony from 1852 to 1945.

FURTHER RESOURCES

Web sites

Australian Government: Department of Foreign Affairs and Trade. "Ancient Heritage, Modern Society." <http://www.dfat.gov.au/aib/history.html> Jan. 20, 2006 (accessed March 2, 2006).

The New South Wales Government's Archives and Records Management Authority. "Welcome to State Records NSW." <http://www.records.nsw.gov.au/staterecords/welcome_to_state_records_nsw_1556.asp> 2006 (accessed March 2, 2006).

Address of John Brown to the Virginia Court at Charles Town, Virginia on November 2, 1859

Speech

By: John Brown

Date: November 2, 1859

Source: John Brown. "Address of John Brown to the Virginia Court at Charles Town, Virginia on November 2, 1859." Charles Town, W.V.: 1859.

About the Author: John Brown, an abolitionist, was born in Torrington, Connecticut on May 9, 1800. A tanner by trade, he moved to Richmond, Pennsylvania in 1826 to set up a tannery and use his barn as a station for the Underground Railroad. A succession of business failures forced him to move frequently. In 1855, Brown moved to Kansas to help establish a free state.

This structure, originally a firehouse, is the site of John Brown's barricade after raiding the local armory during the Harper's Ferry Insurrection of 1859. © CORBIS

Along with his sons, he murdered five pro-slavery settlers in 1856 at Pottawatomie Creek. Forced out of Kansas, Brown then decided to attack the army arsenal at Harper's Ferry as part of an effort to liberate slaves. In October 1859, he captured the arsenal. During the assault, Brown's group killed five people and lost ten men. Brown was tried for murder, treason, and conspiring with slaves to rebel. He was hanged in Charles Town, Virginia (now Charles Town, West Virginia) on December 2, 1859.

INTRODUCTION

John Brown was one of many abolitionists who risked their lives in an attempt to end slavery. More successful and more violent than most, he became a martyr to the abolitionist cause. His death prefaced the United States Civil War.

Raised by an abolitionist family, Brown was a devout Calvinist who believed that abolition was God's cause. In 1851, Brown helped found the League of Gileadites, which attracted progressive whites, free blacks, and runaway slaves. The primary aim of this radical group was to encourage physical resistance to the Fugitive Slave Act of 1850 and to protect runaway slaves from pursuing slaveowners. Despite this activism, Brown's violent streak did not fully emerge until his journey to Kansas.

In Kansas, supporters and opponents of slavery debated with guns whether Kansas would enter the Union as a free or slave state. After one failed attempt to destroy Lawrence, a free-state town, proslavery forces attacked again on May 21, 1856, and destroyed it. Three days later, Brown and his group sought out five Southern settlers along Pottawatomie Creek and butchered them. Brown picked up the nickname of "Pottawatomie Brown" and came to symbolize a holy crusade against slavery. He firmly believed that God had chosen him for a special destiny, that of ending slavery.

Brown decided that God wanted him to liberate the slaves by invading the South and inciting a slave uprising. As he gathered a handful of conspirators behind him, he vindicated his war on slavery on several grounds: the institution was a barbaric and unjustifiable war on blacks, it violated God's Commandments, and it contradicted the cherished ideals of the Declaration of Independence. By the late 1850s, Brown contended, slavery had become so entrenched in the U.S. that only violent revolution could eradicate it.

The federal armory at Harper's Ferry in northern Virginia was well stocked with arms and strategically well placed for easy access to the South through the Appalachian Mountain range. Brown planned to establish a free state in the mountains to use as a base to attack slaveowners. With twenty-one followers including two former slaves, Brown assaulted the arsenal on October 16, 1859. The raid was well planned but not well executed. Thirty-six hours later and after fifteen deaths, including several of his own sons, Brown was captured by Colonel Robert E. Lee. Taken to Charles Town, Brown impressed many people in the South and the North with the courage that he displayed as he went to his death on the scaffold.

▮ PRIMARY SOURCE

I have, may it please the court, a few words to say.

In the first place, I deny everything but what I have all along admitted—the design on my part to free slaves. I intended certainly to have made a clean thing of that matter, as I did last winter, when I went into Missouri and took slaves without the snapping of a gun on either side, moved them through the country, and finally left them in Canada. I designed to do the same thing again, on a larger scale. That was all I intended. I never did intend murder, or treason, or the destruction of property, or to excite or incite slaves to rebellion, or to make insurrection.

I have another objection; and that is, it is unjust that I should suffer such a penalty. Had I interfered in the manner which I admit, and which I admit has been fairly proved (for I admire the truthfulness and candor of the greater portion of the witnesses who have testified in this case)—had I so interfered in behalf of the rich, the powerful, the intelligent, the so-called great, or in behalf of any of their friends—either father, mother, sister, wife, or children, or any of that class—and suffered and sacrificed what I have in this interference, it would have been

all right; and every man in this court would have deemed it an act worthy of reward rather than punishment.

The court acknowledges, as I suppose, the validity of the law of God. I see a book kissed here which I suppose to be the Bible, or at least the New Testament. That teaches me that all things whatsoever I would that men should do to me, I should do even so to them. It teaches me further to "remember them that are in bonds, as bound with them." I endeavored to act up to that instruction. I say, I am too young to understand that God is any respecter of persons. I believe that to have interfered as I have done—as I have always freely admitted I have done—in behalf of His despied poor, was not wrong, but right. Now if it is deemed necessary that I should forfeit my life for the furtherance of the ends of justice, and mingle my blood further with the blood of my children and with the blood of millions in this slave country whose rights are disregarded by wicked, cruel, and unjust enactments.—I submit; so let it be done!

Let me say one word further.

I feel entirely satisfied with the treatment I have received on my trial. Considering all the circumstances, it has been more generous than I expected. I feel no consciousness of my guilt. I have stated from the first what was my intention, and what was not. I never had any design against the life of any person, nor any disposition to commit treason, or excite slaves to rebel, or make any general insurrection. I never encouraged any man to do so, but always discouraged any idea of any kind.

Let me say also, a word in regard to the statements made by some to those connected with me. I hear it has been said by some of them that I have induced them to join me. But the contrary is true. I do not say this to injure them, but as regretting their weakness. There is not one of them but joined me of his own accord, and the greater part of them at their own expense. A number of them I never saw, and never had a word of conversation with, till the day they came to me; and that was for the purpose I have stated.

Now I have done.

▮ SIGNIFICANCE

John Brown's attack on Harper's Ferry in 1859 helped set the stage for the Civil War. As he noted, the crimes of the United States would only be purged away by blood.

Upon his execution for attempting to free slaves, Brown became a martyr to the abolitionist cause. The letters that he had written from jail gave him the image of being a Christ-like man willing to die for the sins of others. He assumed especially heroic proportions among African Americans because of his commitment to the cause of black freedom.

The execution of Brown underlined that no matter how much Southerners claimed that they were fighting for states' rights, slavery was at the heart of the sectional crisis. Southerners would use the events at Harper's Ferry to muster popular support for secession from the Union.

While most Northerners praised Brown's principles, they disagreed with his methods. However, "John Brown's Body," sung to a Methodist hymn became a popular song among the Union troops. In 1862, Julia Ward Howe used some of the lyrics of "John Brown's Body" to create the "Battle Hymn of the Republic." The song, especially the line, "John Brown's body lies a-mouldering in the grave, but his soul goes marching on," became synonymous with the Union cause.

FURTHER RESOURCES

Books

DeVillers, David. *The John Brown Slavery Revolt Trial: A Headline Court Case.* Berkeley Heights, N.J.: Enslow Publishers, 2000.

His Soul Goes Marching On: Responses to John Brown and the Harpers Ferry Raid, edited by Paul Finkelman. Charlottesville, Va.: University Press of Virginia, 1995.

Toledo, Gregory. *The Hanging of Old Brown: A Story of Slaves, Statesmen, and Redemption.* Westport, Conn.: Praeger, 2002.

Municipal Government in 1879

Statement of the Majority of the Board of Selectmen

Government report

By: William Westphal, Thomas J. Blake, and A. L. Sissok

Date: January 16, 1880

Source: Westphal, William, Thomas J. Blake, and A. L. Sissok. "Statment of a Majority of the Board of Selectmen for the Year 1879." Available at: Trinity College, Hartford Studies Project, <http://caribou.cc.trincoll.edu/depts_hartstud/1879%20Selectmen.pdf> (accessed February 1, 2006).

About the Author: The Board of Selectmen was elected by the town meeting in Hartford, Connecticut. Among other things, the Board was responsible for the administration of the almshouse.

INTRODUCTION

European immigration and rapid industrialization following the Civil War were key drivers for the many social changes that occurred in Hartford, Connecticut, during the 1800s. The potato famine brought many Irish to Hartford, and, by 1870, approximately twenty-five percent of the population had been born overseas, with many more residents who were first-generation Americans. The large population increase provided much of the labor to build factories, roads, railways, and other infrastructure needed to transform the city into a large industrial center. However, the rapid population growth and urbanization also brought poverty, crime, and other problems, such as prostitution and public drunkenness, to Hartford. The residents of Hartford expected the city's elected officials, who were more experienced in rural issues, to find solutions to many of these problems. The city did have a budget for providing social services to help poorer residents, and the local almshouse, which was administered by the Board of Selectmen, provided shelter to those who could not afford housing.

Traditionally, local residents of communities in Connecticut, and throughout New England, gathered annually to vote on budgets, policy changes, and other pressing issues during official Town Meetings, while the day-to-day functioning of these towns were the responsibility of individual citizens. However, as towns grew and became more complex, it was necessary for communities to have more control over the intricacies of daily operations, to ensure that trade, services, and other operations functioned smoothly. For this task, many towns elected a Board of Selectmen (usually three to nine members) that was responsible for monitoring many of the town's municipal needs and making decisions necessary to maintain civil order. The Board of Selectmen organized the official Town Meetings, kept citizens aware of important issues, and addressed citizens' concerns regarding town business and activities. The Boards were often expected to address civil disturbances when they arose.

As the economy shifted from agricultural to industrial, the residents of Hartford utilized the manpower provided with the arrival of European immigrants and other outsiders to develop an infrastructure of large industrial factories to replace smaller shops. However, families that had arrived in Connecticut several generations previously were concerned about

In Hartford, Connecticut, as in most of the country, the poor who received public assistance were required to live in housing units like the Blackwell's Island Alms House for Females, shown here in an 1890 photograph. © BETTMANN/CORBIS religious and cultural differences, as well as the poverty of the immigrants. In addition, people were moving in large numbers into Hartford from rural areas of Connecticut. Improving the educational infrastructure, and dealing with crime and mental illness challenged elected officials. Child labor, dangerous working conditions, and the demand for equal rights by women and African-Americans, added to the issues of crime and poverty that reformers were pressing the Board of Selectmen and other elected officials to address.

PRIMARY SOURCE

To the Voters of the Town of Hartford:

We, the undersigned, of the Board of Selectmen of the Town of Hartford for the year 1879, in view of the purposes for which this meeting is called, deem it proper to bring to the attention of our fellow-citizens certain facts concerning the management of the Alms House during the superintendency of George Goyt, which came to our knowledge in the course of our administration of the affairs of the town.

Our duties as selectmen, and the legally constituted overseers of the poor, necessarily brought us into intimate relations with the affairs of the Alms House, with its management, and with Mr. Goyt.

It is apparent that in the management of so large an institution there are a multitude of transactions, large and small, affording many opportunities for improper and improvident conduct, not to speak of corrupt practice and favoritism in business dealings, to the detriment of the town.

The range of the Superintendent's duties is wide. Of course, in our positions, we could not be cognizant of all these matters. We could not know all that the Superintendent was doing. But many facts came to our knowledge which it is but right that the people of the town should know, and without knowing which they can not act intelligently in the matter now under discussion.

Mr. Goyt assumed the duties of the superintendency on or about the 28th day of January, 1879. He employed for his assistant Mr. Hyde, who was under the pay of the town.

For the period of five months, beginning about June 28, they kept upon the farm, and upon fodder either raised thereon, or bought by the town, a trotting horse. This horse was not used for the purposes of the town, but for the pleasure of Mr. Hyde. This horse was regularly trained as a trotter, exercised upon the road, and at Charter Oak Park, and was entered and trotted in races at Providence, Brooklyn, Meriden and Hartford. All this was at the expense of the town, and was under the immediate charge of Mr. Hyde, who accompanied the horse in these trotting tours. At the same time Mr. Hyde was drawing pay from the town for his services.

Again: Mr. Goyt presented to the Selectmen, for payment, bills for oats, meal, claimed to have been consumed on the farm, which could not be accounted for, and which were largely in excess of amounts actually required and used. Upon being called upon for explanation, he was utterly unable to give any.

Mr. Goyt also paid for meal, from 5 to 10 cents per hundred above the market rates, and persisted in so doing, even after responsible parties repeatedly offered and asked to supply the same at the lower and ruling rates.

During the year, it became necessary to purchase wood. One of the Board of Selectmen went and looked at some, and the same was offered to him for a certain price per cord. Mr. Goyt subsequently went and purchased the same wood—ninety-five cords—and paid therefor 50 cents per cord more, although he knew full well that it could be purchased for a lower price.

In the management of the farm, Mr. Goyt has bought cattle and stock, which were placed there and fed for beef, and then sold for much less than their original cost, and much less than their actual value. This he has done without consultation with any of the Board, and upon his own motion.

He has shown no disposition to obtain advice, or inform himself of the wishes of the Board in the matter, although he well knew that at least one of the Board was in a position to give him both advice and aid.

Such are some of the facts which came to our personal knowledge. How many other similar instances there are we know not. It would be strange if more than a small proportion were, known to us. However that may be, the facts within our knowledge have convinced us that Mr. Goyt is not sufficiently capable, reliable and efficient, and not a proper man for the position held.

WILLIAM WESTPHAL.
THOS. J. BLAKE.
A. L. SISSOK.

Dated at Hartford the 16th day of January, 1880.

SIGNIFICANCE

To address the issue of poverty, the government worked to increase the number of people who could live in almshouses, while the jobless were placed in institutions to receive better training. The state government charged the Selectmen in each town with addressing the problems of the poor and providing them with resources. State law required that people receiving full assistance from towns be located in the town's almshouse. Almshouses, which still exist in modern times, provided an affordable residence for poor people. The state of Connecticut also required that the almshouses be administered by the Selectmen of a town. During the 1880s and 1890s, however, there was some concern that people were taking advantage of the Hartford almshouse. Research showed that Hartford was spending $2.07 per poor person, while the rest of the state spent $1.22 per poor person. In addition, some citizens were concerned that immigrant votes were being bought with the aid that public officials provided them (the largest number of people receiving aid came from the immigrant communities).

In the late 1800s and early 1900s, additional laws were enacted to address prostitution, saloon operations, and labor problems. An anti-vice raid was launched by the mayor of Hartford in 1911, which shutdown popular locations known for being places of prostitution. Free lunches in saloons, which were traditionally provided at the price of a drink, became illegal in 1913. These laws were considered by some residents to instill social values, but also aimed to clean up some of the activities that were associated with poverty in Hartford.

Boards of Selectmen continue to exist in the present day. Depending on the location, they are often responsible for hiring employees, determining certain municipal fees, overseeing appointed committees, and creating regulations. Frequently, city managers also are members of the Board of Selectmen. However, in some cities, such as in Hartford, the Board of Selectmen has been replaced by a modern City Council.

FURTHER RESOURCES
Books
Elson, Henry William. "Colonial Government." Chap. 10 in *History of the United States of America*. New York: MacMillan, 1904. Available at: <http://www.usgennet.org/usa/topic/colonial/book/chap10_5.html> (accessed February 1, 2006).

U.S. Dept. of Commerce and Labor, Bureau of the Census. "Paupers in Almshouses 1904." Washington, D.C., U.S. Government Printing Office, 1906. Available at: <http://www.poorhousestory.com/LegalSummaryCover.htm> (accessed February 1, 2006).

Web sites
Connecticut's Heritage Gateway. "An Orderly and Descent Government." <http://www.ctheritage.org/aodg/index.html> (accessed February 1, 2006).

The Reader's Companion to American History. "New England Colonies." <http://college.hmco.com/history/readerscomp/rcah/html/ah_064300_newenglandco.htm> (accessed February 1, 2006).

Trinity College. Trinity Center for Neighborhoods. "The Saloons of Hartford's East Side 1870–1910." <http://www.trincoll.edu/depts/tcn/Research_Reports/60.htm> (accessed February 1, 2006).

Emmeline Pankhurst, Suffragette, Carried by Officer

Photograph

By: Anonymous

Date: June 1914

Source: "Emmeline Pankhurst, Suffragette, Carried by Officer." Corbis, 1914.

About the Photographer: This image is part of the stock collection at Corbis photo agency. The photographer is not known.

INTRODUCTION
While British women gained the right to vote in local elections in 1868, British authorities did not believe that women should be allowed to cast a ballot on national matters. Men were the heads of families and the ones expected to go to war, so men were the only ones allowed to vote. In response, British women created several suffrage organizations. The best-known group was the Women's Social and Political Union (WSPU) founded by Emmeline Pankhurst in 1903.

Pankhurst, born Emmeline Goulden in Manchester, England in 1858, came from a politically active family. Her father supported the anti-slavery movement and her mother took Emmeline to her first suffrage meeting. After attending school in Paris, she married a barrister who was also a social reformer. Pankhurst joined her husband in campaigning for women to have the right to control their own property. She became a member of the Liberal Party as well as the Manchester Women's Suffrage Committee

Emmeline Pankhurst, Suffragette, Carried by Officer: Emmeline Pankhurst is carried away by a policeman after leading a group of suffragettes in an attempt to present a petition to King George V at Buckingham Palace in 1914. © BETTMANN/CORBIS

but soon became disenchanted with traditional politics.

Pankhurst believed that the existing women's suffrage organizations were too timid. She left the Liberal Party in 1907 and began an aggressive plan to win the vote. Starting in 1907, the WSPU held parades in English cities. Male spectators responded by violently attacking the marchers, who were then arrested by the police for disturbing the peace. Pankhurst began to argue that only direct, violent action would secure women the vote since men would do nothing unless their property was threatened.

Pankhurst's militancy brought enormous publicity to the suffrage cause. Along with her daughters, Christabel and Sylvia, Pankhurst etched slogans with

acid in golf greens and set fires in mailboxes. In 1908, she was arrested after issuing a manifesto calling upon people to storm the House of Parliament in support of women's suffrage. When Prime Minister Herbert Asquith refused to endorse women's suffrage in 1911, Pankhurst led a systematic assault on London's most exclusive shops, breaking windows to get attention for suffrage. She received a nine-month prison sentence and, upon her release, continued the violence. For plotting to bomb David Lloyd George, Chancellor of the Exchequer in Asquith's cabinet, Pankhurst earned a three-year prison term. To the dismay of government authorities, Pankhurst drew additional publicity by conducting repeated hunger strikes during her prison stay.

With the outbreak of World War I, Pankhurst suspended the operations of the WSPU and engaged in recruitment tours in Great Britain and the United States on behalf of the war effort. Many of the other militant suffragists regarded such moves as a betrayal of the women's movement. Following the war, Pankhurst lived in Canada while working as a lecturer in social hygiene for the National Council for Combating Venereal Diseases. She returned to England in 1925 and died in 1928.

EMMELINE PANKHURST, SUFFRAGETTE, CARRIED BY OFFICER

See primary source image.

SIGNIFICANCE

Women in England at the start of the nineteenth century had more freedom than in most countries. British women could vote for and serve on school and local government boards. Without their volunteer work in schools and charity organizations, the educational and social support system of Britain would have collapsed. Yet women, along with felons and the mentally ill, could not vote for members of Parliament.

The right to vote was central to the privileges and responsibilities of citizenship in parliamentary systems of government. Some women viewed the right to vote as their reward for having served alongside men in the development of modern society, while others saw the ballot as a means of improving social conditions for the oppressed, including women. By the eve of World War I, the suffrage issue had become the foundation for the first mass-based women's political movement. Both enemies and supporters of women's rights criticized the tactics of militants such as Pankhurst. However, Pankhurst succeeded in making the vote for women a public issue that would not go away.

The final victories in the suffragist battle were not won until after World War I. Women had played a major part on the home front in World War I. As a reward, women over the age of thirty gained the right to vote in national elections in 1918. British women gained the right to vote on the same terms as men in 1923. At that time, any woman twenty-one years old and a six-month resident of Great Britain could cast a ballot.

FURTHER RESOURCES

Books

Bartley, Paula. *Emmeline Pankhurst.* New York: Routledge, 2002.

Raeburn, Antonia. *The Militant Suffragettes.* London: Joseph, 1973.

Web sites

The Time 100. "Emmeline Pankhurst: The Victorian Englishwoman Marshaled the Suffragist Movement, Which Won Women the Vote." <http://www.time.com/time/time100/heroes/profile/pankhurst01.html> (accessed February 20, 2006).

Women in Bathing Suits Being Arrested

Photograph

By: Anonymous

Date: July 12, 1922

Source: Bettmann/Corbis

About the Photographer: The photographer is unknown.

INTRODUCTION

The young women in this photograph are being arrested for exposing their legs in one-piece bathing suits, which was forbidden by ordinances in many U.S. commmunities in the 1920s. These women were probably either fined or released soon after arrest without charge: few women (or none) served jail time for wearing bathing outfits that violated indecent exposure or "public indecency" laws. Many violators of beach dress codes were fined on the spot by special enforcement officers, "beach censors," rather than being arrested.

Thousands of women were arrested in the 1920s for wearing leg-revealing swimming suits, which were a new development in the history of human clothing. In antiquity, swimming suits did not exist: bathing was done in the nude. However, for most of the last two thousand years open-water bathing or immersion for pleasure essentially did not exist in European societies. In the 1700s, ocean-shore bathing began to come into vogue and elaborate body-covering costumes were devised for both men and women. Men's costumes, like their everyday cloths, were more or less form-fitting; women's costumes resembled ankle-length gowns complete with bonnets, shoes, long sleeves, and gloves to prevent the skin from being browned by sun exposure. At the time, sun-darkened skin was seen as coarse or unattractive, the reverse of today's usual beauty standard for light-skinned persons in European cultures. Some South Asian cultures retain the earlier European standard, and many women guard themselves from the sun to avoid darkening.

Throughout the nineteenth century, bathing costumes remained bulky and restrictive for women, often made out of flannel or other opaque fabrics and even weighted with lead to keep the skirts from floating upward in the water. "Bathing machines" were standard at seaside resorts in England the United States, essentially closets or booths on wheels that could be rolled down to the water's edge to minimize exposure to the public gaze. By the 1920s, women's bathing skirts had shortened, in many cases, to just above or below the knee. Further, several forms of gender equality were being sought at the time: the vote, more equitable divorce laws, and broader career choices for women. To some women, it seemed unjust that men should be allowed to wear one-piece bathing suits that exposed their legs to the upper thigh while women must still wear skirts. (Men's bathing suits did not yet commonly expose the upper body either.) Crystal Eastman, one of the founders of the American Civil Liberties Union, wrote in 1927 that as early as 1900, as a young girl, she "was a ringleader in the rebellion against skirts and stockings for swimming" in their summer community, and shocked her father by wearing a man's one-piece costume into the water. Yet he allowed her to do so: "he himself had been a swimmer," Eastman wrote, and "he knew he would not want to swim in skirt and stockings. Why then should I?"

PRIMARY SOURCE

Women in Bathing Suits Being Arrested: Bathing beauties being arrested in 1922 for defying a Chicago edict banning abbreviated bathing suits on beaches. © BETTMANN/CORBIS

PRIMARY SOURCE

WOMEN IN BATHING SUITS BEING ARRESTED
   See primary source image.

SIGNIFICANCE

The primary social driving force behind the movement toward the one-piece bathing suit in the 1920s was not athletic freedom of movement but sexuality. Many or most of the women wearing the new, more revealing costumes could not even swim: they wore them on public beaches in order to be, in the language of the original caption of the photo shown here, "bathing beauties" The idea of being sexually admirable in a bathing costume was glamorized by the movies, for which the term "bathing beauty" had been invented: ordinary young women wanted to emulate the stars. In the late 1910s, beauty contests were organized for the first time in which the contestants wore bathing costumes. The first Miss American pageant was held on the beach at Atlantic City, New Jersey in 1921, featuring a parade of young women wearing one-piece bathing suits similar to those seen here. Bathing-beauty pageants proliferated throughout the 1920s, greatly enhancing the popularity of the one-piece, leg-revealing bathing suit for women.

Social conservatives in both the United States and Europe deplored the trend. In Italy under Mussolini, the National Federation of Catholic Men cooperated with the police to identify indecent dress at resorts and effect arrests. In the French city of Biarritz, rules required, as the *New York Times* for July 24, 1925 described, that "Women's bathing dresses must reach from the neck to below the knees. All décolleté [low-neck] effects are prohibited."

In the United States, numerous ordinances were passed and enforced to combat the trend toward female leg exposure. "Beach censors" were empowered to arrest people—usually women—on beaches who violated the codes describing what could be shown and what could not. Palm Beach, Florida, forbade "flesh-colored" or white stockings but had trouble enforcing the ban because a precise definition of "flesh-colored" proved elusive. Eventually, the beach censor was equipped with a set of color cards that could be used to test suspect stockings.

Massive disobedience of these laws defeated them. Eventually, public standards shifted. The old regulations came to be seen as absurd and were repealed. Public exposure or indecency laws today mostly ban the exposure of genitalia, not of other body parts: restaurants and other public places are allowed by law to require the wearing of shirts and shoes. A major exception is that in most U.S. communities it is still illegal for women to expose their breasts other than for the purpose of breast-feeding: thus, women can still be fined or arrested on most U.S. beaches for not wearing sufficiently concealing bathing costumes. This may change: a "topfree" movement in the United States and Canada seeks legalized toplessness for both sexes. In California, where public breastfeeding was not legalized until 1998, the public defender of Ventura County, Liana Johnson, asked the state legislature in 2005 to make topless sunbathing legal, equalizing male and female breasts under the law. California law presently forbids exposure of "any portion of the breast at or below the upper edge of the areola of any female person." Johnson's efforts have given rise to disputes over whether female toplessness is, under California law, "lewd"—a sex crime—or merely "indecent," a misdemeanor. At least one California court has ruled that even persons convicted of misdemeanor indecent exposure must register as sex offenders under California's Megan's Law, which requires the identities of such offenders to be made public on the Internet. Female toplessness on beaches is legal today in many European countries.

FURTHER RESOURCES
Periodicals
Salladay, Robert. "Woman Promotes Right to Go Topless." *Los Angeles times.* January 22, 2005. <http://www.save-california.com/getpluggedin/latimes_12205.php> (accessed March 8, 2006).

Web sites
Assumption College. "Revues and other Vanities: The Commodification of Fantasy in the 1920s." Undated. <http://www.assumption.edu/ahc/Vanities/default.html> (accessed March 8, 2006).

The Scopes Trial, 1925

Darrow's Eloquent Appeal

Newspaper article

By: Henry L. Menken

Date: July 14, 1925

Source: Mencken, H. L. "Darrow's Eloquent Appeal Wasted on Ears That Heed Only Bryan, Says Mencken." *Baltimore Evening Sun*, July 14, 1925.

About the Author: H. L. Mencken (1880–1956) was a prolific and a pre-eminent American journalist, editor, and social commentator. A life-long resident of Baltimore, Maryland, Mencken's commentaries combined an often biting wit with keen analyses regarding American life. Mencken paid particular attention to those public issues where morality or personal freedoms were engaged, such as the influence of the Klu Klux Klan in national politics in the 1920s and 1930s, the role of organized religion in American society, and the impact of Prohibition (1919–1933) on national life. Two lasting testaments to Mencken's lengthy career are his unparalleled coverage of every American presidential nomination convention between 1920 and 1948 and his insights regarding the conduct of the Scopes "Monkey Trial" in 1925.

INTRODUCTION
In 1925, the United States was a nation of remarkably divergent views concerning the interrelated issues of public morality and religion. The Volstead Act of 1919, which prohibited the purchase, distribution, or consumption of alcohol in the United States, had been a victory for America's conservative, fundamentalist constituency, while the so called "Jazz Age" of increasing social freedoms was in full swing in the nation's cities. Important national issues, such as those of education and religion, were approached in distinctly regional ways across America.

The predominately rural state of Tennessee was a leading example of such regional diversity. Tennessee was a part of America for which H. L. Mencken coined the phrase the "Bible Belt," a swath of the American heartland where fundamentalist religion and conservative social values were usually powerful forces in politics, public education, and social life. The prosecution of John Scopes (1900–1970) for teaching the theories of Charles Darwin (1809–1882) and evolution in his Dayton, Tennessee, classroom brought into focus, for the first time on a national stage, the relationship between education and religious teachings in public schools

By 1925, Mencken was an established journalist, with a following of his daily columns in the *Baltimore Sun* newspaper that went beyond the then usual local impact of an urban political newspaper reporter. His series of reports from the Scopes trial describe not only the daily battles between two American titans, William Jennings Bryan (1860–1925) and Clarence Darrow (1857–1938), but also Mencken's personal contempt for what he perceived as the largely negative impact of fundamentalist religious thought on the community at large.

The blunt and often acerbic language employed by Mencken in describing the Scopes trial is remarkable, considering the more conservative journalistic temper of those times. He refers to the local people variously as hillbillies and peasants and Dayton as a place where religion was hammered into the heads of an unsophisticated population. Mencken makes no attempt to provide balanced, even-handed reporting of this event; he clearly sides with the arguments advanced by Darrow for the teaching of evolution. However, the strength of the Mencken commentary is in his skill as an observer. As personally repellant the person and the arguments of William Jennings Bryan were to Mencken, he gave each significant play. The underpinnings of the fundamentalist Christian faith in Tennessee and elsewhere, both as a religious fact and as a part of the social fabric, were the subject of extensive comment in the Mencken trial articles.

▮ PRIMARY SOURCE

Dayton, Tenn., July 14— The net effect of Clarence Darrow's great speech yesterday seems to be precisely the same as if he had bawled it up a rainspout in the interior of Afghanistan. That is, locally, upon the process against the infidel Scopes, upon the so-called minds of these fundamentalists of upland Tennessee. You have but a dim notion of it who have only read it. It was not designed for reading, but for hearing. The clanging of it was as important as the logic. It rose like a wind and ended like a flourish of bugles. The very judge on the bench, toward the end of it, began to look uneasy. But the morons in the audience, when it was over, simply hissed it.

During the whole time of its delivery the old mountebank, Bryan, sat tight-lipped and unmoved. There is, of course, no reason why it should have shaken him. He has those hill billies locked up in his pen and he knows it. His brand is on them. He is at home among them. Since his earliest days, indeed, his chief strength has been among the folk of remote hills and forlorn and lonely farms. Now with his political aspirations all gone to pot, he turns to them for religious consolations. They understand his peculiar imbecilities. His nonsense is their ideal of sense. When he deluges them with his theological bilge they rejoice like pilgrims disporting in the river Jordan.

The town whisper is that the local attorney-general, Stewart, is not a fundamentalist, and hence has no stomach for his job. It seems not improbable. He is a man of evident education, and his argument yesterday was confined very strictly to the constitutional points—the argument of a competent and conscientious lawyer, and to me, at least very persuasive.

But Stewart, after all, is a foreigner here, almost as much so as Darrow or Hays or Malone. He is doing his job and that is all. The real animus of the prosecution centers in Bryan. He is the plaintiff and prosecutor. The local lawyers are simply bottle-holders for him. He will win the case, not by academic appeals to law and precedent, but by direct and powerful appeals to the immemorial fears and superstitions of man. It is no wonder that he is hot against Scopes. Five years of Scopes and even these mountaineers would begin to laugh at Bryan. Ten years and they would ride him out of town on a rail, with one Baptist parson in front of him and another behind.

But there will be no ten years of Scopes, nor five years, nor even one year.

Such brash young fellows, debauched by the enlightenment, must be disposed of before they become dangerous, and Bryan is here, with his tight lips and hard eyes, to see that this one is disposed of. The talk of the lawyers, even the magnificent talk of Darrow, is so much idle wind music. The case will not be decided by logic, nor even by eloquence. It will be decided by counting noses—and for every nose in these hills that has ever thrust itself into any book save the Bible there are a hundred adorned with the brass ring of Bryan. These are his people. They understand him when he speaks in tongues. The same dark face that is in his own eyes is in theirs, too. They feel with him, and they relish him.

I sincerely hope that the nobility and gentry of the lowlands will not make the colossal mistake of viewing this trial of Scopes as a trivial farce. Full of rustic japes and in bad taste, it is, to be sure, somewhat comic on the surface. One laughs to see lawyers sweat. The jury, marched down Broadway, would set New York by the ears. But all of that is only skin deep.

Deeper down there are the beginnings of a struggle that may go on to melodrama of the first caliber, and when the curtain falls at least all the laughter may be coming from the yokels. You probably laughed at the prohibitionists, say, back in 1914. Well, don't make the same error twice.

As I have said, Bryan understands these peasants, and they understand him. He is a bit mangey and flea-bitten, but no means ready for his harp. He may last five years, ten years or even longer. What he may accomplish in that time, seen here at close range, looms up immensely larger than it appears to a city man five hundred miles away. The fellow is full of such bitter, implacable hatreds that they radiate from him like heat from a stove. He hates the learning that he cannot grasp. He hates those who sneer at him. He hates, in general, all who stand apart from his own pathetic commonness. And the yokels hate with him, some of them almost as bitterly as he does himself. They are willing and eager to follow him—and he has already given them a taste of blood.

Darrow's peroration yesterday was interrupted by Judge Raulston, but the force of it got into the air nevertheless. This year it is a misdemeanor for a country school teacher to flout the archaic nonsense of Genesis. Next year it will be a felony. The year after the net will be spread wider. Pedagogues, after all, are small game; there are larger birds to snare—larger and juicier. Bryan has his fishy eye on them. He will fetch them if his mind lasts, and the lamp holds out to burn. No man with a mouth like that ever lets go. Nor ever lacks followers.

Tennessee is bearing the brunt of the first attack simply because the civilized minority, down here, is extraordinarily pusillanimous.

I have met no educated man who is not ashamed of the ridicule that has fallen upon the State, and I have met none, save only judge Neal, who had the courage to speak out while it was yet time. No Tennessee counsel of any importance came into the case until yesterday and then they came in stepping very softly as if taking a brief for sense were a dangerous matter. When Bryan did his first rampaging here all these men were silent.

They had known for years what was going on in the hills. They knew what the country preachers were preaching—what degraded nonsense was being rammed and hammered into yokel skulls. But they were afraid to go out against the imposture while it was in the making, and when any outsider denounced it they fell upon him violently as an enemy of Tennessee.

Now Tennessee is paying for that poltroonery. The State is smiling and beautiful, and of late it has begun to be rich. I know of no American city that is set in more lovely scenery than Chattanooga, or that has more charming homes. The civilized minority is as large here, I believe, as anywhere else.

It has made a city of splendid material comforts and kept it in order. But it has neglected in the past the unpleasant business of following what was going on in the cross roads Little Bethels.

The Baptist preachers ranted unchallenged.

Their buffooneries were mistaken for humor. Now the clowns turn out to be armed, and have begun to shoot.

In his argument yesterday judge Neal had to admit pathetically that it was hopeless to fight for a repeal of the anti-evolution law. The Legislature of Tennessee, like the Legislature of every other American state, is made up of cheap job-seekers and ignoramuses.

The Governor of the State is a politician ten times cheaper and trashier. It is vain to look for relief from such men. If the State is to be saved at all, it must be saved by the courts. For one, I have little hope of relief in that direction, despite Hays' logic and Darrow's eloquence. Constitutions, in America, no longer mean what they say. To mention the Bill of Rights is to be damned as a Red.

The rabble is in the saddle, and down here it makes its first campaign under a general beside whom Wat Tylor seems like a wart beside the Matterhorn.

SIGNIFICANCE

The Scopes trial is a remarkable study of both the structure, as well as the tensions, present in American society in 1925. It is equally significant that the same issues that percolated through the so called "Monkey Trial" are the subject of renewed interest today throughout the Unites States.

Rural Tennessee in 1925 was a fitting battleground for the battle between fundamentalist religion and educational freedoms. John Scopes, a twenty-four-year-old high school science teacher in Dayton, Tennessee, was determined that his students would be prepared for a wider world, and he believed that preparation should include the evolutionary theories of Charles Darwin. Such teachings conflicted with the law of Tennessee, known as the Butler Act, which had enacted a blanket prohibition against any public educational instruction that contradicted creationism, the word of God as set out in the Bible in the book of Genesis. Many southern American states had similar legislation in place in 1925.

The state prosecution of Scopes at Dayton was a classic test case, where each of the intermingled concepts of church and state, the freedoms of expression, religion, and education, the letter of the law, and rural versus urban ways of American life, would come into play. Ironically, these broad and compelling interests

Lawyer Clarence Darrow pleads against religious bigotry before a jury in Dayton, Tennessee, during the Scopes Trial in 1925. © BETTMANN/CORBIS

all arose in a matter where the maximum penalty was a one-hundred-dollar fine.

The potential for national impact from this local Tennessee prosecution was also reflected in its two chief combatants, William Jennings Bryan for the prosecution, and Clarence Darrow for the defense. A national figure, Bryan had run unsuccessfully for President three times; known as the "Great Commoner," his constituency was composed largely of religious fundamentalists. Bryan thrust himself into this conflict first by filing the formal complaint against Scopes and then leading the prosecution.

Clarence Darrow was a living legend, the most famed American lawyer of the age. Darrow's initial involvement in the Scopes defense had been facilitated by the American Civil Liberties Union, who saw an opportunity to advance their views of freedom of expression through Scopes to a national audience. In one of many footnotes to the Scopes trial, Darrow's remarkable address to the Scopes jury was later immortalized in the movie *Inherit the Wind*.

The trial reports of H. L. Mencken make it plain he saw the Scopes conviction as a foregone conclusion, given the fiercely conservative nature of the Dayton community, as reflected in the jury and the presiding judge. Mencken's observations were confirmed when the jury returned a guilty verdict in eight minutes after the conclusion of the twelve-day trial. In one sense, the Scopes result confirmed the ability of the state to impose educational rules that both advanced and protected traditional Christian values and beliefs.

From a vantage point of an observer in 1975, the Scopes ruling would have appeared somewhat archaic, even faintly humorous. Fifty years after Scopes's conviction, the exclusion of Darwin and his evolutionary theories from an American high school biology curriculum, in favor of the teaching of creationism, would have seemed nonsensical. By 1975, other aspects of religious instruction, such as the saying of the Lord's Prayer in classrooms, or religious education in public schools, had disappeared as a result of various high court rulings that held such practices to violate the United States constitutional rules regarding the separation of religion and public-funded institutions.

However, more than eighty years later, there is a profound, ever increasing significance to the arguments advanced by both sides in the Scopes trial. The rise of home schooling as a preferred method of education in America, particularly among members of conservative Christian denominations, is one example. Further, there has been a resurgence in the public debate concerning whether the teaching of evolution in American classrooms must necessarily exclude instruction in the principles "Intelligent Design," a modern rendering of creationism that is endorsed by many Christian fundamentalists in the United States.

FURTHER RESOURCES

Books

Larson, Edward. *Trial and Error: The American Controversy Over Creation and Evolution.* New York, Oxford University Press, 2003.

Rogers, Mary Elizabeth, ed. *The Impossible H. L. Mencken.* New York: Doubleday, 1991.

Web sites

Famous Trials in American History. "Tennessee vs. John Scopes: The 'Monkey Trial', 1925." <http://www.law.umkc.edu/faculty/projects/ftrials/scopes/scopes.htm> (accessed November 1, 2005).

Public Viewing of John Dillinger's Body

Photograph

By: Anonymous

Date: ca. 1934

Source: "Public Viewing of John Dillinger's Body." Corbis, ca. 1934.

About the Photographer: This photograph is part of the stock collection at Corbis photo agency, headquartered in Seattle and provider of images for magazine, films, television, and advertisements. The photographer is not known.

INTRODUCTION

John Dillinger was a depression-era bank robber who instigated a crime wave in 1933–34 of daring and brutality. Lasting just months, a succession of bank robberies led by Dillinger made him the FBI's Public Enemy Number One and a figure who was both feared by his victims and idealized and admired by the downtrodden of depression-hit America. His death after a shootout with police outside a Chicago cinema in July 1934 gave way to a score of myths and legends.

Born John Herbert Dillinger to a middle-class Indianapolis family in June 1903, on leaving school the young Dillinger struggled to settle into working life. He could not hold down a regular job and later deserted from the U.S. Navy, from which he was eventually dishonorably discharged. His marriage to a local girl, Beryl Hovious, lasted just several months over 1923–24 as Dillinger increasingly retreated to the speakeasies and dives of Indianapolis.

After a drinking binge in 1924, Dillinger assaulted and robbed a local drugstore owner. He was caught and sentenced to ten years imprisonment. Serving time in Indiana's prisons changed the petty lawbreaker and drifter into a hardened criminal. Dillinger fell in with a gang of seasoned bank robbers who planned a massive crime spree upon their eventual release.

Dillinger served nine years of his sentence before being released on parole in May 1933, following the intercession of his father and the judge who had sentenced him. Almost immediately he resumed his criminal career with a series of petty robberies in Indianapolis. This earned him enough cash to buy a fast car and guns, enabling him to turn to the more lucrative pursuit of bank robberies. Within three months of his release from prison, three bank raids had yielded him more than $40,000.

Using this new wealth, Dillinger plotted the release of his jailbird friends. He smuggled arms into the jail where he had spent so much of his life, and using those weapons ten men escaped from Indiana State Prison on September 22, 1933. Four days before that breakout, Dillinger had himself been picked up by police in Indianapolis and sent to Lima, Ohio to face trial on bank robbery charges. One of his freed friends first acts was to reciprocate the favor and raid Lima Jail, killing a sheriff and freeing Dillinger.

The daring and brutality with which these jailbreaks were executed brought Dillinger additional fame and notoriety. He had become the criminal that no upholder of the law could touch, a famed desperado who used his renown to justify his crime spree in Robin-hood-like terms to newspapermen who caught up with him and who he actively courted. He was, he

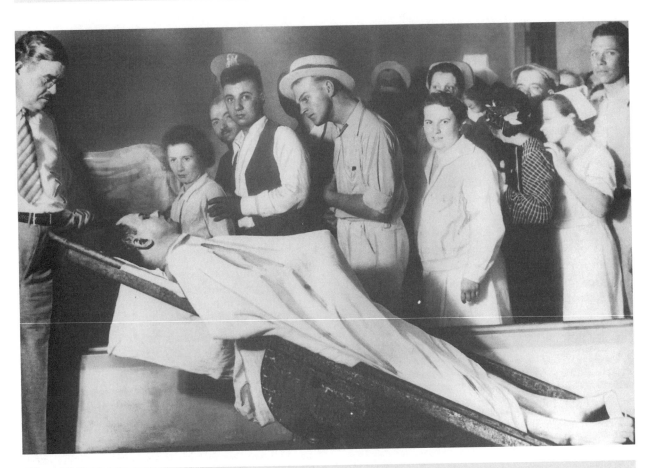

PRIMARY SOURCE

Public Viewing of John Dillinger's Body: The bullet-riddled body of bank robber John Dillinger is put on public display in the Chicago morgue after he was ambushed and shot to death by the FBI and police. © BETTMANN/CORBIS

explained, only stealing wealth from bankers who had themselves stolen from the good people of America. In a depression-hit country, where incomes had halved in just a few years, his anti-establishment rhetoric struck many a chord, although there is little—except vague anecdotal evidence—that suggests he ever shared any of his newfound wealth.

Throughout the remainder of 1933, the bank robberies continued across the Midwest, although the Dillinger gang were also often blamed for crimes they had not committed. His reputation widened as tales of his daring and near misses from police assumed mythical proportions. On one occasion, police caught him coming out of a Chicago doctor's surgery, but he drove away through a hail of bullets. Yet when police did finally catch up with him, vacationing in Tucson, Arizona in January 1934, his arrest passed quietly.

This was not the end of Dillinger's story. On March 3, 1934, Dillinger bluffed his way out of Indi-

ana's Crown Point jail brandishing a wooden gun and escaping in a sheriff's car (evidence has since shown that it is likely that Dillinger bribed his captors and used the wooden gun as cover for his methods).

Now with the title of the FBI's Public Enemy Number One, Dillinger reunited with his gang, who waged a desperate path across the Midwest, trying to avoid detection, but also funding their exploits with further robberies. More close encounters with the law added to the fugitive's reputation. At one point he was cornered in a St. Paul apartment, but equipped with a machine gun, sprayed his way to freedom. At a Wisconsin roadhouse, FBI agents killed one of his gang members and wounded another two, but not Dillinger.

Finally, on July 22, 1934, Dillinger met his end. Attending the film *Manhattan Melodrama* at a Chicago cinema with his girlfriend, Polly Hamilton, and a brothel owner, Mrs. Anna Sage (also known as Ana

Cumpanas), he was betrayed to police by Sage, who was seeking to avoid deportation to her native Romania by striking a deal. On leaving the cinema, Sage tipped off agents who opened fire into Dillinger's back, killing him instantly.

PRIMARY SOURCE

PUBLIC VIEWING OF JOHN DILLINGER'S BODY

See primary source image.

SIGNIFICANCE

When the FBI released Dillinger's body a week later, a hearse rode his body to the home of his sister outside Indianapolis. There, 2,500 mourners filed past the dead criminal before he was buried a few days later before an attendance of family members, pressmen, and sympathetic members of the public. This show of sympathy was instructive of how Dillinger had captured the public's imagination, despite being a reckless and violent criminal.

But why was John Dillinger revered by so many people? He certainly wasn't the first career criminal to divide American opinion. Only a few years earlier, Al Capone, a Chicago bootlegger and smuggler, had become one of the most famous men in the world for, as he liked to put it, giving "the people what they want"—namely booze during the prohibition era. In a sense, Dillinger did just that: in a country transfixed by the poverty depression had brought, Dillinger's claim that he was a modern-day Jesse James and recovering from bankers what they had "stolen" from the people carried huge resonance. It was a myth that Dillinger was the Midwest's answer to Robin Hood, but so inculcated by poverty were most people that they believed him to be a kind of savior, a decent man battling against the same authorities that could not alleviate their plight.

By degrees, crime had been "normalized" during America's prohibition era, as the country's drinkers engaged in the largest binge of civil disobedience in history in the nation's speakeasies and blind tigers. It was also a time when gangsters were making an imprint on popular culture. In comic books and particularly movies, such as *The Public Enemy* (1931) and *Scarface* (1932), the glamorization of crime meant real-life crooks were becoming anti-heroes. Dillinger, who modeled himself on Douglas Fairbanks (the star of *Robin Hood*), seemed a real-life incarnation of one of these silver-screen stars. He would even add a few film-star flourishes to his bank raids, such as vaulting over counters and treating female bank employees courteously while robbing them. Of course, all this added to his allure.

The final layer of mystique came after Dillinger's death, when rumors and myths about his prowess perpetuated. Most notable amongst these was that he had actually escaped and a different body had been buried—this despite the very public display of his corpse.

Dillinger's fame and infamy has continued partly because of such myths, but also because he has been immortalized on film so often. Starting with the FBI's propagandist newsreel *John Dillinger: Public Enemy Number One* (1934), a number of movies and TV series have been made about him. These include: *Dillinger* (1945), *Appointment with Destiny* (1971), *Dillinger* (1972), *The Lady in Red* (1979), and *John Dillinger* (2005). Such interest has been added to with numerous books published about his brief life.

FURTHER RESOURCES

Books

Matera, Dary. *John Dillinger: The Life and Death of America's First Celebrity Criminal.*. New York: Carroll and Graf, 2005.

Toland, John. *The Dillinger Days*. New York: Random House, 1971.

Web sites

CrimeLibrary.com. "Little Bohemia." <http://www.crimelibrary.com/gangsters_outlaws/outlaws/dillinger/1.html> (accessed February 25, 2006).

Bogart with the Maltese Falcon

Photograph

By: Anonymous

Date: 1941

Source: "Bogart with The Maltese Falcon." Corbis, 1941.

About the Author: This photograph is part of the stock collection at Corbis photo agency, headquartered in Seattle and provider of images for magazine, films, television, and advertisements. The photographer is not known.

PRIMARY SOURCE

Bogart with the Maltese Falcon: A still from the film noir classic *The Maltese Falcon* shows star Humphrey Bogart holding the falcon. © JOHN SPRINGER COLLECTION/CORBIS

INTRODUCTION

Crime has always been a popular theme in film and *The Maltese Falcon* (1941) is a classic. It belongs to the "film noir" genre, which arose in the 1940s and is characterized by a moral and psychological darkness, both in theme and visual elements. *The Maltese Falcon* is based upon a story by Dashiell Hammett (1894–1961), the American novelist and screenwriter. The film was the first work of the great director John Huston and starred the legendary Humphrey Bogart (1899–1957), who is depicted in the photograph here.

Bogart's character is Sam Spade, a private investigator who investigates the death of his partner. He is hounded by the police himself when he gets involved in the pursuit of the valuable statuette that gives the story its name. Huston's Maltese Falcon was actually the third remake of the film and, according to film historians, easily the best version with its fine acting and

stylish direction. It is faithful in most respects to Hammett's 1929 story, which was published as a serial in a detective fiction magazine called Black Mask. The film is peopled with corrupt low-life villains, deceitful women and tough heroes like the cool, cynical Spade, who lives by his own rules. It received three Oscar nominations but won no awards.

Bogart went on to play another "hard boiled" detective, Philip Marlowe, in *The Big Sleep* (1946). Marlowe was the creation of Raymond Chandler (1888–1959) and the film, another "noir" classic, involves seven killings, gambling, pornography and generalized vice and corruption. Spade and Marlowe are both men who prefer action—even if it includes violence—to the careful investigation of the evidence. As such, they form a sharp contrast with that earlier detective hero, Sherlock Holmes, who favored a more gentlemanly and analytical approach to crime.

PRIMARY SOURCE

BOGART WITH THE MALTESE FALCON

See primary source image.

SIGNIFICANCE

Film noir is an important trend in the cinematic portrayal of crime and punishment. The word "noir" is French for "black" and was coined by the French film critic Frank Nino in 1946. During World War II, France had been under Nazi occupation and Hollywood film imports were forbidden. Accordingly, when the conflict ended, the critics and the cinema-going public had several years of Hollywood output to catch up on. They were startled by how the theme and content of American films had changed during the 1940s. Before they had been optimistic and straightforward; now, they were dark and full of foreboding.

Film noir was probably rooted in the German expressionism of émigré directors such as Fritz Lang, which proved an ideal vehicle for a U.S. society troubled by the war. This was coupled with the introspection of psychoanalysis, also popular in artistic circles around this time, to create troubled, yet cynical, heroes. The absence of men at war had left women in charge on the domestic front. These social changes were reflected by the "femme fatale" characters that often appeared in film noir—independent, demanding and likely to trap the hero in a web of deceit.

The visual elements of film noir reflected both theme and content and, to a large extent, the budgetary restraints of the war years. Tilted camera angles, long shadows and high-contrast imagery all helped to create a mood of paranoia and alienation. Sets often involved streets, rain, flashing neon lights, and hotel rooms, all contributing to the gloomy atmosphere. Plot lines were bleak and fatalistic, where one false move could plunge the hero into a nightmarish vortex of intrigue. Film noir was in its heyday in the late 1940s, where it continued to reflect troubling changes in American society—unemployment after the war, race riots, strikes, rationing, and the start of the Cold War. The genre reached Europe with, for example, *The Third Man* (1949) from the British director Carol Reed, which ends with a shootout in the distinctly "noir" setting of an underground sewer.

Filmmaking has changed a great deal in the last fifty years, but the classics of film noir are still popular. There have been certain films since the heyday of film noir that seem to have many of its elements, such as Roman Polanski's *Chinatown* (1974), Ridley Scott's *Bladerunner* (1982), and Curtis Hanson's *LA Confiden-* *tial* (1997). A sub-genre known as tech-noir, which combines science fiction with classic film noir, is exemplified by films such as Andy and Larry Wachowski's *The Matrix* (1999) and Steven Spielberg's *Minority Report* (2002). Film noir, it seems, continually re-invents itself, playing on the public's fascination with crime and punishment.

FURTHER RESOURCES

Books

Film Noir: An Encyclopedic Reference to the American Style, 3rd ed. Edited by Alain Silver and Elizabeth Ward. Woodstock, N.Y.: Overlook Press, 1993.

Web sites

Crime Culture. "Film Noir." <http://www.crimeculture.com/Contents/Film%20Noir.html> (accessed February 26, 2006).

Filmsite.org. "Film Noir." <http://www.filmsite.org/filmnoir.html> (accessed February 26, 2006).

D.A. McCall, Secretary of the Mississippi Baptist Convention Board, Baptizes Convicts on a Prison Farm near Parchman on 18 August 1946

Photograph

By: Anonymous

Date: August 18, 1946

Source: "D.A. McCall, Secretary of the Mississippi Baptist Convention Board, Baptizes Convicts on a Prison Farm near Parchman on 18 August 1946." Alamy Images, August 18, 1946.

About the Photographer: This image is part of the stock collection of Alamy Images. The photographer is unknown.

INTRODUCTION

Parchman Farm began in 1907 as one of Mississippi's penal farms. The subject of numerous blues songs and a central character in such novels as William Faulkner's 1948 *Old Man* and Eudora Welty's 1970

Losing Battles, it became the best-known of all the penal farms in the United States.

Parchman was a prison operated on an agricultural system. Set in the Yazoo Delta in isolated Sunflower County, the farm benefited from exceptionally rich Delta soil. It was a typical Delta plantation, consisting of 15,500 acres (6,270 hectares) planted in cotton, corn, and assorted vegetables, with cotton as the leading crop. Parchman usually had fewer than two thousand convicts. The prisoners, separated into small groups, lived in camps and were largely self-supporting. A brickyard, a machine shop, a gin, and a storage plant were operated by convict labor. From the beginning, the prison made enough money to be self-supporting. For the first fifty years of its existence, Parchman's agricultural yield provided Mississippi with its greatest sources of income other than tax revenue.

The inmates toiled under conditions that shocked most people. The cages were unfit for human habitation, especially the showers, where convicts often stood ankle-deep in raw sewage. Within the rat-infested barracks, a convict hierarchy reigned supreme, reportedly inflicting atrocities at will. In the cotton rows, "trusty-shooters" guarded convict field hands with 30-30 Winchester rifles, and stories of slaughter had filtered out of the penitentiary for years. At "Little Alcatraz," the prison's maximum security unit, naked men were confined in darkness, knocked about by water propelled through high-pressure hoses, and deprived of adequate food for days on end.

With its vast cotton acreage, black field hands, and white overseers, the plantation would have been quite at home in the Mississippi of 1860. The brutality also seemed like something out of the antebellum

PRIMARY SOURCE

D.A. McCall, Secretary of the Mississippi Baptist Convention Board, Baptizes Convicts on a Prison Farm near Parchman on 18 August 1946: Secretary of the Mississippi Baptist Convention Board D. A. McCall baptizes convicts on a prison farm near Parchman, Mississippi, in 1946 © BLACK STAR/ALAMY

era. Both media accounts and gossipy tales told of the punishments inflicted to keep the long line of convicts chopping and picking in the cotton fields. Guards maintained control through the notorious strap, "Black Annie," bloodhounds and German shepherds, and the fabled "trusty-shooters," convicted murderers who were assigned to guard and sometimes shoot dead convicts in the fields.

In 1972, District Judge William C. Keady held in *Gates v. Collier* that Mississippi violated the First, Eighth, and Fourteenth Amendments as well as several provisions of its own state law mandating minimal standards at Parchman Farm. The court subsequently issued 150 orders for relief. By 1976, Parchman Farm had been fully dismantled.

PRIMARY SOURCE

D.A. MCCALL, SECRETARY OF THE MISSISSIPPI BAPTIST CONVENTION BOARD, BAPTIZES CONVICTS ON A PRISON FARM NEAR PARCHMAN ON 18 AUGUST 1946

See primary source image.

SIGNIFICANCE

Parchman Farm was the product of a prison movement that began in the United States in the 1820s. Prior to this time, Americans of the colonial and early national periods viewed crime as a normal part of life. They did not attempt to eliminate crime since sin was a predictable and inevitable result of the corruption of humans. This religious perspective did not lead to humane treatment of offenders. Harsh corporal and capital punishments were common in this early era.

The direction of American punishment took a new and sudden turn during the presidency of Andrew Jackson in the 1820s. The rise of the market economy and the extension of the vote to all white men created a world that was dramatically and disturbingly different from previous eras. Traditional forms of social control were now believed to be inadequate in a complex society threatened by imminent social disorder. Crime was suddenly viewed as a social problem instead of a religious one.

In response to growing fears, penitentiaries were constructed as institutions for criminals. The penitentiary, with its emphasis on architecture, internal arrangement, and daily routine, reflected the American vision of what a well-ordered society should be. In contrast to colonial Americans, who used institutions

only as a last resort, Jacksonians viewed prisons as a first resort to combat social problems.

Jacksonians developed two systems of prison discipline. Both the Pennsylvania and Auburn models enforced silence, attempted spiritual reform, and emphasized societal obedience. Only the Auburn system included work programs and striped suits. Inmates worked side by side in silence. The impressive rate of productivity made the Auburn model popular. No one questioned the institutional incarceration as primary strategy for crime control.

By the late twentieth century, the Auburn model had become barbaric to many influential Americans. Prisons that emphasized work programs and incarceration instead of reform came under very heavy attack. A number of influential scholars theorized that the ruling class used the criminal justice system to oppress, regulate, and coerce the working class. The existence of Parchman Farm, a predominantly black labor camp that financially profited the state of Alabama, gave support to this argument. The prison had to change because it no longer fit American ideas about social control. It had become the most famous example of primitive justice and a place out of step with the nation's evolving sense of decency.

FURTHER RESOURCES

Books

Taylor, William Banks. *Down on Parchman Farm: The Great Prison in the Mississippi Delta*. Columbus, Ohio: Ohio State University Press, 1999.

Welch, Michael. *Punishment in America: Social Control and the Ironies of Imprisonment*. Thousand Oaks, Calif.: Sage, 1999.

Gangs in Perspective

Book excerpt

By: Gilbert Geis

Date: June 1965

Source: Gilbert Geis. *Juvenile Gangs*. Washington D.C.: U.S. Government Printing Office, 1965.

About the Author: A retired professor from the University of California at Irvine, Gilbert Geis received his doctorate from the University of Wisconsin at Madison. He has researched and written extensively on topics

Gang members in New York City flee the scene after a fight, 1962. © BETTMANN/CORBIS

related to criminology and juvenile delinquency. More than 350 of his articles have been published and he is a past president of the American Society of Criminology.

INTRODUCTION

Gang violence in the major urban centers continues to be one of the greatest sources of criminal activity in the United States. Gangs, despite ongoing efforts on the part of law enforcement to limit their growth, continue to attract youth particularly in inner city areas with large minority communities. Violence connected to gangs is believed to have led to the deaths of more than 25,000 people over the last two decades. Gangs of various sizes can be found in more than 800 cities around the United States.

During the 1990s, the rise in gang activity and related crimes served as the basis for enhanced legislation directly focused upon limiting the spread of gangs. While gang violence among juveniles is a problem that is most prevalent in the United States, similar phenomena exist in other Western democracies.

Sociology and criminology experts maintain that the rise of gang activity is linked to a general ethical mood prevalent in the greater society. Youth are generally attracted to the life styles offered by gangs because they present juveniles with a sense of belonging and camaraderie as well as excitement.

While the number of gangs and the number of gang members continue to rise, the intensity and nature of the violent activities with which they are involved are not believed to have grown worse as compared to similar groups in history. The types of criminal activity with which gangs in modern society are involved are similar to the illegal or antisocial activities with which such groups have been involved throughout history. It is believed that the renewed focus on gangs has come about with the gradual breakdown of social barriers between classes in Western democracies, allowing the threats posed by gangs to become more visible.

Efforts aimed at combating gang violence focus on a combination of enhanced law enforcement and educational and social programming. Specific attention is paid by the judicial system towards rehabilitating gang members while they are in prison with the intent that upon release they will be able to find new, non-criminal activities.

PRIMARY SOURCE

The conclusions of the Mead study and similar inquiries force us to look closely at the social structure in which gangs form and in which they operate in order to obtain an indication of the functions which gangs serve. The conclusions of these studies also lead us to an appreciation of the fact that gangs need not exist—that they are not necessary products of something inherent in the nature of young men. And finally, anthropological research reminds us, lest we be inclined to forget, that the basic ingredients of gang existence probably lie deeply embedded within the fabric of a society, and that products of its social structure and ordering will continue to remain relatively impervious to major alterations so long as dominant social motifs persist.

In the United States, the emphasis on competition and individualism, for instance, which is basic to our way of life, probably could not be altered drastically without social surgery that might be extremely injurious to the general vitality and attractiveness of many aspects of our existence. At the same time, if juvenile delinquency and gang activity are most basically responses to the ethos of the society in which they are found, it is also unlikely that either will be eradicated in any dramatic fashion in the United States in the near future.

Cross-Cultural Perspective.—Albert K. Cohen, a sociologist at the University of Connecticut, has pointed out that "the sad truth is that the comparative study of juvenile delinquency does not exist." Cohen's call for such research is based upon a desire to gather cross-cultural material in order, among other things, to understand better similar behavior in our own society. He quotes two Italian researchers who have indicated that gangs as we know them are rare in their country and, where they do exist, they seldom attack other adolescents but direct their activity against adults. "If this is so," Cohen suggests, "the tendency for delinquents to coalesce into gangs and for gangs to war on other gangs, so common in our country, is not necessarily implicit in the idea of delinquency."

The material that we do have from foreign countries regarding delinquent and gang behavior is quite suggestive in terms of broadening our understanding of the full panorama of such activity. It also helps to provide additional clues to the cultural roots of delinquency since it is often through noting similarities and variations to the thing that interests us that we come to a clearer understanding of its generic attributes. Thus, for instance, a study of race relations in the Union of South Africa, where conditions are worse, as well as in Hawaii and Brazil, where they are better, will contribute considerably to an appreciation of the nature of America's racial situation today.

It is worth noting initially that the present state of gang behavior in the United States hardly indicates the total depravity of our society. Nor is it accurate to maintain that conditions today are worse than they were in the romanticized past of human history. Daniel Bell, among other social commentators, has tried to show that crime was probably appreciably higher and more brutal during America's frontier period than it is today. Bell believes that the general breakdown of social barriers between classes has brought about the myth that the country is more ridden with illegality now than earlier in its history. Previously, persons in the middle class were merely better shielded, because of communication and transportation obstacles, from evidence of violence and theft.

Throughout recorded history, individuals and groups have always failed to adhere to demands for conformity to the general dictates of their society, and they have resorted to acts which were outlawed or disapproved. It is very difficult to specify with precision those conditions which have particularly encouraged or discouraged illegal aggression or depredations in any society at any time in history. A lack of consensus regarding proper social behavior among all members of the society is, of course, virtually by definition an underlying factor in disruptive activity. The real and the perceived ability and efficiency of retaliatory forces, either secular or theological, have also undoubtedly influenced the extent and form of antisocial behavior. Deprivation alone, however, is hardly adequate to account for phenomena such as crime and gang violence; nor, for that matter, neither is any other single isolated factor sufficient unto itself as an explanation. But it again needs to be emphasized that gang behavior today hardly points to a state of degeneracy and decline in contemporary civilization. Note, for instance, the following vivid portrayal of gang activity in the 18th century by William Lecky, the noted historian of bygone manners and morals:

> The impunity with which outrages were committed in the ill-lit and ill-guarded streets of London during the first half of the eighteenth century can now hardly be realized. In 1712, a club of young men of the higher classes, who assumed the name of Mohocks, were accustomed nightly to sally out drunk into the streets to hunt the passers-by and to subject them in mere wantonness to the most atrocious outrages. One of

their favorite amusements, called "tipping the lion," was to sqeeze the nose of their victim flat upon his face and to bore out his eyes with their fingers. Among them were the "sweaters" who formed a circle round their prisoner and pricked him with their swords until he sank exhausted to the ground, the "dancing masters" so-called from their skill in making men caper by thrusting swords into their legs, the "tumblers," whose favorite amusement was to set women on their heads and to commit various indecencies and barbarities on the limbs that were exposed. Maid servants, as they opened their masters' doors, were waylaid, beaten and their faces cut. Matrons enclosed in barrels were rolled down the steep and stony incline of Snow Hill. Watchmen were beaten unmercifully and their noses slit. Country gentlemen went to the theater as if in time of war, accompanied by their armed retainers.Such behavior makes most contemporary juvenile gangs appear by comparison to be composed of gentle and mild-mannered lads out for a playful romp. It is usually reassuring and always fruitful to try to gain a clearer perspective of current events by looking back into historical annals and archives.

The two most noteworthy parallels to American gang activity in recent European history appear in prewar Germany and in the post-revolutionary Soviet Union. Both seem to indicate a combination of social upheaval and ideological disruption as major ingredients in the emergence of juvenile gangs.

Following the Soviet revolution of 1917, large groups of youths, finding themselves in a socially disorganized society, which was still groping for political order, and also finding themselves without adequate adult supervision because of the death or dislocation of their parents and relatives, formed marauding bands, housing themselves in cellars and similar makeshift shelters in or near the large urban centers.

Attempts to incorporate these youths into the majority society after the regime had become more stabilized were unsuccessful at first, and the explanation offered, "that children who had lived for more than a year on the streets found it difficult to adapt themselves to the new life" because they had been "influenced by the picaresque life of the vagabond," has relevance to work with gangs in the United States. It suggests the importance of appreciating fully the attractions of gang existence, the camaraderie, the self-indulgence, the luxury, and the excitement of gang life that must be weighed with the disadvantages so that a better understanding is achieved of both the lures and the fears connected with gang membership.

The major stress in Soviet efforts to reform the habits of the bezprizornye (literally, "the neglected"), who

numbered more than 524,000 by 1921, was placed upon training for factory employment. Special use was made of the honor code of the boys, a code somewhat similar to that found among members of American gangs:

> In the beginning we made many mistakes, but now we know that, above all, we must teach these children by appealing to their sense of honor. Strange to say, a sense of honor is much more strongly developed amongst the bezprizornye than it is in normal children. Locks are of no use at all, for they can easily pick them, so we give them keys. They are really astonished that they are treated like ordinary children.

The Soviets inaugurated a rule that no questions be asked of a boy concerning his past life or record, unless he initiated the subject. They also attempted to put group pressure upon individual boys who would not abide by the rules and to instill a sense of shame through ritualized examples of disapproval:

> The children have meetings every evening, and those who have not worked well, or who have done something wrong, are called to account. The unfortunate delinquent has to stand in the middle of a circle and submit to a fire of questions. The worst punishment is temporary forfeiture of the badge of the community.

The use of peers to impose sanctions, in ways similar to that described above, has traditionally been one of the most effective techniques in working with any group. This is particularly true when the peers themselves have at one time occupied the same position as those whom they are now trying to influence. But the technique also contains many subtle pitfalls and much potential for boomeranging upon a program, unless it is employed with considerable care and understanding. In fact, as we shall shortly see, despite their apparent success with the bezprizornye, the Soviets actually still have not resolved the problem of youthful rebellion and continue to grope for adequate methods for dealing with it.

The German adolescents, the Vandervogel, had a considerably more formal and formidable structure than the Russian youths and resembled in some respects the Boy Scouts in the United States. Their generally middle-class background adds a different note to the study of rebellious gangs, which usually are formed in working-class settings. The Vandervogel, unlike our Boy Scouts, however, were in strong opposition to the values of their parents, whom they viewed as stolid burgher types, unexciting and hardly worthy of emulation. As Becker has noted:

> German youth loathed and hated the world of their elders, and were ready to follow any Pied Piper whose mystery and power held promise of a new realm where longings found fruition. Definite promises,

clear-cut goals, purposeful methods were unnecessary—indeed, no small part of the revulsion against adult life was against its very planfulness, its readiness to cast aside the joys of spontaneity in favor of crafty money-getting and the ribbon to stick to the coat. It was a rebellion against flabby school routine, insincere church attendance, flatulent concerns, boring parties designed for display and climbing, repellent counsel about ways of getting on in the world—to escapes making you feel that adventure was still possible.

The German Vandervogel groups tended to be led by individuals who have been characterized as "eternal adolescents"—unstable of purpose, diffusely emotional, dogmatically idealistic, intellectually fuzzy, and erotically fixated on leaders or followers—Becker thus describes them, and believes that "they found the gates of the adult world too high to scale or too forbidding to enter." The Vandervogel were also characterized by a strong homosexual tinge, a trait that may not be receiving adequate attention in studies of American gang behavior, in which personal adornment and fanciful hair styles, normally considered the province of female plumage, often represent the trademark of the gang member. The Vandervogel, however, were considerably more monastic than their American counterparts, which often have girl auxiliaries and extensive heterosexual involvement.

The Vandervogel engaged in numerous outings and camping expeditions, sometimes traveling to neighboring countries, where they acquired experience and information that later was to prove of considerable value to invading German troops during the second World War. It was during the course of the War, in fact, often as gestapo members, that Vandervogel initiates found a sympathetic response to their previous social protest, and it was in the gestapo that they often discovered a satisfying role to play and a niche that was able to provide them with the rewards and the recognition they desired.

The German and Russian material on gangs points consistently to the relationship between social conditions and the appearance of juvenile groups of a particular nature. The political and middle-class coloration of the German gangs and the prevalent pattern of mobility among the dispossessed Soviet youth are both adaptations different from the phenomenon of today's American urban, insular, and apolitical working-class gangs. It may be that we are soon to witness the birth of political awareness among American gangs, particularly as racial issues blaze in urban areas, and it may be that middle-class youths will revolt more pronouncedly against social pressures and gather together in defiant groups in order to render their protest more effective. If so, we will have to trace the origins of these movements to social conditions and base attempts to ameliorate them upon an understanding and interpretation of such conditions.

The lesson that might be read from the history of the German and Soviet youth movements is that there are at least two general ways of "reforming" gangs—one is to make them by one means or another conform more closely to the values of the major social system, while the other is to have that system move more closely toward their values. It would seem perhaps to be the better part of social wisdom, granting these choices, to aim for some sort of an intermediate condition: To offer to the gang member some acceptable use and outlet for his talents, feelings, and aspirations by effecting some alterations in the social system or in his ability to cope with it. In response to such widened opportunity, presumably the gang member will come to abandon some of his more unacceptable behavior.

SIGNIFICANCE

While gangs have become an entrenched part of American society and there is a direct link between juvenile delinquency and gang violence, this article suggests that gangs need not be a necessary problem in all U.S. cities and that there are ways of combating them. Yet, the author contends that, given the nature of the societies in which gangs have been allowed to flourish, reducing the frequency of gang crimes will not be easily achieved.

Gang violence is linked to serious crimes like armed robbery and homicides, generally precipitated by one gang infringing on the territory of another. Despite the violent nature of these gangs, this article highlights that in relation to other criminally inspired groups in history, modern day gangs in the United States are relatively mild. The primary causes for the growth of gangs in society have historically been linked to major social upheaval. Using this argument, the article suggests that gangs are as much a reflection of a lack of general moral norms in society as opposed to evidence of growing juvenile delinquency.

The Soviet Union in the post-revolution years and Germany just prior to the World War II, are prime examples of environments in which social disharmony contributed to the growth of youth gangs. While this article was written in 1965, a period of considerably more social unrest than later decades, its thesis is significant—addressing the broader society is key to fixing the growing problems of juvenile delinquency.

The solutions offered by this article focus on motivating the broader American society to reach out to gang members and encourage them to use their talents and emotions for positive purposes. The article supports a method of treatment towards gang members based on respect rather than harsh discipline. It is believed that when gang members see themselves as more respectable youth rather than neglected citizens, they will feel more appreciated and be less prone to violence. This approach asserts that if gang members recognize that society is developing constructive opportunities for them, they will, in some part, abandon their criminal activities in favor of more lawful behavior.

FURTHER RESOURCES

Books

Christensen, Loren W. *Gangbangers: Understanding the Deadly Minds of America's Street Gangs.* Boulder, Colo.: Paladin Press, 1999.

Hernandez, Arturo. *Peace in the Streets: Breaking the Cycle of Gang Violence.* Washington, D.C.: Child Welfare League of America, 1998.

Web sites

Safe Youth.org. "Youth Gangs." <http://www.safeyouth.org/scripts/teens/gangs.asp> (accessed February 7, 2006).

Motorcycle Gangs: Losers and Outsiders

Magazine article

By: Hunter S. Thompson

Date: May 17, 1965

Source: Thompson, Hunter S. "Motorcycle Gangs: Losers and Outsiders." *The Nation* (May 17, 1965).

About the Author: Hunter S. Thompson (1937–2005) is best known as the founder of "gonzo" journalism, an irreverent style of reporting in which the distinction between the subject of an article and the writer's personal perspectives is often difficult to distinguish. Thompson's work began to find favor with American and international audiences in the late 1960s. Thompson had earned a precarious living as a journalist prior to 1964, the year that he immersed himself in the nascent Hells Angels biker culture of California. As a frequent contributor to *Rolling Stone* magazine, Thompson achieved status as both a counter cultural icon, as well as notoriety as a fierce critic of President Richard Nixon. Thompson was also a best-selling author, with works that included *The Hells Angels* and *The Great Shark Hunt*. Thompson's later work

A member of the Hell's Angels Motorcycle Club experiences engine trouble during the funeral procession in 1966 of fellow member James "Mother" Miles in Sacramento, California, who was killed when his cycle collided with a car. The funeral services were held over a coffin draped by two black leather jackets. © BETTMANN/CORBIS

expressed a deep disenchantment with American society. Thompson took his own life in 2005.

INTRODUCTION

In 1965, the public perception of the motorcycle gang was not the entirely dark and overtly criminal image that this phrase conveys today. The Hells Angels, as then chronicled by Hunter S. Thompson, appear to share more attitudes in common with the drunken brawlers who had ridden their motorcycles into Hollister, California, to briefly take over that town for a weekend in 1947, than with the fearsome modern public persona of the Angels, that of an organized, efficient criminal association.

The California Hells Angels of 1965 were inspired by the image created by the Hollister types— wild, brawling comrades, in search of fun on powerful machines, loud and free spirited, with manners calculated to upset conventional American society. The seed for this archetype was planted at Hollister and then cultivated to cult status by Marlon Brando's portrayal of a motorcycle gang leader in the 1954 film *The Wild One*, a production loosely based on the Hollister incident.

Between 1947 and 1964, motorcycle gangs and their membership were perceived as a small, decidedly fringe element in American society. Three events that occurred in the months prior to the publication of Thompson's 1965 article triggered a process by which this public view point was significantly altered. The first two developments were successive magazine articles, published in *Time* and *Newsweek* respectively, that detailed the problems associated with the behavior of motorcycle gangs in California. These articles were the first national media attention directed at the California motorcycle gang subculture, and they cast its members in a highly negative, anti-social light.

The third event that impacted the public opinion of motorcycle gangs in advance of Thompson's article was the allegation that four members of the California Hells Angles, with whom Thompson consorted in the course of his research, were involved in the gang rape of two young women near Monterey, California over the Labor Day weekend of 1964. Thompson's observations of the gang members are, thus, made at a time in the history of the Hells Angels when the perception of the bikers as simply rowdy, Harley Davidson motorcycle aficionados was beginning to give way to that of the biker as a dangerous criminal.

PRIMARY SOURCE

San Francisco

Last Labor Day weekend newspapers all over California gave front-page reports of a heinous gang rape in the moonlit sand dunes near the town of Seaside on the Monterey Peninsula. Two girls, aged 14 and 15, were allegedly taken from their dates by a gang of filthy, frenzied, boozed-up motorcycle hoodlums called "Hell's Angels," and dragged off to be "repeatedly assaulted."

A deputy sheriff, summoned by one of the erstwhile dates, said he "arrived at the beach and saw a huge bonfire surrounded by cyclists of both sexes. Then the two sobbing, near-hysterical girls staggered out of the darkness, begging for help. One was completely nude and the other had on only a torn sweater."

Some 300 Hell's Angels were gathered in the Seaside-Monterey area at the time, having convened, they said, for the purpose of raising funds among themselves to send the body of a former member, killed in an accident, back to his mother in North Carolina. One of the Angels, hip enough to falsely identify himself as "Frenchy of San Bernardino," told a reporter who came out to meet the cyclists: "We chose Monterey because we get treated good here; most other places we get thrown out of town."

But Frenchy spoke too soon. The Angels weren't on the peninsula twenty-four hours before four of them were in jail for rape, and the rest of the troop was being escorted to the county line by a large police contingent. Several were quoted, somewhat derisively, as saying: "That rape charge against our guys is phony and it won't stick."

It turned out to be true, but that was another story and certainly no headliner. The difference between the Hell's Angels in the paper and the Hell's Angels for real is enough to make a man wonder what newsprint is for. It also raises a question as to who are the real hell's angels.

Ever since World War II, California has been strangely plagued by wild men on motorcycles. They usually travel in groups of ten to thirty, booming along the highways and stopping here and there to get drunk and raise hell. In 1947, hundreds of them ran amok in the town of Hollister, an hour's fast drive south of San Francisco, and got enough press to inspire a film called *The Wild One*, starring Marlon Brando. The film had a massive effect on thousands of young California motorcycle buffs; in many ways, it was their version of *The Sun Also Rises*.

The California climate is perfect for motorcycles, as well as surfboards, swimming pools and convertibles. Most of the cyclists are harmless weekend types, members of the American Motorcycle Association, and no more dangerous than skiers or skin divers. But a few belong to what the others call "outlaw clubs," and these are the ones who—especially on weekends and holidays—are likely to turn up almost anywhere in the state, looking for action. Despite everything the psychiatrists and Freudian casuists have to say about them, they are tough, mean and potentially as dangerous as a pack of wild boar. When push comes to shove, any leather fetishes or inadequacy feelings that may be involved are entirely beside the point, as anyone who has ever tangled with these boys will sadly testify. When you get in an argument with a group of outlaw motorcyclists, you can generally count your chances of emerging unmaimed by the number of heavy-handed allies you can muster in the time it takes to smash a beer bottle. In this league, sportsmanship is for old liberals and young fools. "I smashed his face," one of them said to me of a man he'd never seen until the swinging started. "He got wise. He called me a punk. He must have been stupid."

The most notorious of these outlaw groups is the Hell's Angels, supposedly headquartered in San Bernardino, just east of Los Angeles, and with branches all over the state. As a result of the infamous "Labor Day gang rape," the Attorney General of California has recently issued an official report on the Hell's Angels. According to the report, they are easily identified:

The emblem of the Hell's Angels, termed "colors," consists of an embroidered patch of a winged skull wearing a motorcycle helmet. Just below the wing of the emblem are the letters "MC." Over this is a band bearing the words "Hell's Angels." Below the emblem is another patch bearing the local chapter name, which is usually an abbreviation for the city or locality. These patches are sewn on the back of a usually sleeveless denim jacket. In addition, members have been observed wearing various types of Luftwaffe insignia and reproductions of German iron crosses.* (*Purely for decorative and shock effect. The Hell's Angels are apolitical and no more racist than other ignorant young thugs.) Many affect beards and their hair is usually long and unkempt. Some wear a single earring in a pierced ear lobe. Frequently they have been observed to wear metal belts made of a length of polished motorcycle drive chain which can be unhooked and used as a flexible bludgeon... Probably the most universal common denominator in identification of Hell's Angels is generally their filthy condition. Investigating officers consistently report these people, both club members and their female associates, seem badly in need of a bath. Fingerprints are a very effective means of identification because a high percentage of Hell's Angels have criminal records.

In addition to the patches on the back of Hell's Angel's jackets, the "One Percenters" wear a patch reading "1%-er." Another badge worn by some members bears the number "13." It is reported to represent the 13th letter of the alphabet, "M," which in turn stands for marijuana and indicates the wearer thereof is a user of the drug.

The Attorney General's report was colorful, interesting, heavily biased and consistently alarming—just the sort of thing, in fact, to make a clanging good article for a national news magazine. Which it did; in both barrels. *Newsweek* led with a left hook titled "The Wild Ones," *Time* crossed right, inevitably titled "The Wilder Ones." The Hell's Angels, cursing the implications of this new attack, retreated to the bar of the DePau Hotel near the San Francisco waterfront and planned a weekend beach party. I showed them the articles. Hell's Angels do not normally read the news magazines. "I'd go nuts if I read that stuff all the time," said one. "It's all bullshit."

Newsweek was relatively circumspect. It offered local color, flashy quotes and "evidence" carefully attributed to the official report but unaccountably said the report accused the Hell's Angels of homosexuality, whereas the report said just the opposite. *Time* leaped into the fray with a flurry of blood, booze and semen-flecked wordage that amounted, in the end, to a classic of supercharged hokum: "Drug-induced stupors... no act is too degrading... swap girls, drugs and motorcycles with equal abandon... stealing forays... then ride off again to seek some new nadir in sordid behavior..."

Where does all this leave the Hell's Angels and the thousands of shuddering Californians (according to *Time*) who are worried sick about them? Are these outlaws really going to be busted, routed and cooled, as the news magazines implied? Are California highways any safer as a result of this published uproar? Can honest merchants once again walk the streets in peace? The answer is that nothing has changed except that a few people calling themselves the Hell's Angels have a new sense of identity and importance.

After two weeks of intensive dealings with the Hell's Angels phenomenon, both in print and in person, I'm convinced the net result of the general howl and publicity has been to obscure and avoid the real issues by invoking a savage conspiracy of bogeymen and conning the public into thinking all will be "business as usual" once this fearsome snake is scotched, as it surely will be by hard and ready minions of the Establishment.

Meanwhile, according to Attorney General Thomas C. Lynch's own figures, California's true crime picture makes the Hell's Angels look like a gang of petty jack rollers. The police count 463 Hell's Angels: 205 around L.A. and 233 in the San Francisco-Oakland area. I don't know about L.A. but the real figures for the Bay Area are thirty or so in Oakland and exactly eleven—with one facing expulsion—in San Francisco. This disparity makes it hard to accept other police statistics. The dubious package also shows convictions on 1,023 misdemeanor counts and 151 felonies—primarily vehicle theft, burglary and assault. This is for all years and all alleged members.

California's overall figures for 1963 list 1,116 homicides, 12,448 aggravated assaults, 6,257 sex offenses, and 24,532 burglaries. In 1962, the state listed 4,121 traffic deaths, up from 3,839 in 1961. Drug arrest figures for 1964 showed a 101 percent increase in juvenile marijuana arrests over 1963, and a recent back-page story in the *San Francisco Examiner* said, "The venereal disease rate among [the city's] teen-agers from 15–19 has more than doubled in the past four years." Even allowing for the annual population jump, juvenile arrests in all categories are rising by 10 percent or more each year.

Against this background, would it make any difference to the safety and peace of mind of the average Californian if every motorcycle outlaw in the state (all 901, according to the state) were garroted within twenty-four hours? This is not to say that a group like the Hell's Angels has no meaning. The generally bizarre flavor of their offenses and their insistence on identifying themselves make good copy, but usually overwhelm—in print, at least—the unnerving truth that they represent, in colorful microcosm, what is quietly and anonymously growing all around us every day of the week.

"We're bastards to the world and they're bastards to us," one of the Oakland Angels told a *Newsweek* reporter. "When you walk into a place where people can see you, you want to look as repulsive and repugnant as possible. We are complete social outcasts—outsiders against society."

A lot of this is a pose, but anyone who believes that's all it is has been on thin ice since the death of Jay Gatsby. The vast majority of motorcycle outlaws are uneducated, unskilled men between 20 and 30, and most have no credentials except a police record. So at the root of their sad stance is a lot more than a wistful yearning for acceptance in a world they never made; their real motivation is an instinctive certainty as to what the score really is. They are out of the ball game and they know it—and that is their meaning; for unlike most losers in today's society, the Hell's Angels not only know but spitefully proclaim exactly where they stand.

I went to one of their meetings recently, and half-way through the night I thought of Joe Hill on his way to face a Utah firing squad and saying his final words: "Don't mourn, organize." It is safe to say that no Hell's Angel has ever heard of Joe Hill or would know a Wobbly from a Bushmaster, but nevertheless they are somehow related. The I.W.W. had serious plans for running the world, while the Hell's Angels mean only to defy the world's machinery. But instead of losing quietly, one by one, they have banded together with a mindless kind of loyalty and moved outside the framework, for good or ill. There is nothing particularly romantic or admirable about it; that's just the way it is, strength in unity. They don't mind telling you that running fast and loud on their customized Harley 74s gives them a power and a purpose that nothing else seems to offer.

Beyond that, their position as self-proclaimed outlaws elicits a certain popular appeal, however reluctant. That is especially true in the West and even in California where the outlaw tradition is still honored. The unarticulated link between the Hell's Angels and the millions of losers and outsiders who don't wear any colors is the key to their notoriety and the ambivalent reactions they inspire. There are several other keys, having to do with politicians, policemen and journalists, but for this we have to go back to Monterey and the Labor Day "gang rape."

SIGNIFICANCE

The chief importance of the observations of Hunter S. Thompson regarding the California Hells Angels as they existed in 1965 is that his work represents the preservation of a historical artifact. The characterizations of the bikers and their community by Thompson is akin to a prehistoric insect being encased in amber, as the modern, multi-national, and highly structured Hells Angels bear very little resemblance to the undisciplined rowdy rabble depicted here.

Thompson refers to an unspoken identification that he perceived as existing between the Hells Angels and the lower strata of male American society, each possessing the same limited talents and abilities. The bikers were only a sample of these millions of losers and outsiders. This is a far more difficult relationship to imagine as existing today between biker gangs and society, given the widespread negative publicity such gangs have attracted, primarily through high profile prosecutions for drug trafficking, murder, extortion, and other serious crime.

A second, purely journalistic significance to Thompson's work is the fact that his fresh, candid perspective was due to what today would be inconceivable—unfettered, daily access to the Hells Angels membership. This access gives Thompson's work a breadth of perspective that is reflected in his scathing criticism of both the police attitudes towards the Hells Angels and the loser that he sees as the dominant component of Hells Angels membership. The richness of Thompson's narrative is a product of the closeness of his associations with his subject.

Thompson's use of the term "outlaw" to characterize the Hells Angels membership was not the first example in American journalism of this usage. The Hollister biker incident in 1947 was labeled an outlaw occurrence at that time. However, the description of the Hollister participants as outlaws was a reflexive usage of the term, unsupported by any analysis of whom or what these rowdy, drunken persons represented. In contrast, Thompson's description of the outlaw mentality of the Hells Angels in 1965 was both timely and prescient. It was clear that the Hells Angels perceived themselves as beyond the reach of conventional society and its laws; it is equally beyond question that "outlaw" is today the accepted label for all such motorcycle organizations. In 1965, the term conveyed a notion of non-conformist, unconventional behavior, linked to the freedom of the open road; the modern outlaw motorcycle gang is associated with little beyond criminality.

Thompson also clearly articulates a viewpoint that has remained the mantra for the public relations arms of the organized motorcycle gangs today—that their membership is not a threat to anyone, that they are, at heart, simply like-minded motorcycle enthusiasts, and that as Thompson describes it, the police-inspired fears of bikers are just a "big con."

Thompson supports his thesis of the Hells Angels as an overstated threat to society from a number of angles. In addition to his derisive attitude concerning the sophistication and capabilities of the membership, Thompson sees the bikers fundamentally as striking a pose, with the club colors, patches, and paraphernalia all calculated to create an image of rebellion, when in fact the bikers yearn for societal acceptance. Thompson describes the motivation to become a Hells Angels member as apparently mindless, the banding together of men who are motivated by a perverse loyalty to one another, as if these people had no greater imagination to do anything else.

A compelling irony to Thompson's work is the fact that he lived long enough (he died in February 2005) to observe the rise of the Hells Angels and other gangs, such as the Detroit-based Banditos, from local aggregations to powerful, multi-national, chapter-based organizations that are linked to the international criminal world.

FURTHER RESOURCES

Books

Dubois, Judith. *Media Coverage of Organized Crime: Impact on Public Opinion?* Ottawa: Research and Evaluation Branch, Royal Canadian Mounted Police, June, 2002. Available at: <http://www.rcmp-grc.gc.ca/ccaps/media_e.htm> (accessed November 2, 2005).

Thompson, Hunter S. *Hells Angels.* New York: Ballantine Books, 1966.

Web sites

Hells Angels Motor Cycle Club—Sweden. <http://www.hells-angels.se> (accessed November 2, 2005).

Antiwar Demonstrator Throwing Tear Gas

Photograph

By: Anonymous

Date: May 5, 1970

Source: Bettman/Corbis.

About the Photographer: The photographer is unknown.

INTRODUCTION

During the Vietnam War the United States supported the South Vietnamese government in its opposition to the communist-led North Vietnamese, who wanted to unite the two countries under a soviet-style government. Beginning in the mid-1950s, when the U.S. first sent a handful of military advisors, American military involvement grew rapidly in the 1960s. By 1969 over 500,000 combat troops were stationed in Vietnam.

While most Americans supported the war effort, a minority vocally opposed it. This minority grew larger and more aggressive as the war expanded. Pacifists began to protest American involvement in Southeast Asia as early as 1963. They emphasized acts of personal witness, particularly civil disobedience, which carried the risk of arrest and jail. As the war escalated, President Lyndon B. Johnson launched massive bombing raids and substantially increased the number of U.S. troops in Vietnam. Johnson's policies sparked protests on college campuses, and students quickly became the most visible group in the antiwar movement. In part this was because the draft brought the war home to male students in a very personal way, becoming the focus of widespread resistance.

After Johnson declined to run for reelection, Nixon's expansion of the war into neighboring Cambodia set off more protests. At Kent State University in Ohio, students held a mock funeral for the Constitution and burned a Reserve Officer Training Corps building. The mayor of Kent declared a state of emergency and requested assistance from Ohio Governor James Rhodes, who sent the National Guard to restore order. On May 4, 1970, during a scheduled protest, the guardsmen attempted to disperse the crowd. During the chaos that followed, the guardsmen fired a thirteen-second volley that killed four students and injured nine. Kent State immediately closed for the remainder of the school year, while demonstrations in response to the shooting forced almost 500 other universities to suspend classes.

PRIMARY SOURCE

ANTIWAR DEMONSTRATOR THROWING TEAR GAS
See primary source image.

Antiwar protests persisted through the early 1970s and attracted much media coverage wherever they were held. Conservatives blamed the student protesters and the media for giving aid and comfort to the enemy by undermining the war effort. Activists challenged U.S. support of an apparently never-ending and increasingly unpopular war. In 1972, Democratic presidential candidate George McGovern openly stated his plans to withdraw American forces from Vietnam. By the time the Paris Peace Accords were signed in 1973, more than 60 percent of Americans opposed the war. American involvement ended in 1975 when the U.S. withdrew the last of its forces from South Vietnam, and the nation fell to the communist North Vietnamese.

The anger over Vietnam has never truly disappeared from American politics with liberals and conservatives at the millennium still debating the merits of American involvement. Opposition to U.S. military intervention overseas has remained strong. In the wake of Vietnam, presidents hesitated to send troops to foreign hotspots for fear that the U.S. would become trapped in another quagmire that would again badly split the nation.

FURTHER RESOURCES

Books

DeBenedetti, Charles. *An American Ordeal: The Antiwar Movement of the Vietnam Era.* Syracuse, NY: Syracuse University Press, 1997.

De Groot, Gerard J. *A Noble Cause?: America and the Vietnam War.* New York: Pearson Education, 2000.

PRIMARY SOURCE

Antiwar Demonstrator Throwing Tear Gas: An anti-war demonstrator at the University of California, Berkeley, throws a tear gas cannister at police during a student strike on May 5, 1971 to protest the killing the previous day of four students at Kent State University by National Guardsmen. © BETTMANN/CORBIS

SIGNIFICANCE

In 1979 the state of Ohio settled a civil suit with the families of the four dead students; Governor Rhodes signed a statement that the incident was a tragedy that should never have occurred.

Rubin "Hurricane" Carter Gripping Jail Bars

Photograph

By: Anonymous

Date: 1975

Source: Bettmann Archives, Corbis Corporation.

About the Photographer: This image is owned by Corbis a photo agency headquartered in Seattle, Washingtong. Corbis licenses images for use in magazines, films, television, and advertisements. The photographer is unknown.

INTRODUCTION

Rubin Carter (1937–) acquired the nickname "Hurricane" when he was an aspiring middleweight boxer, battling his way to international prominence from the rugged environs of Paterson, New Jersey. In 1966, Carter was a ranked middleweight contender, with aspirations of becoming a world boxing champion. On June 17, 1966, Carter and a friend, John Artis, were intending to spend the evening in a local Paterson tavern. At a nearby establishment, the Lafayette Bar and Grill, two black men burst into the lounge, each armed with a gun and clearly intent on a robbery. The Lafayette did not serve blacks and it had an all white clientele. In the struggle, two people were shot and killed by the robbers, who fled the scene. Carter and Artis were stopped in Carter's vehicle not far from the Lafayette. A subsequent investigation located two live rounds in Carter's vehicle that matched the caliber of the murder weapon used at the Lafayette. Carter and Artis were identified by eyewitnesses from the Lafayette as the perpetrators; a number of these witness statements were later recanted or otherwise undermined. Carter provided an alibi after his arrest, which was later established to be false.

Race was a dominant theme in the proceedings against Rubin Carter from the time of his arrest. Carter and Artis were black, as were the robbers observed by the eyewitnesses. The police investigators and all of the key prosecution witnesses were white. Carter maintained, in a variety of ways, that he and Artis were the victims of a police frame-up. In the first trial, all available witnesses testified, including those whose stories had changed in any fashion between the night of the murders and date of the prosecution. Carter and Artis were convicted of murder in May 1967, and they faced the death penalty as a result.

The racial overtones of the trial were precipitating factors in the increasing publicity concerning Rubin Carter and what was seen by many as a wrongful conviction. Carter launched an appeal, a process that spanned a period of more than eight years. Numerous issues regarding trial and procedural fairness were raised on appeal, and the New Jersey Supreme Court ordered a new trial. The second trial was held in June 1976, and a jury again convicted Carter and Artis of the robbery and the murders at the Lafayette. The essential foundation for the prosecution case in the second trial was unchanged from the 1967 proceedings—a combination of eye-witness identification, the live ammunition, and Carter's apparently false alibi.

The second trial and conviction of Carter did not silence public outrage; in the minds of many, Carter was a symbol of all that was wrong with the American justice system, which was widely seen as discriminatory in its treatment of the black population. Carter's circumstances became an international *cause célèbre*, and support from a number of international groups galvanized around him. With such assistance, Carter successfully appealed his second conviction in 1985, with the New Jersey Supreme Court again ordering a new trial, highlighting further procedural errors made at the second trial. The state decided that it would not prosecute Carter a third time; he had spent nineteen years in prison between the time of his arrest and the final decision of the prosecution.

Carter and his supporters claimed the outcome was an exoneration; no such official or legal pronouncement has ever been made regarding the case. Carter moved to Canada, where he was a member of the Association in Defense of the Wrongfully Convicted (ACWYC), based in Toronto. He resigned from this organization, amidst dissension with its Canadian leadership, in 2004.

PRIMARY SOURCE

RUBIN "HURRICANE" CARTER GRIPPING JAIL BARS

See primary source image.

SIGNIFICANCE

In 1975, singer Bob Dylan recorded the song, "Hurricane" (the first stanza is quoted below) both in tribute to Carter and as a condemnation of the perceived police racism that had worked against him. The popular song captured an ethos and a sensibility that was evident throughout much of the United States in 1975:

> Pistol shots ring out in the barroom night
> Enter Patty Valentine from the upper hall.
> She sees the bartender in a pool of blood,
> Cries out, "My God, they killed them all!"
> Here comes the story of the Hurricane,
> The man the authorities came to blame
> For somethin' that he never done.
> Put in a prison cell, but one time he could-a been
> The champion of the world.

Although the events are unconnected, the notion of a wrong to be righted for Rubin Carter—a racially rooted sin to be redressed—carried with it for his supporters the same moral imperative that flooded from the Watergate scandals.

As with many prosecutions where an accused person is held up as a symbol of an injustice like racism,

PRIMARY SOURCE

Rubin "Hurricane" Carter Gripping Jail Bars: Boxer Rubin "Hurricane" Carter, who was arrested and imprisoned along with John Artis for a bar room murder in 1966. He was released in 1985 when a judge finally decreed that the arrest and conviction had been based on racial prejudice and not on facts. © BETTMANN/CORBIS

the cause is often far more attractive than the purported victim himself. Rubin Carter became an international symbol of what was wrong with American justice; the drive to free him focused on his race and policing attitudes towards blacks, while setting aside two jury verdicts reached on the basis of the physical evidence of live ammunition, a false alibi, and a number of eyewitnesses, however tainted. There was an undoubted racial divide in America in 1975; whether that divide and Carter's guilt intersected is a significant issue that remains current.

In addition to the spotlight that the Carter prosecution cast upon race in the justice system, the broader issue of wrongful conviction and its consequences, which was the motivation for many seeking Carter's freedom, is cast in a different light today. Scientific testing—both DNA evidence and sophisticated ballistics analysis—often level a playing field tilted by racial

inequality and intolerance. The Lafayette Lounge murder scene in 1966 would be approached by investigators today more systematically and scientifically; the evidence gathered at such scenes today is subjected to forensic analysis in the hope that science can provide definitive answers regarding guilt and innocence. Science has not eradicated issues of race in criminal investigations, but it has provided a measure of objectivity absent in 1966 America.

Rubin Carter moved to Toronto after his 1985 release from prison in New Jersey. He became an evocative symbol for the Canadian group, the Association in Defense of the Wrongly Convicted, and a member of the ADWYC board. The ADWYC, which were engaged in their own high profile Canadian causes, were quick to capitalize on the fame of Rubin Carter as a purported symbol of a wrongly convicted person. It is significant that Carter has never been exonerated by the legal system or otherwise declared innocent of the Lafayette murders. The fact that he can credibly be held up as such a symbol is more a testament to the characterizations of Carter presented by the media and his celebrity supporters, than to any conclusions drawn from a close examination of the facts of the killings.

Today, DNA technology is a powerful tool in the re-examination of doubtful convictions. An equally notorious 1982 murder case resulted in the conviction and 1992 execution of Richard Coleman by the state of Virginia. This case was the subject of worldwide commentary, including a plea for Coleman's life by Pope John Paul II. Richard Coleman, like Rubin Carter, was held up by opponents of the death penalty as a man convicted (and in Coleman's case, executed) for a crime he did not commit, and proof of the need for the abolition of the death penalty. DNA testing definitively established that Coleman was the murderer in January 2006.

FURTHER RESOURCES

Books

Hirsh, James S. *Hurricane: the Miraculous Journey of Rubin Carter.* New York: Houghton Mifflin, 2000.

Wice, Paul B. *Rubin "Hurricane" Carter and the American Justice System.* New Brunswick, N.J.: Rutgers University Press, 1998.

Web sites

The Graphic Witness. "Hurricane Carter: The Other Side of the Story." <http://www.graphicwitness.com/carter/index.html> (accessed January 13, 2006).

University of Washington School of Law. "The Hurricane." <http://lib.law.washington.edu/ref/hurricane.htm> (accessed January 11, 2006).

The Mob was the City's Watchdog During Giuliani Cleanup

Newspaper article

By: Tom Robbins

Date: March 28, 2003

Source: Robbins, Tom. "The Mob was the City's Watchdog During Giuliani Cleanup." *The Village Voice* (March 28, 2003).

About the Author: Tom Robbins is a staff reporter for *The Village Voice*. He writes about politics and local government in New York City.

INTRODUCTION

During the time he served as mayor of New York City, Rudolph Giuliani (1944–) set himself the task of eliminating organized crime from a number of the city's businesses that had been traditionally under the control of the mob. These included the Fulton Fish Market, the San Gennaro Festival, the garbage disposal industry, and those responsible for unloading trucks across the city. Giuliani included these goals as a major point in his campaign when he was running for office, and once elected, he was vocal about following through with his plans. However, even as Giuliani had members of these businesses questioned regarding their activities in an effort to root out anyone with ties to organized crime, the Department of Finance hired a private security firm to insure the safety of their offices—a security firm with connections to an organized crime family in the Bronx.

PRIMARY SOURCE

In 1996, then mayor Rudy Giuliani was in the midst of a fervent drive to rid the city's private carting and wholesale fish industries of mob influence. Garbagemen, seafood workers, and truck unloaders were interviewed, fingerprinted, and confronted with any evidence of unsavory associations.

"We're sending the clear and unequivocal message," the prosecutor-turned-politician said in a speech, "that we do not tolerate organized crime in the Fulton Fish Market, the carting industry, the San Gennaro festival, or anywhere."

That same year, the Department of Finance quietly signed a three-year contract with a private security firm to provide guards for its offices. The $3 million deal went to the Explorer Investigation Agency, a state-licensed company based in a small, two-story brick building at 601 West 51st Street on the far West Side. The company's chief executive is a white-haired 67-year-old man named Anthony Negri Sr. His contract called for Explorer to provide more than 40 guards at 15 locations around the city, including the finance department's main offices in Lower Manhattan and Brooklyn. The company did well enough to win a renewal of its contract in 1999, this time for $4 million.

At the same time that Negri's firm was being paid to watchdog the offices where much of the city's $23 billion in tax revenue is handled, however, city police detectives assigned to an organized-crime investigation were watching Negri. On three separate occasions over the summer and fall of 1998, they watched Negri pull up in his white Mercury SUV to Joe & Joe's Restaurant on Castle Hill Avenue in the north Bronx, where he met with organized-crime figures. Among them was the then acting boss of the Genovese crime family, Dominick "Quiet Dom" Cirillo.

Detectives were impressed to see Cirillo sit down with Negri and others for several reasons. For one thing, Cirillo, whose nickname reflects his soft-spoken manner, is notoriously careful about whom he meets with. Such caution has helped the 73-year-old gangster, whose only conviction is a 1952 heroin sales rap, stay out of trouble. For another, the acting boss had suffered a recent heart attack, and police weren't sure he was up to managing mob business.

Also sitting with Cirillo and Negri was Michael Crimi, a 66-year-old labor consultant who was the immediate target of the investigation by the office of Manhattan District Attorney Robert Morgenthau and the School Construction Authority. Crimi, although never charged in the probe, was believed to be serving as the mob's "middleman" for a group of corrupt roofing contractors and union officials (see "The Man Who Got Away," March 12–18).

Detectives overheard the trio discuss construction deadlines and the cost of union labor, according to court affidavits filed in conjunction with the case. They caught only intriguing snatches of conversation, among them this comment by Crimi to Negri: "The broad owes him $20,000. He wants to kill her."

The cops weren't the only ones in Joe & Joe's who knew these weren't ordinary businessmen. When Cirillo walked out of the restaurant after a July meeting, one patron was overheard to say, "He is walking alone. He is lucky no one has shot him yet."

Like Crimi, Negri was never charged in the case. But detectives learned through wiretaps and surveillance that the two men were close friends who spoke often about business. Crimi was a regular visitor to Negri's offices on West 51st Street and even used the security firm owner to help arbitrate disputes with business associates. An analysis of Crimi's phone records showed that he called Negri constantly, at work and at his Rockland County home.

Indeed, the men were such good pals, court records show, that Crimi arranged for Negri's son-in-law to get a job with Princeton Restoration, a major roofing contractor that was allegedly secretly paying Crimi $500 a week to arrange favorable union deals.

Detectives also took note that Negri's security firm shares offices in the small building on the corner of Eleventh Avenue and 51st Street with a tiny, 85-member local of the mob-ridden International Longshoremen's Association. There were dozens of calls between Crimi and the offices of ILA Local 976, which represents production and warehouse workers. Inside the same small office, the ILA officials also preside over a much larger union, not affiliated with the AFL-CIO, called the United Construction Trades & Industrial Employees. That union has been accused by other labor organizations of signing low-cost, sweetheart contracts with employers facing legitimate employee organizing drives.

None of those troublesome associations, however, hindered Negri's work for the city. His company was paid a total of $7.5 million for its six years of service to the finance department, records show. It hit just one bad patch, when one of its security guards was caught last August submitting phony time sheets with the help of a finance agency clerk. The city's investigations department nailed that one, and the two men later pled guilty. But even that was considered an isolated incident, and the only reason Explorer Investigation lost a second contract renewal last fall, city officials said, was because another company underbid it. Explorer had a little more trouble with a separate contract, this one with the Port Authority, to guard some piers in Red Hook, Brooklyn. A three-year contract signed in 2001 was canceled last year after a dispute over wage rates. Explorer also holds two other contracts with the Port Authority worth more than $2 million. Negri, as well as his son Anthony Negri Jr., who handles day-to-day affairs for the security firm, failed to return repeated calls.

As long as its investigation into construction corruption was under way, the D.A.'s office had good reason not to tell the city about any shadowy vendors that turned up during its probe. To do so could have jeopardized the secrecy of ongoing, fruitful wiretaps. But the construction probe ended in July 2000 with indictments of 13 people, including top contractors in the roofing business and union officials. All of the D.A.'s secret wiretap information was turned over to defendants and their lawyers. Even Negri would have been notified that he had been overheard on them. But no one remembers doing anything about the fact that a Genovese crime family associate was guarding the city's revenue offices. "There is no cut-and-dried policy on this," said one official in Morgenthau's office. "You don't disclose things during an investigation unless there is imminent harm. Whether you do later is decided on an ad hoc basis." In this case, the official added, "we saw no crimes relating to the guard company."

Negri's mob ties, however, are well known to other law enforcement authorities as well. After federal prosecutors in Brooklyn indicted a group of high-level Genovese gangsters last year, they put Negri's name on a list of mob-tied people the defendants were prohibited from contacting. Nor does law enforcement have any doubts about the security firm owner's mob pedigree. "We believed Negri had more juice than Crimi," said one prosecutor. "It's our understanding that if they ever open the [mob membership] books again, he will be one of the first ones inducted." That level of law enforcement intelligence provided the basis for many of the decisions made by city licensing officials during the Giuliani administration's push to chase wiseguys out of the Fulton Fish Market, the private carting business, and later, the San Gennaro festival. Giuliani's aides, many of them ex-prosecutors themselves, confronted license seekers with city, state, and federal evidence of any contacts with organized crime, often in the form of wiretaps and surveillance photos.

"God forbid anyone in the fish market should have shown up in a social club somewhere," said Gerald McMahon, an attorney who represented more than two dozen fish wholesalers and loading firms that were denied licenses under the system. "That was it for their license." Let alone having been spotted meeting regularly with the acting boss of the Genovese crime family.

SIGNIFICANCE

Prior to becoming the mayor of New York, Rudolph Giuliani built a solid reputation as someone who was tough on crime, particularly anything having to do with the trafficking of drugs. As a lawyer with

Then-U.S. Attorney Rudolph Giuliani (left) and FBI Director William Webster look at chart of "The Commission" of La Cosa Nostra during the 1985 press conference at which reputed godfathers of the nation's five most powerful Mafia families were indicted. © BETTMANN/CORBIS

the U.S. Attorney's office, he served as chief of the Narcotics Unit. Later, as Associate Attorney General, he was responsible for all of the U.S. Attorney's federal law enforcement agencies—the Drug Enforcement Agency, the Bureau of Corrections, and the U.S. Marshals. Once he became mayor, Giuliani turned his attention to improving the safety of New York City, which included taking a stand against organized crime. He wanted to eliminate the tax imposed on numerous businesses by the mob, thereby improving the economy of the city by restoring a fair-market system and allowing business owners to profit from their hard work without having to turn a share of those profits over to organized crime families. As a result, Giuliani was ultimately responsible for the conviction of numerous crime bosses. He succeeded in lowering both the overall crime rate and the incidents of murder by more than half, and New York's methods of crime prevention became an example for other cities across the nation.

Giuliani passed Local Law 50, which changed the way the Fulton Fish Market ran, despite various threats and set backs, including an arson fire that damaged the oldest building in the market. As a result, more fish was delivered to the market, and the cost of unloading that fish was reduced by twenty percent. The price of loading was reduced even further, by seventy percent. Giuliani ended the organized crime monopoly on the carting of refuse by having the city set the maximum rate that any company can charge for garbage removal services. He put an end to illegal gambling and extortion during the annual San Gennaro Festival by requiring the city to grant a new permit each year, one that is withheld until festival promoters agree to a city-appointed monitor who is in charge of making sure the festival operates within legal guidelines. As a result, the amount of money the festival earns each year for charity has risen substantially.

However, even with his ambitious goals and determination, Giuliani was unable to completely control the spread of organized crime in the city. When the Department of Finance hired the Explorer Investigation Agency to handle their security, they awarded a multi-million dollar contract to an organization run by Anthony Negri Sr., a man who was under investigation by New York City police detectives due to his regular association with Dominick "Quiet Dom" Cirillo of the Genovese crime family. Michael Crimi, a labor consultant under suspicion by the Manhattan District Attorney, also met with Negri and Cirillo. Conversations were taped regularly, making it unlikely that the Department of Finance remained ignorant of Negri's ties, even if they were unaware of them in the beginning. However, Negri continued to provide security services, and the contract with Explorer Investigation was renewed once before they were eventually underbid by another firm. The strict attention directed toward those areas of New York targeted by Giuliani's agenda was not applied equally to all areas of business.

This raises the question as to whether certain levels of organized crime were considered acceptable, or whether it was simply a case of an institution being so widespread that it was impossible to eliminate it entirely. In the case of Negri, the Explorer Investigation Agency appeared to be performing the job they were paid for, and at no time was there any indication that illegal activities were taking place in or around the offices of the Department of Finance. If that is the case, then the elimination of organized crime in the areas specifically targeted by Giuliani had a higher priority, given that they were directly affecting the economy and ongoing prosperity of New York City.

FURTHER RESOURCES

Books

Giuliani, Rudolph W., and Kevin Kurson. *Leadership*. New York: Miramax Books, 2004.

Web sites

New York City web site. "Biography of Rudolph Giuliani." <http://www.nyc.gov/html/records/rwg/html/bio.html> (accessed January 12, 2006).

New York City web site. "Freeing the Economy from Organized Crime and Restoring Open, Competitive Markets." <http://www.nyc.gov/html/rwg/html/97/orgcrime.html> (accessed January 12, 2006).

La Cosa Nostra in the United States

Government report

By: James O. Finkenauer

Date: October 1, 2005

Source: Finckenauer, James O. "La Cosa Nostra in the United States." Available at: <http://www.ojp.gov/nij/international/lcn.html> (accessed January 8, 2006).

About the Author: James O. Finckenauer, Ph.D, is a member of the National Institute of Justice (NIJ), which is based in Washington, D.C. The NIJ is the research, evaluation, and development agency of the U.S. Department of Justice. The NIJ has a number of responsibilities, the most comprehensive of which is the assessment of national criminal justice programs and technologies. The NIJ also plays an ongoing role in relation to Homeland Security initiatives, and it also maintains relationships with international organizations such as the United Nations.

INTRODUCTION

La Cosa Nostra (LCN) is one of three popular synonyms for organized crime in the United States; it is an expression used interchangeably with the terms "Mafia" and "the Mob." These terms refer to the place that organized criminals of Italian-American descent have occupied in both the criminal underworld, as well as broader American society, for almost a century. The acronym LCN has been the official term employed by law enforcement officials since 1970, when then Attorney General John Mitchell (1913–1988) ordered federal law enforcement personnel to refrain from all references to the Mafia and its ethnic origins in all official correspondence.

La Cosa Nostra, which took its name in America from the Italian phrase meaning "Our Concern," is an organization with roots in the Sicilian Mafia, a semi-secret criminal organization that rose to prominence in the ports of Sicily in the mid-nineteenth century. Large scale Italian immigration to the United States in the early 1900s, particularly to the cities of New York and Chicago, was the impetus for the establishment of the American variant.

The Volstead Act of 1919 prohibited the sale and distribution of alcohol throughout the United States; the sale of illegal liquor during Prohibition provided the primary stimulus for the growth of the LCN.

FBI Agents and technicians from the New York City Medical Examiners' office search for the bodies of three victims who vanished without a trace. This deserted industrial area of Ozone Park has been known as "The Hole" for over fifty years and is reputed to be the final resting place for a number of mob figures. © RICHARD COHEN/CORBIS

Mobsters such as Al "Scarface" Capone (1899–1947) and the Gambino family of New York were public and notorious figures. The strict hierarchical nature of the LCN, with each "family" headed by a don whose control was virtually absolute, created strict lines of authority within each LCN organization. Violations of the rules of the family were swiftly resolved on an internal and often violent basis. Gambling, extortion, prostitution, and protection became the cornerstones of all organized crime business when Prohibition was repealed in 1933. By the 1960s, the LCN had grown to wield national influence; elements of the LCN not only directed the expansion of the city of Las Vegas and its gambling-based economy but also exercised de facto control of pre-Castro Havana in the 1950s. The suspected involvement of the LCN in the assassination of President John F. Kennedy in 1963 and the disappearance of Teamsters Union president Jimmy Hoffa (1913–1975?) in 1975 has been the subject of intense and persistent national commentary.

As with many successful corporate enterprises, the LCN was quick to seize any available opportunities that were consistent with its core business. The largest of these diversifications was the entry of the LCN into the international drug trade in the 1960s, spearheaded by Charles "Lucky" Luciano(1897–1962).

For the first several decades of its existence, the LCN had thwarted most law enforcement efforts aimed against it, in part due to its ability to corrupt various police and prosecutorial agencies. The passage of the Racketeer Influenced and Corrupt Organizations Act of 1970, better known as RICO, was the first coordinated federal government effort to deal assertively with organized crime. A number of LCN members have been successfully prosecuted under this act, the most notable being the "Teflon Don," John Gotti.

ORGANIZATIONAL STRUCTURE

La Cosa Nostra or LCN—also known as the Mafia, the mob, the outfit, the office—is a collection of Italian-American organized crime "families" that has been operating in the United States since the 1920s. For nearly three quarters of a century, beginning during the time of Prohibition and extending into the 1990s, the LCN was clearly the most prominent criminal organization in the U.S. Indeed, it was synonymous with organized crime. In recent years, the LCN has been severely crippled by law enforcement, and over the past decade has been challenged in a number of its criminal markets by other organized crime groups. Nevertheless, with respect to those criteria that best define the harm capacity of criminal organizations, it is still pre-eminent. The LCN has greater capacity to gain monopoly control over criminal markets, to use or threaten violence to maintain that control, and to corrupt law enforcement and the political system than does any of its competitors. As one eminent scholar has also pointed out, "no other criminal organization [in the United States] has controlled labor unions, organized employer cartels, operated as a rationalizing force in major industries, and functioned as a bridge between the upperworld and the underworld" (Jacobs, 1999: 128). It is this capacity that distinguishes the LCN from all other criminal organizations in the U.S.

Each of the so-called families that make up the LCN has roughly the same organizational structure. There is a boss who controls the family and makes executive decisions. There is an underboss who is second in command. There is a senior advisor or consigliere. And then there are a number of "capos" (capo-regimes) who supervise crews made up of "soldiers," who are "made members" of Cosa Nostra. The capos and those above them receive shares of the proceeds from crimes committed by the soldiers and associates.

Made members, sometimes called good fellows or wise guys, are all male and all of Italian descent. The estimated made membership of the LCN is 1,100 nationwide, with roughly eighty percent of the members operating in the New York metropolitan area. There are five crime families that make up the LCN in New York City: the Bonanno, the Colombo, the Genovese, the Gambino, and the Lucchese families. There is also LCN operational activity in Boston, Chicago, Philadelphia, and the Miami\South Florida area, but much less so than in New York. In other previous strongholds such as Cleveland, Detroit, Kansas City, Las Vegas, Los Angeles, New Orleans, and Pittsburgh, the LCN is now weak or nonexistent. In addition to the made members, there are approximately 10,000 associate members who work for the families. Until the recent demise of much of its leadership, there was a Commission of the bosses of New York's five LCN families that coordinated control of labor unions, construction, trucking and garbage hauling companies, and that resolved disputes between families.

La Cosa Nostra does not enjoy general social acceptance and support. With the exception of a few ethnic Italian neighborhoods where certain of the more brazen exploits and some of the community "good deeds" of bosses are admired, Italian organized crime reinforces a stigma that most Italian-Americans want to get rid of. Along with the effectiveness of law enforcement, the absence of support for the LCN means that recruitment has become difficult. Some families have disappeared, and others are only 50 percent to as little as 10 percent of their size 30 years ago. At the same time however, as with all organized crime, it is the community's desire for illicit goods and services that continues to help fuel the survival of the LCN.

Becoming a made member of LCN requires serving an apprenticeship and then being proposed by a Boss. This is followed by gaining approval for membership from all the other families. Once approved, there is a secret, ritualized induction ceremony. Made membership means both honor and increased income. It also, however, entails responsibilities—in particular taking an oath of omerta. Omerta demands silence to the outside world about the criminal affairs of the family, never betraying anyone in the family, and never revealing to law enforcement anything that might incriminate anyone in organized crime. The penalty for violating this oath is death. Any wise guy who takes a plea without authorization by the family runs the risk of the death penalty. That death is indeed used to enforce internal discipline is evidenced by the execution in 1998 of a capo in the Genovese crime family for pocketing money that should have been passed on to his superiors. An underworld source said about this missing capo: "The people they're looking to send a message to is not the general public. It's the mob itself, which totally understands that the guy is gone." At the same time, the fact that there are over a hundred members in the Federal witness protection program suggests that omerta is not nearly as effective as it once was.

VIOLENCE

La Cosa Nostra, over many years, established its reputation for the ruthless use of violence. This violence has occurred mostly in the form of beatings and killings. Personal violence, and to a lesser degree violence against property, e.g., bombings, arson, explosions, is the typical pattern of the systematic use of violence as a tool of doing business.

That violence continues to be an LCN tool is evidenced in several cases within the past three years. The first two incidents were carried out at the behest of the former head of the Gambino crime family in New York, John Gotti. In a 1997 trial, a member of the Gambino family testified about a torture killing that had been ordered by Gotti. The victim had apparently fired a shot at Gotti. He was tortured with lighted cigarettes and a knife, shot in the buttocks, carried in the trunk of a car, and ultimately killed with five shots to the head. In the second example, the same John Gotti, from his federal prison cell, contracted with two members of the white supremacist group the Aryan Brotherhood to kill the former consigliere of the Gambino crime family who had threatened to kill him.

ECONOMIC RESOURCES

Jacobs (1999) believes that one of the LCN's major assets is its general business acumen. They are best described, he says, as being entrepreneurial, opportunistic, and adaptable. They find ways to exploit market vulnerabilities, while at the same time maintaining the necessary stability and predictability that business requires to be profitable. One of the ways they do this is by taking over only a piece of a legitimate business—and providing a service in return—rather than taking over the whole business. The latter would, of course, require a management responsibility that they do not want and possibly could not handle, and that would in addition likely upset the business climate necessary for success.

La Cosa Nostra's illegal activities cover a wide range. Gambling and drugs have traditionally been their biggest money makers. Loan sharking is often linked with the gambling and drugs, and is an area that exemplifies the role played by the credible use of violence. The same is true of extortion. The other more traditional crimes also include hijacking, air cargo theft, and of course murder.

Then there are a set of crimes that have become specialties of the LCN, and are unique to them in the United States. Although some of these criminal activities have had national effects, they have been carried out almost exclusively by the five crime families in New York City since LCN penetration of the legitimate economy elsewhere in the U.S. is minimal. The specialties of the New York families include labor racketeering, various kinds of business racketeering, bid-rigging, business frauds, and industry cartels. It is in these areas that the LCN demonstrates its most aggressive and effective penetration of the legitimate economy. Labor racketeering involves organized crime control of labor unions. With this control, gained by the threat and use of violence, vast sums of money are siphoned from union pension funds, businesses are extorted in return for labor peace and an absence of strikes, and bribes are solicited for sweetheart contracts. Another speciality, business racketeering, has occurred in New York City in the construction, music, and garbage industries. The LCN controls unions, bars, strip joints, restaurants, and trucking firms. The five families have also controlled at various times the Fulton Fish Market, the Javits Convention Center, the New York Coliseum, and air cargo operations at JFK International Airport, among other targets. Again the principal tools of control are extortion and the use of violence.

One of the best examples of an LCN cartel was their monopoly of the waste hauling industry in New York City for almost 50 years. La Cosa Nostra used its control of local unions to set up a cartel (Jacobs & Hortis, 1998). The cartel monopolized the industry by threatening business disruption, labor problems, and personal violence. As a result of its monopoly control, the LCN forced participants and consumers to pay inflated prices for waste hauling—a practice known as a "mob tax." Over the years this mob tax cost the industry hundreds of millions of dollars.

In part in reaction to effective law enforcement actions in many of the areas mentioned above, La Cosa Nostra has diversified its activities and extended its penetration in legal markets by switching to white-collar crimes in recent years (Raab, 1997). They have carried out multimillion dollar frauds in three areas in particular: health insurance, prepaid telephone cards, and through victimizing small Wall Street brokerage houses.

POLITICAL RESOURCES

As has already been indicated, La Cosa Nostra is today much less powerful and pervasive than it was in the past. A loss of political influence has accompanied its general decline. In its heyday, the LCN exercised its political influence mostly at the local level, through its connections with the political machines that operated in certain U.S. cities such as New York, New Orleans, Chicago, Kansas City, and Philadelphia. With the demise of those machines, and with the advent of political reforms stressing open and ethical government, many of the avenues for corrupt influence were substantially closed. Today, the LCN exercises political influence in certain selected areas and with respect to certain selected issues. For example, it has attempted to influence the passage of legislation regulating legalized gambling in states such as Louisiana.

In one of the most notorious cases in recent years, in Boston a former FBI supervisor admitted (under a grant of immunity) to accepting $7,000 in payoffs from two FBI mob informants. The two mobsters were major figures in the New England Cosa Nostra. A second FBI agent was subsequently convicted in the case in 1999. The two FBI agents were charged with alerting the informants to investigations in which they were targets, and with protecting them from prosecution.

There has never been any evidence that La Cosa Nostra has had direct representation in the Congress of the United States, nor in the U.S. executive or diplomatic service. Neither is there any evidence that it has ever been allied with such armed opposition groups as terrorists, guerrillas, or death squads. In this respect, the LCN exemplifies one of the traditional defining characteristics of organized crime in that its goal is an economic rather than a political one. Where there has been political involvement, it has been for the purposes of furthering economic objectives.

RESPONSES OF LAW ENFORCEMENT AGENCIES TO ORGANIZED CRIME

Law enforcement, and particularly federal law enforcement, has been tremendously successful in combating La Cosa Nostra over the past 10 years. Crime families have been infiltrated by informants and undercover agents, and special investigating grand juries have been employed in state and local jurisdictions. Especially effective use has been made of investigative and prosecutorial techniques that were designed specifically for use against organized crime, and in particular against La Cosa Nostra. These latter techniques include electronic surveillance, the witness protection program, and the Racketeer-Influenced and Corrupt Organizations Act (RICO). The RICO statute has clearly been the single most powerful tool against the LCN. There are now state RICO statutes as well as the federal one. RICO enables law enforcement to attack the organizational structure of organized crime and to levy severe criminal and civil penalties, including forfeitures. It is the threat of these penalties that has convinced many made members of the LCN to become informants and/or to seek immunity from prosecution in return for becoming a cooperating witness. They are then placed in the witness protection program. Civil remedies have included the court-appointment of monitors and trustees to administer businesses and unions that had been taken over by the LCN, to insure that these enterprises remain cleansed of corrupt influences.

Two of the latest weapons against La Cosa Nostra penetration of sectors of the legitimate economy are regulatory initiatives. Because La Cosa Nostra is mainly a domestic operation, there is little international cooperation in its investigation and prosecution.

SIGNIFICANCE

The rise of La Cosa Nostra is an event of remarkable significance in American social and legal history. From a localized Italian immigrant protection organization in eastern American cities, the Mafia acquired a public reputation not simply as a criminal element, but as an entity that transcended all conventional American legal structures—the Mob was essentially a law unto itself.

The LCN achieved its position in society through the combination of old country traditions of honor and brotherhood, sometimes referred to as the omerta, and the application of time honored business principles. In every city where it has operated, the LCN created a strict organizational structure, operating businesses that sold commodities (such as alcohol) and services (including prostitution, gambling, and protection) that had an obvious and definable market. It was an LCN strength that the general public was rarely affected in a direct fashion by the more violent aspects of their operations; most Mafia violence was internal, and the illegal sale of alcohol, as an example, was to willing buyers.

The LCN prospered because it was operated with discipline; the Mafia family structure, in addition to the preferences given to members of Italian descent, placed the concepts of obedience, honor, and respect above all others. This tradition runs counter to the individual-based, almost libertarian views of modern business and society at large.

One of the most significant aspects of the Mafia's rise through the mid-twentieth century was the manner in which it became rooted in the consciousness of the American public—not only as a synonym for organized crime, but also as an efficient, influential organization that attracted a measure of admiration and respect. The 1974 motion picture *The Godfather* does not glorify either crime or the LCN, but there is no question of the aura of presumed power and influence that radiates from the criminal world it portrays. Later Hollywood films that have popularized Mafia methods and influence include *Good Fellas* and *Get Shorty*.

This perception of the LCN has not been restricted to Hollywood. An enduring irony of American law enforcement and prosecutorial history is that the most notorious Mafia gangster in history, Al Capone, operated a vast and notorious bootlegging and multi-dimensional criminal empire in Chicago and elsewhere for many years; he was never prosecuted for any of the serious crimes associated with his organization, including numerous killings of Mafia rivals. Al Capone was indicted and successfully prosecuted for the more pedestrian offence of income tax evasion.

The lingering significance of the Mafia has been diminished to a degree by more zealous federal prosecutions of high-level LCN leaders since 1970. RICO is a part of that initiative. However, the modern Mafia also must be considered in the context of a much changed American society. As adaptable as the Mafia has been—its beginnings in simple protection rackets transformed into holdings in the trucking, construction, and technology industries—America is increasingly less homogenous. The cultural diversity of modern America has diminished the ability of the LCN to achieve both notoriety and respect. However, the Mafia has left one certain legacy—in the American lexicon. There are now references to the "Russian Mafia" and "Chinese Mafia"; the Mafia has become a descriptor for any ethnically based crime group, a testament to the influence of this original American criminal organization.

FURTHER RESOURCES

Books

Cummings, John. *Goombata: The Rise and Fall of John Gotti and his Gang.* New York: Little, Brown, 1990.

Mass, Peter. *The Valachi Papers.* New York: Harper Collins, 1968.

Pileggi, Nicholas. *Wise Guys.* New York: Simon and Schuster, 1985.

A Group of Men Sing in Australia's Northern Territory

Photograph

By: Mission Australia

Date: April 8, 2004

Source: Mission Australia/Handout/Reuters/Corbis

About the Photographer: This photograph was supplied by a nondenominational Christian missionary organization, Mission Australia, that organizes volunteer patrols to pick up people intoxicated in public and take them to alternative accommodations.

INTRODUCTION

The men in this undated photograph are indigenous Australians, often known as "Aborigines," living in the Northern Territory of Australia. They are making music in a public place; at the time the picture was taken a volunteer patrol known as a Community Day Patrol was nearby (it is not shown). The patrol was organized by a nondenominational Christian missionary organization, Mission Australia. The purpose of Community Day and Night Patrols is to pick up people who are intoxicated in public and take them to alternative accommodations such as the Caryota Sobering Up Shelter in the city of Darwin, which is partly funded by the Australian Department of Health and Community Services. The purpose of the Patrols is crime prevention. By taking intoxicated persons to shelters, the Patrols attempt to prevent violent behavior and subsequent arrest. There is no sign that the men in this photograph are intoxicated: rather, they represent the sort of peaceful social activity that is threatened by high addiction and crime rates among indigenous Australians.

Not all community patrols are run by Mission Australia. A Day Patrol was instituted in the small community of Ali-Curung in the Northern Territory in August, 1998, following the adoption by the Territory in 1996 of its Aboriginal Law and Justice Strategy. This is an attempt, in the words of the territorial government, at "not just a simple revitalisation of customary law, but also the use of culturally-relevant decision-making, combined with mainstream law and justice processes." The patrol in Ali-Curing is made up of local women, mostly Aborigines, one of whom describes the operation of the Patrols in the context of the community authority structure as follows: "We use the Elders [of the tribe] to come in and support Night Patrol in the community. If it gets worse and the person won't listen to the Elders, well we call in traditional owners then. They come and talk with the Elders and the Night Patrol about this person who's causing too much trouble. They then decide, the Elders and the traditional owners, what to do with the troublemaker. So this is just sorting out problems in this community meeting."

▓ **PRIMARY SOURCE**

A GROUP OF MEN SING IN AUSTRALIA'S NORTHERN TERRITORY

See primary source image

PRIMARY SOURCE

A Group of Men Sing in Australia's Northern Territory: A group of men sing in Australia's Northern Territory in this 2004 photograph. With indiginous women 45 times more likely to suffer domestic violence, some Northern Territory communities are fighting to end the cycle of abuse and the sense of hopelessness bought by alcoholism and domestic violence endemic to aboriginal communites across the country. © MISSION AUSTRALIA/HANDOUT/REUTERS/CORBIS

SIGNIFICANCE

The Aborigines of Australia are descended today from peoples who inhabited that continent prior to its colonization by Europeans beginning in the late eighteenth century. As of 2002, twice as many indigenous Australians were victims of physical violence annually than were non-indigenous Australians. Thirty-five percent of Aborigines fifteen years or older had been charged with a crime at some time in their lives and about 16 percent had been arrested during the previous five years. Although comprising only about 1.4 percent of the Australian population, Aborigines were 20 percent of the national prison population in 2003 (up from 14.5 percent in 1986), making an Aborigine about ten times likelier to be in prison than a non-Aborigine. Life expectancy is approximately twenty years less for Aborigines than for other Australians, alcoholism is common among Aboriginal adults, and sniffing gasoline, which causes permanent brain damage, is a problem among Aboriginal children. Alcohol use, according to the Australian Institute of Criminology (AIC, a government body), was in 1988 "the most significant feature of serious crime committed by Aboriginal and Torres Strait Islanders" (a distinct group of indigenous Australians). This explains the focus of the Day and Night Patrols, which seek to intervene non-violently before alcohol-intoxicated persons have clashed with the law.

The disproportionate incarceration rates, poor health, poverty, and addiction problems of the Aborigines are a consequence of several centuries of colonization. By 1900, disease and displacement (plus some direct violence) had killed off about 90 percent of the original population of Australia, and the survivors' descendents remained second-class citizens until relatively recently. For example, Aborigines did not have the right to vote in national elections until 1962. In 1986, the Australian Federal Government recommended that "the Aboriginal legal services be restructured to achieve greater involvement of Aboriginal communities in the day-to-day delivery of [legal] services," and in 1986 the AIC recommended, among other measures, the "empowerment of the Aboriginal people in areas of community regulation, crime prevention, and alcohol and offender rehabilitation . . ." Starting in the 1990s, these recommendations have reflected in such efforts as the Aboriginal Law and Justice Strategy of the Northern Territory.

The crime and alcohol problems of the Aborigines of Australia are by no means unique among aboriginal peoples who have been reduced by colonization to small minorities and relegated, for the most part, to remote reservations. Statistics for North American Indians (the term used for Native Americans by the U.S. Department of Justice) are similar in this respect to those for Australian Aborigines: American Indians suffer over twice the general U.S. rate of violent victimization, are more than twice as likely as members of other races to be arrested for alcohol-related offences, and are more than twice as likely to fall below the Federally defined poverty line.

FURTHER RESOURCES

Web sites

Australian Bureau of Statistics. "Aboriginal and Torres Strait Islander Peoples: Contact with the Law." <http://www.abs.gov.au/ausstats/> Jan. 20, 2006 (accessed March 2, 2006).

U.S. Bureau of Justice Statistics. "American Indians and Crime." <http://www.ojp.usdoj.gov/bjs/abstract/aic.htm> Feb. 14, 1999 (accessed March 2, 2006).

Australian Human Rights and Equal Opportunity Commission. "Aboriginal and Torres Strait Islander Social Justice." <http://www.hreoc.gov.au/social_justice/croc/sub3.htm> Sep. 11, 2003 (accessed March 2, 2006).

Attitudes Toward the Death Penalty for Persons Convicted of Murder

United States, Selected Years 1953–2003.

Chart

By: The Gallup Organization

Date: 2005

Source: *Sourcebook of Criminal Justice Statistics 2003.* Reprinted by permission.

About the Author: This chart was created for the U.S. Department of Justice by the Gallup Organization. The Gallup Organization is an American firm that provides market research, health care, and consulting services on a global scale. It routinely conducts polls to gauge public opinion on various issues. Since its establishment in 1958 by American statistician George Gallup (1901–1984), it has become a respected indicator of public opinion.

INTRODUCTION

The U.S. Department of Justice regularly commissions survey organizations such as the Gallup Organization, which conducted this survey of attitudes toward the death penalty, to assess public attitudes toward crime and punishment issues. The survey results, along with results from the analysis of other primary and secondary information gathering activities, are compiled into an annual *Sourcebook of Criminal Justice Statistics* and made available to the public online.

The survey of public attitudes toward the death penalty has been conducted sporadically over the past half-century; in recent years it has been conducted nearly annually. The question at issue, "Are you in favor of the death penalty for a person convicted of murder?" is one of the central questions in public debate over criminal justice policies in the United States. The U.S. is one of the few industrialized democracies that continues to impose the death penalty (on a state-by-state basis), and understanding the amount of public support for the death penalty is important as state and federal governments review the appropriateness of their criminal justice codes. Having a criminal code that is out of step with public attitudes is not a viable option in American democracy.

Attitudes toward the death penalty for persons convicted of murder

UNITED STATES, SELECTED YEARS 1953–2003[a]

Question: "Are you in favor of the death penalty for a person convicted of murder?"

	Yes, in favor	No, not in favor	Don't now/ refused[b]
1953	68%	25%	7%
1956	53%	34%	13%
1957	47%	34%	18%
1960	53%	36%	11%
1965	45%	43%	12%
1966	42%	47%	11%
1967	54%	38%	8%
1969	51%	40%	9%
1971	49%	40%	11%
March 1972	50%	41%	9%
November 1972	57%	32%	11%
1976	66%	26%	8%
1978	62%	27%	11%
1981	66%	25%	9%
January 1985	72%	20%	8%
November 1985	75%	17%	8%
1986	70%	22%	8%
1988	79%	16%	5%
1991	76%	18%	6%
1994	80%	16%	4%
1995	77%	13%	10%
1999	71%	22%	7%
2000	66%	28%	6%
2001	68%	26%	6%
2002	70%	25%	5%
May 2003	70%	28%	2%
October 2003	64%	32%	4%

[a]Percents may not add to 100 because of rounding.
[b]May include other response categories such as "depends".

SOURCE: The Gallup Organization, Inc., *The Gallup Poll* [online]. Available: http://www.gallup.com/poll/ [June 11,2003]; and data provided by The Gallup Organization, Inc. Table adapted by Sourcebook staff. Reprinted by permission.

■ PRIMARY SOURCE

Attitudes Toward the Death Penalty for Persons Convicted of Murder While Americans have generally been in favor of the death penalty for murder, the rate at which they support it has varied considerably over the past 50 years. *SOURCEBOOK OF CRIMINAL JUSTICE STATISTICS 2003.* REPRINTED BY PERMISSION.

■ PRIMARY SOURCE

ATTITUDES TOWARD THE DEATH PENALTY FOR PERSONS CONVICTED OF MURDER

See primary source image.

SIGNIFICANCE

Overall, at least a plurality and usually a majority of the American public has been in favor of the death penalty since the survey of death penalty attitudes was inaugurated more than fifty years ago. However, attitudes for and against the death penalty have followed a sinuous trend over that time, and public support for executions briefly dipped below fifty percent of survey respondents in the 1960s and early 1970s.

Examination of the trends in public attitudes for and against the death penalty for persons convicted of murder shows that attitudes favoring the death penalty dropped from initially high levels in the early 1950s and reached a nadir in the mid-to-late 1960s and early 1970s. This nadir coincides with the so-called "countercultural" phenomenon in the mid-to-late 1960s. However, this downward trend in favorable attitudes was reversed, and approval of the death penalty began to increase, reaching record high levels in the mid-1990s. Since that time, approval of the death penalty has decreased fairly steadily, and at last reading had fallen to percentages not seen since the mid-to-late 1970s.

Notably, the trend toward increasing approval of the death penalty up to the mid–1990s cut across racial and gender categories according to a report posted on the University of Alaska web site. Presumably, the current decline in approval does as well. However, while trends of increase in death penalty support have cut across racial and gender categories, the absolute level of support for the death penalty among blacks, Hispanics, and women is far below that of white males. The difference between whites and blacks in the prevalence of death penalty support appears to be due to the fact that blacks are far more likely to believe that a high proportion of innocent people are executed. Hispanics are about midway between blacks and whites on this issue.

Uncertainty about one's attitude as measured by the "Don't know/Refused" category, seems generally to have decreased since the early years of the survey. This gives the impression that people who had been uncertain have by now largely decided against the death penalty, and that the public has become increasingly polarized about the issue. Apart from this shift away from "fence sitting," the trend in unfavorable attitudes against the death penalty is approximately the reverse of the favorable attitudes. Unfavorable attitudes were highly prevalent in the late 1950s and 1960s, but began to fall in the 1970s and reached a nadir in the 1980s and 1990s. However, over the past ten years unfavorable attitudes have increased steadily.

Anti-death penalty demonstrators march through the streets of Terre Haute, Indiana, on June 10, 2001 on their way to the Federal Penitentiary to protest the execution of Oklahoma City bomber Timothy McVeigh. McVeigh's was the first federal execution since 1963. © REUTERS/CORBIS

The Death Penalty Information Center (DPIC) has been able to shed more light on public attitudes by asking the public using the Gallup Poll whether they supported the death penalty or life in prison without parole. The DPIC asked, "Which is the better penalty for murder, death or life imprisonment?" According to survey results, over the years since 1985, "support for the sentence of 'Life without Parole' as an alternative to the death penalty has steadily increased, to the point where now the country is evenly split on capital punishment. In 1994, only thirty-two percent favored Life, with 50% favoring death. In 2004, support for life without parole had grown to forty-six percent."

Furthermore, the DPIC attempts to show that the basic rationale for the death penalty, that it can deter criminals from murdering people, lacks credibility among the public. Once again the DPIC points to a declining trend in public support: "In less than 20 years, public opinion regarding the deterrent effect of the death penalty—long the backbone of its support—

has reversed itself. In 1986, 61% believed the punishment to be an effective deterrent. In 2004, 62% believed that the death penalty did not deter crime." Adding victim restitution to the mix further erodes public support for the death penalty in the context of the Gallup Poll. If public support for the death penalty is compared to support for life imprisonment combined with restitution to the victim's family, support for the latter alternative rises to forty-four percent versus forty-one percent for the death penalty.

Although the DPIC has demonstrated that there is considerable "softness" in the public's support for capital punishment, and that it is possible in a survey context to reduce public support for the death penalty below its support for some hypothetical alternative, the contention that death penalty support can be reduced much below fifty percent seems to be a long shot. Currently, there appears to be a cultural norm in the U.S. of about sixty percent approval of the death penalty, and attitudes favoring executions fluctuate within ten to fifteen percentage points of this sixty-percent level. Fluctuations appear to depend on sociodemographic trends, such as the rise and maturation of the baby boomer generation or the intensity of the war on drugs. Economic cycles may play a role in which economic upturns are correlated with more forgiving attitudes toward criminals. Currently, the U.S. is experiencing a drop in pro-execution attitudes in the midst of a long-term increase (albeit with some hiccups). This could be due to decreasing crime rates in times of prosperity, which reduce the numbers of people affected by crime. The reduction in the number of crime victims could lead to more "forgiving" attitudes toward criminals.

The American Psychological Association has weighed in on the question of why people have certain moral attitudes, saying that human genetics may play a role. According to a 2001 APA press release, "Attitudes are learned, but new research [studies of twins raised together and apart] shows that differences between people in many attitudes are also partly attributable to genetic factors. These include attitudes as diverse as whether one likes roller coaster rides to controversial social issues such as attitudes toward abortion and the death penalty for murder." A biological component to such attitudes—in the context of American culture—could help explain their relative stability over time. According to a 2004 Harris Poll, "Support for the death penalty remains very strong in the United States, even though almost everyone believes that innocent people are sometimes convicted of murder, and only a minority believes it is a deterrent." In other words, support for executing killers seems to depend on a "gut feeling" that is not well connected to evidence about the effectiveness or accuracy of capital punishment.

Attitudes toward the death penalty appear to be more related to a person's emotional reaction when faced with the reality that one person has taken another person's life. There is a yawning gulf between the response of one observer who feels outrage that a murderer could have deprived another of existence and the response of another observer who seeks explanations that could be applied to preventing future murders. Thus, the death penalty advocate views murder as the ultimate transgression against the sacredness of human life, for which the only fit punishment is to suffer the same fate. The death penalty opponent might consider the victim as a victim of human ignorance and looks to a more enlightened future by applying "lessons learned" without "sinking to the level of the murderer" by executing him or her.

Viewed in this way, the pro-death penalty perspective appears to devalue the criminal, while the anti-death penalty perspective appears to devalue the victim. It is no wonder that biological or behavioral genetics explanations have been advanced to explain why people have trouble bridging such a gulf. Different people appear predisposed by temperament to identify with the victim or the offender. Reason can make only marginal differences, while major cultural and socioeconomic trends can make larger, but still non-decisive, shifts in attitudes toward this fundamental question of life and death.

FURTHER RESOURCES
Web sites

American Psychological Association. "Study With Twins Finds Differences In Certain Attitudes Partly Due To Genetic Factors." <http://www.trinity.edu/~mkearl/death-5.html> (accessed February 10, 2006).

Death Penalty Information Center. "Public Opinion About the Death Penalty." <http://www.deathpenaltyinfo.org/article/> (accessed February 10, 2006).

Harris Interactive. "More Than Two-Thirds of Americans Continue to Support the Death Penalty." <http://www.harrisinteractive.com/harris_poll/index.asp?PID=431> (accessed February 10, 2006).

Trinity University. "Moral Debates of Our Times." <http://www.trinity.edu/~mkearl/death-5.html> (accessed February 10, 2006).

University of Alaska Anchorage. Justice Center. "Death Penalty Statistics." <http://justice.uaa.alaska.edu/death/stats.html> (accessed February 10, 2006).

Sexual Assault Statistics

Website

By: Men Against Sexual Assault

Date: 2003

Source: *Men Against Sexual Assault at the University of Rochester.* "Sexual Assault Statistics." <http://sa.rochester.edu/masa/stats.phpl> (March 13, 2006).

About the Author: Men Against Sexual Assault (MASA) is an advocacy and activist organization that started near the end of the twentieth century at the University of Rochester in New York. Its stated mission was to put an end to sexual violence against women through education and public dissemination of information regarding violent crimes against women. Although their initial target audience was exclusively male, they provide educational materials (brochures, seminars, workshops, and the like) without regard to gender.

INTRODUCTION

The University of Rochester chapter of Men Against Sexual Assault (MASA) was started by a woman and a group of four men in 1997 to empower men to end violence against women. Their aim was to begin at a grassroots level and spread their message across the campus primarily through workshops and campus discussion groups. Within a relatively short period of time, the group shifted from faculty to student leadership, and broadened its target audience enormously through the use of the Internet. By creating an informational Web site, the group has been able to reach beyond the University of Rochester to support and encourage other student groups involved in the movement to end violence and sexual assault against women.

The Internet has revolutionized much of American (and global) culture. It has, in particular, provided a forum for heretofore local interest groups who can now use the World Wide Web to spread their message across the globe, reaching potentially tens of millions of viewers in seconds (or less). Where private interest groups might once have had to hold many meetings, send out mass mailings, put up posters and flyers, engage local media, and canvass whole areas to spread their particular message, they can now accomplish far more with keywords, blogs, and links to professionally (and often inexpensively) created websites.

Through the Internet groups can attract new members, communicate with a nearly unlimited audience, catalyze vast numbers of people to change behaviors or perform specific advocacy actions, and attract global funding. Groups can exist with limited space, staffing, or resources—other than a computer with internet access, a printer, adequate software, and a webmaster. The Internet also offers the unprecedented ability to disseminate swift and targeted responses to queries or information requests. In the past, it would have been necessary to return telephone calls or to provide written responses via the postal system (now referred to as "snail mail"); responses can now be nearly instantaneous.

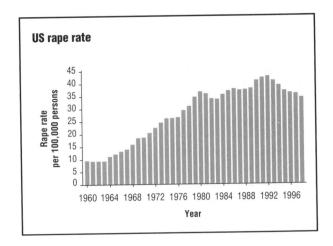

US rape rate

Sexual Assault Statistics: This bar graph shows the rate of rapes per 100,000 people from 1960 through 1998.
FEDERAL BUREAU OF INVESTIGATIONS, UNIFORM CRIME REPORTS

Occurrence of Rape

Rape is a serious problem in the United States today. The United States has the highest rape rate among countries which report such statistics. It is **4 times** higher than that of Germany, **13 times** higher than that of England and **20 times** higher than that of Japan.

Above is a chart showing the estimated rape rate per 100,000 people in the United States between 1960 and 1998. The rape rate in the US in 1998 was **34.4 per 100,000** persons. In 1997 there was a decrease of **7%** in the overall crime rate, but the rate of rape and sexual assault did not decline at all. (National Crime Victimization Survey, 1997)

Women are **10 times** more likely than men to be victims of sexual assault (National Crime Victimization Survey, 1997). A study among college women has shown that **1 out of every 5** college age women report being forced to have sexual intercourse. (1995 National College Health Risk Behavior Survey) **22%** of all women say that they have been forced to do sexual things against their will, where only **3%** of men admit to ever forcing themselves on a woman. (Laumann, 1994)

Reporting Statistics

Only **16%** of rapes and sexual assaults are reported to the police (Rape in America: A Report to the Nation. 1992). In 1995 there were **97,460** rapes reported to law enforcement officials. At a 16% reporting rate, this means that there were actually closer to **649,733** rapes in the United States. Along the same lines, the number of rapes reported in New York state in 1996 was **20,911.** At a 16% reporting rate, this means the actual number of rapes was closer to **139,406.** (Computerized Criminal History, Feb. 1998)

The rate of false reports of rape is approximately **2 - 3%** which is no different than that for other crimes. This is different than the **8%** of reports which are unfounded. This means that in 8% of the rape cases reported the investigators or prosecutors deemed that the case was not prosecutable for any number of reasons. Only **2 - 3%** of the reports however were fabricated stories.

Victim Characteristics

1 in 3 sexual assault victims are under the age of 12 (Snyder & Sickmund, 1999) and convicted rape and sexual assault offenders report that **2/3** of their victims were under the age of 18. Among victims age 18 - 29, **two thirds** had a prior relationship with the rapist. (National Crime Victimization Survey, Criminal Victimization, 1996)

18% of women who reported being raped before age 18 said they were also raped after age 18. (Violence Against Women Survey, 1998)

Perpetrator Characteristics

In 1997, **68.3%** were perpetrated by someone who knew the victim. (Bureau of Justice's National Crime Victimization Survey, 1997) **78%** of women raped or physically assaulted since they turned 18 were assaulted by a current or former husband, live-in partner or date. **17%** were victimized by an acquaintance, **9%** by a relative other than a husband and only **14%** were assaulted by a stranger. (National Violence Against Women Survey, 1998)

Assault Characteristics

Rape and sexual assault are not crimes that usually occur in dark alleys or in deserted areas at night. As a matter of fact **6 out of 10** sexual assaults occur in the home of the victim or the home of a friend, neighbor or relative. (Greenfeld, 1997) **43.4%** of rapes and sexual assaults occur between the hours of 6PM and midnight Greenfeld, 1997) and about **two thirds** occur between the hours of 6 PM and 6 AM (Greenfeld, 1997).

Impact of Rape

Rape is a violent crime which has many severe effects on the victim both in the long term and in the short term. For example, **36%** of women who are injured during a rape require medical attention (National Violence Against Women Survey, Nov.1998). **25 - 45%** of rape survivors suffer from non-genital trauma, **19 - 22%** suffer from genital trauma, up to **40%** obtain STDs and **1 - 5%** become pregnant as a result of the rape. There are an estimated **32,000** rape related pregnancies in the United

States annually. (Holmes, 1996) Sexual assault survivors' visits to their physicians increase by **18%** the year of the assault, **56%** the year after and **31%** the second year after the assault. (Koss, 1993)

The consequences of rape are not always physical though, and are not always immediate. **80%** of rape victims will suffer from chronic physical or psychological conditions over time. (Strategies for the Treatment and Prevention of Sexual Assault. 1995) Rape survivors are also **13 times** more likely to attempt suicide than not crime victims and **6 times** more likely than victims of other crimes. (Rape in America: A Report to the Nation, 1992) **26%** of women with bulimia nervosa were raped at some point in their lives. The mental health costs of sexual assault victims are very high, studies have shown that **25 - 50%** of rape and child sexual abuse victims receive some sort of mental health treatment as a result of the victimization. (Miller, 1996)

Overall, rape has the highest annual victim cost of any crime. The annual victim costs are **$127 billion** (excluding child sex abuse cases). This is followed by assault at **$93 billion** per year, murder (excluding arson and drunk driving) at **$61 billion** and child abuse at **$56 billion** per year. (Miller, 1996)

Conviction and Sentencing

Less than half of those arrested for rape are convicted, **54%** of all rape prosecutions end in either dismissal or acquittal. The conviction rate for those arrested for murder is **69%** and all other felons is **54%**. (The Response to Rape: Detours on the Road to Equal Justice) **21%** of convicted rapists are never sentenced to jail or prison time, and **24%** receive time in local jail which means that they spend an average of **less than 11 months** behind bars. (The Response to Rape: Detours on the Road to Equal Justice)

SIGNIFICANCE

Men Against Sexual Assault is a relatively new version of a paradigm that got its start in the United States during the second wave of feminism in the 1970s. One of the earliest organizations created in concert with feminism was the National Organization for Men Against Sexism (NOMAS). During the 1970s there was an upsurge in the creation of men's studies programs at colleges and universities, as well as limited participation by males in women's studies programs. A series of annual conferences on men and masculinity were held at college campuses, which grew into a somewhat amorphous nonorganization based on support for feminism as well as nonstereotypic, gay-affirmative ideas of masculinity.

Young women test their drinks for date rape drugs at a pub in San Jose, California in 2002. AP IMAGES

Over time, the group evolved into an antisexist group first called the National Organization for Changing Men, later renamed NOMAS. Although it has many goals and objectives, central among them are activism to encourage the abolition of sexism and the establishment of a system that they consider true equality: racial, gender, cultural, religious and spiritual, sexual–affectional orientation, social class, and the like. The group is explicitly profeminist, antiracist, and gay affirming.

In addition to encouraging men to take significant responsibility for ending violence of all types, advocacy groups dedicated to the eradication of violence against women challenge stereotypic concepts of masculinity with an explicit assumption that cultural pressures on men to embody traditional ideals of masculinity have led to social acceptance, and inherent decriminalization, of the violence and brutality of rape and sexual assault.

Men Can Stop Rape (MCSR) is another large group utilizing both traditional forms of local activism and the Internet to spread its message. It began in the 1980s as a profeminist organization dedicated to ending male violence toward women. By the end of the twentieth century it had grown in size and political stature to become a 501(c)3 nonprofit organization dedicated to ending violence of all kinds, and to the creation of a peaceful society characterized by justice and equality. The group teaches that it is not necessary to control or to dominate others, that violence is not a necessary behavior, and that compassion and nonviolence are characteristics of people with bravery and integrity. MCSR aims to prevent the development of violence and to create an atmosphere supportive of positive social change.

FURTHER RESOURCES

Books

Goldrick-Jones, Amanda. *Men Who Believe in Feminism*. Westport, Connecticut: Praeger 2002.

McLean, Christopher, Maggie Carey, and Cheryl White, eds. *Men's Ways of Being*. Boulder, Colorado: Westview Press 1996.

Web sites

National Organization for Men Against Sexism. "A Brief History of NOMAS" <http://www.nomas.org/briefhistory.html> (accessed March 13, 2006).

Men Against Sexual Assault at the University of Rochester. "About Men Against Sexual Assault." <http://sa.rochester.edu/masa/about.php> (accessed March 13, 2006).

Chronicle of Philanthropy: Philanthropy Careers. "Advocacy Groups Discover the Power of Blogs to Spread Their Messages." <http://philanthropy.com/jobs/2004/08/19/20040819-32353.htm> (accessed March 13, 2006).

Inlet. "National Advocacy Groups." <http://inlet.org/guide/advocacy.shtml> (accessed March 13, 2006).

Men Can Stop Rape. "Making Our Communities Stronger." <http://www.mencanstoprape.org/index.htm> (accessed March 13, 2006).

University of Southern California. Annenberg Online Journalism Review. "Net Changes Game of Political Advocacy for Groups on the Right and Left." <http://www.ojr.org/ojr/glaser/1073429305.php> (accessed March 13, 2006).

What Happened When I Did Tell

Book excerpt

By: Carolyn Ainscough and Kay Toon

Date: 2000

Source: Ainscough, Carolyn, and Kay Toon. *Surviving Childhood Sexual Abuse*. United Kingdom: Fisher Books, 2000.

About the Author: Coauthors Carolyn Ainscough and Kay Toon both attended Leeds University in England, where they met while training as clinical psychologists. After graduating, they went to work for the Wakefield Health Authority. Ainscough and Toon specialize in the effects of sexual abuse, and have presented numerous workshops, lectures, and interviews

on the subject, both in the United Kingdom and around the world.

INTRODUCTION

Sexual abuse, especially when the victim is a child, can not only have serious, long-term effects on a person's ability to have a normal sexual relationship, but also on the ways in which a person relates to others in general. Sexual abuse survivors have many reasons to avoid discussing their experiences, but high among them is a fear that if they admit what happened and try to discuss the abuse with a friend or advisor, that person will either refuse to believe them or will make light of their suffering and thereby invalidate the experience. Many survivors do find that the first, second, or even the tenth person they tell about their abuse proves unable to give them the help they want and need. However, there are people willing and able to assist abuse survivors, and it is important for people who have suffered from sexual abuse to continue to tell their stories until they find the support they require.

PRIMARY SOURCE

Once survivors stop feeling ashamed and blaming themselves for the abuse, they begin talking about it to other people. Survivors are frequently surprised to find that many of their friends and family tell them that they too, have been sexually abused, sometimes by the same abuser.

Nowadays the sexual abuse of children is in the news. More people know about it. More people are ready to listen and act to protect children and help adults. People are still around who won't listen, won't believe, will deny it, won't protect, and will abuse. However, there are more and more people around who will help. Try to find one of these people....

Ingrid's story

Ingrid first told a childhood friend about the abuse and wasn't believed. She continued to tell different people for more than thirty years until, at last, she got a sympathetic response and some help:

I think I may have told some friends at school, when I was still a child, but I don't have a clear memory of that. I know that later I told my first husband, before I married him, when I was seventeen. I didn't like sex and thought it may have had something to do with my past. He believed me but put little importance on the fact I had been abused. He beat me and took me in a sexual way that showed no love, no concern, no care for me. During my seven-year marriage to him, my problems increased. At times I became introverted and tried to analyze my problems to find a way to solve them. I couldn't do it on my own. I knew that only outside help could help me get rid of the memories that still haunted me. Very early in my marriage I realized I wouldn't get help from my husband, so I went to my primary-care doctor in Germany and told him, asking him to help me. His words: "Too bad, but forget about it, it's in the past." I had trusted him completely before, but when he could not respond to my need, not even see my need, I lost that trust. It took a few months for me to recover from the shock….

My husband had many affairs, which made me feel even more inferior, and again I realized that I needed to sort out my life before I could sort out my marriage. I made an appointment with a marriage counselor, not to complain about my husband's behavior, but to tell the female counselor about the abuse and my consequent dislike for sex. She said what I liked or didn't like was not important, and if I wanted my husband to remain faithful I would have to satisfy him in bed. She thought it was silly of me to make such a fuss over something so long in the past.

Again I walked home feeling empty and degraded. I spoke to no more people in the medical profession, people who should have known that professional help was needed. Always the response was, "Forget about it. He won't do it any more, so why do you worry about it?" By then I'd realized that more problems had developed, not only my distaste for sex. Every time I tried to tell someone who might be able to help, I also explained the effects the abuse had on me. I got no help. Maybe I told the wrong people? I asked my brother to help me, begging my abuser to help me overcome the damage he did, by keeping out of my way. I was trying to avoid him. He didn't help me. He came to my house when he wanted to. Because my first husband had become friends with him and the lover of my brother's wife (with my brother's approval), I saw him frequently. I could not tell my parents. I felt I had to protect them from knowledge of what their son had done. But I talked to my sister, two cousins and an aunt and told them what he had done. They may have believed me, I don't know, but they looked at me in disgust and said, "He's got his faults, but he's also got his good sides, you shouldn't always see bad in people. He is our brother!" I was made to feel ashamed for telling the truth.

I withdrew into myself for a while and wondered if it was worth the bother. By belittling something that I felt had destroyed the value of my life they belittled me. One problem increased—the feeling of being worthless and of no importance. Not even my…family seemed to care about my pain, and nobody was going to help me.

I stopped telling anybody for about two years after my divorce while I tried to find out who I was and what direction to [take] in my life. When I met my second husband and knew I was going to marry him, I told him about my childhood experiences… If he has a problem, he ignores it and pretends it goes away. He believes me but is completely unwilling to listen to me talk about the past or my problems. So again, no help.

Because my regular primary-care doctor in Wakefield wasn't available, I saw someone else in his office when I went in with a minor health problem. I had not spoken about the abuse for about three years, apart from when I told my second husband. It was time to try again, because I knew I needed help. I didn't want to risk this marriage breaking up because I was an unfeeling partner during lovemaking. I don't think the doctor even heard what I was telling him. He never looked up from writing a prescription. He didn't say a word. By now I'd learned that if I wanted to tell someone about the abuse, I had to put all those years, all the pain and all the effects the abuse had on me into two or three sentences. I never got more time than that to talk about it. I was always interrupted with some patronizing remark. This time I didn't wait to recover from being rejected in my need for help. Within days I saw a female doctor in the family planning clinic and told her the same story. Her advice to overcome my dislike of physical contact was to "satisfy myself…" if I couldn't find pleasure with a man. To a victim of sexual abuse who looks on sex as dirty and degrading, this is the most unhelpful suggestion there is.

Every time I told someone, the emptiness in me grew. I was so eager to find some response, someone who would say, "Tell me about it, I'll help you." I knew what my brother did was wrong. I wanted reassurance that it was wrong, someone to reinforce my belief that it was his fault that I wasn't feeling the way other women feel.

I tried to talk about it a few more times to people, mostly friends. They hardly acknowledged what they heard; none of them was supportive. Then I gave up. I resigned myself to never being able to enjoy sex; always having thoughts that I was less worthy than others; never losing the fear that my son would abuse his sisters; and all the other problems that I knew resulted from the sexual abuse I suffered as a child.

Suddenly I had some personal tragedies, which had nothing to do with my past. They came within a few weeks of each other and I became depressed. After three weeks, I went to see one of the [doctors] to get some drugs to help. I gave her all the reasons why I thought things were getting too much for me. Again I mentioned… that I was abused as a child. For the first time in my life someone looked at me with sympathy,

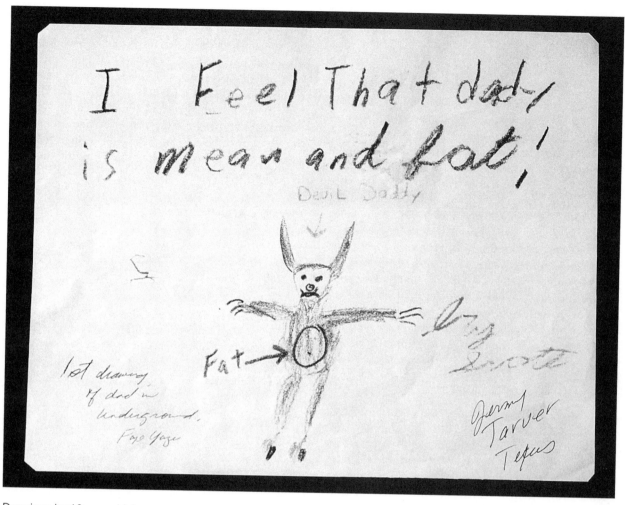

Drawings by 10-year-old Jeremy purport to reveal the link between the sexual act and a satanic ritual. The drawing says "I feel that Daddy is mean and fat." Fay Yager, who set up a network for child victims of sexual abuse, has added her remarks to the drawing. © SOPHIE ELBAZ/SYGMA/CORBIS

encouraging me to keep talking about it. We talked for about ten minutes. Never before was I allowed to say so much about how I felt…She told me about the Survivors group and asked if [I would] be interested in joining them. I almost cried with relief…. I was interested!

The new group had just started, so I had to wait three months before I could join, but from that day onward I felt protected. I saw that even though more than thirty years had passed since I first asked for help, it was not too late. We can change our lives, no matter how long it takes. The hardest part for me was always the moments just after telling someone, when I was not believed or [told] to forget it. But whenever I felt close to giving up I thought…somewhere, someone must care. I just had to find that person. Now I think that persever-ance was the right way for me. If I had given up trying, I

would not be the woman I am now. I am happier now and more fulfilled than I have ever been before.

SIGNIFICANCE

Sexual abuse by an older person against a child takes many forms, including sexual kissing, touching, and oral, vaginal, or anal intercourse. It can also exist in the form of non-physical sexual behavior, such as nude photography, revealing the adult's genital areas, or verbal threats of a sexual nature. In the majority of sexual abuse cases, the perpetrator knows the child, but is not a relative. Instead they are neighbors, fam-ily friends, a babysitter, or some other person who has easy contact. Only approximately thirty percent of known instances of sexual child abuse take place with a family member, and approximately ten percent with a stranger.

Because the adult abusing the child is so frequently a person that child knows and trusts, it becomes very difficult for a child to speak about the abuse to someone else. The abuser, simply by taking advantage of their relationship to the child, has automatically damaged that child's ability to trust other adults, forcing them to question their own judgment as to whether a person is actually trustworthy. Children in this situation wonder if any adult can be relied upon to protect them from their abuser, or even if any adult will believe their world over that of another grown up. Additionally, the abuser often plays upon their age and relationship with the child to pressure him or her into remaining silent about the abuse. By stressing their relationship to the child, the adult makes the child an active participant in keeping the abuse quiet, making it a game or a secret between the two of them. Conversely, the adult might threaten the child, stating that something bad might happen to them or to their loved ones if they tell the truth, thereby using fear and guilt to keep the child from reporting the abusive behavior.

Sexual child abuse, if not treated early, can have long-term effects on the child that continue into adulthood. Signs that a child might be experiencing sexual abuse include nightmares or trouble sleeping, unusual interest in things of a sexual nature, depression or withdrawal from friends and family, an inappropriate seductiveness for their age, secrecy, a refusal to go to school, increased aggressive behavior, and even suicidal tendencies. Poor self-esteem, depression, sexual anxiety and disorders, and additional unhealthy behavior such as alcoholism, drug use, eating disorders, and self mutilation, can continue to haunt victims of abuse as they grow older. In addition, survivors of abuse often have an unrealistic outlook when it comes to relationships. They frequently find that they continue to nurture abusive relationships into their adult lives, even though the abuse is not necessarily still sexual in nature. That dynamic has become normal to them, and they need to relearn ways to relate to people in order to find themselves in healthier friendships and/or marriages.

It is vitally important that children who have been sexually abused receive the care and support they need to overcome this abuse. Although the survivor might have trouble bringing themselves to talk about the abuse, it is necessary for their recovery. Even if a person rejects their appeal for help, a survivor needs to continue trying to talk about their problems. If the first person cannot help them, they must remain per-

sistent and move on to the next person. There are doctors and support groups trained to handle the emotional backlash that results from being abused sexually as a child, and survivors wishing support need to seek out these resources. Likewise, anyone who discovers that a friend or family member is struggling with the aftermath of sexual abuse, needs to be supportive of that person, even if they do not understand the best way to help them. Simply believing the abuse survivor is the first step in helping them find the support they require.

FURTHER RESOURCES

Books

Bass, Ellen, and Laura Davis. *The Courage to Heal: A Guide for Women Survivors of Child Sexual Abuse*. New York: Collins Books 1994.

Web sites

American Academy of Child and Adolescent Psychiatry. "Child Sexual Abuse No. 9." <httphttp://www.aacap.org/publications/factsfam/sexabuse.htm> (accessed March 2, 2006).

National Center for Post-Traumatic Stress Syndrome. "Child Sexual Abuse." <http://www.ncptsd.va.gov/facts/specific/fs_child_sexual_abuse.html> (accessed March 2, 2006).

Prevent Abuse Now.com. "Sexual Abuse." <http://www.prevent-abuse-now.com/> (accessed March 4, 2006).

Sex Crimes Cover-up By Vatican?

Newspaper article

By: Vince Gonzales

Date: August 6, 2003

Source: Vince Gonzales. *CBS News*. "Sex Crimes Cover-up by Vatican?" <http://www.cbsnews.com/stories/2003/08/06/eveningnews/main566978.shtml> (accessed March 10, 2006).

About the Author: In 1990, Vince Gonzales graduated from the State University of New York, Brockport with a bachelor's degree in political science and communications/journalism. He then studied journalism at Columbia University Graduate School. Gonzales then participated in a training program with CBS affiliates until he joined CBS News as a correspondent

Barbara Blaine, founder of the Survivors Network of those Abused by Priests, displays a picture of herself at the age of 12, center left, while protesting outside St. Peter's Square, Rome, Monday, April 11, 2005. AP IMAGES

in 1998. He was awarded two Columbia University awards, an Emmy, and awards from the Society for Professional Journalists.

INTRODUCTION

In 2002, claims began to surface regarding alleged sex abuses by Catholic priests, many dating back several decades. Though claims of sex abuse against priests certainly did not begin in 2002, their number skyrocketed that year, leading to a public outcry and eventually a response by the Vatican. The first allegations began to surface in 1985, when Reverend Thomas Doyle, a canon lawyer for the Vatican, wrote a confidential memo to the bishops of the United States citing thirty cases and one hundred victims of alleged sex crimes perpetrated by priests. He estimated a cost of $1 billion over ten years to the church. At the same time, writing for the *National Catholic*

Reporter, Jason Berry published a nationwide examination of the allegations against priests. Four years later, in 1989, Joseph Ferrario became the first American bishop accused of molestation. These charges were eventually dismissed by the court. By 1992, the U.S. bishops agreed on a set of principles by which to handle accusations of sex abuse. At the same time, Berry continued to document the cases against priests, which by this time numbered over four hundred cases.

January of 2002 brought a floodgate of charges against priests, beginning with the conviction of defrocked Boston priest John Geoghan. He was accused of abusing over 130 children and faced charges of indecent assault and battery. As Geoghan was sentenced to nine to ten years' incarceration, the archdiocese began to face accusations of cover-up due to the number of priests involved and the documentation of claims against priests. In April 2002, Pope John

Paul II called a meeting of the U.S. cardinals and tasked them with the creation of a policy to handle allegations and prevent future cases from occurring. The pope stated, "There is no place in the priesthood and religious life for those who would harm the young." In response to the pope's admonishing, the U.S. bishops met in June of 2002 and agreed on a policy which would remove accused clergy from their positions, but not automatically defrock them from the priesthood. Priests who have become "notorious and [are] guilty of the serial, predatory sexual abuse of minors" would be submitted to a special process whose role is to defrock the priest. The Vatican initially rejected this document and in November of 2002, the bishops passed an amendment which would immediately remove any priest convicted of engaging in the sexual abuse of a minor. By this time, over 325 of the nation's 46,000 priests had been reassigned due to allegations of sexual misconduct. By December, the Vatican accepted the new policy toward sexual predators within the priesthood. In addition, Cardinal Bernard Law, of the Boston Archdiocese, resigned his position under pressure from the public.

In 2004, the U.S. Catholic bishops created the National Review Board to act as an overseer of the new policies. The board released two studies regarding the sexual abuse cases that had faced the church. One study covered the alleged abuses between 1950 and 2002, finding 10,667 cases against priests. The second study placed the responsibility for the continued abuse on the U.S. bishops for insufficiently addressing allegations.

PRIMARY SOURCE

For decades, priests in this country abused children in parish after parish while their superiors covered it all up. Now it turns out the orders for this cover up were written in Rome at the highest levels of the Vatican.

CBS News Correspondent Vince Gonzales has uncovered a church document kept secret for 40 years.

The confidential Vatican document, obtained by CBS News, lays out a church policy that calls for absolute secrecy when it comes to sexual abuse by priests—anyone who speaks out could be thrown out of the church.

The policy was written in 1962 by Cardinal Alfredo Ottaviani.

The document, once "stored in the secret archives" of the Vatican, focuses on crimes initiated as part of the confessional relationship and what it calls the "worst crime": sexual assault committed by a priest or "attempted by him with youths of either sex or with brute animals."

Bishops are instructed to pursue these cases "in the most secretive way ... restrained by a perpetual silence ... and everyone (including the alleged victim) ... is to observe the strictest secret, which is commonly regarded as a secret of the Holy Office ... under the penalty of excommunication."

Larry Drivon, a lawyer who represents alleged victims, said, "This document is significant because it's a blueprint for deception."

Drivon said this proves what he has alleged on behalf of victims in priest-abuse lawsuits: that the church engaged in a crime—racketeering.

"It's an instruction manual on how to deceive and how to protect pedophiles," Drivon said. "And exactly how to avoid the truth coming out."

The U.S. Conference of Catholic Bishops said the document is being taken out of context, that it's a church law that deals only with religious crimes and sins. And that the secrecy is meant to protect the faithful from scandal.

"The idea that this is some sort of blueprint to keep this secret is simply wrong," said Msgr. Francis Maniscalco, a spokesman for the Conference.

"This is a system of law which is complete in itself and is not telling the bishops in any way about how to handle these crimes when they are considered as civil crimes," Maniscalco said.

But Richard Sipe, a former priest who has written about sex abuse and secrecy in the church, said the document sends a chilling message.

"This is the code for how you must deal with sex by priests. You keep it secret at all costs," Sipe said. "And that's what's happened. It's happened in every diocese in this country."

According to church records, the document was a bedrock of Catholic sex abuse policy until America's bishops met last summer and drafted new policies to address the crisis in the church.

SIGNIFICANCE

In 1962, Cardinal Alfredo Ottaviani held the position of Prefect of the Holy Office, which is now known as the Congregation for the Doctrine of Faith. Ottaviani's office oversaw the creation of the document titled "Instruction on proceeding in cases of solicitation." According to the Catholic Church, the document is not, as the CBS report suggests, a blueprint for the cover-up of sexual abuses by priests. The document, according to the *Catholic World News*, deals with the act of solicitation on the part of the priest, an act considered an ecclesiastical crime. The intent of the document is to create a procedure to investigate priests who are accused of using the Sacrament of Penance (or confession) to entice a penitent, or parishioner, to engage in sexual activity. If the act of solicitation results in actual sexual activity, the rules of secrecy provided in the document no longer apply. The document cites in section 18 that every Catholic has a duty to bring charges against a priest who engages in solicitation, not, as the report suggests, that an accuser will be excommunicated. The church asserts that the document allows for criminal charges to be brought against a priest, while at the same time the priest could be charged in an ecclesiastical court. It also holds that the procedure outlined in the document is intended to protect the secrecy of the confessional, not the actions of an errant priest.

FURTHER RESOURCES

Web sites

Catholic World News. "CBS News Distorts 1962 Vatican Document." <http://www.cwnews.com/news/viewstory.cfm?recnum=24023> (accessed March 10, 2006).

CBS News. "Instruction on the Manner of Proceeding in Cases of Solicitation." <http://www.cbsnews.com/htdocs/pdf/Criminales.pdf> (accessed March 10, 2006).

CBS News. "Taint of Church Sex Scandal Lingers." <http://www.cbsnews.com/stories/2002/04/19/national/main506674.shtml> (accessed March 10, 2006).

Hurricane Katrina Aftermath

To Protect and Serve

Photograph

By: Rick Wilking

Date: September 1, 2005

Source: Rick Wilking. "Hurricane Katrina: To Protect and Serve." Corbis, 2005.

About the Photographer: Rick Wilking is a freelance photographer best known for his twelve years on the White House staff as an official photographer to the President of the United States.

INTRODUCTION

On the morning of August 29, 2005, Hurricane Katrina, the strongest hurricane ever recorded in the Gulf of Mexico (Hurricane Rita, later on that season, would outdo its ferocity), hit the coastlines of Louisiana, Mississippi and Alabama. For nearly twenty-four hours it would batter the three southern states, causing catastrophic damage estimated at $75 billion. In total the hurricane killed more than 1,400 people, making it the deadliest storm to hit America in nearly eighty years.

By far the most seriously impacted area was the city of New Orleans. Levees, which had previously protected the low-lying city from Lake Pontchartrain, were breached by floodwater, causing devastation across large parts of the city and leaving many districts under water. Around one million people had been displaced or evacuated because of Katrina, including most of the population of New Orleans. But evacuation had not been mandatory and up to 150,000 people—the old, the poor, the infirm, the stubborn, and the naive—remained in the ruined city for the duration of the storm, and once there could not get out afterwards. This included up to 30,000 people at the city's official shelters at the Superdome Stadium and Convention Center.

Within hours of Katrina abating, the natural chaos wrought by the storm had given way to mayhem of a manmade complexion. Only a skeleton service of police and national guardsmen remained in New Orleans, and they were immediately overwhelmed by the scale of the devastation with which they were faced. Substantial numbers of reinforcements would not arrive for days, leaving the city in a state of lawlessness. Looters began roaming the streets, some stealing food and water out of necessity; but many others taking a more opportunistic view and stealing electrical equipment, consumer goods and anything else they could get their hands on. New Orleans' French Quarter was sacked by looters and some remaining store owners became involved in shootouts with looters.

Darker rumors also began to surface from the Superdome, from where stories of rape, assault, and murder began to emerge. Many of these stories assumed exaggerated importance and were distorted in the chaos in the days following Katrina, but more than forty sexual assaults were reported in New Orleans during this time. Moreover, rescue helicopters arriving at the Superdome on September 1 were reportedly shot upon by refugees, delaying the rescue effort even further. A form of martial law was invoked, although depleted ranks of police and National Guard

PRIMARY SOURCE

Hurricane Katrina Aftermath: A Louisiana state policeman carries a five-day-old baby, an evacuee brought for treatment to a location near the Superdome (background) in downtown New Orleans, Louisiana, on September 1, 2005. The baby's mother said she had been trapped in her home after Hurricane Katrina hit. Authorities struggled to evacuate thousands of people from hurricane-battered New Orleans as food and water grew scarce and looters raided stores. © RICK WILKING/REUTERS/CORBIS

were seemingly in no position to universally enforce it.

By that stage the world's media, who seemed to be in the wrecked city in greater numbers than rescue teams and police and National Guard, were almost universally describing New Orleans as being in "a state of anarchy." Anger at the apparent inertia of the federal government was widespread both in New Orleans and across the world. Longstanding rivals of the U.S. government, such as Venezuela and Cuba, made offers of relief aid, while President Bush seemed to struggle to keep pace with events. Ray Nagin, New Orleans Mayor, repeatedly showed his frustration at Washington's failure to respond to the unfolding scenes of lawlessness, accusing the federal government of "feeding the people a line of bull and spinning [while] people are dying" and imploring Washington to "get off your asses and let's do something."

Finally, on Friday September 2, large numbers of National Guard reserves arrived in New Orleans to help bring order to the city. Louisiana governor Kathleen Blanco warned that "they know how to shoot to kill." Several shootouts occurred between guards and looters, including a fatal incident at Danziger Bridge on September 4, when eight armed men began shooting at contractors, and the National Guardsmen protecting them opened fire, killing five of the assailants. The influx of the National Guard over the weekend of September 3–4 quickly brought the New Orleans state of "anarchy" under control. They were able to assist in bussing out survivors, control looting, and protect contractors brought in to rebuild the breached levees and pump out flood water.

PRIMARY SOURCE

HURRICANE KATRINA AFTERMATH

See primary source image.

SIGNIFICANCE

The wake of Hurricane Katrina was a political disaster for President Bush, with his approval ratings falling lower than those of any president since records began. He was roundly criticized for his failure to grasp the extent of the tragedy; America's occupation of Iraq—ordered by Bush—was blamed for diverting thousands of National Guard troops away from the disaster; his benign record on environmental issues was invoked; and many of his political opponents, pointing out that many of Katrina's victims were black and poor, used the catastrophe as evidence that President Bush cared nothing for marginalized sections of American society. The question of racism was brought into play too: setting the tone, Reverend Jesse Jackson, inspecting the pavement outside New Orleans Convention Center, said "This looks like the hull of a slave ship."

More than anything else, however, it was the delay between the hurricane and the rescue effort starting in earnest that caused the most anger. The state of anarchy and imminent sense of danger prevalent in New Orleans in the days after Katrina served to exacerbate negative feelings towards the federal government, but it was by no means the cause.

On September 9, Federal Emergency Management Agency (FEMA) director Michael Brown was dismissed from his role of managing the Hurricane Katrina relief effort. Brown had been criticized for his management of the tragedy, but many felt that he was made a scapegoat for wider failings within the Bush administration.

By September 12, a fortnight after Katrina had struck, New Orleans had effectively turned into an army camp, with 70,000 national guardsmen and active-duty soldiers based in the region, accompanying thousands of local, state, and federal law enforcement officers. They were accompanied by hundreds of mercenaries, drafted in by the city's wealthiest families to protect their homes from looters.

Assessments of media coverage of Katrina in the weeks and months following the disaster brought accusations that the media had exaggerated the prevalence of crime in New Orleans. In actuality the worst they had usually done was report misleading eyewitness statements as fact. A prime example was Police Chief Eddie Compass reporting on September 1 of the Superdome: "We have individuals who are getting raped; we have individuals who are getting beaten." Five days later, he told Oprah Winfrey that babies were being raped. The first example turned out to be a substantial over-exaggeration; the latter wholly unsubstantiated.

Elsewhere in America, communities that had accepted Katrina refugees claimed that the influx of these newcomers had led to crime waves in their cities in the months following the disaster. In Houston, which took in 150,000 New Orleans refugees, murders were up fifty percent year on year for January 2006. "These guys are hooking up with friends and old rivalries are beginning again," Sergeant Brian Harris, a Houston Gang Murder Squad investigator, told *Time* magazine. Fraudulent relief and insurance claims have also come under scrutiny from law enforcement agencies at local, state, and federal level. Six months after the hurricane, reports of arrests and prosecutions for fraud were occurring on almost a weekly basis.

FURTHER RESOURCES

Web sites

CNN.com. "Big Questions for the Big Easy." <http://www.cnn.com/SPECIALS/2005/katrina> (accessed March 5, 2006).

Federal Emergency Management Agency. "Louisiana Hurricane KatrinaDeclared August 29, 2005." <http://www.fema.gov/news/event.fema?id=4808> (accessed March 5, 2006).

Guardian Unlimited. "Special Report: Hurricane Katrina." <http://www.guardian.co.uk/katrina/0,16441,1560620,00.html> (accessed March 5, 2006).

Looters Make Off With Merchandise

Photograph

By: Eric Gay

Date: August 30, 2005

Source: Eric Gay/AP Photo

About the Photographer: This photograph was taken by the Associated Press photographer Eric Gay soon after Hurricane Katrina struck the U.S. and several Latin American nations in August, 2005.

INTRODUCTION

This photograph was taken on a street in the city of New Orleans. On August 29, 2005, Hurricane Katrina, a Category three storm, made landfall not far to the east of New Orleans. An official order had already been given to evacuate the city, but this was not possible for thousands of residents, especially those too poor to own cars. As engineers had often warned could happen, the hurricane's storm surge (rise in water level caused by high winds and low barometric pressure) breached several levees keeping the salty waters of Lake Pontchartrain out of the city. About eighty percent of the city was flooded, some in water several stories deep, some in water only a few feet or inches deep. Aid from Federal and State sources did not reach the city for days, and some residents took what they needed from stores, including such items as food, dry socks and shoes, disposable diapers, and bot-

PRIMARY SOURCE

Looters Make Off With Merchandise: Looters make off with merchandise from several downtown businesses in New Orleans after Hurricane Katrina hit the area in 2005. AP IMAGES

tled water. There was also opportunistic theft of jewelry, alcohol, and weapons.

Reports of chaotic violence in New Orleans were widespread in the immediate aftermath of Hurricane Katrina. "Rape and Anarchy in New Orleans," read the cover story of the *New York Post* for September 2, 2005; "Despair and Lawlessness Grip New Orleans," read the front-page banner headline of the *New York Times* for the same day. Reports of snipers firing at rescue helicopters and ambulances, rampant murder, rape gangs, and the like appeared on numerous TV network news programs, including those of CNN, Fox, and ABC. The words "looting and violence" were often used together. A New Orleans SWAT (Special Weapons and Tactics) police team commander was quoted in the *New York Times* for September 11, 2005 as saying that "murders were occurring" and that persons who had taken refuge in the city's Convention Center were being terrorized "every night" by "armed groups of men" and rape gangs.

PRIMARY SOURCE

LOOTERS MAKE OFF WITH MERCHANDISE
See primary source image

SIGNIFICANCE

Media coverage of the social aftermath of Katrina is in some ways typified by this picture. Although the persons in this photograph are denoted "looters" by the Associated Press, there is no way to tell from the photo exactly what they are taking or why. Widespread use of the term "looting" to describe people taking items that they needed for survival as well as those seizing luxuries or weapons helped foster a distorted nationwide impression of total civil breakdown in New Orleans during the flood period: a *USA Today* headline for Sep. 2, 2005 read, "'The Looters, They're Like Cockroaches'." Reports did appear, though relatively rarely, noting that some of the "looting" was driven by necessity. For example, on August 31 the Canadian TV network CTV reported an interview with two New Orleans police officers who were standing guard as employees of the Ritz-Carlton Hotel filled laundry bins with snack foods, medicines, and bottled water taken from a drugstore. "This is for the sick," an Officer Jeff Jacob was quoted as saying. "We can commandeer whatever we see fit, whatever is necessary to maintain law."

Eventually, stories appeared that discredited almost all of the more extreme reports of anarchy in New Orleans. The *New Orleans Picayune* reported on September 26 that the official police count of violent deaths in the city during the flood period totaled only four—not particularly high for that span of time, given that New Orleans would normally see approximately two hundred homicides in a year. Over a month after the floods subsided, representatives of the Air Force, Coast Guard, Department of Homeland Security, and Louisiana National Guard could not confirm a single incident of guns being fired at rescue helicopters, although reports of such events were widely credited during rescue efforts. Stories of ambulances being fired at were also retracted. One crime category in which the stories of disorder may have been less exaggerated is rape: reports have emerged suggesting that over forty rapes may have taken place in the city during the flood period.

Because dramatic stories tend to be more marketable, crime is chronically overreported in the U.S. media, and not only during extraordinary emergencies such as the flooding of New Orleans. Between 1990 and 1998, American TV network news time devoted to crime stories increased by a factor of 4.73 even while actual crime rates were flat or declined in almost all categories; homicide arrests, for example, dropped 32.9% in the same period. Homicides account for only .1 to .2 percent of arrests, but approximately twenty-eight percent of all crimes reported on evening news programs are homicides. Similarly, much of the "looting" reported in New Orleans—no one knows how much—was survival-driven commandeering of supplies in a context where aid from Federal and other sources had broken down so badly that bipartisan Congressional hearings were held to investigate.

Reporting patterns have a strong influence on public perceptions of crime. In June 1993, only five percent of those polled by the *Washington Post* and ABC named crime as "the most important issue facing the country." In the next few months (October 1993 to January 1994), the number of minutes devoted to crime by network TV news jumped from sixty-seven minutes a month to 157 minutes a month; when polled in February 1994, thirty-one percent of those polled named crime as the biggest issue in the country, a six fold increase. Yet crime itself had remained approximately flat in this period. In forming an accurate concept of crime patterns, whether national trends or local surges, quantity of media coverage is not a reliable metric. Scholars rely on sources such as the FBI's Uniform Crime Reports and (often cited as more reliable because based on more uniform methods of data collection) the Bureau of Justice Statistics annual National Crime Victimization Survey. Although these sources also must be handled skeptically, they are evidence-based rather than ratings-driven.

FURTHER RESOURCES
Web sites

CTV.ca news staff. "Looters Take Advantage of Katrina Devastation." Aug. 31, 2005. <http://www.ctv.ca/servlet/ArticleNews/story/CTVNews/20050830_hurricane_katrina_050830/> (accessed March 7, 2006).

Jackson, Janine, and Jim Naureckas. "Crime Contradictions: U.S. News Illustrates Flaws in Crime Coverage." *Extra!* May/June 1994. <http://www.fair.org/index/> (accessed March 7, 2006).

Yassin, Jaime Omar. "Demonizing the Victims of Katrina: Coverage painted hurricane survivors as looters, snipers and rapists." *Extra!* November/December 2005. <http://www.fair.org/index/> (accessed March 7, 2006).

6 Forensics and Criminology

Forensics and Criminology

Forensic science is a "hands on" science, often engaged in crime solving at the molecular level. Criminology is a more theoretical practice, seeking to understand the cause of crime, and studying criminal behavior in the context of societal impacts and responses. Criminologists seek to prevent crime, as well as to improve the workings of the criminal justice and correctional systems.

Forensic science utilizes scientific disciplines in relation to specific questions of law. When they are working in the field, forensic scientists seek to establish a positive trace or link between a suspect and a crime scene or victim, by means of physical evidence, such as fibers, textile fragments, tire or shoe imprints, tool or die markings, or materials used to create incendiary devices or to start fires.

Forensic scientists bring an increasingly sophisticated array of tools to their task. They examine physiological evidence such as blood, semen, fingerprints (see "Is Fingerprint Identification a 'Science'"), ear prints, other bodily fluids or cellular materials, and hair samples, taken from the scene or left on the victim, and attempt to generate plausible lists of suspected perpetrators.

Modern molecular biology in the form of DNA analysis has proved a powerful tool (see "DNA Evidence and Miscarriages of Justice", providing powerful evidence to convict, acquit, prove, or even exhonorate.

Forensic scientists identify weapons and ammunition or projectiles by means of ballistics studies and a ballistic database. (See "Does the United States Need a National Database for Ballistic Fingerprints?".)

Forensic scientists also examine questioned documents for authenticity and provenance and use highly specialized techniques and equipment. In "Computer Forensics," the new science of digital forensics is introduced, which involves the systematic recovery of data from digital storage devices such as computer discs, iPods, cell phones, digital cameras, and personal digital assistants, for use in law enforcement.

Criminologists utilize the social, behavioral, and physical sciences as framework for engaging in study of the underlying causes of criminal behavior; they examine the demographics, environmental variables, socioeconomics, cognitive, and psychological precursors to the development of criminal behavior. For an early application of these techniques see "A Comparative Study of the Intelligence of Delinquent Girls."

Deputy John Fletcher

Photograph

By: John C.H. Grabill

Date: 1887

Source: John C.H. Grabill. "Deputy John Fletcher." Corbis, 1887.

About the Photographer: One of the better-known photographers of the Old West, John C.H. Grabill first set up a commercial photography studio in 1866 in Sturgis, present-day South Dakota. He moved throughout the West, chiefly photographing Indians, miners, soldiers, wagon trains, and landscapes.

INTRODUCTION

In the American West, the years after the Civil War were marked by lawlessness and feuds. Settlers poured into the region too quickly for the legal system to adapt. The nearest courts and sheriffs were often two or more days away. The absence of law enforcement forced Westerners to create their own form of policing, and they chose the age-old system of an eye for an eye. Additionally, everyone had at least one gun. As a result, bloody feuds between two families or factions became common. Texas was the leading state for personal wars, with the region between San Antonio

■ PRIMARY SOURCE

Deputy John Fletcher: Deputy John Fletcher, on horseback in cowboy apparel, prepares to leave Flagstaff, Arizona in 1887. He is on his way to intervene in the Graham-Tewksbury feud, also known as the Pleasant Valley War. © BETTMANN/CORBIS

and Houston labeled the Pure Feud Belt. However, all of the Western states had episodes of violence.

The Pleasant Valley War of the Graham-Tewksbury feud broke out in Arizona. It soon became big enough and bloody enough to claim national attention. At a conservative estimate, thirty deaths were attributed to the feud with the heaviest losses occurring in 1887. Some of the men involved went mysteriously missing, never to be heard from again.

The trouble in Pleasant Valley began with a charge of cattle rustling against the Tewksbury family in 1883. The three angry men who rode up to the Tewksbury ranch to make the charge suddenly exchanged shots with the Tewksbury men. One rider died and one was badly injured. Subpoenaed to testify at the trial of John and Ed Tewksbury for murder, Frank Tewksbury could not stand the stress of days of travel. He died of tuberculosis, with his brothers blaming the Graham brothers for his death. The Grahams and their supporters then killed a Tewksbury shepherd and drove a herd of Tewksbury sheep over a cliff. John Tewksbury and a friend were then murdered. Tewksbury's pregnant widow, Mary, was prevented by John Graham from stopping wild hogs from eating her husband's remains. Tewksbury supporters then shot John Graham and some Graham supporters. More shootings and a mob lynching of three Graham men followed. The last death occurred when Ed Tewksbury shot Tom Graham in 1892 as Graham rode in his wagon. Tewksbury became the last principal combatant still standing. Never convicted of the crime, Tewksbury died of tuberculosis in 1904.

The violence in Arizona became intolerable as more people moved into the territory. For the sake of the safety of their families and their possessions, Arizonans wanted law and order. They sought some sort of codified justice.

Additionally, by the 1880s, vigilantism brought a taint upon the community involved in the violence. It damaged the reputation of Arizona among the people in the rest of the United States by giving the impression that all Arizonans were barbarians who were too bloodthirsty to rely upon the legal system. In short, the Pleasant Valley War hurt the statehood hopes of Arizonans. For the sake of the future, Arizonans increasingly wanted peace at any price.

No major feud occurred in the Arizona Territory after the end of the Graham-Tewksbury war. While the conflict was glamorized in Zane Grey's 1922 novel, *To The Last Man*, it was a nightmare both for the families involved and the Pleasant Valley community. No one wanted a similar resurgence of violence.

FURTHER RESOURCES
Books

Dedera, Don. *A Little War of Our Own: The Pleasant Valley Feud Revisited*. Flagstaff, Ariz.: Northland Press, 1988.

Hanchett, Leland J., Jr. *Arizona's Graham-Tewksbury Feud*. Cave Creek, Ariz.: Pine Rim Publishing, 1994.

Web sites

Smith, Mark. *Americanwest.com*. "The Pleasant Valley War." <http://www.americanwest.com/vispages/msmith1.htm> (accessed February 17, 2006).

PRIMARY SOURCE

DEPUTY JOHN FLETCHER
See primary source image.

SIGNIFICANCE

The Pleasant Valley War was not exceptional in history. Feuds happen whenever the law is absent or powerless and conditions become intolerable. In centuries past, it was considered a family obligation to avenge the killing of a relative. Anglo-Saxons could substitute money for blood (wergeld) and prevent the killing, but the English had to wait until the Middle Ages for murder to be defined as a crime against the state. Relics of these old attitudes appeared in more civilized times and places such as Arizona in the late nineteenth century.

A Comparative Study of the Intelligence of Delinquent Girls

Book excerpt

By: Agusta F. Bronner

Date: 1914

Source: Bronner, Augusta F. *A Comparative Study of the Intelligence of Delinquent Girls*. New York: Columbia University Teacher's College, 1914.

About the Author: During the early part of the twentieth century, Dr. Augusta F. Bronner performed extensive research into the possible causes of criminal behavior, particularly in young women. She worked in conjunction with Dr. William Healy, and together they studied the circumstances in which people fell into delinquent or criminal behavior. Their studies included a series of tests to determine whether natural intelligence (or its lack) played a part in a person's moral development.

INTRODUCTION

Scientists and sociologists have long studied the factors that determine a person's behavior, including genetics, environment, and the influence of others. In the early twentieth century, Dr. Augusta F. Bronner began to investigate the causes of delinquent behavior in young women. She acknowledged that it was unlikely that any one cause was solely responsible for girls becoming involved in criminal lifestyles, but she was particularly interested in whether a girl's intellectual abilities contributed to this type of behavior. Bronner questioned whether a girl with diminished mental faculties was more likely to become a delinquent because she was simply incapable of understanding that this behavior was wrong, or, alternatively, because her lower intelligence made it easier for other people to convince her to participate in criminal activities. She also wished to determine whether those girls falling into delinquent behavior were intellectually incapable of supporting themselves through honest means.

PRIMARY SOURCE

PART I

1. THE PROBLEM

The question of the delinquent girl is one that has aroused much interest of late. Varied are the explanations that have been given as to the causes that have led to the beginning of her career. Vice Commissions have attempted to investigate the economic and social conditions that are involved. In several places, notably at the Laboratory for Social Hygiene, Bedford Hills, and in Chicago, under the direction of Dr. William Healy, the mental status is being delved into as well. In the latter instance, the delinquent is being studied from every possible viewpoint—mental and physical, as well as environmental and social. These latter investigations tend to show that the problem is no simple one; there is no one ever-present and only cause, but a number of inter-related factors whose relative importance varies with each individual case.

However, apart from those who are working experimentally and scientifically, we find many social workers and, indeed, many of the general public who have expressed their views on the subject. Very many of these have stated it as their opinion that delinquency is due very largely to the fact that the offenders are not sufficiently intelligent to care for themselves without running into difficulties, in fact that the large majority are subnormal or feeble minded.

Whether every feeble-minded girl is a potential offender, is easily led, the tool of a stronger-minded, more gifted person, is one question. But it is an entirely different question from the one we have in mind, namely, whether all social and moral offenders are mentally ill or mentally unfit.

Are these offenders so lacking in capacity that they are unable to earn a livelihood in legitimate vocations? Is it because they are "industrial inefficients" that they begin careers of wrong doing? Or is it because their lack of ability means lack of moral stamina as well that they are easily influenced, persuaded readily, to join the ranks of offenders?

How do they compare in general intelligence with their sisters who have never come in conflict with the law, with those who are leading lives where, at least, criminal tendencies, should they exist, are controlled?

Of course, one can not compare them with those offenders so much cleverer, or so much luckier, that they can offend without the offense being detected or known. For it must be remembered that in all studies of delinquents, it is only the caught delinquent that is discussed. Who knows aught of the many unknown law-breakers—perhaps equally or more culpable—who are clever enough to mingle with their fellows, unsuspected even of guilt. Because the feeble-minded girl is so much more readily—and therefore so much more often—detected and brought into court, is she the more likely to predominate in institutions where investigations are being carried on.

In this study that same selective factor is operative among the delinquents investigated. They form one of the four groups that are compared. The second group is made up of students in the Freshman and Sophomore classes of Teachers College and Barnard College of Columbia University. The third is composed of girls who are members of evening clubs at settlements and branches of the Y. W. C. A. in the same districts of New York City from which the delinquent girls here studied largely came.

The delinquent and college groups vary widely, of course, in many ways—probably in hereditary and environmental forces. It is conceivable that members of the two groups are equally well endowed intellectually; on the other hand, do certain tests differentiate the two groups, should this not be true?

In the third group, though the environmental factors, at least such as living conditions and educational opportunities, are more nearly the same as in the first group, there is another point to be considered. Those who compose this group are again selected after a fashion. For it is only the brighter, the more ambitious, probably, who join the classes that are available to all, and we have, therefore, subjects for testing who are not chosen at random from among the residents of these neighborhoods, but a group selected by certain ideals.

In order to compare the delinquents with a group not selected for intellectual attainments, it was desired to use as a fourth group, subjects who are doing work of a character where no intellectual standard obtains. It was believed that this requirement would best be found by using a group of those engaged in domestic service.

The problem, then, that is undertaken in this study, is to determine the intellectual status of a group of delinquent girls as compared with the intellectual status of several other groups that represent varying degrees of education and that are engaged in occupations requiring varied degrees of intelligence and ability.

If the delinquent is less capable than the college girl or even than the girl who, though working daily, yet desires to improve herself by study at night, how does she compare with those who, though pursuing a vocation that demands less skill and training, yet earn a livelihood and are economically independent?

2. CONCLUSIONS

As a result of these experiments, we may conclude that certain tests serve to define the intellectual status of various groups of individuals, so that they can be compared one with the other. The tests for general intelligence which have been found, in other studies, to throw light on the capacity of different individuals, prove of value when applied to a problem such as the one dealt with in this study. They enable one to form some judgment of the general ability of the members of the groups, and to compare groups as a whole with each other. If now we attempt to answer our original question, "Are these thirty delinquent girls so lacking in intellectual capacity that they are unable to earn a livelihood in legitimate vocations?" we must answer, in the light of our findings, "No more so than others who are succeeding in doing so."

Compared with the group of college students, we find the delinquents much less capable; compared with members of evening classes as represented by our group, we find the delinquents still the less capable of the two. Undoubtedly the delinquent group, as a whole, is poor in ability, yet it is composed of girls who vary greatly among themselves, for the best in the group is six times as successful as the poorest in the group, averaging the results on the six general intelligence tests. The poorest members of the group are very poor indeed.

But the results attained by Group S show that this lack of capacity, in and of itself, does not explain the fact of delinquency, for Group S, though no more gifted, yet contains only members who are not and have not been delinquent as far as known.

Since Groups D and S, when compared, prove to be quite on a par as far as general intelligence is concerned, we must conclude that the explanation of the delinquent tendencies shown by members of Group D is something other than the intellectual status alone. This does not mean, of course, that the mentality may not be one factor; but, at least, there must be other factors as well which cause these individuals to engage in careers that lead them into conflict with the law, while others of like mentality experience no such difficulties.

Just what these other factors may be requires much more elaborate study. One does not know what part is played by home conditions, nor what has been the influence and example of parents and associates; one can not tell without special investigation how much or how little the environment has sheltered the individual girl; nor does one know the shocks and temptations to which each has been subjected. Education, companionship, wholesome interests and recreations—all these and many other forces combine to make each person what he is. Perhaps physical factors are involved as well; perhaps, too, the emotional make-up of different individuals varies so that what is temptation for one is not equally so for another.

At any rate, the results of these experiments tend to show that in a study of the causative factors involved in the beginnings of careers such as our delinquent group represents, it is not sufficient to give mental tests alone, essential as these are; nor can one lay all the blame for delinquencies in behavior at the door of poor mental gifts.

SIGNIFICANCE

In setting up her study, Dr. Bronner could not take all factors into account. She noted that she had no way of determining whether there was a portion of the delinquent population that was highly intelligent and, because of this, had been able to elude detection as they engaged in criminal activities. The group of delinquents she studied, therefore, might simply have been the least intelligent portion of this demographic, and, as a result, they had been unable to escape arrest

Helen Golstein, 20, and Mildred Luonce, 19, charged with aiding thieves in New York City, are held by police without bail after a raid at East 18th Street in 1924. © BETTMANN/CORBIS

she found that while it was possible to determine the intellectual abilities of individuals and then to compare them based on these tests, there was nothing to prove that intellectual abilities were an underlying factor in the delinquent behavior of the girls being tested. Within the delinquent group itself, intelligence varied greatly, and while some proved to be less intelligent than those girls with similar backgrounds who were successfully supporting themselves in domestic service, others were of equal or greater intelligence. When compared to the group of college students, the delinquents proved to be less intelligent overall. However, Bronner was forced to acknowledge that there was no way to be certain that there were not other delinquent girls who had evaded capture through the very intelligence that would have allowed them to score on par with the college students. At the end of her experiments, Bronner concluded that intelligence tests alone were not sufficient to determine what caused girls to enter into delinquent behavior. In all likelihood, factors such as environment, family background, circumstance, and outside influences also contributed to whether or not a girl became a delinquent.

The question as to how and why girls become delinquents has prompted further research in the decades that followed, including studies as to why girls appear to be less likely to participate in criminal activities than boys, and how classic theories in criminology relate differently to women. Key influences have been determined to include early delinquency, at a time when a child is unaware that their behavior is unacceptable; reaction to conflict, such as falling into patterns of self-defense in violent situations that eventually become the normal means of behavior; learned behavior, where a person is taught to participate in delinquent behavior early in life and that behavior is reinforced through a reward system; and social reinforcement, where a person is encouraged by peers to participate in behavior they might otherwise consider to be wrong. In the case of women, self-defense against sexist mores or sexual aggression can also play a role in developing delinquent behavior. The variety of potential influences makes it difficult to prevent the development of such behavior. Since there are so many factors to take into consideration, it is nearly impossible to determine what combination of circumstances will trigger the development of delinquent behavior.

and/or prosecution. However, she proceeded with the experiment, comparing the group of delinquent girls to a group that attended college, another group that came from a similar background to the delinquents and yet used their evenings to attend classes at the Y.W.C.A., and another group from the same background who, rather than falling into criminal behavior, worked in domestic positions.

As Bronner anticipated, the intelligence test scores of the college students were far higher than the scores of the girls in the delinquent group, a result she believed was due both to a difference in family and in the environments in which they were raised. But comparing the other groups proved difficult once Bronner started examining other differences in circumstance. Those girls taking evening classes were the most ambitious in their groups, and therefore exhibited an ability to choose to improve their situations, which seemed to indicate that they already had superior intellect.

Bronner determined that the comparison between the delinquent girls and those girls working in domestic service—and therefore not pursuing an intellectual path—proved to be the most fair. Ultimately, however,

FURTHER RESOURCES
Books

Knupfer, Anne Meis. *Reform and Resistance: Gender, Delinquency, and America's First Juvenile Court*. New York: Routledge, 2001.

Sutherland, E. H. *Social Attitudes: Mental Deficiency and Crime*. New York: Henry Holt, 1931.

Web sites

Juvenile Forensic Evaluation Resource Center. "Female Juvenile Delinquency: Risk Factors and Promising Interventions." <http://www.ilppp.virginia.edu/Juvenile_Forensic_Fact_Sheets/FemJuv.html> (accessed January 12, 2006).

Juvenile Justice. "Contemporary Theories Explaining Deviancy." <http://husky1.stmarys.ca/~evanderveen/wvdv/Juvenile_justice/contemporary_theories_deviancy.htm> (accessed January 12, 2006).

An Early Lie Detector Test

Photograph

By: Anonymous

Date: 1915

Source: Corbis

About the Photographer: This photograph, originally from the Bettmann Archive, is currently owned by Corbis, a photo agency headquartered in Seattle, Washington. Corbis licenses images for use in magazines, films, television, and advertisements.

INTRODUCTION

Crime investigators have always been concerned with determining whether or not a suspect is telling the truth. When people lie, they tend to undergo certain characteristic physiological changes such as fidgeting, facial flushing, and avoidance of eye contact. If these physiological changes could be measured accurately, then scientifically based lie detection might be possible, and the results presented as evidence in a trial.

Cesare Lombroso (1835–1909), a pioneering figure in criminology, was the first person to use a machine that could measure changes in blood pressure and pulse as a means to assess a suspect's honesty. During World War I, William Marston (1893–1947), a graduate of Harvard University, developed a similar machine for use in detecting espionage and helped introduce its use into the American legal system.

The modern polygraph was invented by police officer John Larson. It measures blood pressure, respiration, and pulse while a suspect is being questioned.

PRIMARY SOURCE

An Early Lie Detector Test: A prisoner undergoes psychological testing by a primitive lie detector in 1915 as a guard stands behind him with a pistol. © BETTMANN/CORBIS

The multiple outputs of the device produce several lines on graph paper, which is the source of the device's name—polygraph. In 1939, Leonard Keeler, a student of Larson's, added measurement of skin conductance to the polygraph and, thus, introduced the version of the instrument that is still used today. The photograph below shows a suspect being interrogated using a primitive polygraph, probably based on blood pressure and pulse measurements.

PRIMARY SOURCE

AN EARLY LIE DETECTOR TEST

See primary source image.

SIGNIFICANCE

The status of the polygraph evidence in U.S. courts has always been somewhat controversial. Generally, evidence from a polygraph test is only admissible by prior agreement. In 1923, a defendant named James T. Frye appealed his murder conviction on the grounds that the court had not taken into account results of a blood pressure test. His conviction was, however, upheld, and, as a result, the federal court instituted the "Frye Test," which requires the scientific community to judge the validity of new methods, such as the polygraph test. Experts were required to prove the value of forensic tests outside the court before these tests could be used as evidence.

The Frye case did not deter the developers of the polygraph, and they continued to refine the device. As the device came into wider use, it became clear that the skill of the examiner and the questions asked are as important as the performance of the device itself. One important aspect of a polygraph examination is the use of a neutral control question as a baseline. The assumption is that this neutral question will elicit a lower response than questions related to the crime. Even with the use of the control question, the possibility remained that innocent people might be angry and frightened while being interrogated, causing their polygraph results to resemble those expected of a guilty person.

The modern polygraph is a small portable device. Rubber tubes are placed on the chest and abdomen of the suspect, a blood pressure cuff is placed on the arm, and small metal plates are applied to the fingers. When each question is asked input from three physiological responses—skin resistance, blood pressure, and respiration—is recorded as traces on a chart. A scoring system is used, based upon deviations from baseline on the chart. From this, the examiner decides whether the suspect is telling the truth, is lying, or whether the result is inconclusive.

The American Polygraph Association claims a high degree of accuracy for the device, as long as the examiner is skilled and a reliable instrument is used with a validated testing and scoring system. However, one study showed an error rate of eighteen to fifty-five percent among a group of six interpreters. Another, which used actual criminal investigation data, showed the examiners were right sixty-three to seventy-six percent of the time. These studies seem to show that the accuracy of polygraph results can depend heavily on the skill of the examiner. Some defendants, desperate to prove their innocence, may call for a polygraph test only to fail the test due to the stress of the experience. Others, who are guilty, may give a performance on the polygraph that makes them appear to be innocent because they are not very emotionally responsive.

The case of Roger Keith Coleman, convicted of rape and murder in 1982, illustrates the importance of timing and setting when administering a polygraph test. Coleman asked for a polygraph test to prove his innocence, but was only allowed to take the test on the day set for his execution. No second opinion was allowed nor was a second test permitted. It is hardly surprising that Coleman "failed" the test, given the stress he must have been under. He was executed later that day.

The polygraph also has been used in employment screening, but this application of the device was outlawed in the U.S. in 1988, except for certain sensitive positions. It is also sometimes used in civil litigation. While other forms of lie detection, such as hypnosis and the use of hypnotic drugs or "truth serum" have limited credibility, a new truth-detection technique that does look promising is brain fingerprinting. This technique involves recording brain activity in response to questions about crime details of which only the perpetrator would have knowledge. Studies have not yet compared the accuracy of the polygraph with brain fingerprinting but, when they do, the results should be fascinating.

FURTHER RESOURCES

Web sites

North Carolina Wesleyan College. "Scientific Lie Detection." <http://faculty.ncwc.edu/mstevens/425/lecture21.htm> (accessed February 11, 2006).

Ramsland, Katharine. "The Polygraph." *Crime Library,* <http://www.crimelibrary.com/forensics/polygraph/> (accessed February 11, 2006).

Lindbergh Baby Kidnapping Poster, 1932

Poster

By: H. Norman Schwarzkopf

Date: March 11, 1932

Source: Bettmann/Corbis

About the Artist: H. Norman Schwarzkopf was the superintendent of the New Jersey Police at the time of the Lindbergh kidnapping. He created the poster displayed below. The Famous Trials Project, from which the poster is drawn, is a website compiled by Douglas O. Linder, professor of law at the University of Missouri at Kansas City, as an educational resource of law students and scholars.

INTRODUCTION

The kidnapping of the son of famous American aviator Charles A. Lindbergh was, perhaps, one of the most famous cases of the twentieth century. On the night of March 1, 1932, the infant son of Colonel Charles A. Lindbergh and his wife Anne was abducted from the second-floor nursery of his home in Hopewell, New Jersey. In May 1927 Lindbergh had become the first person to fly solo across the Atlantic Ocean. He was an American hero and the reasons for the kidnapping became clear when a ransom note was found at the scene of the crime. That, and a home-made ladder leading up to the nursery, were the two prime clues in the crime.

On March 5, the kidnapper communicated with the Lindberghs for the first time. Then, John F. Condon, a public school principal, offered a reward for the return of the child, publishing a letter to this effect in the *Bronx Home News*. The kidnapper responded the next day and the Lindberghs agreed to have Condon act as a mediator. It was at this crucial time that the poster shown below appeared.

PRIMARY SOURCE

LINDBERGH BABY KIDNAPPING POSTER, 1932
See primary source image

SIGNIFICANCE

On March 12, Condon met with the kidnapper and soon after turned over $50,000 in ransom money. He was told that the child could be found on a boat near Martha's Vineyard Island, but it turned out that no such boat existed. The hunt continued and on May 12, the body of the child was found in a woodland near the Lindbergh's home. Forensic evidence pointed to asphyxiation or blunt force injury as the cause of death.

Analysis of the ransom note had suggested a perpetrator of poor education and of German descent. The homemade ladder suggested that the kidnapper was skilled in carpentry. A forensic expert said that four different types of wood—Ponderosa pine, North Carolina pine, birch, and fir—had been used in its construction. The fir was particularly significant and

WANTED
INFORMATION AS TO THE WHEREABOUTS OF

CHAS. A. LINDBERGH, JR.
OF HOPEWELL, N. J.
SON OF COL. CHAS. A. LINDBERGH
World-Famous Aviator

This child was kidnaped from his home in Hopewell, N. J., between 8 and 10 p. m. on Tuesday, March 1, 1932.

DESCRIPTION:

Age, 20 months	**Hair, blond, curly**
Weight, 27 to 30 lbs.	**Eyes, dark blue**
Height, 29 inches	**Complexion, light**

**Deep dimple in center of chin
Dressed in one-piece coverall night suit**

**ADDRESS ALL COMMUNICATIONS TO
COL. H. N. SCHWARZKOPF, TRENTON, N. J., or
COL. CHAS. A. LINDBERGH, HOPEWELL, N. J.**

ALL COMMUNICATIONS WILL BE TREATED IN CONFIDENCE

March 11, 1932
COL. H. NORMAN SCHWARZKOPF
Supt. New Jersey State Police, Trenton, N. J.

PRIMARY SOURCE

Lindbergh Baby Kidnapping Poster, 1932: A poster distributed during the infamous Lindbergh baby kidnapping case titled "Wanted: Information as to the whereabouts of Chas. A. Lindbergh, Jr." It was distributed by the U.S. Department of Justice on March 11, 1932. The poster shows two pictures of the Lindbergh baby and describes his physical characteristics and last known whereabouts. © BETTMANN/CORBIS

was likely a piece of flooring that had been used to finish off the job when the carpenter ran out of wood. Next, distinctive marks were found on the wood that suggested a planing machine had been used for smoothing the side rails of the ladder.

Planed wood samples from more than 1,500 mills all over the country tracked the material used in the

Police in Mount Rose, New Jersey, sift for clues at the site where the body of the murdered Lindbergh baby was found, September 1934. © BETTMANN/CORBIS

ladder to a company in the Bronx where, coincidentally, many of the ransom notes had turned up. All of this led to the arrest of Bruno Richard Hauptmann, a German immigrant and carpenter. He was found with some of the ransom money in his possession, although he claimed he was taking care of it for a friend. He had lain low for three years, but the police had meanwhile been tracking the serial numbers of the ransom notes. In Hauptmann's home, police found a missing floorboard that corresponded to the piece used in the construction of the ladder. There was also a defective wood plane that could have been responsible for the marks on the ladder.

Hauptmann's trial for murder and kidnapping began in January 1935; he was convicted and sentenced to death. Two appeals and a stay of execution were turned down and Hauptmann was executed on April 3, 1936. However, his widow Anna continued to protest his innocence and campaigned to clear his name until the mid-1980s.

The Lindbergh case had a lasting effect on U.S. law. In the 1920s, kidnapping had become a major criminal activity in the U.S. The usual way of dealing with it was to pay the ransom and then let the police investigate. Children were not the only victims. Indeed, some gangs would kidnap a rich businessman, which aroused less public hostility. Hauptmann's execution brought an end to the kidnapping "boom" as new legislation known as the "Little Lindbergh" laws came into effect in several states. These laws made it a capital offense to carry out kidnapping if any physical harm came to the victim. Even sending a ransom note might result in a penalty of twenty years imprisonment, a fine of $5,000, or both.

FURTHER RESOURCES
Books

Lyle, Douglas. *Forensics for Dummies.* Hoboken, N.J.: Wiley, 2004.

Wilson, Colin. *The Mammoth Book of True Crime.* London: Robinson, 1998.

Handwriting Evidence from Lindbergh Case

Photograph

By: Anonymous

Date: September 21, 1934

Source: "Handwriting Evidence from Lindbergh Case." Corbis, 1934.

About the Photographer: This photograph is part of the stock collection at Corbis photo agency, headquartered in Seattle and provider of images for magazine, films, television, and advertisements. The photographer is not known.

INTRODUCTION

On the night of March 1, 1932, the infant son of the American aviator Colonel Charles A. Lindbergh and his wife Anne was abducted from the second-floor nursery of his home in Hopewell, New Jersey. Lindbergh was considered an American hero, for in May 1927 he had become the first person to fly solo across the Atlantic. As a high-profile person, he and his family were vulnerable to kidnapping because the perpetrators felt large sums of ransom money could be extracted. Sure enough, a ransom note was soon found at the scene of the crime. That, and a homemade ladder leading up to the nursery, were the two prime clues in the case.

There were as many as twelve ransom notes, demanding different sums of money. One of these is depicted in the primary source below. On March 5, the kidnapper sent a note direct to the Lindberghs for the first time. Then, John F. Condon, a public school principal, offered a reward for the return of the child, publishing a letter to this effect in the Bronx Home News. The kidnapper responded the next day and the Lindberghs agreed to have Condon act as mediator.

On March 12, Condon met with the kidnapper and soon after turned over $50,000 in ransom money. He was told the child could be found on a boat near Martha's Vineyard Island, but it turned out that no such boat existed. The hunt continued and on May 12, the body of the child was found in woodland near the Lindbergh's home. Forensic evidence pointed to asphyxiation or blunt force injury as the cause of death.

PRIMARY SOURCE

HANDWRITING EVIDENCE FROM LINDBERGH CASE
See primary source image.

SIGNIFICANCE

Analysis of the ransom notes had suggested a perpetrator of poor education and of German descent. A ladder found at the scene of the crime was another important piece of evidence, leading to the arrest of Bruno Richard Hauptmann, a German immigrant and carpenter. He was found with some of the ransom money in his possession, although he claimed he was taking care of it for a friend. On his arrest, samples of his handwriting were sent to the FBI laboratory in Washington, D.C. for comparison with the ransom notes. One such comparison is shown in the illustration above. Hauptmann's signature has been reconstructed from letters in one of the notes and compared with that appearing on his auto registration card. It was to prove a damning piece of evidence.

Hauptmann's trial for murder and kidnapping began in January 1935; he was convicted and sentenced to death. Two appeals and a stay of execution were turned down and Hauptmann was executed on April 3, 1936. However, his widow Anna continued to protest his innocence and campaigned to clear his name up until the mid-1980s. Some say that the ransom notes were a hoax but that was not the view of the FBI.

Handwriting analysis, of the sort that helped to convict Hauptmann, is an important tool in forensic science. The expert looks for various points of similarity and difference between two documents—in this case Hauptmann's writing and the ransom notes. The overall form is important—the size, shape, and slant of the different letters are vital features of this overview. Spacing between letters and words will also be noted. Content, too, gives vital clues. Also, are there wrong spellings, or mistakes in punctuation or grammar that can indicate level of education and ethnic origin?

The written ransom note might be a rich source of evidence, but it is not very common in the twenty-first century. Handwriting examiners spend more time looking at printed documents and photocopies which are, of course, revealing in their own way. The ransom note is not common because kidnapping itself has

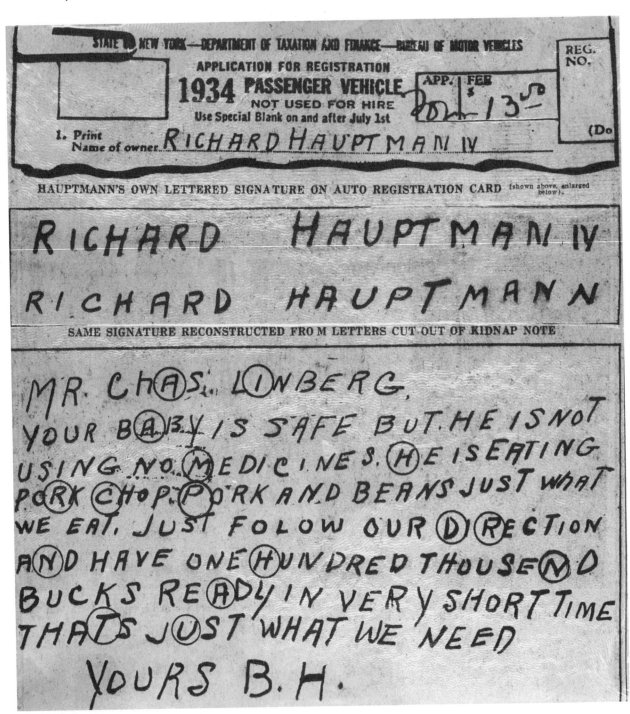

HAUPTMANN'S OWN LETTERED SIGNATURE ON AUTO REGISTRATION CARD (shown above, enlarged below).

SAME SIGNATURE RECONSTRUCTED FROM LETTERS CUT OUT OF KIDNAP NOTE

PRIMARY SOURCE

Handwriting Evidence from Lindbergh Case: Handwriting evidence submitted in 1934 against Bruno Richard Hauptmann, the convicted kidnapper of the Lindbergh baby. At the top is Hauptmann's own lettered signature on an auto registration card copied at the motor vehicle bureau, and below is a ransom note. © BETTMANN/CORBIS rather gone out of fashion—at the time of the Lindbergh case, it was accepted that huge ransom sums could be paid to resolve the matter. That is no longer the case, at least publicly, as has been seen from the spate of kidnappings in Iraq in recent years. But forgery and fraud still provide ample work for the handwriting forensic analyst.

FURTHER RESOURCES

Books

Lyle, Douglas. *Forensics for Dummies*. Hoboken, N.J.: Wiley, 2004.

Web sites

CharlesLindbergh.com. "Charles A. Lindbergh Jr. Kidnapping, March 1, 1932." <http://www.charleslindbergh.com/kidnap/index.asp> (accessed February 25, 2006).

Federal Bureau of Investigation. "Famous Cases: Lindbergh Kidnapping." <http://www.fbi.gov/libref/historic/famcases/lindber/lindbernew.htm> (accessed February 25, 2006).

Forensic Experts Unearth Mass Grave

Photograph

By: Danilo Krstanovic

Date: July 25, 2002

Source: Reuters/Corbis

About the Photographer: This photograph was taken by Danilo Krstanovic, a photographer for Reuters (newswire service), on July 25, 2002, at a mass graves for victims of the 1995 massacre in Srebrenica.

INTRODUCTION

In the summer of 1995, as part of a program of "ethnic cleansing" being carried out by Serbia in the country of Bosnia and Herzogovina, Serb military forces executed some 8,100 Muslim males civilians, from teenagers to elders, near the town of Srebrenica. Bodies from the massacre—actually a series of massacres, not all committed one day or in one place—were buried in several mass graves. Several months later, in an effort to conceal these facts, Serb military forces used earth-moving machinery to excavate the mass graves and move the bodies to fresh graves in

more remote locations. This picture shows a member of an international team excavating one of these secondary graves in 2002 as part of a project to identify the victims.

Following the G-7 summit in Lyon, France in 1996, the International Commission on Missing Persons (ICMP) was formed to uncover information about persons who had disappeared in the various wars and conflicts that had occurred in the Balkan states in the early 1990s. (The G-7 or "Group of Seven" consisted of Canada, France, Germany, Italy, Japan, the U.K., and the U.S.A, who together represent about half the world's economy; it has since

PRIMARY SOURCE

Forensic Experts Unearth Mass Grave: Polish anthropologist Eva Klonowski inspects bodily remains found in a mass grave near the town of Zvornik, close to the Bosnian border with Serbia. Experts believe that the mass grave holds up to 100 bodies of Bosnian Muslims from Srebrenica massacred by Serb forces in 1995. © REUTERS/CORBIS

become the G-8, with the addition of the Russian Federation. The G-8 meets periodically to discuss economic and other issues.) The ICMP's operations were later expanded to cover missing-persons cases from Macedonia and Kosovo, where conflicts had also occurred. The ICMP has also assisted in identifying human remains from the tsunami of 2004.

PRIMARY SOURCE

FORENSIC EXPERTS UNEARTH MASS GRAVE
See primary source image.

SIGNIFICANCE

The main activities of the ICMP are carried out by its Forensic Science Department, which, in the ICMP's words, "has the primary responsibility within ICMP for developing, implementing and managing the technical process of assisting governments in exhumations, examinations, and identifications of persons missing as a result of violent conflicts." Exhumations are a primary activity because many of the people who are disappeared in these conflicts are buried after being shot. The ICMP's Forensic Science Department has three divisions:

(1) Excavations and Examination Program. This is the division at work in the photograph. This division detects burial sites and excavates them to recover human remains and all possible information about their origin, identity, and circumstances of interment. "Anthropological examination" of the remains and any artifacts found with them is one of the methods used in collecting this information, hence the presence of an anthropologist in the photo.

(2) Identification Coordination Division. Many of the people murdered and buried in the conflicts studied by the ICMP left surviving relatives. Identifying victims' remains depends largely on matching DNA from bone marrow in mass graves with the DNA of living relatives. Moving the Srebrenica bodies with power machinery to secondary mass graves tended to tear them apart and mingle them, making DNA identification of remains particularly needful. To match DNA of victims to living relatives, DNA from those relatives is also needed, so the Identification Coordination Division of the ICMP has carried out an extensive program of collecting blood samples in order to construct a DNA database.

(3) DNA Laboratories. This division extracts DNA from the samples dug up by the Excavations and Examination Program and subjects them to analysis.

The ICMP has become an acknowledged world leader in forensic DNA extraction and matching.

The Srebrenica massacre, because of its magnitude, has been the largest single project of the ICMP. Human remains from Srebrenica recovered by the ICMP are transported to a dedicated mortuary and examination facility in Tuzla in eastern Bosnia. Thousands of body bags containing remains of victims of the Srebrenica massacre are kept on shelves in this refrigerated facility, pending identification and burial.

The ICMP program has been notably successful. As of the end of 2001, at which time ICMP made its first DNA match, only about 100 Srebrenica victims had been identified; since that time the ICMP has identified about 3,500 of the massacre's 8,100 victims through DNA matching. As of 2006, the work was continuing

State terror in the form of "disappearance"—meaning abduction, torture (often), execution, and clandestine burial (usually)—has been used by a number of governments in the last several decades, including Argentina, El Salvador, Guatemala, Serbia, and others. The goal of clandestine burial is to erase evidence of the perpetrators' actions and terrorize the surrounding population with fears of disappearance and presumed death. The ICMP strives, by undoing the anonymity of some victims, to reduce the effectiveness of "enforced disappearance as a tool of war." Also, by documenting the numbers and identities of victims, the ICMP provides scientific information that can be used to refute revisionist claims about the number and identity of the victims. For example, politically motivated claims have been made to the effect that the Srebrenica massacre did not really happen, or was not as large as claimed, or that the dead were soldiers killed in combat, not murdered civilians. A recent report issued by the government of Serbia claimed, for example, that only 1,800 soldiers had been buried at Srebrenica, not 8,100 civilians. The ICMP's data precisely and scientifically refute these claims.

FURTHER RESOURCES

Periodicals

Rohde, David. "Graves Found that Confirm Bosnia Massacre." *Christian Science Monitor*. Nov. 16, 1995. Available at <http://www.pulitzer.org/year/1996/international-reporting/works/ROHDE-NOV16.html> (accessed March 23, 2006).

Web sites

International Commission on Missing Persons. <http://www.ic-mp.org/> (accessed March 23, 2006).

Does the United States Need a National Database for Ballistic Fingerprints?

Magazine article

By: Stephen P. Halbrook

Date: November 26, 2002

Source: Halbrook, Stephen P. "Does the United States Need a National Database for Ballistic Fingerprints?" *Insight Magazine* (November 26, 2002).

About the Author: Stephen P. Halbrook, Ph.D., an attorney in Fairfax, Va., and a research fellow at the Independent Institute in Oakland, Calif., is author of *That Every Man Be Armed* and *Freedmen, the Fourteenth Amendment, and the Right to Bear Arms.*

INTRODUCTION

Guns are a common tool of crime—they are used to kill, injure, and establish control over victims in crimes such as rape, armed robbery, and abduction. They are also a rich source of forensic evidence that can often lead investigators to a perpetrator. The gun itself, its bullets, casings, and the marks left on a bullet after it's fired can reveal a great deal about what happened at the crime scene.

It is unusual to find the weapon itself at the crime scene, but bullets or bullet fragments can often be retrieved and linked to the weapon used. Sometimes the casing—the part of the cartridge left when the bullet has been fired—is the only piece of evidence left. Both casings and bullets bear characteristic marks related to the gun and how it has been fired. In the hands of a skilled firearms and ballistics examiner, these can yield a great deal of information.

The Bureau of Alcohol, Tobacco, Firearms, and Explosives (BATFE) has established the National Integrated Ballistic Information Network (NIBIN), which contains data on bullets and casings used in crimes. Since bullets fired from the same gun have very similar markings, a database match can link crimes and criminals together. A national ballistic fingerprinting database was proposed in the wake of the 2002 Washington, D.C. sniper killings. It's a contentious issue, with strong arguments and opinions on both sides.

State Senator Jack Scott, D-Altadena, announces the introduction of legislation in 2002 that would require manufacturers and importers to collect "ballistic fingerprints" on all firearms manufactured and sold in the state of California. AP IMAGES

▮ PRIMARY SOURCE

DOES THE UNITED STATES NEED A NATIONAL DATABASE FOR BALLISTIC FINGERPRINTS?

No: Don't Start a Boondoggle Bullet Library that Will Become a Stealth Gun Registry

November 26, 2002

Stephen Halbrook

Insight Magazine

Apprehending the snipers who recently terrorized the Washington area took place through old-fashioned gumshoe police work and citizen involvement. That did not, however, prevent the murders from sparking a new gun-control debate, this time over whether firearms should be "fingerprinted" through use of ballistic imaging.

The hijackers of Sept. 11, armed with box cutters and then with airliners, proved terrorists don't need firearms. John Allen Muhammad and John Lee Malvo were vocal sympathizers of the hijackers. Muhammad told Harjeet Singh that he planned to shoot a fuel tanker and cause it to explode on the freeway, and then to snipe at motorists. He also intended to kill a police officer and then blow up the mourners at the funeral home. Last June, Singh disclosed these conversations to police and an FBI agent, who did nothing.

Media discussion highlights that Muhammad had been in the U.S. military and had rifle training, and that the great satan—the National Rifle Association (NRA)—has blocked "commonsense" gun legislation. Muhammad's terrorist sympathies and plans are barely mentioned.

During the same period that the snipers played their deadly game, drug traffickers firebombed the Baltimore row house of a neighborhood antidrug activist, killing her, her husband and her five children. These murders prompted zero legislative panaceas.

But, for those focused on the single-minded agenda of regulating American citizens who own firearms, the serial sniper rejuvenated S 3096, the Ballistics, Law Assistance and Safety Technology Act, sponsored by Sens. Herb Kohl (D–Wis.), Dianne Feinstein (D–Calif.), Charles Schumer (D–N.Y.) and Jack Reed (D–R.I.); and HR 408, sponsored by Reps. Anna Eshoo (D–Calif.) and John Conyers (D–Mich.). This legislation would require ballistics testing of all firearms manufactured.

The bills would require manufacturers and importers to test-fire all firearms, prepare ballistics images of the bullets and cartridge casings (which must then be stored) and provide the records to the Bureau of Alcohol, Tobacco, and Firearms (ATF) [now the Bureau of Alcohol, Tobacco, Firearms, and Explosives—BATFE] for its computerized database which law-enforcement agencies can access. Agencies will work with industry "to curb firearm-related crime and illegal firearm trafficking." The bills allocate $20 million to get things started.

The bills end with an unlikely section entitled "Privacy Rights of Law-Abiding Citizens," which provides that ballistics information "may not be used for prosecutorial purposes unless law-enforcement officials have a reasonable belief that a crime has been committed and that ballistics information would assist in the investigation of that crime." Indeed not, prosecutions cannot proceed without probable cause to believe these things. This does not restrict surveillance of law-abiding citizens where no prosecution has been initiated.

The scheme is a giant loophole if it does not include the names of the current owners of the 260 million firearms already out there, who must bring their guns in for testing. To be enforceable, felony penalties must be imposed for noncompliance. The gun owners may as well be fingerprinted and photographed while they're at

it—the lack of which is just another loophole. Would criminals, after they obtain their guns through theft or the black market, keep ATF current with their names, addresses and gun descriptions?

Technically, the proposal just isn't feasible as a crime-fighting tool. Fingerprints and DNA do not change, but bullets and shell casings certainly do. Rifling marks on a bullet change as the barrel receives more wear and tear—a couple of scrapes with a file can change the "fingerprint" immediately—and barrels may easily be replaced. Shell-casing marks are made by the breech face or bolt, extractor, ejector, and firing pin. Again, a swipe with a file, normal wear, or parts replacement creates a new "fingerprint." Ammunition made by different manufacturers give dissimilar images. Shotguns shoot ball shot through a smooth bore, so there's no bullet to test; revolvers and single-shot rifles leave no ejection marks. Only semiautomatics eject shell casings, but a brass catcher can be attached. A criminal could leave someone else's fired brass (perhaps from a shooting range) at a crime scene.

To be sure, ballistics testing can be useful on a limited basis to help solve crimes, chiefly when a crime gun is seized. A shell casing from the seized firearm may be compared with a casing from the scene of an unsolved crime. After a close match is found through use of the database, an examiner then must make visual comparisons using optical devices. By limiting the database to crime guns, the evidence is pinpointed, and the system is not overloaded with images of casings from countless firearms held by the public at large. The National Integrated Ballistic Information Network (NIBIN), administered by the ATF, conducts this type of testing.

The Bureau of Forensic Services of the California Department of Justice conducted tests and concluded: "When applying this technology to the concept of mass sampling of manufactured firearms, a huge inventory of potential candidates will be generated for manual review. This study indicates that this number of candidate cases will be so large as to be impractical and likely will create logistic complications so great that they can not be effectively addressed." A database of shell casings from all firearms would generate so many "hits" that the information would be useless.

The Ballistic Imaging Evaluation and Study Act (HR 3941 and S 2581), sponsored in the U.S. House of Representatives by Republican Rep. Melissa Hart of Pennsylvania and in the Senate by Democratic Sen. Zell Miller of Georgia, would provide for further study by the National Academy of Sciences. The bills are supported by the NRA and the National Shooting Sports Foundation.

Maryland and New York are the only states which require ballistic imaging for all new handguns sold in those states. Neither has solved a single crime with these programs. After defunding programs that put cops on the beat, Maryland spent $5 million to test 2,000 handgun shell casings. As the sniper struck in the D.C. suburbs, the FBI disclosed that Maryland had halted certain background checks on gun buyers because funds had run out.

When the sniper was on the loose, we saw an illustration of how police are spread too thin when every citizen is a suspect. While cops halted all traffic to search white vans, ATF went into every gun store in the Maryland suburbs and got the identity of every purchaser of a 0.223-caliber rifle. Cops then beat on the doors of every such person—there were hundreds—and seized the rifles for ballistic testing. All the while the sniper cruised around in his blue Chevy Caprice sedan with his rifle purchased on the West Coast.

While current bills in Congress would require ballistic testing only of new guns, the system would be worthless without testing of all guns and registration of all gun owners. Any transfer of a gun would require notice to ATF. The replacement of any parts, whether a barrel or firing pin, would necessitate new ballistic testing. Thus, the sale of firearm replacement parts would need to be regulated—they would need serial numbers and would require an ATF permit to acquire. New crimes with new felony penalties must be legislated.

The above is not a slippery-slope prediction; rather it is the only logical path of the current push for governmental omniscience regarding gun owners. Every new control has inherent "loopholes" allowing "circumvention," and these defects will continue until perfect knowledge by the authorities is attained. Gun controllers insist that knowing who owns every gun and the fingerprints of every gun would have led police immediately to Muhammad. As claimed by the Brady Campaign to Prevent Gun Violence, ballistic fingerprinting would have "solved this crime after the first shooting."

Yet, in all but one of the shootings, no shell casing was found since Muhammad and/or Malvo were shooting from inside a car trunk, where there were openings for the barrel and the scope. The casings were ejected into the trunk. Perhaps the Brady group will suggest a further panacea—making it illegal to shoot from car trunks.

While prohibitionist groups deny that ballistic-fingerprinting programs would require registration of firearm owners, they simultaneously are calling for bans on ordinary rifles. More typically—as experiences from Nazi Germany to current England and New York City verify—registration is enacted first, and then confiscation. Today's approach is more direct: "Tougher restrictions must be placed on so-called sniper rifles, such as the 0.50, 0.308 and 0.223 calibers," says Tom Diaz of the

Violence Policy Center. Rep. John Conyers (D–Mich.) urges the Federal Trade Commission to investigate the marketing of rifles to civilians, arguing that "Sniper weapons are different from standard hunting rifles because they are designed to strike a target from a distance."

Factually, the 0.308 is a "high-caliber" rifle that hunters typically equip with a scope to strike deer "from a distance." The 0.223 rifle is the most popular caliber for varmint hunting. "Sniper" rifle is a pejorative substitute for "hunting" rifle.

Since only one shot was fired in each of the D.C. area murders, the murder weapon could have just as well been a single-shot. In fact it was a Bushmaster XM15 semiautomatic. Contrary to media reports, that rifle is not an "assault weapon" as defined by federal law. Yet prohibitionists already are appealing to the recent killing spree to argue for reenactment of the federal assault-weapon ban which sunsets in 2004.

The proposal for universal ballistic fingerprinting is just one more scheme to register, regulate, and potentially incarcerate law-abiding firearm owners. It offers no true benefit for law enforcement—as the Fraternal Order of Police puts it: "With such small chances that it would be used to solve a firearm crime . . . these are law-enforcement dollars best spent elsewhere." Instead of pinpointing likely suspects, it overextends the net and makes a suspect out of every American citizen who chooses to own a firearm.

SIGNIFICANCE

Although gun dealers and manufacturers have recorded sales records and serial numbers since the 1968 Gun Control Act, the proposed database would require manufacturers or the BATFE to store digital images of each new gun's ballistic fingerprint. Ideally, if a bullet or casing found at a crime scene matched one in the database, it could be traced to the weapon and original purchaser. Of course, the weapon could have been sold—perhaps more than once—or stolen before falling into the perpetrator's hands. But proponents believe such a system would have the potential to give investigators a lead.

To gauge the potential benefit of such a database, a 2002 NIBIN study showed that for 166,672 entries, there were 264 hits, or 0.16 percent, in criminal investigations. For casing entries, there were 4,395 hits from 351,194 entries, or 1.25 percent. How many of these led to a conviction is not known. This is an expensive way to investigate a crime, although it's possible that costs might decrease enough over time to make it a more viable method.

DNA fingerprinting technology has proven invaluable in the investigation of many serious crimes. It remains to be seen whether a national ballistic fingerprinting database could serve forensic science and still protect individual rights and liberties.

FURTHER RESOURCES

Books

Lyle, Douglas P. *Forensics for Dummies*. Hoboken, NJ: Wiley, 2004.

Web sites

National Center for Policy Analysis. "Ballistic Imaging: Not Ready for Prime Time." <http://www.ncpa.org/pub/bg/bg160> (accessed February 24, 2006).

DNA Evidence and Miscarriages of Justice

Internet article

By: Bernie Matthews

Date: March 18, 2005

Source: Bernie Matthews. *On Line Opinion—Australia's e-Journal of Social and Political Debate*. <http://www.onlineopinion.com.au/view.asp?article=3258> (accessed February 26, 2006).

About the Author: Bernie Matthews is a convicted bank robber and prison escapee who has served time for armed robbery and prison escapes in New South Wales (1969–1980) and Queensland (1996–2000). He is now a journalist.

INTRODUCTION

Biological evidence, such as blood grouping and fingerprints, has long been used as forensic evidence. DNA fingerprinting was introduced into American courts as admissible evidence in 1988 and has given new meaning to the concept of establishing the identity of a suspect from a trace of biological material left at the scene of a crime.

DNA is a very long molecule found in the nucleus of cells which contains the genetic blueprint in the form of a chemical code. Research in the 1960s showed that the code consists of the sequence of the

four chemical 'letters' (known for short as A, C, G and T) making up the DNA molecule. Apart from identical twins, each individual has a different DNA sequence. This was exploited by Alec Jeffreys and his team at Leicester University, England, in the 1980s. They developed a way of comparing these differences in DNA between individuals—a technology generally known as DNA fingerprinting.

The methods used in DNA fingerprinting are advancing all the time but generally they focus upon two types of variations seen in DNA. Variable Number Tandem Repeats (VNTR) are sections of sequence that are repeated all along the DNA molecule in various locations (known as loci). One person may have five copies of a VNTR at a particular locus, while someone else has eight. The other variation is called the Short Tandem Repeat (STR) which, as the name suggests, is a much shorter piece of sequence—typically just three to seven letters long. The value of the STR is that the repeats are found over much shorter segments of the DNA molecule so technicians can use even fragments of a DNA molecule (useful when a sample has been degraded at the crime scene) to make an analysis.

Typically, in a DNA fingerprint, VNTRs or STRs are several loci will be examined. If only one was investigated, the chances of getting a unique match between two samples (sample at crime scene and sample taken from suspect) would not be great. It may be that one percent of the population shares the pattern at that locus. But when more loci are examined and matches are still found, then the chance of the pattern belonging to someone other than the suspect soon become extremely small—of the order of one in several million. DNA is therefore a very powerful forensic tool for establishing identity and has been used to secure convictions all over the world in the last two decades. But, as the article below describes, sometimes the technology goes wrong.

PRIMARY SOURCE

DNA EVIDENCE AND MISCARRIAGES OF JUSTICE

The exposure of flawed DNA testing procedures at Queensland's John Tonge Centre contained in a leaked internal report, compiled by Ms Deanna Belzer on February 12, 2005, reinforced repeated claims made during the past six years by convicted bank robber Marc Andre Renton, that he had been wrongfully convicted on the strength of flawed DNA evidence. Renton's claims were substantiated by Australia's foremost DNA expert Professor Barry Boettcher.

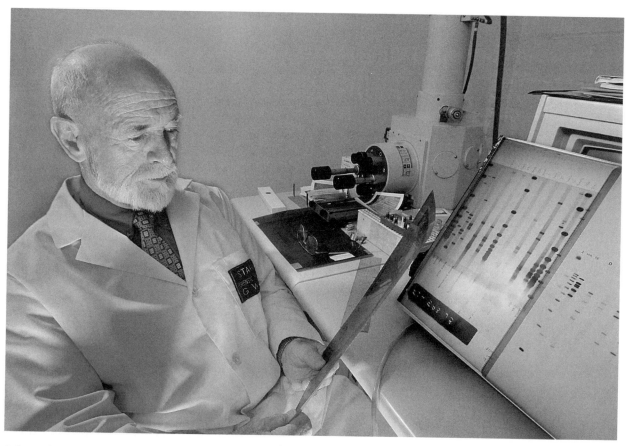

A forensic scientist at George Washington University studies DNA evidence in a laboratory. © RICHARD T. NOWITZ/CORBIS

Renton is not the only Queensland prisoner who has claimed he is suffering a miscarriage of justice resulting from the flawed testing procedures or the scientific interpretation of DNA evidence offered to Queensland courts by staff from the John Tonge Centre.

The Wayne Edward Butler case

The brutal murder of Natasha Douty, a Queensland resort worker who was bashed to death on a secluded beach on Brampton Island in 1983, remained unsolved for 18 years. Sydney businessman, Wayne Edward Butler, was holidaying on Brampton Island when Douty was killed but claimed he was jogging around the island unaccompanied for four hours at the time of the murder. He was originally eliminated as a suspect after he submitted to a blood test. Without an eyewitness account or confessional evidence the crime remained unsolved until Butler's arrest and conviction in 2001.

Butler's conviction became a flagship for DNA profiling in Queensland, after staff from the John Tonge Centre testified that semen found on a towel at the crime scene in 1983 matched Butler's DNA profile. That evidence was coupled with testimony that the chance of someone else having the same DNA profile as Butler was forty-three trillion to one. The ABO or blood grouping technology that originally cleared Butler as a suspect in 1983 was rejected by the jury in preference to the DNA evidence.

The Queensland Court of Criminal Appeal supported the jury's verdict and said the jury was justified in rejecting the results of the 1983 blood test on the grounds that DNA provides a more certain result and the blood samples may have been degraded. Despite the supposedly irrefutable DNA evidence, which convicted Butler, and later upheld by the Queensland Criminal Court of Appeal, he has steadfastly maintained his innocence of the crime.

Butler's protestations of innocence have again been reinforced by scientific conclusions from Australia's foremost DNA expert, Professor Barry Boettcher, who questions the DNA evidence put before the jury and the opinion of the Queensland Criminal Court of Appeal when it dismissed Butler's appeal. Professor Boettcher disagrees that an ABO test is forensically less certain than a DNA test and claimed "the only difference between an ABO test and a DNA test is that it is less discriminatory".

Professor Boettcher's scientific opinion is supported by his conclusion that it is not Butler's semen on the towel. The semen on the towel came from a man with blood Group "O". Wayne Butler is blood group "B". Professor Boettcher suggested that the errors in the DNA testing process relating to the Butler case could have resulted from the mislabelling of test tubes inside the John Tonge Centre—a fact that was substantiated during Butler's trial when staff from the John Tonge Centre admitted making labelling errors during the DNA testing process.

The Robert Paul Hytch case

Disputed DNA evidence in another Queensland murder case resulted with Robert Paul Hytch, 29, being freed from prison after he was acquitted of killing missing 16-year-old Bowen schoolgirl Rachael Antonio. A previous 1999 Townsville Supreme Court jury had found him guilty for the manslaughter of the missing Bowen teenager and he was jailed for nine years.

DNA evidence used to convict Hytch during his 1999 trial involved a spot of blood found on his sandal which forensic experts claimed was 900,000–1 chance of being from Antonio. It was argued at his appeal that the DNA evidence was so powerful, from an emotional sense, it had to impact on the jury decision but it should have been ruled inadmissible hearsay because the witness who gave the evidence during the trial merely read a report of work done by others.

The defence was not able to cross-examine those who did the actual work about the possibility of contamination or degradation of DNA samples. The blood found on Hytch's sandal could not be aged. The blood could have got there any time and there was no evidence to support the theory that she bled before she died because the body has not been found.

At his second trial Hytch's defence lawyer, Harvey Walters, argued that the whole case against his client hinged on dodgy scientific evidence. The defence called its own forensic expert who disputed the DNA evidence linking Ms Antonio to a sandal worn by Hytch on the night of her disappearance and the jury subsequently acquitted him.

Flawed DNA testing procedures and the questionable interpretation of DNA evidence is not solely confined to the Queensland legal system.

The Nick Lisoff Case

In NSW the spectre of planted DNA evidence surfaced when Nick Lisoff and two other men were arrested over a brutal 1996 bashing in which the victim lost a considerable amount of blood and required urgent blood transfusions to survive. The victim was rushed to hospital in a critical condition where he received a life-saving blood transfusion. Police went to the hospital and took a sample of the victim's blood to assist their investigations.

When the three men were arrested two of them pleaded guilty to the attack but Lisoff continued to protest his innocence. Police confiscated the track-suit pants Lisoff was wearing on the day of the attack to determine if there was any DNA evidence that could tie him to the crime.

An inspection of the track-suit pants revealed traces of blood splashed on them and when NSW forensic scientist, Bob Goetz, compared samples from the track-suit pants with that from the victim by using an automated DNA profiling system he concluded that the sample from Lisoff's track-suit matched the sample from the victim. Goetz calculated that the chance of the blood on Lisoff's track-suit coming from someone other than the victim was less than one in ten billion. It was conclusive and irrefutable scientific evidence but Lisoff continued to challenge it and protested his innocence with an alibi to the crime.

Lisoff's lawyers solved the impasse by hiring an independent DNA specialist, Dr Brian McDonald, to analyse the blood samples. McDonald analysed the blood samples using a different DNA profiling technique called "silver staining" and compared the victim's blood taken at the hospital, the blood from Lisoff's track-suit pants and blood taken from the victim several months later.

Dr McDonald discovered two weak bands indicating another person's DNA present in the samples taken from the victim in hospital and the same two weak bands were present in the sample from the track-suit pants. Those two weak bands were not present in the blood sample taken from the victim months after the attack. McDonald concluded that the two weak DNA bands came from the person who donated blood for the victim's blood transfusion because the police had taken their blood sample at the hospital after the blood transfusion had been performed.

Dr McDonald's scientific conclusions raised serious questions about the quality protocols and storage of DNA evidence. How did the victim's post transfusion blood sample get on the track-suit pants after he had been taken to hospital?

Lisoff's defense lawyer, Phil Hogan, summed up the situation during the June 27, 2002 ABC TV *Catalyst* program "A Shadow of Doubt":

To put it in a nutshell, people don't have a blood transfusion immediately before being assaulted and so the theory was that the blood on the track pants could only have got there after the victim had had the blood transfusions because the presence of all the extraneous DNA and therefore again the theory was that those blood traces on the clothes must have been planted. But how? For two weeks the track pants and the blood sample from the victim had been stored in the same police evidence room.

In the end it was decided that the scientific evidence was too complicated for a jury to decide upon so the case was heard before a single judge. The judge felt that there was a theoretical possibility that the evidence could have been tampered with although there was no firm evidence that a police officer had tampered with it. The judge determined he could not be satisfied beyond reasonable doubt and he acquitted Lisoff.

The Janine Balding Case

Twenty-year-old Sydney bank teller, Janine Balding, was abducted, raped and murdered in 1988 by a group of street kids. Stephen Wayne "Shorty" Jamieson is one of three men convicted for the crime but Jamieson has consistently denied any involvement in the murder. Those assertions are supported by two other men convicted for the crime who have also consistently claimed from the time of their 1988 arrest that it was not "Shorty" Jamieson who was with them when Janine Balding was murdered.

They have claimed it was another street kid named "Shorty"' Wells but investigating detectives were convinced they had the right "Shorty"' when they arrested Jamieson on the Gold Coast and extradited him back to NSW.

"Shorty" Jamieson was not convicted on forensic evidence. He was convicted on the testimony of a prison informer who has since died, the transcript of a police interview signed by Jamieson but disputed by his defence lawyers in court, and an eyewitness who said he had seen Jamieson with the co-offenders after the attack.

In 2001 the NSW Carr Government enacted legislation to cement ten of the State's worst criminals in their cells by marking their files "NTBR—Never To Be Released". "Shorty" Jamieson was among those targeted by the new legislation along with the other two Janine Balding murderers who were 14 and 16 respectively at the time of the murder.

In 2003 the NSW Premier, Bob Carr, announced the formation of an "Innocence Panel" in NSW comprising representatives of police, the Director of Public Prosecutions, the Privacy Commissioner and victims of crime. It was the first official body in Australia to review convictions where new DNA evidence had come to light and claims of innocence from prisoners could either be established or refuted. The purpose of the panel was to look at the material and where it thought the prisoner might have

a reasonable case, to send that case back into the court system.

The panel swiftly ran aground after "Shorty" Jamieson made an application to have his murder conviction reviewed.

Despite the lack of forensic evidence at his trial Jamieson was the only person convicted of having anal intercourse with Janine Balding prior to her death. He applied to the Innocence Panel to have her underwear, and swabs from the rape kit tested for DNA. The Innocence Panel recommended the new DNA tests be carried out.

The results of the new DNA tests came through simultaneously with an announcement from the NSW Minister for Police, Mr John Watkins, that the Innocence Panel would be immediately suspended. Mr Watkins published a press release that said:

"Mr Jamieson's case before the Innocence Panel is a matter of great concern because of the effect on the family of the victim and as a result of issues raised in the Jamieson case that they hadn't considered, the panel would henceforth be suspended."

The DNA test results showed evidence that two people had anally raped the deceased. "Shorty" Jamieson was not one of them. The NSW Innocence Panel was suspended as a result of the findings while the political implications dictated that a convicted killer with his papers marked "NTBR" remains in jail with a letter confirming DNA evidence points to someone else being responsible for the crime he was imprisoned for.

"Shorty" Jamieson sought independent legal advice and he is now seeking a judicial inquiry into his conviction.

SIGNIFICANCE

There are standard procedures for carrying out DNA fingerprinting. Put simply, the DNA is first extracted from the biological sample—blood, semen, skin, sweat or hair—chopped into fragments which are then separated to give a pattern of bands on a slab of gel. The VNTR or STRs are tagged with a radioactive probe molecule, after transferring the bands to a nylon membrane. The pattern of the two samples are visualized by placing the membrane between two pieces of X-ray film. A direct comparison between the two can then be made.

Needless to say, there is plenty of scope for error in the above process—from mislabeling samples to keeping the sample at the wrong temperature (all biological samples are prone to degradation). In a properly accredited lab, staffed by trained technicians who understand the procedures, mistakes should not happen. But, as the article above points out, there have been many cases where the DNA evidence has been challenged on technical grounds. Added to the potential lab errors outlined above, there may be questions over the matching and interpretation of DNA fingerprints. Given that many countries are now in the process of setting up DNA databases to aid criminal investigation, it is increasingly important that standards of testing and interpretation are as high as possible.

While there is rightly concern that the innocent may be falsely convicted on the grounds of faulty DNA evidence, it should not be forgotten that the opposite is sometimes true. That is, DNA evidence has been used to grant people their freedom. The Innocence Project is a U.S. advocacy group that has promoted the use of DNA testing, post-conviction, to prove the innocence of 174 people wrongly convicted of sexual assault and murder. Several of those shown to be wrongly convicted were on Death Row and some within only hours of execution. In an interesting twist to this kind of work, DNA testing has shown, recently, that Roger Keith Coleman was indeed guilty of the rape and murder for which he was executed in Virginia in 1992. Coleman had vigorously protested his innocence during a very high-profile campaign.

FURTHER RESOURCES

Books

Jackson, Andrew R.W., and Julie M. Jackson. *Forensic Science.* Harlow, England: Pearson, 2004.

Lyle, Douglas. *Forensics for Dummies.* Hoboken, N.J., Wiley, 2004.

Web sites

The Innocence Project. <http://www.innocenceproject.org> (accessed February 26, 2006).

USA Today. "Increasing DNA Exonerations Contradict Predictions." <http://www.usatoday.com/news/health/2002-01-18-dna.htm> (accessed February 26, 2006).

Not Guilty. "The Brain Never Lies."

Newspaper article

By: Anne McIlroy

Date: November 5, 2005

Source: McIlroy, Anne, "Not Guilty. 'The Brain Never Lies.'" *Toronto Globe and Mail* (Saturday, November 5, 2005) F6.

About the Author: Anne McIlroy is the science reporter for the *Toronto Globe and Mail*, Canada's leading daily newspaper, founded in the 1840s, with a circulation of over one million.

INTRODUCTION

The search for truth is as old as civilization itself. The basis of modern "lie detection" is the polygraph, which measures the emotional and physiological changes that occur when most people tell a lie. In medieval times, however, little was understood about how the body and brain work, and courts of that era believed divine intervention would indicate if a suspect was, or was not, telling the truth. It was believed that God would protect an innocent and truthful person from coming to harm in any "test" of their veracity. So, for instance, the suspect would have to carry a red hot iron bar or walk over hot coals. If they were burned, it was proof they were lying and they could be hanged without further ado. In an ordeal by water, the accused was tied into a sack and tossed into a pond. If they floated, they were lying, if they sank—and possibly drowned—they were telling the truth.

By the 1600s, however, such ordeals gave way to a more objective investigation of statements and evidence. Suspects would be questioned in detail, with logical and scientific reasoning applied to what they said. This was the origin of modern legal cross-examination and the presumption that the truth is being told, unless guilt can be proved beyond reasonable doubt. Skilful questioning, debate, and the presentation of evidence were thought sufficient to determine the suspect's truthfulness.

In the nineteenth century, the pseudo-science of phrenology—in which the shape of a person's skull was thought to indicate moral character, intelligence, and criminal tendencies—became an accepted type of "evidence" in criminal courts. Phrenology has long been discredited, but it may have been the first biological attempt at lie detection. Another, the administration of "truth serum," used barbiturates such as scopolamine, sodium amytal, or sodium pentothal, which were thought to "rewire" the brain and compel the suspect to tell the truth. In 1963, however, the U.S. Supreme Court ruled that extracting confessions in this manner was a form of torture and the practice was ruled unconstitutional.

The polygraph, or lie detector, first used in 1924, uses sensors to record changes in breathing rate, blood pressure, and perspiration during questioning. While polygraphs are routinely used in American criminal investigations, suspects and defendants cannot be forced to take them, because the accuracy and interpretation of such results have long been debated. The brain fingerprint, as described in the article below, may have the potential to supersede the polygraph as a technique for determining truth from falsehood.

PRIMARY SOURCE

Not Guilty: "The Brain Never Lies"

By ANNE MCILROY

Saturday, November 5, 2005 Page F6

BRAIN FINGERPRINTING: All of convicted killer Terry Harrington's protestations of innocence fell on deaf ears. So he turned to a mind-reading technique to help prove he didn't do it. ANNE McILROY reports.

For two decades, Terry Harrington protested his innocence from his Iowa prison cell, insisting that he had not shot and killed a retired police officer when he was 17 years old.

Then he decided to try brain fingerprinting. It's a computerized mind-reading technique developed by Jerry Farwell, an American researcher and entrepreneur who says he can tell if the details of a crime scene are stored in a suspect's brain. If Mr. Harrington were innocent, the test would show that his brain did not recognize details about the murder, details the killer would know.

"The brain never lies," Dr. Farwell says.

For decades, researchers have been searching for the Holy Grail of police work, a way to know if suspects are telling the truth when they declare their innocence.

Polygraphs, which measure heart rate, sweat, and other physiological responses, don't work well in many situations and can be manipulated.

Brain scans have potential, and preliminary findings show that different parts of our brains are at work when we fib than when we tell the truth.

It may be that our faces don't lie. Researchers have spent years analyzing and categorizing rapid-fire facial "micro-expressions" that telegraph emotions such as anger and fear that can dramatically contradict what someone is saying.

But the scientists involved in these two new approaches say it is far too early to use them in court.

Brain fingerprinting is ready to go, Dr. Farwell says, and in a decade or so will be as revolutionary as DNA evidence in helping police investigate crimes and helping the wrongfully convicted clear their names.

In preparation for testing Mr. Harrington, the scientist gathered information about the shooting of John Schweer, a night watchman at a car dealership whose body was found on railway tracks in Council Bluffs, Iowa, on a summer morning in 1977. Police and prosecutors had relied heavily on the testimony of a witness, Kevin Hughes, who said he and Mr. Harrington had gone to the city the night of the killing to steal a car.

Mr. Harrington had an alibi. He says he was at an outdoor concert in north Omaha, about 32 kilometres away. Several witnesses, including his high-school football coach, testified that they had seen him.

Who was telling the truth? The jury believed Mr. Hughes, who said he had seen Mr. Harrington running out from behind a building after the shooting.

There was a field of grass and weeds behind the building, and if Mr. Harrington had committed the crime, he would have had to run across it to get to his car. These were the kinds of details Dr. Farwell was looking for.

Brain fingerprinting, which the scientist has been working on for more than 15 years, involves showing someone accused or convicted of an offence pictures of the crime scene or flashing key words about the crime on a computer screen. The suspect has electrodes attached to his scalp that measure his brain's electrical response.

If a suspect recognizes the information, Dr. Farwell says, there is a split-second jump in electrical activity, a particular "ah ha" moment, a type of brain wave that says, "I know this."

Mr. Harrington was hooked up to the system, and the phrase "weeds and grass" flashed on the screen, along with other words connected to the crime, and neutral phrases to provide a comparison. In a second test, details about his alibi were also flashed on the screen.

"The result clearly indicated that the record stored in his brain didn't match the crime scene and did match the alibi," Dr. Farwell says. "He turned to me and said, 'For all these years, I've known I was innocent, and now someone else knows it too.'"

But would a convicted murder's response to phrases such as "weeds and grass" indicate if he was telling the truth? Would a court accept that a scientist can determine if the memory of a crime is stored in someone's brain like footage in a video library? For Mr. Harrington, it was a worth a shot.

A long shot, according the critics such as Emanuel Donchin, who in the late eighties made the original discovery of the "ah ha brainwave," on which the brain fingerprinting test is based. He was working with Dr. Farwell, then a graduate student at the University of Illinois. At the time, he said more research was needed before it could be used in real life." Unfortunately, the necessary research has never been conducted," Dr. Donchin says.

John Turtle, a Ryerson University associate professor who is an expert in the fallibility of memories, says everyone distorts memories over time.

And that is just one potential problem. Drugs, alcohol, sleep deprivation, and strong emotions can also have an impact on whether memories are stored in the first place. So can trauma. In the process of committing a violent crime, the perpetrator might not register what colour sweater the victim was wearing or where in the house she died. Criminals who commit more than one offence would be at risk of mixing up details. Psychopaths may respond differently when presented with details of a crime they committed.

Still, Dr. Turtle says Dr. Farwell's approach, while it may seem outlandish, has potential. That's what Anne Danaher thought. The prison barber, she had worked tirelessly on Mr. Harrington's appeals for a new trial. She was the one who contacted Dr. Farwell, and persuaded him to perform the test on Mr. Harrington. She also helped him gather the details he needed.

In the course of her research, she found potentially exculpatory police reports about another suspect that were never given to Mr. Harrington's lawyer. Now, they had those reports and a brain-fingerprinting test that showed Mr. Harrington had not been there when Mr. Schweer was killed.

But there was still the damaging testimony from Mr. Hughes.

Dr. Farwell tracked him down with the help of a private detective, and they made a surprise visit. Mr. Hughes stuck to his story for an hour, while Dr. Farwell repeated that Mr. Harrington's brain was telling them something different. Then came the confession. "I wasn't there, Harrington wasn't there. I don't know anything about it. I don't know who did it. I was afraid they'd convict me of the crime, so I made up the story about Harrington," Dr. Farwell recalls Mr. Hughes saying.

He and the private investigator put him in a car and drove him to a court reporter, where he made a videotaped statement.

It was time to go to court. The judge accepted the results of the brain-fingerprinting test, the new testimony from Mr. Hughes and the suppressed police reports, but ruled against giving Mr. Harrington a new trial. Mr. Harrington appealed, and in February 2003, the Iowa Supreme Court overturned his conviction, and ordered a new trial.

By then, he had been in prison for 25 years. He was allowed to go free while prosecutors prepared for a second trial. He rode a motorcycle, watched a football game and began evening classes at a community college.

Prosecutors offered him a deal: Plead guilty to second-degree murder and his ordeal would be over. But Mr. Harrington wanted to clear his name. He was rearrested, and went back to jail briefly, then posted bail and was released. In October 2003, the charges were officially dropped.

Mr. Harrington, who is suing the police, is not giving interviews on the advice of his lawyer, Tom Frerichs.

Dr. Farwell claims only a modest role in getting justice for Mr. Harrington, and says Ms. Danaher deserves most of the credit. It wasn't brain fingerprinting that got him out of jail, he says, although it played a role in getting the confession from Mr. Hughes.

While Ms. Danaher is convinced of Mr. Harrington's innocence, she is skeptical about whether brain fingerprinting really works. But Mr. Frerichs thinks that it does. "I think the science behind it is valid—and a little scary."

Dr. Farwell says his test has never failed. In 1999, he says, it helped to get a confession out of James Grinder, who asked to take the test, and then confessed when he was told that it showed he had knowledge of the rape and murder of Julie Helton 15 years earlier. He later confessed to several other murders.

But it didn't save Jimmy Ray Slaughter, a former Gulf War veteran convicted of a particularly sadistic double homicide. The test found that key details about the murder of his former girlfriend and their baby daughter weren't stored in his brain, but it didn't help his appeal for clemency. He was executed in Oklahoma City this year.

Mr. Slaughter wasn't an ideal client, even as convicted murderers go. Prosecutors said he shot and paralyzed his former girlfriend, Melody Wuertz, and that she probably watched, helpless, while he shot their 11-month-old baby, Jessica.

Ms. Weurtz's family would have been outraged if Mr. Slaughter's execution had been stayed because of his response to the phrase "living room," which is one of the probes Dr. Farwell used to see if he knew where his baby's body was found.

More than one phrase is used, of course. The test depends on a consistent recognition of a series of details that the perpetrator of a crime would know.

Still, it seems too simplistic for an organ as mysterious and complicated as the human brain. Scientists don't understand the basic operating system, how memories are made or stored. That makes it difficult to accept that anyone can really tell whether a particular memory exists by monitoring the brain's reaction to phrases such as "weeds and grass" or "living room."

Exonerated by a computerized brain-scanning technique, Terry Harrington, center, leaves the Clarinda (Iowa) Correctional Facility with his mother, left, and daughter, right, after Iowa Governor Tom Vilsack signed a reprieve for Harrington, who had served twenty-five years of a life without parole sentence. AP IMAGES

Dr. Farwell insists that he can. Ten years from now, he says, people accused of crimes they didn't commit will demand that police not tell them any details, so they can be brain fingerprinted and prove their innocence. Imagine how you would feel to be charged with a killing you didn't commit. Brain fingerprinting might be worth a shot.

SIGNIFICANCE

Brain fingerprinting is a forensic investigation technique built upon scientific knowledge of memory and the brain. When a suspect is exposed to details of a crime scene, these inevitably trigger a measurable and specific response in the brain known as a MER-MER (memory and encoding related multifaceted electroencephalographic response). The MERMER is recorded by electrodes applied to the suspect's scalp and recorded along with the rest of the brain's electrical activity in an electroencephalogram (EEG) trace.

An important feature of EEGs are *event-related potentials*—spikes of activity that appear after the subject is exposed to specific sounds or sights related to the crime scene. Event-related potentials occur at various periods after the exposure and signify various aspects of brain processing. An evoked potential occurring between 300 and 1,000 milliseconds after exposure is known as a P300 and indicates recognition of information presented in the stimulus.

Used correctly, brain fingerprinting could be an extremely powerful technique to establish truth in criminal investigations. One obvious drawback, however, is that knowledge of the crime scene may be stored in a suspect's brain and may be revealed by the fingerprint, but does not, in itself, establish guilt unless the exposure contains details that could only be known to the perpetrator. An innocent person could easily be aware of crime scene details through court proceedings or media coverage.

Brain fingerprinting could also be used in crime prevention to pinpoint those who have knowledge of plans and plots. For instance, terror suspects might be identified before being allowed entry to a country if their brain fingerprint shows awareness of details of planned attacks.

FURTHER RESOURCES

Periodicals

Burke, Tod W. "Brain fingerprinting: Latest tool for law enforcement." *Law & Order* June 30, 1999: (47) 6, 28–31.

Web sites

BBC News. "A Brief History of Lying." <http://news.bbc.co.uk/1/hi/uk/1740746.stm> (accessed January 13, 2006).

Brain Fingerprinting Laboratories "A New Paradigm." <http://www.brainwavescience.com> (accessed January 13, 2006).

Yorkshire Ripper Hoax Suspect Arrested After 25 Years

Wearside Man, 49, Taken to Leeds for Questioning: *Letters and Sneering Tape Put Police off Sutcliffe Trail*

Magazine article

By: Martin Wainwright

Date: October 19, 2005

Source: *Guardian Unlimited.* "Yorkshire Ripper Hoax Suspect Arrested After 25 Years." <http://www.guardian.co.uk/uk_news/story/0,,1595544,00.html> (accessed March 4, 2006).

About the Author: Martin Wainwright writes for the British daily newspaper the *Guardian.*

INTRODUCTION

Peter Sutcliffe, the notorious Yorkshire Ripper, convicted of the murders of thirteen women, several of them prostitutes, has been held in Broadmoor Special Hospital, a secure psychiatric facility, for many years. The case has uncanny echoes of Jack the Ripper, who stalked and killed prostitutes in London's East End in 1888.

Police hunting for the Yorkshire Ripper believed him to be the author of a tape and letters that taunted them for failing to catch him. The killer was eventually caught, but "Wearside Jack"—who actually sent the letters and tape—remained at large. In October 2005, however, a man was arrested after almost a quarter century of investigation.

■ **PRIMARY SOURCE**

Yorkshire Ripper Hoax Suspect Arrested After 25 Years

Wearside Man, 49, Taken to Leeds for Questioning

Letters and Sneering Tape Put Police off Sutcliffe Trail

Martin Wainwright

Wednesday October 19, 2005

A man was arrested yesterday on suspicion of perpetrating one of the most notorious and lethal hoaxes in British criminal history—the "I'm Jack" tape and letters which sabotaged the hunt for the Yorkshire Ripper.

Twenty-five years of stop–start police inquiries culminated with a knock on the door of a 49-year-old in Wearside, Sunderland, who was taken by detectives to Leeds for questioning. Today he faces a battery of forensic evidence concerning three letters and a tape recording sent to the head of the Ripper inquiry, Superintendent George Oldfield.

The false information, purporting to come from a killer, derailed a huge hunt for the sadistic murderer of 10 women, a murderer who killed a further three women in or after the 18-month period while resources were poured into the red herring of tracking down the non-existent murderer, identified as having a strong Wearside accent, two unusual speech defects, and a distinctive blood group traced from an envelope.

The fatal shift of focus may have helped the true killer, Peter Sutcliffe, who was interviewed by police three times and released, before finally he was caught by chance in Sheffield in April 1981 while searching for a 14th victim.

The Bradford lorry driver had had what were apparently firm alibis, but his local accent, quite unlike that of the tape, played a part in downgrading him as a realistic suspect.

West Yorkshire police have several times officially announced they had abandoned their hunt for the hoax perpetrator. As recently as July, they said an audit had failed to turn up the original cassette and letters, thought to have handwriting carefully disguised.

But copies exist, published and broadcast nationally in June 1979 when Mr Oldfield excitedly told a press conference of a major development in the Ripper hunt. The tape offered chilling taunts: "I'm Jack ... You're no nearer catching me now than four years ago when I started."

Police said last night: "Officers from West Yorkshire this afternoon travelled to the Sunderland area where they arrested a 49-year-old local man on suspicion of attempting to pervert the course of justice. This relates to the hoax letters and tape that was sent to police during the Yorkshire Ripper murder investigation."

The hoaxer's disastrous success has infuriated police for years; in 1983 the West Yorkshire chief constable during the Ripper hunt, Ron Gregory, expressed his frustration in his memoirs: 40,000 people had been interviewed in an attempt to identify the tape; speech experts at Glasgow University detected a hidden stammer, and a mispronunciation of the letter 's', but were very surprised that no one recognised the voice and came forward.

Mr Gregory also believed in a possible link between the hoaxer and the rape and murder of Joan Harrison, 20, in Preston in 1975. Sutcliffe was later questioned; his O blood group differed from the rarer B group in forensic evidence at Preston and also on the hoaxer's envelope.

In 2002 the Sunderland Echo focused on a 46-year-old former soldier. Voice tests narrowed the hoaxer's likely home to the Castletown area, and the Echo's suspect, said by then to be overseas, allegedly matched 10 of 12 features. A West Yorkshire investigation in 1987 found no evidence to support repeated allegations the hoaxer was a disgruntled police officer.

Sutcliffe was jailed in 1981 after admitting to 13 murders and the attempted murder of seven other women between 1978 and 1980. He was later ruled criminally insane and committed to Broadmoor.

SIGNIFICANCE

Hoaxes are fairly common after major crimes that generate a lot of publicity. The perpetrators are usually attention seekers, people with a grudge of some kind, who may be mentally ill or delusional and perhaps really believe they did commit the crime. Police often appeal to the public for help in solving serious crimes and are obliged to follow every lead. Consequently, a hoaxer can waste a great deal of police time—a significant matter when resources and manpower are limited and a serial killer is at large. The Yorkshire Ripper hoax, described above, is a good example of how a clever hoax may even cost lives.

Most hoaxers have no connection with the true perpetrator. However, "Wearside Jack" may have been known to Peter Sutcliffe through the Joan Harrison murder. The way he deliberately misled the police suggested he could perhaps have been an accomplice, covering up for the killer. Indeed, he may have mur-

dered Harrison himself; some investigators suggest he could also have been responsible for the unsolved murder of Julie Perigo in 1986, when Sutcliffe was behind bars.

One witness to Wearside Jack's connection with Sutcliffe may be Olive Curry, a former waitress in a North Shields canteen, says that in the summer of 1978 Sutcliffe used to come in with a companion that may have been the hoaxer. One day Sutcliffe told her that both were lorry drivers—he from Bradford, his friend from Sunderland, Wearside Jack's home town. Curry has visited Sutcliffe in prison to discuss the matter, but he refuses to give any information.

Because the letters and tape had disappeared for a while, a theory evolved that the hoaxer was a disgruntled police officer who wished to embarrass colleagues involved in the case. This may also explain, at least partly, why the investigation stalled for so long.

In October 2005 police arrested 49-year-old John Humble of Sunderland, an unemployed alcoholic laborer and charged him with perverting the course of justice by sending the Wearside Jack letters and tape. A DNA profile obtained from the saliva on the envelopes led police to Humble, who had submitted a DNA sample after a motor vehicle arrest five years previously. Although he originally pleaded not guilty to the charges, on February 24, 2006, he confessed to perpetrating the hoax, although he claimed he had wanted only to help police, not distract them.

FURTHER RESOURCES
Books
Lavelle, Patrick. *Shadow of the Ripper: The Secret Story of the Man who Helped the Ripper to Kill and Kill Again.* London: John Blake Publishing, 2003

Web sites
The Hunt for Wearside Jack <http://www.execulink.com/~kbrannen/wearside.htm> (accessed January 24, 2006).

FBI Agents Often Break Informant Rules

Newspaper article

By: Dan Eggen

Date: October 12, 2005

Source: Eggen, Dan. "FBI Agents Often Break Informant Rules." *Washington Post*, October 12, 2005, <http://www.washingtonpost.com/wp-dyn/content/article/2005/09/12/AR2005091201825.html> (accessed February 11, 2006).

About the Author: Dan Eggen is a staff writer for the *Washington Post* newspaper. The *Washington Post*, first published in 1877, is regarded as one of America's leading daily newspapers.

INTRODUCTION

The use of an informant is the seamy reality faced by law enforcement agencies that conduct investigations into many types of serious criminal activity. Terrorism, drug trafficking, loan sharking, protection rings, and similar activities are often perpetrated within the realm of the organized criminal. The hallmark of any successful organized criminal venture is secrecy.

The wall of silence surrounding a criminal venture is breached in one of two ways—through undercover police operatives or through the cultivation of confidential informants. The grooming of inside informants to provide information concerning the operations of La Cosa Nostra (the LCN, or Mafia) or motorcycle gangs such as the Banditos or the Hell's Angels is a time-honored investigative practice.

Police agencies worldwide use informants. The aphorism "to find an outlaw you have to use an outlaw" is a restatement of a broader principle—the end justifies the means. The extreme secrecy employed by most criminal organizations makes the use of an undercover operative, working inside the target organization, a dangerous, difficult, and time consuming undertaking. A well-placed informant can often provide a steady stream of useful information.

Since its creation in 1936, the FBI developed a number of internal practices regarding the cultivation and protection of informants. As a result of public pressure concerning the relationships between FBI field agents and confidential informants, the federal Attorney General has—since 1976—regularly published detailed guidelines to regulate the FBI in its confidential informant relationships, with mixed success.

Former Ku Klux Klansman Mitchell Burns didn't have much sympathy for blacks and the civil rights movement when the Sixteenth Street Baptist Church was bombed in 1963. But something within him changed when an FBI agent showed him morgue photographs of the four black girls killed and asked for help finding the killers. Burns, shown here in 2001, became a confidential, paid informant known by the pseudonym Tom Dooly. AP IMAGES

FBI excesses in terms of permitted confidential informant conduct were the impetus to the latest guidelines advanced by the Attorney General. The most notorious example was that of Boston mobster James "Whitey" Bulger—permitted to flee Boston by his FBI handlers in advance of a racketeering indictment. Bulger was the suspected head of organized crime in South Boston for many years. While the FBI's informant practices had long overlooked the commission of minor crime by its designated informants, the FBI had a responsibility to exercise more care regarding the treatment of serious criminals.

The informant world is the intersection of crime detection and investigative expediency; if the information secured from an informant is the only evidence upon which a case against a criminal kingpin is founded, the issue of prosecutorial transparency will follow. What was offered? What was promised? What was given? These are the questions that will be pivotal to any successful prosecution that is founded on the word of a confidential informant. Where the entire relationship between FBI agent and an informant is not documented and cross-checked, an acquittal at trial is likely to result.

PRIMARY SOURCE

Many FBI agents have ignored Justice Department rules for handling confidential informants that were established in the wake of several high-profile scandals, according to a study released yesterday.

In an analysis of 120 informant files from around the country, the Justice Department's inspector general, Glenn A. Fine, found that FBI agents violated procedures in 87 percent of the cases, including some in which informants allegedly engaged in illegal activity without proper oversight or permission.

"We found significant problems with the FBI's compliance with the attorney general's guidelines on confidential informants," Fine said in a statement. "We are concerned that the FBI has not taken the necessary steps to ensure that FBI agents and their supervisors adhere to these important requirements."

The report, parts of which are redacted because they involve classified material, also faults FBI agents for in some cases failing to notify officials in Washington about the initiation of criminal intelligence probes and for consistently failing to obtain advance approval to listen in on informants' conversations.

FBI Director Robert S. Mueller III told Fine's investigators that many agents found it difficult to comply with complicated paperwork requirements for confidential informants. The FBI said in a statement yesterday that many of Fine's recommendations for reform have been implemented and that the FBI is reworking procedures to make it easier for agents to comply with the rules.

"Confidential informants and other confidential human sources are critical to the FBI's ability to carry out our counterterrorism, national security and criminal law enforcement missions," the FBI statement said. "A source can have a singular piece of information we could not otherwise obtain, enabling us to prevent a terrorist act or crime, or apprehend a fugitive."

Among the violations Fine highlighted were a handful of cases involving "otherwise illegal activity," referring to cases in which the FBI permits informants to commit an act—such as engaging in conversations about a conspiracy or handling money as part of a controlled drug purchase—that would otherwise be a crime.

Fine's report listed two cases in which agents allegedly failed to properly inform prosecutors when an informant was allowed to engage in illegal activity and five others in which agents failed to tell prosecutors that an informant had committed a crime not authorized by his FBI handlers. FBI field agents also often failed to properly review an informant's performance or notify senior officials when an informant had been "deactivated," according to the report.

Fine's report comes more than four years after the FBI revised its rules in the wake of several incidents involving informants. Perhaps the most infamous involved former FBI agent John J. Connolly Jr., who allowed Boston mobster and FBI informant James J. "Whitey" Bulger to flee by tipping him off to an imminent federal racketeering indictment.

Kevin R. Brock, assistant director of the FBI's Office of Intelligence, said in an interview that many of the cases cited by Fine involved administrative violations or honest disagreements about legal definitions. Some acts involving minor crimes, for example, can be authorized internally without involving a U.S. attorney's office.

"Most of these are administrative failures and we are working to address those," Brock said. "It's not like we had sources running around, willy-nilly breaking the law."

SIGNIFICANCE

The dramatic incidence of breaches of the Attorney General's guidelines in the handling of FBI informants underscores the greatest difficulty in the conduct of high level, often sensitive, criminal investigations that occur in the murk of the dark, fluid underworld. The desire to remain attentive to the public interest—as it is manifested by 100 percent transparent law enforcement practices and adherence to investigative rules—is contrasted with the often compelling pressure to solve cases through the use of confidential informants, even where that solution will render a serious criminal as legally untouchable.

The Bulger case is a worst-case example. By any reckoning, the relationship between Boston FBI agents and James "Whitey" Bulger and his Winter Hill Gang associate Stephen "The Rifleman" was a wholesale bypassing of the Attorney General's directives. It was a story with a particularly bad ending, since Bulger was evidently tipped off about a pending murder and racketering indictment. He disappeared, and his FBI handler received ten years in prison. In addition, the FBI were the target of numerous civil wrongful death law suits, advanced by the families of persons allegedly murdered by Bulger while he worked with the FBI.

Public reaction to the revelation that FBI agents do not always adhere to their mandated guidelines in confidential informant relations is not likely to resound as loudly as would a complaint that the FBI decided to not pursue certain investigative leads due to the restrictions of bureaucratic guidelines. The use of informants in organized crime investigations is so well entrenched that the public is somewhat inured to such administrative breaches. The fact that the excesses of the Bulger case did not generate a public firestorm is proof that the practice is valued.

The FBI confidential informant methods survived the adverse public opinion generated by the notorious COINTPRO investigations into alleged subversive groups in the 1950s and 1960s. An FBI informant received blanket immunity and $150,000 in fees for what would have been chicanery anywhere else in the notorious ABSCAM sting in the 1980s. It is a notable feature of FBI/informant dealings that there are only guidelines, not federal statutes, to mandate the way in which FBI agents must conduct themselves in confidential informant relations.

As a national police agency, the FBI has a larger-than-life reputation in the minds of American citizens. If this gold standard law enforcement agency, operating with the weight of the national government behind its activities, fails to abide by its own rules, what of the three person detective office in a small American town, operating with far less scrutiny?

Where America has operated with guidelines and Inspector General reviews, other jurisdictions have added further measures of insulation between the informant and the judicial process. In the province of Ontario, Canada, all cases that propose to use the tes-timony of a "jailhouse informant" are vetted by a com-mittee of prosecutors prior to trial. There is a fear in many countries that the use of a police informant will lead to miscarriages of justice, especially wrongful convictions.

FURTHER RESOURCES

Books

Ranalli, Ralph. *Deadly Alliance: The FBI's Secret Partnership With the Mob.* New York: Harper Collins, 2001.

Periodicals

U. S. Department of Justice. Office of the Inspector General. "Federal Bureau of Investigation Compliance with Attorney General's Investigative Guidelines." September 2005.

Web sites

Truth in Justice. "FBI Informant System Called a Failure." <http://www.truthinjustice.org/corrupt-FBI.htm> (accessed February 13, 2006).

Identification Evidence

Is Fingerprint Identification A "Science"

Internet article

By: Andre A. Moenssens

Date: April 19, 2005

Source: Forensic-Evidence.com

About the Author: Andre Moenssens is the editor of Forensic-Evidence.com, an information center in forensic science, law, education and public policy for lawyers, forensic scientists, educators and public officials. He is emeritus professor of Criminal Law at the University of Missouri and has written many books on forensic science.

INTRODUCTION

Humans and other primates are unique in having thickened, roughened, skin on their fingertips, toes, palms, and soles of the feet. These skin surfaces, when magnified, look like a plowed field, with ridges and furrows, and allow us the useful ability to grip things. Forensic scientists refer to this feature of skin as friction ridges. Skin is never completely dry or clean; grime, oil and sweat on the fingerpads create an impression of the ridge pattern, known as a finger-

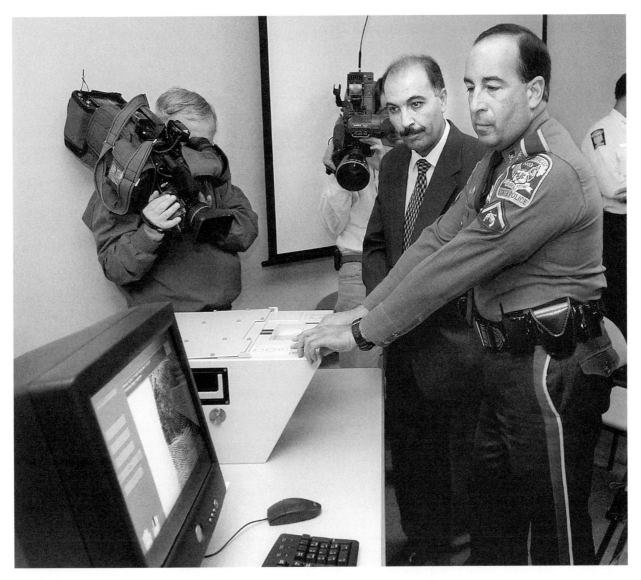

With the Automated Fingerprint Identification System, introduced in 2003, a fingerprint check on an individual can be cut from as much as four to six months to minutes or hours. AP IMAGES

print, whenever someone touches something. Fingerprints have been recovered from all kinds of surfaces, although it has proved hard to detect them on human skin, which would be a very useful source of evidence if it could be done.

Fingerprints are said to be unique to the individual, as discussed in the article below, and have been admissible evidence in court for over one hundred years. The first person to be convicted on fingerprint evidence was Francesca Rojas, an Argentinian woman who killed her two children in 1892. In the United States, the first conviction on fingerprint evidence was of Thomas Jennings, in Chicago, who was executed

for murder in 1912. In the early days, fingerprint investigators had to sort manually through records of prints to find a match. Now fingerprint matching is done by a computer program. The Federal Bureau of Investigation began to automate fingerprint analysis with the Automated Fingerprint Identification System (AFIS) in the 1960s. The AFIS computer scans and digitally encodes fingerprint records into a database. It can match a sample by searching through the database very rapidly—the speed currently is 500,000 prints a second. But even with its long tradition, coupled with new technology, fingerprinting is being questioned as a scientific technique.

PRIMARY SOURCE

Fingerprint identification has been around for a long time. It has nearly a century of court acceptance in the United States. Yet, in the aftermath of United States Supreme Court cases like Daubert v. Merrell Dow Pharmaceuticals (1993) and Kumho Tire v. Carmichael (1999), requiring courts to determine the reliability (validity) of underlying techniques before admitting expert opinion based on it, questions are bound to be raised about the scientific legitimacy of many of the techniques commonly used in crime laboratories, fingerprint identification among them.

Skilled examiners of fingerprint evidence agree that the process of comparing latent fingerprints of unknown origin with inked impressions of known origin is an "art," rather than a science. It requires an examiner to assess, on the basis of experience in dealing with thousands of fingerprints, what parts of an incomplete and partially blurred latent print show visible friction ridge detail that can be used for identification purposes. But whether fingerprint identification is "art" or "science" is clearly no longer relevant to a Daubert inquiry. What needs to be examined is whether the underlying premises upon which fingerprint identification are based have been empirically validated. And these premises are three-fold: (1) the friction ridge detail of the epidermis on the palm side of the hands remains unchanged during the lifetime of an individual, except for accidental or intentional scarification or alteration; (2) friction ridge pattern areas exhibit so much variety of detail that no two patterns are ever found to be exactly the same on the digits (or palms or soles of feet) of one individual or on the digits (or palms or soles of feet) of other individuals; (3) while these friction ridge patterns exhibit an infinite variety of detail, they nevertheless fall within certain broad classes or categories that permit police to store and retrieve millions of prints according to classification formulae.

Premise one has clearly stood the test of time and experience. It has been established in over 100 years of accumulated experience that friction ridge patterns remain unchanged naturally in their ridge detail during the lifetime of an individual. The ridge patterns begin to form during pre-natal life and are fully formed by the seventh month of fetal life.

Premise three has equally proved to be true by verification and experience. We have been able to deal with millions of accumulated fingerprint cards by devising classification formulae based on pattern types and subgroups until the advent of automated computer and retrieval systems, referred to generically as AFIS systems in "the trade," made such classification formulae unnecessary.

Premise number two, that all fingerprints are unique and never duplicated in the universe, is a premise that is harder to prove empirically, despite the fact that all fingerprint examiners fervently believe in it. However, in all of the human experience with fingerprints world-wide, no two fingerprints from different digits have ever been found to match exactly. It has been argued that, since millions of sets of prints have been stored in fingerprint files as voluminous as, say, the FBI Identification Section and no exact duplication of friction skin detail has been encountered in these fingerprint repositories, individuality is clearly proved. The problem with this assertion is that it does not stand the test of reason. The millions of sets of prints were never compared against one another for possible duplication of friction ridge patterns. Filing and retrieving prints from such a massive file only results in an examination of a comparatively small number of sets of prints: those with a matching, or approximately matching, classification formula.

There is, however, respectable empirically established evidence of the uniqueness of fingerprint patterns. Studies done by many examiners have shown that the fingerprints of identical twins are different, as are the prints of triplets, quadruplets, and quintuplets. In that sense, fingerprint identification has been found to be even more discriminating than the vaunted DNA (deoxyribonucleic acid) "fingerprinting" method, which cannot distinguish, by today's technology, between the DNA of identical twins. Since inherited traits for similarity in patterns and sub-pattern types are the most common among people who are very closely related, the difference in the prints of such persons certainly can be taken as empirical evidence of fingerprint individuality. Might we not infer from that experience that all fingerprints of different digits are, indeed, different?

Persons skilled in fingerprint identification, who have literally viewed, scanned, and studied tens—if not hundreds—of thousands of individual patterns, do not doubt this. Clearly, if exact pattern duplication were to exist in the world, at least a single instance of this would have been discovered by now. While such claims have been made often, every case, when examined, has established that the prints of different digits that were allegedly "the same" exhibited indeed clearly visible differences that would not have lead an examiner to an erroneous identification. There simply was no duplication of individual ridge detail in prints from different digits.

At the time when fingerprint evidence was first admitted by courts, such empirical evidence or experience in dealing with millions of fingerprint records was not available. If the courts at that era which confronted fingerprint identification evidence first [in Argentina (1892), India (1897), France (1902), and subsequently in England and the United States] had been required to satisfy a Daubert-like decision, perhaps fingerprint identifications would not have been deemed admissible in those early years. With the data that is available today, however, it would be rather ludicrous to argue that the premises underlying fingerprint identification have not been scientifically validated in the face of the accumulated experience of the millions of fingerprints that have been scrutinized by experts.

But there is, today, an opportunity to prove the underlying principle of individuality empirically in a manner that was not available in the past. The tremendous computer databases holding millions of individual finger impressions can today be searched to determine whether pattern duplication exists. While experience has dictated such research is not necessary, the purists (or skeptics) could be satisfied by a rather simple research program that asks our AFIS systems to search, say, a partial individual print of a known person and compare the print against the entire data base. Competent fingerprint examiners feel confident that when the "statistical matches" the computer is bound to throw up are visually examined by them for concordance of individual ridge detail, no two prints from different digits will be found to match.

SIGNIFICANCE

Scientific validity of evidence that may convict a suspect is, of course, crucial. The fact that the majority of forensic scientists believe in fingerprints and that it has a long tradition is not enough, in itself, to establish their validity. Further experiments, such as the one involving AFIS as suggested by Professor Moenssens, would strengthen confidence in this kind of evidence. Fingerprint theory has hardly been examined using the standard blinded approach which is traditional in science. When an examiner gives a second opinion on a match found during an investigation, he or she is usually aware of the judgement given by the first examiner. This, in itself, introduces a bias, however impartial the second examiner believes themselves to be.

Although computer databases play a huge role in fingerprint analysis, the human element—both in protecting the evidence and examining it—remains indispensable. Recent challenges to fingerprint evidence suggest that the approach is really an applied science, with a artistic or subjective component to it, rather than a pure science like chemistry or mathematics. For instance, Oregon attorney Brandon Mayfield was identified as a suspect in the 2004 terrorist bombings in Spain. Later, Spanish police arrested an Algerian suspect and Mayfield was released without charge. Investigation of the case showed a number of concerns over the identification of Mayfield's fingerprints on a

bag of detonators linked to the attacks. One was the enormous size of the Integrated AFIS system which can apparently pull out confusingly similar candidate prints for further examination. The sheer power of the database can, it seems, work against the investigation process at times.

In another recent case, Stephan Cowans was sentenced to 35 to 50 years in prison for shooting a police officer in 1997 after a positive identification from a fingerprint on a drinking glass. But DNA evidence found at the scene later exonerated him. Poor training on the part of fingerprint analysts led to errors that were not discovered by either the verification examiner or Cowans' own defense team. These are just two cases—there may be many more and they demonstrate that fingerprint evidence is not as infallible as the experts might have us believe. So far, there have been 42 Daubert challenges to fingerprints—demanding more scientific validation, as described in the article above. None has been successful, showing that it may be difficult to get the experts to accept a need for further research. But scientific investigation into fingerprint evidence may help tighten up procedures and show the best way of using fingerprint evidence, in the interests of justice being done to suspects and victims alike.

FURTHER RESOURCES

Books

Jackson, Andrew, and Julie Jackson. *Forensic Science*. Harlow, England: Pearson, 2004.

James, Stuart, and Jon Nordby, eds. *Forensic Science*. Boca Raton: CRC Press, 2003.

Web sites

Massachusetts Bar Association. "Lawyer's Journal: Fingerprint Identification and its Aura of Infallibility." <http:// www.massbar.org/publications/lawyersjournal/article/> (accessed March 28, 2006).

Computer Forensics

Photograph

By: Kim Kulish

Date: January 7, 2005

Source: Corbis

About the Photographer: This photograph was taken at the opening of the Silicon Valley Regional Computer

Forensics Lab in Menlo Park, California, on January 7, 2005 by Kim Kulish, a photographer for the Corbis photo agency.

INTRODUCTION

Computer forensics, also called digital forensics, is the systematic recovery of data from digital storage devices—computer discs, iPods, cell phones, digital cameras, personal digital assistants, and the like—for use in law enforcement.

This photograph was taken on the opening day of the Silicon Valley Regional Computer Forensics Lab (RCFL) in Menlo Park, California. The facility, which cost two million dollars, measures 17,000 square feet, and is located in a business park, employed eight dorensic digital examiners who were equipped with a wide array of tools for the extraction and decryption of information from digital devices. The Silicon Valley

RCFL was the latest in a network of FBI-sponsored regional computer forensics laboratories across the U.S., with the others (as of 2006) being in Centennial (CO), Chicago, Dallas, Hamilton (NJ), Houston (TX), Kansas City (MO), Portland (OR), Salt Lake City (UT), Buffalo (NY), Dayton (OH), Philadelphia (PA), and Louisville (KY).

Each RCFL serves a specific geographic area and is jointly funded and utilized by the Federal Bureau of Investigation and the other federal, state, and local law enforcement agencies in the area that it serves. The National Program Office of the RCFL program states that "An RCFL is a one-stop, single service forensics laboratory and training [facility] devoted to the examination of digital evidence in support of criminal investigations and to the detection and prevention of terrorist acts." The Silicon Valley RCFL also function as a school training up to one thousand police officers a year in the proper collection and handling of digital

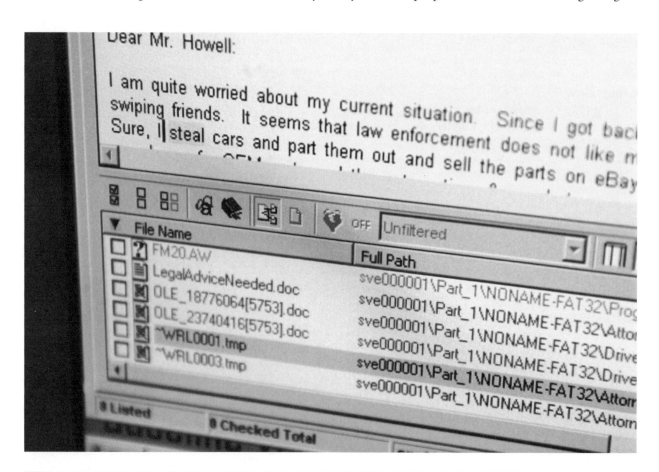

PRIMARY SOURCE

Computer Forensics: This email message, displayed at the Silicon Valley Regional Computer Forensics Lab in 2005 in Menlo Park, California, is an example of the sort of electronic evidence that the lab works to recover and provide to law enforcement agencies. © KIM KULISH/CORBIS

evidence. Staff members of the facility may also participate directly in the physical collection of digital evidence, as in going to crime scenes or helping to execute search warrants. A typical RCFL is staffed by ten to twelve examiners, a director, and a secretary ("administrative support person").

The work of the RCFL facilities is distinct from the eavesdropping, decryption, and other computer- and communications-related technical activities carried out by the Central Intelligence Agency, National Security Agency, and other government agencies. The RCFL network is tasked to obtain evidence so that it that can be presented publicly in courts of law.

▮ PRIMARY SOURCE

COMPUTER FORENSICS

See primary source image.

SIGNIFICANCE

Devices that store digital information have become ubiquitous in business, banking, personal communications, and daily life. They have therefore also become ubiquitous in crime. Criminals receive and send e-mails, both encrypted and in the clear, and store incriminating information on their computers; hackers break into computerized banking systems to steal cash or account numbers; the creation of computer viruses is an inherently digital crime; downloading child pornography is a crime that depends entirely on digital communications and storage devices; and so on.

Digital evidence, like all other evidence gained by intrusive means (property searches, wiretaps, etc.) can only be obtained legally in the U.S. and many other countries if a warrant has been issued or if the material can be acquired by police without searching private property or eavesdropping. (If a letter, optical disc, or hard drive is thrown out as trash, it is fair game for police to examine.)

Applications of computer forensics to real-world cases are numerous. In one notorious case, a woman who murdered a pregnant woman and stole the baby out of the victim's body was tracked by analyzing e-mails saved on the victim's computer. (The baby was recovered alive.) Often, digital devices or files contain more information than users are aware of, which may be used against them. In 2006, the *Washington Post* posted to its website a picture of a spam-generating hacker. The picture had been doctored to conceal the hacker's identity but the file contained "meta-information"—information about information, in this case

information about the digital photograph—that revealed where it was taken, potentially leading to identification of the hacker by police or others. In Italy in 2005, computer records of cell-phone calls made in Rome were the basis for arrest warrants issued for nineteen C.I.A. agents allegedly involved in kidnapping a Muslim cleric: in the Italian cell phone system, each phone transmits a unique code that allows its location at the time to be determined later, sometimes with a precision of several yards. In 2005, the U.S. Justice Department subpoenaed records kept by the Google Corporation on billions of searches performed by Internet users, not as part of any particular investigation but in order, it said, to demonstrate the frequency of searches for child pornography. Google refused, fearful that demands for more sensitive information—such as which searches originated from which users—might be demanded next.

Countermeasures are available to those who are concerned that their data might be acquired by police. Although the police are equipped to defeat many forms of encryption, some publicly available encryption schemes, such as the Pretty Good Privacy public-key system, are reputedly quite difficult to crack. Misleading data can be planted for apparent discovery by investigators. Not storing incriminating data at all is a particularly effective way to defeat computer forensics, if it can be managed. Simply deleting files, however, does not protect them from recovery: a hard drive must be thoroughly wiped or physically destroyed to prevent recovery.

Like all law-enforcement tools, the methods of computer forensics can be used not only against criminals, but also against political dissidents. In some countries, such as China, digital forensics methods are used to jail persons who access pro-democracy websites. In 2005, the Internet company Yahoo! supplied computer records on Internet user activity to the Chinese government that helped it apprehend and jail at least two Internet users who criticized Chinese human rights abuses and corruption online.

FURTHER RESOURCES

Periodicals

Tsai, Alice. "Computer Forensics: Electronic Trail of Evidence." *NHSCPA [New Hampshire Society of Certified Public Accountants] E-News.* May, 2002. Available at <http://www.nhscpa.org/May2002News/forensics.htm > (accessed March 23, 2006).

Web sites

"Silicon Valley Regional Computer Forensics Laboratory." Home page. <http://www.svrcfl.org/> (accessed March 23, 2006).

Justice and Punishment

In many countries there is a fundamental and ancient division of the law into civil and criminal law (see "Code Civil des Français"); each system has its own procedures and penalties. Although there are exceptions, civil law (also called private law in some countries) generally deals with administrative matters and contractual or property disputes between citizens. Theft, fraud, crimes of violence, etc. fall into the domain of the criminal justice system.

According to data published by the Bureau of Justice Statistics, the majority of crimes in the United States remain unsolved (and statistics are similar in most other countries). Arrests, however, lead to a highly defined judicial process, and upon conviction, a range of proscribed punishments.

If an arrest occurs and a suspect is charged with the crime, a judge must then decide whether to hold the suspect in custody or release the suspect on bail. Depending on the type and severity of crime, a range of proceedings then further determine whether there is sufficient evidence to put a suspect on trial for potential loss of property and liberty. In the United States, by law, a suspect is presumed to be innocent until proven guilty (convicted by a jury of peers). At any stage in the judicial process, however, a plea of guilty by the accused changes the process to one designed to assign appropriate punishment in the form of probation, diversionary program, fine and/or incarceration.

To give adequate coverage to all judicial systems this book would need several additional volumes devoted to that subject. There are profound differences in judicial systems and in the ultimate punishment for crime. In some countries, for example, corporal punishment in the form of beatings or caning is still considered appropriate punishment for crimes that might merit only a small fine in the United States.

Although abolished in many Western nations, capital punishment is still used in many states within the U.S. The issue and practice merits wide coverage in the following section. Despite attempts to make the processes as clinical and painless as possible (see "Execution by Lethal Injection: Missouri" and "Execution by Electrocution") the death penalty remains contentious—even as punishment for crimes of treason (see "Must They Die?"), and especially when possible inequities in sentencing or errors in conviction are clearly demonstrable (see "Illinois Stops Executions"). Other countries, however, expand the use and forms of capital punishment (see "Use of Beheading and Amputation in Saudi Penal System").

The judicial system in the United States came under intense scrutiny following the trial of former American football star O.J. Simpson. The trial was widely televised and critics argue that it showed critical weaknesses of the jury system when average citizens are asked to weigh technical forensic evidence. The trial started a wave of televised trials and turned courtroom drama into the ultimate "reality series", at times with life and death at stake. Critics argue that the trial of the once wealthy and popular Simpson also provided evidence of the persuasiveness of powerful and skilled attorneys and thus laid bare the reality of a two-tiered level of justice: that available to the rich as opposed to that available for the poor.

Code Civil des Français

Photograph

By: Anonymous

Date: 1804

Source: Réunion des Musées Nationaux/Art Resource, NY

About the Photographer: This undated photograph shows the title page of the Napoleonic Code or *Code Civil des Français*, first edition (1804).

INTRODUCTION

The *Code Civil des Français* (Civil Code of France), more commonly known as the Napoleonic Code, was first published in 1804. This image shows the title page of the first edition (*édition originale*). The Code is a systematic collection of laws meant to cover all aspects of private law. It is a "civil" code because it is distinct from criminal, religious, military, and other forms of law, restricting itself to matters of property, marriage, inheritance, loans, and the like.

The Code was promulgated by Emperor Napoleon Bonaparte (1769—1821), who was originally a general of the radically egalitarian, anti-royalist French Revolution (1789–1799) but later elevated himself to absolute ruler of France. The Code was devised by an expert commission led by Jean-Etienne-Marie Portalis under Napoleon's personal direction in order to clean up the legal chaos that existed in France at the time. Before the Revolution, over 400 local legal codes existed in France; the committees of the Revolution added to the confusion by enacting over 14,000 additional laws in just a few years. The Code, modeled on the civil code of Roman Emperor Justinian (483–565 A.D.) and on existing French law, systematically laid down rules governing all aspects of personal identity (citizenship, guardianship, paternity adoption, marriage, etc.) and all aspects of property: types of property, inheritance, loans, mortgages, contracts, and so on. The Code did not specify criminal law (i.e., types of murder, assault, theft, and the like or their punishments). These and other aspects of law were dealt with in the Code of Civil Procedure (1806), Commercial Code (1807), Criminal Code (1808), Code of Criminal Procedure (1808), and Penal Code (1810).

PRIMARY SOURCE

CODE CIVIL DES FRANÇAIS

See primary source image.

SIGNIFICANCE

The 1804 *Code Civil des Français* established a uniform French system of civil law, that is, a system of law based on a codified body of fixed rules that are interpreted in court by individual judges. A legal code of this type is distinct from a constitution, which describes how laws are made and what kinds of laws can and cannot be made. (The First Amendment of the U.S. Constitution, for example, forbids Congress from making any law establishing or restricting religion, abridging the freedom of speech, and so forth.) A legal system based on civil and other codes is distinct from a common law system, which is based on binding precedents laid down by decisions in specific court cases. The United States is governed by a common law tradition with substantial statutory law.

However, civil law systems are common in Europe and elsewhere today, partly because of Napoleon Bonaparte's military success. In a ten-year span, Napoleon conquered most of continental Europe, incorporating conquered territories into a French Empire and imposing French law, including the *Code Civil des Français*, throughout. The Code was also imposed in French colonial territories worldwide. After Napoleon's defeat and the breakup of the Empire, most formerly conquered countries retained the Code as the basis of their legal system.

The area that now includes the U.S. state of Louisiana was first a French colony and then a Spanish colony, and was finally acquired by Napoleon from Spain in 1800. Only three years later he sold Louisiana to the United States, but an early version of the *Code Civil des Français* had already been imposed. The Napoleonic Code thus became a unique feature of Louisiana state law and remains so to this day, though the distinctive character of Louisiana has been eroding over time.

Although the Napoleonic Code is often considered enlightened or progressive—it did not criminalize same-sex acts, for example—it did codify the repression of women in important ways, reversing the more gender-egalitarian laws set up immediately after the French Revolution. For example, under the Code, a woman had to reside where her husband resided. Women were forbidden to participate in lawsuits, act as court witnesses, or act as witnesses to births, deaths, and marriages. Married women had little or no con-

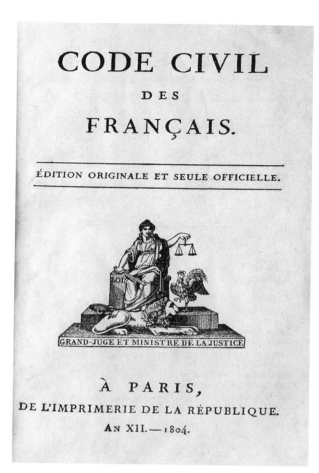

CODE CIVIL

DES

FRANÇAIS.

ÉDITION ORIGINALE ET SEULE OFFICIELLE.

À PARIS,

DE L'IMPRIMERIE DE LA RÉPUBLIQUE.

AN XII.—1804.

■ PRIMARY SOURCE

Code Civil des Français: The title page of the Code Civil des Francais. REUNUION DES MUSEES NATIONAUX/ART RESOURCE, NY

trol over their own property; wages earned by working women became the property of their husbands. Men were absolved from paternity suits and from the support of children born out of wedlock. Adultery by a woman was punished by fines and imprisonment, but adultery by a man was not punished unless he brought his sexual partner home to live with him. The Code did, however, forbid marriage without consent and allow divorce by mutual consent. No women participated in the writing of the Code.

FURTHER RESOURCES

Web sites

The Civil Code (English translation of the *Code Civil des Français*). "Information Sheet 80: Piracy." <http://www.napoleon-series.org/research/government/c_code.html> (accessed March 8, 2006).

La-Legal.com. "How the Code Napoleon makes Louisiana law different." <http://www.la-legal.com/history_louisiana_law.htm> (accessed March 8, 2006).

Female Convicts During the Silent Hour at Brixton Prison, London

All Prisoners Were Required to Sit Quietly Outside Their Cell

Illustration

By: Henry Mayhew and John Binny

Date: 1862

Source: "Female Convicts During the Silent Hour at Brixton Prison, London." Illustration from *The Criminal Prisons of London and Scenes of Prison Life* by Henry Mayhew and John Binny. Griffin, Bohn, and Co.: London, 1862.

About the Illustrator: Henry Mayhew and John Binny were journalists in nineteenth century England with an interest in social issues. This engraving comes from their work on London prisons and the criminal justice system. Mayhew is also known for being one of the cofounders of *Punch*.

INTRODUCTION

In England, the Industrial Revolution and the massive growth in the population of cities like London led to great social change, including an increase in the crime rate. Traditionally, criminals were either executed or transported to Australia. But society gradually realized that capital punishment and transportation were too harsh for all but the most serious of crimes, and demand for reforms mounted.

Incarceration was increasingly seen as an alternative punishment to execution or transportation. As a result, old prisons were expanded and new ones were built. They were cold, damp, unhealthy places that housed men, women and children. There was no segregation by seriousness of offence—the insane, hardened criminals, petty thieves, those awaiting trial, and debtors were all locked up together. Many died or were released out only to reoffend.

FEMALE CONVICTS AT WORK, DURING THE SILENT HOUR, IN BRIXTON PRISON.
(From a Photograph by Herbert Watkins, 179, Regent Street.)

Female Convicts During the Silent Hour at Brixton Prison, London: An illustration from *The Criminal Prisons of London and Scenes of Prison Life,* an 1860 publication by Henry Mayhew and John Binny. It depicts female prisoners at Brixton Prison. The prisoners are sitting quietly outside their cells, as required during the silent hour. PRIVATE COLLECTION/BRIDGEMAN ART LIBRARY/THE STAPELTON COLLECTION

Prison reform led to some changes in the nineteenth century. Elizabeth Fry (1780–1845),who worked mainly with women prisoners, argued that being in prison was punishment enough in itself. As a Quaker, she believed that people should be treated decently, no matter what they had done. Other reformers hoped that better conditions might reform the criminal

Victorian prisons were an improvement, but they were still unpleasant. One common practice was to keep the prisoners in silence and even solitary confinement so they could reflect on their crimes. Brixton Prison in South London was built in 1819 and still stands today. It became a women-only prison in 1862, the year the illustration below was produced. It shows the women being supervised outside their cells as they observe the rule of silence.

FEMALE CONVICTS DURING THE SILENT HOUR AT BRIXTON PRISON, LONDON

See primary source image.

SIGNIFICANCE

The silent system was imposed in response to a strong contemporary belief that criminals were born, not made, and that rehabilitation was impossible. If their will were broken in prison, it was thought, they would be too frightened to reoffend. Conditions had to be hard under this rubric, and in some prisons, convicts were kept in total silence. This was not as bad, however, as solitary confinement, which was common in the 1840s. Many prisoners went mad after being kept in isolation. Another practise was to make prisoners do hard, meaningless labor—walking on a treadmill or picking oakum—separating strands of rope—for hours on end. The treadmill was not banned until 1902.

Even though conditions were harsh, life in Victorian jails may have been easier than on the teeming streets of London. Prisoners were, on the whole, fed, warm, and safe. In 1865, however, a new Prisons Act was passed to appease the public, who clearly thought that not enough punishment was being meted out. The assistant director of prisons, Sir Edmund du Cane, promised "Hard labour, hard fare, and hard board." The hard labor was the treadmill, hard fare was deliberately monotonous—although adequate— food. The hard board was a wooden plank bed, which replaced the hammocks that prisoners had slept on before.

Today arguments about prison reform continue. Many prisoners are mentally ill and have been jailed for relatively minor offenses. This is particularly true where women are concerned. There is often a case for having a convict serve their sentence in the community rather than locking them in prison. If they can, at the same time, render some service to the community, so much the better. Of course, the public is entitled to protection from dangerous criminals and these people do need to be locked away until it is deemed they are harmless. There is also a natural desire for justice, of which seeing someone punished for their crime is a natural part. But so many convicts come out of prison only to reoffend that it is hard to see whether imprisonment as a form of punishment really serves society in the long term.

FURTHER RESOURCES

Web sites

The National Archives. "Victorian Prisons: Why Were Victorian Prisons So Tough?" <http://www.learningcurve.gov.uk/snapshots/snapshot24/snapshot24.htm> (accessed February 14, 2006).

Victorian Web. "The Cornhill, Great Expectations, and the Convict System in Nineteenth-Century England" <http://www.victorianweb.org/authors/dickens/ge/convicts.html > (accessed February 14, 2006).

J'accuse!

Letter

By: Émile Zola

Date: January 13, 1898

Source: Zola, Émile. "J'accuse!"

About the Author: Émile Zola (1840–1902) was a prominent French writer who helped popularize naturalism, a literary school that desired to reflect everyday realities in writing. An activist for liberalizing reforms, Zola was also active in French politics. He published his letter, "J'acccuse!" (I accuse!) in the Parisian daily publication, L'Aurore (The Dawn).

INTRODUCTION

In 1894, the French government tried and convicted military officer Alfred Dreyfus with treason. Dreyfus was convicted of passing intelligence secrets to German officials at the German Embassy in Paris. At the time of his trial, Dreyfus was the highest-ranking Jewish officer in the French Army. As the case against Dreyfus progressed, French authorities realized they had scant evidence that implicated Dreyfus in the espionage plot. The realizations came too late, as other officials feared public outrage if the trail were to be withdrawn. Dreyfus's trial continued. Suspicious and secretive evidence in the form of a sealed dossier was provided to prosecutors, but not the defense. Other errors of evidence and investigation also marred the case.

Dreyfus was convicted and stripped of his commission and all military honors. Friends and family of Dreyfus waged a campaign to exhonorate him, citing anti-Semitism as a leading factor in the the government's prosecution of Dreyfus. Dreyfus was sentenced to life in prison on the infamous penal colony on Devil's Island. He remained in prison until 1899 when he agreed to a plea bargain of a tacit admission of guilt in exchange for relaease.

Dreyfus was exhonorated of all charges in 1906. He chose to rejoin the army when his commission was reinstated and later served in World War I.

J'ACCUSE!

See primary source image.

■

SIGNIFICANCE

French writer Émile Zola helped bring the Dreyfus Affair into the public spotlight. Zola believed that Dreyfus was the victim of growing anti-Semitism in both French government and society. Zola risked his liberty to speak publically on behalf of Dreyfus. On January 13, 1898, Zola published his rebuke of the government's handling of the Dreyfus case in the form of an open letter to French President, Félix Faure.

Zola titled the letter "I accuse!" In the piece, he accused the french government of hiding the truth, lying about key evidence, and forming a conspiracy to frame Dreyfus. "We are horrified by the terrible light the Dreyfus affair has cast upon it all, this human sacrifice of an unfortunate man, 'a dirty Jew.' Ah, what a cesspool of folly and foolishness, what preposterous fantasies, what corrupt police tactics, what inquisitorial, tyrannical practices! What petty whims of a few higher-ups trampling the nation under their boots, ramming back down their throats the people's cries for truth and justice, with the travesty of state security as a pretext," Zola wrote. While the letter called attention to Dreyfus's plight, helping to turn public opinion in his favor, Zola was convicted of libel mere weeks after its publication. Zola then fled to England to avoid inprisonment. He continued to campaign for Dreyfus's freedom.

Deuxième Année. — Numéro 87

Cinq Centimes

JEUDI 13 JANVIER 1898

Directeur
ERNEST VAUGHAN

L'AURORE

Littéraire, Artistique, Sociale

Directeur
ERNEST VAUGHAN

LES ANNONCES SONT REÇUES :
142 — Rue Montmartre — 142

Les manuscrits non insérés ne sont pas rendus

Téléphone : 102-88

J'Accuse...!

LETTRE AU PRÉSIDENT DE LA RÉPUBLIQUE

Par ÉMILE ZOLA

LETTRE A M. FÉLIX FAURE

Président de la République

Monsieur le Président,

Me permettez-vous, dans ma gratitude pour le bienveillant accueil que vous m'avez fait un jour, d'avoir le souci de votre juste gloire et de vous dire que votre étoile, si heureuse jusqu'ici, est menacée de la plus honteuse, de la plus ineffaçable des taches?

PRIMARY SOURCE

J'accuse!: The front page of the *L'Aurore* newspaper on January 13, 1898, showing Emile Zola's famous letter "J'Accuse!," condemning the conviction of Captain Dreyfus. SNARK/ART RESOURCE, NY

FURTHER RESOURCES
Books
Burns, Michael. *France and the Dreyfus Affair: A Brief Documentary History* . Bedford / St. Martin, 1998.

Web sites
La Société Littéraire des Amis d ' É Zola . "The Alfred Dreyfus Affair" <http://www.dreyfuscase.com/index.html> (March 28, 2006).

General Li Hung Chang's Reminder to the Lawless

Photograph

By: Anonymous

Date: c. 1900

Source: Corbis

About the Photographer: The photographer is unknown.

INTRODUCTION

In this picture, the severed heads of several pirates are hung in wooden cages over a high wall, probably that of a prison, apparently to deter crimes by others. This photograph is one half of a stereoscopic pair meant to be seen as a three-dimensional image. The original caption, supplied by the European or American manufacturer of the stereoscopic card, emphasizes the purpose of the display: "Li Hung Chang's reminder to the lawless."

Li Hung Chang (1823–1901) was a diplomat, statesman, and general during the later years of the Manchu or Qing (Chi'ng) Dynasty in China. He was noted for his diplomatic skills. At the age of 80 he was appointed viceroy of the southern region of Canton by the dowager empress of China. The Canton area was plagued by murderous pirates—not swashbuckling clichés, but violent Chinese outlaws. Large gangs of 50 or more would swarm large British merchant vessels, or disguise themselves as a pleasure party, hiring a launch for the day and taking along a gaily-dressed young woman or two as a distraction. The Empress sent her best man, Li Hung Chang, to correct the situation.

Beheading was standard punishment in China at that time for crimes such as murder and piracy.

Viceroy Ts'en, a successor of Li Hung Chang in Canton in the early twentieth century, wrote in response to British complaints of continuing piracy, "Have I not already decapitated over 15,000 robbers since my appointment[?] I executed 50 only two days ago and this does not include many shot and otherwise destroyed. Am I not honestly doing my best?"

PRIMARY SOURCE

GENERAL LI HUNG CHANG'S REMINDER TO THE LAWLESS
See primary source image.

SIGNIFICANCE

Li Hung Chang relied on increased pursuit and execution of pirates and thieves to protect trade relations with Western nations. Problems protecting trade goods led him to pursue a policy of railroad construction and military reform. Despite these modernization plans, Li Hung Chang relied on traditional-and sometimes brutal-forms of punishment for capital crimes.

Beheadings themselves were often public events, performed either in the city-center or immediately outside of the city boundaries. Sometimes, the accused were shamed by having their queues or pigtails cut off before being beheaded. In many parts of China, beheadings were infrequent occurrences. An American missionary in Kiukiang in 1876 noted in a letter describing a public execution that the city had not executed a prisoner for many years.

The public display of heads was intended to deter capital crime. Whether it actually had that effect, however, may be questioned. Years later, piracy continued and Li Hung Chang's successor Ts'en executed thousands of criminals.

FURTHER RESOURCES
Periodicals
Goertzel, Ted. "Capital Punishment and Homicide: Sociological Realities and Econometric Illusions." *Skeptical Inquirer*.

Web sites
Death Penalty Information Center. Fagan, Jeffrey. "Deterrence and the Death Penalty: A Critical Review of New Evidence." <http://www.deathpenaltyinfo.org/FaganTestimony.pdf> (accessed March 7, 2006).

Pro-Death Penalty.Org. "Standing United for the Death Penalty." <http://www.prodeathpenalty.org/> (accessed March 7, 2006).

PRIMARY SOURCE

General Li Hung Chang's Reminder to the Lawless: General Li Hung Chang's reminder to the lawless: the heads of five pirates hang over the wall at Honam, China. © CORBIS

Censored Guillotine Scene

Photograph

By: Anonymous

Date: 1904

Source: "Censored Guillotine Scene." Corbis, 1904.

About the Photographer: The source photograph is a still from a movie by Georges Méliès, the first film scene ever to be suppressed by the police. The photographer is unknown.

INTRODUCTION

The guillotine is best known for creating a sea of blood during the French Revolution of the 1790s. The French did not invent the device though. Crude versions of the guillotine existed as early as the fifteenth and sixteenth centuries in Italy, England, Scotland, Naples, Holland, and Germany. Its use represented an exceptional aristocratic privilege. The victim avoided the contaminating hands of the working class hangman while the execution was performed with mechanical efficiency. The executioner only pulled up the razor-sharp blade by a cord and then released it to chop off the victim's head in a flash.

PRIMARY SOURCE

The guillotine's mechanical efficiency fascinated people as much as it repelled them. This still from a 1904 movie by Georges Méliès shows a man being prepared for the guillotine. It is the first film scene ever to be suppressed by police.
© HULTON-DEUTSCH COLLECTION/CORBIS

For most of the population, execution remained a imprecise and gruesome affair. Executioners who wielded axes sometimes failed to kill with the first blow, forcing the condemned to endure multiple slices. Hangmen occasionally failed to employ proper counterweights, with the result that the condemned person's neck did not break immediately and the prisoner slowly strangled to death. In 1757, the Damiens Affair shocked France. Robert-François Damiens was sentenced to be publicly hanged, drawn, and quartered for attempting to kill the king. He was briefly choked in a noose and his genitalia were cut off before four horses attempted to pull him apart. The horses were unable to dismember him and Damiens was finally cut apart with a knife. While drawing and quartering was comparatively rare, France in the eighteenth century still broke non-nobility on the wheel and burned them at the stake.

Equalization of the death penalty was first proposed by Joseph Ignace Guillotin (1738–1814), a professor of anatomy and a deputy for the Third Estate in the French National Assembly. Guillotin, a Jesuit who left the order to become a physician, was a humanitarian. He wanted to retain the deterrent value of capital punishment while ending the torture associated with it. The guillotine reduced the pain of the victim and limited the spectacle of public execution to a sudden spurt of blood. The Assembly decreed decapitation as the death penalty in June 1791 and another physician, A. Louis, actually invented the guillotine. The machine began operation in April 1792. Nicknamed "The Widow," it remained in use in France until 1981.

PRIMARY SOURCE

CENSORED GUILLOTINE SCENE
See primary source image.

SIGNIFICANCE

Public executions in France ended in 1939. Execution increasingly became a relatively rare form of punishment, for only the most heinous of crimes. Between 1965 and 1981, only eight men were guillotined. The last use of a guillotine in France occurred on September 10, 1977, when an Algerian named Hamida Djandoubi was executed for murdering a woman in Marseille. After 1977, President Valery Giscard d'Estaing gave life sentences to prisoners condemned to death.

By the end of the twentieth century, the guillotine increasingly came to be seen as an antique device from an uncivilized era. The Giscard government considered abolishing its use, but no alternative could be found. Proposals for sending convicted murderers to isolated South Sea islands or to bleak Antarctic wastelands were rejected as either too nice for the convicts or too nasty for the jailers. The issue of the death penalty created such high feelings on both sides that no solution could be found.

On September 20, 1981, France's National Assembly voted overwhelmingly by 369–116 to abolish the death penalty. The Socialist Party, newly in power, fulfilled its campaign promise to end execution. A majority of the French public disagreed with the government. The French people supported the continued use of execution as a deterrent to rising crime. At the time of the vote, 52 percent of the French public supported the death penalty while 42 percent opposed it.

The decision, which sent the nation's two guillotines to museums, made France the last country in Western Europe to end the death penalty. The Socialists believed that it made no difference to society whether criminals were executed or sentenced to life imprisonment. Passage of the law automatically commuted the sentences of the six men on death row.

FURTHER RESOURCES
Books

Arasse, Daniel. *The Guillotine and The Terror*. London: Allen Lane/Penguin Press, 1989.

Bryan, Geoffrey. *Off With His Head!*. London: Hutchinson, 1934.

Opie, Robert Frederick. *Guillotine: The Timbers of Justice*. Stroud, U.K.: Sutton Publishing, 2003.

Chain Gangs

Photograph

By: Anonymous

Date: circa 1905

Source: "Southern chain gang." The Library of Congress.

About the Photographer: This image comes from the Library of Congress's collection. The photographer is unknown.

INTRODUCTION

The proliferation in the United States of chain gangs, so called because they consisted of small groups (usually numbering between four and six individuals) of prisoners who were shackled together at the ankles, were used as a means of low-cost labor from the end of the Civil War through the end of World War II in the United States. Interestingly, the use of chain gangs grew from a prison reform effort. Prior to the last quarter of the nineteenth century, extreme maltreatment, abuse, and frequent use of capital punishment for comparatively minor offenses of prisoners was common, even tacitly condoned. William Penn sought to put an end to the miseries experienced by prisoners, and advocated allowing them gainful employment and access to the outdoors. The rapid upshot of that was the development and proliferation of chain gangs in which groups of incarcerated felons were shackled together at the ankles and sent out to perform hard labor, generally involving repetitive, physically challenging menial tasks. Prison labor was felt to be in the public good for two primary reasons: the abolition of slavery and the need to rebuild the South, along with the dominant fundamentalist ethic that advocated hard work as a means of making societal restitution for criminal misdeeds (punishment plus payment).

Ultimately, prison laborers, particularly those on chain gangs, became a saleable commodity: they would be leased to private individuals or businesses in exchange for a sufficient sum so as to ensure that the prison systems were economically viable. The penal system did not have to supervise or maintain the working prisoners, and the lease owners got incredibly cheap labor that could be made to work, quite literally, until they dropped—from exhaustion or worse. The inmates were reputed to be treated abominably, with cruel and malevolent supervisors who overworked and underfed them, often beating or physically punishing those who refused, or were unable, to be sufficiently productive. Many inmates on chain gangs perished—in some areas of the country, it was nearly fifty percent of those sent out on lease details.

In 1934, the lease system throughout the United States was abolished by Congressional mandate. This did not eliminate the use of chain gangs; it merely prevented individuals and private corporations from exploiting the use of exceptionally cheap labor. The inmates could still be made to work on public lands and utilities, and to perform labor that would remunerate the system for the cost of feeding and housing them. Chain gangs, by the start of America's Great Depression, had been put to work maintaining public highways, building new roadways, and supplying labor

PRIMARY SOURCE

Chain Gangs: A Southern chain gang, circa 1905. Prisoners in a chain gang would be linked to each other with chains and sent out into the community under guard to do manual labor. These men are doing road work. THE LIBRARY OF CONGRESS

for the farms and public enterprises that provided their food and clothing. By the height of the Great Depression, chain gangs had been largely disbanded in an effort to allow as many needy free men and women (non-incarcerated individuals) to earn a living as possible.

PRIMARY SOURCE

CHAIN GANGS

See primary source image.

SIGNIFICANCE

After World War II, the number of states employing chain gangs significantly declined. Virtually no northern states continued the practice. Many of the states, particularly those in the northern regions of the country, reportedly put an end to chain gangs because of their reputed similarity to the indignities, cruelties, and atrocities associated with slavery, to which this practice was likened. The parallel was reinforced by the fact that the vast majority of the chain gangs were composed nearly exclusively of African-Americans. The states utilizing this means of employing inmates justified their actions by stating that it was cost-effective: many workers could be sent to a particular area to perform demanding physical labor with a minimum of supervisory manpower. By increasing the size of the inmate workforce, it was possible to increase both productivity and profit margin.

The harsh, often brutal, conditions under which chain gangs labored attracted public attention in 1967, when it was revealed that the conditions of Georgia work camps, which utilized chain gangs as laborers, were so dreadful that the prisoners began doing themselves grievous bodily harm in order to avoid work. The use of work camps was terminated shortly thereafter.

During the decades in which the prison populations of the United States remained relatively stable, there was neither financial nor spatial need to consider reinstituting labor camps or chain gangs. The correctional climate took a definite turn in the 1990s, however, in the aftermath of the "get tough on crime" and "three strikes and you're out" legislation. Prisons and jails were filling at previously unheard-of rates, overcrowding was common, and the financial resources necessary to feed, clothe, and shelter the burgeoning population of inmates were being overstretched. At the same time, the political climate of the country was one of intolerance of crime and the perpetrators thereof, along with a return to the much earlier philosophy of punishment rather than rehabilitation as a deterrent for future criminal behavior. Criminals were made partially accountable for the costs of their confinement; their personal funds were extremely limited, and used for court costs, victim restitution, and their own personal hygiene (shampoo, soaps, deodorant, lotions, etc.) or commissary (coffee, tea, snack foods) products. They were given mandatory jobs, depending on their security level, at the facility in which they were housed (either in prison industries or by private corporations), and paid infinitesimal wages, most of which were used to support the costs of their housing. Lower-security inmates were often assigned to outdoor work details, in which they were taken in brightly uniformed (typically, neon jumpsuits with D.O.C. insignia emblazoned across the front and back) groups to do highway cleanup, road maintenance, logging,

farming, or similar physically challenging tasks that required minimal skills.

As a means of deterring crime, as well as a means of keeping down the cost of supporting inmates who were contributing to prison overcrowding (rather than simply continuing to build more and more prisons), a few states (Alabama, Florida, and Arizona) reinstituted the practice of assigning relatively low-security prisoners, and sometimes first offenders, to chain gangs in the mid-1990s. Inmates on these work details may only legally be assigned to public works such as the cleanup, maintenance, and construction of highways, bridges, and overpasses.

Convicted felons may be sentenced to specific periods of work on chain gangs, or they may be remanded to them as part of a disciplinary action. In either case, the term of service is required to be finite, and the conditions of work, sustenance, and shelter are supposed to be strictly regulated so as to fall within the Constitutional rights of the individual prisoner. However, there has been considerable public outcry at the reactivation of the practice, asserting that it subjects inmates to cruel and unusual punishment; deprives them of the right to congregate and socialize; denies them contact and visitation with family and other significant persons; violates their privacy by forcing them to relieve themselves in public; and subjects inmates to dangerous working conditions that impose unacceptable levels of emotional and physical stress. Countering those assertions, the Alabama Department of Corrections has asserted that it is a highly effective deterrent to future criminal behavior.

FURTHER RESOURCES
Books

Braithwaite, J. *Crime, Shame and Reintegration*. Cambridge, Mass.: Cambridge University Press, 1992.

Elikann, Peter T. *The Tough-On-Crime Myth: Real Solutions to Cut Crime*. New York: Insight Books, 1996.

Whitman, James O. *Harsh Justice: Criminal Punishment and the Widening Divide Between America and Europe*. New York: Oxford University Press, 2003.

Periodicals

Anderson, J., and L. Dyson. "A Tracking Investigation To Determine Boot Camp Success And Offender Risk Assessment For CRIPP Participants." *Journal of Crime and Justice* 19, 1 (1996): 179–190.

Brownstein, Rhonda. "Chain Gangs are Cruel and Unusual Punishment." *Corrections Today* (April 1996): 179.

Cohen, Warren. "Need Work? Go to Jail." *US News & World Report* (December 9, 1996): 76–77.

Reynolds, Marylee N. "Back On the Chain Gang." *Corrections Today* (April, 1996): 180–184.

Sellin, T. "A Look at Prison History." *Federal Probation* 31, 3 (1967): 18–23.

Two Reports on the Reorganization & Reconstruction of the New York City Prison System

Book excerpt

By: Hastings Hornell Hart

Date: January 1925

Source: Hart, Hastings Hornell. *Two Reports on the Reorganization & Reconstruction of the New York City Prison System.* New York: Prison Association of New York, 1925.

About the Author: Hastings Hornell Hart (1851–1932), served as the consultant on correctional institutions for the regional plan of New York to the Prison Association of New York. Today known as the Correctional Association of New York, the Prison Association was founded in 1844 and acts as an independent, nonprofit organization to monitor activities in the state's prisons and report their findings to the government, the media, and the general public. The association is involved in research, public education, and development of policy recommendations aimed at ensuring the New York prison system is run efficiently, fairly, and humanely.

INTRODUCTION

The prison system in the state of New York is the fourth largest penal system in the United States. Today more than $2 billion dollars each year are spent in the state's prisons. The prison system operates seventy different prisons housing more than 65,000 inmates. Among nations that report statistics on imprisonment, the United States records the highest per capita rate of people living in prison. The high numbers are attributed to a number of factors, including longer prison terms and the war on drugs, which has imprisoned large numbers of inmates whose criminal records are otherwise non-violent.

While conditions in prisons have improved significantly in recent decades as a result of efforts from human rights and other non-governmental organizations, many prisons remain extremely violent and dangerous places. Critics of the penal system have argued that the harsh conditions in prisons contribute to hardening criminals and to a high rate of recidivism (released inmates re-enter society only to commit crimes and be returned to prisons). Prisons in the United States have long been centers of gang activity—gang members retain their memberships inside prison and are imprisoned together with fellow members of their gangs.

Like most governmental activities in the United States, the prison system is divided into the local, state, and federal levels. Prisoners are sent to one of these three levels depending upon the nature of their crime and where it was committed. Local and county governments usually operate only smaller prisons or jails for inmates awaiting trials. State prisons house inmates facing longer sentences, including prisoners on death row for having committed homicidal crimes. Depending upon the specific state, prisoners who are given sentences without the chance for parole will either spend the remainder of their lives on death row or be eligible for the death penalty. Federal prisons house prisoners who have committed crimes against the laws of the United States government or, in other specific cases, offenses that are considered federal crimes because they have taken place in more than one state.

Prisons constructed today are ultra-modern facilities that rely on technological advances to supervise and confine prisoners. Prisons vary in level of confinement between minimum security institutions where inmates share dormitory-like housing and work in public service projects outside of the facilities, to supermax security institutions where inmates are all housed separately and have little contact with other prisoners.

PRIMARY SOURCE

HART'S ISLAND

The Branch Penitentiary, Hart's Island.—This prison is still called "The Reformatory Prison," although it has for several years been a branch of the Penitentiary. It receives male prisoners under penitentiary sentences, with a maximum of three years, and 29 prisoners under workhouse sentences with a maximum of two years, both classes of prisoners being subject to parole. On the date of my visit, February 28, 1924, there were present

692 prisoners under penitentiary sentences, 157 under workhouse sentences, and two under reformatory sentences; total, 851. The buildings are: administration building with four dormitories; hospital building with general and tuberculosis wards, capacity 40 patients, containing also dormitories for 74 officers; also one dormitory for prisoners (both these buildings are practically fireproof); a wood and brick dining hall containing three dormitories which are dangerous fire traps; a disciplinary building, power house, store house, stable and several residences. The old men's department (not included above) consists of a group of antiquated wooden cottages built for veterans of the Civil War. These buildings are worn-out, rotten fire-traps in which the beds of the old men are crowded together. They contain no day rooms, and the poor old men lead a wretched existence in winter and in stormy weather. These inmates are worn-out old men, no longer capable of inflicting any serious damage upon society. Many of them are of the vagrant and intemperate classes. It is cruelty to turn such men loose on the streets of New York, and they sometimes secrete themselves when they are about to be discharged, because they prefer even this unhappy condition to vagrancy in the great city. The Commissioner of Correction has urged legislation whereby men of this class can be transferred to the Almshouse instead of being committed and re-committed. The Island contains about 77 acres of land, of which four acres belong to private parties, a fact which promotes escapes and the smuggling of drugs and other contraband materials. This land should be acquired by the city through condemnation proceedings in order to prevent these evils.

Hart's Island has been used for the past 50 years as a potter's field for the burial of the paupers. Already 241,000 burials have been made. During the past 10 years, 1914 to 1923, 58,273 bodies have been interred, a yearly average of 5,828. The bodies are buried in trenches 40 x 16 feet, three deep. The boxes containing the bodies are placed side by side in double rows, 25 in a row, so that 500 bodies of adults are interred in a space 40 x 16 feet, which is equal to 640 square feet. If we leave a space of only two feet 30 between trenches, it will make 112 square feet additional or a total of 752 feet for each trench containing 150 bodies, which is five square feet for each body. The bodies of children, especially those of infants, occupy a much smaller space. It is estimated that the 241,000 bodies already interred occupy about 15 acres. The burials at the present rate occupy probably about one-half acre yearly. The city owns approximately 77 acres of ground on Hart's Island. Some of this ground is low and wet. Only a small portion is fit for gardening. I learned that about 16 acres are under cultivation, but this garden spot is gradually being absorbed for burial purposes, and if the present rate of burials continues it will probably be all used up in another 30 years.

There are a few old shop buildings on Hart's Island, but they are entirely inadequate for the employment of 700 prisoners. Immediate provision should be made for suitable shops with modern equipment to permit of the employment of the prisoners on the state's use plan. Such shops should have available from 2 to 6 acres of space, according to the kinds of industries to be pursued. As already stated, the present capacity of the dormitories is 700 prisoners. The minimum amount of ground required for prison buildings, shops, storehouses, stables, and so forth for 700 prisoners, exclusive of gardens and recreation grounds, would be about 16 acres, or one acre for every 44 prisoners. Under these circumstances it is evidently impracticable to provide additional prison facilities on Hart's Island unless the use of the Island as a burial place should be discontinued. An effort was made some years ago to substitute cremation for burial, which would be a most desirable change from every practical point of view. I understand that this plan was not actively opposed by the religious authorities of the various sects, but it was impossible to obtain unanimous agreement and the proposition was finally dropped. If the bodies already interred on Hart's Island could be removed and cremated, the Island would furnish a good site for an industrial prison for not more than 700 prisoners. If the bodies are not removed and burials on the Island are continued, the number of prisoners should be reduced as the available land decreases; otherwise it will be impossible to provide the shop room, exercise grounds and gardens which are indispensable to a well-conducted modern prison and to the employment of the prisoners in such a way as to preserve their physical and moral health, to give them some degree of vocational training, and to permit them to earn at least a portion of the cost of their maintenance.

SIGNIFICANCE

Films and works of fiction have often depicted prisons of the early half of the twentieth century as dark and dangerous places, where conditions for prisoners fostered violence and depression. This excerpt, written in 1925, serves to reinforce that picture and presents New York's prisons as institutions in need of repair and renovation. This report highlights the impact of bureaucratic and budgetary constraints on the decisions that prison authorities are able to make—constraints that continue to the present day.

The author speaks about overcrowding in the prison and notes that the prison should be expanded to

View of prison buildings on Welfare (now Roosevelt) Island in New York City, 1932, referenced in the Hart prison report.
© BETTMANN/CORBIS

ensure that the rights of prisoners are being preserved. The report was issued under the auspices of a non-governmental agency, the Prison Association of New York, and it demonstrates the efforts taken to monitor the conditions of prisons and the treatment of inmates in 1925.

The Branch Penitentiary on Hart's Island was a facility for prisoners who had committed less serious crimes. Three years was the maximum sentence any prisoner served and all the prisoners were eligible for parole. Yet the conditions at this prison were harsher than the inmates' crimes would seem to have warranted. It may, then, be safe to assume that conditions

in prisons housing more violent inmates were far worse at that time.

Even though prisons in the United States are designed to punish inmates for the crimes that they have committed, they are also intended to be run with a sense of discipline that prevents correctional officers from torturing or mistreating prisoners. This requirement is established by the U.S. Constitution's prohibition of the use of "cruel or unusual punishment" of prisoners. It reflects the democratic values of the country. These values maintain that even those who break the law must be treated with decency and granted their rights as humans.

FURTHER RESOURCES

Books

Carlson, Peter M. and Judith Simon Garrett. *Prison and Jail Administration: Practice and Theory.* Gaithersburg, Md: Aspen Publishers, 1999.

Ross, Jeffrey Ian and Steven Ian Richards. *Behind Bars: Surviving Prison.* New York: Alpha, 2002.

Web sites

New York State Department of Correctional Services. <http://www.docs.state.ny.us/> (accessed February 10, 2006).

Devil's Island Fugitives

Penal Colonies

Photograph

By: Anonymous

Date: 1938

Source: AP Images

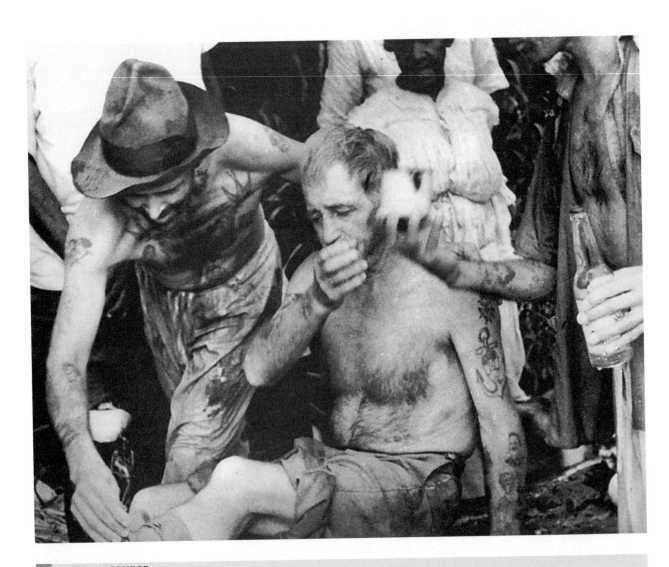

PRIMARY SOURCE

Devil's Island Fugitives: One of seven fugitives who fled from France's Devil's Island penal colony in Cayenne, French Guiana, in January 1938. He is shown here receiving water and assistance after arriving in Port-of-Spain, Trinidad, after a 600-mile, 18-day journey in an open boat, the last four days without food or water. AP IMAGES

About the Photographer: The photograph was taken by an anonymous Associated Press photographer.

INTRODUCTION

Both Great Britain and France sought to rid themselves of criminals by banishing them to the New World. Great Britain used Australia while France operated a penal colony known as Devil's Island in French Guiana from 1852 to 1945.

Prison sentences for criminals were rare in England before the late eighteenth century. Punishment more typically took the form of hanging or whipping. Faced with a growing and unruly population of petty criminals and political rebels, however, the British government began shipping them to colonies in North America and the Caribbean. The scale of the operation was modest, about 700 felons per year. Beginning in 1787, however, after the American Revolution, Britain began sending prisoners to Australia. In all, about 160,000 British convicts went to Australia before transportation stopped in 1868.

France developed penal colonies relatively late. The French empire did not cover as much territory as the British, making it difficult to find the right isolated spot. Additionally, the French had a functioning police force and an effective penal system at home. Yet the Australian model prompted the French to consider the option. The French sought a place with a healthy climate, fertile ground, and that was far enough away to create an obstacle to escape yet close enough that transporting criminals there would not be too expensive.

French Guiana had the right location and good soil but possessed a deadly climate. Between 1852 and 1938, over 56,000 mostly male prisoners went to Ile du Diable or Devil's Island; 90 percent of them died there of disease and abuse. The underfed naked convicts often were forced to work in water up to their waists. Prisoners sentenced to a term of less than eight years had to spend an equal period of time living in the colony after their release. Prisoners with sentences of more than eight years had to remain in the colony permanently. Although escape was difficult and the punishments severe, prisoners frequently tried to escape.

PRIMARY SOURCE

DEVIL'S ISLAND FUGITIVES

See primary source image.

SIGNIFICANCE

The French government believed that sending prisoners to French Guiana would help stabilize the colony's population and make it into the same sort of success as Australia. But the prisoners' high death rate did little to help the colony's numbers.

After waves of bad publicity and the election of the Popular Front government in France, the French stopped exporting prisoners to Devil's Island in 1938. World War II and the German occupation of France delayed closure of the base until 1946. By that time, however, it had gained everlasting notoriety for the prisoners who passed through it, including the wrongly convicted French army officer Alfred Dreyfus.

French Guiana is still part of France. Unlike the peoples of other European colonies in the Caribbean who demanded independence after 1945, the people of French Guiana wanted to remain part of the French nation. As a result, they enjoy one of the highest standards of living in the Caribbean.

FURTHER RESOURCES

Books

Miles, Anthony. *Devil's Island: Colony of the Damned.* Berkeley, CA: Ten Speed Press, 1988.

Redfield, Peter. *Space in the Tropics: From Convicts to Rockets in French Guiana.* Berkeley: University of California Press, 2000.-//Gale Research//DTD Document V2.0//EN">

Must They Die?

Photograph

By: William A. Reuben

Date: March 6, 1951

Source: Reuben, William A. "To Secure Justice in the Rosenberg Case." New York: National Committee to Secure Justice in the Rosenberg Case, 1951.

About the Photographer: William A. Reuben wrote a seven-part series of articles for the socialist journal *National Guardian*, which were published along with letters from the Rosenbergs in the pamphlet "To Secure Justice in the Rosenberg Case."

INTRODUCTION

Charged under the Espionage Act of 1917, Julius and Ethel Rosenberg were accused of giving critical information about nuclear and other weapons development to the Soviet Union. Following their conviction in 1951 and execution in 1953, critics claimed their sentence was excessive and that the Rosenbergs were victims of a growing fear of communism in the U.S.

Julius Rosenberg, born to Polish immigrant parents in 1918, studied electrical engineering at the City College of New York, where he became active in the Young Communist League. Ethel Greenglass, a social activist fellow member of the Young Communist League, was several years older than Rosenberg. After they married, the couple became full members of the American Communist Party. They left the party in 1943, claiming they wanted to spend more time with their family. In reality, however, it allowed them to pursue espionage activities. Julius was fired from his civilian job with the U.S. Army Signal Corps when it was discovered that he had lied about his membership in the Communist Party.

In 1950 the Rosenbergs were accused of giving the Soviets sketches of atomic weaponry components and other crucial technical information from the Manhattan project, the secret government program that developed America's atomic bomb. Rosenberg's brother-in-law, David Greenglass, also a socialist, worked as a military machinist on the project. He confessed that he had agreed to provide information to Julius, who then passed it on to Soviet intelligence.

Aleksandr Feklisov, a KGB intelligence officer who worked in the Russian consulate office in New York, recruited and ran a network of spies in the U.S. He first met Julius Rosenberg in 1943 and claimed to have had over 50 meetings with him from 1943 to 1946. In 1997 Feklisov revealed that Rosenberg had given the Russians the information that enabled them to build a proximity fuse—a device necessary for several weapons, including one that shot down an American U2 spy plane in 1960.

The U.S. Federal Bureau of Investigation (FBI) began to unravel the arrangements between Greenglass and Rosenberg when they arrested Harry Gold, a courier for the Soviet spy ring who in turn sent the information to Anatoly Yakolev, vice-consul at the Soviet embassy in New York City.

The authorities charged Ethel Rosenberg hoping to pressure her husband into confessing and naming his coconspirators, even though evidence against her was minimal. Throughout their trials, and up to the time of their execution, the Rosenbergs vehemently

Julius and Ethel Rosenberg leave federal court in New York City after being arraigned on charges of espionage, August 23, 1950. © CORBIS

asserted their innocence. Gold and Greenglass received prison sentences, not the death penalty, in exchange for their cooperation with authorities and testimony. Greenglass later admitted that he lied about his sister Ethel's involvement to protect his own wife. Ethel Rosenburg became the first woman killed in the U.S. since Mary Surratt, convicted of complicity in the assassination of Abraham Lincoln, was hanged.

PRIMARY SOURCE

MUST THEY DIE?

See primary source image.

SIGNIFICANCE

The Rosenbergs' appeals ended in the U.S. Supreme Court, when the justices, in special session, voted 6–3 to permit their execution. For two years there was a tremendous amount of support on their

ETHEL AND JULIUS ROSENBERG
Victims of a cold war Sacco-Vanzetti case?

MUST THEY DIE?

By William A. Reuben

ON March 6, 1951, in a federal courtroom at Foley Square in New York City, this nation's first atom-bomb spy trial began, when the clerk-of-court solemnly intoned:

"The United States of America versus Julius Rosenberg, Ethel Rosenberg and Morton Sobell."

U.S. Atty. Irving Saypol announced that the government was ready.

Julius and Ethel Rosenberg were defended by Emanuel H. Bloch and his father, Alexander Bloch; Sobell was represented by Edward M. Kuntz and Harold M. Phillips.

Nearly 300 talesmen were questioned before a jury of 12 plus four alternates could be seated. It is singular that in a city more than 30% Jewish in population, not a single talesman of Jewish extraction survived the day and a half of questioning before a jury was seated.

TRIAL BY PRESS: The government announced it would call 118 witnesses. Among them were to be top nuclear physicists Dr. J. Robert Oppenheimer and Dr. Harold C. Urey and Lieut. Gen. Leslie Groves, head of the war-time atomic bomb project.

PRIMARY SOURCE

Must They Die?: Ethel and Julius Rosenberg during their trial for espionage, followed by part of an article titled "Must They Die?" by William A. Reuben. PUBLIC DOMAIN behalf, with thousands of people in the U.S. and in Europe marching in protest. The Rosenbergs' two young sons, Michael and Robert, carried signs that read, "Don't Kill My Mommy and Daddy." The White House received many letters asking for clemency, which was denied by both Presidents Truman and Eisenhower.

In the years following their executions, Rosenberg supporters claimed the couple had been victims of a McCarthy-era witch-hunt. But in his posthumously published memoirs, Kruschev himself praised the Rosenbergs for hastening Soviet development of atomic weapons. And in 1995 the U.S. National Security Agency released transcripts of the Venona Project, a 1940s intelligence operation in which Soviet espionage cables were intercepted and decrypted. The cables proved decisively that Julius Rosenberg had spied for the Soviet Union. Strong evidence against Ethel Rosenberg, however, has never been conclusive.

FURTHER RESOURCES

Books

Haynes, J.E., and H. Klehr. *Venona: Decoding Soviet Espionage in America*. Yale University Nota Bene, 1999.

Radosh, R., and J. Milton. *The Rosenberg File*. 2nd ed. Holt, Rinehart, and Winston, 1997.

Reuben, W.A. *To Secure Justice in the Rosenberg Case*. New York: National Committee to Secure Justice in the Rosenberg Case, 1951. Michigan State University Library Archives. <http://archive.lib.msu.edu/AFS/dmc/radicalism/public/all/securejusticerosenberg/> (accessed January 28, 2006).

Roberts, S. *The Brother: The Untold Story of the Rosenberg Case*. Random House, 2001.

Web sites

BBC. "Wars and Conflict: The Cold War." <http://www.bbc.co.uk/history/war/coldwar> (accessed January 28, 2006).

City College of New York Libraries. Reference and Research. "Government Views of the Rosenberg Spy Case." <http://www.ccny.cuny.edu/library/Divisions/Government/rosenbergs.html> (accessed January 28, 2006).

NOVA Online. Tyson, Peter. "Read Venona Intercepts" <http://www.pbs.org/wgbh/nova/venona/intercepts.html> (accessed January 28, 2006).

University of Missouri–Kansas City School of Law. "Famous Trials: The Rosenberg Trial." <http://www.law.umkc.edu/faculty/projects/ftrials/rosenb/ROSENB.HTM; (accessed January 28, 2006).

Not To My Heart's Liking

Book excerpt

By: Bo Lozoff

Date: 1985

Source: Lozoff, Bo. *We're All Doing Time: A Guide to Getting Free*. Durham, NC: Human Kindness Foundation, 1985.

About the Author: Bo Lozoff, along with his wife, Sita, founded the Prison-Ashram Project in 1973, with the help of Ram Dass. The initial premise of the project entailed going into prisons and offering educational programs involving yoga and meditation, spirituality, and self-awareness. Their Human Kindness Foundation, as well as the book *We're All Doing Time* stemmed from the same philosophy of kindness, compassion, self-awareness, and a sincere belief in the possibility of rehabilitation from a criminal lifestyle.

INTRODUCTION

Bo Lozoff was an early advocate of a paradigm similar to that utilized in prison's with faith-based cell blocks, in which incarcerated felons are permitted to live in housing units aligned with specific spiritual practices, and to encourage the embodiment of that religious or spiritual philosophy in their rehabilitation and educational efforts as well as in their day-to-day functioning within the prison system.

In the early 1970s, Lozoff sought to create meditation and spiritual practice groups in high security correctional facilities, and was not permitted to do so. In collaboration with Ram Dass, he decided to try to create an analogous movement within the United States prison system in which prisoners could shift their thinking about incarceration, turning their cells into virtual *ashrams*. It was their (Lozoff and Ram Dass) intention to create a program of education and spiritual teaching, tailored to the needs of incarcerated individuals. Lozoff began a widespread project in which he contacted inmates and sought their feedback and guidance on the generation of a curriculum that would be suited to their needs. In addition, he and his wife, Sita, began to put together materials for a series of workshops that could be incorporated into the inmate programming at lower security facilities. The Prison-Ashram Project was well underway by the mid–1970s, and the philosophy of prison as ashram was being practiced by inmates all over the country.

Lozoff's book, *We're All Doing Time*, has been sent to individual convicts as well as prison libraries throughout the country, and in several countries around the world. It has been translated into the more widely spoken global languages (Spanish, Italian, and French). The book is available to incarcerated individuals without any cost, through the auspices of the Human Kindness Foundation. The objectives of the Prison-Ashram Project entail encouraging individuals to take full responsibility for their own behavior (past as well as current and future), to engage in inner-directed spiritual practice, and to become positive forces of change within themselves, their immediate environment, and the world.

One of the major concerns expressed by those involved in Lozoff's charitable organization, the Human Kindness Foundation (HKF) is that persons who are incarcerated, are not involved in rehabilitation efforts, and that a system based on retributive, rather than restorative, justice, ultimately creates more violence and crime than it corrects. The HKF posits that many jails and prisons are very effective at instilling bitterness and violence among those incarcerated, and that one way of quelling this would be to completely separate violent from nonviolent inmates. Robin Casarjian's Houses of Healing program is similar to that proposed by the HKF. It encourages inmates to look for the stillness within themselves, and to find a place of peace, rather than one of anger and violence. Both types of (prison) program advocate shifting to a life that is inner-directed and founded on peaceful interaction and higher meaning as the most effective means of achieving rehabilitation. The letter below is from a prisoner on death row in Idaho who is seeking help in obtaining peace in the context of his crimes and incarceration.

PRIMARY SOURCE

Dear Friends,

I'm searching for my spiritual awakening that so far I've not been able to find, and my life has come to a point where I need to find myself before I'm lost in the terrible maze of unknowing.

Let me take a few minutes to tell you a little about myself and my present situation. Hopefully it will help you to know what it is I'm trying to find. I'm twenty-seven years old, born Sept. 8, 1950. I'm presently in the Idaho State Prison for first-degree murder, two counts. I was sentenced to death in March 1976, but the Idaho Supreme Court vacated my death penalty. (Tommy's death penalty

has been reinstated, and at this time [1985] he's back on death row.) These two charges in Idaho aren't the only ones I have. There are even more in other states. Please let me explain why I did these cold-blooded, without any mercy, killings.

In April of 1974, eleven men entered my home in Portland, Oregon, raped my seventeen-year-old wife, who was three months pregnant at the time, then threw her four stories out our apartment window.

You see, I had been running drugs and guns for some people out of Nevada. My wife had asked me to stop so I tried to get out but they said no. On my next run I kept the goods I was to deliver and told them I'd turn it over to the feds if they tried causing me any trouble. I never would have, but they thought I was serious. Well, they set me up on a phony bust to get me out of the way thinking I had told my wife where I had stashed the stuff. I never did!

So, when they went to our house, after beating her and realizing she really didn't know where I put the stuff, they gang-raped her and threw her out the window. By some freak accident she lived for several months after that, long enough to tell me who most of the eleven were. She committed suicide while in a state mental institution, as her body was so crippled up from the fall, she had lost all hope and just wanted to die. In August of 1974, I went after the eleven guys who did it and caught nine of them in several different states. I was unable to complete my death mission and get the last two because I got caught here in Idaho.

Since all of this happened, I've had no inner peace at all. All I can think of is my wife, the only person who ever loved me and all I had in this world. I can see the men I killed and the look of pure fear and disbelief that I'd found them, as I took their lives. I'm not saying I was right for what I did, and I can't really say I'm sorry. I only know that I have no peace, happiness, or love, but at times I feel that I can have, but I just don't know where to look. I need help but I have nobody to turn to. My family has turned from me and I have nobody to write to or to visit me. I can't carry my burden alone anymore, so I ask you from the deepest of my heart, please send me any material that you think might help me. I am in maximum-security, solitary confinement and have been for almost four years.

Really, all I want to do is find that something that I know for a fact exists that will free me from all my burdens.

Sincerely yours, Tommy/Idaho

Indiana Governor Mitch Daniels, right, is surrounded by a group of inmates after speaking at an open house for the first Faith and Character-Based Purposeful Living Units at the Correctional Industrial Facility in Pendleton, Indiana, 2005. AP IMAGES

SIGNIFICANCE

America has become a country noted for its crime rate, its exceptionally high degree of interpersonal violence, and the number of individuals incarcerated at any given time. Since the institution of the truth in sentencing and "three strikes and you're out" laws, the number of persons incarcerated in the United States has increased exponentially. As a consequence, prisons have become crowded, and educational, vocational, and rehabilitative programming have all suffered. Many sociologists have described American prisons, particularly higher-security facilities, as human warehouses, where inmates have a great deal of time, every day, to dwell on their anger and beliefs about injustices perpetrated upon them. It is the belief of Bo Lozoff and others like him that prisons encourage anger and negative behavior, that they do not require inmates to look inward and to take personal responsibility for their criminal actions, and that they do not mandate any form of reparative justice or restitution for wrongdoing. It is Lozoff's belief that there is no place for the concept of compassion within the present criminal justice system—neither for nor by the inmates. In jails and prisons set up to accommodate general populations—those in which the inmates are permitted to move about within portions of the facility and are not confined exclusively to their cells—violent and nonviolent offenders are typically mixed within the same housing units. There is considerable between-inmate violence in many prisons, and gangs are very active within the walls. In some jails and prisons, there is significant predatory violence, in which young, "soft"(either overtly homosexual, or not stereotypically hard-core masculine inmates), nonviolent, easily intimidated inmates are harassed, bullied, or brutalized (physically, sexually, or both).

The spiritual underpinnings of the Human Kindness Foundation and Houses of Healing paradigms are centered on the concepts of personal responsibility, reconciliation, compassion, and forgiveness. The premise of the prison cell as ashram suggests embarking on an inward (spiritual) journey in which inmates can use meditation and spiritual practice in order to transform and improve themselves. It is Lozoff's assertion that the prison cell can be likened to a monastery, as there are limited trappings of society, and few distractions to prevent the fostering of spiritual growth. Inmates can use their time to grow and develop as peaceful spiritual beings who are potentially capable of making positive contributions to society, whether from within or outside the prison walls.

Much of the HKF's work is founded on the restorative justice model, which holds that any criminal act impacts the whole of the community, which then must be repaired and restored to wholeness. They would suggest that the criminal offender, if possible, be returned to the community (after a period of incarceration, if that is adjudicated) and encouraged to make a positive contribution by becoming a viable, employed, proactive member of society. From a practical standpoint, this is often a difficult ideal to achieve, as it is extremely difficult for convicted felons to obtain and keep gainful employment.

The Human Kindness Foundation has created a sort of halfway house called the Kindness House on their North Carolina grounds, in which returning prisoners can obtain transitional housing, engage in spiritual practice, and become involved in human service activities. One of the larger tasks to be accomplished while in residence is the acquisition of job-related skills: the ability to adhere to a fixed daily schedule, to meet personal responsibilities, to work for another person, and to acquire some basic employability training. Lozoff has also created a source of direct employment and job training, by opening a biodiesel refinery to be staffed primarily by former inmates. In addition to his direct work with inmates and former prisoners, Lozoff advocates that all people show kindness and compassion toward former inmates and recovering addicts (drugs and alcohol) who are striving to turn their lives around and participate in society in a meaningful fashion.

FURTHER RESOURCES

Books

Casarjian, Robin. *Houses of Healing: A Prisoner's Guide to Inner Power and Freedom.* Boston, Massachusetts: The Lionheart Foundation, 1995.

Kipnis, Aaron. *Angry Young Men: How Parents, Teachers and Counselors Can Help "Bad Boys" Become Good Men.* San Francisco, CA: Jossey-Bass, 1999.

Lozoff, Bo. *It's a Meaningful Life, It Just Takes Practice.* New York, New York: Penguin Compass, 2000.

Web sites

Human Kindness Foundation. "Prison-Ashram Project." <http://www.humankindness.org/project.html> (accessed March 11, 2006).

Shambhala Sun Online. "A Nation Behind Bars." <http://www.shambhalasun.com/Archives/Columnists/> (accessed March 11, 2006).

Death by Lethal Injection: Missouri

Book excerpt

By: Fred A. Leuchter

Date: October 15, 1988

Source: Fred A. Leuchter. "Death by Lethal Injection: Missouri." In *Lethal Injection Machine Manual: State of Missouri.* Boston, Mass.: Fred A. Leuchter Associates, 1988.

About the Author: Fred A. Leuchter ran a company which specialized in the design and manufacture of execution equipment, including devices for delivering execution and lethal injection. Leuchter famously argued that the Holocaust could not have taken place after traveling to concentration camps to carry out research into gas chambers. In 1990, he was exposed as having no formal engineering qualifications, even though he sold his equipment to several states, including Missouri, as detailed below.

INTRODUCTION

Lethal injection was introduced into the United States as a means of execution when it was adopted by the state of Oklahoma in 1977. The first person to be executed by lethal injection was Charles Brooks, in Texas, in 1982. Since then, 842 people have been executed by lethal injection in the United States. It has

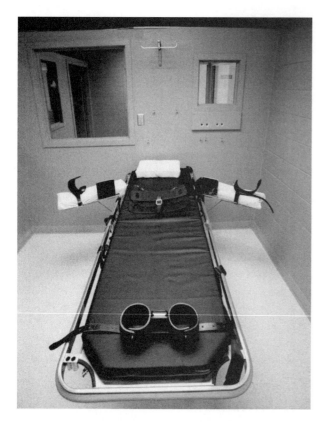

The lethal injection equipment at the Orgeon State Penitentiary, 1997. Subjects are strapped to the table and connected a a machine in another room with tubes, through which the letal chemicals are injected. AP IMAGES.

become the leading form of execution, used by thirty-seven of the thirty-eight states that have the death penalty. The concept of execution by lethal injection arose after a number of botched hangings in New York in the late 19th century. A committee was set up to consider alternatives to hanging and came out in favor of electrocution, as lethal injection was strongly disapproved of by the medical profession. The subject came up again at the start of the modern era of the death penalty, when it was ruled constitutional again in 1976 by the Supreme Court. By that time, modern medical technology made the idea of lethal injection more of a practical proposition.

Death by lethal injection involves three different drugs. The prisoner is strapped down to a gurney and two needles attached to long tubes are inserted into veins in the arms. The tubes are connected to several intravenous drips though a hole in a cement block wall. One drip contains saline and this is started first. At a signal from the warder, a curtain is raised so the prisoner is exposed to witnesses in an adjoining room. Then a drip with an anesthetic, sodium thiopental, is

started and the prisoner is put to sleep. Next, a drug called pancuronium bromide (Pavulon) is injected. This paralyzes all the muscles so the prisoner stops breathing. Finally, potassium chloride is injected and this stops the heart. Therefore, the condemned prisoner dies from a combination of anaesthetic overdose and respiratory and cardiac arrest. Sodium thiopental and pancuronium bromide are both used clinically, but the doses used in lethal injection are far higher than the therapeutic doses. The manual extract below describes the lethal injection process in more detail.

PRIMARY SOURCE

EXECUTION BY LETHAL INJECTION: MISSOURI

The Fred A. Leuchter Associates, Inc. Modular Lethal Injection Machine is designed to sequentially deliver variable quantities of three solutions at variable time periods. Utilizing standard 60cc disposable syringes, it is essentially driven by weighted pistons depressing the syringe plungers. It is designed to sequentially deliver the solutions at time intervals controlled by an electrical, solid-state, timing system powered by a sealed battery which receives its charge from the power line. The system is designed to be activated by two executioners: a solid-state digital circuit will randomly determine which executioner controls the system, but will not retain the chosen executioner in memory. Since it operates from battery power, it is not subject to power line failure. Three electrical solenoids cause the weighted pistons to depress the respective syringe plungers. Chemical delivery is via a single intravenous line, commoned by an eight-port stainless steel manifold with luer lock entry ports. This line joins with a standard intravenous administration set dispensing saline solution on a continuous basis into the subject. Three solid state timers operate the solenoids and the stages are initiated by switch-controlled relays monitoring the volume of solution in each syringe.

In the event of a timing system failure, an electrical override is provided to control the solenoid operation. Two switches are used to control the depression of each successive plunger. Any one, or all three plungers, may be controlled, depending upon the problem encountered. The controlling switch group is preset during machine makeready. Thus, the system still functions as a one-of-two executioner controlled system. In the event of total electrical failure, or a partial mechanical failure of the Prime System, a second Back-up System, which is strictly mechanical, is employed. This system consists of a redundant set of piston driven syringes and is operated by three sets of double pull knobs. Determination of which executioner will control the system is made during makeready. Both knobs of each set are pulled in tandem sequentially and the system operates as a one-of-two executioner system. The use of either back-up system requires that sequential timing between successive plunger actuations be determined by clock and command. All three systems have been engineered with a minimal amount of components for trouble free operation, and it is unlikely that a systems failure should occur in any of the three systems. However, should failure occur, the redundant systems should insure a problem-free execution.

Provision is made for systems purge via two saline filled syringes and an external saline supply is utilized to prevent coagulation at the needle tip, in the usual manner. The system is designed to accept eight 60cc syringes; two for saline, two for Pentathol, two for Pancuronium Bromide, and two for Potassium Chloride. Each of the six functional syringes has a positive piston stop pin to prevent premature operation of the system.

The system consists of two modules; The Control Module and The Delivery Module. The Control Module is made up of the power, sequential timing and control circuitry. The Delivery Module consists of the electro-mechanical and mechanical drive assemblies, syringes, and manifold, to ensure proper fluid delivery.

THE CONTROL MODULE

The Control Module is designed utilizing state-of-the-art, solid-state, power, digital and timing circuitry and conventional electrical switches. The on/off and function switches are key controlled to prevent accidental operation. The battery, power supply and charging circuit are also part of this package.

The Control Panel itself contains the Key-controlled on/off switch and two executioner switches (which are pushed simultaneously) for the prime system; the key-controlled function switch for the electrical back-up system (to determine which executioner activates the system) and six operating switches, arranged in three pairs, for the back-up system. These switches are thrown simultaneously by the executioners and control the sequential dispensing of the fluids, individually. Each pair is thrown simultaneously with the proper time interval between operations when the electrical back-up system is utilized.

There are two sets of monitoring lights, one on The Control Module and a redundant set on The Delivery Module. A system-on light indicates power on. Each syringe is monitored by a three light sequence. Red indicates Ready, Yellow indicates Operating and Green indicates Completion. The sequence occurs three times, once for each syringe. The Control Module shall be in The Control Room.

THE DELIVERY MODULE

The Delivery Module consists of an eight inlet, one outlet stainless steel manifold containing two purge syringes filled with saline solution, two syringes filled with Sodium Pentathol, two syringes filled with Pancuronium Bromide, and two syringes filled with Potassium Chloride. The outlet is connected to a disposable intravenous administration set terminating in a needle tip and connected to a saline dispensing bag a short distance from the manifold. Additional hardware includes the cylinder matrix for supporting the syringe assembly, three electrical solenoids, three solenoid pull rods, six mechanical pull knobs, six connecting cables, six weight stop pins, six weighted pistons, six cylinders, and nine indicator lights. A total of eight disposable 60cc syringes are utilized in the system. During system makeready, all three solenoid pull rods are used, but only three of the six connecting cables, one for each set of two. The pull knobs are arranged in three pairs and both from each pair are pulled, one by each executioner, but only one from each pair is connected (either all odd or all even numbers). All manifold inlet connections are accomplished by luer lock fittings. Two purge syringe back flow stop brackets and twelve piston spaces are also part of The Delivery Module.

During makeready, the two saline syringes are used to bleed the system, the other syringes are installed, after filling, in the proper order, as assemblies, with the weighted piston, cylinder and piston stop pin. The cables are connected in the proper sequence and the solenoid pull rods inserted into the pistons. The Delivery Module shall be in the Execution Chamber.

PROCEDURE

It is suggested that the following procedure might be followed to facilitate a smooth execution. These dosages are established, although not recommended, through consultation with pharmaceutical manufacturers. We at Fred A. Leuchter Associates, Inc., not being pharmacologists, do not recommend, or in any way guarantee the efficacy of these chemicals or dosages, but simply communicate the recommendations of the manufacturers.

1. Pre-injection 10cc antihistamine, one half hour prior to execution.
2. Pre-injection 8cc 2% Sodium Pentathol (5 grams/250 ml, Abbott Labs #6108-01) five minutes prior to transmittal of subject to death chamber.
3. Machine injection 15cc Sodium Pentathol 2% Solution (as above) delivered over a ten second time period.
4. One minute wait.
5. Machine injection 15cc Pancuronium Bromide (Pavulon, Organon Drug Co., 2ml/2mg/ml) over a ten second time period.
6. One minute wait.
7. Machine injection 15cc Potassium Chloride (KCl Injectable solution).
8. Two minute wait.
9. Execution over.

SYSTEM NOTES

Times may be varied up to two and one half minutes by setting the timer in The Control Module.

Volumes to be dispensed may be varied by reducing the volumes in the syringe and utilizing the appropriate piston spacer.

Speeds of injection may be varied by using needles of different sizes. It is recommended not to exceed a twelve gauge. Fourteen gauge angiocaths are supplied.

The battery contains sufficient power at full charge to sustain operation for at least six usages of the system at fifteen minute time intervals before recharge is necessary. A uniform, slow-rate charge circuit, designed to guarantee a maximum battery life, will completely charge the battery over a 14 hour time period from 110 vac line power. The battery is a 12-volt 15-ampere hour battery.

DISCLAIMER

Fred A. Leuchter Associates, Inc. assumes no liability for the intended or actual use of this device.

OPERATIONAL PROCEDURE

PRE-SETUP

1. Charge battery for 18 hours or more prior to usage. To charge battery, plug unit into 110 vac and turn key switch to charge position.
2. Remove all cylinders and pistons. This is IMPORTANT.
3. Test electrical operation. Turn both key switches to ARMED.
4. Pull solenoid pins forward.
5. Push both actuator switches and watch solenoid rods pull in sequence. One minute will occur between successive pulls. Depress each syringe switch located in Delivery Module after its solenoid rod has pulled.
6. Repeat using override switches, twice: once for left and once for right position.
7. Check syringe switches for proper clearance with piston disk in down position. Adjust switch up or down, with locknuts, for clearance at proper dosage. In all cases, switch must be set with piston resting on depressed syringe plunger (zero cc), with syringe properly installed in cylinder and on luer lock connection. If spacer is required for dosage, spacer must be affixed to piston. After height is determined, switch is locked into position with nuts; actuator arm at maximum position under switch disk, but not bent or flexed beyond proper depression point.
8. Verify switch operation by manually dropping pistons on switches in sequence while repeating step 5.
9. Recharge.

SETUP

1. Remove all six pistons and cylinders from Delivery Module.
2. Cylinders are numbered from right to left from 1 thru 6, with the two end syringes for purge.
3. Consult chart for dosages and spacers.
4. Assemble pistons and spacer with velcro pads.
5. Fill purge syringes with 60cc saline solution and install on manifold by inserting into bracket and gently pushing luer lock tip into mating inlet with graduations on syringe facing operator. Turn one full turn to the right (clockwise from top).
6. Depress both purge syringes until fluid escapes from all manifold inlets. Pinch outlet on extension set.
7. Fill syringes with proper chemical dosages. Insert proper cylinder and lock proper syringe into cylinder retaining ring (slot) with graduations facing operator. Lift cylinder/syringe assemble and set luer lock tip of syringe into mating inlet. Pushing gently down, twist assemble one full turn to the right (clockwise from top) until graduations face operator. Install in order of 1 thru 6 from right. Install piston and stop pin after each cylinder/syringe installation. Note: cylinders 2, 4 and 6 use pistons with switch disk. Cylinders 1 & 2, Pentathol; cylinders 3 & 4, Pavulon; cylinders 5 & 6, KCl.
8. Unpinch iv extension and depress both purge syringes until fluid escapes from outlet in iv extension. Install purge syringe back flow stop brackets. Pinch iv extension outlet.
9. Slip solenoid pull rods through piston holes, cylinders 2, 4 & 6. Twist cylinder to check insertion. If it will not twist, insertion was proper. This is IMPORTANT.
10. Install pull cable through piston holes cylinders 1, 3 & 5. Verify insertion visually. This is IMPORTANT. Use cables 1, 3 & 5 or 2, 4 & 6. STOP. Are the necessary spacers in place and backflow brackets installed? If so, proceed. When ready, remove piston stop pins. DANGER. System is now ARMED. Close door. See item 5 under use.
11. Spacers and back flow stop brackets MUST be used as described.

USE

After completing test procedure and setup of Delivery Module, proceed as follows:

1. Pre-inject subject with 10cc antihistamine one half hour before execution.
2. Pre-inject subject with 8cc Pentathol 5 minutes before execution.
3. Strap subject to gurney and install iv, 1000ml 0.9 % sodium chloride via 14 gauge x 1.5 inch angiocath and start iv.

4. Transmit subject to execution chamber and connect Delivery Module iv to saline iv.

5. Remove piston stop pins from Delivery Module cylinders.

6. Turn both key switches to armed.

7. Begin execution on command by depressing both station buttons.

8. After activation, the following will occur:

   A. First syringe begins 4 seconds after start and a yellow light will light.

   B. Green light will indicate first stage complete in approximately 10 seconds.

   C. Second syringe will activate with yellow light one minute after first green light and will deliver solution and green light in approximately 10 seconds.

   D. Third syringe will activate with yellow light one minute after second green light and a third green light will indicate completion in approximately 10 seconds.

   E. After third green light, turn main switch to off. One minute later the execution will be completed.

(Approximate total time, 4 minutes.)

Note: if a malfunction occurs, it should be handled in the following manner:

   1. Any yellow light fails to operate.
   Cause: Timer malfunction.
   Remedy: Continue execution using electrical override switches. If the first yellow light fails, use all switches. If second yellow light fails, use switches two and three. If third yellow light fails, then use switch three.

   2. Any green light fails to operate.
   Cause: Defective syringe.
   Remedy: Continue execution using mechanical pull knobs. If the first green light fails, use all six knobs. If second green light fails, use phase two knobs. If third green light fails, then use only phase three knobs.

Note: Mechanical override can be used alone by pulling both knobs marked phase one and waiting 70 seconds, then pulling both knobs marked phase two and waiting 70 seconds, then pulling both knobs marked phase three.

9. After subject has been removed, remove back flow stop brackets from purge syringes and depress completely to purge system.

SIGNIFICANCE

Lethal injection is supposed to be more humane than other forms of execution. It may, therefore, have allowed executions to take place which would not otherwise have happened. Although the idea of putting someone to sleep, as one would an injured animal, may add some weight to the arguments of those supporting the death penalty, lethal injection is still associated with some serious drawbacks.

First, the condemned prisoner still undergoes the severe physical and mental stress associated with being on Death Row, especially as the execution time approaches. Second, the medicalization of execution gives rise to serious ethical and practical problems. Two of the three drugs used in lethal injection have genuine therapeutic uses. To use them to kill appears perverse and creates real ethical problems for doctors and nurses. Many professional medical associations, such as the American Medical Association, the World Medical Association, and the International Council of Nurses, have declared that taking part in executions is strictly against their ethical code. The fact that doctors and nurses are dedicated to healing the sick is a deeper issue than the misuse of the drugs used in lethal injection. To carry out tasks related to execution is a clear perversion of their duty, according to many professional organizations.

Yet lethal injection is a medical procedure and to be done correctly, some input is needed from medical personnel, argue prison authorities. This conflict has led to various legal actions being taken by doctors, their professional associations, and even prisoners against prison authorities in various states. In general, a doctor will at least certify that the prisoner is dead following lethal injection.

Although prison technicians can be trained in lethal injection, they are more likely to get it wrong than someone who is medically qualified. For instance, they may inject into a muscle instead of a vein, which can cause extreme pain, as can a clogged needle. Many prisoners have damaged veins because of previous intravenous drug use and it can be difficult to find a suitable vein for carrying out the lethal injection. This can lead to long and extremely stressful delays while the prisoner is still strapped in position, waiting for the procedure to begin.

The arguments against lethal injection are strengthened by a number of botched executions in recent years. In 1985, Stephen Peter Morin, who had a history of drug abuse, experienced a delay of forty-five minutes before his execution in Texas as technicians searched for a suitable vein. Also in Texas, the execution of Raymond Landry in 1988 was interrupted when the syringe came out of his vein, spraying the deadly chemicals all over the room. The syringe had to be re-inserted but this apparently took several minutes and was done without witness observation. Finally, the manual extract above refers to a lethal injection machine used in Missouri, the state where Bert Leroy Hunter suffered a botched execution in 2000. He had an unusual reaction to the drugs and one witness reported his violent convulsions during the injection process. Another Missouri execution went wrong in 1995, when the chemicals stopped circulating during the lethal injection of Emmitt Foster. The straps binding him to the gurney had been fixed too tight—the coroner had to step into the death chamber, diagnose the problem and order the straps to be loosened so the execution could proceed; death did not occur until half an hour after the process began.

FURTHER RESOURCES

Books

Web sites

Amnesty International. "Lethal Injection: The Medical Technology of Execution." <http://web.amnesty.org/library/Index/engACT500011998> (accessed February 26, 2006).

BBC News. "New Rules for U.S. Lethal Injection." <http://news.bbc.co.uk/2/hi/americas/4715034.stm> (accessed February 26, 2006).

Death Penalty Information Center. "Methods of Execution." <http://www.deathpenaltyinfo.org/article.php?scid=8&did=245> (accessed February 26, 2006).

Execution by Electrocution

Book excerpt

By: Fred A. Leuchter

Date: November 27, 1989

Source: Fred A. Leuchter. "Execution by Electrocution" In *Modular Electrocution System Manual: State of Tennessee*. Boston, Mass.: Fred A. Leuchter Associates, 1989.

About the Author: Fred A. Leuchter ran a company which specialized in the design and manufacture of execution equipment, including devices for delivering execution by electrocution. Leuchter famously argued

that the Holocaust could not have taken place after traveling to concentration camps to carry out research into gas chambers. In 1990, he was exposed as having no formal engineering qualifications, even though he sold his equipment to several states, starting in Tennessee.

INTRODUCTION

The methods of execution that are allowed in the United States are: lethal injection, electrocution, gas chamber, hanging, and firing squad. Lethal injection is, increasingly, the preferred method. Electrocution, however, is still used in ten states, although it is the sole method used in Nebraska. In Illinois and Oklahoma, electrocution is held in reserve in case lethal injection were to be ruled unconstitutional. In Tennessee, where the electric chair described below was first used, all those sentenced to death after January 1, 1999, will be executed by lethal injection. Those sentenced before choose between lethal injection and electrocution.

The electric chair was first introduced in New York in 1888, supposedly as a more humane method of execution than hanging. It was used to execute one William Kemmler in 1890 and other states began to adopt the method. Since 1976, 152 people have been executed by electrocution in the electric chair, compared to 841 by lethal injection, eleven in the gas chamber, three by hanging and two by firing squad.

Even when carried out correctly, electrocution is a gruesome process. The condemned person is shaved and strapped into the chair with belts crossing his body. A skullcap-shaped electrode is placed on the scalp and forehead and a second electrode fixed to the leg. Electricity will pass through his body between the two electrodes.

The prisoner is blindfolded and the execution team withdraws to the observation room. A warden signals the executioner to pull a handle which connects to the power supply. An electric shock of 500 to 2000 volts passes through the prisoner's body, lasting for about thirty seconds. The current is then turned off and, once the body has cooled, doctors check to see if the heart has stopped. If not, then another jolt is applied and the process continues until the prisoner is dead. The manual extract below describes the equipment and process in more detail.

The electric chair at Somers, Connecticut, 1987. © UPI/
CORBIS-BETTMANN.

PRIMARY SOURCE

EXECUTION BY ELECTROCUTION: TENNESSEE

THE FRED A. LEUCHTER ASSOCIATES, INC. MODULAR
ELECTROCUTION SYSTEM

The design of an electrocution system involves the
consideration of a few, but very significant, requirements.
Voltage, current, connections, duration and number of
current applications (jolts).

Requirements

First, the system should contain three (3) electrodes. The
head should be fitted with a tightly fitting cap containing
an electrode with a saline solution moistened sponge. It
is through this electrode that the current is introduced.
Second, each ankle should be tightly fitted with an electrode, causing the current to divide and guaranteeing passage through the complete trunk of the subjects body.
Use of one (1) ankle electrode (instead of two [2]) will
almost always ensure a longer and more difficult electrocution. These two (2) ankle electrodes are the return path
of the current. Contact should be enhanced by using
saline salve or a sponge moistened with a saline solution
at each of the ankle connections. It is of the utmost
importance that good circuit continuity, with a minimum

amount of resistance, be maintained at the electrode
contacts. Further, a minimum of 2000 volts ac must be
maintained, after voltage drop, to guarantee permanent
disruption of the functioning of the autonomic nervous
system. Voltages lower than 2000 volts ac, at saturation,
cannot guarantee heart death and are, thus, not adequate
for electrocution, in that they may cause unnecessary
trauma to the subject prior to death. Failure to adhere to
these basic requirements could result in pain to the subject and failure to achieve heart death, leaving a brain
dead subject in the chair.

Medical Description

During electrocution there are two (2) factors that must
be considered: the conscious and the autonomic nervous
systems. Voltages in excess of 1500 volts ac are generally sufficient to destroy the conscious nervous system,
that which controls pain and understanding. Generally,
unconsciousness occurs in 4.16 milliseconds, which is
1/240 part of a second. This is twenty-four (24) times as
fast as the subjects conscious nervous system can
record pain. The autonomic nervous system is a little
more difficult, however, and generally requires in excess
of 2000 volts ac to seize the pacemaker in the subjects
heart. Generally, we compute the voltage at 2000 volts ac
plus 20%. After the voltage is applied and the subjects
body saturates, the voltage has dropped about 10%
(depending upon the resistance of the electrode contacts
and that of the subject body) and this should be taken into
consideration, as well. Current should be kept under six
(6) amperes to minimize body damage (cooking).

Ideally, the voltage is calculated thus:

The average man weighing 70 kilos (154 lbs.) requires
2000 volts ac to seize the heart.

Increase the voltage by 20% to accommodate subjects
with greater resistance.

2000 volts ac plus 20% equals 2400 volts ac. Increase
voltage by 10% for drop at saturation.

2400 volts ac plus 10% equals 2640 volts ac.

Thus, the voltage should be 2640 volts ac.

This 2640 volts ac should be applied in two (2) jolts of one
(1) minute each, spaced at a ten (10) second interval. On
occasion, the subjects heart will spasm, instead of seizing, during the first application of current and the application of the second jolt will generally eliminate this
problem. This spasm is due to excessive chemical build-
up (acetylcholine and sympathin) at the nerve junctions
and the ten (10) second wait generally allows for dissipa-
tion of the chemicals.

System Description

Fred A. Leuchter Associates, Inc. manufactures a low-
cost, state-of-the-art modular system for electrocution.

The system utilizes solid state circuitry for control and timing, current regulation to five (50) milliamperes (1%) and single and two (2) station control for operation. It is designed with plug-in components for ease in repair and maintenance, and because of its modular design can be installed in very little time by untrained personnel.

The control system is designed for a timing sequence which will deliver two (2) one (1) minute jolts at minimum of 2400 volts ac spaced ten (10) seconds apart. To guarantee fail-safe operation, a redundant system's timer activates and shuts down the system if any of the sequential timers fail. Additionally, there are two (2) modes of operation: single station and two (2) station. In single station, one (1) push button switch controls the operation. In two (2) station, two (2) switches are utilized and logic (computer) circuitry determines which switch causes operation. The two (2) station mode precludes the use of an executioner, since no one knows which of the two (2) switches activated the system. The system does not retain the operating switch in memory. Further, since the controls are operated electronically, the operator handles only low voltage equipment, being completely isolated from the high voltage, guaranteeing operator safety.

The high voltage circuitry is designed to deliver 2640 volts ac upon activation and, as the load saturates and the current increases, the voltage stabilizes at (or above) 2400 volts ac. The current is limited to five (5) amperes, maximum, by a current regulator. The voltage, in accordance with the standard formula for admittance, will drop approximately 10% or 240 volts, but the current will never exceed five (5) amperes with 1% (five [50] milliampere) regulation. A current limiting breaker protects the load in the event of a regulator failure and will open the circuit at six (6) amperes. The equipment is protected by a ninety (90) ampere overcurrent breaker.

The Power Supply

The power supply consists of a 208 volt ac primary, 2640 volt ac secondary transformer coupled to a saturable reactor with current monitoring circuitry, two (2) overcurrent limits and a high voltage contactor.

It is designed to deliver five (5) amperes at 1% (fifty [50] milliampere) regulation at 2400 volts ac, plus 10% (240 volts ac). This means that when the circuit is closed, 2640 volts ac is fed into the load. As the load saturates, the current increases and the voltage drops. At approximately ten (10) seconds into operation, the load is fully saturated and will appear to be approaching a direct short circuit. The current regulator, however, limits the current to five (5) amperes at the saturation voltage point of 2400 (minimum) volts ac. If the current regulator fails, an overcurrent breaker is set to trip at six (6) amperes.

The system operates by monitoring output current, processing it in a direct current amplifier, and applying it to a direct current coil which controls the flux density in the core of the reactor. It is, essentially, a highly accurate magnetic amplifier.

Additionally, the power supply contains overcurrent protection for both the equipment and the load and an output contactor for closing the high voltage circuit to the Electric Chair. All connections to the power supply, except those for the 208 volts ac in, which are terminal block, are via two (2) military-type circular connectors.

The Control Console

The control console is a sloped metal panel cabinet containing the timing circuitry, computer controlled switching circuitry and controls for the system operation. It contains two (2) key switches for circuit control and a key-controlled fail-safe switch for high voltage output.

The timing sequence is accomplished with two (2) solid-state one (1) minute timers and one (1) ten (10) second timer cascaded from a system's timer of 130 seconds, guaranteeing system shutdown after 130 seconds even in the event of a sequential timer failure. Timer activation is all by precision relay.

One (1) and two (2) station control is standard and is facilitated by solid-state circuitry. In single station control, one (1) switch operates an electronic relay and activates the system. In two (2) station control, two (2) switches are utilized and the logic (computer) circuitry chooses the switch which will activate the relay. This insures that no one will know which operator controlled the circuit, as with a firing squad. The system does not retain the operating switch in memory.

The Electric Chair

The electric chair consists of an oaken chair with an adjustable backrest, inherent leg electrodes, a leather and sponge helmet with electrode, a drip pan, a plexiglass seat and a non-incremental restraint system. It is covered with a high gloss epoxy paint similar to that which is used in the space program. It is connected to the power supply via one military type connector. This chair was fabricated in part with wood from Tennessee's original electric chair.

The ankle electrodes, which are fabricated onto the leg stock, are turned of solid brass. They accommodate a #6 conductor and are paralleled to ground.

The helmet consists of an outer helmet of leather and an inner helmet of copper mesh and sponge. It will disassemble for repair and the electrode will accommodate a #6 conductor.

The chair design includes a removable drip pan. The straps are of nylon aircraft construction and consist of two (2) ankle straps, two (2) wrist straps and one (1) cross-the-chest harness, all with quick release fasteners. All fasteners comprising the restraints are non-incremental, enabling a tighter fit.

The entire system, because of its modular design, may be installed by non-technical people in several hours and is fully field repairable.

SPECIFICATIONS

Power Supply

Voltage: 208 volts ac in, 2400 volts ac plus 10% or 2640 volts ac out.

Current: five (5) amperes at 1% (fifty [50] milliampere) regulation.

Overcurrent protection: six (6) amperes; ninety (90) amperes; load and equipment respectively.

Input: 208 volts ac, 75 Amp, 60 Hz, 15.5 VA.

Disconnect rated 208 volts ac, 100 Amp.

Main Transformer: Primary-195 volts ac, 68 amps, 13.2 KVA. Secondary-2640 volts ac, 5 amp.

Saturable reactor: 75 amp, 15 KVA.

Control Transformer: Primary-208 volts ac.Secondary-110 volts ac, 50-60 Hz, 750 KVA.Meters: 1 volt, 1 amp.

Terminations: two (2) MS (military-type) circular connectors, console and high voltage output. Terminal block, 208 volts ac input.

Enclosure: NEMA 12.

Control Console

Voltage: 110 volts ac.

Overcurrent protection: one (1) ampere; three (3) ampere.

Timing: sequential—one (1) minute; ten (10) seconds; one (1) minute. All solid-state with a 130 second system's timer.

Switches: three (3) lock type—two (2) for circuit control operation, one (1) for system fail-safe; two (2) operator switches.

Terminations: one (1) MS (military-type) circular connector.

Electric Chair

Material: oak.

Electrodes: all turned of solid brass, two (2) leg, one (1) helmet.

Helmet: leather, copper mesh and sponge.

Straps: nylon, aircraft-type; quick release.

DISCLAIMER

Fred A. Leuchter Associates, Inc. assumes no liability for the intended or actual use of this device.

SET-UP

1. Determine that the main disconnect is off. If not, turn off.

2. Determine that the Power Supply input circuit breaker is off. If not, turn off.

3. Determine that all switches on the Control Console are off: POWER ON switch and COMPUTER ON switch in left off position. Note specifically that ELECTRIC CHAIR FAILSAFE switch is in center off position.

4. Connect control cable between the Power Supply and the Control Console by inserting the polarized connectors and tightening the connector nuts. Connect the Control Console end first. The power is now supplied to the Control Console.

5. Verify power at the Control Console by turning Power On switch to right and verify SYSTEM ON light. Turn COMPUTER ON switch to right and verify COMPUTER ON light.

6. Verify ELECTRIC CHAIR FAILSAFE SWITCH by turning switch to left (OPERATION POSITION). Note that the ELECTRIC CHAIR ENERGIZED light is not on. If light is on, there is a system malfunction or someone activated the timing sequence. VERIFY. Turn the ELECTRIC CHAIR FAILSAFE SWITCH off (center) and then to the left (TEST POSITION). Verify ELECTRIC CHAIR ENERGIZED light on. Output contactor on Power Supply is closed. Turn all switches off in reverse sequence. Turn off the power supply input circuit breaker and the main disconnect, in that order.

Note Well: do not proceed unless the ELECTRIC CHAIR ENERGIZED light is OFF.

7. Complete test of Control Console as per instructions.

8. Complete test of Power Supply as per instructions.

9. Complete test of Electric Chair as per instructions.

10. Connect power cable between the Power Supply and the Electric Chair by inserting polarized connectors and tightening the connector nuts. Connect Electric Chair end first.

11. Turn on main disconnect.

12. Turn on Power Supply input circuit breaker. The Electrocution System is now ENERGIZED and ready for use.

NOTE WELL: Turn off both main disconnect and input circuit breaker when not using chair.

DANGER THE SYSTEM IS LIVE. Follow to Operational Procedure.

OPERATIONAL PROCEDURE

1. Steps 1. through 12. of SET UP should have been completed earlier.

2. Determine that the main disconnect is off and that the input circuit breaker to the Power Supply is off. Remove all keys to the Control Console and determine that all switches are off. If not, turn off. Determine that the Electric Chair Energized light is off. If not, shut electric chair failsafe switch to off (center position). DO NOT PROCEED UNLESS ELECTRIC CHAIR ENERGIZED LIGHT IS OFF. Only one key is to be used for operation.

3. Prepare subject for electrocution: Shave approximately a three Inch (3") diameter spot on the top of executee's head. Cut pants off to knees, slit pants to knees or supply subject with short pants.

4. Mix a saturated saline (salt water) solution (add salt until it will no longer mix to lukewarm water).

5. Wet sponge in helmet (saturate).

6. Wet ankle sponges if a determination is made that they are to be utilized. Use of sponges is recommended in most cases.

7. Loosen all adjustments in restraint system and move backrest all the way back.

8. Refer to special Protocol for logistic procedure.

9. Sedate subject either orally or with injection if permissible. A 5cc Injection of Versed (Midazolam HCL) 1 mg/ml has been used in the past for sedating executees. Orally, two (2) 50mg capsules of Nembutal Sodium (Pentobarbital sodium USP) Abbott Pharmaceuticals NDC 0074-3150-11. Another alternative would be 1.5 oz. of an 80 proof whiskey. This should be done one half (1/2) hour prior to the execution.

10. Curtain on witness window should be opened.

11. Subject must walk into execution chamber and speak to show he is alive.

12. Curtain on witness window should be closed.

13. Executee should be strapped into chair in the following manner:

A. Connect and tighten waist harness.

B. Tighten shoulder adjustments.

NOTE WELL: All connectors should be kept centered by adjusting both sides of adjustors.

C. Connect and tighten arm restraints, centering connectors.

D. Insert subject's legs into electrodes on leg stock and connect and adjust the restraints keeping the connectors in the center. The saturated saline sponges are recommended and may be placed behind the subject's leg between the leg and the electrode.

NOTE WELL: All adjustment should be as tight as possible at this time.

E. Install saline saturated helmet on the executee's head and tighten chin strap as tight as possible. The face curtain is optional and may be installed at this time.

F. Insert helmet conductor into electrode on helmet and tighten handscrew. Tighten further with allen wrench.

G. Loosen backrest adjuster, pull backrest as far forward as possible (tightening the subject) and tighten backrest adjuster locking the backrest in place.

NOTE WELL: Subject is now ready for execution.

14. Open the witness window curtain.

15. The Doctor should now examine the subject and certify that he is alive.

16. Turn on main disconnect.

17. Turn on input circuit breaker to the Power Supply.

18. On order from the Warden, the key will be inserted and the Power On switch will be turned on. The System On Light will be verified. The key will be removed.

19. On order from the Warden, the key will be inserted and the Computer On switch will be turned on only if a two operator procedure is to be utilized. The Computer On (Double) light will be verified. The key will be removed.

20. When the Warden determines that the execution will proceed, he will order that the key will be inserted and the Electric Chair Failsafe switch will be turned from center position to the Operation position to the left.

WARNING: THE SYSTEM IS NOW ARMED. DO NOT TOUCH THE ACTIVATION BUTTONS (SINGLE OR DOUBLE).

21. On order from the Warden, the execution will commence. One (1) or two (2) executioners will push either the SINGLE or DOUBLE buttons, simultaneously, if two. Verify the Electric Chair Energized light.

NOTE: The system will now deliver Two (2) Jolts of current, each for one (1) minute with a ten (10) second off time separating the two (2) Jolts. If a failure occurs on Double operation, simply activate the Single button and the timing sequence will proceed. If a further failure occurs, operate the system in manual by turning the Electric Chair Failsafe switch to TEST position (right) and time with a watch or clock: Sixty (60) seconds on; Ten (10) seconds off; Sixty (60) seconds on. Upon completion, turn Electric Chair Failsafe switch to off (center) position. Proceed with step twenty-two (22).

22. Upon completion of the timing sequence the subject should be dead. Turn off the Electric Chair Failsafe switch (center position) and VERIFY that the Electric Chair Ener-

gized light is off. Do NOT proceed unless the Electric Chair Energized light is off.

23. Use key to shut off Computer On switch and Power On switch, both to the left in this order.

24. Shut off input circuit breaker to the Power Supply and the main disconnect, in this order.

NOTE: If Electric Chair Energized light is not off, turn off main disconnect.

25. The Doctor should now verify heart death of the executee.

NOTE: If death has not occurred, Proceed with steps sixteen (16) through Twenty-five (25) again.

26. The execution is now over.

27. Close witness window curtain and remove witnesses.

28. Verify that all switches are off and the key removed. Verify that the input circuit breaker to the Power Supply is off. Verify that the main disconnect is off. Do NOT proceed until this step is complete and the Electric Chair Energized light is off.

28. The Executee should be removed from the chair in the following manner:

A. Disconnect helmet in reverse procedure of thirteen (13) F. Loosen and remove Helmet.

B. Pull release on ankle fasteners and pull legs forward.

C. Pull release on arm fasteners and free arms.

D. Pull release on chest harness fastener and subject's body will slump forward and hang in harness.

E. Remove subjects body to storage or pick-up location.

29. Clean chair seat with lysol or similar disinfectant and mild soap. Clean electrodes and with mild soap and water. Thoroughly dry chair. Wash and dry leg sponges.

30. Remove and dump drip pan; wash, dry and replace.

31. Clean helmet with clear water and dry. Store on styrofoam head.

32. Re-connect restraint system fasteners and partially tighten.

33. Verify all switches and power off.

34. Disconnect both the control cable and the power cable and coil for storage.

35. Remove all Keys.

SIGNIFICANCE

Witnessing an electrocution must be difficult for all concerned. Supreme Court Justice William Brennan described how the prisoner's eyeballs may pop out and he may vomit blood, urinate, and defecate as the electric shock passes through his body. The flesh, meanwhile, turns bright red as its temperature rises and he may even catch fire. Witnesses hear a sound like bacon frying and the unmistakable odor of burning flesh permeates the chamber. At post-mortem, the body is hot enough to blister the doctor's skin and so examination has to wait until the internal organs cool down. Mostly the brain has a "cooked" appearance.

Judge Brennan argued that electrocution was as cruel and inhumane as more ancient methods of execution such as disemboweling when alive, public dissection, burning alive at the stake, crucifixion, and breaking at the wheel. The prisoner is boiled alive from the inside; for the body contains a large proportion of water in its tissues. Indeed, the temperature in the brain itself is thought to reach the boiling point of water during an electrocution.

Concern over the ethics of using electrocution as a method of execution has led to developments in several states in recent years. In 2003, Judge Joseph Bataillon, speaking of a death row inmate in Nebraska, ruled "In light of evidence and evolving standards of decency, the court would find that a death penalty sentence imposed on a defendant in a state that provides electrocution as its only method of execution is an unnecessary and wanton infliction of pain." The sentence was changed to life imprisonment.

In 2001, Georgia's highest court ruled that the electric chair was a cruel and unusual punishment in violation of the state's constitution. The courts said that electrocution "inflicts purposeless physical violence and needless mutilation that makes no measurable contribution to accepted goals of punishment. In Kentucky, condemned inmates have the unenviable choice between electrocution and the electric chair, with those sentenced after 1998 to be executed by injection.

Electrocution is traumatic enough for the prisoner even if all goes to plan. However, there have been reports of several botched executions where even more suffering must have been inflicted. For example, the execution of John Evans in Alabama in 1983 took fourteen minutes—a third jolt of electricity was applied, despite the pleas of the prisoner's lawyers, leaving his body charred and smoldering. During the process, sparks and smoke came out of the hood covering Evans' head. The electrocution of William Vandiver in Indiana in 1985 took seventeen minutes and five jolts of electricity.

In 1997, a crown of foot-high flames leapt from the headpiece when Pedro Medina was executed in Florida, and smoke filled the chamber, gagging the witnesses. The technician threw the switch to cut off the power and Medina's chest was seen to heave until the flames stopped and he eventually died. The sponge, designed to conduct electricity, had been improperly applied to the prisoner's head, concluded a later investigation. While lethal injection is felt to be more humane, there are several reports of botched executions using this process as well.

FURTHER RESOURCES

Books

Brandon, Craig. *The Electric Chair: An Unnatural American History*. Jefferson, N.C.: McFarland & Company, 1999.

Web sites

Death Penalty Information Center. "Methods of Execution." <http://www.deathpenaltyinfo.org/article.php?scid=8> (accessed February 27, 2006).

The Vincentian Center for Church and Society. "Legal Arguments Against the Death Penalty." <http://www.vincenter.org/95/gregory.html> (accessed February 27, 2006).

An Execution and its Aftermath

Book excerpt

By: Robert Johnson

Date: 1990

Source: Robert Johnson. *Death Work: A Study of the Modern Execution Process*. Pacific Grove, Calif.: Brooks Cole, 1990.

About the Author: Robert Johnson is a professor at the American University's (Washington, D.C.) School of Public Affairs. He has written several books about different aspects of the prison system. He had studied the concept of death by execution, in the context of the prison setting, for more than a decade when he wrote the book from which this piece is excerpted.

INTRODUCTION

There are many crimes for which the death penalty may be imposed at the state or federal level, but premeditated murder (accompanied by a variety of extenuating conditions or circumstances) is chief among them. Thirty-eight states have a provision for capital punishment (although it is "on the books" in

New York, the death penalty was ruled unconstitutional in that state in 2004), although many of them have rarely employed it. The typical inmate remains on death row for ten to twenty years. During that time, appeals are repeatedly argued, continually delaying the execution date. Death row inmates are nearly always excluded from the general prisoner population, generally living in what is termed "administrative segregation" or in Special Housing Units (SHUs). Such inmates are confined to their cells for twenty-three hours per day, leaving then only for a brief (generally five minutes) shower and scheduled recreation time. Segregated inmates recreate individually, and many penitentiaries confine them to "recreation cages"—fully enclosed mesh, wire, or chain link outdoor cages that are only slightly larger than their cells. They rarely have access to educational or training programs, even by correspondence, and have limited visitation and telephone privileges. Inmates given the death penalty must learn to cope with the quite significant stress of waiting to be executed and the uncertainty of not knowing when, or if, that will occur.

Between 1972 and 1976, the Supreme Court of the United States imposed a ban on prison executions in America. Since the ban was lifted in 1976, more than 1,000 executions have been carried out in prisons across the country. Of those, about eighty-three percent have been accomplished by lethal injection, fifteen percent by electrocution, one percent by lethal gas (also called the gas chamber), and the remainder evenly divided between hanging and the employment of a firing squad. All of the states employing the death penalty but one—Nebraska, carries out all executions by the use of electrocution (the electric chair)—use lethal injections, which have been considered the most humane form of execution until rather recently. The Constitution of the United States prohibits the use of "cruel and unusual punishment," mandating that a death sentence be carried out as compassionately as possible.

In addition to execution by lethal injection and by electrocution (described in considerable detail below), death row inmates in America may still be executed by the use of lethal gas, hanging, and by firing squad. In brief, execution in a gas chamber entails securing the inmate in a chair within a sealed chamber. A bucket of sulfuric acid is located under the chair and the executioner triggers the release of sodium cyanide into the pail, causing a chemical reaction that releases cyanide gas into the air. The inmate breathes in the gas, and, after several minutes, dies of asphyxiation as a result of oxygen deprivation. Execution by firing squad entails strapping the inmate into a chair that is surrounded by absorbent containers (often, sand bags). The inmate's face is covered, and a target is pinned over the heart area. Several shooters are stationed behind a wall at a distance of about twenty feet. Historically, one or more of them have "blanks" rather than live ammunition in their rifles. When the signal is given, the firing squad aims and fires at the target. The inmate dies of blood loss and vital organ destruction. Depending on the accuracy of the shots, death may be nearly instantaneous or may take several minutes.

▮ PRIMARY SOURCE

WITNESS TO AN EXECUTION

At eight in the evening, about the time the prisoner is shaved in preparation for the execution, the witnesses were assembled. Eleven in all, we included three newspaper and two television reporters, a state trooper, two police officers, a magistrate, a businessman, and myself. We were picked up in the parking lot behind the main office of the Department of Corrections. There was nothing unusual or even memorable about any of this. Gothic touches were notable by their absence. It wasn't a dark and stormy night; no one emerged from the shadows to lead us to the prison gates.

Mundane consideration prevailed. The van sent for us was missing a few rows of seats, so there wasn't enough room for the group. Obliging prison officials volunteered their cars. Our rather ordinary cavalcade reached the prison only after getting lost. Once within the prison's walls, we were sequestered for some two hours in a bare and almost shabby administrative conference room. A public information officer was assigned to accompany us and answer our questions, but when we grilled him about the prisoners and the execution procedure the prisoner would shortly undergo, he confessed ignorance regarding the most basic points. Disgruntled at this and increasingly anxious, we made small talk and drank coffee. We didn't psych up as the execution team did, but we did tense up as the execution time approached.

At 10:40, roughly two and a half hours after we assembled and only twenty minutes before the execution was scheduled to occur, we were taken to the basement of the prison's administration building, frisked, then led down an alley that ran along the outside of the building. We entered a neighboring cell block and were admitted to a vestibule adjoining the death chamber. Each of us signed a log, and we were then led to the witness area off to our right. To our left and around a corner, some thirty feet away, sat Jones in the condemned cell. He couldn't see us, but I'm quite certain he could hear us. It occurred to me that our arrival was a fateful reminder for the prisoner. The next group would be led by the warden, and it would be coming for him.

We entered the witness area, a room within the death chamber, and were escorted to our seats. Through the picture window filling the front wall of the witness room, we had a clear view of the electric chair, which was about twelve feet away and well illuminated. A large, high-back, solid-oak structure with imposing black straps, the chair easily dominated the death chamber. The electric chair is larger than life, a paradox that no doubt derives from its sole purpose as an instrument of death. The warden had told me, "It's the biggest chair you'll ever see," and he was right. Behind the electric chair, on the back wall, was an open panel full of coils and lights; over the chair, two domed light fixtures were strung from the ceiling. Peeling paint hung from the ceiling and walls, which were stained from persistent water leaks. (The walls have since been painted, but the leaks remain.) A stark and lonely tableau, I assure you.

Two substantial officers—one a huge, hulking figure weighing some four hundred pounds, the other not much smaller—stood beside the electric chair. The deterrent message to the approaching inmate was clear. As one of these officers put it, "You got seven hundred or so pounds waiting for you at the chair, so don't go thinking about bucking." Each officer had his hands crossed at the lap and wore a forbidding blank expression. The witnesses gazed at them and the chair, absorbed by the scene, scribbling notes furiously. We did this, I suppose, as much to record the experience as to distract ourselves from the growing tension.

A correctional officer entered the room and announced a trial run of the machinery. Seconds later, lights flashed on the control panel behind the chair, as the officer had said they would, indicating that the chair was in working order. A white curtain, open for the test, separated the chair and the witness area. After the test, the curtain was drawn, allowing the officers to prepare the cap and mask that would be placed on the prisoner once he was secured in the chair. (It was thought that observing the staff preparing these paraphernalia would needlessly upset the witnesses. The impression the team wished to leave with the witnesses, at this point at least, was that executions simply happen.) The curtain was then reopened, to be left open until the execution was over. Then it would be closed to allow the officers to discreetly remove the prisoner's body.

Several high-level correctional officers were present in the death chamber, standing just outside the witness area. There were two regional administrators, the director of the Department of Corrections, and the warden. Also present were Jones's chaplain and lawyer. Other than the chaplain's black religious garb, subdued grey pinstripes and bland correctional uniforms prevailed. All parties were quite solemn.

I knew from my research that Jones was a man with a tragic past. Grossly abused at home, he went on to become grossly abusive of others. (His crime, committed when he was on drugs, was a gruesome murder of an elderly woman.) I was told he could not describe his life, from childhood on, without talking about fighting to defend his precarious sense of self—at home, in school, on the streets, in the prison yard. Belittled by life and choking with rage, he remained hungry to be noticed, even if notoriety was all he might hope for. Paradoxically, Jones the condemned prisoner had found his moment in the spotlight—though it was a dim and unflattering light cast before a small and unappreciative audience. "He'd pose for cameras in the chair—for the attention," I'd been told earlier that day by a member of the prison's psychological treatment unit. Yet the plain truth was that Jones had to endure one more losing confrontation, this time with the state. He won't be smiling, I thought, and there will be no cameras.

Virtually no one holds up well in the face of an execution, and Jones was no exception. But Jones, like many other prisoners before him, did cope for a time, with the help of the outsiders the warden described as adjuncts to his team. In Jones's case, this group included two attorneys in addition to his personal counselor. Jones thought of his attorneys as allies and friends. His counselor, who had helped a number of other condemned men face their end, was known for her matter-of-fact, cut-and-dried approach. Jones called her by her last name, mixing affection and respect. He also spoke by phone with a journalist covering his story, with whom he had become close. These sources provided an inside view of Jones's efforts to hold himself together in the face of his impending execution.

THE EXECUTION

At 10:58, Jones entered the death chamber. He walked quickly and silently toward the chair, his escort officers in tow. Three officers maintained contact with Jones at all times, offering him physical support. Two were stationed at his elbows; a third brought up the rear, holding Jones's back pockets. The officers waiting at the chair described the approaching Jones as "staring off in a trance, with no meaning in his stares. It was like he didn't want to think about it." His eyes were cast downward. His expression was glazed, but worry and apprehension were apparent in the tightly creased lines that ran across his forehead. He did not shake with nerves, nor did he crack under pressure. One could say, as did a fellow witness, "Anybody who writes anything will have to say he took it like a man." But a scared and defeated man, surely. His shaven head and haggard face added to the impression of vulnerability, even frailty.

Like some before him, Jones had threatened to stage a last stand. But that was lifetimes ago, on death row, with his fellow condemned to lean on. In the death house, alone, Jones joined the humble bunch and kept to the executioner's schedule. At the end, resistance of any kind seemed unthinkable. Like so many of those before him, Jones appeared to have given up on life before he died in the chair. His execution, like those of the men who preceded him, was largely a matter of procedure.

The procedure, set up to take life, had a life of its own. En route to the chair, Jones stumbled slightly, as if the momentum of the event had overtaken him, causing him to lose control. Were he not held secure by three officers, he might have fallen. Were the routine to be broken in this or, indeed, any other way, the officers believe, the prisoner might faint or panic or become violent, and have to be forcibly restrained. Perhaps as a precaution, when Jones reached the chair, he did not turn on his own but rather was turned, firmly but without malice, by the officers in his escort. Once Jones was seated, again with help, the officers strapped him in.

The execution team worked with machine precision. Like a disciplined swarm, they enveloped Jones, strapping and then buckling down his forearms, elbows, ankles, waist, and chest in a matter of seconds. Once his body was secured, with the electrode connected to Jones's exposed right leg, the two officers stationed behind the chair went to work. One of them attached the cap to the man's head, then connected the cap to an electrode located above the chair. The other secured the face mask. This was buckled behind the chair, so that Jones's head, like the rest of his body, was rendered immobile.

Only one officer on the team made eye contact with Jones (as he was affixing the face mask), and he came to regret it. The others attended to their tasks with a most narrow focus. Before the mask was secured, Jones asked if the electrocution would hurt. Several of the officers mumbled "no" or simply shook their heads, neither pausing nor looking up. Each officer left the death chamber after he finished his task. One officer, by assignment, stayed behind for a moment to check the straps. He mopped Jones's brow, then touched his hand in a gesture of farewell. This personal touch in the midst of an impersonal procedure was, in the warden's opinion, an attempt to help the officer himself live with the death penalty. The warden noted that it also by implication helped the team of which he was a part. "It's out of our hands," the gesture seemed to imply. "We're only doing our job."

During the brief procession to the electric chair Jones was attended by a chaplain from a local church, not the prison. The chaplain, upset, leaned over Jones as he was being strapped in the chair. As the execution team worked feverishly to secure Jones's body, the chaplain put his forehead against Jones's, whispering urgently. The priest might have been praying, but I had the impression he was consoling Jones, perhaps assuring him that a forgiving God awaited him in the next life. If Jones heard the chaplain, I doubt that he comprehended his message. At least, he didn't seem comforted. Rather, he looked stricken and appeared to be in shock. Perhaps the priest's urgent ministrations betrayed his doubts that Jones could hold himself together. The chaplain then withdrew at the warden's request, allowing the officers to affix the mask.

The strapped and masked figure sat before us, utterly alone, waiting to be killed. The cap and mask dominated his face. The cap was nothing more than a sponge encased in a leather shell, topped with a metal receptacle for an electrode. Fashioned in 1979 in replica of a cap dating back to the turn of the century, it appeared decrepit, presumably from sitting in brine for a number of years. It resembled a cheap, ill-fitting toupee. "It don't fit like a normal hat," said the officer responsible for securing this piece of hardware to the prisoner, in a matter of fact tone, "it's for a person with no hair." The mask, also created in 1979 and modeled on a turn of the century original, was made entirely of leather. Somehow, it, too, looked well-worn, perhaps because it was burned in places—from saliva that had spilled from the mouths of some of the executed prisoners, then been brought to a boil by the heat of the electricity coursing through the chair and its appurtenances. The mask had two parts. The bottom part covered the chin and mouth; the top, the eyes and lower forehead. Only the nose was exposed. The effect of the rigidly restrained body, together with the bizarre cap and the protruding nose, was nothing short of grotesque.

A faceless man breathed before us in a tragicomic trance, waiting for a blast of electricity that would extinguish his life. The internal dynamics of an electrocution are quite profound. As the electrician affiliated with the team made clear to anyone who would listen, in one swift and violent instant twenty-five hundred volts of electricity, at five to seven amps, shoot through the body, starting at the head, passing through the brain, then on to the heart and other internal organs, some of which explode, before the current comes to ground through the ankle. Jones presumably did not know the details, but the general picture is vividly impressed in the minds of all condemned prisoners facing death by electrocution.

Endless, agonizing seconds passed. Jones's last act was to swallow, nervously, pathetically, his Adam's apple bobbing. I was struck by that simple movement then and cannot forget it even now. It told me, as nothing else did, that in Jones's restrained body, behind that mask, lurked a fellow human being who, at some level, however primitive, knew or sensed himself to be moments from death.

Jones sat perfectly still for what seemed an eternity but was in fact no more than thirty seconds. Finally, the electricity hit him. His body stiffened spasmodically, though only briefly. A thin swirl of smoke trailed away from his head, then dissipated quickly. (People outside the witness room could hear crackling and burning; a faint smell of burned flesh lingered in the air, mildly nauseating some people.) The body remained taut, with the right foot raised slightly at the heel, seemingly frozen there. A brief pause, then another minute of shock. When it was over, the body was inert.

Three minutes passed while officials let the body cool. (Immediately after the execution, I'm told, the body would be too hot to touch and would blister anyone who did.) All eyes were riveted to the chair; I felt trapped in my witness seat, at once transfixed and yet eager for release. I can't recall any clear thoughts from this time. One of the officers later volunteered that he shared this experience of staring blankly at the execution scene. Laughing nervously, he said,

> It's a long three minutes. It hits him and then you wait. The (current) goes on a couple of times. And you wait three minutes after the machine goes off; the doctor comes in and checks him. You just, you just, you just watch the whole thing. There's nothing really (pause) going through your mind. Had Jones's mind been mercifully blank at the end? I hoped so.

An officer walked up to the body, opened the shirt at chest level, then went to get the physician from an adjoining room. The physician listened for a heartbeat. Hearing none, he turned to the warden and said, "This man has expired." The warden, speaking to the director of corrections, solemnly intoned, "Mr. Director, the court order has been fulfilled." The curtain was then drawn, and the witnesses filed out.

The deathwatch team commenced its final duties. Approaching the chair, they found Jones's body frozen in an arched position, his right leg bent and rigid from the force of the electricity. The leg had received second-degree burns where the electrode touched the skin. Jones's head was facing upward, his eyes puffy and closed. This all looked quite grotesque to me, but the warden was of the opinion that Jones had died with a look of peace on his face. (The warden could speak comparatively on this matter. The inmate before Jones had apparently fared much worse. In the warden's words, "It looked like something terrible had reached in and snatched his soul right out through the mouth on his face, like his soul had been yanked from him.") Jones's inert body was lifted from the chair. This took several men, each now wearing protective rubber gloves to shield them from disease. (The officers feared AIDS, though there had been no evidence Jones had had the dread disease. They speculated that germs would proliferate wildly in reaction to the heat generated by the electrocution.) The body was then placed on a gurney and wheeled into a nearby room to cool. Aptly, the room is known as the cooling room.

The team milled around the cooling room, congregating near the body. No one had specific duties at this point, and the mood was subdued. No congratulations were exchanged here, though the feeling seemed to be one of a job well done. The officers were clearly relieved to be finished. For the doctor and his assistants, however, work was just beginning. They used sandbags to flatten Jones's right leg and otherwise prepared the corpse for the morgue. Their labors took some six or seven minutes. By the time they were finished, everyone was ready to go home.

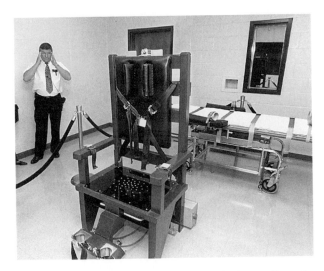

Ricky Bell, the warden at Riverbend Maximum Security Institution in Nashville, Tennessee, gives a tour of the prison's execution chamber in 1999. AP IMAGES

SIGNIFICANCE

The current controversy around lethal injection centers upon the use of one agent: pancuronium bromide. It is a muscle paralyzing agent that causes respiration to cease. Essentially, the process is this: the inmate is strapped to a gurney, and an intravenous saline drip is started in a large vein in each arm. At the prescribed time, sodium thiopental is injected, which sedates the inmate to the point unconsciousness. Pancuronium bromide is then injected, in order to paralyze the large muscles and extinguish respiration. Finally, potassium chloride is injected, which stops the heart. After the inmate is pronounced dead by the attending physician—who is legally (and ethically) prohibited from participating in the execution—an autopsy is performed. There have been numerous recent instances in which it was determined that death was caused by asphyxiation. This suggested that the inmate had not been deeply enough sedated at the time the second drug was administered and was likely to have suffered significant pain, dying essentially as the result of suffocation. One of the many concerns raised by this information is that the action of pancuronium bromide paralyzes muscles without affecting the brain. As a result, the inmate would have an awareness of suffocating—but be unable to signal suffering in any way—for the several minutes it took him to die.

Research evidence obtained during a study of autopsy and toxicology reports among executed inmates strongly suggested that nearly fifty percent of those tested were not fully anesthetized during the lethal injection process, and would have experienced high levels of pain while dying. In a study published by *The Lancet* in April 2005, it was concluded that many inmates were conscious during execution. This was thought to be due, in part, to the fact that drug administration occurred outside of the room in which the inmate was located, making it impossible to directly monitor the inmate's condition. In addition, the drug was administered by non-medical personnel who were almost certainly lacking in training and experience with drug administration, intravenous line placement, and individual titration of drug dosages. Pancuronium bromide, marketed as Pavulon, was previously used in animal euthanization, but its use was banned by the American Veterinary Medical Association. It was banned due to evidence that it could mask indications that the sedation had failed to effectively anesthetize the animal and that the animal could experience severe pain during the process. The authors of *The Lancet* study advocated a suspension of executions by lethal injection until a thorough review was done of the available results, and until public and judicial commentary could be obtained.

There are competing theories regarding the effect of capital punishment on potential criminals. The deterrence theory states that the individuals most likely to commit capital crimes do not act spontaneously (by definition, first degree murder must have been planned in advance and the same is true for most other capital offenses). They plan their crimes and contemplate the hierarchy of potential outcomes. If the deterrence theory is true, there should be a decrease in the capital crime or first degree murder rate in the period immediately following an execution that has received considerable media coverage. Conversely, the brutalization theory suggests that executions graphically demonstrate to the criminal population that human life has little or no value. This theory holds that the number of premeditated murders occurring in the aftermath of an execution is likely to increase. The brutalization theory is based on social learning theory suggesting that the modeling (exposure to a role model who performs the behavior being studied) of aggression encourages others who are easily influenced to behave in a similar way. Although there are study results consistent with both theories, there is somewhat more evidence in favor of the deterrence hypothesis, providing the execution receives significant media attention. In situations in which there is little or no media coverage, death by execution has no discernible effect on capital crime rates. There is a current move in America to abolish the death penalty by attempting to mount conclusive evidence that it violates Eighth Amendment ("cruel and unusual punishment") rights.

FURTHER RESOURCES

Books

Zimring, Franklin E. *The Contradictions of American Capital Punishment*. New York: Oxford University Press, 2003.

Periodicals

Grant, Robert. "Capital Punishment and Violence." *The Humanist* 64 (January–February 2004): 25–30.

Koniaris, L. G., et al. "Inadequate Anesthesia in Lethal Injection for Execution." *The Lancet* 365 (April 16, 2005): 1412–1414.

Stolzenberg, Lisa, and Stewart D'Alessio. "Capital Punishment, Execution Publicity and Murder in Houston, Texas." *Journal of Criminal Law and Criminology* 94 (2004): 351–387.

Tremoglie, Michael. "Capital-Punishment Canards." *Insight on the News* 19 (March 4, 2003): 52.

Web sites

Death Penalty Information Center (DPIC). "Crimes Punishable by the Death Penalty." <http://www.deathpenalty-info.org/article.php?scid=10> (accessed February 2, 2006).

Dead Man Walking

Photograph

By: Anonymous

Date: 1995

Source: "Dead Man Walking." MGM, 1995.

About the Photographer: This image is part of the photo library at Metro-Goldwyn-Mayer (MGM), a prominent American media company. Founded in 1924, MGM is a Hollywood-based producer and distributor of films and television programs.

INTRODUCTION

Sister Helen Prejean was born in Baton Rouge, Louisiana in April 1939. She joined the Sisters of St. Joseph of Medaille at the age of eighteen and later settled in New Orleans, where she devoted her life to working among its poor. In 1981 she began her prison ministry, also serving on the board of the National Coalition to Abolish the Death Penalty between 1985 and 1995. It was for this work that Prejean would become most widely recognized.

Prejean published *Dead Man Walking: An Eyewitness Account of the Death Penalty* in 1993, an account of her relationship with Patrick Sonnier, who was executed in April 1984. Hitherto a petty criminal, Sonnier had been convicted of the 1977 rape and double murder of David Leblanc and Loretta Ann Bourque, a high school couple, in Iberia Parish, Louisiana. His brother, Eddie James Sonnier, had also been found guilty, but his death sentence was later reduced to life without parole.

Patrick Sonnier began a correspondence with Prejean in 1982, and the nun eventually became his spiritual adviser. It was this relationship that formed the basis of *Dead Man Walking*, although far from being exclusively about Sonnier or the story of his redemption, it was a more philosophical reflection on the societal impact of the death penalty. According to Prejean it was a "sustained meditation on love, criminal violence, and capital punishment. In a larger sense, it is about life and death itself. Are we here to persecute our brothers or bring compassion into a world that is cruel without reason? "

Her book became an international bestseller and catapulted Prejean to international fame. *Dead Man Walking* was on the *New York Times* bestseller list for

PRIMARY SOURCE

Dead Man Walking: Sister Helen Prejean, played by Susan Sarandon in the 1995 film *Dead Man Walking*, serves as a spiritual advisor to condemmed murderer Matthew Poncelet, played by actor Sean Penn. WORKING TITLE/HAVOC/THE KOBAL COLLECTION/TODD, DEMMIE

thirty-one weeks and nominated for the Pulitzer Prize. It was also translated into ten different languages.

In 1994, Susan Sarandon and her partner Tim Robbins bought the film rights to *Dead Man Walking*, which was released a year later to popular acclaim. The film closely followed the book, although certain details were fictionalized. Robbins wrote and directed it, while Sarandon played Prejean. Sean Penn played Matthew Poncelot, a character based on Patrick Sonnier. It was nominated for four Oscars at the 1996 Academy Awards Ceremony, including best director, best actor, and best actress. Sarandon collected the latter award.

PRIMARY SOURCE

DEAD MAN WALKING
See primary source image.

SIGNIFICANCE

Dead Man Walking was the latest in a series of critically and commercially successful films that brought marginalized political issues into mainstream public debate. Just as *Mississippi Burning* (1988) tackled racism in the south, *Philadelphia* (1993) highlighted prejudice against homosexuals in corporate America, or *The Shawshank Redemption* (1994) dealt with the brutality of America's prison system, so too did *Dead Man Walking* bring capital punishment to public attention. Yet while each of these films heightened public interest in issues that were previously widely disregarded, it was not matched by a clamor for legislative change that followed, for instance, the nineteenth century plays *Ten Nights in a Barroom* (prohibition), *Uncle Tom's Cabin* (slavery), or Harper Lee's 1960 novel, *To Kill a Mockingbird* (segregation). Indeed from 1993, the year Helen Prejean's book was first published, the number of death penalties carried out has risen dramatically, roughly doubling.

Tim Robbins and Susan Sarandon had long been among Hollywood's most outspoken campaigners on social issues and were well known for their liberal views. *Dead Man Walking* was widely regarded as a statement against the death penalty, although that view disregarded the film's inherent subtlety. Several reviewers wrote of being undecided on where Robbins stood on the death penalty, such was the emotional neutrality he took in directing it.

Nevertheless, *Dead Man Walking* heightened the position of Robbins and Sarandon as the so-called conscience of Hollywood. Over subsequent years they used their standpoint to speak out on issues ranging from animal rights to domestic violence. In 2002 and 2003, they were among President George W. Bush's most vocal and fervent critics when he led the United States into war in Iraq, views that were acclaimed and derided by the American public in equal measure.

The film release of *Dead Man Walking* changed Sister Helen Prejean's life too. Already globally famous after the publication of her international best-seller, Sarandon's immortalization of her on film made her the world's leading opponent of capital punishment. Her crusade against the death penalty has come to incorporate many facets, and she has sought to learn from the experiences of not just the criminal, but victims and their families, and even executioners. One of her more contended arguments is that the effect of capital punishment on the men who administer it is as destructive as it is on the individual sentenced to death.

Since his election in 2000, President Bush has been among Prejean's principal targets. During his six years as Texas governor Bush presided over 152 death penalties and scrutiny of the way justice was carried out in Texas has suggested that justice was sometimes applied unfairly and that Bush was less than diligent in the way in which he dealt with appeals for clemency. Prejean has accused Bush of using execution as a tool to boost his political fortunes and of "callous indifference to human suffering." He had, she wrote in the *New York Review of Books*, "no quality of mercy."

Such attacks have continued to win her admirers, but she has also been the target of criticism and vitriol. Advocates of the death penalty and some victims groups have made her the target of letter-writing campaigns and protests to her archdiocese. She has also been verbally abused by supporters of the death penalty.

While Sister Helen Prejean attracted considerable and widening support following the success of her book and her depiction in film, America seems no more likely to end its use of capital punishment. The death penalty "isn't and never will be [acceptable] because of what it does to us," she told *Time* magazine in 2005. "There's a death of innocence in all of us...I say, for our own sake as a society, let's take death off the table. We can't handle it."

FURTHER RESOURCES

Books

Hood, Roger. *The Death Penalty: A Worldwide Perspective*. Oxford, U.K.: Oxford University Press, 2004.

Prejean, Helen. *Dead Man Walking*, film tie-in edition. London: Zondervan Publishing House, 1996.

Web sites

Helen Prejean, CSJ. <http://www.prejean.org> (accessed March 12, 2006).

Sister Helen Prejean (personal blog). <http://sisterhelen.type-pad.com> (accessed March 12, 2006).

If It Doesn't Fit, You Must Acquit

Photograph

By: Sam Mircovich

Date: 1995

Source: AP Worldwide Images

About the Photographer: This photograph was taken on June 15, 1995, by photographer Sam Mircovich, in the courtroom where O.J. Simpson was being tried for murder. Mircovich is now the entertainment pictures editor for the international news agency Reuters.

INTRODUCTION

On June 12, 1994, Nicole Brown Simpson, former wife of football star Orenthal James Simpson

(O.J. Simpson, 1947–) was murdered at the Simpson home in Los Angeles. Also murdered was her acquaintance, Ronald Goldman. The subsequent trial of O.J. Simpson for murder made legal and cultural history and ended in his acquittal. During the trial, the prosecution asked Simpson to don a blood-soaked glove found outside his house shortly after the murder: Simpson struggled with the glove, as shown here, and said, "They don't fit. See? They don't fit." Defense lawyer Johnnie Cochran (1937–2005) later told the jury, "If it doesn't fit, you must acquit." Many legal experts hold that Simpson was guilty of the murder, but was acquitted because of incompetent prosecution, faulty police work, and racial factors. Some argue that the jury's decision was correct because the prosecution failed to prove Simpson's guilt beyond a "reasonable doubt," the standard that juries are ordered to consider.

The day after the murder, Simpson was questioned by police and gave confused replies, including a denial of knowing how he had received a fresh cut on his right hand (the murders had been committed with a knife). He was later to claim that he had smashed a glass in grief upon hearing of his wife's death, cutting his hand. A warrant was issued for his arrest, but he failed to present himself at police headquarters. Instead, on June 17, Simpson took to the road in a white Bronco owned by a friend. Simpson wandered the streets of Los Angeles at low speed for many minutes, chased on the ground by numerous police and filmed from above by television cameras. He eventually returned to his own house and was arrested.

O.J. Simpson had played professional football from 1969 to 1979 and was inducted into the Pro Football Hall of Fame in 1985. Nicole and O.J. were married in 1985 and divorced in 1992. At that time, O.J. pled "no contest" to charges of domestic abuse. During the trial, Nicole's sister testified to having seen Simpson throw Nicole against a wall and commit other abusive acts, and a tape was played of a harrowing 911 call made by Nicole during an assault by O.J.

The evidence against Simpson was strong. There was his proven history of abuse, his confused alibi, the fresh cut on his hand, his strange ride in the Bronco (with a fake beard and mustache, a loaded gun, thousands of dollars in cash, and a passport on board), hairs consistent with O.J.'s on the body of one victim, and other evidence both physical and circumstantial. Genetic evidence indicated that O.J.'s blood was on a glove matching one at the murder scene and that his wife's blood was on a pair of socks, both articles of clothing found in or near O.J.'s house. However, the police and prosecution made grave blunders. The

behavior of Los Angeles police officer Mark Fuhrman, who said he had found the blood-soaked glove outside O.J.'s house, was particularly damaging for the prosecution. Fuhrman said on the stand, under oath, that he had never used "the 'n' word," that is, "nigger," but tapes were produced showing that this was a lie. Fuhrman admitted on the same tapes to planting evidence in past cases to help produce convictions. A key police witness was, therefore, a proven liar and confessed evidence-planter. The defense suggested that O.J. was framed by the police. During his summation, defense lawyer Cochran compared Fuhrman to Hitler.

One hundred and thirty-three days of courtroom proceedings were televised to an estimated ninety-five million viewers, making his trial one of the most avidly watched TV events in history. When the jury verdict of "not guilty" was read on October 3, 1995, over ninety percent of all TV viewers were watching the broadcast.

O.J. Simpson was also sued in civil court by the families of Nicole Brown Simpson and Ronald Goldman. The standards of evidence are lower in a civil suit than they are in criminal proceedings. The jury in the civil trial only had to find that a preponderance of the evidence indicated he had caused the deaths in order to find him liable. In 1997, the civil court found Simpson to be guilty of wrongfully causing the two deaths and ordered to pay both compensatory damages ($8.5 million) and punitive damages ($25 million). Probably the most important new evidence of O.J.'s guilt presented at this trial were photos of him wearing a pair of shoes whose prints matched those at the crime scene and which he had denied owning.

In 1998, Simpson said to an interviewer: "Let's say I committed this crime….Even if I did do this, it would have been because I loved [Nicole] very much, right?"

PRIMARY SOURCE

IF IT DOESN'T FIT, YOU MUST ACQUIT
See primary source image.

SIGNIFICANCE

Race was an important factor in the Simpson trial and in the public reaction to it. Among the general public, opinion on O.J.'s guilt was (and, as of 2005, remained) deeply divided along racial lines, with approximately two thirds of black Americans believing that O.J. was innocent and two thirds of white Americans believing that he was guilty.

PRIMARY SOURCE

If It Doesn't Fit, You Must Acquit: Murder defendant O. J. Simpson tries on one of the leather gloves prosecutors say he wore the night his ex-wife Nicole Brown Simpson and Ron Goldman were murdered, during his double-murder trial in Los Angeles in 1995. AP IMAGES

Race was an explicit issue during the trial itself. The brutality of white police toward blacks was (and remains) a major problem in many parts of the United States. Cases of evidence planted by police have been discovered in some cities, and cases of police using excessive violence against black suspects have emerged since the Simpson trial. The jury in the Simpson trial was mostly black. The defense lawyer, also black, explicitly asked the jury to consider the racist beliefs of detective Fuhrman in making their decision. Across the U.S., many black Americans believed that O.J.'s case was yet another case of a black man being framed by bigoted police—only this time, the black man had the power and fame to fight back and win in court. Many white Americans, on the other hand, tended to

assume O.J.'s guilt and to downplay or not realize the country's longstanding history of injustice against black defendants.

Even black Americans who believe in O.J.'s guilt tend to be keenly aware of the historic unfairness of the legal system toward black defendants: "They framed a guilty man—that's all it was," said a Los Angeles barber interviewed for the PBS program *Frontline* ten years after the trial. On these terms, the Simpson not-guilty verdict was perceived by many people as not so much a victory for justice (the acquittal of an innocent man) as a defeat for injustice (a setback for a corrupt justice system).

The O.J. trial turned a public spotlight on these race-linked differences in perception. It also motivated many police departments and court systems, including those in Los Angeles, to enact more demanding policies in their handling of evidence and witnesses.

FURTHER RESOURCES

Web sites

Liebovich, Laurie. "The Mystery of O.J. Simpson." *Salon.com.* Feb. 3, 1998. <http://www.salon.com/media/1998/02/03media.html> (accessed March 20, 2006).

Linder, Doug (professor at University of Missouri—Kansas City School of Law). *Famous American Trials: The O.J. Simpson Trial, 1995.* Includes links to court documents. <http://www.law.umkc.edu/faculty/projects/ftrials/Simpson/simpson.htm> (accessed March 20, 2006).

Public Broadcasting System (PBS). "The O.J. Verdict." *Frontline.* Oct. 10, 2005. <http://www.pbs.org/wgbh/pages/frontline/oj/view/> (accessed March 20, 2006).

Sentence Enhancements Statute

Government document

By: California Legislature

Date: 1998

Source: California Penal Code § 666.7. (12) (1998).

About the Author: The California Legislature is the body elected to enact laws for the state of California.

INTRODUCTION

After a trial is completed and a guilty verdict returned, or when a defendant enters a guilty or no contest plea, the sentencing phase of the adjudication process begins. Federal and state guidelines for the type and term of sentence imposed are based on the nature of the crime and its surrounding circumstances. There are five possible outcomes: Depending on the nature and severity of the felony offense, the offender can be: 1) ordered to make restitution to the victim, pay a fine, or both; 2) given a suspended sentence with no mandatory reporting requirements; 3) made to serve a period of probation, under specific conditions for a particular period of time; 4) remanded to community service, to a specific form and type of treatment program, or otherwise given a specific time and

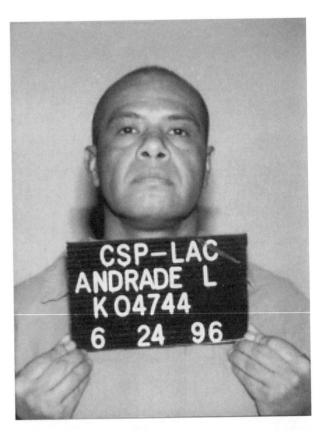

A police mug shot of Leandro Andrade. Andrade received a sentence of 50 years to life in prison for stealing less than $200 worth of video tapes, a consequence of his prior thefts and California's "three strikes" sentence enhancement laws. AP IMAGES

task combination that must be performed according to precise conditions; or 5) sentenced to a period of incarceration.

Procedures for the trial phase and the sentencing portion are notably different. Before conviction or the entering of a plea, the defendant is entitled to all of the rights and privileges of due process. Defendant and attorney are entitled to see all the evidence to be put forth, to examine and rebut witnesses, and to offer argument, proof, and witnesses of their own. In the trial or plea portion of the proceedings, it is only the behavior or specific actions of the defendant that are under consideration for the decision of guilt or innocence.

The sentencing phase is somewhat more arbitrary, in that the judge considers not only the behavior of the now-convicted felon in arriving at a decision, but also how the crime occurred—whether substance abuse was involved, whether the trafficking of illegal substances occurred, or whether drugs or alcohol played a part in the commission of the crime; the amount of drugs or money involved; whether weapons were used at all, as a threat, or actually discharged; whether and to what extent bodily harm was caused— as well as various aspects of the offender's personality and past actions (within the framework of the standards of acceptable legal practice).

Some aspects considered for sentencing are: whether the defendant has a prior criminal history, and, if so, what the prior convictions concerned (violent or nonviolent crimes, number of prior offenses or criminal convictions, age at prior offenses), whether and how many prior incarcerations there were, current age, education and employment history, and family and social history.

In brief, the trial and conviction phases are concerned with the establishment of criminal behavior, and the attribution (based on a preponderance of evidence and beyond a reasonable doubt or on an admission of guilt) of the criminal offense to the specific defendant, and the decision that the establishment of guilt to the alleged offender constitutes a crime that necessitates some sort of punishment. The sentencing phase assesses the relationship between convicted offender and criminal behavior to ascertain the appropriate type and duration of punishment.

PRIMARY SOURCE

666.7. It is the intent of the Legislature that this section serve merely as a nonsubstantive comparative reference of current sentence enhancement provisions. Nothing in this section shall have any substantive effect on the application of any sentence enhancement contained in any provision of law, including, but not limited to, all of the following: omission of any sentence enhancement provision, inclusion of any obsolete sentence enhancement provision, or inaccurate reference or summary of a sentence enhancement provision.

It is the intent of the Legislature to amend this section as necessary to accurately reflect current sentence enhancement provisions, including the addition of new provisions and the deletion of obsolete provisions.

For the purposes of this section, the term "sentence enhancement" means an additional term of imprisonment in the state prison added to the base term for the underlying offense. A sentence enhancement is imposed because of the nature of the offense at the time the offense was committed or because the defendant suffered a qualifying prior conviction before committing the current offense....

(b) The provisions listed in this subdivision imposing a sentence enhancement of one, two, or three years' imprisonment in the state prison may be referenced as Schedule B.

(1) Commission or attempted commission of a felony hate crime (subd. (a), Sec. 422.75, Pen. C.).

(2) Commission or attempted commission of a felony against the property of a public or private institution because the property is associated with a person or group of identifiable race, color, religion, nationality, country of origin, ancestry, gender, disability, or sexual orientation (subd. (b), Sec. 422.75, Pen. C.).

(3) Felony conviction of unlawfully causing a fire of any structure, forest land, or property when the defendant has been previously convicted of arson or unlawfully causing a fire, or when a firefighter, peace officer, or emergency personnel suffered great bodily injury, or when the defendant proximately caused great bodily injury to more than one victim, or caused multiple structures to burn (subd. (a), Sec. 452.1, Pen. C.).

(4) Carrying a loaded or unloaded firearm during the commission or attempted commission of any felony street gang crime (subd. (a), Sec. 12021.5, Pen. C.).

(5) Personally using a deadly or dangerous weapon in the commission of carjacking or attempted carjacking (para. (2), subd. (b), Sec. 12022, Pen. C.).

(6) Being a principal in the commission or attempted commission of any specified drug offense, knowing that another principal is personally armed with a firearm (subd. (d), Sec. 12022, Pen. C.).

(7) Furnishing or offering to furnish a firearm to another for the purpose of aiding, abetting, or enabling that person or any other person to commit a felony (Sec. 12022.4, Pen. C.).

(8) Selling, supplying, delivering, or giving possession or control of a firearm to any person within a prohibited class or to a minor when the firearm is used in the subsequent commission of a felony (para. (4), subd. (g), Sec. 12072, Pen. C.).

(9) Inducing, employing, or using a minor who is at least four years younger than the defendant to commit a drug offense involving any specified controlled substance, including, but not limited to, heroin, cocaine, and cocaine base, or unlawfully providing one of these controlled substances to a minor (para. (3), subd. (a), Sec. 11353.1, H.& S.C.).

(10) Prior conviction of inducing, employing, or using a minor to commit a drug offense involving cocaine base, or unlawfully providing cocaine base to a minor that resulted in a prison sentence with a current conviction of the same offense (subd. (a), Sec. 11353.4, H.& S.C.).

(11) Prior conviction of inducing, employing, or using a minor to commit a drug offense involving cocaine base, or unlawfully providing cocaine base to a minor with a current conviction of the same offense involving a minor who is 14 years of age or younger (subd. (b), Sec. 11353.4, H.& S.C.).

(12) Inducing, employing, or using a minor who is at least four years younger than the defendant to commit a drug offense involving any specified controlled substance, including, but not limited to, phencyclidine (PCP), methamphetamine, and lysergic acid diethylamide (LSD), or unlawfully providing one of these controlled substances to a minor (para. (3), subd. (a), Sec. 11380.1, H.& S.C.).

(13) Causing great bodily injury or a substantial probability that death could result by the knowing disposal, transport, treatment, storage, burning, or incineration of any hazardous waste at a facility without permits or at an unauthorized point (subd. (e), Sec. 25189.5, and subd. (c), Sec. 25189.7, H.& S.C.).

(c) The provisions listed in this subdivision imposing a sentence enhancement of one, two, or five years' imprisonment in the state prison may be referenced as Schedule C.

(1) Wearing a bullet-resistant body vest in the commission or attempted commission of a violent offense (subd. (b), Sec. 12022.2, Pen. C.).

(2) Commission or attempted commission of any specified sex offense while armed with a firearm or deadly weapon (subd. (b), Sec. 12022.3, Pen. C.).

...(s) The provisions listed in this subdivision imposing a sentence enhancement of 15 years' imprisonment in the state prison may be referenced as Schedule S.

(1) Kidnapping a victim under 14 years of age for the purpose of committing any specified felony sex offense (subd. (b), Sec. 667.8, Pen. C.).

(2) Commission of any specified drug offense involving a substance containing heroin, cocaine base, cocaine, methamphetamine, amphetamine, or phencyclidine (PCP), when the substance exceeds 20 kilograms or 400 liters (para. (4), subd. (a), and para. (4), subd. (b), Sec. 11370.4, H.& S.C.).

(3) Manufacturing, compounding, converting, producing, deriving, processing, or preparing any substance containing amphetamine, methamphetamine, or phencyclidine (PCP) or its analogs or precursors, or attempting to commit any of those acts, when the substance exceeds 105 gallons or 44 pounds (para. (4), subd. (a), Sec. 11379.8, H.& S.C.).

(t) The provisions listed in this subdivision imposing a sentence enhancement of 20 years' imprisonment in the state prison may be referenced as Schedule T.

(1) Intentionally and personally discharging a firearm in the commission or attempted commission of any specified felony offense (subd. (c), Sec. 12022.53, Pen. C.).

(2) Commission of any specified drug offense involving a substance containing heroin, cocaine base, or cocaine, when the substance exceeds 40 kilograms (para. (5), subd. (a), Sec. 11370.4, H.& S.C.).

(u) The provisions listed in this subdivision imposing a sentence enhancement of 25 years' imprisonment in the state prison may be referenced as Schedule U.

(1) Commission of any specified drug offense involving a substance containing heroin, cocaine base, or cocaine, when the substance exceeds 80 kilograms (para. (6), subd. (a), Sec. 11370.4, H.& S.C.).

(v) The provisions listed in this subdivision imposing a sentence enhancement of 25 years to life imprisonment in the state prison may be referenced as Schedule V.

(1) Intentionally and personally discharging a firearm in the commission or attempted commission of any specified felony offense and proximately causing great bodily injury.

SIGNIFICANCE

The underlying premise of state and federal sentencing enhancements is that they augment a sentence that would, of necessity, have been imposed—that is, they do not *cause* a person to be sentenced to a correctional institution, they merely add time to what would have been imposed in any case. Sentence enhancements are intended to deter future criminal activity, since felons are less affected by the fact of incarceration than they are by the duration of the sentence and the type of facility in which they serve it: Being sentenced to a super-maximum security facility, in which a convicted felon spends twenty-three hours per day in a cell, and exits only to shower and recreate in a "cage" is far more arduous than being in a medium security facility where there are educational opportunities, jobs to engage in, and congregate time for meals and recreation.

Every state in America has enacted some form of sentence enhancement legislation. Many use enhancements for repeat offenders to lengthen the mandatory sentence and increase the severity (or level) of punishment as well as move the offender from a minimum or facility to a maximum or supermaximum prison. The Violent Crime Control and Law Enforcement Act of 1994 framed the "three strikes and you're out" policy to mandate life without parole for the felons convicted for the third time of violent (including sexual assault and rape) or significant drug-related offenses. "Truth in sentencing" legislation requires that convicted violent or major drug-related offenders serve at least eighty-five percent of their imposed sentences before they can be considered for parole or early release.

Another type of sentence enhancement occurs when an individual is convicted of a "hate crime," in which a victim or crime location is chosen because of what it represents. That is, targeting a victim based on (actual or perceived) ethnicity, culture, race, religion, sexual orientation, gender, age, or disability status. Hate crime sentencing enhancements were intended to augment federal and state sentencing enhancement legislation ratified in 1994.

FURTHER RESOURCES
Books

Tonry, Michael, ed. *The Handbook of Crime and Punishment.* New York: Oxford University Press, 2000.

Walker, Samuel. *Taming the System: The Control of Discretion in Criminal Justice, 1950–1990.* New York: Oxford University Press, 1993.

Zimring, Franklin, Gordon Hawkins, and Sam Kamin. *Punishment and Democracy: Three Strikes and You're Out in California.* New York: Oxford University Press, 2001.

Let the Litigation Begin
Columbine Massacre Lawsuits

Internet article

By: Dave Cullen

Date: May 28, 1999

Source: *Salon.* "Let the Litigation Begin." <http://www.salon.com/news/feature/1999/05/28/families> (accessed January 10, 2006).

About the Author: Dave Cullen is a Denver-based author and journalist who writes for Salon.com and the *New York Times.* His account of the Columbine massacres—*A Lasting Impression on the World: The Definitive Account of Columbine and its Aftermath*—will be published in 2007.

INTRODUCTION

On Tuesday, April 20, 1999, teenage students Eric Harris and Dylan Klebold went on a shooting rampage at Columbine High School, near Denver. Armed with sawn-off shotguns, a semiautomatic pistol, and an array of pipe bombs, they began their spree at 11:20 A.M. During the next 45 minutes they shot and killed twelve students and a teacher and wounded 34 others before turning the guns on themselves. The death toll would surely have been higher had a 20-pound propane bomb in the cafeteria detonated.

The Columbine massacre became the most closely followed story of the decade. Yet morbid fascination gave way to searching questions. As details of Harris's and Klebold's fixation with violent video games like Doom, heavy metal music, and bloody films like *Natural Born Killers* emerged, the role of such cultural influences in American society were examined. Whether white supremacist views (the attack occurred on the hundred and tenth anniversary of Hitler's birth) fueled their rampage is unknown; they did, however, target students with religious beliefs.

With Harris and Klebold dead, soul-searching gave way to questions of greater responsibility. Was anyone else responsible for the Columbine massacre? Were the boys' parents at fault? Could the school have protected its students from such an attack? Should the police, who knew of the teens' violent website, threats against other students, and arrest records, have intervened before the massacre? Were the weapons manufacturers to blame?

In the years following the massacre these questions were to be argued in courts across America. But the parents of Isaiah Shoels, the only African-American victim of Harris and Klebold, filed the first lawsuit—against the killers' parents—just five weeks after their son's death, beginning a period of lengthy litigation.

PRIMARY SOURCE

LET THE LITIGATION BEGIN

Kevorkian's lawyer's suit against the Columbine killers' parents is just the beginning.

By Dave Cullen

May 28, 1999

"This is not about money!"

So declared Michael Shoels as he announced his family's $250 million wrongful death lawsuit against the parents of Columbine killers Eric Harris and Dylan Klebold. "This lawsuit is about change!" Shoels insisted. "That's the only way you get change, if you go rattling their pocketbooks."

Welcome to Round Two of the Columbine Tragedy, where the action shifts to the courtroom, but the focus remains squarely on the media.

Fresh from victory in the sensational Jenny Jones tabloid television trial, and several assisted-suicide cases for Dr. Jack Kevorkian before that, attorney Geoffrey Fieger flew to Denver to represent the parents of Isaiah Shoels, the only African-American killed in the April 20 attack that left 15 dead. The suit filed Thursday in Denver's District Court charges the killers' parents with five counts of parental negligence.

Fieger said the suit against the killers' parents is just the beginning: He plans to eventually target police, school authorities, gun manufacturers, accessories to the murders and "any individual who directly contributed to two sick children possessing an arsenal and access to the school."

The lawsuit was not filed in Jefferson County, where the murders occurred, but in Denver, Feiger said, because the Shoels family moved to Colorado's largest city since the killings to flee ongoing racial discrimination and intimidation. Michael Shoels said that days after his son was murdered, a young man in a trench coat showed up in his yard, and his wife Vonda "was terrified about continuing in that location." He said the police response was, "This is happening all over the neighborhood."

The legal wrangling might have begun sooner, if not for an anti-ambulance-chaser statute in Colorado, which forbids attorneys from contacting families until one month after the death of a victim. Technically, the moratorium did not apply in this case, as the family initiated contact with Fieger. Local reaction Thursday was fiercely negative, with talk radio dominated by anti-lawsuit sentiment, leveled generally against the lawyers rather than the Shoels family.

Fieger acknowledged "there will be cynics" who think the lawsuit is "about greed." But Colorado law limits awards in wrongful death cases to $250,000—state law restricts suits against governmental entities like the school district even further, to $150,000—and Fieger insists he'll spend more mounting the case than he can ever hope to recover. He admitted one goal of the lawsuit would be to overturn those dollar limits, which may involve additional suits in other jurisdictions. "This lawsuit is a symbol," he said. "This lawsuit is to serve as a living memorial to Isaiah Shoels."

The first lawsuit targeted the killers' parents, Fieger added, because it will give him time to develop the case against the other parties. He said he may even turn to federal courts to take advantage of this week's Supreme Court decision holding schools responsible for sexual harassment. "I can't believe that the Supreme Court would hold that immunity is gone from sexual harassment, but not for the loss of human life," he said.

The suit charges each of the four parents with five counts of parental negligence, which involve their allowing their sons to amass a cache of semiautomatic weapons; stockpile bombs and explosives; continue to hang out together, since each was "a coconspirator and accomplice in a prior criminal act"; to "author extremist writings of a hateful nature" and to continue to grant their sons "extraordinary privileges despite knowledge that [they] had been engaged in prior serious criminal activity."

But Fieger and the Shoelses seemed to have divergent agendas for their crusade. Fieger, who recently staged an unsuccessful run for governor of Michigan, delivered an impassioned opening statement that sounded like a stump speech for a third-party candidate for president. He ripped into "the excesses of liberal social engineering" that have "contributed to the erosion of personal responsibility and an excessive preoccupation with self-indulgent and material pursuits." But then he quickly turned on "conservatives" who he charged "destroyed the social safety net," including access to quality medical care and mental health treatment, "made the reality of a living wage unlikely" and destroyed our future with "mindless rhetoric about Second Amendment rights." He acknowledged that he developed his agenda independently of the Shoels family. "Those were my statements. The family doesn't tell me how to try the lawsuit. I think they agree with them. I ran them by them."

Michael Shoels, by contrast, ticked off a priority list that included morality in the home, prayer in the schools, and an end to all forms of hate, including but not limited to pervasive racial bigotry. He repeatedly returned to the racial abuse his family suffered before and after the shootings, which he says went unanswered by law enforcement. Vonda Shoels remained quiet through most of the proceedings, but responded quickly and forcefully when asked what she hopes to accomplish with the suit: "Change! Because no one should have to suffer like we had to suffer."

None of the other families have announced lawsuits yet, and none had immediate reactions to the Shoelses' suit. Neither the Harris nor Klebold families commented on it, directly or through attorneys.

The lawsuit isn't the only wrangling about money in the wake of the Columbine tragedy. Locally there's been growing tension about the use of a $2.3 million Healing Fund, donated by strangers around the country to help the Columbine victims' families, as well as the 23 wounded survivors. Very little of that money has actually been distributed.

In the past few days, there have been local news reports detailing how victims' parents are upset about the way the money will be distributed. Several parents complained of mounting medical bills, and one mother told of being unable to work since the trauma, and having to beg for money to cover rent. A Wednesday meeting between families and Jefferson County District Attorney Dave Thomas, who serves as co-chairman of the fund, seemed to ease some of the tension. Thomas announced that the funds would be used primarily to assist victims' families, with a much smaller allotment for the community. A survey will be distributed to families to resolve details, particularly whether the money should be divided equally, or based on need.

Meanwhile, victim Cassie Bernall's family declined to seek riches when they chose a publisher to tell the story of their daughter's conversion from troubled teen to Christian martyr. Despite interest from major mainstream publishers, they sold the book, titled *She Said Yes,* to a small Christian publishing firm.

SIGNIFICANCE

The Shoels's case reached court in November 2000. By then they had been joined by twelve other families of the dead or injured. The core of their case was that Harris's and Klebold's families had "breached their duty of care" by allowing their sons to amass a

The parents of Isaiah Eamon Shoels, who was killed in the April 1999 Columbine High School massacre, stand next to their son's grave marker. © LISS, STEVE/CORBIS SYGMA

cache of illegal weapons. Their lawsuit also claimed that Harris had planned the attack for 14 months and that his family should have been aware of this. The families rejected these accusations, but settled the suit for $1.6 million raised through homeowner insurance policies. This money was eventually divided between thirty-one families. An additional $900,000 came from Mark Manes, who sold guns to the pair.

In July 2004, however, the Shoels were back in court, this time before the U.S. Tenth Circuit Court of Appeals. They claimed that their family had accepted the deal in error, because of a mistake at their lawyer's office. The court ruled that the Shoels could not back out of the settlement they'd reached with the Harris and Klebold families.

Lawsuits accusing Columbine High School of failing its duty of care were dismissed, as were suits that alleged that a Denver police officer accidentally killed one of the victims, and another filed against eleven video game manufacturers and two film studios. A case brought against the makers of Solvay, an antidepressant used by Eric Harris, was settled out of court in April 2003, when the drug company agreed to make a $10,000 donation to the American Cancer Society.

Commenting on litigation spawned by the tragedy, *Christian Science Monitor* writer Jeff Kass mused: "Converting grief into legalese is something of an American trademark from plane crashes to SUV rollovers, the courts are a popular venue to help pinpoint blame and act as an emotional salve for those affected by tragedy." He also quoted Richard Lieberman, a Los Angeles–based psychologist and member of the National Association of School Psychologists National Emergency Assistance Team, who said that litigation was a double-edged sword. It keeps "people looking backward ... [when] the key to healing is moving forward,"; but Kass acknowledged that "lawsuits can bring order to chaos, and change laws for the better."

Despite all this legal action, however, little—other than the relatively small settlement with the Harris and Klebold families—was achieved. Contributing to a collection of essays, *Suing the Gun Industry: A Battle at the Crossroads of Gun Control and Mass Torts*, Howard M. Erichson suggests that more useful litigation would have pressed for "trigger locks to prevent accidental shootings and for smart gun technology to prevent unauthorized use by nonowners."

Yet the Columbine killings did reawaken a debate about America's gun control laws, and the massacre proved an important cultural touchpoint, influencing both Gus Van Sant's 2003 film *Elephant* and Douglas Coupland's novel, *Hey Nostradamus!*

Perhaps the best-known and most controversial work inspired by the tragedy was the 2002 polemic *Bowling for Columbine* directed by Michael Moore, which argued that American culture is innately violent. The film won an Academy Award for best documentary in 2003, but did little to change America's gun laws and, ironically, made Moore himself the target of yet more litigation.

FURTHER RESOURCES

Books

Lytton, Timothy D., ed. *Suing the Gun Industry: A Battle at the Crossroads of Gun Control and Mass Torts*. Ann Arbor, MI: University of Michigan Press, 2005.

Web sites

Christian Science Monitor. "Columbine Seeks Slosure—Out of Court." < http://www.csmonitor.com/2001/1129/p2s1-usju.html> (Jan 10, 2006).

Illinois Stops Executions

Magazine article

By: Anonymous

Date: February 2000

Source: "Illinois Stops Executions." *The New Abolitionist* 14 (February 2000).

About the Author: This article was published without a byline, and was written by a staff writer for *The New Abolitionist*, a periodical written and run by the Campaign To End The Death Penalty, an organization based in Chicago, Illinois.

INTRODUCTION

The history of the death penalty has been fraught with controversy for decades, since the Supreme Court eliminated its use in all states as a means of criminal punishment in June of 1972. At that time, the Court pronounced the death penalty to be random and proven to be racially discriminatory. In November 1973, however, the state of Illinois reinstated the death penalty when then-Governor Dan Walker signed a new, supposedly improved law into effect. By 1975, the Illinois Supreme Court nullified the new law as invalid. So began an ongoing debate as to whether or not the death penalty could be considered a just and practical means of punishment—and whether any judicial body had the legal and moral right to enforce it—or whether the chance of putting an innocent person to death was too great to risk, questions that reflect similar debates around the world.

PRIMARY SOURCE

"It's clear that the system is broken."

This is how an aide to Illinois Gov. George Ryan described the death-penalty system in Illinois. On January 31, Ryan said he was stopping all executions in Illinois because the system is "fraught with error and has come so close to the ultimate nightmare... Until I can be sure with moral certainty that no innocent man or woman is facing a lethal injection, no one will meet that fate."

There is no time limit on Ryan's action, but it is similar to the proposals for a moratorium on capital punishment that abolitionists have been fighting for.

Ryan is a Republican who still supports the death penalty. He only called a moratorium because of growing pressure. Two weeks earlier, Steve Manning became the 13th innocent man to be released from Illinois' death row. His conviction was based mainly on the testimony of a jailhouse snitch—which was proved false by FBI investigators.

With Manning's release, Illinois has freed more men from death row than it has executed since 1977. And there is growing talk that a 14th innocent man will be released—Edgar Hope.

Ryan's action is the first halt on executions in any state. Over the last year, lawmakers in six other states proposed moratoriums, but none became law. Illinois' action will add momentum to the moratorium movement.

This is a victory for abolitionists. But it is only a first step. Ryan wants to create a special panel to study the death-penalty system. If he packs it with fellow Republicans, the moratorium will be short-lived. The commission should be made up of people who know the true face of this system—like Dennis Williams and Darby Tillis, two of the 13 innocent ex-death row prisoners.

George Ryan, governor of Illinois, announces a moratorium on executions in his state on January 31, 2000. AP IMAGES

SIGNIFICANCE

There are many arguments against the use of the death penalty. Foremost is the fact that it negates a human being's right to life, and that it is completely irrevocable. This is of particular concern because there is a strong chance that an innocent person might be executed before the truth of the case comes to light. In addition to these concerns, there is no indication that the death penalty has proven to act as a deterrent against the types of violent crimes that result in its application.

On an international level, the death penalty has lost popularity over the last thirty years. Amnesty International, an organization dedicated to the protection of human rights, sponsored the International Conference on the Death Penalty in 1977, in Stockholm, Sweden, in an attempt to encourage the participating nations to consider alternate forms of punishment and to stop the use of the death penalty. At that time, sixteen countries had abolished the death penalty. Over the next three decades, an additional seventy nations eliminated the use of corporal punishment. Since the late 1990s, the United Nations Commission on Human Rights has also taken an active stance against the death penalty, passing an annual resolution encouraging member nations to at least establish a moratorium on executions.

In the United States, the death penalty remains an available means of punishment in thirty-eight out of fifty states, as of early 2006. Despite the elimination of corporal punishment by the Supreme Court in the 1970s, numerous states enacted laws that reinstated the death penalty, and between 1977 and 2005, 1,004 individuals were executed. The state of Illinois experienced several reversals by various courts in their attempt to reinstate the death penalty, but ultimately succeeded in reviving it. On September 12, 1990, death row inmate Charles Walker ceased to appeal his sentence and became the first person to be executed in Illinois under the new legislation. On May 10, 1994, convicted serial killer John Wayne Gacy became the first involuntary execution in Illinois in the seventeen years since the death penalty was reinstated.

By 2000, however, more Illinois death row inmates had been exonerated than had actually been executed, adding fuel to the argument that there is a real risk of sending innocent individuals to their deaths. By declaring a moratorium on executions in January 2000, Illinois Governor George Ryan took a stand that indicated it was unacceptable to take that risk, no matter how many guilty people escaped execution as a result. Ryan proceeded to form the Commission on Capital Punishment, whose purpose was to examine the weaknesses in the Illinois death penalty administration, and to determine how it might be reformed.

Various committees continued to find further indications that it was unlikely that the death penalty could continue without the potential for miscarriages of justice. In May of 2001, the Center on Wrongful Convictions reported that forty-six innocent Americans had been convicted of crimes based on either mistaken or deliberately false eyewitness testimony, and sent to death row as a result. A later report stated that since the 1950s, twenty-six wrongful executions had been carried out, based on convictions that were the results of false confessions.

In June of 2001, lawyers in charge of capital appeals for the Office of the State Appellate Defender decided to start the process of attempting to gain clemency for the death row inmates in the state of Illinois. While deals were being considered, Governor Ryan suggested that he himself might offer clemency to the inmates in question. This potential plan is a natural continuation of his earlier moratorium on executions. Ryan continued to consider the idea for several years, meanwhile granting pardons or clemency to several death row inmates. Then in January 2003, shortly before leaving office, Ryan announced his decision to go through with his intentions, and proceeded to provide all death row inmates in Illinois with clemency.

FURTHER RESOURCES
Web sites

Amnesty International. "The Death Penalty." <http://web.amnesty.org/pages/deathpenalty-index-eng> (accessed February 27, 2006).

DeathPenaltyInfo.org. <http://www.deathpenaltyinfo.org> (accessed February 27, 2006).

History of the Death Penalty in Illinois. "30 Years of the Death Penalty." <http://www.truthinjustice.org/dphistory-IL.htm> (accessed February 27, 2006).

World Socialist Web Site. "Illinois Death Penalty Report Reveals Widespread Abuse." <http://www.wsws.org/articles/2002/apr2002/illi-a27.shtml> (accessed February 27, 2006).

Saudi Arabia: Execution of Nigerian Men and Women

Use of Beheading and Amputation in Saudi Penal System

Report excerpt

By: Amnesty International

Date: June 15, 2000

Source: Amnesty International. "Saudi Arabia: Execution of Nigerian Men and Women." London: Amnesty International, June 15, 2000. Available online at <http://web.amnesty.org/library/print/>. (accessed January 20, 2006).

About the Author: Amnesty International (AI) is a human rights watchdog organization that engages in research and activities to prevent and end human rights abuses. AI operates as an organization independent from government, politics, and religion.

INTRODUCTION

During the beginning of the twentieth century, Abd al Aziz and the House of Saud forged Saudi Arabia into a unified kingdom. In a culture largely ruled by familial alliances, Abd al Aziz successfully created a state with loyalty to Al Saud. In order to create this loyalty and stability, Abd al Aziz used a code of behavior and a security force to instill respect and obedience to the law. Abd al Aziz created the modern day penal system in Saudi Arabia based upon the sharia, specifically the Hanbali school of Sunni Islam. The Hanbali School is based on the teachings of Imam Ahmad ibn Hanbal, one of the founders of Sunni Islamic Law. Hanbal was an expert on the traditions concerning the life of the Prophet Muhammad. The Hanbali judicial system is based on the traditions, sayings and life of Muhammad. This system of law outlines three types of crimes: crimes explicitly defined by the sharia, implicitly defined crimes found in the prohibitions of the sharia, and emerging more recently through governmental decrees, those crimes dealing with corporate law, taxation, immigration, and oil and gas.

For crimes that are explicitly defined by the sharia—homicide, assault, adultery, theft, and robbery—a *hadd*, or penalty, is also outlined. Homicide, for example, is determined by the sharia as a crime against an individual rather than the western view of crime against society. As such, the victim's family has the right to enact punishment, which can range from granting clemency to demanding *diya*, or compensatory payment, or even the victim's next of kin enacting the same bodily injury. Those accused of a crime are not afforded the same basic rights as those in western societies. In certain situations, namely cases involving death and grievous injury, the court holds the accused without bail or communication with an attorney. Although lawyers can advise the accused, criminal trials in Saudi Arabia are generally held without the benefit of council. The trials are closed and for trials involving foreign nationals, consular access is generally not allowed. A judge, considering the accounts of witnesses and the defendant's sworn testimony, determines the guilt or innocence of the accused, at which point a sentence is imposed. In the case of appeal, the Ministry of Justice examines a judge's decision, except for those sentences of death or amputation. In cases with a sentence of death or amputation, appeals are directed to a panel of five judges. The king automatically reviews the findings of this appellate court in all cases of capital punishment.

▮ PRIMARY SOURCE

Saudi Arabia has one of the highest rates of capital punishment in the world. Of the 766 executions recorded by Amnesty International between 1990 and 1999, over half were of migrant workers and other foreign nationals. While a high proportion of those were Asian migrant workers mainly from Pakistan, Bangladesh, India, Indonesia, the Philippines and Nepal—who comprise between sixty and eighty per cent of Saudi Arabia's workforce—at least seventy-two were Nigerians, mostly convicted for drug smuggling or armed robbery. By mid-June 2000 Saudi Arabia had executed fifty-three people, twenty-five of them in May: nineteen were Saudi Arabian nationals and thirty were foreign nationals, including from Nigeria, India, Pakistan, Sudan, Eritrea, Yemen, the Philippines, Ethiopia, Egypt and Iraq. Migrant workers and other foreign nationals have faced discriminatory treatment under the criminal justice system in Saudi Arabia.

Saudi Arabia has expanded the scope of the death penalty to cover a wide range of offences, including offences without lethal consequences such as apostasy, drug dealing, sodomy and 'witchcraft'. The scores of people who are executed every year, many for non-violent crimes, are put to death after summary trials that offer them no opportunity to defend themselves and almost no protection against miscarriages of justice.

Execution is by public beheading for men and, according to reports, by firing squad or beheading for women, sometimes in public. Foreign nationals are sometimes not even aware that they have been sen-tenced to death and neither they nor their families are warned in advance of the date of execution. They are rarely if ever allowed to see their loved ones before they are executed.

For those in prison who fear they face execution, the psychological torment is extreme. A former prisoner released from a women's prison in 1999 described to Amnesty International the fear of a fellow woman prisoner accused of murder: 'Every time a guard opens her cell door she gets very scared [thinking] that they will come to take her out for execution.'

Relatives of those executed in many cases receive no formal notification that the execution has taken place. The governments of foreign nationals executed in Saudi Arabia are also not always informed.

Amnesty International is also concerned at the high levels of judicial amputation carried out in Saudi Arabia, which it considers to be a form of torture as defined under the United Nations Convention Against Torture and Other Cruel, Inhuman, and Degrading Treatment or Punishment, to which Saudi Arabia became a state party in 1997. So far this year twenty-three amputations have been recorded, compared with two in the whole of 1999. Seven of these were 'cross amputations' (amputation of the right hand and left foot). On 13 May 2000 cross amputations were carried out on Kindi Amoro Muhammad, Nurayn Aladi Amos and Abdullah Abu-Bakr Muhammad, Nigerian nationals convicted of armed robbery and assault with seven Nigerians executed on the same day (see above). In June two Nigerian men had their right hands amputated following conviction for theft: on 1 June Muhammad Othman Adam in Mecca, and on 4 June Sanussi Sani Muhammad.

▮

SIGNIFICANCE

A 1999 review by Human Rights Watch (HRW) determined that "The government of Saudi Arabia, an absolute monarchy, continued to violate a broad array of civil and political rights, allowing no criticism of the government, no political parties, nor any other potential challenges to its system of government. Arbitrary arrest, detention without trial, torture, and corporal and capital punishment remained the norm in both political and common criminal cases, with at least twenty-two executions and three judicial amputations of the hand carried out by mid-October. Human rights abuses were facilitated by the absence of an independent judiciary and the lack of public scrutiny by an elected representative body or a free press." The study also determined that women face discrimination within the penal code. For example, it takes the testimony of two women to equal the testimony of one man. HRW also cites that although the penal code is based on teachings of Imam Ahmad ibn Hanbal, few laws are published. The Saudi monarchy possesses the power to "appoint and dismiss judges and to create special courts, undermining judicial independence. In addition, judges [enjoy] broad discretion in defining criminal offences and setting punishments, which [includes] severe floggings, amputations and beheadings." The report also asserts that Saudi allows for convictions based on uncorroborated confessions.

The crime rate in Saudi Arabia is relatively low and the increase in crime rates coincided with the presence of foreign workers. As a result, supporters of severe punishment, such as amputations and beheadings, attribute the low crime rate to the prevailing system.

FURTHER RESOURCES

Web sites

Human Rights Watch. "Saudi Arabia." <http://www.hrw.org/worldreport99/mideast/saudi.html> (accessed January 6, 2005).

Global Security. "Hanbali Islam." <http://www.globalsecurity.org/military/intro/islam-hanbali.htm> (accessed January 6, 2005).

The Case for Legalisation

Magazine article

By: Anonymous

Date: July 26, 2001

Source: "The Case for Legalisation." *The Economist Newspaper, Ltd.* (July 26, 2001).

About the Author: *The Economist* is a London-based, international news weekly in print since 1843. Articles most frequently appear in *The Economist* without author bylines. The magazine claims to be "writ[ten]by many hands but it speaks with a collective voice." The editorial staff asserts that author anonymity focuses the reader on the content of an article, not its writer.

INTRODUCTION

There have been arguments in support of, and against, the legalization of *street drugs* since the days of the alleged *opium dens* —and probably long before that. Perhaps the controversy began when the first person developed an addiction that interfered with daily functioning, and it had an impact on local society. In general, drug legislation and interdiction laws have been at least as concerned with the prevention of drug trafficking and importation, and all of the criminal behavior associated therewith as they have been with the public health and the negative societal impacts of drug abuse and addiction.

The American *war on drugs* technically dates back to 1875, when opium use was outlawed in northern California. Initially, it was intended as a means of shutting down local *opium dens;* the legislation was quickly broadened to include laws restricting opium from being smoked, and sharply curtailing (smoking opium) importation, and trafficking, particularly by persons of Chinese ethnicity or descent. This represents a very early instance of racial disparity in the *policing* of *dangerous street drugs.*

The Harrison Act, passed in 1914, was written in such as way as to afford legislative control over the manufacture, sales, importation, distribution, and taxation of cocaine and opium, and products made from them, but did not intend to prohibit their use. The same can basically be said for the 1937 Marijuana Tax Act. In effect, both of these laws intended to provide a framework for the licensure of professionals who were to be permitted to distribute or manufacture those drugs. The Harrison Act contained a clause in which it specifically provided for the medical use of cocaine and opium.

The central ethical issue involved in the legislation of drug manufacture and distribution has always been one of personal privacy: is it acceptable for a country founded on a democratic premise to legislate what can and cannot be ingested by its private citizens? If so, where is the line drawn? Why is it acceptable for people to be able to easily purchase and use tobacco products, for which there is a vast body of research data indicating potential for lethality, but not to do the same for cannabis sativa products? A similar parallel can be drawn for alcohol consumption and the use of cocaine (or other illegal drugs of similar genre).

There is much scholarly, research, and public data suggesting that the costs associated with drug use in America are enormous. The Office of National Drug Control Policy (ONDCP) estimates that roughly fourteen million United States citizens frequently use illegal drugs, and this is believed to have remained fairly stable for a decade or so. The NODCP estimates that nearly twenty billion dollars are spent annually in America to fight the *war on drugs.* In addition, drugs cost the country countless billions more each year in arrests, incarceration, litigation, loss of life, crimes associated in some way with drug use or drug-seeking behaviors, time spent in recovery and rehabilitation programs, time lost from work, decreased work productivity, and the like.

PRIMARY SOURCE

It is every parent's nightmare. A youngster slithers inexorably from a few puffs on a joint, to a snort of cocaine, to the needle and addiction. It was the flesh-creeping heart of "Traffic," a film about the descent into heroin hell of a pretty young middle-class girl, and it is the terror that keeps drug laws in place. It explains why even those politicians who puffed at a joint or two in their youth hesitate to put the case for legalising drugs.

The terror is not irrational. For the first thing that must be said about legalising drugs, a cause The Economist has long advocated and returns to this week (see survey), is that it would lead to a rise in their use, and therefore to a rise in the number of people dependent on them. Some argue that drug laws have no impact, because drugs are widely available. Untrue: drugs are expensive—a kilo of heroin sells in America for as much as a new Rolls-Royce—partly because their price reflects the dangers involved in distributing and buying them. It is much harder and riskier to pick up a dose of cocaine than it is to buy a bottle of whisky. Remove such constraints, make drugs accessible and very much cheaper, and more people will experiment with them.

A rise in drug-taking will inevitably mean that more people will become dependent—inevitably, because drugs offer a pleasurable experience that people seek to repeat. In the case of most drugs, that dependency may be no more than a psychological craving and affect fewer than one in five users; in the case of heroin, it is physical and affects maybe one in three. Even a psychological craving can be debilitating. Addicted gamblers and drinkers bring misery to themselves and their families. In addition, drugs have lasting physical effects and some, taken incompetently, can kill. This is true both for some "hard" drugs and for some that people think of as "soft": too much heroin can trigger a strong adverse reaction, but so can ecstasy. The same goes for gin or aspirin, of course: but many voters reasonably wonder whether it would be right to add to the list of harmful substances that are legally available.

The case for doing so rests on two arguments: one of principle, one practical. The principles were set out, a century and a half ago, by John Stuart Mill, a British liberal philosopher, who urged that the state had no right to intervene to prevent individuals from doing something that harmed them, if no harm was thereby done to the rest of society. "Over himself, over his own body and mind, the individual is sovereign," Mill famously proclaimed. This is a view that The Economist has always espoused, and one to which most democratic governments adhere, up to a point. They allow the individual to undertake all manner of dangerous activities unchallenged, from mountaineering to smoking to riding bicycles through city streets. Such pursuits alarm insurance companies and mothers, but are rightly tolerated by the state.

True, Mill argued that some social groups, especially children, required extra protection. And some argue that drug-takers are also a special class: once addicted, they can no longer make rational choices about whether to continue to harm themselves. Yet not only are dependent users a minority of all users; in addition, society has rejected this argument in the case of alcohol—and of nicotine (whose addictive power is greater than that of heroin). The important thing here is for governments to spend adequately on health education.

The practical case for a liberal approach rests on the harms that spring from drug bans, and the benefits that would accompany legalisation. At present, the harms fall disproportionately on poor countries and on poor people in rich countries. In producer and entrepot countries, the drugs trade finances powerful gangs who threaten the state and corrupt political institutions. Colombia is the most egregious example, but Mexico too wrestles with the threat to the police and political honesty. The attempt to kill illicit crops poisons land and people. Drug money helps to prop up vile regimes in Myanmar and Afghanistan. And drug production encourages local drug-taking, which (in the case of heroin) gives a helping hand to the spread of HIV/AIDS.

In the rich world, it is the poor who are most likely to become involved in the drugs trade (the risks may be high, but drug-dealers tend to be equal-opportunity employers), and therefore end up in jail. Nowhere is this more shamefully true than in the United States, where roughly one in four prisoners is locked up for a (mainly non-violent) drugs offence. America's imprisonment rate for drugs offences now exceeds that for all crimes in most West European countries. Moreover, although whites take drugs almost as freely as blacks and Hispanics, a vastly disproportionate number of those arrested, sentenced and imprisoned are non-white. Drugs policy in the United States is thus breeding a generation of men and women from disadvantaged backgrounds whose main training for life has been in the violence of prison.

Removing these harms would bring with it another benefit. Precisely because the drugs market is illegal, it cannot be regulated. Laws cannot discriminate between availability to children and adults. Governments cannot insist on minimum quality standards for cocaine; or warn asthma sufferers to avoid ecstasy; or demand that distributors take responsibility for the way their products are sold. With alcohol and tobacco, such restrictions are possible; with drugs, not. This increases the dangers to users, and especially to young or incompetent users. Illegality also puts a premium on selling strength: if each purchase is risky, then it makes sense to buy drugs in concentrated form. In the same way, Prohibition in the United States in the 1920s led to a fall in beer consumption but a rise in the drinking of hard liquor.

How, if governments accepted the case for legalisation, to get from here to there? When, in the 18th century, a powerful new intoxicant became available, the impact was disastrous: it took years of education for gin to cease to be a social threat. That is a strong reason to proceed gradually: it will take time for conventions governing sensible drug-taking to develop. Meanwhile, a century of illegality has deprived governments of much information that good policy requires. Impartial academic research is difficult. As a result, nobody knows how demand may respond to lower prices, and understanding of the physical effects of most drugs is hazy.

And how, if drugs were legal, might they be distributed? The thought of heroin on supermarket shelves understandably adds to the terror of the prospect. Just as legal drugs are available through different channels—caffeine from any cafe, alcohol only with proof of age, Prozac only on prescription—so the drugs that are now illegal might one day be distributed in different ways, based on knowledge about their potential for harm. Moreover, different countries should experiment with different solutions: at present, many are bound by a United Nations convention that hampers even the most modest moves towards liberalisation, and that clearly needs amendment.

To legalise will not be easy. Drug-taking entails risks, and societies are increasingly risk-averse. But the role of government should be to prevent the most chaotic drug-users from harming others—by robbing or by driving while drugged, for instance—and to regulate drug markets to ensure minimum quality and safe distribution. The first task is hard if law enforcers are preoccupied with stopping all drug use; the second, impossible as long as drugs are illegal. A legal market is the best guarantee that drug-taking will be no more dangerous than drinking alcohol or smoking tobacco. And, just as countries rightly tolerate those two vices, so they should tolerate those who sell and take drugs.

SIGNIFICANCE

Although fourteen or fifteen million people in the United States use illegal drugs (which includes the use of legal drugs for non-medical purposes and legal drugs that are obtained via illegal means) fairly regularly, a very small percentage of them are actually addicted, or are suffering the effects thereof. For those individuals, the needs for treatment are both urgent and lasting, as addiction treatment is ineffective without long-term follow-up and the inclusion of a variety of social support systems (treatment resources, health care coverage, education, job training, childcare, safe housing, and so forth). For those with addiction issues, interaction with the law enforcement system is common, as is poverty, lack of health care resources, adequate housing, and unemployment or underemployment. For those living in impoverished or inner city areas (or both), crime and drugs are often the only ways for poorly educated youth to make a reasonable living. For many, there is far more appeal in the money and elevated lifestyle sometimes associated with the drug trade than there is in the abject poverty and despair of life in housing projects.

The modern *war on drugs* got its start in the 1970s, under then-President Richard Nixon. It gained momentum with former President Ronald Reagan's creation of the Office of National Drug Control Policy as well as with then First Lady Nancy Reagan's *Just Say No (to drugs)* campaign.

Legislators (and others) argue against drug legalization, stating that it will cause an enormous upsurge in drug use, and ensuing addiction, among the general population. There are concerns for the deleterious health effects of drugs as a result of long-term or improper usage. Proponents of legalization argue that while use may peak briefly, it will level off rapidly, and the costs associated with public regulation will be far less than those associated with fighting the *war on drugs*. They also assert that some legal drugs have exceedingly harmful potential effects—as has been robustly documented in the case of alcohol and tobacco use. Those who argue that more crimes will be committed as a result of drug use are countered by those who assert that enormous amounts will be saved by the sharp decline in drug-related arrests, prosecutions, and incarcerations, if drugs are no longer illegal.

If the impact of educational programs on the overall number of smokers in America is an indication of the most effective approach to limiting initial and long-term exposure to potentially lethal substances, then it strongly suggests that the best route to preventing substance abuse in general is by effective,

Demonstrators march down Broadway to New York City Hall in 1998 to protest the use of surveillance cameras in Washington Square Park and to call for the legalization of marijuana. AP IMAGES

dle exchange programs could be implemented on a large-scale, and manufacture could be made to adhere to governmentally-regulated health and safety standards. Prison and jail populations would decrease exponentially, and potentially productive citizens could be returned to the workforce. The incentives to work in illegal drug trade would be all but absent, and the cost of drugs would likely drop considerably with free trade and open market competition. The American population would have ready access to drugs for which there are considerable therapeutic benefits under certain medical circumstances. Substance abuse and dependence would shift from being a legal justice and law enforcement issue to a physical and behavioral health concern. It would appear that there is much to be gained by ending the *war on drugs* and considering a new, and potentially more effective, paradigm.

FURTHER RESOURCES

Books

Moffitt, Arnol, John Malouf, and Craig Thompson. *Drug Precipice: Illicit Drugs, Organised Crime, Fallacies of Legalisation, Worsening Problems, Solutions.* Sydney, New South Wales: University of New South Wales Press, 1998.

Szasz, Thomas. *Our Right to Drugs: The Case for a Free Market.* Westport, Connecticut: Praeger, 1992.

Web sites

Schaffer Library of Drug Policy. "End the War (Anthony Lewis, New York Times, November 3, 1995)." <http://www.druglibrary.org/Schaffer/debate/mcn/mcn3.htm> (accessed March 28, 2006).

Kids Against Drugs—Campaign for Drug-Free Families. "Home Page and Statement of Purpose." <http://www.kidsagainstdrugs.com/> (accessed March 28, 2006).

Justice Policy Institute. "New national report shows that drug-free zone laws fail to protect youth from drug sales, worsen racial disparity in prisons: Growing movement to change ineffective laws finds support among lawmakers and law enforcement officials." <http://www.justice-policy.org/article.php?id=571> (accessed March 28, 2006).

Drug War Chronicle. "Raising awareness of the consequences of drug prohibition." <http://stopthedrugwar.org/index.shtml> (accessed March 28, 2006).

Schaffer Library of Drug Policy. "The Consumers Union Report—Licit and Illicit Drugs." <http://www.druglibrary.org/SCHAFFER/library/studies/cu/cumenu.htm> (accessed March 28, 2006).

thoughtful, targeted, and well-placed educational efforts.

There is little objective evidence to suggest that the *war on drugs* is being won in America—indeed, the explosion in incarceration and criminal recidivism over the past several decades indicates just the opposite. In fact, the costs to the American economy and population are staggering; this suggests that there might be benefit in considering alternative means to the same end: decreasing the importation, manufacture, distribution, and use of potentially harmful (whether legal or illegal) drugs by the American population. By considering sweeping legalization and decriminalization of drugs for personal use, substance abuse treatment could be made readily available, nee-

Requests for Immunity by Federal Prosecutors, 1973–2003

Government report

By: Department of Justice, Bureau of Justice Statistics

Date: June 11, 2003

Source: "Requests for Immunity by Federal Prosecutors, 1973—2003." *Sourcebook of Criminal Justice Statistics Online* , vol. 31. Washington, D.C.: Department of Justice, Bureau of Justice Statistics, 2003.

About the Author: The United States Department of Justice is responsible for the conduct of all legal proceedings, both civil and criminal, authorized by American federal statues. The Bureau of Justice Statistics is the branch of the Department of Justice responsible for the compilation and publication of all data in relation to the function of the Department.

INTRODUCTION

Immunity from prosecution is far more notorious in the court of public opinion than it is actually utilized in the American criminal trial process. Immunity has acquired a measure of public notoriety because it is a device only employed in high-profile proceedings, such as those involving organized crime.

As the thirty-year statistics published by the Department of Justice reveal, requests for immunity by Federal prosecutors for witnesses are very rare, relative to the volume of prosecutions conducted across the United States. Immunity requests are advanced in less than one percent of all criminal proceedings per year; an even smaller fraction are made in other federal proceedings, such as income tax and immigration cases.

Immunity is a virtually impenetrable protective barrier from prosecution when provided to a person of interest. Most typically, immunity is sought for a particular witness as a part of the larger resolution of their dealings with the state. A plea bargain regarding other criminal charges, admission into a Witness Protection program, or relocation measures often form a part of immunity discussions.

Unlike countries such as Great Britain or Canada, which share a common legal heritage with the United States, the immunity sought by an American prosecutor for a witness is formally authorized by way of a judicial order. Once conferred, the immunized witness must testify or face contempt of court charges.

Immunity is founded upon the broadest and the most flexible of legal principles, the *public interest*. The Department of Justice prosecutors who advance an immunity request must assess the public interest by applying the following considerations:

1. The importance of the prosecution: a murder or high level drug conspiracy might attract an immunity request; the robbery of a tavern will not.
2. The value of the anticipated evidence from the witness: if the case can be proven by other means, the witness will not attract immunity.
3. The likelihood of the witness complying with a request to testify in the ordinary course.
4. The witness' level of participation in the offense that is the subject of the prosecution: in conspiracy cases, the target witness is often highly placed.
5. The criminal history of the witness.
6. The likelihood of a successful prosecution.
7. The likelihood of adverse collateral consequences to the witness; these usually relate to threats of death or bodily harm to the target witness or family.

It is a fact of prosecutorial life that in many cases, immunity will be sought and obtained for otherwise highly unsavory persons. Investigators and prosecutors have long recognized that granting immunity to such individuals is sometimes the price they have to pay in order to secure their help in prosecuting even more serious crimes.

PRIMARY SOURCE

REQUESTS FOR IMMUNITY BY FEDERAL PROSECUTORS, 1973–2003

See primary source image.

SIGNIFICANCE

Transparency is the hallmark of an effective justice system—the ancient maxim, justice must not simply be done, justice must be seen to be done, exemplifies this fact. Transparency and its brother, accountability, only live when the public are given the tools with which to measure the overall performance of the law in relation to society.

The first significance of the published data concerning requests for witness immunity is the fact that it exists at all. Thirty years of records is an unimpeach-

Requests for immunity by Federal prosecutors to the U.S. Attorney General and witnesses involved in these requests

BY ORIGIN OF REQUEST, FISCAL YEARS 1973–2003

	Requests			Witnesses		
	Total number	Criminal Division Number	Percent	Total number	Criminal Division Number	Percent
1973	1,160	769	66%	2,715	1,598	59%
1974	1,410	1,121	80%	3,655	2,055	56%
1975	1,632	1,259	77%	3,733	2,183	58%
1976	1,789	1,361	76%	3,923	2,366	60%
1977	1,798	1,250	70%	4,413	1,969	45%
1978	1,445	959	66%	2,997	1,403	47%
1979	1,596	1,163	73%	3,204	1,816	57%
1980	1,653	1,207	73%	3,530	1,892	54%
1981	1,686	1,252	74%	3,271	2,032	62%
1982	1,836	1,394	76%	3,810	2,233	59%
1983	1,986	1,425	72%	4,226	2,243	53%
1984	2,378	1,838	77%	4,784	2,858	60%
1985	2,451	1,898	77%	5,146	3,329	65%
1986	2,550	1.948	76%	5,013	3,267	65%
1987	2,359	1,869	79%	4,603	3,249	71%
1988	2,359	1,821	77%	4,702	3,205	68%
1989	2,301	1,807	79%	4,495	3,249	72%
1990	2,049	1,694	83%	3,735	2,905	78%
1991	1,953	1,561	80%	3,377	2,449	73%
1992	1,819	1,417	78%	3,242	2,309	71%
1993	1,959	1,466	75%	3,521	2,393	68%
1994	1,717	1,262	74%	3,279	2,225	68%
1995	1,520	1,182	78%	2,776	1,987	72%
1996	1,493	1,135	76%	2,806	2,066	74%
1997	1,502	1,108	74%	2,737	1,953	71%
1998	1,340	1,017	76%	2,300	1,616	70%
1999	1,196	908	76%	2,059	1,444	70%
2000	1,206	955	79%	2,164	1,584	73%
2001	1,132	929	82%	1,986	1,558	78%
2002	901	717	80%	1,546	1,084	70%
2003	913	743	81%	1,613	1,175	73%

Note: These data reflect requests received from Federal prosecutors under 18 U.S.C. 6001-6005, the statue that governs the granting of use immunity. 18 U.S.C. 6003 requires all Federal prosecuting attorneys to receive authorization from the U.S. Attorney General (or representative) before seeking a court order for witness immunity. It should be noted that in some cases in which the authorization is obtained, the prosecutor may decide not to seek the immunity order from the courts. Therefore, the number of witnesses actually granted immunity is probably lower than the data in the table indicate. It should also be noted that data for 1973 and 1974 include a total of 11 requests and 27 witness, and 7 requests and 11 witnesses, respectively, falling under an older statute, 18 U.S.C. 2514, which was repealed. "Criminal Division" includes the Criminal division of the U.S. Department of Justice and the U.S. attorneys. Other requests, not pertaining to the Criminal division, come from the remaining divisions of the U.S. Department of Justice (e.g., Antitrust, Tax, Civil Division, Civil Rights, and Environment and Natural Resources), as well as from the other Federal agencies (e.g., Federal Trade Commission, Securities and Exchange Commission, and Department of the Army) and from Congress, all of which may request immunity for witnesses. Some data have been revised by the Source and may differ from previous editions of Sourcebook.

SOURCE: Table constructed by Sourcebook staff from data provided by the U.S. Department of Justice, Criminal Division.

■ **PRIMARY SOURCE**

Requests for Immunity by Federal Prosecutors, 1973–2003 *SOURCEBOOK OF CRIMINAL JUSTICE STATISTICS 2003.* REPRINTED BY PERMISSION.

Former major league baseball player Jose Canseco raises his hand to be sworn in for testimony before a 2005 congressional hearing on the use of steroids by baseball players. Canseco refused to testify without the immunity he had requested. © JASON REED/REUTERS/CORBIS

able measuring stick with which to assess this corner of the federal justice system.

Immunity from prosecution is closely linked to its criminal litigation cousin, the plea bargain. For many prospective protected persons, any arrangement with the prosecution that is distilled to "If I talk, you don't prosecute me" is as good as an acquittal. The reality of major crime prosecutions is that in many cases, to achieve an ultimate goal, there must be compromises; grants of immunity to otherwise undesirable people are a means to an end.

Like the plea bargain, the grant of immunity from prosecution is a dark, ever-present reality to the conduct of major criminal trials. The serious crimes typically prosecuted by the Federal Department of Justice typically involve sophisticated and often well-funded defendants. Terrorism and other crimes against the 2001 Patriot Act, the multinational drug trade, and the traditional organized crime of La Cosa Nostra or outlaw motorcycle gangs are perpetrated by disparate groups that operate with a common denominator—secrecy. Conventional prosecutorial theory means if one unsavory person must be granted immunity to penetrate the veil of secrecy to secure the conviction of a larger or more dangerous group, the prosecution has made a wise investment on behalf of the public.

The figures described in the Department of Justice table do not convey the full import of the immunity application to the reader. Immunity when sought by the federal authorities will almost always be a form of *transactional immunity* , in which the recipient will be protected from any consequences of his actions that lead to the immunity agreement being sought, save for perjury when testifying pursuant to the immunity order.

The other chief significance of an immunity request is that unlike a plea bargain, immunity will ultimately be tested in a public courtroom. Once a witness testifies under an immunity order, they may be cross-examined with respect to all that was promised and proffered to secure the cooperation of the witness with the state. Many criminal trials become credibility contests between opposing unsavory persons, one of whom is charged, the other immunized into the foundation of the prosecution case.

The thirty years of data does not reveal a discernable pattern of requests. The numbers fluctuate. The one constant factor has been the presence of the Racketeer Influenced Corrupt Organizations Act of 1970, better known by its acronym, RICO. Aimed at the activities of organized criminals, RICO-related prosecutions by their nature have been a stimulus for witness immunity applications.

The Department of Justice figures highlight a fundamental distinction between the resources of the state and those of the defense. The state must prove its case in a criminal proceeding beyond a reasonable doubt; the ability of the state to procure witnesses on the strength of an offer of prosecutorial immunity is a significant weapon. The defense has no corresponding ability to offer such protection to any of its prospective witnesses, a disparity that has never been addressed in American criminal procedure.

FURTHER RESOURCES

Books

Goldfarb, Ronald. *Perfect Villains, Imperfect Heroes: Robert F. Kennedy's War Against Organised Crime.* Sterling, Va.: Capital Books, 2002.

Morse, Christopher J. *New York Criminal Procedure.* Durham, N.C.: Carolina Academic Press, 2004.

Web sites

Department of Justice. "United States Attorneys Manual." <http://www.usdoj.gov/usao/eousa> (accessed February 27, 2006).

University of Arkansas. "No Immunity Request by Local Attorney Could Land Her Tough Sanctions, Maybe Jail." <http://law.uark.edu/library/finals/brill/web/the-client/marksway2.htm> (accessed February 27, 2006).

Michael Jackson Booked

Photograph

By: Anonymous

Date: November 20, 2003

Source: AP Images

About the Photographer: The photographer who took this booking photograph (mug shot) of Michael Jackson for the Santa Barbara, California, Sherrif's Deptartment is unknown.

INTRODUCTION

Having lived most of his life in the glare of media spotlight, Michael Jackson's eccentric lifestyle has frequently been scrutinized. He became the world's most famous singer after launching his solo career with *Off The Wall* in 1979. Three years later *Thriller* became the biggest-selling album of all time with 51 million albums sold since 1982.

Dubbed "Wacko Jacko" by the British tabloid media, Jackson became as famous for his eccentric behavior as he was for his music. Much attention was focused on his extensive plastic surgery, his penchant for exotic pets and other strange purchases, as well as his perpetually childish demeanor. Jackson cultivated this Peter Pan image, even calling his massive California ranch "Neverland" and filling it with fairground equipment.

However this reputation for eccentricity took on a darker complexion when Jackson was accused of sex abuse. In 1993 Jordan Chandler, the teenage son of a Beverly Hills dentist, accused Jackson of molestation. Police investigating the case raided the Neverland Ranch, but the Chandler family settled out of court with Jackson and never filed criminal charges. The settlement was said to be in excess of $20 million.

Santa Barbara County Sheriff's Dept.

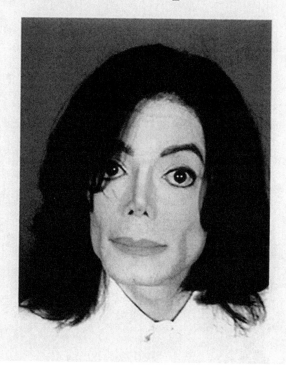

11/20/2003
Photo Image of:
NAME: JACKSON, MICHAEL
RAC: B   SEX: M
DOB: 8/29/1958   AGE: 45
HGT: 511   WGT: 120
BLD: CMP:
HAI: BLK   EYE: BRO
MKS:
BOOKING #:   621785

PRIMARY SOURCE

Michael Jackson Booked: A 2003 booking card from the Santa Barbara County Sheriff's Department displaying Michael Jackson's photo and vital statistics. AP IMAGES

After the Chandler case Jackson's career began to decline. In 2003 the British broadcaster Martin Bashir, who had built his reputation with celebrity interviews, was granted unprecedented access to Jackson's home to make the documentary *Living with Michael Jackson.* The film was an extraordinary portrayal of a seemingly troubled man, but the most incredible part was when children whom Jackson had befriended were interviewed. They admitted to attending "sleepovers" he hosted and to sharing his bed. Given the pop star's inherent childishness this did not by itself point to child abuse, but it begged a fundamental question: What 44-year-old man attended sleepover parties with young boys?

Living with Michael Jackson created a storm of headlines. After its screening one of the children interviewed by Bashir, Gavin Arvizo, came forward with new allegations of sexual molestation. Like the Chandler family, the Arvizo's were represented by

Larry Feldman; and as before the investigation was launched by District Attorney Tom Sneddon.

Jackson was arrested in November 2003, booked in Santa Barbara County, California, and brought to trial in spring 2005. He faced ten charges ranging from child abduction, false imprisonment, and extortion to administering alcohol to and committing of a lewd act on a minor. On June 13, 2005, Jackson was acquitted of all charges.

PRIMARY SOURCE

MICHAEL JACKSON BOOKED

See primary source image.

SIGNIFICANCE

Booking photographs (mug shots) are taken during every booking after arrest, and often contain addi-

Michael Jackson exits the Santa Barbara County courthouse on March 21, 2005, during his trial for child molestation.
© CARLO ALLEGRI/POOL/REUTERS/CORBIS

tional identifying information as in this case, the height, weight, race, hair color, eye color, and sex of Michael Jackson. Whether the individual is eventually acquitted or found guilty, a record of the mug shot remains and is kept available to share among other law enforcement agencies.

Jackson's acquittal owed as much to the lack of firm evidence as it did to the defense's discrediting of the main prosecution witness, Janet Arvizo.

Accusations that Jackson kept a "suitcase" full of pornography in the bedroom he shared with young boys on his controversial sleepovers were found to be unsubstantiated. When it was suggested that he kept and shared pornographic material on his computers,

the judge examined the material but agreed with the defense that it may have been automatically stored by the computers and "there wouldn't be any way of knowing if anyone looked at the material or not." The judge also agreed that the material did not match the time period of the alleged crimes. The judge tired of hearing outlandish charges not backed up with evidence. When Mrs. Arvizo told the jury that "Neverland is all about booze, pornography and sex with boys" the judge admonished her for her outburst. Charges that Jackson regularly served children alcohol were also never substantiated.

It was the discrediting of Mrs. Arvizo, in fact, that proved the turning point. The Jackson defense team had hired a private detective to uncover information about her and then successfully turned the trial into an examination of her credibility, portraying her as venal and money-grubbing. Her aggressive manner also riled the jurors. One juror, Melissa Herard, told the *Guardian*, "A lot of the parts of her testimony, I just wanted to break out laughing, but I couldn't. She was just up and down, up and down."

After the trial, one juror told CNN's Larry King that he believed Jackson had "probably molested boys" but that the evidence presented had not been sufficient to warrant a conviction. Although the jurors believed a crime may have been committed, the prosecution had not satisfied its burden of proof "beyond reasonable doubt". On that basis Jackson had been found not guilty.

Critics argued that some jurors may have used the trial aftermath as an ego trip; others questioned whether they had found Mr. Jackson innocent because of his celebrity and their dislike for the accuser's mother. Eleanor Cook, a 79-year-old juror, criticized Janet Arvizo for snapping her fingers while evidence was being given and said that her attitude was "intimidatoray".

After the trial Jackson vowed to change his ways and promised to be more guarded in his interaction with children. Since the trial Jackson has been living in Bahrain and his Neverland ranch was closed in March of 2006.

Despite having his name cleared, plummeting record sales that followed the original accusations, combined with his extravagant lifestyle and the Arvizo trial left Michael Jackson financially ruined and his career in tatters. His previous studio album, *Blood on the Dance Floor* released in 2003, sold just 900,000 copies, a fraction of the millions he sold in the 1980s. Despite owning a substantial portion of publishing rights to songs by the Beatles, Jackson was left in financial turmoil with post-trial debts said to total $150m.

FURTHER RESOURCES
Web sites

Guardian Unlimited. "Special Report: Michael Jackson Trial" <http://www.guardian.co.uk/jackson/0,15819, 1428022,00.html> (accessed: Jan 11, 2006).

Sony Music Entertainment, Inc. "Michael Jackson Official Web Site" <http://www.michaeljackson.com/> (accessed: Jan 11, 2006).

Parolees in Revolving Door

Newspaper article

By: Jim H. Zamora

Date: December 23, 2002

Source: Zamora, Jim H. "Parolees in Revolving Door." *San Francisco Chronicle*, December 23, 2002, <http://www.sfgate.com/> (accessed January 31, 2006).

About the Author: Jim Herron Zamora is a journalist on the staff of the *San Francisco Chronicle*. He is currently assigned to the Metro and Oakland Bureaus, writing on topics concerning crime and the criminal justice system, and their impact on residents and life in the East Bay region.

INTRODUCTION

Although statistics vary somewhat from state to state, one of the single largest contributing factors to the ever-growing American prison population is the extraordinarily high recidivism rate. Based on the most current statistics available from the Western Prison Project, more than 700 people are in prison for each 100,000 members of the American population. That figure represents the highest rate among all of the countries in the world for which such statistics are collected. The number of incarcerated Americans has increased by more than sixty percent since 1973. In addition to the roughly two million individuals serving time in the American correctional system, there are approximately four times as many people either on probation or parole, or who have completed their sentence requirements.

A very large number of those serving time in the correctional system are repeat offenders who are back in the system as a result of parole or probation violations. As legally defined, probation is a sentencing term that allows a convicted offender to be released into the community with stipulations involving program attendance, community service, gainful employment, and generally remaining clear of the criminal justice system for a specified period of time. In brief, probation involves suspending all or part of the prison term imposed at sentencing, pending successful completion of the specified probation conditions. An individual may be given a wholly suspended sentence (serving no period of incarceration) or may be sentenced to incarceration followed by probation. Probation is usually given to individuals who are young,

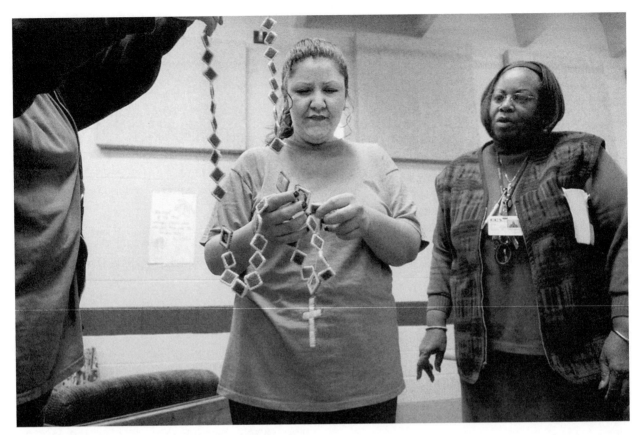

With Chaplain Shirley Compton, right, standing beside her, an inmate, center, in the Life Principles Community/ Crossings program at the New Mexico Women's Correctional Facility holds a handmade rosary with sewn-in pictures of her four children, her mother, and herself. The program seeks to help women avoid returning to prison. AP IMAGES

non-violent, first-time offenders, or otherwise likely to benefit more from rehabilitation efforts or programming than from exposure to the prison system and its inhabitants. By federal statute, the upper limit for allowable probation time is sixty months. Supervision by a probation and parole officer is always a part of the process, and can vary in level of contact and intensity of requirements. Often, both probation and parole programs involve quite frequent contacts, either by telephone or in person, with the assigned officer, as well as blood or urine drug and alcohol screens. If the offender violates the conditions of the probation in any significant way, the suspension of the sentence can be revoked, and the offender sent to prison to serve his term (after the appropriate legal actions are taken to assure that no violation of constitutional rights has occurred).

Parole is the legal term for release from prison or jail before the offender has served the full term of the sentence imposed, based on the accrual of sufficient "good time." Good time is defined as prison time served without sanctions or disciplinary actions. Its

calculation is based on a very specific formula that considers the nature of the crime, length of sentence, type of conviction, level of incarceration, and various other factors, depending on location and whether the inmate is housed in a county, state, or federal jail or prison. Parole always involves the service of a term of incarceration, and the parolee is therefore considered a higher risk for the community than the probationer. Parole is typically more stringent than probation, and imposes more conditions in terms of meetings with the assigned parole officer, increased frequency of drug and alcohol screening, mandatory program participation, and extensive supervision of the entire re-entry process for a prolonged period of time. Violation of parole also reactivates the initial sentencing time, but the process is somewhat different than that which applies to probation. An allegation of a probation violation sets a judicial review process in motion. If the parolee commits a significant violation of the release conditions or commits a new crime for which he is apprehended and convicted, the parolee appears before the Parole Board for consideration of revocation of the parole period and re-institution of the original sentencing requirements.

Recidivism can involve the revocation of probation or parole, conviction for a new offense while in the community, or conviction of a crime while incarcerated, necessitating an additional period of incarceration to be served at the end of the current term.

■ PRIMARY SOURCE

Since his first arrest at age 19, Gary Johnson has been in prison six times, mainly for drugs or minor parole violations. On the streets, he's been shot twice. Behind bars he was stabbed twice by other inmates.

But he's not a murderer, rapist or robber—just a two-bit drug offender who keeps offending and then returning home to his mom's couch.

"I don't really have any big dreams," said Johnson, 42, who began a new drug counseling program last month after parole agents spotted him hanging out on a street corner. "I'd be very happy if I could just stay outside (prison), maybe get some kind of job. I'm too old for this: It's wearing on me."

With ex-cons being blamed for helping drive up crime across California, a growing number of critics point to California's revolving-door prison policy—which does little to help nonviolent drug offenders back into society. "About half of inmates are going to reoffend and end up incarcerated no matter what you do," said Mario Paparozzi, former chairman of the New Jersey Parole Board. "The hard part of our business is what do you do with that other half." Last year, 126,000 prisoners in California were released—six times more than in 1975—and most of them had little preparation for life on the outside.

Before the mid–1970s, most sentences were indeterminate, meaning that most inmates could get off much earlier than their original sentence if they completed vocational or academic classes in addition to good behavior.

The state replaced that system with one lacking an incentive for inmates to take classes or get counseling to help them prepare for life outside prison.

Now, virtually everyone released from prison spends three years on parole. Most—about 71 percent—end up back in prison within 18 months—the nation's highest recidivism rate and nearly double the average of all other states.

But their average stay back in prison is only five months, and some experts wonder whether California is just postponing crime rather than solving it. "If you put somebody back in prison for only a few months, all you have done is postponed the inevitable return to the streets of a convict who is unprepared for society," said Paparozzi, now a criminology professor at the College of New Jersey.

STATE PRISONS' MISSION

The mission of the California Department of Corrections is to protect the public from criminals—not rehabilitate offenders, notes department spokeswoman Terry Thornton.

"California law dictates that the purpose of prison is punishment," she said. "We offer opportunities for those willing to change. Those willing to take responsibility for their actions are the ones who improve, and we will help them." But critics say other states, including New York and Texas, have succeeded in being tough on violent criminals while reducing recidivism among nonviolent drug offenders.

"We are trying get the violent felons into prison and use other sanctions for the nonviolent offenders," said Tom Grant, spokesman of the New York Division of Parole. "A dirty drug test would not send you back into a correctional setting in New York. It might get you into drug treatment program."

PAROLEES FILL PRISONS

California is one of three states in which most people who enter prison each year are not new offenders but parolees who either commit new crimes or so-called technical violations of their parole terms, such as failing a drug test or missing appointments with their case agent.

"Having a zero-tolerance approach to technical violations really means you've given up on preparing these inmates for life outside prison," said Paparozzi. "With this approach, California may want to just abolish parole and keep everyone in prison for a couple more years."

In 1980, 21 percent of those entering prison were parole violators, evenly split between technical violations and new offenses. By 2000, 69 percent of those entering in prison were parolees; 57 percent for technical parole violations and 12 percent for new felony convictions.

That overall rate is about double the national average for parolees re-entering state prison. And California is the only state where most people entering prison are not there for committing new crimes.

"(We are) looking at ways to reduce the high number of parolees that return to prison for technical violations," said Nancy Lyons, deputy executive director of Little Hoover Commission, an independent state oversight agency. "California stands alone from all the other states when it comes to revocation rates." The commission plans hearings on parole reforms Jan. 23 and Feb. 27 in Sacramento.

"California made an expensive policy choice to put more people in prison instead of trying other alternatives," said Jeremy Travis of the Urban Institute, a Washington, D.C., think tank, who has co-authored several recent studies on recidivism and parole in California.

"The question is really whether you can afford that policy anymore.... I don't think California can afford to build more prisons in the current economic environment."

From the late 1970s to the late 1990s, California added more prison cells than any state in U.S. history. But spending on parole agents lagged, according to state data analyzed by UC Irvine Professor Joan Petersilia.

In 1997, California cut spending on parole services by 44 percent, nearly doubling parole caseloads to more than 70-to-1, according to Petersilia's 2000 report for the California Policy Research Center.

That leaves agents little time for anything but rounding up violators. Statewide, authorities have lost track of 1 in 5 parolees.

Only 5 percent of California's prisoners complete a re-entry program before they are released from prison, and fewer than a quarter of them get education or vocational training while in prison, according to Petersilia's study.

"So many people come out of prison with nothing but $200 and a head full of anger," said Ron Owens, an ex-convict who now counsels parolees. "They don't learn to be better people on the outside. They only know how to function on the inside."

Oakland has more nonprofits to help inmates and their families than any other city in California, parole officials said.

Every Wednesday, representatives from a dozen organizations make presentations to 50 newly released inmates who are required to attend.

But parole agents cannot force the ex-convicts to participate. Most show initial interest but about 90 percent fail to follow though.

Parolees, agents and counselors said inmates who go directly from highly structured and regulated life in prison back to their old neighborhoods lack the self-discipline to change.

"In prison, we are willing to beg for a job flipping pancakes for 6 cents an hour, but outside we'll never think of filling out a job application at an IHOP," said Kevin Grant, an ex-convict who oversees a re-entry program.

"Inside we know how to be good prisoners, follow the rules. But outside, we just lose it all and act like fool kids again."

Ex-convicts say it's tough to change their stripes. Gary Johnson has lost count of how many re-entry programs he has quit.

"I've wasted a lot of time in programs that didn't really help me," he said. "But I've wasted a lot more time on street corners."

SIGNIFICANCE

During the 1990s, there was a significant change in the American system of jurisprudence regarding both sentencing and time served. Prior to that time, there was considerably more leniency in probation, parole, and even in discharged sentences (acquittal rates, dismissal of charges, etc.). The American justice system has characterized itself as being "tough on crime," meaning that first-time or non-violent offenders are more likely to be sentenced to prison terms, and repeat offenders are likely to get far longer sentences than would probably have been the case in the past (depending on the severity and nature of the offense for which the individual has been convicted). One of the concomitant problems with the system, along with recidivism, is the failure of the penal system to rehabilitate convicted felons, or render them more likely to become productive, law-abiding citizens upon release from prison than they were before serving their sentences. Very few prison systems incorporate a thorough education and recidivism reduction curriculum into their prison education programs. There are few job-training or work-release systems in effect, and few systems, whether public or privatized (prisons run by private correctional corporations) are able to budget for that type of programming. The problems created by the lack of re-entry training or recidivism reduction programs are significant contributing factors to repeat offending. Inmates have few skills and little motivation to acquire them when they leave prison; they have no training or education with which to secure reasonable (earning sufficient income to deter them from returning to their former criminal occupations), gainful employment; and they are likely to be barred from securing skilled or lucrative jobs. Since most job applications ask whether the applicant has a past felony conviction, former inmates are either forced to lie or they are unable to qualify for many higher-paying jobs.

Many of the individuals who become unsuccessful criminals (i.e., those who get arrested and convicted) are from lower socioeconomic backgrounds, are poorly or minimally educated—many had learning difficulties, behavior problems, or poor school attendance as children—and are members of minority groups. The vast majority of inmates are male, nearly two-thirds of them are Black or Hispanic, and between fifty and sixty percent of them are in prison on a second or third (frequently many more than that) conviction. Slightly more than a third of all inmates incarcerated at any given time are doing time as the result of a violent offense. Depending on the area, from one-third to three-fourths of all incarcerated felons have a history of substance abuse and are in prison (or jail) for substance-related offenses (buying, selling, trafficking, or any of the related offenses, such as prostitution and weapons charges). The U.S. Bureau of Justice Statistics reports that nearly seventy percent of those who have served time for a felony are rearrested for a significant crime within three years of release. The vast majority of convicted felons who serve jail or prison time have a history of multiple arrests, often starting as youthful offenders. The average number of arrests (again, this varies by age and geographic location) is between seventeen and twenty—either with or without attendant incarceration. Innmates generally are young, and the overwhelming majority are below the age of thirty-five. Older inmates are generally those who are serving long terms, and have been incarcerated for a prolonged period. It is common for incarcerated felons to refer to crime as "a young man's game" that they will either "outgrow or be killed by."

FURTHER RESOURCES
Books
Perry, Robert J., Dona Wilpolt, and Charles A. King. *Getting Free Behind the Walls: Comprehensive Addictions Treatment.* Santa Fe, N. Mex.: New Mexico Corrections Department, 2000.

Soering, Jens. *An Expensive Way to Make Bad People Worse: An Essay on Prison Reform from an Insider's Perspective.* New York: Lantern Books, 2004.

Web sites
Economist.com. "Crime in the United States." <http://www.economist.com/background/displayBackground.cfm?story_id=1270755> (accessed February 2, 2006).

Economist.com. "Prison and Beyond: A Stigma That Never Fades." <http://www.economist.com/world/na/displayStory.cfm?story_id=1270755> (accessed February 2, 2006).

Prison Policy Initiative. "The Prison Index. " <http://www.prisonpolicy.org/articles/prisonindex_highincarceration.pdf> (accessed February 2, 2006).

U. S. Department of Justice. Bureau of Justice Statistics. "Criminal Offender Statistics." <http://www.ojp.usdoj.gov/bjs/crimoff.htm> (accessed February 2, 2006).

Wagner, Peter. "Incarceration Is Not an Equal Opportunity Punishment." *Prison Policy Initiative,* June 28, 2005, <http://www.prisonpolicy.org/articles/notequal.shtml> (accessed February 2, 2006).

Megan's Law Poorly Enforced

Newspaper article

By: Anonymous

Date: April 3, 2004

Source: *The Washington Times.* "Megan's Law Poorly Enforced." April 3, 2004. <http://www.washtimes.com/national/20040403-113759-4539r.htm> (accessed September 22, 2005).

About the Author: This article was written without attribution by a staff writer for the *Washington Times;* a daily newspaper published in Washington, D.C. with an average daily circulation of 103,017.

INTRODUCTION
On July 29, 1994, seven-year-old Megan Kanka of Hamilton Township, New Jersey, was sexually assaulted and murdered by her neighbor Jesse Timmendequas, a twice-convicted sex offender free on parole.

The incident prompted Governor Christine Todd Whitman to sign the first "Megan's Law," which requires community notification when convicted sexual offenders are released into a neighborhood.

When the federal Megan's Law was signed by President Bill Clinton in May 1996, it became applicable nationwide. The law has two components: States must register convicted pedophiles and must make information on them available to the public. The New Jersey version requires active community notification, which means that law enforcement officers must inform communities directly about sex offenders released into a neighborhood. The federal version requires only that the information be made public. A newspaper notice would be deemed sufficient.

In addition, if the offender is deemed to pose only a moderate risk, federal law requires merely that at-risk schools and community groups be identified; for high-risk offenders, however, the community must be informed. Every state has its own procedure for disclosing such information, but given the discrepancies in standards and notification, many critics claim that Megan's Law is not being enforced effectively.

The article below, detailing inadequate enforcement of Megan's Law and lax management of registered sex offenders in the state of Pennsylvania, was posted on the *Washington Times* web site in April 2004.

■ PRIMARY SOURCE

MEGAN'S LAW POORLY ENFORCED

A review of state police monitoring of sexually violent predators under Megan's Law found that community notification about these felons is often "incorrect, late and ineffective," Pennsylvania's chief auditor says.

The head of the state police says the agency is making efforts to improve the administration of the Megan's Law registry.

Convicted sex offenders classified as sexually violent predators are considered to have a mental abnormality or personality disorder that makes them likely to reoffend. They are subject to more stringent monitoring than the wider class of 6,210 sex offenders in Pennsylvania.

The review identified shortcomings in notifying the public on the whereabouts of 13 out of 17 sexually violent predators who had home addresses in the state during a nine-month period that ended in January, state Auditor General Robert P. Casey Jr. said Friday. Currently, Pennsylvania has 31 sexually violent predators, but 12 of them are in state prisons.

In seven of the 17 cases, the study found that schools and child care centers had not been told a violent predator was living nearby. One predator came to the attention of police only when he contacted them. In another instance, state police told local police about a violent predator only after he had left the area.

Notice was eventually made about all 17, but Mr. Casey said delays—in one case, notification was more than nine months late—violated the law's requirement for timely notice.

Mr. Casey urged the state police to review its management of the Megan's Law registry, improve training and establish a toll-free hot line to help communities implement the law.

"The state police should not wait for the audit to be done to bring about changes to the sexually violent predator category," Mr. Casey said.

State police Commissioner Jeffrey B. Miller said Friday the agency is working to improve the program.

A fourth officer will move to the department's Megan's Law bureau, and the agency is working to free up headquarters staff to focus on notification.

Commissioner Miller also said the department is seeking a change in state law so that judges will provide sexual offenders' sentencing orders to state police immediately.

Mr. Casey recently lost an attempt to force state police to disclose details about its monitoring of all Megan's Law sex offenders. A court ruled that the state's Megan's Law requires public release of information only about sexually violent predators.

Mr. Casey sought the records after the Associated Press reported in January 2003 that California had lost track of more than 33,000 convicted sex offenders, despite a law requiring rapists and child molesters to register each year.

The child-advocacy group Parents for Megan's Law since then has found that states across the country have lost track of thousands of sex offenders.

Megan's Law is named for a 7-year-old New Jersey girl who was kidnapped, raped and killed in 1994 by a convicted sex offender who lived in her neighborhood.

■ SIGNIFICANCE

On October 22, 1989, eleven-year-old Jacob Wetterling was kidnapped at gun-point by a suspected sex offender when he, along with his brother and a friend were returning to their Minnesota home from a convenience store. He has never been found.

Until 1989, law enforcement agencies in the United States did not have a comprehensive list of sex offenders. In 1994, the Jacob Wetterling Crimes Against Children and Sex Offender Registration Act, or the Wetterling Act, was passed (around the same time when New Jersey's Megan's Law was signed) making it mandatory for each state to establish an effective registration program for convicted sex offenders. Each state was also required to maintain a registry that included a list of pedophiles and others who committed crimes against children.

According to the Wetterling Act, however, the information was to be kept confidential. Law enforcement agencies could determine whether or not to make the information public at their discretion. Critics argue that a number of sex offenders escaped scrutiny because they were not considered dangerous enough, or the information was not released for fear of community unrest. The federal Megan's Law—an amendment to the Wetterling Act—allowed (but did not require) registry information to be disclosed for

San Jose, California, police officers, from left, Raul Martinez, Andrew Harsany, and Eric Dragoo search through the residence motel room of a paroled sex offender during a routine parole violation check in 2002. Despite a state law requiring rapists and child molesters to register each year and be included in the Megan's Law database, California has lost track of nearly half of its sex offenders. AP IMAGES

any permissible state purpose. Because the federal law does not mandate proactive notification, opponents believe the law's effectiveness is diminished.

In the years since the federal Megan's Law was passed, most states have established searchable sex offender databases. More often than not, however, it is the community's responsibility to obtain information about convicts released into their neighborhoods. Information in the state's registry, however, is often updated only when the offender personally notifies the registry of an address change. Law enforcement agencies cannot routinely inspect the activities of thousands of offenders under their jurisdiction. Consequently, parents, school authorities, and day care providers must read their state's sex offender registry to learn if an offender has moved into their neighborhoods. Criminal background checks, including a search of the sex offender registry, are essential before hiring anyone who would be working close to young children.

Media reports, such as the one above, claim that poor enforcement of Megan's Law fails to give parents and communities correct and timely notification about sex offenders in their vicinities. Advocates for better enforcement claim that the law should require active notification, instead of making the public check for such information. This can be done by direct mailings, door-to-door notifications, community meetings, notices in local media, information released to schools, youth organizations, churches, and day care centers.

FURTHER RESOURCES
Web sites

KlaasKids Foundation. "Megan's Law by State"<http://www.klaaskids.org/pg-legmeg.htm> (accessed January 14, 2006).

New Jersey Law Network. " Megan's Law" <http://www.njlawnet.com/megan.html> (accessed January 14, 2006).

State of New Jersey. Office of the Attorney General. Department of Public Safety. New Jersey State Police. New Jersey Sex Offender Internet Registry. "Megan's Law"<http://www.nj.gov/njsp/info/reg_sexoffend.html> (accessed January 14, 2006).

Parents for Megan's Law. " Commonly Asked Questions: Megan's Law"<http://www.parentsformeganslaw.com/html/questions.lasso> (accessed January 14, 2006).

Sanctioning and Supervising Impaired Drivers

Article

By: National Commission Against Drunk Driving (NCADD)

Date: 2005

Source: *NCADD: National Commission Against Drunk Driving.*"Sanctioning and Supervising Impaired Drivers." <http://www.ncadd.com/sanction_iis.cfm> (accessed January 14, 2006).

About the Author: The National Commission Against Drunk Driving (NCADD) is a consortium of private and public groups. It is a nonprofit publicly funded agency established to educate the public about the hazards, legal risks, and social implications of drunk driving. The organization lobbies for greater awareness about drunk driving and urges the use of technology to strengthen enforcement of "driving under the influence" (DUI) laws. It is the successor to the National Commission of Drunk Driving that was established as the first such national body by President Ronald Reagan to examine the problem of drunk driving.

INTRODUCTION

Driving under the influence (DUI), or driving while intoxicated (DWI), is a major driving and transportation safety issue because drivers impaired by alcohol or drugs cause a significant number of accidents, many of them fatal or critical. DUI is a serious offense, and all fifty states have passed strict laws to discourage drunk driving and get offenders off the road. This includes raising the legal drinking age to twenty-one and adopting a zero-tolerance approach toward drivers caught under the influence of drugs or alcohol.

Drivers who behave erratically can be stopped by a police officer and questioned about their alcohol consumption. If the officer notices a strong alcohol odor, slurred or incoherent speech, or uncooperative behavior, drivers can be asked to undergo a field sobriety test that shows whether they have consumed enough alcohol or other drugs to impair their motor functions. Drivers suspected of drunk driving may also be asked to undergo a breath alcohol test, which gives an approximation of their blood alcohol content (BAC). They can be arrested if their BAC registers above the legal limit. A driver who is suspected of being intoxicated can have his drivers license suspended immediately, booked for drunk driving, and taken to a holding a cell until he is sober.

"Sanctioning and Supervising Impaired Drivers" describes a system known as the ignition interlock system, which is intended to detect and prevent drunk driving by those with previous DUI convictions. The article explains how the system works and also details some of the stumbling blocks in integrating the technology into existing DUI monitoring programs.

■ PRIMARY SOURCE

Sanctioning and Supervising Impaired Drivers

Technology Overview—Ignition Interlock Systems

What Is an Ignition Interlock System?

An ignition interlock is a sophisticated system that tests for alcohol on a driver's breath. It is a device that requires a vehicle operator to blow into a small handheld alcohol sensor unit that is attached to a vehicle's dashboard. The car cannot be started if a BAC is above a preset level (usually 0.02 to 0.04). Alcohol safety interlocks that meet the standards issued by NHTSA (see the See [sic] NHTSA Conforming Products List and Technical Information Regarding Alcohol and Drug Law Enforcement Technology) not only require a test to start the engine, but also require a test every few minutes while driving. Called the "rolling or running retest," it prevents a friend from starting the car and then allowing an impaired driver from taking [sic] over the wheel (NHTSA guidelines call for only one subsequent test and the Alberta, Canada standard calls for multiple running retests). With modern safeguards, alcohol safety interlocks are extremely difficult to circumvent when properly installed and monitored every 30 to 60 days.

When used by the courts or state motor vehicle departments in conjunction with a monitoring, reporting, and support program, the ignition interlock system provides DWI offenders with an alternative to full license suspension. Its use has spread rapidly across the country

Sweden has the world's lowest allowable levels of blood alcohol (.02 percent), and 98 percent of those caught over that level will loose their driving license for two months to a year. One truck driver stopped by police had half of a light beer with dinner, and almost didn't pass a sobriety test. © GEORGE STEINMETZ/CORBIS

and as of late 1999, 37 states have enacted legislation providing for its integration into the DWI adjudication and sentencing process.

Who Uses This Technology?

All DUI offenders have the potential to benefit from the use of the ignition interlock—it's [sic] installation allows offenders to maintain their responsibilities while also reminding them that their behavior has a direct impact on their right to drive. Court systems and motor vehicle administrations agree that it is a valuable tool because it deters individuals from driving while intoxicated while the device is installed. Additionally, when its use is required as a provision of probation/parole, the threat of doing jail time better ensures that DUI offenders will correctly use the device each and every time he/she [sic] gets behind the wheel. DUI offenders benefit from the device as well. Their lives, and those of family members who share the use of the car, can remain relatively undisrupted—individuals can go to work, pick up children, run errands, etc.

Legislators and government officials like this program because in most cases, the installation and maintenance fees, which run about $60 per month, are paid for by the DUI offenders. Thus, the program can be self-sustaining and does not necessarily affect taxpayers.

The Federal government, in the Transportation Equity Act for the 21st Century (TEA-21), supports the use of the ignition interlock. Section 164 of the TEA-21 Restoration Act indicates that state laws regarding second and subsequent convictions for driving while intoxicated or driving under the influence of alcohol (DWI/DUI) must, among other provisions, "Require that all motor vehicles of repeat intoxicated drivers be impounded or immobilized for some period of time during the license suspension period, or require the installation of an ignition interlock system on all motor vehicles of such drivers for some period of time after the end of the suspension." TEA-21 requires that states have such repeat intoxicated driver laws in place by October 1, 2000. States without these laws will have a portion of their Federal-aid highway construction funds redirected into other state safety activities, beginning in Fiscal Year 2001.

Does This Technology Work?

Yes. Not only can ignition interlocks reduce recidivism while they are installed, but the data that is recorded by them can also be used to predict future behaviors of DUI offenders—their recording devices can show patterns of abuse that can lead to DWI/DUIs (offers insight into offender behaviors). For example, the most frequent time of day for recording elevated BAC levels is 7AM. This figure indicates a night of heavy drinking. Additionally, their use can stop individuals from driving drunk during high-risk time periods—from 12AM–3AM.

Are There Major Stumbling Blocks to Technology Integration?

Yes. While "breath alcohol ignition interlock devices, when embedded in a comprehensive monitoring program, lead to 40–95 percent reductions in the rate of repeat DWI offenses of convicted DWI offenders,"[11] the technology has not been widely integrated into the field. According to Dr. Paul Marques in his position paper, Alcohol Ignition Interlock Devices, published for the International Council on Alcohol, Drugs and Traffic Safety, a number of stumbling blocks are present, including:

- The protective effect of the interlock lasts only as long as it remains installed on the vehicle. The likelihood of repeat DUI offenses rises back to previous levels once it is removed from the car.

- Only a small percentage of eligible offenders ever enter an interlock program. As a result, interlocks have not yet made a large contribution to highway safety (at the population level). This may change when many more states, provinces, and nations adopt interlock programs.

- The most dangerous repeat DWI offenders only rarely become eligible for an interlock and then only

Tim Hallford, a contractor who installs ignition interlock devices, holds one that will be installed in the car of a DWI offender in Albuquerque, New Mexico, in 2002. Before starting the vehicle a driver has to blow into the tube and is prevented from starting the vehicle when the device registers above a certain level of intoxication. AP IMAGES for a brief period of time because of the manner in which interlocks are assigned to prior DWI offenders (interlock use is not necessarily widespread and sentencing procedures are inconsistent). Research is called for that would evaluate the impact of lowering the threshold for entry into an interlock program and raising the threshold for exit from an interlock program. If such an approach was successful, it could put more of the most dangerous repeat offenders under the control of a program and retain them until evidence was available documenting their readiness to drive without an external monitor.

- Not all drivers of interlock-equipped vehicles will be equally motivated to comply with interlock restriction and monitoring requirements. Authorities need to be attentive to these differences. The evidence base for interlock effectiveness in reducing DWI is strong but most studies to date have evaluated the effects of interlocks on offenders who are motivated to be compliant with the law.

- The majority of convicted DWI offenders whose licenses are suspended choose to drive anyway, and since an alcohol interlock program can improve monitoring and prevent impaired driving, it is worth evaluating the public safety impact of an early or immediate post-conviction interlock requirement relative to simply suspending the driver's license.

- It is impractical to require that an interlock system be installed on every vehicle owned by someone who will be required to use an interlock device. As an alternative the driver license of such drivers should be clearly marked showing that the driving privilege is exclusively contingent upon use of interlock vehicles.

- In the future, the interlock may become an integral part of advanced driver recognition and control systems. In the meantime it is very easy for a driver to circumvent the interlock by using a different vehicle without the interlock. Accordingly, at the current stage of technological development, an offender's motivation for compliance with the interlock restriction is expected to be a prime factor in determining effectiveness. Brief motivational interventions delivered while drivers are captive in the interlock program may help improve motivation for making lasting behavior changes.

SIGNIFICANCE

A high percentage of traffic accidents in the United States are caused by intoxicated drivers, because alcohol consumption significantly diminishes motor skills. Besides being hampered by impaired vision, intoxicated drivers have much more trouble understanding traffic signals, reading sign boards, observing traffic, and controlling or altering their own movements.

Driving under the influence is a crime, yet according to the NCADD website, it is one of the most common offenses in the country, resulting in a vehicle crash every thirty-three minutes somewhere in the United States and causing around 16,000 fatalities every year. A University of Chicago survey indicated that DUI cases have increased markedly since 1997.

Law-enforcement agencies have developed various means of deterring drunk driving. Applying for a driver's license, for example, implies automatic consent to alcohol-detection tests requested by an officer, including breath, blood, and urine tests. A variety of other technologies and screenings can also detect alcohol in the driver's system. These include passive breath and saliva screening, breath alcohol test calibration, and evidential breath alcohol testing. Proactive measures include vehicle ignition interlock systems and remote monitoring technology for repeat offenders.

Typical DUI offender programs can include deferred prosecution, in which an offender is awarded a deferred trial; being jailed for a day or two to be educated about the hazards of DWI; and being subjected to a victim panel of drunk driving accident victims' relatives. Drivers licenses can be reinstated if no repeat offense occurs in a stated time frame.

FURTHER RESOURCES

Web sites

About.com: Alcoholism/Substance Abuse. "Drunk Driving Increases, Study Shows"<http://alcoholism.about.com/od/dui/a/dui050420.htm> (accessed January 14, 2006).

About.com: Alcoholism/Substance Abuse. "Penalties for Drunk Driving"<http://alcoholism.about.com/cs/drive/a/aa082797.htm> (accessed January 14, 2006).

America's Health Insurance Plans. "Highway and Traffic Safety in Managed Care Toolkit"<http://www.ahip.org/links/NHTSA_Site/resources.html> (accessed January 14, 2006).

NCADD: National Commission Against Drunk Driving. "Alcohol Technology Resource Center"< http://www.ncadd.com/alcohol_tech_reso_center.cfm > (accessed January 14, 2006).

Capital Punishment Statistics

Summary Findings

Government report

By: Bureau of Justice Statistics

Date: January 13, 2005

Source: "Capital Punishment Statistics: Summary Findings." Bureau of Justice Statistics, 2005. <http://www.ojp.usdoj.gov/bjs/cp.htm> (accessed February 27, 2006).

About the Author: Founded in 1979, the Bureau of Justice Statistics is part of the U.S. Department of Justice. Its role is to collect, analyze, publish and disseminate information on crime, offenders, victims, and operation of the justice system at all levels of government.

INTRODUCTION

Death by execution has played an important role in human justice. Many countries have now abolished capital punishment, although the concept continues to attract some public support. In the United States, thirty-eight states still have capital punishment, although it was ruled unconstitutional in Kansas and New York in 2004. Twelve states, including Maine,

Rhode Island, Alaska, and Hawaii, do not have the death penalty.

There is a clear geographical, and maybe cultural and political, influence on how and if the death penalty operates in the United States. There are many states who have not executed anyone in the last thirty years—such as New Hampshire, New Jersey, and South Dakota. In this time, Texas has executed 357, followed by Virginia with 94, while Wyoming, Tennessee, and several other states have executed only one person during this time. There have been some changes in the law relating to the death penalty in recent years. In 2005, the death penalty was outlawed for juveniles and in 2002 for those who are mentally retarded.

Hangings, beheadings—and worse—used to be a public spectacle and entertainment. Execution today is a more private matter, although witnesses are still necessary. If execution is necessary, today's ethics ask it be done in a humane way. Accordingly, the majority of death penalties in the United States over the last thirty years have been carried out by lethal injection, followed by electrocution and gas. There is a trend towards using the lethal injection as the sole means of execution. For instance, Utah banned death by firing squad in 2004 in favor of the lethal injection. The

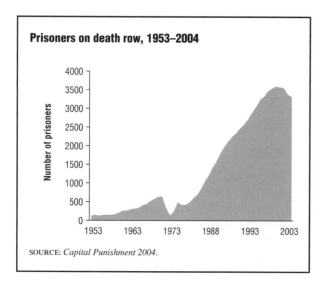

Prisoners on death row, 1953–2004

SOURCE: *Capital Punishment 2004.*

Based on information from the U.S. Bureau of Justice Statistics, this graph shows that the number of prisoners awaiting execution in the United States rose consistently from the 1970s until the early 2000s. U.S. DEPARTMENT OF JUSTICE; OFFICE OF JUSTICE PROGRAMS; BUREAU OF JUSTICE STATISTICS

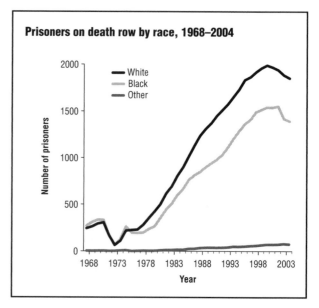

Prisoners on death row by race, 1968–2004

Although the days when African-Americans outnumbered whites on death row are in the past, minorities still make up a disproportionate share of death row inmates when compared to their share of the U.S. population. U.S. DEPARTMENT OF JUSTICE; OFFICE OF JUSTICE PROGRAMS; BUREAU OF JUSTICE STATISTICS

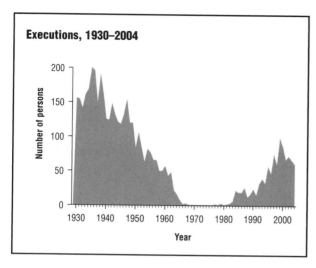

Executions, 1930–2004

Number of persons (y-axis)
Year (x-axis)

This U.S. Bureau of Justice Statistics graph shows the number of executions in the United States between 1930 and 2004. Supreme Court rulings against the death penalty meant that very few executions took place in the late 1960s and 1970s. U.S. DEPARTMENT OF JUSTICE; OFFICE OF JUSTICE PROGRAMS; BUREAU OF JUSTICE STATISTICS

extract below summarizes the latest statistics on the death penalty in the United States.

■ **PRIMARY SOURCE**

CAPITAL PUNISHMENT STATISTICS

Summary Findings: Executions 2003—2004

Executions

In 2004, 59 inmates were executed, 6 fewer than in 2003.

In 2003, 65 persons in 11 States and the Federal system were executed—24 in Texas; 14 in Oklahoma, 7 in North Carolina; 3 each in Alabama, Florida, Georgia, and Ohio; 2 each in Indiana, Missouri, and Virginia; and 1 each in Arkansas and the Federal system.

Of persons executed in 2003:

- 41 were white
- 20 were black
- 3 were Hispanic (all white)
- 1 American Indian

Of those executed in 2003:

- 65 were men

Lethal injection accounted for 64 of the executions; 1 was carried out by electrocution.

Thirty-eight States and the Federal government in 2003 had capital statutes.

Prisoners under sentence of death

The number of prisoners under sentence of death at yearend 2003 decreased for the third consecutive year.

At yearend 2003, 37 States and the Federal prison system held 3,374 prisoners under sentence of death, 188 fewer than at yearend 2002.

Since the death penalty was reinstated by the Supreme Court in 1976, white inmates have made up more than half of the number under sentence of death.

Of persons under sentence of death in 2003:

- 1,878 were white
- 1,418 were black
- 29 were American Indian
- 35 were Asian
- 14 were of unknown race.

Forty-seven women were under a sentence of death.

The 369 Hispanic inmates under sentence of death accounted for 12% of inmates with a known ethnicity.

Among inmates under sentence of death and with available criminal histories:

- nearly 2 in 3 had a prior felony conviction
- about 1 in 12 had a prior homicide conviction.

Among persons for whom arrest information was available, the average age at time of arrest was 28; 2% of inmates were age 17 or younger.

At year end, the youngest inmate under sentence of death was 19; the oldest was 88.

SIGNIFICANCE

South Korea and Japan are the only other democratic societies in the world retaining the death penalty. In the United States, there have been around 13,000 legal executions since colonial times. In the 1930s, there were around 150 executions a year. After that, the public and the justice system seemed to turn against capital punishment and the number of executions was down to almost zero by 1967. The Supreme Court actually banned the death penalty in 1972, but it was brought back in 1976. The peak year for executions in the United States in recent times was 2000, when ninety-eight people received the death penalty. Since 1976, there has been a total of 1,009 executions. The number of death sentences handed out has, however, gone down dramatically since 1999 when it was 276. In 2004, the figure was 125 and at its peak, in 1995 and 1996, it was 317.

Anti-death penalty demonstrators rally at the State Capitol in Austin, Texas, on January 17, 1998. They are protesting the planned execution of Karla Faye Tucker. Tucker was executed by lethal injection on February 3rd. AP IMAGES

There is an issue over race and the death penalty in the United States, which various research studies have sought to penetrate. The data shows that thirty-four percent of those executed since 1976 have been black compared to fifty-eight percent white. If data on victims in crimes attracting the death penalty is analyzed, then seventy-nine percent were white and fourteen percent black. Interracial murder is a strong factor in death penalties ordered by judges but there is a clear racial disparity. There have been twelve executions involving a white defendant and a black victim and 209 involving a black defendant and a white victim. There is also a large geographical divide in murder and death penalty statistics. The Southern states have the highest murder rate (6.6 per 100,000 in 2004) and account for over eighty percent of all executions. In the Northeastern States, the murder rate is lowest at 4.2 per 100,000 and these states have less than one percent of all executions.

Opponents of capital punishment often argue about the risk of executing an innocent person. The statistics do lend some credence to this argument. Over 120 people have been released from Death Row since 1973 with evidence of their innocence, following successful appeals. There are currently over 3,000 inmates awaiting the death sentence in the United States, most of them in California, Texas, and Florida. Around half are white and half are black. Only forty-nine of them are women.

Even if the death penalty carries the risk of executing an innocent person, it could still have some value to society if it acts as a deterrent. However, a recent survey of criminologists had eighty-four percent of them rejecting this idea, as do a majority of police chiefs. But public support for capital punishment remains strong. A Gallup poll done in 2005 found sixty-four percent in favor, compared with eighty percent in 1994. However, if there was the option of life without parole, the proportion in favor of the death penalty went down to fifty percent. Many faith groups, including the Catholic Church, are strongly opposed to the death penalty.

FURTHER RESOURCES

Books

Vila, Bryan, and Cynthia Morris. *Capital Punishment in the United States: A Documentary History*. Westport, Conn.: Greenwood, 1997.

Web sites

Death Penalty Information Center. "Facts about the Death Penalty." <http://www.deathpenaltyinfo.org> (accessed February 26, 2006).

MegaLaw.com. "Death Penalty/Capital Punishment Law." <http://www.megalaw.com/top/deathpenalty.php> (accessed February 26, 2006).

The Court and Law Enforcement

Magazine article

By: William J. Stuntz

Date: July 25, 2005

Source: *The New Republic Online*. "The Court and Law Enforcement." <https://ssl.tnr.com/p/docsub/> (accessed March 28, 2006).

About the Author: William J. Stuntz is a professor at Harvard University's School of Law. He is also a prolific writer, whose areas of particular interest are criminal policy and procedure, crime law, and the relationship between the law and Christianity.

INTRODUCTION

The Supreme Court is the highest legal authority in the United States. Its mission, overall, is the protection, preservation, and interpretation of the Constitution (and, thereby, is also the ultimate authority on Constitutional law). The United States has the oldest written Constitution still in active use.

The Supreme Court is tasked with the ultimate ability to discern whether or not legislation or court procedural decisions (lower courts) in any way conflict with the text or the spirit of the Constitution. If that is found to be the case, the Court has the authority to

take action in order to preserve the law of the land, whether that means overturning a lower court decision or vacating a piece of legislation.

The judicial system in the United States is set up along two parallel tracks: state and federal court systems. Within each of those, there are two more parallel processes, for civil and criminal proceedings. A significant portion of the strength and power of the United States government lies with the states, with discrete authority and oversight left for the federal government. State law violations, which account for the vast majority of matters that go before the criminal justice system, are litigated within the state courts; federal violations are tried at the federal level. Illegal activity can be prosecuted at either the civil or criminal level, each of which has different policies and procedures, as well as varying standards of proof and types of punishment. The rules of evidence are quite similar across both types of proceedings. Among the greatest differences between civil and criminal trials are the burdens of proof: in a civil trial, guilt need only be determined *by a preponderance of evidence;* the criminal code requires certainty *beyond a reasonable doubt*. In a criminal trial, there is very little right to appeal an unfavorable outcome for the prosecution; that is not the case in a civil suit. Criminal convictions can carry sentences involving incarceration, civil penalties are typically limited to monetary judgments.

Both state and federal court system have three levels. At the state level, courts are arranged by geographic locale, as well as by level of authority. The trial court is at the lowest, or first level, in which cases are tried before a judge, a jury may be utilized, witnesses and evidence are presented, and the final arbiter (judge, or sometimes a jury) decides the facts of the case and determines an outcome based on the law(s) under consideration. The next level is the court of appeals, employed primarily to adjudicate disputed decisions. The highest court in the state is the State Supreme Court, which is considered the highest authority on interpretation of state law.

In the federal system, courts are organized both by locality and by hierarchy (district court, court of appeals, and federal supreme court). At the lowest level are the district courts, which adjudicate basic civil and criminal proceedings. The federal court of appeals generally hears cases in which the losing party believes that there has been an error made in interpretation or application of the relevant law. If the judges at the federal court of appeals are in disagreement (there are three judges per case at that level), the parties engaged in litigation may request a hearing by the members of the Supreme Court. The highest court in

U.S. Chief Justice John Roberts waits for his family on the steps of the Supreme Court after his investiture ceremony in Washington, D.C., on October 3, 2005. © BROOKS KRAFT/CORBIS

the nation has nine judges, at least four of which must agree that a case should be heard in order for it to be accepted.

■ PRIMARY SOURCE

Supreme Court appointments are like "Law & Order" episodes: The cast of characters changes, but the dialogue always sounds the same. Whoever the nominees are, the script for the inevitable confirmation battles has already been written. Abortion, church and state, more abortion, gay rights, and still more abortion—interest groups and senators are setting the table, and that's the

menu. It's strangely disconnected from what the Supreme Court actually does and from the places where the justices really exercise power. If *Roe v. Wade* goes by the boards, abortion law will stay roughly the same. Nor will American life change much if the Ten Commandments start dropping off courthouse walls.

By contrast, another aspect of the Court's work affects lots of lives. The United States incarcerates more than two million people in its prisons and jails today, roughly seven times the number held in 1970 and five times the 1980 figure. For the past forty years, the Supreme Court has helped shape the process that puts those men and women behind bars. When can police officers frisk suspects on the street or search their cars? When do police have to give *Miranda* warnings? How hard can they push suspects to confess—and how hard can prosecutors push defendants to plead guilty? How must juries be selected? Which sentencing procedures are permissible, and which ones aren't? Supreme Court justices answer all these questions and dozens more like them.

The answers matter enormously. Which means that the Supreme Court's most important job is not managing the culture wars. Regulating the never-ending war on crime is a much bigger task. Alas, it may also be the job the court does worst.

Civilizations define themselves by when, how, and whom they punish. Those choices are especially important in a society like ours, with a long history of both criminal violence and official racism. Forty-five percent of American prisoners are black. The imprisonment rate—the number of prison inmates per 100,000 people—stood at 482 in 2003. Among black males, the figure was 3,405. For black men in their late twenties, the number exceeds nine thousand. Court decisions that help shape those numbers are vastly more important than the latest church-state fight.

And the justices *do* shape those numbers, both by what they regulate and by what they leave alone. Fourth Amendment case law makes it easy to justify police stops and frisks in the inner-city neighborhoods where many of those young black men live. In one recent case, a Chicago man saw a police van and ran. According to the justices, that was reason enough to seize him. The results in *Illinois v. Wardlow* sounds obvious to middle-class suburbanites. But, to people in neighborhoods like Wardlow's running from the cops may be more a survival skill than a sign of guilt.

Another recent case, *Kyllo v. United States,* involved a defendant who was growing marijuana inside his house on Rhododendron Drive (no kidding) in Florence, Oregon. Using a thermal imager, officers discovered that one wing of the house was a lot warmer than the rest. Inside, they found more than one hundred marijuana plants. The Supreme Court held that the thermal imager violated the defendant's rights. Decisions like *Wardlow* and *Kyllo* make it a good deal easier for the police to make drug busts on poor city streets than in the suburbs.

That's not all. Criminal trials have grown so cumbersome (and budgets so strained) that hardly anyone uses them. Nineteen out of every twenty felony convictions stem from guilty pleas. What does the Supreme Court have to do with that? Plenty. The Court has imposed elaborate rules governing nearly every aspect of criminal trials, from jury selection to sentencing. That makes trials more expensive. Worse, the justices keep refining procedural rules—making them so nuanced that no one can understand them. The examples are endless. The prosecutors in *Miller-El v. Dretke* struck almost all the blacks from the defendant's jury. You're not supposed to do that. A straightforward case, right? Not when Justice David Souter was through with it. His majority opinion went on for thirty-three pages of mind-numbing detail, muddying the waters. And, because lawyers can't tell what the law requires, they waste more time and energy arguing about it, which makes trials more costly still.

It gets worse. Last January, in *United States v. Booker,* the justices handed down a decision that rewrote key federal sentencing statutes. *Booker* provided dueling majority opinions by two opposing blocs of justices. Ruth Bader Ginsburg, the only justice to sign both, didn't explain her views. Lawyers and judges were left scratching their heads.

Procedures should be clear and simple. For criminal trials, they are anything but. That breeds uncertainty. It also breeds litigation that focuses on the process, rather than on the question that criminal trials are supposed to answer: whether the defendant committed the crime.

Poor defendants can't afford all that procedural litigation—hence the high guilty plea rate. Cash-strapped district attorneys know that and charge accordingly. So the universe of criminal defendants grows steadily poorer. In a society where race and class often coincide, these class biases tend to produce racial biases. This may explain why blacks, who were one-third of the total prison population in 1960, now make up nearly half.

These sound like liberal complaints. But conservatives have a lot to complain about, too, as they would know if they paid attention to anything other than the culture wars. *Miranda* doctrine bars the police from even the most genteel questioning of suspects who say the magic words—"I want to see a lawyer"—after they hear the famous warnings. That is a valuable gift to sophisticated criminals who know enough to keep their mouths shut. Not coincidentally, it is also a large gift to terrorists—which is why the government does not want to abide by

U.S. law when questioning suspected Al Qaeda members.

Why does the Court do such a bad job in this area? The answer may be simple ignorance. The criminal justice system is a massively complex enterprise. Figuring out the effects of the latest abortion ruling is child's play compared with unpacking the consequences of decisions like *Wardlow* and *Kyllo* on policing or the effects of cases like *Miller-El* and *Booker* on criminal trials and plea bargains. Getting those consequences right would be hard even for experts. And the highest court in the land is not filled with experts. Souter is the only sitting justice with substantial experience in criminal litigation—and that was on the not-exactly mean streets of New Hampshire. Frontline urban prosecutors and defense attorneys rarely end up on federal appeals courts, the breeding ground for future justices. So they never make it to presidential short lists.

Justices who have never seen the inside of a police station are happy to expound on the virtues and vices of different kinds of drug enforcement. If they knew more, they might say less. Veterans of the criminal justice trenches understand that, when it happens, productive change comes from the men and women who serve in those trenches. Community policing and crime labs, drug courts and faith-based prison initiatives, "broken windows" policing and partnerships with inner-city churches—all the best ideas in contemporary criminal law enforcement bubbled up from below. None stemmed from judicial edicts.

Judging from the names bandied about in press, the next couple of Supreme Court picks will be like the ones who have gone before. That's a shame, but it need not be a tragedy. The justices—both old and new—need to remind themselves of a few simple truths. The Constitution guarantees a fair criminal process. That should mean a modest number of basic guarantees, defined as clearly as possible. Beyond the basics, legislators, prosecutors, and police officers should be free to experiment. The criminal justice system desperately needs innovation. Constitutionalizing everything five justices can agree on stifles innovation. If President Bush wants good results in this piece of the legal landscape, he should appoint justices who will let the real reformers do their jobs.

SIGNIFICANCE

The Supreme Court is in session from the first Monday in October of each year until the end of June or the early part of July of the following year. Each session is called a "Term", which is composed of alternating two week long sittings and recesses. When the Supreme Court justices are sitting, they are actively hearing cases and proffering their expert legal opinions. When they are in recess, they are writing decisions and engaging in the administrative business of the Court. The process is very different at the level of the Supreme Court than it is at other judicial levels; in the initial phase, the justices do not call witnesses or see evidence presented live; there is no jury, and they generally receive written files for review, rather than actually hearing cases, when making their decisions regarding which of the vast number of cases proposed they should fully hear and consider offering their opinions on. For the selected cases, they initially review and consider all prior decisions and legal opinions rendered, as well as a short statement containing the facts and arguments of the case (called a "brief"), as presented by the attorneys for each side. When the cases are actually being heard, each side has thirty minutes to present and argue its case. At the end of each week (no cases are heard on Fridays), the justices meet to discuss the week's cases; opinions are rendered on Tuesday and Wednesday mornings, as well as on the third Monday of each sitting.

The Court is comprised of a Chief Justice and eight Associate Justices. Each person is proposed for nomination by a sitting president, and goes through a senatorial approval process. Once ratified and approved, they sit on the bench for life, unless they are impeached and removed (this has never happened in the United States), or choose to retire. There is considerable public debate regarding whether the majority opinions of the incumbent justices are reflective of the dominant political climate of the moment, or whether they are more in line with the prevailing public sentiment.

There are no formal educational, professional, prior judicial, or experiential requirements for potential nominees to the Supreme Court, the president is empowered to select virtually anyone he or she deems suitable. However, the Senate Judiciary Committee questions each candidate at considerable length, and makes the final decisions regarding acceptance or rejection of nominees. The Supreme Court justices need not be expert in any area of the law, or in their understanding of the tenets of the Constitution, when they are seated, although they study those matters in great detail during their tenure, and particularly so in the rendering of opinions. The decisions of the federal Supreme Court, which was created by Article III of the Constitution of the United States, are final—there are no further appeals. Decisions made by the Supreme Court are typically based upon the principles of common law and by reference to precedent set in previous instances of similar legal cases. Opinions

need not be unanimous, they need only reach majority. Both majority and dissenting opinions are rendered in written form and published for public review.

FURTHER RESOURCES

Books

Lively, Donald E. *Foreshadows of the Law: Supreme Court Dissents and Constitutional Development.* Westport, Connecticut: Praeger 1992.

Smolla, Rodney A. (Editor). *A Year in the Life of the Supreme Court.* Durham, North Carolina: Duke University Press 1995.

Web sites

CNN.com. "Law Center: High court bars Internet porn law enforcement" <http://www.cnn.com/2004/LAW/06/29/scotus.web.indecency/> (accessed March 28, 2006).

Supreme Court of the United States. "The Court and Constitutional Interpretation." <http://www.supremecourtus.gov/about/constitutional.pdf> (accessed March 28, 2006).

Crime and Sentencing 10-20-Life Felons

Government report

By: Florida Department of Corrections

Date: August 2005

Source: Florida Department of Corrections. "10-20-Life Prisoners Sentenced to Florida's Prisons." August 2005. <http://www.dc.state.fl.us/pub/10-20-life/index.html> (accessed February 8, 2006).

About the Author: This report was created by the Florida Department of Corrections under the direction of Governor Jeb Bush, Lt. Governor Toni Jennings, and Secretary James V. Crosby, Jr. The Florida Department of Corrections is responsible for the administration of all correctional sentences in the state of Florida and for the operation and maintenance of Florida's prisons.

INTRODUCTION

In 1999 the Florida Legislature enacted one of the toughest gun-crime laws in the United States, the 10-20-Life law. Proposed by Governor Jeb Bush, 10-20-Life mandates fixed minimum sentences for felony offenses committed with a firearm. The law provides for a mandatory minimum sentence of ten years for producing a firearm during the commission of an offense, twenty years for firing the gun, and twenty-five years to life for injuring or killing an individual by firing the gun. Additionally, under this legislation mere possession or ownership of a firearm by a convicted felon is also subject to a mandatory minimum sentence of 3 years in prison. Since its inception in 1999, more than four thousand offenders have been sentenced under Florida's 10-20-Life law.

The excerpt below is taken from a complete statistical report on the impact of Florida's 10-20-Life legislation on correctional sentences.

PRIMARY SOURCE

10-20-LIFE PRISONERS SENTENCED TO FLORIDA'S PRISONS

Maximum Prison Sentence Length

The maximum (total) sentence received may be greater than the longest mandatory 10-20-Life sentence imposed for offenders. For example, 154 felons whose longest 10-20-Life mandatory was 10 years received total sentences of life in prison. In many cases, the longer total sentence reflects these felons' more serious criminal histories.

Three-fifths (60.6%) of those convicted as felons possessing guns received a total sentence of 3 years, the same length as the mandatory minimum sentence imposed under 10-20-Life; but 11.5% (221 of 1,914) received a total sentence of 10 years or longer.

Almost three-fourths (71.6%) of felons who pulled a gun, but did not fire it (10-year mandatory) received total sentences of at least 10 years and less than 20 years; but one-fifth (20.7%) received a total sentence of 25 years or longer, including 154 (9.4%) who were sentenced to life in prison.

About three-fifths (61.2%) of felons who fired a gun without causing injury or death (20-year mandatory) received total sentences of at least 20 years and less than 25 years; and almost two-fifths (38.8%) received total sentences of 25 years or longer, including 26 (12.9%) who were sentenced to life in prison.

More than two-fifths (45.1%) of felons who injured or killed a victim using a gun (25-year to life mandatory) were sentenced to life in prison; and more than half (54.9%) received total sentences of 25 years of longer.

Maximum prison sentence length

| | Maximum mandatory sentence | | | | |
	3 yr	10 yr	20 yr	25–Life	Total
Under 3	0	0	0	0	0
3	1,159	0	0	0	1,159
3+ to 9+	534	0	0	0	534
10 to 19+	183	1,171	0	0	1,354
20 to 24+	12	127	123	0	262
25+	26	184	52	217	479
Life	0	154	26	178	358
Total	1,914	1,636	201	395	4,146

PRIMARY SOURCE

Crime and Sentencing 10-20-Life Felons This table shows sentences imposed on felons in Florida who possessed a gun or committed a gun-related crime. "CRIME AND SENTENCING OF 10-20-LIFE FELONS," *FLORIDA DEPARTMENT OF CORRECTIONS*, AUGUST 2005. REPRODUCED BY PERMISSION.

SIGNIFICANCE

Within its longer report, the Florida Department of Corrections claims that the 10-20-Life law has contributed to a thirty-percent decrease in rates of violent gun crime in the six years since it was enacted. Careful consideration of this claim reveals that the impact is in fact not as great as they suggest.

The reported number of violent offences involving a firearm in 1998 was 31,643 while in 2002, the number was 26,346: a decrease of 5,297. The claimed "thirty percent decline" was in fact calculated by assuming that the crime rate would have remained at the 1998 level in subsequent years and by adding up the sum total of crimes "not committed" due to the 10-20-Life law. Thus, the Florida Department of Corrections claims that the 10-20-Life law has prevented thirty percent of the crimes that would have been committed if this legislation did not exist.

Consideration of trends in violent gun crime and violent crime in general in Florida, however, shows that these rates have been dropping since the late 1980s, a full decade before the enactment of this legislation. Further, the number of violent crimes committed with a firearm actually increased slightly from 2000 to 2002 during the 10-20-Life era before resuming its downward trend. The decrease in violent gun crime from 1998 to 2004 does not necessarily indicate the success of the 10-20-Life legislation so much as a continuation of the earlier downward trend in violent crime rates. Despite the 2.7-million-dollar public service campaign that warned would-be criminals,

A group of prison inmates start boot camp by marching in line at the Sumter County Florida Correctional Institution, 1989. © BETTMANN/CORBIS

"Use a gun and you're done," there is no evidence of a significant decrease in crime attributable to the 10-20-Life law.

The implications of the 10-20-Life legislation for the Florida correctional system are great. The penalties required by this law are the minimum that may be imposed and much lengthier sentences are often handed down as consecutive sentences may be given for multiple convictions. The existence of a previous criminal record may also prompt a judge to order a prison term that is longer than the mandatory minimum sentence. As indicated by the statistics above, this judicial discretion to order sentences that are longer than the mandatory minimum is frequently exercised. Nearly forty percent of individuals subject to a mandatory minimum sentence of three years were sentenced to more than the minimum. Twenty-eight percent of convictions subject to a ten-year minimum sentence received a sentence of more than twenty years. Given that the legislation does not appear to have a significant deterrent effect, and much longer

sentences are being handed down, one can expect to see an exponential increase in the number of individuals incarcerated for a lengthy period or for life in Florida. This trend toward longer periods of incarceration is certain to necessitate the construction of additional and larger prison facilities to accommodate the growth of the prison population.

The "get tough on crime" approach remains popular among Republican policy makers, despite increasing evidence that harsher sentences have little influence on the reduction of crime rates. Studies on similar forms of legislation in both Washington State and in California, known as "Three Strikes" legislation, have indicated that such laws are largely ineffective in reducing crime rates or decreasing the cost of enforcement: court costs as well as the number of those incarcerated are skyrocketing.

Burgeoning prison populations are costing taxpayers a hefty annual sum with an average price tag of more than $25,000 per inmate, per year. The United States spends tens of billions of dollars every year on

Close-up of a man's hands grippings the bars of his prison cell. © ROYALTY-FREE/CORBIS

Web sites

Florida Department of Law Enforcement. "Firearm Involved Violent Crimes." <http://www.fdle.state.fl.us/FSAC/Crime_Trends/violent/Reg_FA_2004.ppt> (accessed February 28, 2006).

Update: Killer's Retardation Case Reprised

Newspaper article

By: Anonymous

Date: October 9, 2005

Source: Update: Killer's Retardation Case Reprised." *Washington Post* (October 9, 2005): C02. Available at: <http://www.washingtonpost.com/wp-dyn/content/article/2005/> (accessed January 14, 2006).

About the Author: The *Washington Post* is a leading front-line media conglomerate in the United States. Launched in December 1877 as a four-page publication on rag paper, it will complete 130 years of eventful and successful existence in 2007. Its operations currently include print, cable, interactive and educational media, broadcasting, and magazine publications.

INTRODUCTION

According to news reports, on August 16, 1996, two friends—Daryl Atkins and William Jones—spent a day of drinking and smoking marijuana. Later that night, Atkins borrowed a friend's gun and went to a 7-11 convenience store in Hampton, Virginia, to buy beer. However, discovering that he was broke, Atkins began panhandling people for money. A little while later, Eric Nesbitt, a twenty-one-year-old Air Force mechanic stationed at Langley Air Force Base, Hampton, Virginia, also came to the store. As Nesbitt was leaving the store, Atkins and Jones forced themselves into Nesbitt's truck at gunpoint and hijacked it. They also stole sixty dollars from his wallet and later forced him to withdraw two hundred dollars from a drive-through ATM. Reportedly, they drove Nesbitt to a secluded spot a few miles away in York County where Atkins shot Nesbitt eight times and killed him. Atkins also sustained two bullet injuries in the foot.

criminal justice and corrections, yet for all this outlay of tax dollars, the U.S. maintains the highest rate of incarceration in the world and one of the highest crime rates per capita.

However, the implementation of lengthier sentences and the perception of a tough justice system is one that resonates with U.S. citizens who are increasingly fearful of crime and victimization and thus see imprisonment as a quick and viable solution. Clearly the 10-20-Life legislation and similar types of laws across the United States are direct policy responses to public concern about violent crime. However, a brief cost-benefit analysis of this type of legislation reveals that the expense of administering and enforcing these laws yields little result beyond the illusion of security for the American public.

FURTHER RESOURCES

Periodicals

Kovandzic, Tomislav V., John J. Sloan, and Lynne M. Vieraitis. "'Striking Out' as Crime Reduction Policy: The Impact of 'Three Strikes' Laws on Crime Rates in U.S. Cities." *Justice Quarterly*. 21, 2 (2004): 207–239.

Piquero, Alex. "Reliable Information and Rational Policy Decisions: Does Gun Research Fit the Bill?" *Criminology and Public Policy* 4, 4 (2005): 779–798.

After their arrest in the same year, Jones and Atkins were both indicted for capital murder under Virginia law. But in a deal with the prosecution a year later, Jones pleaded guilty to first degree murder and testified against Atkins who pleaded not guilty. During this trial, the jury was presented with a record of Atkins's previous felonies, as well as a history of Atkins's academic performance that displayed a string of academic failures and extremely poor performance during school.

At this point, the defense called Dr. Evan Nelson, a forensic psychologist, as a witness. Dr. Nelson had previously administered a standard psychometric test (Wechsler Adult Intelligence Scale or WAIS III) to Atkins to measure his IQ. As Dr. Nelson testified, this test measured Atkins's IQ at fifty-nine, a score that classified him as mildly retarded.

Eventually, the jury sentenced Jones to life in prison, but sentenced Atkins to death because Virginia law specifies that the person who pulled the trigger is eligible for the death penalty. The Virginia Supreme Court upheld this decision, but the death sentence was reversed because of a procedural error and a second sentencing hearing was ordered.

During this hearing in 1999, Dr. Nelson testified again. However, the state of Virginia called another psychologist, Dr. Stanton Samenow, as a witness and Dr. Samenow rebutted Dr. Nelson's findings. Based on a series of tests called the Wechsler tests, as well as on further investigation of Atkins's general knowledge, understanding, and awareness of current events, Dr. Samenow concluded that Atkins had at least average intelligence and understanding. At this hearing, Atkins was again sentenced to death, and this sentence was again affirmed by the Virginia Supreme Court.

In 2002, the U.S. Supreme Court was prompted to issue a writ of certiorari (a decision to hear an appeal from a lower court) to the Supreme Court of Virginia to examine the case. Eventually, the U. S. Supreme Court decided that sentencing retarded individuals to death was unconstitutional and unallowable. This finding is considered by many to be a landmark ruling.

The U.S. Supreme Court only ruled that retarded individuals could not be sentenced to death. It, however, did not comment on whether Atkins was mentally retarded or not. As a result, in August 2005, the York County court deemed Atkins was not mentally retarded and set his execution date for December 2005. The defense counsel for Atkins filed an appeal in September 2005 against this decision. As of 2006, the execution is stayed as the case is slated to come up for appellate hearing again.

The primary source is a news story that appeared in the October 9, 2005, issue of the *Washington Post*. The article reported that Atkins's attorneys filed an appeal in the Virginia State Supreme Court against the ruling of the York County court that declared Atkins was not mentally retarded.

PRIMARY SOURCE

Attorneys for Virginia death row inmate Daryl Renard Atkins have filed an appeal in his case, which made legal history in 2002 when the U.S. Supreme Court used it to outlaw executions of mentally retarded prisoners.

The high court did not determine whether Atkins met the definition for mental retardation, and this summer, a trial was held in York County on that question. In an unusual proceeding that drew national attention, more than 50 witnesses testified about Atkins's IQ scores, school records and childhood abilities. Prosecutors have long argued that Atkins is not mentally retarded and should be put to death for the 1996 carjacking and murder of Eric Nesbitt, 21, an Air Force mechanic.

After 13 hours of deliberation, jurors concluded that Atkins was not mentally retarded. Execution was set for Dec. 2. The notice of appeal was filed in mid-September, Atkins's execution will be stayed and new legal briefs will be drafted, his attorneys said. Arguments before the state Supreme Court probably will occur next year.

Joseph Migliozzi Jr., lead counsel for Atkins, contended in an interview that the trial in York County was tainted when the judge gave jurors information about Atkins's previous conviction and told them Atkins had already been given a death sentence. Migliozzi also contended that Virginia's law on mental retardation is constitutionally flawed. The law, passed after the U.S. Supreme Court ruling, violates due process rights, he said, places the burden of proof on the defendant and fails to outline procedural issues, including whether to probe jurors for their opinions about the death penalty and what would happen in the case of a hung jury.

"I feel strongly that he was denied a fair trial," Migliozzi said.

Emily L. Lucier, a spokeswoman for Virginia Attorney General Judith W. Jagdmann, said the state would not comment while the case is pending.

Daryl Atkins, third left, sits with his defense attorneys, Joseph Migliozzi, Jr., left, Mark Oliver, second left, and Richard Burr, right, in a courtroom in Yorktown, Virginia, in 2005. Atkins, a death row inmate whose case led to the Supreme Court's ban on executing the mentally retarded, was nonetheless found mentally competent by a Virginia jury and scheduled for execution. AP IMAGES

SIGNIFICANCE

The death penalty is the subject of a raging debate in the United States. After a sustained campaign to eradicate its use, the U.S. Supreme Court banned it in 1972. But the death penalty was reinstated in 1976 after a brief prohibition of only four years. As of April 2005, thirty-eight states in the United States authorize the death penalty. Twelve states have completely abolished it. Seven states allow the death penalty, but have not executed any felon since 1976. Texas has executed the largest number of prisoners in the United States since 1976, while California has the largest number of prisoners on death row.

According to a Human Rights Watch Report, the United States is one of only a few constitutional democracies in the world that allows the death penalty. In December 2005, it joined China, Vietnam, and Iran as the country with the highest number of executions carried out since 1994.

Since the late 1990s, some reports suggest that the trend in the United States is moving toward abolish-

ing capital punishment. The Atkins case is regarded by many as a landmark case in the ongoing death penalty debate. In 2002, as mentioned earlier, the U.S. Supreme Court abolished the death penalty for mentally handicapped individuals when it heard this case on appeal. However, it is important to note that the U.S. Supreme Court did not define mental retardation when it issued its judgment (or, in other words, determine whether Atkins should be considered mentally retarded or not). Instead, the court left it for the individual states to establish a definition of mental retardation independently.

Since the 2002 U.S. Supreme Court ruling that declared the death penalty for mentally retarded individuals was unconstitutional, several cases have been prosecuted in which the accused was deemed mentally handicapped and, therefore, not eligible for the death penalty. In most of these cases, the landmark 2002 U.S. Supreme Court ruling was cited. However, many feel that it is extremely difficult to come to a decision regarding whether or not a defendant is mentally retarded. Finally, it should be noted that Daryl Atkins has not benefited from the 2002 U.S. Supreme Court ruling, since he was judged mentally fit by the York County court.

FURTHER RESOURCES

Periodicals

Glod, Maria. "Va. Killer Isn't Retarded, Jury Says; Execution Set." *Washington Post* (August 6, 2005): A01.

Web sites

Amnesty International. "The Death Penalty." <http://web.amnesty.org/pages/deathpenalty-index-eng> (accessed January 14, 2006).

CNN. "Supreme Court Bars Executing Mentally Retarded." <http://archives.cnn.com/2002/LAW/06/20/scotus.executions/> (accessed January 14, 2006).

Human Rights Watch. "U.S.: 1,000th Execution Scheduled for Friday." <http://hrw.org/english/docs/2005/11/30/usdom12117_txt.htm> (accessed January 14, 2006).

The International Justice Project. "Daryl Renard Atkins." <http://www.internationaljusticeproject.org/retardationDatkins.cfm> (accessed January 14, 2006).

Legal Information Institute, Cornell University. "Atkins v. Virginia." <http://supct.law.cornell.edu/supct/html/00-8452.ZS.html> (accessed January 14, 2006).

Pro-death Penalty.com. "Who Speaks for the Victims of Those We Execute?" <http://www.prodeathpenalty.com/> (accessed January 14, 2006).

8 Social Issues and Future Trends

Social Issues and Future Trends

Opinions about crime and punishment have undergone significant evolution during the last hundred years. At the same time, much of society has changed as well. The globe has become a complicated and densely populated place. While many people enjoy unprecedented health, freedom, and opportunity, in most areas of the world, conflict, poverty, lack of education, epidemic disease, and lack of economic prospect are still powerful social factors.

Individuals who are poorly educated generally lack marketable job skills, and may have a difficult time providing for themselves and their families, making such modern-day group enterprises as gang membership ("Testimony, United States Senate Committee on the Judiciary: Combating Gang Violence in America") and traveling sales crews ("A Road to Trouble") appear attractive to potential participants.

Where there is restriction of personal freedoms by a government, political dissent may be considered suspect or even criminal behavior (see the "Heavy Hand of Secret Police Impeding Reform in Arab World").

After the September 11, 2001 terrorist attack on the World Trade Center in New York, there has been an upsurge in international law enforcement activities, at times coupled with accusations of brutality or lack of regard for the civil rights of the individuals concerned. "CIA Holds Terror Suspects in Secret Prisons" offers insight into the complex issues involved in combating and litigating acts of international terror-

ism. "Racial Profiling in the Age of Terrorism" explores the challenge of racial profiling as a practice, as it continues to be questioned and deliberated by courts and civil libertarians alike.

With the explosion of the Internet and the double-edged sword of freedom and anonymity that it provides, there has been a proliferation of online pornography and crimes against children, described in "On line Vigilantes Hunt Pedophiles" and "Most Feared Internet Crimes: Child Pornography."

Within the United States, there have been sweeping changes in both the prison systems and in legislation governing adjudication and punishment of criminal behavior. Toward the end of the twentieth century, "truth in sentencing" legislation engendered lengthier prison sentences to be served. Laws also mandated lengthy prison sentences for multiple repeat offenders who are convicted of certain types of crimes (typically those involving illegal drugs or violence). For many convicted felons, the conditions of release to parole or probation are so stringent that they find it extremely difficult to remain on "the outside", driving up the rates of recidivism in many geographic areas and resulting in reliance upon state governors to rule on individual release dates. This is explained in "Doors Closing for Lifers—Again."

For all of the advances in criminology, fundamental questions still exist and remain controversial, including the minimum age of legal accountability (see "Old Enough to be a Criminal?").

Old Enough to be a Criminal?

United Nations document

By: UNICEF

Date: 1997

Source: "Old Enough to be a Criminal?" In: *The Progress of Nations, 1997.* <http://www.unicef.org/pon97/p56a.htm> (accessed January 9, 2006).

About the Author: UNICEF (the United Nations Children's Fund) was formed in 1946 to help children affected by World War II. Today UNICEF has over 7,000 people working in 157 countries around the world. The organization's mission is to build a world where the rights of each and every child to health, education, dignity, and justice are fully recognized.

INTRODUCTION

One of the most difficult areas of criminal justice is providing a legal framework to deal with the transition from childhood innocence to full adult maturity. Children and adolescents who commit criminal acts should not, in general, be held, tried, or punished in the same way as an adult committing the same crime. The issue arises because, of course, children do commit crimes. Their behavior is more spontaneous than that of adults and they are more easily influenced or led, which, under some circumstances, can result in their involvement in crime. Generally, these are property offenses, such as theft or criminal damage, but more serious crimes occur from time to time.

Children are, for instance, capable of murder. In 1993, two-year-old James Bulger was murdered in Liverpool, England, by two ten-year-old boys. In 2000, a six-year-old girl in Michigan was shot dead by a six-year-old classmate. Such cases are rare, but they always re-ignite the debate on the age of criminal

Providence, Rhode Island, Police Chief Dean Esserman speaks during a 2003 news conference about child care and crime. Quality early childhood and after-school programs, especially for at-risk children, can help reduce crime later in life, according to a report by a Washington-based law enforcement group. AP IMAGES

responsibility. The precise definition of criminal responsibility varies from place to place but, in general, to be responsible for a criminal act implies the perpetrator must understand what they are doing and that it is wrong.

Clearly, most young children are too immature to fully appreciate the difference between right and wrong. Many countries have fixed an age below which children cannot be held criminally responsible for their actions. Commonly, this age is set at ten years, although the age of criminal responsibility can vary between six and twelve years, according to the country. The article below discusses the call under the U.N. Convention on the Rights of the Child for nations to set a minimum age for criminal responsibility.

PRIMARY SOURCE

Children below a certain age are too young to be held responsible for breaking the law. That concept is spelled out in the Convention on the Rights of the Child, which calls for nations to establish a minimum age "below which children shall be presumed not to have the capacity to infringe the penal law." But the Convention does not set a specific age, and it varies greatly.

International standards, such as the Beijing Rules for juvenile justice, recommend that the age of criminal responsibility be based on emotional, mental and intellectual maturity and that it not be fixed too low.

The Committee on the Rights of the Child, which monitors countries' implementation of the Convention, has recommended that the age be guided by the best interests of the child.

In the US, the age of criminal responsibility is established by state law. Only 13 states have set minimum ages, which range from 6 to 12 years old. Most states rely on common law, which holds that from age 7 to age 14, children cannot be presumed to bear responsibility but can be held responsible.

In Japan, offenders below age 20 are tried in a family court, rather than in the criminal court system. In all Scandinavian countries, the age of criminal responsibility is 15, and adolescents under 18 are subject to a system of justice that is geared mostly towards social services, with incarceration as the last resort. As of April 1997, only 15 juveniles were serving a prison sentence in Sweden.

In China, children from age 14 to 18 are dealt with by the juvenile justice system and may be sentenced to life imprisonment for particularly serious crimes.

In most countries of Latin America, the reform of juvenile justice legislation is under way. As a result, the age of adult criminal responsibility has been raised to 18 in Brazil, Colombia and Peru. Children from age 12 to 18 are held responsible under a system of juvenile justice.

The wide variation in age of criminal responsibility reflects a lack of international consensus, and the number of countries with low ages indicates that many juvenile justice systems do not adequately consider the child's best interests.

Age of criminal responsibility is just one variable influencing how juveniles are treated by justice systems. Other variables include whether there is a separate juvenile law based on child rights; whether a young person is subject to punitive sanctions or only to socio-educational measures; and whether the country has separate court systems and jails for young people. A juvenile justice system provides legal protections and an objective standard for treatment. In its absence, young people may be handled by the adult criminal justice system or be held in lsquo;protectiversquo; custody, where they have no legal protections and may face arbitrary or harsh treatment.

AGE OF CRIMINAL RESPONSIBILITY

Minimum age at which children are subject to penal law in countries with 10 million or more children under 18 years old:

Mexico	*6-12
Bangladesh	7
India	7
Myanmar	7
Nigeria	7
Pakistan	7
South Africa	7
Sudan	7
Tanzania	7
Thailand	7
United States	**7
Indonesia	8
Kenya	8
UK (Scotland)	8
Ethiopia	9
Iran	***9
Philippines	9
Nepal	10
UK (England)	10

UK (Wales) 10

Ukraine 10

Turkey 11

Korea, Rep. 12

Morocco 12

Uganda 12

Algeria. 13

France 13

Poland 13

Uzbekistan 13

China. 14

Germany 14

Italy 14

Japan. 14

Russian Federation 14

Viet Nam 14

Egypt. 15

Argentina. 16

Brazil ****18

Colombia. ****18

Peru. ****18

Congo, Dem. Rep. . . . . -

*Most states 11 or 12 years; age 11 for federal crimes.

**Age determined by state, minimum age is 7 in most states under common law.

***Age 9 for girls, 15 for boys.

****Official age of criminal responsibility, from age 12 children's actions are subject to juvenile legal proceedings.

SIGNIFICANCE

The variation in ages of criminal responsibility listed above are a reflection of the history and culture of a nation. The monitoring committee for the Convention on the Rights of the Child does not actually call for a minimum age of criminal responsibility that will be universally applied. However, it does criticize those countries that make the age twelve or less. The modern approach to setting the age should take account of a child's cognitive, moral, and psychological development. Obviously, this depends upon the individual child and his or her circumstances, but there is a clear danger in setting the age too low. Between the ages of eight and fourteen, for example, a child in Scotland or Kenya may be charged with a crime whose significance is not understood, because he or she was not mature enough to really appreciate the difference between right and wrong. In China, Japan, and Germany, this immaturity in the eyes of the law is recognized. Yet, there is no reason to believe that a child's understanding of a criminal act is a function of the country in which he or she happens to live.

Abolishing the age limit altogether, as was suggested recently in Scotland, is similarly fraught with danger. A child of any age might be brought to trial for an offence he or she did not appreciate having committed and be subjected to legal proceedings he or she does not understand—a clear travesty of justice. Yet the age of criminal responsibility is not considered in a vacuum; rather, it is part of a system. In the Scottish case, the Lord Advocate looks after the interests of those under sixteen and will intervene before they are brought before an adult court. And, in practice, although an age of criminal responsibility of eight seems harsh, only a tiny fraction of child offenders actually come before the courts. The majority are dealt with by the Children's Panel, which is more focused on welfare issues than punishment. In the case of a very young child having to be charged—if the age of criminal responsibility were abolished—then the Lord Advocate would act as a safeguard to ensure that the child is not subject to proceedings he or she cannot understand.

When it comes to punishment, obviously society's need for justice must be satisfied. But, in the case of a child or adolescent, welfare and education are probably more important components of any sentence handed out. The Convention on the Rights of the Child says that no child—that is, person under 18—should ever be subject to capital punishment or imprisonment without prospect of release. Arrest, detention, and imprisonment of a child should always be seen as a last resort and be imposed for the minimum length of time. These are the minimum conditions that a child should be guaranteed should he or she break the law. Balancing the rights and needs of a juvenile offender with those of victims and society at large remains a huge challenge—of which the age of criminal responsibility is just one element.

FURTHER RESOURCES
Books

Wilson, Colin. *The Mammoth Book of True Crime*. London: Robinson, 1998.

Periodicals

Urbas, Gregor. "The Age of Criminal Responsibility." *Trends and Issues in Crime and Criminal Justice* No. 181 (November 2000).

Web sites

BBC News. "Challenge to Age of Criminal Responsibility." <http://news.bbc.co.uk/2/hi/uk_news/scotland/1465782.stm> (accessed January 9, 2006).

U.N. Office of the High Commissioner for Human Rights. "Convention on the Rights of the Child." <http://www.unhchr.ch/html/menu3/b/k2crc.htm> (accessed January 9, 2006).

Child Pornography and Prostitution in the U.S.

The Abused, the Abusers, and Recommendations to Counteract It

United Nations document

By: UN Economic and Social Council

Date: February 7, 1997

Source: "Rights of the Child." UN Economic and Social Council: Commission on Human Rights (53rd Session), 1997.

About the Author: The United Nations Economic and Social Council (ECOSOC) is an intergovernmental body composed of fifty-four member nations. The ECOSOC reports to the General Assembly, making recommendations on human rights matters and otherwise assisting the Assembly in promoting international economic and social development. To assist it in its work, the Council established the subsidiary Commission on Human Rights in 1946.

INTRODUCTION

In 2005, the US Department of Justice estimated that around 293,000 American minors were at risk of becoming victims of commercial sexual exploitation. The majority of these victims tended to be children who had run away from home or who had been turned out by their parents, and generally came from homes where they had been abused. The Justice Department put the average age at which girls become victims of prostitution at 12–14; for boys and transgender youths (largely made up of boys dressed as girls), it was younger at an average age of 11–13. The prevalence of street children engaged in prostitution had reached, the department conceded, "epidemic levels." For example, one Department of Justice study reported that fifty-five percent of homeless girls engage in street prostitution.

Commercial sexual exploitation nevertheless constitutes only a minor part of child sex abuse in the United States. The overwhelming majority of child molestation—up to ninety-six percent—was carried out by persons known to the victim and in the majority of those cases from members of the same family.

■ PRIMARY SOURCE

CHILD PORNOGRAPHY AND PROSTITUTION IN THE U.S.

B. Characteristics

Once children and adolescents have decided to run away from their homes they frequently become caught in a vicious circle of dependence. With no or minimal financial means and no job, and cut off from family contacts, runaways can easily become dependent on older men or protectors who "rescue" them from the streets. This dependence is often exacerbated by dependence on drugs and alcohol, which in turn may lead to their resorting to prostitution and sex for survival. Therefore, the Special Rapporteur is able to detect a direct correlation between runaway and "throwaway" children who end up homeless in the streets and child prostitution. With regard to involvement in child pornography, the correlation is not necessarily so strong since many children lured into pornography are simply recruited from their neighborhoods, nearby schools or acquainted families with children.

The Special Rapporteur also attempted to determine whether children and adolescents are lured away from home into commercial sexual exploitation by professional recruiters or organized rings of pimps/procurers and criminals engaging in trafficking or sale of children for purposes of child prostitution and child pornography. While it seems that small groups of loosely connected individuals sometimes attempt to recruit children into prostitution or to become involved in child pornography, especially in the Mid-West, organized criminal rings involved in trafficking per se are not known to exist in the United States. The "selling" of a prostitute from one pimp to another, however, does occur and the current rate has been estimated at US$ 3,000 per girl; whereas the rate for services by girl prostitutes was estimated at US$ 75 an hour in New York City.

One shocking aspect of child prostitution brought to the attention of the Special Rapporteur relates to "second generation child prostitutes". According to this information, there exist cases where pimps have made their teenage prostitutes pregnant, with a view either to increasing dependency or to being able to put a very young child on the prostitution market in view of the increasing demand for younger, virgin prostitutes.

With regard to child pornography, it seems that in the United States pornographic materials, such as videos and photos, featuring children, are mainly produced by amateurs for the use of paedophiles and only in limited numbers, in view of the severe penalties applicable to the production, dissemination and possession of child pornography in the country.

In connection with substance abuse, it was noted that frequently pimps and procurers try to discourage the use of drugs and alcohol since the prostitute does not "perform" as well when under their influence and consequently does not bring in enough money. On the other hand, the Special Rapporteur was informed that there are an increasing number of "crack prostitutes", predominantly female, who operate without a pimp and sell their body only in exchange for drugs.

In connection with children who have either run away from home or have been lured into the streets, it was pointed out to the Special Rapporteur that, if hospitals and medical centers possessed an electronic recording system for children who seek their help, the chances of identifying and recovering missing children or children controlled by pimps might be increased. It was further emphasized that social workers and hospital staff are not informed enough to link up cases that are treated within their purview with organizations dealing with missing and abducted children. For example, in cases of teenage pregnancies, medical staff are much more likely to inquire into incest and/or abuse within the family than into possibilities of child prostitution.

The Special Rapporteur would like to emphasize that the above analysis applies to both girls and boys, but that the phenomenon of boy prostitution differs from girl prostitution in a number of ways. It was noted several times that young boys prostitute themselves much less openly on the street, partly owing to the social stigma attached to homosexual prostitution, and are more likely to operate independently of pimps. This could result from the fact that often boy prostitutes are not, nor do they consider themselves as, homosexuals and are, therefore, much more in control over their bodies and over the sexual acts they perform or let their clients perform. Consequently, boy prostitutes are, relatively speaking, in a much better bargaining position than their female counterparts and are able to charge a much higher price for their services. The ration of boys to girls in child prostitution in the United States varies by region but, for example, in New York City, 51 per cent of child prostitutes are estimated to be boys and boy prostitutes are largely to be found concentrated in specific places such as San Francisco and New Orleans.

The Special Rapporteur is concerned at reports that the type of prostitution in which girls in particular are involved is becoming increasingly violent, including bondage, sado-macochism and spanking. The sexual act is most likely performed in cars and not, as in the past, in motels or brothels.

Profile of the perpetrator

There exists no doubt that the compulsive behavior of a paedophile is much more difficult to deter or to cure than the behavior of a sporadic "curious" abuser, whether in relation to child pornography or to child prostitution. It is believed that whilst a regular sex offender is known to abuse up to a maximum of 100 children in his lifetime, the rate for paedophiles is suspected to be 400 children. The Special Rapporteur is particularly concerned about the high rate of recidivism to be found among paedophiles. The recidivist rate for a sex offender who only occasionally abuses children is much lower.

The publicizing of successful federal investigations leading to the arrest of offenders in child sex cases should be considered an effective deterrent. The question of rehabilitation of the perpetrators is a very complex one, especially in view of the high coast of treatment of sex offenders. On the other hand, imprisonment for life also poses a considerable financial burden on the community. In connection with the efficacy of chemical sterilization as a punishment, it was held that this would not necessarily result in change of behavior because compulsiveness cannot be physically deterred. Despite sterilization, the ability to have an erection can still exist and/or the abuser might resort to digital and other forms of abuse.

It is interesting to note that the profile of perpetrators and/or clients may vary notable. Whereas the majority of clients looking for prostitutes in New York City are reported to be white, male college students in their early twenties, the average child sex abuser/paedophile is reported to be a successful white businessman, between 30 and 60 years old, often with a family often described as an "outstanding member of the community".

A. International

The convention on the Rights of the Child, which defines a child as a person under 18 years old, is the most important international human rights instrument regulating the protection of children's rights. Of particular relevance to the aspects of commercial sexual exploitation of children discussed in this report, are the provisions referred to below.

Article 32 of the Convention recognizes the right of the child to be protected from economic exploitation and from performing any work that is likely to be hazardous or to interfere with the child's education, or to be harmful to the child's health or physical, mental, spiritual, moral or social development.

Under the Convention, States parties also undertake to protect the child from all forms of sexual exploitation and sexual abuse and are required to take measures to prevent the inducement or coercion of a child to engage in any unlawful sexual activity; the exploitative use of children in prostitution or other unlawful sexual practices and the exploitative use of children in pornographic performances and materials. Article 35 provides that State parties shall take all appropriate measures to prevent the abduction of, the sale of or traffic in children for any purpose or in any form.

The Special Rapporteur notes with regret, however, that the Government of the United States of America is one of only five countries that have not yet ratified the Convention on the Rights of the child. The President of the United States, Mr. Bill Clinton, in his address on Human Rights Day, on 10 December 1996, stated that it was "shameful" that the United States had not yet ratified either the convention on the Elimination of All Forms of Discrimination against Women or the convention on the Rights of the Child. In this connection, the Assistant Secretary of State for Human Rights reassured the Special Rapporteur of the strong commitment of the current Administration to make every effort to overcome the existing strong opposition within the United States Senate, with a view to the ratification of both instruments.

In this connection, the American Bar Association was of the opinion that a concentrated effort to educate and inform the public is needed. To this end and in order to address uninformed fears by state legislators, the Center for Children and Law is currently carrying out research on the legal implications for all states if the United States were to ratify the Convention on the Rights of the Child, for example in the areas of age majority or the right to education

B. National

In view of the highly decentralized state government structure in the United States, this section will mainly address relevant provisions in federal legislation, bearing in mind that state legislation across the country may differ significantly from state to state. Federal law in the United States is applied in all cases that have an interstate character or that are determined to be of particular federal concern. The Special Rapporteur was able to observe, for example, that cases involving child prostitution are investigated by three federal agencies, namely the Federal Bureau of Investigation (FBI), the US Customs Service and the US Postal Service. Child prostitution cases which would, for example, involve the transportation of minors across state borders would also involve federal jurisdiction.

In some cases, both federal and state charges may be brought against the same defendant, but consecutive or concurrent prosecutions for the same conduct would violate federal policy. Some comments on common elements of state legislation in relation to commercial sexual exploitation of children may be of use. The United States Congress and most state legislatures have enacted criminal laws designed to protect children and youth from sexual exploitation by adults through prostitution or pornography. Under certain circumstances, other laws proscribing child sexual abuse or statutory rape can also be used to prosecute adults who sexually exploit children and youth. The mandatory reporting of child sexual abuse and exploitation to law enforcement and child protection agencies by teachers, health-care professionals and others who are in a position to identify potential victims is also required by most state law.

Federal law, and most state law, prohibits the production, distribution, receipt and possession of child pornography. Conspiracy and attempts to violate the federal child pornography laws are also chargeable federal offences. Most statutory laws define child pornography as visual depictions of a minor engaged in "sexual conduct" or in "sexually explicit conduct". Child pornography is considered a criminal offence in the United States because it represents the permanent record of the sexual abuse or exploitation of the actual child.

Some jurisdictions specifically prohibit the use of computers in connection with child pornography. Federal law specifies that persons who knowingly transport visual depictions or advertisement of child pornography "by any means, including by computer" are criminally liable.

In this connection, under the United States Code, Tiltle 18 on Crimes and Criminal Procedure (18 USC.), chapter 110 "Sexual exploitation and other abuse of children", paragraph 2251, states that any person who employs, uses, persuades, induces, entices or coerces a minor to engage in...any sexually explicit conduct for the purpose of producing any visual depiction of such conduct shall be punished if such person knows or has reason to know that such visual depiction will be transported in interstate or foreign commerce or mailed, or if such visual depiction has actually been transported. Paragraph 22252 prohibits the transportation, importation, shipment and receipt of child pornography by an interstate means, including by mail and computer. There is no requirement to show commercial purpose nor any minimum number of visual depictions. Paragraph 2251A prohibits the selling and buying of minors and makes the transfer of custody for purposes of visual depiction or engaging in sexually explicit conduct a criminal offences.

With regard to child prostitution, the Federal Government's primary law criminalizing child prostitution is the Mann Act, part of the Violent Crime Control and Law Enforcement Act 1994. The United States Code, Title 18 on Crimes and Criminal Procedure, chapter 117 "Transportation for illegal sexual activity and related crimes", paragraph 2422 prohibits enticing, persuading and inducing any person to travel across a state boundary for prostitution or for any sexual activity for which any person may be charged with a crime. Paragraph 2423, provides that "a person who knowingly transports any individual under the age of 18 years in inter-state or foreign commerce...with intent that such individual engage in prostitution, or in any sexual activity for which any person can be charged with a criminal offense, shall be fined under this title or imprisoned for not more than 10 years, or both".

SIGNIFICANCE

The 53rd Session of the United Nations Report on the "Rights of The Child" was a not-so-veiled criticism of the United States failure to ratify the UN Convention on the Rights of the Child. Since its creation in 1989 it has been ratified by 192 nations and is the most widely ratified UN Convention in history. Only Somalia and the United States had not signed up to it. Somalia, beset by civil war and under the dominance of local warlords, lacked a recognized government to do so, but the United States had no such mitigating circumstances. Even President Clinton, in 1996, described his country's refusal to ratify the convention as "shameful."

Although the United States signed the Convention on February 16, 1995, the treaty has never been submitted to the U.S. Senate. The United States government has, since the 53rd Session of the United Nations, stated that it has no plans to ratify the convention. Although signing up to it would most likely have a negligible effect on U.S. statutes, campaigners against child sexual exploitation say that it would be a massive symbolic step for the American government and would also raise awareness about a problem that has reached "epidemic" proportions amongst homeless children.

By the very nature of the United States' federal system of governance, measures to limit child prostitution at a national level have largely been limited to cover inter-state trade in minors for purposes of sexual exploitation. This has been a federal offence since

Runaway teenage girl on a subway platform in New York City, 1999. © ROBERT ESSEL NYC/CORBIS

1910. A concerted effort has been made since 2003 to enforce federal statutes prohibiting the transport of minors across state borders for the purpose of committing illegal sexual acts. Operation Innocence Lost is a nationwide initiative to stem the tide of interstate sex trafficking in the United States. As part of this the PROTECT Act was passed in April 2003 to tighten existing legislation and stiffen sentences. Although it has enjoyed some success, its critics state that it doesn't go far enough, nor does it tackle the root problems of child prostitution, which tend to exist at a localized level. Only around a fifth of child prostitution involves interstate trafficking. Federal statutes also cover children brought from outside the United States for the purposes of commercial sexual exploitation. These account for a tiny minority of those involved in the U.S. sex trade.

The success of state statutes, the principal legislation to tackle child prostitution on a local level, has been patchy. Measures are generally preventative—such as the provision of social services to help keep vulnerable children off the street or drug rehabilitation programs to remove dependency away from a pimp or dealer—rather than counteractive. Colorado has received praise from criminologists for differentiating between "prostitution by a child" and "prostitution of a child." The former means the child performing (or offering or agreeing to perform) sexual acts (or any person performing or offering or agreeing to perform such acts with a child) in exchange for money. Prostitution of a child means inducing a child to perform sexual acts by coercion, threat, or intimidation. The distinction removes the burden of criminality away from the child and gives law enforcers an additional piece of legislation with which to attack both abusers and exploiters. Most states, however, do not make such distinctions.

The limitations of counteractive statewide legislation have meant U.S. law enforcement agencies have been unable to keep pace with the rise in the sexual exploitation of children. Since the 1997 publication of the UN Report on the "Rights of The Child," incidents of traditional child prostitution have largely remained static, but different methods of child sexual exploitation have seen overall figures rise. For instance, the advent of the Internet and the emergence of high-speed broadband connections have seen an exponential growth in access to child pornography. Lewd acts and images can now be broadcast over an easily accessible medium and not just from within United States borders, but from anywhere on the planet. Research to indicate whether this has led to an actual increase in child victims is nevertheless still patchy, although anti-pornography campaigners insist that child pornography helps feed—and therefore increase—the demand for child prostitution.

Nevertheless, the Internet's biggest role in increasing child victims of sexual exploitation is in the number of children who have been sexually solicited via the Web. This stood at 1.5 million in 2000, the most recent year for when figures were available, and of these 920,000 were at high risk of actual sexual abuse.

This fits in with highly publicized research which has shown that not only is the problem of child sexual exploitation in the United States on the rise, but that the social class and backgrounds from which child prostitutes are emerging is widening. Research published in 2003 by Richard Estes of the University of Pennsylvania showed a huge rise in children from affluent backgrounds voluntarily engaging in prostitution to help fund their lifestyles. A *Newsweek* investigation published in the wake of these findings focused on the example of "Stacey," a seventeen-year-old from Minneapolis who sold sex to pay for the latest fashions at her local mall. She told *Newsweek*: "Potentially good sex is a small price to pay for the freedom to spend money on what I want." Such incidents nevertheless constitute a minor part of America's child prostitution problem.

FURTHER RESOURCES

Web sites

Missingkids.com. "Prostitution of Children and Child Sex Tourism." <http://www.missingkids.com/en_US/publications/NC73.> (accessed February 28, 2006).

Newsweek. "Nationwide Increase in Teen Prostitution." <http://www.couplescompany.com/Wireservice/Parenting/teenProstitution.htm> (accessed February 28, 2006).

Time. "Running Scared." <http://www.time.com/time/archive/preview/0,10987,981850,00.html> (accessed February 28, 2006).

University of Pennsylvania. "The Commercial Sexual Exploitation of Children In the U.S., Canada and Mexico." <http://caster.ssw.upenn.edu/~restes/CSEC_Files/Exec_Sum_020220.pdf> (accessed February 28, 2006).

Bill Clinton's Death Penalty Waffle

Magazine article

By: Alexander Nguyen

Date: July 2000

Source: Alexander Nguyen. "Bill Clinton's Death Penalty Waffle." *American Prospect* (July 2000).

About the Author: Alexander Nguyen is a former *American Prospect* writing fellow. He is a student at Yale Law School.

INTRODUCTION

Although capital punishment had been an instrument of the American justice system for almost as long as the country is old, it was not until 1930 that statistics on executions were collated on a nationwide basis. Between 1930 and 1967, 3,859 executions were carried out in the United States, the majority of which were for murders, although around twelve percent of this total were executed for rape and a small minority for other crimes.

However, from 1950, the average number of executions carried out each year—which had previously stood at around 150 —began to decline dramatically. This trend reflected a wider societal mood shift away from the use of capital punishment. Although the overall consensus was almost always in favor of the death penalty (according to pollsters Gallup, the only exceptions came in the mid-1960s), public doubts and a number of legal challenges to America's death penalty saw judges increasingly desist from using capital punishment.

In 1967, by which time execution had become almost extinct as a form of punishment, legal challenges led to an unofficial moratorium on the death penalty as the Supreme Court struggled with its constitutional and legal ramifications. These culminated in the 1972 Supreme Court decision *Furman v. Georgia*, which struck down federal and state capital punishment laws permitting wide discretion in the application of capital punishment. The Supreme Court dubbed these laws "arbitrary and capricious" and said that they thus constituted a "cruel and unusual punishment"—a violation of the Eighth Amendment. The Furman ruling saw six hundred death row inmates have their sentences lifted.

More fundamentally, however, those states that still had capital punishment were forced to rewrite their statute books so that they complied with *Furman v. Georgia* and also subsequent rulings, in which the Supreme Court further modified instances in which the death penalty could be handed out. Under these new laws death sentences continued to be handed out, and executions resumed in 1977. Continued legal challenges meant that never more than a handful were carried out for several years. Under President Ronald Reagan (1981–1989), never more than twenty-five executions were carried out in a single year, and sometimes considerably less. This trend largely continued under President George H.W. Bush (1989–1993).

Yet the number of executions carried out did not reflect the dramatic increase in death penalties handed out. During the Reagan and Bush presidencies, the number of prisoners on death row rose fivefold, to more than 2,500. This was partly a reflection on the politicization of law and order issues. During the 1980s, as violent crime plagued American cities, the death penalty and law enforcement became the central political issue of the day. Voters demanded stiffer penalties on convicted criminals and it became increasingly popular for politicians to make capital out of a strong line on crime. Indeed what stronger line could be taken than the death penalty?

For a governor, rejecting a plea for clemency was viewed as a mark of strength; for a prospective candidate, standing against the death penalty was seen as weak and soft on crime. Never was this more apparent than in the differing fortunes of Michael Dukakis and Bill Clinton, Democratic Presidential nominees for 1988 and 1992, respectively. In 1988, Dukakis was asked on live television whether or not he would favor the death penalty for someone who had raped and murdered his wife. Dukakis stumbled in search of an answer, which was "no"; the press and public thereafter viewed him as "weak" and "liberal," and he lost the election. Four years later, Bill Clinton made certain that he took center stage when the execution of Rickey Ray Rector came up in his home state of Arkansas. Rector had been convicted of killing a police officer, but had afterwards turned the gun on himself. Instead of killing himself however, he had blown out one third of his brain, leaving him mentally retarded. Yet Clinton insisted that this was no grounds for clemency and Rector went to the electric chair.

In ensuring Rector's death, Clinton assuaged the doubts of floating voters who had hitherto seen him in similar terms to Michael Dukakis. Many believe this helped Clinton win the Presidential election. Nevertheless, throughout his eight years as President, the issue of the death penalty would be one that his critics consistently raised as an example of Clinton's so-called moral weakness.

PRIMARY SOURCE

Bill Clinton recently spared Juan Raul Garza's life—at least for a little while. On August 5, Garza—a drug trafficker convicted of ordering the murder of three people—would have become the first person executed by the federal government in almost 40 years. Though few question whether Garza is guilty, Clinton wants to give him time to request clemency under new guidelines, which are still being drafted.

Some Republicans have suggested that Clinton did this to make it easier for Al Gore to attack George W. Bush as the murderingest politician (137 served, and counting). But the real story here may be how Bill Clinton has morphed from an opponent of the death penalty to an avid supporter to a near agnostic—and the lessons it may offer for execution's opponents.

In his early days, Clinton opposed the death penalty. And while he and his wife Hillary Rodham Clinton were both teaching at the University of Arkansas Law School, she wrote an appellate brief that helped free a mentally retarded man from execution. "Clinton was against the death penalty," says Arkansas attorney Jeff Rosenzweig, who, like Clinton, grew up in Hot Springs, Arkansas. "He told me so."

As a young governor, Clinton was reluctant to facilitate the executions permitted by his state. Prosecutors often had to pressure Clinton to schedule inmates' executions, according to the Legal Times. By not doing so, he was postponing their deaths indefinitely.

Clinton eventually signed a policy that effectively set the execution dates for him. Nevertheless, he was no Robespierre: During his first term as governor, he freed 70 people from jail, 38 of whom were convicted of first-degree murder. But when one of those murdered again a few months after his release, Clinton suffered a humiliating defeat for re-election to a Republican who accused him of being soft on crime. When Clinton ran again, he publicly apologized for freeing the convicts and vowed not to do so again if re-elected. Since 1983 he has granted only seven requests.

By his second term as governor, Clinton had begun morphing into a death penalty supporter. In 1988 he expressed his support quite mildly, saying that while "many fine people" believed executions to be immoral, "that's just not my view of it." He also told The Arkansas Democrat-Gazette, "I can't say it's an inappropriate punishment for people who are multiple murderers and who are deliberately doing it and who are adjudged to be sane and know what they're doing when they're doing it."

Gradually, Clinton became a more willing executioner. Days before an execution, a lawyer from the American Civil Liberties Union approached Clinton at a tree-planting ceremony. Shaking Clinton's hand, the lawyer confronted him, saying, "You won't remember the tree, but you'll remember the people you executed." Clinton parried, "I remember the people that they killed, too."

On the national stage, something happened that would cement Clinton's support for the death penalty for years to come. Asked during the 1988 debates if Michael Dukakis would support the death penalty if his wife Kitty were raped and murdered, Dukakis stared into the camera, squinted into the lights above, and then said, "I think there are better and more effective ways to deal with violent crime." The answer ruined Dukakis. Bush relentlessly charged Dukakis with being soft on crime, and his

loss changed the landscape of what Democrats could say about the death penalty.

Clinton had learned his lesson. By 1992 the presidential candidate was insisting that Democrats "should no longer feel guilty about protecting the innocent." To make his point, he flew home to Arkansas mid-campaign to watch the execution of Rickey Ray Rector, a 40-year-old black man convicted of killing a black police officer. After shooting the cop, Rector shot himself in the head and damaged his brain.

Though courts decided Rector was mentally competent to be put to death by lethal injection, evidence suggests otherwise. Rector's prison guards called him "the Chickman" because he thought the guards were throwing alligators and chickens into his cell. He would grip the bars and jump up and down like an ape. On the night of his execution, Rector saved the slice of pecan pie to be eaten before bedtime, not realizing his death would come first. He also told his attorney that he would like to vote for Clinton in the fall.

Also executed during the campaign was Steven Douglas Hill, who was convicted of shooting a state police investigator after he and an accomplice escaped from a state prison. Hill confessed to the crime, but his partner Michael Cox has insisted for years that it was he, not Hill, who pulled the trigger. In all, Arkansas executed four people on Clinton's watch.

The executions made Clinton's wish come true. Never again would anyone seriously accuse him of being soft on crime. Never again would anyone challenge his status as a New Democrat.

As president, Clinton continued to endorse the death penalty. In 1994 he pushed a crime bill through Congress that allows prosecutors to seek the federal death penalty in 60 more crimes than they could previously. Later, in his campaign against Bob Dole, Clinton ran a TV ad in which he recommended that in addition to putting more cops on the streets, "expand the death penalty. That's how we'll protect America."

In 1996, prompted by the Oklahoma City bombing, Clinton supported antiterrorism legislation that included an (ultimately unsuccessful) provision that would have curtailed the writ of habeas corpus—the power of federal courts to second-guess state courts on whether or not a fair trial had been given. The law would have allowed inmates only one federal death row appeal filed within one year of exhausting all the possible state appeals.

Quite recently, however, Clinton has changed his position. Expressing some concern that the death penalty was being distributed unequally across racial and geographic lines, his White House has asked the Department of Justice to do a statistical survey. And Clinton promised to delay Garza's execution—a move that contrasts sharply with the bloodthirsty persona he adopted almost two decades ago.

Clinton still officially supports the death penalty and so far has ignored the calls for a national moratorium on federal executions. In fact, when Senator Russell Feingold sent Clinton a letter asking him to suspend federal executions and review the death penalty, the letter went unanswered. Nevertheless, it is important to ask why—in the heat of his vice president's campaign—this poll-driven president would risk backing off the very position that secured his reputation as an electable moderate.

There are several factors giving Clinton wiggle room—and they center on the fact that recent attacks on the death penalty have been formulated not on principle, but on process.

The first empirical argument is the racial disparity. Of the 21 people on federal death row, 17 are black, Asian, or Hispanic. The second, and even more promising, argument is that the specter of putting an innocent person to death is too large. Columbia University released a study that showed that two-thirds of death penalty cases appealed between 1973 and 1995 were so flawed they had to be overturned. In Illinois—where Republican Governor George Ryan recently suspended the death penalty to investigate the fairness of the process—13 death row inmates have been freed and 12 executed since 1977. In Ryan's state, college students were able to dig up evidence exonerating inmates on death row. Since 1993 the availability of DNA testing has also cast much doubt on the certainty of guilt in convictions.

Third—rather than arguing against the death penalty as a whole—opponents have highlighted particular cases. "I don't think that much ground will be gained by sort of generically attacking the institution of the death penalty," Democratic strategist Scott Segal told The Washington Times. "Democrats will gain ground by pointing out specific instances."

Finally, backing off the death penalty has become safer since crime levels dropped so precipitously over the past decade. With the decline in crime, the support for the death penalty has fallen too. Polls place current support at 66 percent, down from 80 percent in 1994. Support falls to only 52 percent if an alternative punishment such as life imprisonment is offered as an option, according to Gallup polls.

But there's a better measure than polls: President Clinton's chameleon-like approach may give observers the best reflection of the political environment of all. And if Clinton is softening his death penalty stance, opponents can be sure that now is the moment to redouble

efforts to chip away at execution's foundation—for they may be able to topple the whole institution.

SIGNIFICANCE

During Clinton's presidency, the number of executions carried out would rise dramatically. In 1993, the first year of his Presidency, thirty-eight executions were carried out nationwide, a figure which itself marked a thirty-year high. In 2000, the last year of his Presidency, this had risen to eighty-five, thirteen fewer than the previous year's record of ninety-eight executions.

While Clinton himself had little input in the majority of these executions, which were all carried out by states, according to his critics his attitude toward capital punishment typified "Clintonism"— the idea that following the polls was more important than being guided by a moral compass. When Clinton had been Governor of Arkansas in the 1970s, he had opposed the death penalty, but when law and order issues came into vogue during the next decade, he switched standpoint and ultimately became an enthusiastic backer. This culminated in his hardline stance over Rickey Ray Rector, the mentally retarded man who was executed in the run-up to the 1992 Presidential election.

Clinton's continued support of the death penalty came at a time when virtually every democracy in the world repealed capital punishment legislation. When his presidency ended in 2001, the death penalty was banned in 108 countries—including every nation besides Belarus in Europe—and the U.S., India, and Japan were the only big democracies that had not desisted in its practice. While Clinton could have argued that this was a reflection of public support for the death penalty, many countries that had banned it still had a majority of popular opinion calling for its return.

Nevertheless, public doubts about the death penalty, similar to many of those held during the 1960s, began to return during the Clinton presidency. The number of death row acquittals after new evidence revealed a conviction to be faulty doubled between 1994 and 2000. This meant that there was one release for every seven executions, causing many people to beg the question that if so many could be reprieved, how many innocents might have been sent to undeserved deaths? By 2000, a Gallup poll revealed that support for the death penalty in the U.S. had fallen to sixty-six percent—the lowest in nineteen years. This fell to just fifty-two percent when the

Protesters against the death penalty reflect outside the Federal Prison at Terre Haute, Indiana, during the morning hours of June 21, 2001, prior to the execution of Mexican-American drug lord and murderer Juan Raul Garza. © REUTERS/CORBIS

option of life imprisonment without parole was offered.

There was also a growing surfeit of evidence that proved the effectiveness of the death penalty. Critics—including, ironically, both those in the pro- and anti-capital punishment camps—argued that executions were applied too haphazardly to put any would-be felon off.

In August 2000, during the last months of his presidency, Clinton gave a stay of execution to Juan Raul Garza, a convicted murderer and drug trafficker who was set to become the first person executed by the federal government in almost forty years. That was ostensibly so that new clemency procedures could be completed, but the move briefly raised vague hopes amongst abolitionists that Clinton was about to switch direction again and lead some sort of moratorium on the death penalty, as had happened in 1967.

No such thing happened and Clinton left the White House the following January. His successor, George W. Bush, as Governor of Texas, oversaw more executions than any other politician in decades. Within months of his inauguration, Garza was executed by lethal injection. Since then, annual executions have continued to be carried out at around the same rate as they had done during the Clinton era.

FURTHER RESOURCES
Books

Hood, Roger. *The Death Penalty: A Worldwide Perspective*. Oxford, U.K.: Oxford University Press, 2004.

Klein, Joe. *The Natural: The Misunderstood Presidency of Bill Clinton*. London: Coronet, 2002.

Web sites

Death Penalty Information Center. "History of the Death Penalty." <http://www.deathpenaltyinfo.org/article. php> (accessed February 27, 2006).

Most Feared Internet Crimes

Child Pornography

Statistical table

By: Pew Research Center

Date: February 2001

Source: The Pew Internet & American Life Project Survey. <http://www.pewinternet.org/pdfs/PIP_Fear_of_crime.pdf>

About the Author: The Pew Research Center is an initiative of the Pew Charitable Trusts, and is charged with informing the public, press, and policy makers on important issues and trends.

INTRODUCTION

During the last few decades, there has been great worldwide concern about child pornography, pedophilia, and related issues. A related aspect of these issues concern ways in which children can be kept safe, since their innocence and naivety can make them unfortunate targets of such crimes. Increasing access to new technology, like video and camera phones, may complicate the problem. Most experts state that instances of child pornography have increased since the advent of the Internet.

The Internet has grown explosively since its inception and now permeates nearly every sphere of modern human activity, including communications, entertainment, news, banking, business, research, and commerce. However, the uses of the Internet have not been without controversy. It has opened up novel means for online crimes like fraud, hacking, and identity theft. In addition, it has provided a new avenue for classic crimes like stealing and swindling, and has given legal authorities worldwide a new subject of concern—cyber-crime. The most unsavory use of the Internet is as a channel for peddling all forms of pornography, including child pornography.

Various reports suggest an increase in online pedophiles who assume that the virtual nature of their crime protects them from detection and prosecution. Some studies link an increase in sex-crimes and crimes of pedophilia to an increase in child pornography on the Internet. New technologies, including Internet-enabled cellular phones, may also give predators increased access to children.

PRIMARY SOURCE

MOST FEARED INTERNET CRIMES
See primary source image.

SIGNIFICANCE

According to the Pew Center, the internet is an entity through which many worries fester for Americans. In fact, the Pew Center study on American's "Most Feared Internet Crimes" lists "child pornography" as the most feared out of eight categories listed. Other feared Internet crimes include organized terrorism, credit card theft, and computer viruses.

Child pornography is a serious issue worldwide. In January 2004, a British Broadcasting Corporation (BBC) report blamed the Internet for the rise in incidents relating to child pornography. According to the report, there was a 1,500 percent rise in such incidents in the United Kingdom since 1988.

Various other sources point out that the global scale of child pornography is massive. These sources suggest that nearly fifty-five percent of the pornographic material originates in the United States, while about twenty-three percent originates in Russia.

The apparent increase in the incidence of child pornography offenses has been linked to the relative ease of distribution and access to these materials on the Internet. Surveys conducted in 2003 suggested that child pornography accounted for nearly twenty-four percent of Internet images searches. Dealing with child pornography has become a priority for police and law enforcement agencies.

The U.S. Congress passed the Child Pornography Prevention Act in 1996. The act stiffened fines and jail time for those convicted of producing and distributing pornographic materials depicting children. The act also criminalized the receipt of child pornography via email or Internet download. A later amendment broadened the definition of child pornography to include computer-generated images. However, the Supreme Court struck down the amendment as unconstitutional asserting that animated or computer-generated images do not involve or injure an actual child.

Canada and Britain, like the United States, prohibit mere possession, accessing, or downloading of child pornography. Britain maintains a ban on simulated and computer-generated pornographic images depicting children. In the early twenty-first century, a number of members of Parliament issued an appeal to Internet service providers in the United Kingdom to

PEW INTERNET & AMERICAN LIFE PROJECT SURVEY "MOST FEARED INTERNET CRIMES" AS OF FEBRUARY 2001*

The percentage of all Americans who say they are most concerned about...

Type of Internet Crime	Percent
Child pornography	50%
Credit card theft	10
Organized terrorism	10
Destructive computer viruses	5
Hackers attacking the government	5
Wide-scale fraud	2
Hackers attacking business	1
Another crime not listed as a choice	13

Source: Pew Internet & American Life Project. "Fear of Online Crime: Americans Support FBI Interception of Criminal Suspects' Email and New Laws to Protect Online Privacy," p. 8. Information available online at http://www.pewinternet.org/reports/toc.asp?Report=32 (cited April 26, 2002).

* Margin of error is ± 2 percent.

PRIMARY SOURCE

Most Feared Internet Crimes As shown in this table, child pornography was by far the "most feared Internet crime" among Americans in 2001. TABLE CREATED FOR THOMSON GALE BY GGS INFORMATION SERVICES.

block child pornography web sites. They urged the government to enact a law compelling these companies to spell out their policies on this issue. It remains to be seen whether such measures will reduce the incidence of child pornography offenses.

FURTHER RESOURCES

Web sites

BBC News. "Extent of Child Net Porn Revealed." <http://news.bbc.co.uk/2/hi/uk_news/3908215.stm> (accessed January 14, 2006).

BBC News. "Porn Ring 'Was Real Child Abuse'." <http://news.bbc.co.uk/2/hi/uk_news/1109787.stm> (accessed January 14, 2006).

Cyber-Rights & Cyber-Liberties. "Regulation of Child Pornography on the Internet." <http://www.cyber-rights.org/reports/child.htm> (accessed January 14, 2006).

LegalDay. "Operation Ore." <http://www.legalday.co.uk/current/ore.htm> (accessed January 14, 2006).

RCMP Gazette. "Just the Facts." <http://www.gazette.rcmp-grc.gc.ca/article-en.html/> (accessed January 14, 2006).

The Register. "Net Blamed for Massive Increase in Child Porn." <http://www.theregister.co.uk/2004/01/12/net_blamed_for_massive_increase/> (accessed January 14, 2006).

U.K. Home Office. "Internet Crime." <http://www.homeoffice.gov.uk/crime-victims/reducing-crime/internet-crime/> (accessed January 14, 2006).

AMBER Alert

Photograph

By: Nati Harnik

Date: December 11, 2002

Source: AP Images

About the Photographer: Nati Harnik is a photographer for the Associated Press news organization.

INTRODUCTION

The AMBER Alert system is a voluntary partnership between U.S. law enforcement and the media that encourages the public to help find abducted children who may be in imminent danger. AMBER stands for America's Missing: Broadcast Emergency Response Plan. Dallas-Forth Worth broadcasters and law enforcement officials jointly developed the warning system in 1997 in memory of nine-year-old Amber Hagerman. Hagerman was kidnapped while riding her bicycle in Arlington, Texas, and brutally murdered. By February 2005, the system had been adopted across the entire United States.

Each state has its own AMBER alert plan and distinct criteria for issuing an alert. However, the U.S. Department of Justice has established some voluntarily guidelines, which suggest than an alert be issued whenever law enforcement concludes that a child age seventeen or younger has been abducted and is danger of being injured or killed. There must be enough descriptive information to create an alert, and the child's name should be entered into the National Crime Information Center database. AMBER alerts should be reserved for the most severe, time-sensitive cases. They are only issued by law enforcement and are not used in the case of runaways. Experts warn that abuse of AMBER alerts could desensitize the community and lead to the program's failure.

When an alert is warranted, descriptions of the child, alleged abductor, and suspected vehicle are quickly distributed to radio and television stations, which interrupt programming with an emergency bulletin similar to those used in the event of severe weather. Alerts can also be posted on the Internet, on lottery tickets, and sent to wireless devices such as cell phones. In some states, the AMBER alert is posted on the electronic highway billboards that normally inform travelers about traffic conditions. People who have information about the child or alleged suspect are asked to immediately call 911 or the telephone number posted with the alert.

On December 11, 2002, nine-month-old Brodjinique Dunn was kidnapped when the car she was riding in was stolen from a gas station. Nebraska issued its first-ever AMBER Alert in response, with messages being broadcast through the media and posted on highway signs. Iowa law enforcement also issued an alert. The car was found, parked, less than two hours later. Brodjinique was unharmed.

PRIMARY SOURCE

AMBER ALERT

See primary source image.

AMBER Alert: Cars pass a sign on Interstate 80 in Omaha, Nebraska showing an "AMBER Alert" for a white 1995 Jeep with Nebraska license plate NDW242. The car was stolen with nine-month-old Brodjinique Dunn in the backseat. She and the car were found unharmed several hours later. AP IMAGES.

SIGNIFICANCE

Time is of the essence when a child is abducted. U.S. Department of Justice data suggest that the majority of children who are abducted and killed die within the first three hours of the kidnapping. The goal of the AMBER alert system is to quickly rouse the community so that the child and alleged abductor are found as soon as possible. Since the program's introduction in 1997, more than 240 children have been safely recovered. The majority of those recoveries occurred after President George W. Bush called for a nationally coordinated effort during the first White House conference on missing, exploited, and runaway children. His administration later appointed Regina B. Schofield as the first national AMBER Alert Coordinator. On April 30, 2003, President Bush signed into law the PROTECT Act. This legislation strengthened laws regarding crimes committed against children, helped facilitate AMBER alert notification and communication systems along U.S. highways, and formally established the national AMBER Alert Coordinator role in the U.S. Department of Justice.

A nationally coordinated effort, widespread interstate use of AMBER alerts, and on-going AMBER alert training conferences have made a dramatic impact on the number of abducted children who are safely recovered. In 2001, two children were safely returned as a result of the AMBER alert system. In 2004, AMBER alerts lead to the safe recovery of seventy-one children. The AMBER alert system is now considered to be one of the most effective tools used to protect America's children.

FURTHER RESOURCES

Web sites

National Center for Missing and Exploited Children. <http://www.missingkids.com> (accessed February 2, 2006).

U.S. Department of Justice. Office of Justice Programs. "Amber Alert." <http://www.amberalert.gov> (accessed February 2, 2006).

Racial Profiling in an Age of Terrorism

Magazine article

By: Peter Siggins

Date: March 12, 2002

Source: Siggins, Peter. "Racial Profiling in an Age of Terrorism." *Ethical Perspectives on the News*, March. 2002, <http://www.scu.edu/ethics/publications/ethicalperspectives/profiling.html> (accessed January 12, 2006).

About the Author: Peter Siggins has served as the Chief Deputy Attorney General for Legal Affairs for the state of California since his appointment to that position in 1999. In that role, he is responsible for all legal work of the California Department of Justice and supervises a staff of more than 900 lawyers who handle all cases in the name of the state of California. Earlier in his career, Siggins was the Senior Assistant Attorney General directing the Correctional Law section of the Attorney General's office. In that post, he supervised defense of all civil litigation cases brought against California's Department of Corrections, the State's Youth Authority, and the Board of Prison Terms.

INTRODUCTION

In the wake of the attacks of September 11, 2001, the United States law enforcement and judicial communities were presented with new questions as to how to best defend the nation from future, similar terrorist attacks. One approach that had long been advocated as effective by law enforcement but opposed by advocates of civil liberties and privacy was known as racial profiling.

Racial profiling refers to a method utilized by police and private investigators where individuals are identified as more likely to be associated with a specific crime because of their race, ethnicity, nationality, or religion. Opponents of this method often refer to a specific application of racial profiling as Driving While Black (DWB), whereby police traffic officers pulled over African Americans at a higher rate only because there is a higher rate of criminal activity by members of their racial group.

Since the terrorist cells that carried out the attacks against the Pentagon and the World Trade Center consisted entirely men of Middle Eastern background who fit a specific physical profile, the issue of racial profiling was placed at the center of the public debate. Opponents of profiling argued that the policy judged people simply based on their personal identities. On the other hand, advocates argued that profiling based on race was an effective crime deterrent, and, in the wake of 9/11, this was a price that needed to be paid for the safety of the nation.

Profiling, while wholly unpopular with many minority groups, was used regularly by both larger police departments and individual security agencies. El Al, the national airline of Israel (a nation that repeatedly has been the target of terror attacks throughout its history), relies on profiling to screen passengers that board its flight. Security analysts say that this method is a major factor that has kept the airline free of any significant security breakdowns, despite being a prime target for an attack. Even while many in the law enforcement and government communities say the method is a necessary tool in fighting terror, it remains one of the more controversial policies that have grown in practice following 9/11.

PRIMARY SOURCE

Earl Warren, 14th Chief Justice of the United States, has become an icon to generations of Americans who believe in the gains for civil rights and personal freedom that were the hallmark of his tenure on the Supreme Court. In 1940, Earl Warren was the attorney general of California, and he delivered a speech where he cautioned against bigotry based upon national origin. He said,

> It should be remembered that practically all aliens have come to this country because they like our land and our institutions better than those from whence they came. They have attached themselves to the life of this country in a manner that they would hate to change and the vast majority of them will, if given a chance, remain the same good neighbors that they have been in the past regardless of what difficulties our nation may have with the country of their birth. History proves this to be true....We must see to it that no race prejudices develop and that there are no petty persecutions of law-abiding people.

Then, in the wake of the attack on Pearl Harbor, by January and February 1942, Attorney General Warren directed the preparation of maps showing all Japanese-owned lands in California, called upon the state's district attorneys to enforce the Alien Land Law against Japanese landowners, and said the presence of Japanese in California provided the opportunity for a repetition of Pearl Harbor. And by March he advocated the exclusion of all Japanese from within 200 miles of the California coast.

Following the attack on Pearl Harbor, the interest in preserving the safety and security of the nation was put in direct conflict with the American democratic ideal of racial equality. The noble cause of equality in that circumstance yielded to our concern for security. Subsequent experience shows that exclusion to be one of the great injustices of WWII visited upon American residents. Congress has since passed laws ordering reparations for those American residents separated from their homes, businesses and lands. Although the Supreme Court's holding in Korematsu, that the Government in time of war had justified racial discrimination in the name of national security is still the law of the land, many lower courts

have recognized the injustice wrought by the Japanese internment and we should not forget it.

It is against this historical backdrop that we encounter post-9/11 efforts to combat terrorist acts on American soil, and examine the role that race should play in an effective effort to deter future attacks. But before assessing whether our government's response to the events of 9/11 betray a pattern of racial profiling, I first want to identify what it is.

In 1968, the Supreme Court decided the landmark case of Terry v. Ohio. Then Chief Justice Warren, joined by seven other members of the Court, held that it is not a violation of the Fourth Amendment for an officer to detain and search a man's person for a weapon in absence of a search warrant, so long as the officer acts upon a reasonable belief based upon objective factors that the man is armed and dangerous. The Court's decision in Terry has been interpreted by lower courts countless times over the years to allow the brief detention and search of persons by law enforcement officials when officers are acting upon reasonable suspicion that criminality is afoot. The lexicon of the criminal justice community now refers very casually to such stop and frisk encounters as "Terry" stops, and over the years these brief detentions have been relied upon by officers with ever increasing frequency to stop and investigate suspicious characters. In 1996 in Whren v. United States, amid growing concern over the use of Terry stops as a prophylactic law enforcement tool, the Supreme Court reiterated the objective nature of the inquiry into a law officer's basis for a Terry stop. The Court held that an officer's subjective motivation has no part to play in the Fourth Amendment analysis of justification for a stop and search when the officer can articulate objective reasons.

Out of the Terry line of cases, as fortified by the Court's decision in Whren, law enforcement agencies all over the country advocated pre-textual stops and encounters with citizens as good proactive policing. The practices are most often deployed through a casual traffic stop occasioned by a burned out taillight or some other minor vehicle code violation. But in recent years, at first anecdotally, then more empirically, it has been demonstrated that the Terry procedure has been used disparately to detain and interrogate black or brown people. In late 1999, the New Jersey state police became the first major law enforcement agency to admit to the stop and detention of disproportionate numbers of black men. Since then, state legislatures all over the country have wrestled with legislation aimed at banning racial profiling, and there has been tremendous outcry to study its effect and occurrence among major law enforcement agencies. For example, the LAPD has been required as part of a consent decree with the USDOJ to collect data that may reveal patterns of racial profiling by officers in traffic stops. Just this year Governor Davis vetoed a bill designed to require local police agencies to report statistics on traffic stops in order to detect patterns of racial profiling. After litigation was filed by the ACLU over the veto of this bill, the Governor and Highway Patrol have instituted the program by executive order. As recently as March 2001, Attorney General Ashcroft condemned racial profiling as "[A]n unconstitutional deprivation of equal protection under our Constitution."

So, racial profiling as the term has been employed in recent public debate, refers to government activity directed at a suspect or group of suspects because of their race, whether intentional or because of the disproportionate numbers of contacts based upon other pretextual reasons. Under Fourth Amendment analysis, objective factors measure whether law enforcement action is constitutional, and under the Fourteenth Amendment challenges to the practice are assessed under the customary strict scrutiny test for racial classifications. It is against this historical and legal backdrop that we should take a look at our law enforcement and internal domestic security response to the horrific acts of September 11th.

In the weeks following September 11, federal, state and local law enforcement officials worked feverishly to investigate those responsible for the most reprehensible crime on American Soil and to assess our state of vulnerability to further acts of terrorism. As part of those efforts conclusions about the ethnicity and national origin of the prime suspects was inescapable. This crime was committed by a group of foreign nationals of middle eastern descent.

Immediately law enforcement officials focused special investigative efforts upon foreign nationals from middle eastern countries, often in disregard of any other factors warranting suspicion. In December, federal investigators began voluntary interviews with more than 5,000 young middle eastern men who entered the United States within the last two years from countries that were linked to terrorism. Federal officials have contacted administrators at more than two hundred colleges and universities to gain information about students from middle eastern countries. What are their majors? Where do they live? How often do they miss class? They have followed up these efforts with unannounced visits and interviews with the students. Some local police chiefs who have worked hard to rebut concerns over racial profiling have resisted cooperation with these federal efforts on the ground that the interviews appear to violate departmental policy or state and local laws.

In California, by September 25, 2001, the governor and attorney general along with the Highway Patrol and the Office of Emergency Services formed the California Anti-Terrorism Information Center. The Center is created to analyze and process the thousands of tips and leads of suspicious activity that began pouring into state law enforcement agencies in the days following September 11th. The effort has been to separate the wheat from the chaff and disseminate to law enforcement information that truly reflects suspicious activity or reliably warrants concern. In just January and February of this year, 1,615 subjects were reported to the database. Two Hundred and twenty eight of them had criminal histories and 330 were the subjects of ongoing investigations. The center services an average of 56 law enforcement agencies per week, and monitors 40 open anti-terrorist investigations.

Significant information continues to be received by the Center every day reporting the conduct of males of apparent Middle East extraction that hardly qualifies for the designation of suspicious or dangerous activity. The job of responsible law enforcement officials is to cull from the many innocuous reports received by the center, those that combine ethnic or national origin with a multiple of indicators to reveal persons who may be a concern or possible threat.

The U.S. Congress, in the days following September 11th, passed The USA Patriot Act, an omnibus bill containing numerous reforms to federal criminal procedure, laws relating to foreign intelligence surveillance, wiretaps and interception of electronic communications, laws relating to the gathering of documentary evidence, and DNA and immigration laws. In a very general sense, the Act makes it easier for federal investigative agencies to obtain wiretaps on multiple electronic devices, and procure electronic and documentary evidence from sources like internet service providers and cable and telephone companies. It also relaxes prohibitions on the sharing of information obtained in investigations by different federal agencies. While the latitude afforded law enforcement activities under the act and relaxed standards for information sharing may give rise to concern for the protection of civil liberties, the provisions most relevant to our discussion today are in the area of immigration and naturalization.

Section 412 of the Patriot Act permits the attorney general of the United States to detain aliens he certifies as threats to national security for up to seven days without bringing charges. The standard to establish grounds for detention is the familiar reasonable suspicion standard enunciated by the Supreme Court in Terry. The certification by the attorney general must set forth that he has "reasonable grounds to believe" the person being detained will commit espionage or sabotage, try to overthrow the government, commit terrorist acts, or otherwise engage in acts that would endanger national security. At the conclusion of seven days, the detention may continue in the event the alien is charged with a crime or violation of visa conditions. But if circumstances prohibit the repatriation of a person for an immigration offense, the detention may continue indefinitely so long as certified by the attorney general every six months. Under the USA Patriot Act, the prospect exists that a person who is confined for a violation of conditions of entry into the US, but cannot be deported to his or her country of origin, may be indefinitely confined here without criminal charges ever filed against them.

Thurgood Marshall wrote that, "History teaches that grave threats to liberty often come in times of urgency, when constitutional rights seem too extravagant to endure." Recent surveys indicate that 66% of whites and 71% of African-Americans support the ethnic profiling of people who look to be of middle-eastern descent. But we also know that hate motivated violence against middle eastern people and members of California's sikh community, often mistakenly thought to be Arabs, spiked in the

weeks after the September 11th attack. There are currently 150 open federal hate crime investigations for incidents following the September 11th attack.

The mission of responsible law enforcement officials in combating domestic terrorism is to take what they know to be true about the ethnic identity of the September 11th assailants, and combine it with other factors developed through investigation and analysis to focus investigative efforts and avoid casting a net too wide. Have the subjects passed bad checks? Do they have multiple forms of identification with different names? Do they live in groups with no visible means of support? Does a subject use credit cards with different names on them? Ethnicity alone is not enough. If ethnic profiling of middle eastern men is enough to warrant disparate treatment, we accept that all or most middle eastern men have a proclivity for terrorism, just as during World War II all resident Japanese had a proclivity for espionage.

Artist Eric Brown discusses his paintings for an art show titled "Homeland Security - An American Profile." The exhibit takes aim at racial profiling in America in the age of terrorism and expresses the fear that under the Patriot Act many Americans will become the targets of profiling. © CHIP EAST/REUTERS/CORBIS

The Israeli airline El Al has a policy of singling out young Arabs for extensive search procedures, but is quick to point out that, in spite of ongoing war in the middle east, it has not had a hijacking in over thirty years. Perhaps there is a need to adjust our expectations in a time of national emergency. Con. Richard Gephardt has said of post-September 11th America that, "We're in a new world where we have to rebalance freedom and security." And Sen. Trent Lott said that, "When you're in this type of conflict, when you're at war, civil liberties are treated differently." The real question for us is how differently and whether differently for all or only a select few.

I agree with the sentiments of Walter Dellinger, former Acting Solicitor General during the Clinton Administration, "I am more willing to entertain restrictions that affect all of us like identity cards and more intrusive X-ray procedures at airports—and am somewhat more skeptical of restrictions that affect only some of us, like those that focus on immigrants or single out people by nationality." It will be impossible to physically protect every location that could be the subject of a terrorist attack. Protection is going to have to be accomplished through infiltration and surveillance, so all of us have to get used to new levels of government intrusion.

SIGNIFICANCE

While the attacks against New York and Washington, D.C. brought the United States into the global war on terror and dramatically changed how the nation tracked terrorists, this document highlights that it was not the first time that the government had to address the question of how to also protect the civil liberties of its citizens in the wake of an attack on the country. The document, in fact, points out that following the attack on Pearl Harbor, the Attorney General of California ordered specific measures to be taken against the Japanese residents of the state to preserve the safety and security of the nation.

This precedent would serve as the basis for many advocates of racial profiling to suggest that, while singling out specific minorities was not a practice usually associated with a democracy, national security concerns superseded the cause of equality. In the wake of the actions taken against the Japanese citizens of the United States during World War II, the Congress ordered that reparations be paid for the loss of property and income incurred by the Japanese. Yet, the United States Supreme Court, in the major precedent decision for the types of racial profiling exacted after 9/11, ruled that racial discrimination in the name of national security was, in fact, justified.

Despite that ruling, racial profiling as a practice continues to be questioned and deliberated by courts and civil libertarians alike. When the acts of 9/11 were carried out by a group of terrorists all bearing roughly the same physical characteristics—young men of Middle Eastern descent—the issue moved to the center of public debate.

As this article suggests, law enforcement agencies focused investigations on broad groups of Middle Eastern men, even when they had little or no reason to suspect them of illegal or terrorist activities. Policies of racial profiling largely enjoyed a high degree of public support in the wake of September 2001 under the assumption—supported by public figures—that the war on terrorism is different than any challenge the United States had faced in the past. Given the new security environment in which the United States finds itself following 9/11, racial profiling, in accordance with the law, has largely been accepted as a necessary form of intelligence gathering. Even though racial profiling is detrimental to some innocent elements of society, it is viewed by many as a means of protection for the nation as a whole.

FURTHER RESOURCES

Books

Harris, David. *Profiles in Injustice: Why Racial Profiling Cannot Work.* New York: W.W. Norton, 2003.

Holbert, Steve, and Lisa Rose. *The Color of Guilt & Innocence: Racial Profiling and Police Practices in America.* San Ramon, Calif.: Page Marque Press, 2004.

Web sites

The American Civil Liberties Union. "Racial Profiling Old and New." <http://www.aclu.org/racialjustice/racialprofiling/index.html> (accessed January 12, 2006).

Testimony, United States Senate Committee on the Judiciary

Combating Gang Violence in America

Testimony

By: Patrick J. Fitzgerald

Date: September 17, 2003

Source: United States Senate Judiciary Committee. *Statement of United States Attorney Patrick J. Fitzgerald,*

Members of a street gang harass a woman. © CREASOURCE/CORBIS

Northern District of Illinois, "Concerning Combating Gang Violence." September 17, 2003.

About the Author: Patrick J. Fitzgerald is the United States Attorney for the Northern District of Illinois, a position he was appointed to in 2001. Since his appointment, he has also participated in the Attorney General's Advisory Committee. He is very involved in the identification and prosecution of international terrorists.

INTRODUCTION

Although "street gangs" have been described in literature and in popular culture since the early years of the twentieth century, they have not been portrayed as constituting a threat to the safety and security of the American public (particularly inner city dwellers) until relatively recently. Until the 1950s and 1960s, gangs were viewed somewhat euphemistically as delinquent youth that patrolled local neighborhoods and defended their turf from rival factions, fighting primarily among themselves, and remaining isolated from

the rest of society in terms of acts of violence (that is, they might aggress against one another, but not against the general public). By the mid-1950s, the concept of "gang wars" had reached public awareness. Still, this was believed to be a relatively isolated phenomenon, with gangs existing in impoverished inner-city neighborhoods, although there was some developing concern about the gangs' growing use of weapons such as knives and handguns. The "wars" were pre-arranged events, with participants, rules of engagement, and weapons identified in advance. Although resulting injuries were common, homicides were not.

During the last quarter of the twentieth century, the gang phenomenon spread outward, moving from a few large cities to many, many cities and towns across the country. As they spread, the gangs themselves became larger and more prolific (myriad new gangs sprang into existence, either by factions splitting off from existing cliques or by the creation of entirely new gang systems). The level of gang-related violence increased exponentially, with the advent of initiation rituals involving aggressive (often criminally so) acts, and street-terrorism-type fighting both within gang factions and between rival local gangs. Gang activity also took on an air akin to that of organized crime, with primary activities involving illicit drug acquisition, production, and trafficking, the development of counterfeiting rings, and the use of increasingly sophisticated weaponry for inter-gang wars.

The incidence and character of gang-related violence has changed dramatically over the past twenty or thirty years: inter- and intra-gang homicide rates have increased exponentially, as have aggravated assaults. Pre-arranged gang fights have been replaced by "show bys," "blow bys," "slashing and bashing," "push-ins," "swarms," "wilding," and "drive bys." Show bys occur when gang members drive through the territory of another gang, brandishing their weapons and posturing in an intimidating manner; a blow by is when the same behavior occurs, but weapons are discharged into the air, without intent to harm anyone. Drive bys are similar to blow bys except that weapons are discharged with the intent to inflict great bodily harm or to kill. Slashing and bashing is when gang members attack non-group members (typically, non-gang members) with chains, pipes, knives, bats, or razors during the course of a gang initiation ritual. Sometimes, prospective gang members are themselves victims of slashing and bashing as part of their initiation—this is also called "beating in." When a clique (usually a term for a subgroup within a gang, but may also be used to refer to the gang in its entirety, especially if it is a prison gang) or gang members engage in push ins or swarms, they invade a house or apartment en masse with the intent of intimidating or threatening the occupants (often family members of an enemy gang) while they are vandalizing, destroying, or robbing the home. Sometimes, female occupants are raped or sexually assaulted during this process. Wilding is analogous to a swarm or a push in, except that the victims have no apparent gang affiliations.

▮ PRIMARY SOURCE

Chairman Hatch, Ranking Member Leahy, and Members of the Committee, I am Patrick Fitzgerald, the United States Attorney for the Northern District of Illinois. It is an honor to have the opportunity to appear before you today to discuss the terrible problem of gangs that grips the nation's third largest city, Chicago, as well as other areas in my district and our nation.

In Chicago, gangs translate into murder and fear. Last year, Chicago's murder rate (homicides per 100,000 residents) was 22; by comparison, New York's was 8. For each of the 648 lives lost last year to homicide in Chicago, countless more lives were ruined for the survivors of those killed, for those wounded but not killed and for the too many thousands who live as prisoners in their homes for fear of walking the streets controlled by gangs. It is fairly estimated that 45% of the homicides in Chicago in 2003 are gang-related. The Chicago Tribune reported last month that one Chicago public school student dies from gunfire every two weeks. Twenty three students died from gun-related deaths between July 2002 and June 2003—none on school property.

But statistics do not paint the full picture. Two incidents in recent months put in perspective the problem we face in Chicago. On July 27th, 9-year old Antonio Campbell was with his mother who had just come home from work at a restaurant and stopped to give her sister a ride home from a party. July 27th happens to be the day the Mickey Cobras gang holds a party to remember a slain gang leader. Antonio Campbell was shot in the head by a stray bullet from gunfire from feuding gang members at that party. A month later, 7-year old Ana Mateo was shot to death by gang gunfire in Chicago. Both victims were children under the age of ten; and both were gunned down by gangs doing what they do—picking up weapons to guard their turf and their profit from their illegal business of drug dealing.

The principal reason for the number of violent deaths in Chicago is the prevalence of street gangs and their entwined involvement with gun violence and drug-trafficking.

Chicago's gangs are numerous, entrenched and organized as well as just plain violent. In 1995, an organizational chart of one Chicago gang—the Gangster Disciples—was recovered in the execution of a federal search warrant; it set out the gang's highly centralized hierarchy which was more sophisticated than many corporations. That gang alone had a force of 7000 members—more than half the size of the Chicago Police Department. That gang dared to form a political action committee, bought legitimate businesses and even sponsored community events.

As if the raw violence is not enough, the gang problem poses unique threats of corruption. The gangs control drug trafficking in Chicago and have at times corrupted police and other law enforcement—some members actually infiltrate law enforcement. Chicago Police Officer Edward Lee Jackson was a high ranking member of the Conservative Vice Lords street gang. Under Officer Jackson's leadership, a tactical team assigned to a police district with heavy drug activity robbed drug dealers who were competing with Traveling Vice Lords and gave the stolen drugs to the Traveling Vice

Lords to distribute until Jackson and his partners were prosecuted in federal court.

Chicago Police Officer Joseph Miedzianowski protected drug dealing by various gangs and robbed drug dealers with the assistance of street gang members, distributing kilograms of crack cocaine himself until he was arrested and convicted. Even in jail, the gangs have power. Just last month, our office charged a corrections officer in an Illinois state prison with smuggling drugs to 9 different gang members in jail, 6 of whom were incarcerated for murder. That corrections officer was a gang member himself. Those gang members who corrupt law enforcement undo the hard and honest work of the overwhelming majority of law enforcement officers.

Law enforcement in Chicago recognizes the severity of the problem and is fighting back, though we need more help. The first part of our strategy has been to focus on guns as part of Project Safe Neighborhoods ("PSN"). Through PSN, we have substantially increased federal prosecution of convicted felons caught carrying a gun and have placed a special emphasis on areas of high violence and on offenders who are gang members. There is an unprecedented partnership between the Bureau of Alcohol, Tobacco, Firearms and Explosives, the Chicago Police Department, the U.S. Attorney's Office, the Cook County State's Attorney's Office, the Illinois Department of Corrections, and local grass roots organizations serving their communities. Whenever a convicted felon with a gun is arrested by Chicago police in targeted police districts, state and federal prosecutors and ATF agents sit down together and decide in which court to prosecute cases. We tap every federal and local law enforcement agency who has relevant knowledge in order to coordinate our attacks on the gangs to which the offenders belong.

In plain terms, our strategy is to go after the worst of the worst. For example, gang leader Earnest Wilson, with prior convictions for attempted first-degree murder, armed robbery, and manslaughter, was stopped while driving a Lincoln Navigator with a Cobray M-11 semi-automatic pistol by his side. The gun had an obliterated serial number and was loaded with 32 rounds. We prosecuted Wilson federally through PSN, and he was sentenced to the mandatory minimum sentence of 15 years without parole, which he is serving far from home in an East Coast prison. Gang member Nathaniel Saunders was found in possession of a gun after having been convicted of several serious felonies and while on parole for murder. We prosecuted him federally through PSN and he was sentenced to 20 years without parole, a sentence that he is serving in a federal prison far from home.

A second part of our strategy to reduce gun violence has been the formation of neighborhood-based Gang Strategy Teams made up of all the law enforcement units—state and federal—that investigate and prosecute gangs. Their mandate is to share more gang intelligence on a regular basis, make greater use of technology, and make coordinated, strategic decisions about how and where to use our limited resources. At our first meetings of the teams, the law enforcement partners put some of their crown jewels—key informants—on the table to share in this battle. A closer partnership will mean deeper, more sustained, more permanent results in fighting gangs. Our success depends on deploying our resources more efficiently, through such techniques as pooling intelligence across agencies and coordinating investigations, jointly targeting the worst offenders for the harsher federal penalties, and refining our investigative and prosecutive strategies to enable us to handle cases more efficiently. And we have done that. I reorganized my Narcotics Unit to recognize the reality that gangs are the drug distribution network for the Chicago area. The Narcotics and Gang section is split in half between prosecutors investigating national and international narcotics rings and those prosecuting the gangs dealing drugs in the Chicago area. But we find that the wiretaps on the gangs have led to wiretaps on members of Mexican cartels who use the gangs to distribute their drugs, and that the wiretaps on international drug traffickers regularly lead to their street gangs who control the distribution of their drugs in this region.

The third part of our strategy for ending the violence caused by street gangs is to focus directly on our ultimate goal, which is not sending people to jail but deterring young men from joining gangs and carrying guns. For many gang members, their affiliation draws attention that passes for respect on the street. We are letting them know that being in a gang will get attention in the police station and the federal courthouse and, then, far less attention in a federal prison in a state far away from their gang. If the word spreads that we are targeting gang members on parole who carry guns in the neighborhoods where people fear going out at night, we can make a difference in the futures of the neighborhoods.

A key part of this same effort at deterrence involves the Illinois Department of Corrections, which has mailed personalized letters to every parolee in the state, advising them that they are being tracked in case they are arrested with a gun and that they face strict federal sentences if caught. The Chicago Police Department's community service arm, Community Alternative Police Strategy ("CAPS"), has placed thousands of posters in targeted neighborhoods warning felons: "Don't Let This Happen To You!" In stark terms, the posters provide details about specific felons from their neighborhoods who were caught carrying guns and are now serving long federal prison sentences.

In addition, in targeted police districts, the PSN partners regularly conduct "parolee forums." Some 30 felons at a time, each convicted of a gun crime and recently paroled into these districts, sit at the same table with law enforcement representatives and community leaders, who present them with the straightforward message that they have a choice in life. For many of these men, when they leave prison, they return to the only things that they know—their neighborhoods, their gangs, their drug dealing. The idea of law enforcement telling each person directly that if he returns to that way of life, the whole community will be watching—the local police, the state prosecutors, federal law enforcement and federal prosecutors—is a direct and difficult message. Yet, the message is sent to let them know that they have a choice. At the same time, they hear community leaders speak about ex-offender job programs, educational opportunities, and substance abuse programs that are available to them. They also hear from a convicted felon, someone who has stood in their shoes, who reiterates the message that the felons can succeed in turning their lives around, showing them that success is an option. And we are seeking and receiving some critical support from corporate Chicago: civic-minded business leaders are helping us to disseminate the deterrent message and we hope will help to underwrite efforts to provide options for ex-offenders other than a return to gangs and violence.

Law enforcement and community leaders in Chicago refuse to accept that nothing can be done about guns, gangs and violence in Chicago. Another city in my district, Joliet, is a city of 100,000. In 1999, state and federal law enforcement agencies began focusing our resources on the worst offenders—mostly gang members—in Joliet. In 2001 and 2002, there were large drops in the most violent crimes committed in Joliet—a 53 percent drop in murders and a 40 percent drop in gang shootings from 2000. The lesson is clear: with a sustained effort, we can lower the murder rate and make a long term difference. We are trying to repeat in Chicago and other cities the success we have seen in Joliet.

One thing that we have learned in our efforts in Chicago and its outlying communities, is that we can not come in and make a splash and then leave. Community groups, citizens, the police, and yes, even the felons, tell us that what we need is a persistent effort to maintain our presence in these areas. We understand that we need to be there for the long run, not just for a sprint. We intend to continue our efforts in the neighborhoods we have targeted first. We intend to extend our efforts to other neighborhoods in need. We intend to expand our project to the school system to work with children in

proactive programs that are already underway and soon to be implemented in the schools. We know that it is only through a constant, persistent, and devoted effort that we will change the way of life on the streets. We are in it for the long haul and so are all of our law enforcement partners. On that note, the fight against gang violence in Chicago has not been a partisan effort. Persons of different party, ethnic, and governmental lines have been setting aside parochial interests to address this crisis. I can say without any hesitation that the Cook County States Attorney is my full partner on the anti-gang effort in Chicago, not a competitor, and our city is safer for that.

I applaud this Committee's efforts to address the war waged against our cities by gangs. Thank you for your time and attention. I appreciate the opportunity to speak on this important and timely matter. I would be pleased to answer any questions the members might have.

SIGNIFICANCE

Gangs have changed in other ways as well. They are frequently now mixed gender groups, although there are still a sizeable number of all-male or exclusively female groups (such as the Latin Ladies, the Lady Rascals, or the Midnite Pearls). They are no longer confined to neighborhoods and may be ideologically or culturally, rather than geographically, affiliated. There are now gangs organized around Asian, Latin, Hispanic, and African-American racial and ethnic groups, such as the Tiny Rascal Gangsters, Asian Boyz, Latin Kings, Mara Salvatrucha, Crips, Bloods, Black Gangster Disciples, and gangs affiliated based on extremist beliefs, such as the Aryan Brotherhood or the Skinheads (white supremacists).

Drugs play a much greater role in gang violence, gang economy, and gang activities than in the past. Gangs often control drug production, distribution, and trafficking, and it may be the primary economic venue for them. Drug use, particularly of heroin, methamphetamine, crack cocaine, and various stimulants is reported to be quite high among gang-affiliated youth. Contemporary gang battles often revolve around drug territory or production infringement. With the economic stakes for gangs rising, the need for protection and defense increases as well. Weapons, particularly guns, have become a valuable commodity for commerce and ownership.

A generation or two ago, street gangs were composed virtually exclusively of adolescents. That, too, has changed. Gang members are now routinely found at the elementary school level, and many youth "grow up" in gangs because older siblings, parents, or other relatives are members, and joining has become an automatic and expected rite of passage. Adolescents no longer "age out" of gang membership. As the gang has taken a firmer hold on society at the local level, offering means of support and employment (drugs, weapons, crime) to those who have little education and few marketable skills, there is little need to move on. Often, in fact, it is not believed possible to leave a gang without serious, often lethal, consequences.

Gangs have extended their reach inside the correctional system—there are now vast gang proliferations, both extensions of street gangs and those that are primarily prison gangs (Mexican Mafia, Neta, Black Guerilla Family, La Nuestra Familia, and the Texas Syndicate, among others) located inside the walls. This means that gang members, or, as they are often called in prison settings, "gangsters," can either maintain gang affiliations and activities while doing time, or they can secure other sources of gang protection while incarcerated. This also adds to the increased upper age ranges for gang members on the streets (incarcerated gang members who maintain their affiliations and return to the active member status upon release).

One aspect of gang membership has not changed: it still has long-lasting negative social, economic, cultural, and personal consequences. Individuals who join gangs have a much higher probability of failing in school and dropping out without obtaining a high school diploma; teen parenthood; early and multiple interactions with the legal and criminal justice system; being involved in violent (often lethal) crime, either as perpetrator or victim; living at or below the poverty level; and failing to acquire job or vocational skills leading to an inability to achieve or maintain steady and profitable employment.

FURTHER RESOURCES

Books

Goldstein, Arnold P. *The Psychology of Group Aggression*. New York: John Wiley & Sons, 2002.

Klein, Malcolm W. *The American Street Gang: Its Nature, Prevalence, and Control*. New York: Oxford University Press, 1997.

Sanders, William B. *Gangbangs and Drive-Bys: Grounded Culture and Juvenile Gang Violence*. New York: Aldine De Gruyter, 1994.

Web sites

Institute for Intergovernmental Research. "National Youth Gang Center (NYGC)." <http://www.iir.com/nygc> (accessed March 5, 2006).

National Gang Crime Research Center. "Gang Profiles." <http://www.ngcrc.com/profile/profile.html> (accessed March 5, 2006).

Road Rage

Honk If You Think I'm Rude

Newspaper article

By: Joseph Siano

Date: February 15, 2004

Source: Siano, Joseph. "Honk If You Think I'm Rude." *New York Times*, February 15, 2004, <http://query.nytimes.com/gst/fullpage.html/> (accessed January 31, 2006).

About the Author: Joseph Siano is a journalist who writes for the *New York Times*. His articles are regularly featured in the Travel section of the newspaper. Siano is perhaps best-known for his contributions to the popular "What's Doing In …?" feature of the Sunday *New York Times* Travel section.

INTRODUCTION

Road rage, a less aggressive form of what has been termed roadway violence, is a nearly ubiquitous experience in America. Virtually every driver (and probably most passengers) has experienced it, whether as the aggressor or as the victim. It can be as benign as quietly grumbling or name-calling when another driver executes a (subjectively) foolish or dangerous vehicular maneuver (backs up without first scanning the immediate area, cuts off another driver by changing lanes abruptly, etc.) or as potentially dangerous as intentionally hitting another driver's vehicle, tailgating another driver for an extended distance, forcing the other driver off the road, or using a weapon to inflict harm to another vehicle or its driver.

Road rage is not a purely American phenomenon. It also has been widely reported (and studied) in the United Kingdom, Australia, Greece, Austria, Ireland, India, China, Japan, and many countries in Europe. Road rage is most likely to occur when there is a confluence of events—bad driving combined with poor road conditions (e.g. rough road surfaces, impaired visibility, traffic congestion, etc.), and an individual predisposition to respond aggressively under circumstances of stress or perceived provocation. There may

A speed camera positioned on the A3 road, fifteen miles southwest of London, England, photographs the license plates of cars that travel faster than 50 miles per hour. Drivers are subsequently ticketed. AP IMAGES

be other factors operating in individual circumstances as well.

The Automobile Association of America (AAA) has issued a very precise definition of road rage, This definition characterizes road rage as a criminal act and draws a sharp distinction between road rage and aggressive driving. Road rage is defined as "an incident in which an angry or impatient motorist or passenger intentionally injures or kills another motorist, passenger, or pedestrian, or attempts or threatens to injure or kill another motorist, passenger, or pedestrian." It must be emphasized that road rage and aggressive driving are not synonymous. Road rage is uncontrolled anger that results in violence or threatened violence on the road; it is criminal behavior. Aggressive driving does not rise to the level of criminal behavior. Aggressive driving includes tailgating, abrupt lane changes, and speeding, alone or in combination. These potentially dangerous behaviors are traffic offenses, but are not criminal behavior.

According to statistics gathered by AAA, incidents of aggressive driving increased by more than fifty percent during the last decade of the twentieth century. The United States Department of Transportation reports that nearly seventy percent of all motor vehicle collisions that result in a fatality can be attributed, at least in part, to aggressive driving. It should be noted, however, that much of the commentary on the incidence of road rage and aggressive driving is derived from anecdotal evidence—subjective statements of individuals involved in motor vehicle accidents, media reports, and the like. There is a relatively small amount of rigorous scientific study of road rage and aggressive driving behavior published in scholarly and scientific literature, in comparison to the large number of reports and articles on road rage appearing in the popular press.

PRIMARY SOURCE

The comedian George Carlin has observed that all the other drivers on the road fall into one of two categories: idiots or lunatics. The former are the slowpokes blocking you; the latter are the leadfoots zooming past you. As unscientific as that conclusion may be, it does demonstrate one speed bump facing any assessment of the state of manners on American highways: while it may be easy to discern what constitutes rude behavior in an airport or on a plane, speed limits, along with a lot of unwritten traffic laws, vary not by state but by driver.

Some things do seem clear. For instance, the fabric of social interaction is a lot less frayed when it has a lighter traffic load running over it. And that which qualifies as rude on the roads in one part of the country can simply be a rule of the road elsewhere.

Consider California, where traffic ranges from the sleep-inducing in rural San Joaquin Valley in the state's heart to the rage-raising in Los Angeles. "We've noticed that the level of frustration that may prompt some less-than-courteous behavior is more likely to occur in those urban areas than, let's say, driving along Interstate 5 in the Central Valley," said Tom Marshall, a California Highway Patrol spokesman.

"I don't think manners are as good in terms of letting pedestrians cross," said Officer Reid Thompson, with the California Highway Patrol in Woodland, west of Sacramento. "People seem a lot busier and more concerned with their own business. But when there's an accident, you still see good Samaritans."

To Mr. Marshall's eye, there appears to be some improvement in the state. Although he has no statistics to back it up, he believes that the state's notoriety as birthplace of road rage (in which drivers would lose control of their emotions and, soon after, their cars, or even start shooting) has subsided. "I base that on the fact that I get a lot less calls from the news media asking for comment on it," he said. "Whether that means it's improving or just isn't noticed as much, I'll leave that up to you."

One survey indicates that at least things may not be getting much worse. David McMillen, a psychology professor and senior research fellow at Mississippi State University's Social Science Research Center, has conducted a series of telephone surveys with questions about driver behavior. They sampled 1,500 people nationwide, chosen by random dialing, with a margin of error of plus or minus 4 percentage points. Participants were asked, for example, whether in the previous 12 months a driver had used a vehicle to make a threatening move toward the one they were in. "In 1999, 28 percent said yes," Professor McMillen said. In spring and summer of 2003, it was 29 percent.

"Of course, that's open to interpretation," he said. "You could be driving down the road, and someone could just not be paying attention and drift into your lane."

Rude gestures are also holding steady, according to Professor McMillen's polling, with 49 percent reporting they or the cars they were in were a target in the previous 12 months in 1999, 41 percent in spring 2003 and 42 percent last summer. These results, he said, don't reflect the shock value of the universal signal of disdain, depending on the neighborhood you're in.

"I think the interpretation and the implied threat is different down here," he said, referring to his fellow Mississippi drivers. "They probably see that as a more aggressive threat." (No, the word "months" was not replaced by "hours" when the rude-gesture question was posed to New Yorkers.)

Professor McMillen's polling shows that, under the wrong circumstances, holding a cellphone to your ear is also a gesture that upsets other drivers.

Last summer, the survey asked motorists if they use a cellphone while driving in heavy traffic; 20 percent said often or sometimes. And we know how all the rest of them feel about it: 80 percent agreed with the statement "When I see other drivers on cellphones, I think they are being unsafe." Professor McMillen observed, purely on anecdotal evidence: "Some people are doing it more and more, and others are becoming more and more upset about it."

His findings also echo the aforementioned Carlin idiot-lunatic paradigm: "Half the people think traffic is moving too slowly and the other half think that it's moving too fast," the professor said.

The AAA Mid-Atlantic office, which covers Delaware, Maryland, Washington and parts of Pennsylvania, New Jersey and Virginia, found out what was bugging drivers in its area last year. It hired R/S/M, professional pollsters, who called a random selection of 1,258 licensed drivers from Philadelphia to Richmond.

Only 11 percent listed drunken drivers as the greatest worry, a fact that worries the AAA, which sees alcohol impairment as the leading danger to drivers.

National Highway Transportation Safety Administration statistics show that alcohol was a factor in 41 percent of fatal crashes and that there were 17,419 alcohol-related traffic deaths in 2002 nationwide. But the largest number of those questioned, about 43 percent (with a 2.8 percentage-point margin of error), said that the greatest threat on the roads was aggressive driving, defined as tailgating, reckless speeding and darting across lanes.

The survey respondents seemed to know where some of the fault lies. About 36 percent (versus 27 percent in 1997) said they were driving at least 20 miles an hour over the limit more often than a few years ago. Another 25 percent or so admitted to tailgating, weaving or abrupt lane changes. About 20 percent (up from 8 percent in 1997) confessed to having made a rude gesture in the previous 12 months. So how do we reconcile that with Professor McMillen's poll, which showed twice that percentage on the receiving end?

Either someone's lying, or we're not all driving on the same roads. Or some people are just too darn sensitive.

SIGNIFICANCE

Although crowded traffic conditions are often cited as a contributory factor to displays of road rage, that is unlikely to be accurate. When traffic is moving slowly—or not at all—there are no opportunities for swerving, rapid lane changes, or cutting off another driver. Those actions can only occur when traffic is moving well, and an impulsive driver can choose to maneuver in dangerous ways in order to "make up time."

There is a tendency for a driver to feel both invincible and anonymous when behind the wheel. Protected by at least a thousand pounds of very responsive and comfortable machinery (we live in the era of programmable, heated seats; custom sound systems; electronically adjustable window locks, doors, and mirrors; deeply tinted windows; onboard navigation systems, and exquisitely responsive automotive engineering), it is easy for a driver to believe that no harm could possibly befall him. Viewing similar vehicles, it is easy to forget that they are driven by fellow humans—possibly even acquaintances, friends, family, or coworkers. In a moment of fury, it is a simple matter for a driver to ignore the possibility that harm can come to anyone and to forget that the other driver is a human being as well. Criminal thinking occurs when perpetrators (those who commit crimes upon the property or person of another) believe that their victims deserve "whatever they get." Victims are dehumanized and treated as if they are incapable of appreciating the severity of their alleged offense against the perpetrator. This type of rationalization makes it very easy for the perpetrator to commit an aggressive act without thinking about its real consequences. In rage behavior, criminal thinking is quite common. The perpetrator does not have to take responsibility for the act, because the other driver "deserved" what he got—in fact, he was "asking for it."

The character of roadway violence is often somewhat different in America than it is in many other countries. Elsewhere in the world, roadway aggression may be fueled by too little space, too many vehicles, and antiquated roadways. In the United States, there is an implicit belief in the concept of manifest destiny—that it is acceptable to defend one's own property (human or material) by whatever means necessary. Americans are explicitly permitted to bear arms and to use them in order to protect that which belongs to them. A motor vehicle is both a costly piece of property and a reflection of the self—therefore doubly essential to protect.

Road rage, as defined in the United States, usually involves a chain of events without any direct expression of interpersonal violence. It is generally initiated by a "bad driving" maneuver by one driver. The perceived victim becomes angry and responds with some form of non-contact aggression, such as horn honking, light flashing, gestures, or shouting. If it ends there, that is simple road rage, and it is not a criminal action. If the behavior escalates, and there is an act of either vehicular violence (using the vehicle as a weapon) or direct interpersonal violence (use of a weapon, fists, etc., to cause bodily harm to the other driver), then it is roadway violence and is considered a criminal assault. Available published research suggests that while road rage is commonly experienced by most drivers (as either victim or aggressor), roadway violence is comparatively rare, contrary to media reports.

FURTHER RESOURCES

Books

Berger, K.T. *Zen Driving*. New York: Ballantine Books, 1988.

Betts, Raymond F. *A History of Popular Culture: More of Everything, Faster, and Brighter*. New York: Routledge, 2004.

Periodicals

Deffenbacher, J. L., et al. "Anger, Aggression and Risky Behavior: A Comparison of High and Low Anger Drivers." *Behavior Research and Therapy* 41 (2003): 701–718.

Deffenbacher, J. L., et al. "Characteristics and Treatment of High-Anger Drivers." *Journal of Counseling Psychology* 47 (2000): 5–17.

Deffenbacher, J. L., et al. "Cognitive-Behavioral Treatment of High Anger Drivers." *Behavior Research and Therapy* 40 (2002): 895–910.

Sharkin, Bruce S. "Road Rage: Risk Factors, Assessment, and Intervention Strategies." *Journal of Counseling and Development* 82 (Spring 2004): 191–198.

Web sites

Davis, Jeanie Lerche. "Getting a Grip on Roadway Anger." *WebMD*, April 1, 2000, <http://www.webmd.com/content/article/35/1728_56860> (accessed January 31, 2006).

Pepper, Mark. "Behavior: Road Rage." *Drivers.com*, June 9, 1997, <http://www.drivers.com/article/167/> (accessed January 31, 2006).

Rathbone, Daniel B., and Jorg C. Huckabee. "Controlling Road Rage: A Literature Review and Pilot Study." *AAA Foundation for Traffic Safety*, June 9, 1999, <http://www.aaafoundation.org/resources/index.cfm?button=roadrage> (accessed January 31, 2006).

On-Line Vigilantes Hunt Pedophiles

Newspaper article

By: Marisa Schultz

Date: March 09, 2004

Source: Schultz, Marisa. "On-line Vigilantes Hunt Pedophiles." *The Detroit News*. (March 09, 2004).

About the Author: Marisa Schultz is a journalist writing for *The Detroit News* and *The Gannett News Service*.

INTRODUCTION

As the world wide web becomes progressively easier to navigate, computer costs plummet and technology proliferates (in homes and in public settings such as libraries, cafes, schools, etc.), and the intimate (in the colloquial sense) chat rooms of the internet become progressively more user-friendly and accessible to juveniles, serious problems are bound to occur.

Children and youth have always been particularly vulnerable to the influence of adults, especially those that they idealize or in some way want to please. The most vulnerable young population is that which is neediest either due to lack of adult or familial supervision or because of a dearth of stability in their home lives. Statistically, those children are the most likely to engage with adults who purport to offer them security and affection, and to be willing to take risks in order to meet the demands of the requestor (whether that be a local meeting, continued contact, secrecy, or even distant travel). The internet makes the job of the pedophile, whether experienced or neophyte, very easy. Message boards and chat rooms abound, and afford relative anonymity.

While it may well be true that the internet renders the predatory behavior of the pedophiles easier and more widespread, so, too, is it the case that the internet has spawned a myriad of watchdog groups and online vigilantes, who, both independently and in concert with a variety of law enforcement agencies (the Federal Bureau of Investigation among them), attempt to ferret out potential or actual predators and either expose them to public humiliation, halt them in their (cyber) tracks, or arrest and prosecute them. Many local and state law enforcement agencies utilize undercover officers whose job it is to lurk on the internet chat rooms and "sting" would-be criminal pedophiles. During the past decade, there have been numerous newspaper, magazine, and television features written by reporters who posed as underage internet surfers and were approached on line by adults (typically males) who attempted to arrange meetings with them for the purpose of engaging in sexual activity with a purported minor.

There are three significant legal and philosophical issues to be raised by these activities: is it entrapment if a person intentionally poses as a juvenile with the expressed purpose of catching adults interested in engaging in sexual behavior with underage persons? Is the behavior of the "posers" such that it might lure a person to commit a criminal act that they might not have considered if a sexually-oriented conversation had not been sought by a provocative (and often sexually-explicitly monikered) "baiter?" Is it a violation of Civil Rights to videotape or publish the chats or photos of the alleged potential perpetrators on the internet or in other media venues, with the intention of using humiliation as a deterrent for future criminal behavior?

PRIMARY SOURCE

Five minutes into his Internet chat with a fourteen-year-old girl, Ray Dooley's conversation turned from snowboarding to sex.

Enticed by "Rachel" of Harper Woods, Dooley, twenty-three, drove fifty miles the next day, apparently expecting to see her in a short leather skirt. Instead, the Port Huron man met a camera crew.

He was caught not by police, but by representatives of the civilian-led vigilante Web site Perverted Justice, who posed in the chat room as Rachel and then posted Dooley's picture, phone number and chat details online.

Dooley is one of about forty Michigan men whom the Web site has embarrassed as "wanna-be pedophiles" in its increasingly controversial effort to keep the Internet safe for kids. While some praise the effort, many law enforcement officials say the site leads to few arrests and may even impede growing efforts to police the Web.

"It helps to educate parents and make them aware how big of a problem this is," said Wayne County Deputy Bill Liczbinski, who is one of four investigators in the county's Internet Crime Unit.

"But from a law enforcement standpoint, those people should be in jail. It's one thing to put their picture up on the Web site and embarrass them, it's another to make them pay for the crime they committed," Liczbinski said.

There's ample evidence of the public safety problem posed by Internet predators.One in five youths ages ten–seventeen received a sexual solicitation over the Internet within the past year, according to a survey by the Crimes Against Children Research Center, based at the University of New Hampshire. One in four kids had an unwanted exposure to pictures of naked people or sex within the last year, the survey found.

The seriousness of Internet crimes was underscored last month when a thirteen-year-old Pontiac girl was taken to West Virginia by a man she met online. Sexual assault charges have been filed against Michael Wiedenbein, 48, of Columbus, Ohio.

Parent Tina Pietrykowski feels Perverted Justice's role is needed now more than ever. She's pushing to have Internet safety taught in her Roseville school district and even has considered volunteering for Perverted Justice.

"Sometimes you have to take the law in your own hands, Pietrykowski said. "I would hate to have what happened to the girl in Pontiac happen again."

Gaining attention

Perverted Justice has gained attention in Metro Detroit for exposing a Warren Mott High School math teacher, and for its partnership with WDIV-Local 4 to broadcast sixteen men within forty hours showing up at doorsteps for what they thought would be sex with minors.

Since the site began in July 2002 in Portland, Ore., 600 men nationally have been exposed. Just a dozen have been arrested.Dooley, who served almost four years in the U.S. Navy before being dishonorably discharged recently for a drunken driving conviction, remains the only Michigan man to be charged after a run-in with Perverted Justice.

Dooley's mother, Louise, said her son shouldn't be charged with a crime: There was no girl and no sex.

"He was not given the opportunity to walk away," said Louise Dooley, whose husband called police to stop the barrage of e-mails and phone calls after their son's

chat was publicized. "No one knows what would have happened."

Others exposed by the site, perverted-justice.com, have lost their jobs and changed their phone numbers.

Brian Graves, the Warren Mott math teacher, will learn this month if the school board will allow him to return to the classroom. Graves, a forty-two-year-old Grosse Pointe resident, was exposed by the site in September for having a sexual conversation with a Perverted Justice volunteer posing as thirteen-year old Keely from Ferndale.

Graves, who is on paid administrative leave, never received an address from Keely to meet her for sex. He was not arrested.

"That creates an interesting dilemma for the school district," Warren Consolidated School District spokesman Bob Freehan said. The site "stops short of a violation of law, and it tosses the decision back to an organization like us."

The Oakland County Sheriff's Department is executing twelve search warrants for men exposed by the site and on WDIV-TV. If police can verify that a crime was committed, arrests could be made, Sheriff Michael Bouchard said.

"We are diligently trying to get the facts and circumstances of those cases," Bouchard said. But "we haven't received one hundred percent cooperation from Perverted Justice."

Perverted Justice officials, who decline to be interviewed using their names, say the group is not opposed to getting pedophiles arrested. Putting men behind bars is not the site's mission, but officials will work with police on arresting men only if the police contact the organization.

Unreliable information

Other police officials say they can't rely on the Perverted Justice chats alone to arrest someone.

"What people don't realize, if a person pulls over drunken drivers and then turns them over to the police (for an arrest), we didn't witness that," Macomb County Sheriff Mark Hackel said. "Same with the chats. We are going to say, 'That's nice. But how do we know who that is with certainly?'"

To fight Internet crimes, Hackel uses volunteers who are trained at catching predators in online chat rooms. Volunteers are needed because the Internet task force, which began in 2001 with five officers, also is busy handling fraud and identity theft cases. These trained civilians are different than Perverted Justice volunteers because their work ultimately will lead to arrests, Hackel said.

A billboard warns of the dangers of on-line sexual predators and solicitation. © ANDREW HOLBROOKE/CORBIS

In Wayne County, investigators have nabbed more than fifty people for computer crimes. They boast a hundred percent conviction rate because, officials say, they are very careful not to initiate contact with the men so that their evidence holds up in court. The unit began in 1998, but was shut down in 2002. After his election, Sheriff Warren Evans re-created the unit in 2003.

Since February, Liczbinski said he lost at least three men he was on the verge of arresting. The men no longer were chatting online. But the fix may just be temporary.

"It's really easy to just log on as someone different," said Tim Lorenzen, law enforcement coordinator for I-SAFE, a nonprofit Internet safety organization. "This site may have the best intentions, but they are going to possibly screw up an investigation. They are trying to expose pedophiles, but they are allowing them to get away without prosecution."

SIGNIFICANCE

Perverted Justice uses trained adult volunteers to surf local (geographically local to the adult volunteer's location) chat rooms, with the explicit objective of ferreting out adults who seek to engage in "live" sexual behavior with juveniles. As stated in their website,

their primary mission is to work cooperatively with law enforcement authorities to accomplish the arrest and prosecution of adults who solicit sex from underage youth (this specific goal comes from the second launch of the site, in July 2003). They report that they will attempt first to work with local law enforcement agencies; in those situations where that venue is not successful (the police department makes a choice not to follow up on the case, for example), they will post the complete and unedited chat log in question on their site and contact the adult who has engaged in same. They do this in order that the adult who has been caught can respond and have equal time to explain his/her perceptions of the interaction. They also verify any telephone numbers sent by the would-be-pedophile during the course of the on-line communications.

Perverted Justice (also known as "Peej") has created a large-scale file exchange repository for use by law enforcement and legal authorities that contains the transcripts of all web chats, any photographs sent by alleged potential perpetrators, identifying information for the poser's and alleged would-be perpetrator's computers, as well as any notes pertaining to individual cases, in an effort to facilitate prosecution of attempted illegal activities (solicitation for sex with an underage person, and similar criminal behaviors). According to information published by Perverted Justice, they have aided in the apprehension, prosecution, and conviction of nearly fifty criminal cases, have an additional 770 (individual) transcripts in their database, and have facilitated the recovery of a juvenile who was abducted, illegally held, and repeatedly sexually assaulted by a man she had met over the internet.

Psychologists and sociologists who specialize in the treatment of sexual dysfunctions and desire disorders refer to the allure of the internet's alleged anonymity (in reality, cyber anonymity is a very relative thing), perhaps lowering inhibitions against acting on desires for (potential) sexual encounters with juveniles. The philosophical case has been made that prior to the advent of the internet, some of those who engage in cyber chats and attempt (sometimes successfully) to meet underage sexual partners might have repressed those desires, or chosen not to act on them. There is also a prevalent belief that the alleged anonymity of the internet lulls would-be perpetrators into the belief that they will not be caught or prosecuted.

As organizations such as Perverted Justice gain media attention, legislators and local law enforcement agencies have begun to seek resources for creating similar venues within their own organizations. There have been a series of undercover stings across the country in recent years, all aimed at capturing and prosecuting internet pedophiles. The Federal Bureau of Investigation has made the investigation of high-technology crimes, particularly those involving the use of the internet for the facilitation of perpetration of illegal sexual acts with children a very high priority issue since the start of the twenty-first century. One of the responsibilities of the FBI's Cyber Crimes Squad is to have agents pose as children or juveniles on the Internet and conduct sting operations in order to capture alleged pedophiles.

There will remain those who have ethical and moral qualms about using adults posing as minors in order to lure actual and potential pedophiles, viewing these activities as a violation of privacy. The law enforcement agencies and volunteer organizations, such as Perverted Justice, who are committed to continuing their work, state that their mission is to reduce the number of sexual predators, and to increase the safety of children and youth. They plan to be a permanent fixture of the cyber landscape.

FURTHER RESOURCES

Books

Glassner, Barry. *The Culture of Fear: Why Americans are Afraid of the Wrong Things*. New York, New York: Basic Books, 1999.

Lipschultz, Jeremy Harris. *Free Expression in the Age of the Internet: Social and Legal Boundaries*. Boulder, Colorado: Westview Press, 2000.

Quayle, Ethel & Max Taylor. *Child Pornography: An Internet Crime*. New York, New York: Brunner-Routledge, 2003.

Web sites

KY-3 News— Springfield, MO. "Sex predator stings spur new legislation." <http://www.ky3.com/news/2293456.html> (accessed March 28, 2006).

News Channel 11—Lubbock, Texas. "Internet Watchdog Group Helps Lubbock Authorities Nab Sexual Predator." <http://www.kcbd.com/Global/story/> (accessed March 28, 2006).

WashingtonBlade.com. "National news: Gays help expose online predators. Internet group asks gays to be more vocal in stopping teen abuse" <http://www.washblade.com/2005/11-25/news/national/> (accessed March 28, 2006).

Worcester Telegram & Gazette News. "Cyber-sleuths target sexual predators." <http://www.telegram.com/apps/pbcs.dll/> (accessed March 28, 2006).

Impeachment

Government document

By: United States Senate

Date: November 7, 2005

Source: *United States Senate*. "Impeachment." <http://www.senate.gov> (November 7, 2005).

About the Author: The United States Senate, which with the House of Representatives comprises the legislative branch of the American government, has two representatives from each state. In addition to its role in proposing and passing laws, the Constitution gives the Senate powers of "advice and consent" to ratify treaties, approve public appointments, and conduct impeachment trials.

President Bill Clinton pauses during a speech on U.S. education spending given at the White House on January 7, 1999. Earlier in the day the U.S. Senate began President Clinton's impeachment trial. © REUTERS/CORBIS

INTRODUCTION

First used in England during the fourteenth century, impeachment is the Constitutional process by which government officials are accused of and tried for criminal acts. The House of Representatives declares the impeachment, and the Senate holds the trial. If convicted, the official is automatically removed from office with no chance for appeal. Because the process is both lengthy and cumbersome, however, only seventeen federal officials have been impeached over the course of the nation's history.

PRIMARY SOURCE

The Senate's Impeachment Role

Under the Constitution, the House of Representatives has the power to impeach a government official, in effect serving as prosecutor. The Senate then holds the impeachment trial, essentially serving as jury and judge, except in the impeachment of a president when the chief justice presides.

The president, vice-president, and all civil officers of the United States are subject to impeachment; conviction means automatic removal from office.

The concept of impeachment originated in England and was adopted by many of the American colonial governments and state constitutions. At the Constitutional Convention, the framers considered several possible models before deciding that the Senate should try impeachments.

Since 1789 only seventeen federal officers have been impeached by the House, fourteen of which were tried by the Senate. Three were dismissed before trial because the individual had left office, 7 ended in acquittal and 7 in conviction. All of those convicted were federal judges.

The United States Constitution provides that the House of Representatives "shall have the sole Power of Impeachment" (Article I, section 2) and that "the Senate shall have the sole Power to try all Impeachments . . . [but] no person shall be convicted without the Concurrence of two-thirds of the Members present" (Article I, section 3).

Impeachment is a very serious affair. It is perhaps the most awesome power of Congress, the ultimate weapon it wields against officials of the federal government. The House of Representatives is the prosecutor. The Senate chamber is the courtroom. The Senate is the jury and also the judge, except in the case of a presidential impeachment trial when the chief justice presides. The final penalty is removal from office. There is no appeal.

So grave is this power of impeachment, and so conscious is the Congress of this solemn power, that impeachment proceedings have been initiated in the House only sixty-two times since 1789. Only seventeen federal officers have been impeached: two presidents, one cabinet officer, one senator and thirteen federal judges. Sixteen cases have reached the Senate. Of these, two were dismissed before trial because the individuals had left office, seven ended in acquittal, and seven in conviction. Each of the seven Senate convictions has involved a federal judge.

Historical Development

Constitutional Origins

In Federalist 65, Alexander Hamilton called impeachment a process designed "as a method of national inquest into the conduct of public men." Hamilton and his colleagues at the Constitutional Convention, who hammered out the provisions for impeachment, knew that the history of impeachment as a constitutional process dated from fourteenth-century England, when the fledgling Parliament sought to make the king's advisers accountable. By the mid-fifteenth century, impeachment had fallen into disuse in England, but, in the early seventeenth century, the excesses of the Stuart kings prompted Parliament to revive its impeachment power. Even as the Constitution's framers toiled in Philadelphia, the impeachment trial of Warren Hastings was in progress in London and avidly followed in America. Hastings, who was eventually acquitted, was charged with oppression, bribery, and fraud as colonial administrator and first governor general in India.

The American colonial governments and early state constitutions followed the British pattern of trial before the upper legislative body on charges brought by the lower house. Despite these precedents, a major controversy arose at the Constitutional Convention about whether the Senate should act as the court of impeachment. Opposing that role for the Senate, James Madison and Charles Cotesworth Pinckney asserted that it would make the president too dependent on the legislative branch. They suggested, as alternative trial bodies, the Supreme Court or the chief justices of the state supreme courts. Hamilton and others argued, however, that such bodies would be too small and susceptible to corruption. In the end, after much wrangling, the framers selected the Senate as the trial forum. To Hamilton fell the task of explaining the convention's decision. In Federalist 65, he argued:

The Convention thought the Senate the most fit depository of this important trust. Where else than in the Senate could have been found a tribunal sufficiently dignified, or sufficiently independent? What other body would be likely to feel confidence enough in its own situation, to preserve unawed and uninfluenced the necessary impartiality between an individual accused, and the representatives of the people, his accusers?

There was also considerable debate at the convention in Philadelphia over the definition of impeachable crimes. In the original proposals, the president was to be removed on impeachment and conviction "formal or corrupt conduct," or for "malpractice or neglect of duty." Later, the wording was changed to "treason, bribery, or corruption," then to "treason or bribery" alone. Contending that "treason or bribery" were too narrow, George Mason proposed adding "mal-administration," but switched to "other high crimes and misdemeanors against the state" when Madison said that "mal-administration" was too broad. A final revision defined impeachable crimes as "treason, bribery or other high crimes and misdemeanors."

In the Constitution, the House is given the "sole power of impeachment." To the Senate is given "the sole power to try all impeachments." Impeachments may be brought against "the President, Vice-President, and all civil officers of the United States." Conviction is automatically followed by "removal from office."

While the framers very clearly envisaged the occasional necessity of initiating impeachment proceedings, they put in place only a very general framework, leaving many questions open to differences of opinion and many details to be filled in. Despite the open-endedness, as Peter Charles Hoffer and N.E.H. Hull note in their book Impeachment in America 1635-1805, thanks to the framers: a tool used in Parliament to curb kings and punish placemen was molded into an efficient legislative check upon executive and judicial wrongdoing. The power of the English House of Commons to impeach anyone, for almost any alleged offense, was restrained; the threat of death and forfeiture upon conviction was lifted; and the interference of the Commons and the House of Lords with the regular courts of justice was limited. American impeachment law shifted, at first inadvertently and then deliberately, from the orbit of English precedent to a native republican course. Federal constitutional provisions for impeachment reflected indigenous experience and revolutionary tenets instead of English tradition.

Impact of Resignation

Throughout the Congress' two hundred years, several major questions have dogged impeachment proceedings. One concerns resignations. In general, the resignation of an official puts an end to impeachment proceedings because the primary objective, removal from office, has been accomplished. This was the case in the impeachment proceedings begun in 1974 against President Richard Nixon. However, resignation has not always been a foolproof way to preclude impeachment, as Secretary of War William Belknap found out in 1876. Belknap, tipped off in advance that a House committee had unearthed information implicating him in the acceptance of bribes in return for lucrative Indian trading posts, rushed to the White House and tearfully begged President Ulysses Grant to accept his resignation at ten o'clock on the morning of March 2, 1876. Around three o'clock that afternoon, representatives, furious at both the president and Belknap for thwarting them, impeached Belknap by voice vote anyway. The Senate debated the question of its jurisdiction, in light of Belknap's resignation, and decided by a vote of 37 to 29 that he could be impeached. But at the end of Belknap's sensational trial in the summer of 1876, he was found not guilty of the charges, not because the senators believed him innocent (most did not), but because most had decided they in fact had no jurisdiction over Belknap, then a private citizen.

Definition of Offenses

Another question, the one debated most hotly by members of Congress, defense attorneys, and legal scholars from the first impeachment trial to the most recent trial of President William Clinton, concerns the issue of what exactly is an impeachable offense. The task of definition left to future legislators by the framers has proved perplexing. Treason and bribery, the two constitutionally designated impeachable crimes, were clear cut. But what were "high crimes and misdemeanors?" Were misdemeanors lesser crimes, or merely misconducts? Did a high crime or misdemeanor have to be a violation of written law? Over the years, "high crimes and misdemeanors" have been anything the prosecutors have wanted them to be. In an unsuccessful attempt to impeach Supreme Court Justice William O. Douglas in 1960, Representative Gerald Ford declared: "An impeachable offense is whatever a majority of the House of Representatives considers it to be at a given moment in history." The phrase is the subject of continuing debate, pitting broad constructionists, who view impeachment as a political weapon, against narrow constructionists, who regard impeachment as being limited to offenses indictable at common law.

Narrow constructionists won a major victory when Supreme Court Justice Samuel Chase was acquitted in 1805, using as his defense the argument that the charges against him were not based on any indictable offense. President Andrew Johnson won acquittal with a similar defense in 1868. But the first two convictions in the twentieth century, those of Judge Robert Archbald in 1913 and Judge Halsted Ritter in 1936, neither of whom had committed indictable offenses, made it clear that the broad constructionists still carried considerable weight. The debate continued during the 1974 investigation into the conduct of President Nixon, with the staff of the House Judiciary Committee arguing for a broad view of "high crimes and misdemeanors" while Nixon's defense attorneys understandably argued for a narrow view.

Influential Impeachment Cases

Over the course of the nation's history, several impeachment cases have been instrumental in the further evolution of the process.

Andrew Johnson

The bitter animosities growing out of the Civil War gave rise to the impeachment trial of President Andrew Johnson, the most famous of all impeachment trials prior to that of President William Clinton in 1999. The first presidential impeachment in American history occurred in 1868. At the heart of the Johnson case, just as in earlier cases, lay issues far larger than the individuals involved.

The Johnson case revolved around the crisis of Reconstruction after the war.

When Johnson succeeded to the presidency in 1865, his ideas for a mild Reconstruction of the southern states clashed with the wishes of a majority of the Congress, controlled by Radical Republicans who favored much stronger action. Throughout 1866, Johnson and Congress were locked in battle.

The Tenure of Office Act, the violation of which was to be the legal basis for impeachment, was passed over Johnson's veto on March 2, 1867. It forbade the president to remove civil officers appointed with the consent of the Senate without the approval of the Senate. Despite the certain consequences, Johnson decided to rid himself of Secretary of War Edwin Stanton, an ally of the Radicals. On August 12, 1867, Johnson suspended Stanton, an act that enraged the Radical Republicans and set in motion events that led the House to vote eleven articles of impeachment against the president.

Johnson's Senate trial began on March 5, 1868, with the defense immediately claiming the necessity of an indictable offense for impeachment. On May 16, after weeks of venomous argument, the Senate took a test vote on Article XI, a catch-all charge thought by the House managers most likely to produce a vote for conviction. The drama of the vote has become legendary. With 36 "guiltys" needed for conviction, the final count was guilty, 35; not guilty, 19. Seven Republicans joined the twelve Democrats in supporting Johnson. Stunned by the setback, the Radicals postponed voting until May 26, when votes on Articles II and III produced identical 35-to-19 tallies. To head off further defeats, the Radicals moved to adjourn sine die, and the motion was adopted 34 to 16, abruptly ending the impeachment trial of President Andrew Johnson.

Charles Swayne

Florida District Judge Charles Swayne was impeached in 1905. He was accused of filing false travel vouchers, improper use of private railroad cars, unlawfully imprisoning two attorneys for contempt, and living outside of his district. Swayne's trial consumed two-and-a-half months before it ended on February 27, 1905, when the Senate voted acquittal on each of the twelve articles. There was little doubt that Swayne was guilty of some of the offenses charged against him. Indeed, his counsel admitted as much, though calling the lapses "inadvertent." The Senate, however, refused to convict Swayne because its members did not believe his peccadilloes amounted to "high crimes and misdemeanors."

It was during the long Swayne trial that the suggestion first surfaced that a Senate committee, rather than the Senate as a whole, should receive impeachment evidence. Senator George F. Hoar of Massachusetts proposed that the presiding officer should appoint such a committee. While Hoar's proposal would eventually be embodied in Rule XI of the Senate's impeachment rules, in 1905 the resolution was referred to the Rules Committee, which took no action.

Robert W. Archbald

The next impeachment trial was that of Judge Robert W. Archbald of the Commerce Court in 1913. Archbald was charged with numerous and serious acts of misconduct stretching over many years, including using his office to obtain advantageous business deals and free trips to Europe. As in the Swayne case, not one of the thirteen articles charged an indictable offense. Yet, apparently because of the seriousness and extent of his crimes, many of which he acknowledged, Archbald was convicted on five of thirteen articles. Alexander Simpson, Archbald's counsel, noted that the decision "determined that a judge ought not only to be impartial, but he ought so to demean himself, both in and out of the court, that litigants will have no reason to suspect his impartiality; and that repeatedly failing in that respect constituted a 'high misdemeanor'." After the Archbald trial concluded, his counsel also suggested that impeachment evidence be taken by a Senate committee. Simpson argued that many senators were not in attendance when evidence was taken before the full Senate and thus relied on the printed Congressional Record.

Harold Louderback

In 1933, the House Judiciary Committee recommended censure, rather than impeachment, for federal judge Harold Louderback of California. A minority of the committee, however, took the issue to the floor of the House where they persuaded that body to adopt five articles of impeachment, charging Louderback with favoritism and conspiracy in the appointment of bankruptcy receivers. Louderback's Senate trial consumed nearly all of May 1933, during the New Deal's Hundred Days, one of the busiest legislative periods in congressional history. A long parade of witnesses, including a faith healer who had to be brought into the chamber on a stretcher, filed through to testify. Democrats charged Republicans with using the trial to delay a banking reform bill, a charge Republicans denied. Tempers in the Senate frayed as witness after witness cast doubt on the charges. When the Senate finally voted on May 24, 1933, Louderback was acquitted on all five articles. Only on the fifth and last charge, a summation of the preceding four, did the vote even reach a majority, still eight votes short of the two-thirds needed for conviction.

Rule XI

The trial of Judge Louderback again brought to the fore the problem of attendance at impeachment trials. After the trial, Representative Hatton Sumners of Texas, one of the House managers, recalled the scanty attendance: "At one time only three senators were present, and for ten days we presented evidence to what was practically an empty chamber." In 1934, Senator Henry Ashurst of Arizona, chairman of the Judiciary Committee, offered the resolution that became Rule XI after its adoption the following year. The key words of Rule XI provide:

That in the trial of any impeachment the Presiding Officer of the Senate, if the Senate so orders, shall appoint a committee of senators to receive evidence and take testimony at such times and places as the committee may determine . . .

Halsted Ritter

Rule XI was not used in the next impeachment trial, that of Florida District Judge Halsted Ritter in 1936. Ritter was charged with a wide range of improprieties that included practicing law while a judge, filing false income tax returns, extortion, and an omnibus charge of misconduct. Ritter's counsel argued that the judge had committed no offense that could be labeled a high crime or misdemeanor and was guilty only of exercising "poor judgment." In fact, Ritter was found "not guilty" by narrow margins on each of the first six charges. On the seventh, however, the omnibus article combining the previous six, Ritter was found guilty, by exactly the required two-thirds vote, of bringing, by his combined actions, "his court into scandal and disrepute." Said the *New York Times* of the decision: "The Senate is putting judges on notice that they will be removed if the sum total of their crimes shows unfitness for the bench regardless of whether a specific high crime or misdemeanor could be established under ordinary rules of evidence."

Richard Nixon

In the summer of 1974 it looked very much as though there might soon be an impeachment trial for a president of the United States, Richard Nixon. The events of those weeks precipitated a more thorough scrutiny of the Senate's impeachment rules than they had previously undergone. In July 1974, the Senate adopted a resolution directing the Senate Committee on Rules and Administration to review the existing impeachment rules and precedents and recommend revisions. The committee devoted long hours to serious reflection about the solemn duty the Senate believed it might be called upon to perform. The committee was meeting on August 8, when President Nixon announced that he would resign the next day. Nevertheless, the panel continued with its work under a mandate from the Senate to file a report by September 1.

The report contained recommendations that were primarily technical changes in the rules that had been adopted in 1868 for the impeachment trial of Andrew Johnson. With the resignation of President Nixon, no further action was taken. The recommendations, however, were resurrected in 1986 and helped inform the debates on how to conduct the trials that resulted in the removal of three federal judges between 1986 and 1989, and again in 1999 when the Senate faced its second presidential impeachment trial.

William Clinton

On December 19, 1998, the House of Representatives approved two articles of impeachment against President William J. Clinton, claiming the president had "willfully corrupted and manipulated the judicial process." The Senate trial began on January 14, 1999, and once again arguments focused on the definition of "high crimes and misdemeanors." Falling short of the necessary two-thirds vote on either article of impeachment (Article I, 55 to 45; Article II, 50 to 50), the Senate acquitted President Clinton on February 12, 1999.

SIGNIFICANCE

Impeachment is one of the most serious responsibilities given to Congress by the Constitution and is reserved for crimes against the nation. Only the House may impeach a government official, and only the Senate can try that person. Because there is no appeals process, the Senate must convict by a two-thirds majority. Impeachment proceedings are milestones in American political history.

Impeachment differs from criminal and civil trials both in purpose and result. A criminal trial is designed to determine the defendant's guilt or innocence; convictions can lead to jail time or even a death sentence. Civil conviction forces the defendant to make financial restitution. The ramifications of an impeachment conviction are entirely political. Once official misconduct has been determined, the individual is required to leave office and cannot hold a public office again. This protects the country and its citizens from corrupt leadership, allows the government to be held accountable for its actions, and ensures that no single elected official is above the law.

FURTHER RESOURCES

Books

Berger, Raoul. *Impeachment: The Constitutional Problems.* Cambridge: Harvard University Press, 1973.

Gerhardt, Michael J. *The Federal Impeachment Process: A Constitutional and Historical Analysis.* Chicago: University of Chicago Press, 2000.

Web sites

American Bar Association. "FAQs and Web Resources on the Impeachment Process." <http://www.abanet.org/publiced/impeach2.html> (January 14, 2006).

U. S. House of Representatives. "Committee on the Judiciary." <http://judiciary.house.gov/> (January 14, 2006).

Expert Witness Questions Child Porn Jailings

Internet article

By: Iain Thomson

Date: October 4, 2005

Source: Thomson, Iain. "Expert Witness Questions Child Porn Jailings," October 4, 2005. <http//:www.vnunet.com/vnunet/news/2143191/expert-witness-questions-child> (accessed January 7, 2006).

About the Author: Iain Thompson is a journalist who specializes in legal affairs for the Business Publications section of the technology publications website, vnunet.com, based in England.

INTRODUCTION

In the pre-computer age, the manufacture and the distribution of child pornography was the preserve of the stereotypical "dirty old man," a lurking, furtive individual, clad in a trench coat, with a manila folder of obscene photographs tucked under his arm, looking to make a trade with a like-minded person. The technological advances in the processing speed and immense storage capacities of the computer, coupled with the global reach of the Internet, have eradicated the stereotypical pornographer. A child pornography trade based upon digital images has elevated the detection and the apprehension of child pornographers from the realm of traditional police work to a high-technology-based, forensic discipline. The criminal possession of child pornography will now, invariably, involve the use of a computer, a hardware peripheral, or a portable, removable media compatible with computer use.

The law does not move with the same speed as the digital technologies it has sought to regulate. In North

America, computers were a staple of both the corporate world and the typical residence long before the power of the state to authorize comprehensive searches and seizures of computer records was confirmed in legislation. The public and law enforcement agencies alike had difficulty with the concept that data stored in a digital fashion within a computer file should be treated as if it were illegal in the conventional sense. Because computer files could seemingly be made to disappear with the press of a button, computer contents were not characterized as pieces of real, tangible evidence.

The first computer-based child pornography prosecutions of the early 1990s generated a significant change in public attitudes toward the contents of a computer and the concept of criminal possession by digital means. Seizures of tens of thousands of images depicting innocent children in positions of utter depravity became common. Police agencies began to direct significant attention and resources to child pornography investigations. A troubling companion issue arose—was child pornography an isolated perversion, or was it a growing, many-tentacled, social ill?

Because of enhanced resources and greater public awareness, significant penalties now exist for all forms of child pornography possession in countries throughout the Western world. From conduct that was deemed to be a personal peccadillo—a victimless crime—the convicted child pornographer is now subject to incarceration. Penal consequences have driven the development of more sophisticated, technology-based, criminal defenses to counter the results of a seemingly successful forensic computer search.

▮ PRIMARY SOURCE

A witness in computer crime trials has called for the release of individuals convicted of child pornography offences based entirely on material found on their hard drives.

Jason Coombes, who has been involved in computer crime trials since 1994, issued a statement calling on police to be more thorough in their investigations.

The expert contends that third-party control of a PC which is then used to store or view child pornography images could lead to the conviction of innocent people.

"I have seen numerous cases in which the computer forensic evidence proves that a third-party intruder was in control of the suspect's computer," said Coombes.

"Every person convicted of an electronic crime against a child based only on evidence recovered from a hard drive that happened to be in their possession should be immediately released from whatever prison they are now being held."

"There is simply no way for law enforcement to know the difference between innocent and guilty persons based on hard drive data circumstantial evidence."

Coombes added that it was the responsibility of the police to use key-logging and internet wiretaps to prove guilt beyond reasonable doubt.

He also described it as "outrageous" that someone could be convicted of such a crime based solely on the contents of their hard drive.

Coombes highlighted the case of Commodore David White, who was accused of accessing a US child porn website and was relieved of his command despite there being no hard evidence against him. He was found dead in his swimming pool the next day.

Investigations into child pornography have led to 4,000 arrests, 1,600 people charged and 1,200 convictions. In the UK there have been 34 suicides by the accused.

Professor Neil Barrett, professor of computer science at Cranfield University, and himself an expert witness at computer crime trials, said: "I have heard this argument before, predominantly from defence witnesses seeking to poke holes in a case."

"To say that everything [in a child porn prosecution] is to do with a hard drive is unreasonable. We would never bring a case purely on the basis of what's on the computer."

Professor Barrett explained that suspects are interviewed and their stories checked before action is taken. If their computer is clean, for example if someone else was using their credit card number, no action is taken.

He added that the onus is always on the prosecution to prove that the accused directly accessed the images.

▮

SIGNIFICANCE

The chief significance of the debate concerning what constitutes the actual or legal possession of child pornography is rooted in the simple question—is it right to convict someone of a serious crime on the sole basis of what is found in a computer? Computer errors abound in our high technology society, from bank machines to computer-generated statements of all kinds. Identity theft, sometimes furthered through computer access, is another basis for the lingering public distrust of technology as the definitive answer to any question. For these reasons, there are many people—although repulsed by child pornography—who are uncomfortable with the computer search alone as proof of a crime. Jason Coombes is giving voice to that constituency.

Cyber controls, such as "Cybersitter," "My Content Filter," and "Parental Controls," on the Internet block access to selected sites and content. With these tools, parents can keep children from accessing most pornography or other objectionable material on their computers. © ANDREW HOLBROOKE/CORBIS

In very broad terms, the public accepts computer technology as a fundamental ingredient of their daily lives. Law enforcement approaches are largely a reflection of public attitudes. A criminal conviction—a fundamentally permanent conclusion regarding the character of an individual—may be supported in part by a technological device, but the public's comfort level is increased if the computer data is not the only evidence in an investigation that supports guilt.

In the Anglo-American tradition of criminal law, wrongful possession of an object is determined by the proof beyond a reasonable doubt of two separate, but related, components—a knowledge of the criminal nature of a particular item and control of it. A person driving a stolen motor vehicle is clearly in control of it; if he honestly did not know that the vehicle was stolen, a charge of possession of stolen property will fail. The same approach has been advanced in computer crimes involving child pornography. The discovery of obscene images stored on a person's computer is not conclusive proof that the owner knew that the images were there. However, there is a fear implicit in the concerns of Jason Coombes that society may be prepared to accept such evidence alone—without other corroboration—to determine guilt, given the foul nature of the material seized.

The comments of Professor Barrett echo the defenses raised in many child pornography trials. Proof as to who was actually using a computer when the image was stored or received may be difficult to establish in some circumstances. This line of reasoning is significant because it raises its own potential solution—is child pornography such a compelling social issue that it warrants its own law to define possession? Should child pornography or the possession of any contraband on a computer be resolved through different, more draconian legal rules, founded on the reverse of the old maxim, "Possession is nine-tenths of the law?". Law enforcement resources also reflect public sentiment. The public wants safety and security, but begrudges the tax increases required to fund additional police resources. Eliminating other suspects in child pornography investigations—who may have taken control of or otherwise accessed a computer to store pornographic images—carries a substantial cost.

The debate concerning police methods in child pornography investigations raises a related, significant issue. With a greater number of child pornography cases coming to light, have the number of such deviant persons increased, or is technology simply allowing child pornographers to be more easily identified? This troublesome question involves a number of issues, including whether the Internet has fostered a climate where such persons feel comfortable.

FURTHER RESOURCES

Books

Taylor, Max. *Child Pornography: An Internet Crime*. New York: Brunner-Routledge, 2003.

Web sites

Sherriff, Lucy. "U.S. Rules All Porn Is Child Porn," *The Register*, June 24, 2005. <http://www.theregister.co.uk/2005/06/24/us_law_2257/> (accessed January 9, 2006).

United States Department of Justice. "Child Pornography." <http://www.usdoj.gov/criminal/ceos/childporn.html> (accessed January 11, 2006).

Thought Crime

Newspaper article

By: Kathleen Taylor

Date: October 8, 2005

Source: Taylor, Kathleen. "Thought Crime." *Guardian Unlimited*, October 8, 2005, <http://books.guardian.co.uk/departments/healthmindandbody/story/0,,1587653,00.html> (accessed February 5, 2006).

About the Author: Kathleen Taylor is a research scientist at the University of Oxford. Until 2002, Taylor studied the effects of dyslexia, but, since that time, she has been studying issues relating to brainwashing, thought control, and interpersonal influence. Her book, *Brainwashing: The Science of Thought Control*, brought together psychological and social issues to assess why groups in history have tried to influence and control the thoughts of others and how that process has impacted society.

INTRODUCTION

With the spread of terrorism into Western democracies and large metropolitan cities, profiling a "typical" terrorist has become increasingly difficult. The challenge was compounded when it was shown that some of the actors behind these terrorist actions were, in fact, citizens of the very nations and communities they were attacking.

The attacks against London's transit system on July 7, 2005, served as one of the clearest examples of the phenomenon of the "home-grown" terrorist in the current war on terror. Included among the suicide bombers who carried out the attacks on London's subways and busses were young British citizens who had grown up, worked, and raised families in British cities.

Brainwashing—a term coined by the CIA in the 1950s—is one explanation that has been advanced in an attempt to understand why people turn to terror. This phenomenon, which has been seen in societies of many types all over the globe, attributes a person's willingness to commit certain acts to an alteration of their free will after they have been subjected to certain specific conditions.

It is argued that isolating a person and then controlling his actions are the two necessary first steps used by terrorists to start new recruits on the road toward martyrdom for their cause. The final steps in the brainwashing of recruits involve planting uncertainty about the person's previously held beliefs, constant repetition of the ideologies of the terrorist group, and manipulation of the person's emotions. These brainwashing tactics are known to have been practiced by groups like Al Qaeda, allowing them to succeed in developing large groups of followers around the world.

The ability of terrorist agencies to use these approaches to recruit followers poses an added risk, since it makes it far easier to conceal terrorists within society. Identifying and thus combating this form of "thought crime" is now being recognized as an important objective for law enforcement and national governments taking part in the war on terror.

PRIMARY SOURCE

Three months ago, on July 7, London suffered its 9/11. An attack on the capital had long been predicted and, mercifully, far fewer people were killed than in the Twin

Towers. But that was no consolation in the chaos. The 52 innocent and unlucky dead, from a striking variety of faiths and backgrounds, left many more distraught friends and relatives, more than 700 injured, a city wounded and a nation in shock.

And then we learned that the bombers were "home-grown." That incongruous word, more often applied to talent, or vegetables, seemed completely at odds with the horror of that summer Thursday and what one bereaved father called its "totally evil" perpetrators. Bemused commentators cast about, desperate to understand how young British men—men such as Mohammad Sidique Khan, married with a job and a baby, living in one of the freest and most fortunate societies on earth—could come to turn their hate on their homeland, and blow themselves to pieces to express that hate.

Once we would have blamed the devil and called those four young suicides "possessed." But in 1950, when the United States confronted Mao Zedong's China in the Korean war, a chilling new word became available. That word, coined by the CIA man Edward Hunter, is "brainwashing." It is a propagandistic, rough-and-ready translation of what the Chinese Communist regime called szu-hsiang kai-tsao: a process of "thought reform" or "re-education." Thought reform was used in academies to make students into good communists and in prison camps to "cleanse" the "wrong thoughts" of political dissidents, foreign citizens and enemy soldiers. After undergoing thought reform, some Americans converted to communism and strongly denounced the US, a spectacle as unnerving to most Americans then as suicide bombers' video testaments are to us today.

Brainwashing threatens cherished notions of free will. It seems to suggest that we may not be safe anywhere, not even inside our own skulls. Since Korea it has been invoked whenever people do something especially incomprehensible. In 1974, the heiress and kidnap victim Patty Hearst joined her abductors in a murderous bank robbery. Four years later the followers of the preacher and paranoid socialist Jim Jones willingly drank sugar-flavoured cyanide. On each occasion, as after Waco, 9/11 and other atrocities, the concept of brainwashing re-emerged into popular consciousness. Sure enough, following 7/7, Khan's shattered family insisted that he must have been brainwashed. How else could a kind and loving man become a suicide bomber?

Say the word "brainwashing," and chances are we think of the Manchurian Candidate, of some mysterious process that installs malevolent new beliefs in people's minds—as if ideologies were just like versions of Windows. This horror-movie view of brainwashing is alarming, but also comforting. It scares us with one of the most frightening visions we can contemplate: the utter loss of

free will as our minds are "turned" or "poisoned," our core identity subjugated to some evil-minded fanatic. But unlike its predecessor possession, brainwashing blames people, not demons. In doing so it offers reassurance, lifting the curse of moral responsibility from the bomber's shoulders—and, by extension, ours—and placing it firmly in Osama bin Laden's lap. Bin Laden is the evil genius with the power to control minds at will. We are the victims, gathering our resources to fight back.

But brains are not computers, and there is no Button X that Osama and his ilk can press to turn a man from good to evil. Giving a name to the pathway from "normal" to "killer" may make us feel better, but it doesn't help us prevent any future bombings. All it offers by way of solutions are the age-old reactions to evil: exorcism or destruction. Exorcism, needless to say, doesn't work on Islamist radicals. Destruction, given our ignorance of where to aim our weapons, runs a high risk of wiping out the wrong targets, as the family of Jean Charles de Menezes has learned.

What we need is not aggression but comprehension: not total evil but graspable human wickedness. We need to think of brainwashing more realistically: not as black magic but in secular, scientific terms, as a set of techniques that can act on a human brain to produce belief change. People do, in certain circumstances, undergo dramatic changes of belief over startlingly short periods of time. Sometimes the new beliefs are frankly bizarre. Sometimes they are lethal: when Jonestown imploded more than 900 people died. But the strangeness or moral repugnance of a belief is no bar to understanding how it can be stamped on a person's mind.

One striking fact about brainwashing is its consistency. Whether the context is a prisoner-of-war camp, a cult's headquarters or a radical mosque, five core techniques keep cropping up: isolation, control, uncertainty, repetition and emotional manipulation. To see how these work, let us imagine a situation in which Mr X, the leader of a small group of ideologues committed to violence, is attempting to brainwash a young man—let's call him Adam.

Mr X has an immediate problem: the message he wants Adam to believe goes against some of Adam's own beliefs, as well as contradicting many beliefs that Adam may not have thought much about, but which are widespread in British society. Adam may, for instance, have friends who Mr X thinks are immoral. Whenever Adam enjoys their company his belief that such friendships are acceptable is reinforced. To contradict that belief, Mr X first needs to weaken it by isolating Adam from his former friends. Indeed, his aim is to isolate Adam as far as possible from every enjoyable aspect of his former life. Jim Jones achieved isolation by physically moving himself and his followers to the Guyanan jungle. More recently, al-Qaida has sent British recruits to remote training camps. If total isolation is not possible, then Mr X will encourage Adam to strengthen his commitments to the group.

Along with isolation goes the second technique: control of what Adam sees, hears and thinks about. Like isolation, control squeezes Adam's mental horizons, narrowing his field of view so that everything becomes interpreted through the one ideological lens. Brains, even well-brought-up, adult brains, depend heavily on the information reaching them via their senses. Beliefs confirmed by that information are reinforced and grow stronger, while beliefs contradicted by it tend to weaken. Mr X will therefore aim to make sure, as far as he can, that Adam spends plenty of time with group members pondering the new ideology and contrasting it favourably with Adam's former beliefs. Adam's media consumption will also be regulated: fewer aspirational Hollywood fantasies and adverts promoting western consumer lifestyles; more about the west's selfish greed, its neglect of its own disadvantaged, and the atrocities that emerge whenever Europe or the US bungles foreign policy.

Adam, however, may still be quite attached to his former beliefs, in which case Mr X will need to challenge them directly. This is where uncertainty comes in, because uncertainty is a potent source of stress: ask any relative of a murder victim whose body cannot be found. If Mr X can make Adam doubt beliefs he used to take for granted, he will look for alternative certainties to replace them—and the brainwasher stands ready to assist, offering a simple, coherent, unified belief system. Mr X wants Adam to look to him for answers to every problem, so he will emphasise his authority and expertise. He will also claim that his ideology is a total system, capable of judging any issue and relevant to every walk of life. Not only does this make Mr X seem more powerful; it also helps stop Adam protecting favourite former beliefs by classifying them as beyond Mr X's ideological remit.

The contrast between the complicated, fragmented muddle of the unbeliever's life and the pure simplicity of true belief is often emphasised by ideologues who understand the power of uncertainty to frighten and unnerve people who may already feel that their lives are out of control. Sayyid Qutb, a founding father of radical Islamism, used the Islamic term jahiliyyah—literally, ignorance—to describe western existence, a word with connotations of darkness, complexity and moral chaos. Qutb's west is not so much the Great Satan as the Great Void: relativist, postmodern and meaningless. Mr X, wanting Adam to find certainty with him and his group, will trade on similar associations to demonise his opponents. By contrast, he will emphasise how clear and simple his basic rules are by making his core message brief, coherent and easy to understand and remember. Every ideology has its soundbites.

Mr X's fourth technique is repetition. The more often Adam hears the core message, the more comfortable and familiar it will feel to him and the more likely he is to take it on board. In Maoist China, thought-reform academies scheduled hours of lectures and discussion, from early in the morning to late at night, for days, weeks, months or even years on end. When not attending lectures, groups of students engaged in a process called "struggle": one person was accused of, or confessed to, having "wrong thoughts" or beliefs; then other group members showed their loyalty by competing to challenge and condemn the unfortunate victim and reiterate the communist message. Students also had to keep detailed, publicly available diaries of what they were thinking: lengthy confessions of thoughtcrime, in effect. Diaries, struggle groups, lectures, debates—and always the same message, hammering into the skull again and again, breaking down resistance.

Isolation, control, uncertainty and repetition will help Mr X and his group to damp down Adam's old beliefs and introduce his brain to new ones. But for the transplant to take, he will need the final weapon in a brainwasher's armoury: emotion. Until the late 20th century scientists largely ignored emotion; science has its fashions like everything else. In recent years, emotion has become a much hotter topic. For ideologues, however, understanding emotions has always been essential. They know, either instinctively or because they have studied their predecessors, that rational argument, though it may please a logician, is a weak tool for gaining followers—or whipping up a mob.

Adam may find Mr X's arguments convincing, but we all have beliefs we never act on. To act, we have to care. Mr X will try to stir up emotions in Adam that make him care: positive feelings when he talks about the new beliefs; negative ones whenever he thinks of old ideas. To do this, he uses the human brain's own power of association to manipulate it. Association allows us to link two brain events (be they perceptions, thoughts, or emotions) if they happen simultaneously. If a cat, for instance, is seen and heard at the same time, its image and meow become associated, so that next time we hear the sound we visualise the animal.

The brain's response to signals from hearing or vision is rapid and transient; when the meow stops, or something more interesting comes along, the person no longer hears the sound of meowing. This allows brains to keep up with a fast-changing world. Emotions, however, tend to linger, especially strongly negative emotions, because they have evolved as override signals triggered by the threat of danger. It didn't matter if your distant ancestor was still shaking 10 minutes later, as long as her reactions were quick enough to get her out of the predator's way in time.

But then human beings invented symbols, and symbolic thinking changes everything. Nowadays Mr X and his like can use symbols—words or images, the more shocking the better—to trigger extremely strong negative emotions in Adam. All Mr X needs to do is mention his enemy the west at the same time, and the association will form in Adam's brain, if it isn't there already. Likewise for positive emotions: when Mr X speaks of peace, love and brotherhood he will be sure to emphasise his group's beliefs as well.

Every human being needs emotional sustenance from others. Mr X will aim to ensure that he and his group become Adam's main or only source for these positive feelings. Kindness and concern, laughter, friendship and contentment will be constantly on offer from them; the rest of the universe will fade into a hateful darkness. As

Adam becomes more dependent, it will be easier to raise the most challenging of issues: suicide bombing. Or, as Mr X will undoubtedly call it, sacrifice, for the good of Adam's now-beloved group.

If Mr X is adept at what he does, Adam will not pause to reject the twisted terrorist logic that says it's OK to kill D because D supports A, who sent in the soldiers who killed B, whom I care about. Adam will not care that D may not have voted for A; that B's death may be due to human error or military savagery, which A condemns; that D has no way of changing A's behaviour; or that Mr X's goals are completely unrealistic. Adam will not stop to ask the difficult questions or to remember the long list of radicals whose fire was doused, of necessity, once they gained power and realised just how muddled and compromised the real world is. Adam would certainly never admit that terrorism springs not so much from evil as from immaturity: the lazy or callous or desperate short-sightedness of people who, like an angry toddler, want their demands met, now, however stupid those demands may be. He may understand the terrorist's grievances,

A poster on a wall in the Jenin refugee camp in the West Bank glorifies Palestinian suicide bomber Shadi Zakaria. In a March 2002 attack, Zakaria killed 16 people in Haifa. Suicide bombings had grown so much in appeal and popularity among Palestinians that a cult, complete with what could pass for rituals, evolved around them. AP IMAGES

but he cannot see the multiple, competing strands of political opinion that so often leave western governments complicit or ethically inert. He will also fail to grasp that each atrocity loses Mr X more friends among those with the power to help his cause. Least of all can Adam bring himself to laugh, albeit angrily and with disgust, at Mr X's ludicrous determination to take himself seriously.

Brainwashed Adam is no longer able to think any of these thoughts. But we can, and that freedom gives us a great advantage over him: the ability to understand what makes Adam and others like him behave the way they do. Whether—and how well—we use that knowledge is up to us.

SIGNIFICANCE

This article highlights a new aspect of the threat posed by international terrorism, whereby terrorist groups succeed in manipulating the thoughts and desires of recruits through the process of brainwashing. While this phenomenon is not impossible to combat, it can not be fought with traditional law enforcement tools or military action and, thus, serves as a new challenge in the war on terror.

Brainwashing is not a new practice and has been used throughout history to different degrees to advance religious, political, and social ideologies. Yet, the spread of global terrorism has raised awareness of its use by terror groups for recruitment purposes.

Since some terrorist groups incite their members to kill themselves and others in the name of the terrorist ideology, complete mental control is considered a necessary prerequisite in developing a terrorist willing to become a martyr for the cause. The article reproduced above explains that brainwashing is, in fact, a scientific process that employs a series of discrete techniques to mold recruits toward a desired end. When all these techniques are employed, the terrorist group can successfully cause individuals to commit extreme acts that they would never have considered before being brainwashed.

The use of these brainwashing techniques requires a willingness on the part of the person being brainwashed combined with environmental conditions that allow the person to see the thoughts being introduced as valid. By isolating and then controlling the information that a person can access, the terrorists are able to begin infiltrating that person's thought processes. The eventual result is to encourage participation in a terrorist attack. As these approaches can theoretically succeed in all nations around the world, international terrorist groups are becoming increas-

ingly reliant on brainwashing to expand their networks with new terrorists who can easily infiltrate a given society. By recognizing the specific dangers of brainwashing, nations will be better prepared to fight the recruitment efforts of terrorists within their own borders.

FURTHER RESOURCES

Books

Pape, Robert A. *Dying to Win: The Strategic Logic of Suicide Terrorism.* New York: Random House, 2005.

Web sites

Atran, Scott. "Genesis and Future of Suicide Terrorism." *Interdisciplines,* <http://www.interdisciplines.org/terrorism/papers/1/6> (accessed February 5, 2006).

A Road To Trouble

Newspaper article

By: Anne Constable

Date: October 11, 2005

Source: Constable, Anne. "A Road to Trouble." *Santa Fe New Mexican* (November 13, 2005): A1, A6.

About the Author: Anne Constable is a staff writer for the *Santa Fe New Mexican* newspaper. She has won first- (feature story) and second-place (news feature) awards from the Association of Alternative Newsweeklies in 2000.

INTRODUCTION

The concept of the door-to-door salesperson has been a mainstay of American culture since the end of the Second World War in 1945. The Kirby vacuum company, Fuller Brush, Tupperware, Avon, and Encyclopedia Britannica all employed traveling salespeople during the middle of the twentieth century. People sold household sundries, books, magazines, cleaning products, knives and kitchen utensils, foodstuffs, and self-care items door-to-door during a time when streets were considered safe and neighborhood crime was low. By the 1970s and 1980s, the demographics of the traveling sales industry had changed (as had the tenor of the country): there were far fewer mature adult professional traveling salespeople, and a burgeoning number of adolescents and young adults being recruited into large-scale door-to-door sales crews.

The young sales crews often travel in groups of twenty-five to fifty, moving from area to area, then state to state. Typically, the crews are recruited by means of newspaper ads promising good pay and the opportunity to travel. They are given minimal training and even less supervision, and housed in groups in inexpensive motels. The sales crews are dropped into neighborhoods, instructed to set out door-to-door to carry out direct sales, and told to earn a specific quota, which generally translates into a targeted dollar amount of sales. If the quota isn't met, the sales representative does not earn any money, and may be subject to a variety of punitive consequences and deprived of privileges such as meal money, use of a telephone, and subjected to verbal abuse by the crew leader(s). When the quota is met, the sales representative may still not be paid as promised, may be given a small meal allowance, and may not be permitted to use a telephone to contact friends or family.

In the case of magazine sales, the subscriptions are sold at significantly higher prices than are available though tear-out response cards inserted in the periodicals themselves, and a hefty processing fee is tagged on to the final cost. The recipient is told that the subscription will not commence for three to four months—although many people never receive their magazines at all, according to data published by observer groups such as Parent Watch and Traveling Sales Watch. The young sales people sometimes report being encouraged to lie to consumers, telling them that they are competing for trips, scholarships, and money for higher educational programs. They are also sometimes reportedly told to lie about where they are from, where they are staying at present, and what their future plans are.

PRIMARY SOURCE

When Carol Salter of Colorado Springs, Colo., heard about the arrest of five door-to-door magazine salesmen in connection with the death of a Santa Fe man late last month, she got a big knot in her stomach.

Salter's eighteen-year-old daughter, LeAnn, had joined a similar crew selling subscriptions door-to-door in Denver and Colorado Springs.

LeAnn had quit the crew two weeks earlier, but Salter couldn't help but think how close her daughter had come to being in Santa Fe at the time of the killing.

In late October, two crews selling subscriptions through the same company had been staying at a Ramada Inn in the Denver area. According to LeAnn, her crew was preparing to go to Utah when she quit. The other crew was headed to Santa Fe.

While LeAnn said in a telephone interview last week that she didn't know any of the people arrested in Santa Fe, she said the traveling-sales environment was often rough. "I'd walk into the hotel room and twenty people would be smoking marijuana and drinking alcohol," she said. "I didn't feel safe."

One night, LeAnn said, the crew tried to persuade her and her boyfriend to go bowling, even suggesting it was mandatory. She declined, saying she was too tired.

LeAnn's crew and the Santa Fe crew both were independent contractors selling subscriptions through Michigan-based World Wide Circulation, one of many clearing houses in the United States involved in door-to-door magazine sales.

Under this system, both the crew managers and crew members are independent contractors. The clearing houses aren't responsible for the actions of crew members or subject to laws governing direct employers.

There is a high turnover among the crews. Managers are constantly recruiting new members, often through ads in local papers promising young people they will have the opportunity to make a lot of money and travel the country. Most salesmen are hired with little or no background checks.

The job doesn't usually appeal to high-school graduates heading for college. But "if you're a small-town kid and you want to travel and you can't find a job, the ads in the newspapers look pretty good," said Earlene Williams, director of an advocacy group called Parent Watch Inc. Williams often helps distraught parents find their children and bring them home.

LeAnn had graduated from Liberty High School and was looking for work for some time when she saw the ad in the local daily newspaper. In addition to travel, it said she could earn $200 a week.

She jumped at the chance to go to Denver for an interview. The company hired her and her boyfriend on the spot. That, Carol Salter said, was her first indication that something wasn't quite right.

LeAnn joined one of the crews and began working neighborhoods in Denver and Colorado Springs. She was told she needed to sell eight subscriptions a day. And when she didn't make her quota, the crew manager warned she could be fired.

According to LeAnn, a trainer advised her to fabricate a story about living in the neighborhood, attending a local university, and needing to raise money for a college trip.

"When she told me that, another flag went up," her mother said. She warned her daughter that she could be arrested for misrepresenting herself.

Carol Salter also went online and began reading about missing kids who had joined traveling sales crews. She saw reports on crimes involving crew members—or crimes committed against them.

She encouraged her daughter to get out. But at that time, LeAnn said, she was excited about going to California.

Salter said her husband, a local sheriff's deputy, also checked out the company with the Better Business Bureau and then contacted LeAnn's team boss in Denver. She said he warned the boss he would bring some heat down on the operation if they tried to prevent his daughter from going home.

The Salters also talked with Charles Leaf, an investigative reporter with a local Fox News channel who was working on a story about traveling sales crews. Leaf later aired a story showing a tussle between his film crew and LeAnn's team at the Denver motel.

Today, LeAnn is working for a local crafts store in Colorado Springs.

"I'm very glad she got out of this before she ended up traveling (to another state,)" said Salter.

Life on a crew

At any one time, as many as fifty thousand young people like LeAnn—and the group of young men accused of killing a Santa Fe man last month—are traveling around the country selling perfume, candy, and jewelry, as well as magazines and books. Most are between eighteen and twenty-four years old.

Crews of fifteen to twenty young people, and sometimes as many as thirty, travel by van from city to city. Typically, about four times a day, the car handler drops them in a new neighborhood and arranges to pick them up at a specific time and place. The manager sets quotas for each crew member.

"Most kids sweat to make the quota," Williams of Parent Watch said of the practices of some sales crews, "and if they make it, it will go up a little."

Crew members who don't fulfill their quotas might find themselves at a late-night meeting, where the manager berates them, she said. Williams said she is aware of one company that forces crew members who don't make their quotas to box one another.

At the end of the day, crew members turn proceeds from sales over to the crew manager. The manager might give a salesman ten dollars or twenty dollars to pay for food and other personal expenses and then keep a record of what percentage of sales is earned by each member.

But a person who wants to leave the crew and asks the manager for money might not get any, Williams said.

Buyers from some itinerant crews don't always get their magazines, either, Williams said, because "a lot can happen between the sale of the magazine and the publishers."

But she said the publishers are not particularly concerned about sales revenues anyway. They are more interested in boosting circulation so they can charge advertisers higher rates. Most of the money earned by such crews stays with the manager and the clearing house, she said.

Some of the kids are satisfied with getting just enough to buy food for the night. Even when they say they were mistreated, some report they made some of the best friends of their lives among the other members of the traveling crews. And a few come from such poor backgrounds that they're glad to have a roof over their heads, Williams said.

On the road, salesmen are assigned four to a room (and two to a bed) with couples often rooming together. LeAnn said she was chewed out by a hotel manager and her crew manager because one of her roommates had spray-painted a message about loving pot on the roof of a hotel balcony—even though she had nothing to do with the vandalism, she said. On another occasion, she said a roommate fired a BB gun in the room. The BB ricocheted and hit her chin.

LeAnn said she finally had enough. The job didn't seem like something she wanted to do. And during her life, she said, she had kept away from drugs and alcohol. When the manager tried to get her to work, even though she was sick, she quit. The crew manager returned her car key, and she drove home. Her boyfriend came back the next day. She was never paid.

Victims and victimizers

Life on the road is sometimes dangerous for traveling sales crews. They can be victims and victimizers.

The Parent Watch and traveling-salescrew.info Web sites contain many news reports of crimes by and against traveling crews. Although not all of them have a bad reputation, door-to-door sales people have been implicated in more than a dozen cases of rape or sexual assault and at least four murder cases since 2000, according to the watchdog group Parent Watch.

In Boston, one salesman was convicted of raping an eighteen-year-old in her home, and two others are facing trial on similar charges.

In 2002, a door-to-door salesman raped and stabbed to death a Knox County, Tenn., grandmother, and two years later, a salesman with the same company raped a LaVergne mother in front of her two-month-old son, according to The Associated Press. All three men had criminal histories.

And a Fort Wayne, Ind., man was killed in a drunken brawl that resulted in the conviction of one traveling salesman for murder and another for involuntary manslaughter in 2002, according to a story in a local newspaper, *The Journal Gazette.*

Civil lawsuits have also been filed around the country claiming companies were negligent in hiring criminals as door-to-door salesmen.

There are also reports of crew members being abused by co-workers and by customers.

Parent Watch and other groups are pushing for legislation that would require traveling crews to register with local authorities. Although some municipalities such as Santa Fe require them to purchase a permit, crews often flout the law. (The crew involved in the Santa Fe homicide did not have a permit to solicit.)

Several bills to bring traveling sales crews under the protection of federal labor standards have failed in Congress. But after seven teenage employees of an Oklahoma-based magazine group were killed and others were injured in a 1999 crash in Wisconsin, lawmakers there introduced a bill that Williams hopes will become a national model. The legislation, which is pending, would require registration, would prohibit the use of independent contractors as crew members and would require at least semi-monthly payment of all wages earned.

None of the Santa Fe crew, including manager Dewell Keith LaFleur, a thirty-year-old ex-Marine formerly from Louisiana, responded to requests for interviews made through their lawyers. Calls placed to World Wide Circulation in Saint Clair Shores, Mich., were not returned.

Jerry Long of Liberty, Mo., declined to talk about his son, who is charged in the Santa Fe case. But he said in a message, "Andrew is a young man with plenty of fine qualities that we love and support."

Unlike this boy selling magazines door-to-door in the 1950s, today's young magazine salespeople travel from city to city in organized groups and must fill high-pressure quotas from their employers. © BETTMANN/CORBIS

SIGNIFICANCE

The Better Business Bureau (BBB) reports that there are extremely large numbers of complaints lodged against the largest direct magazine sales organizations. The BBB posts warnings, particularly to youth, to be wary of seeking or accepting employment with the traveling sales crews. They report that consumers have filed complaints regarding failure to receive promised goods and services, as well as intentional misrepresentation of sales practices (crew members have claimed that they attend local high schools and were trying to earn points to go on school trip, and similarly inaccurate stories). In addition, each of the above-mentioned websites (Parent Watch, magcrews, and Traveling Sales Watch) lists strong warnings about the potential dangers posed to the crews as well as to consumers whose homes are visited and who may lose significant sums of money or their personal safety to the traveling salespeople.

Sales representatives are typically hired at the conclusion of the interview, if one occurs, and background checks rarely, if ever, occur. Because the crew members hired are considered independent contractors, there is no process of insuring or bonding them that takes place. The hiring company has no responsibility, therefore, to protect either the crews or the public (who may potentially be victimized by unscrupulous or criminal crew members). Crew members receive no legal protection for their employment conditions, and accrue no benefits. They do not receive medical or dental insurance, and have no written contracts specifying frequency or method of payment. Many of the former crew members whose stories are posted on the websites report never having been paid, or of leaving the job while being owed thousands of dollars. Former sales crew members report that the majority of money earned by them goes directly to those above them—crew managers, and the owners of the traveling sales company. Law enforcement officials estimate that many abuses, injuries, and victimizations involving traveling sales crews go unreported.

The Child Labor Coalition has published statistics estimating that, at any given time, there are approximately fifty thousand juveniles working door-to-door sales, earning the companies for which they are employed somewhere in the neighborhood of one billion dollars per year. They offer an extensive list of unsafe business practices engaged in by many of the sales companies, and term the work *dangerous and exploitative.*

FURTHER RESOURCES

Books

Short, Jr., James F. *Poverty, Ethnicity, and Violent Crime.* Boulder, Colorado: Westview Press, 1997.

Web sites

The Child Labor Coalition. "Youth Peddling Crews: Sweatshops of the Streets." <http://www.stopchildlabor.org/teensandstudents/doortodoor.htm> (accessed March 05, 2006).

Direct Selling Education Foundation. "Is that traveling sales job for you?." <http://www.dsef.org/information2175/information_show.htm?doc_id=29943> (accessed March 05, 2006).

MagCrew.com. "The Official MagCrew Site: Did you or do you currently sell magazines or soap door-to-door?" <http://www.magcrew.com/> (accessed March 05, 2006).

Parent Watch Inc.: A Clearinghouse for Information on Traveling Sales Crews. "Missing Persons." <http://www.parentwatch.org/missing/missing.html> (accessed March 05, 2006).

Traveling Sales Crews Information Web Site. "Traveling door-to-door sales." <http://www.travelingsalescrews.info//> (accessed March 05, 2006).

Doors Closing for Lifers— Again

Newspaper editorial

By: Staff

Date: October 17, 2005

Source: "Editorial: Doors Closing for Lifers—Again." *San Francisco Chronicle*, October 17, 2005, <http://sfgate.com/cgi-bin/article.cgi?f=/c/a/2005/10/17/EDGDKF8ODH1.DTL> (accessed January 31, 2006).

About the Author: The *San Francisco Chronicle* is the largest newspaper in northern California, with a daily circulation of over 500,000. It was founded in 1865 by Charles and Michael de Young and is currently owned by Hearst Communications.

INTRODUCTION

The concept of a life sentence varies from country to country, as well as from state to state in the United States. Since the "tough on crime" (TOC) laws were enacted in the 1970s, there has been a dramatic rise in the number of persons serving sentences in jails and prisons across America. In conjunction with the TOC legislation, another concept, called truth in sentencing (TIS), has been implemented. TIS involves setting specific sentences for particular crimes, with consideration of the circumstances surrounding them. TIS laws mandate that perpetrators of violent crimes serve a minimum of eighty-five percent of the original sentence before they are eligible for parole. The philosophy underlying both of these types of legislation is that they will act as deterrents for criminals, particularly for those who contemplate committing the most serious of felonies (murder, rape, large-scale drug trafficking, etc.). In fact, the U.S. Bureau of Justice Statistics data support this notion. There has been an overall decrease in murders, sexual assault, and robberies involving the use of a weapon, since these types of legislation were first enacted in the late 1970s.

In general, there are two types of criminal sentences involving actual jail or prison terms—indeterminate and determinate. The judge imposing an indeterminate sentence sets a minimum, and sometimes a maximum, period of prison time to be served, but leaves a wide range in which the actual time served will be determined. An example of an indeterminate sentence for a repeat offense of vehicular manslaughter while under the influence of alcohol might involve sentencing the convicted felon to the state penitentiary for a period of not less than eight but not more than thirty years. A determinate sentence, on the other hand, sets a specific incarceration period. For example, giving a convicted felon a mandatory period of ninety days in the county jail for a second offense of driving while intoxicated is a determinate sentence.

There are several justifications for sending a person to prison: 1) to protect the general population by removing a person who presents a threat to the community until such time as he is no longer deemed a danger; 2) to act as a deterrent to future crimes both for the convicted felon and for others in the community; 3) to give the convicted felon an opportunity to make significant life changes in order to shift from a criminal lifestyle by offering tools such as education and job training; 4) to exact punishment based on the nature of the offense. On the other hand, some members of the public believe that prison time is most effective at creating better criminals. Those who hold this viewpoint maintain that spending years in the company of other convicted offenders in prisons or jails in which there is little or no educational or vocational training only serves to create a subculture of institutionalization. Rather than molding individuals who will have a keen desire to return to society as productive citizens, prison is believed by some to create a "thug mentality" and a belief that a criminal lifestyle is not only desirable, but preferable to the low-paying, low-status job that might be the only apparent available option for a person who has a criminal record. Many convicted offenders come from families with multi-generational cultures of incarceration or criminality—many relatives may have "done time." The offender's neighbors, friends, and acquaintances also may have spent time in prison. When there is a cultural norm of incarceration, its deterrent effect is diminished, and it may be perceived as either desirable—relatively safe and secure—or familiar—a place where the offender knows the rules and fits in.

▮ PRIMARY SOURCE

Earlier this year, we commended Gov. Arnold Schwarzenegger for being willing to grant parole to a greater number of the state's expanding lifer population than his predecessors.

In 2004, he agreed to release 73 lifers recommended for parole by the Board of Prison Terms, recently renamed the Board of Parole Hearings. Although still a tiny fraction of the lifer population, in a single year Schwarzenegger released 12 times more of them than Gov. Gray Davis did during his five years in office. Most had been convicted of first- or second-degree murder decades earlier.

Only 3,168 of California inmates serving life sentences are true lifers. They're the ones sentenced to life without the possibility of parole. The other 27,251 are serving "indeterminate" life sentences. That means that after serving a fixed portion of their sentence—10, 15, 25 years and so on—they are supposed to be given a chance of parole by convincing a historically tough-on-crime parole board that they are fully rehabilitated and deserve to be released.

Yet, Schwarzenegger seems to be backing off on his bold attempt to reduce the state's lifer population, which now constitutes 1 in 4 of all inmates serving life sentences in the nation, at a cost of about $1 billion a year to the California taxpayer. Through Sept. 30 of this year, he agreed to release 29 inmates of the 148 forwarded to him by the parole board, almost all of whose members he appointed. At this rate, he will have released just over half as many inmates in 2004 as in 2005.

These are inmates who, over a period of many years, have participated in a range of programs that have forced them to take responsibility for their crimes. More importantly, they have persuaded parole commissioners—none of whom can be written off as a liberal do-gooder—that they are no longer dangerous.

By contrast, non-lifer inmates serving lesser sentences, who make up the vast majority of California's overflowing prison population, are released automatically on completion of their sentences, without having to convince anyone that they are prepared for life in mainstream society. That's why two-thirds end up back in prison within three years of being released.

The apparent retreat by Schwarzenegger on releasing inmates who have committed capital crimes is undermining his public declaration that "rehabilitation" should be a major focus of the state's correctional system. In July, he even changed the name of the Department of Corrections to the Department of Corrections and Rehabilitation. "Especially at San Quentin, a flagship prison in regards to rehabilitation, you have scores of men coming who, by any set of criteria, are suitable for parole," said Father Steven Barber, the Catholic chaplain at San Quentin State Prison.

"We're not lacking in empathy for victims," said Barber. But at some point, the pain inmates have inflicted on victims and their families "has to be balanced against the number of years someone has to serve paying for it," he said. "When the punishment is satisfied, the next step in a healthy society is forgiveness, a kind of absolution."

A spokesperson for Schwarzenegger denied that his decisions regarding lifers have anything to do with politics. "The governor makes parole decisions on a case-by-case basis, bearing in mind first and foremost what is in the best interests of public safety," a spokesperson told us. But we suspect that the downward trend might be linked to Schwarzenegger's sliding popularity and the backlash his actions provoked from victims' rights groups allied with the powerful California Correctional Peace Officers Association, which represents prison guards and other prison personnel.

Earlier this year, Crime Victims United of California ran a series of television ads attacking Schwarzenegger for allegedly releasing dangerous criminals. Shortly after the ads were aired, the CCPOA staged an emotional rally on the steps of the state Capitol in April. On every side of the crowd were wall-sized displays of photos of victims of violent crime in California. "Perhaps the governor has

listened to some of our concerns," said Harriet Salerno, president of Crime Victims United.

Schwarzenegger's reversal of most of the parole board's recommendations has implications far beyond an individual inmate. It sends a discouraging message to inmates—that no matter how hard they work at rehabilitating themselves, they're unlikely ever to leave prison. "It becomes harder for us to inspire inmates and to serve public safety from the inside," says Jacques Verduin, executive director of the Insight Prison Project, which offers a range of classes in San Quentin for lifers and other inmates.

The law clearly gives lifers serving indeterminate sentences the chance to earn their release. Instead, says Keith Wattley, a staff attorney at the Prison Law Office in San Francisco, "what we have is a law that holds out the illusion of redemption, but in fact denies people any fair chance of living in a free society."

There is no avoiding the serious, often horrific, nature of the crimes committed by every lifer. But what

Adam Riojas, right, laughs in the office of Justin Brooks, left, director of the state Innocence Project, in 2004, in San Diego, California. Riojas, a convicted murderer serving fifteen years to life, was one of more than two dozen people serving possible life terms who were paroled during the first seven months of California Governor Arnold Schwarzenegger's administration. Riojas was paroled after relatives testified that his father confessed to the crime. AP IMAGES

Washington, D.C., homicide detective Mitch Credle, who volunteers as a coach for a Boys & Girls Club team, goes over strategy with his team before a game. Unfortunately, Credle too often sees many of the kids he coaches go to jail. © MARC ASNIN/CORBIS SABA

happened dozens of years ago can't be changed. What can change is the inmate. Until Californians can accept that even a murderer can transform himself or herself, our lifer population will continue to grow, hidden in prisons filled with aging and infirm inmates who no longer threaten our safety.

SIGNIFICANCE

Persons given life sentences may be imprisoned for the remainder of their natural lives without any possibility of parole. At other times, "life" can be part of an indeterminate sentence and may imply the possibility of parole at some future time, as in a sentence of "thirty years to life" for first-degree murder. A third category of life sentencing—generally called "virtual life" or "natural life"—refers to a sentence that so far exceeds the likely lifespan of the offender that parole is not possible. At times, persons are given life sentences, either with or without the possibility of future

parole, as a means of avoiding the imposition of the death penalty. In the state of California, a law popularly referred to as "three strikes and you're out," imposes a mandatory life sentence on repeat offenders who are convicted of a third adjudicated offense. In some cases, all three offenses are considered "minor" felonies involving property or other non-violent crimes. Statistics published by the Sentencing Project, as well as by the U.S. Bureau of Justice Statistics, indicate that nearly ten percent of the U.S. prison population (both federal and state) is serving a life sentence. Of those, more than twenty-five percent are serving a life sentence with no possibility of parole (in several states, all life sentences are for life without parole). This percentage has risen by nearly ten percent since the early 1990s. These statistics present an interesting dichotomy in that the incidence of reported violent crimes has decreased, while the rates at which convicted felons are receiving life sentences have increased considerably over the past two decades.

Parole boards are responsible for weighing all of the factors in an individual situation and making the fairest possible decision based upon all available information. For those with indeterminate life sentences, the possibility of return to the community is decided by a parole board, based on positive changes made by the inmate while in prison, successful efforts at rehabilitation and, perhaps, efforts to make restitution for the crime. Parole boards also consider the nature of the offender's crime, the feelings and beliefs of community members (particularly those of the victim(s) or the victim's family), the potential danger to society posed by the offender's release, the probability of lasting rehabilitation, and financial issues. The financial issues under consideration involve the expense of housing a prisoner for many decades and the increasing costs associated with the incarceration of elderly and sick prisoners.

The changes in sentencing legislation during the final decades of the twentieth century resulted in a marked increase in the amount of time that "lifers" must serve before they are eligible for parole—from about twenty-one years to an average of thirty years. These sentencing changes have led to demographic changes in the prison population as well. The number of inmates over the age of fifty in both federal and state prisons is increasing as a result of the imposition of longer prison terms.

Almost all individuals who receive sentences that approximate the duration of their natural lives have been convicted of heinous crimes; most of the felonies are violent, and the vast majority involve murder (either first- or second-degree), sexual assault, or rape. Many involve the use of weapons or resulted in great bodily harm in some way. Some of the more controversial life sentences are given to individuals who were considered conspirators or co-conspirators in the crime committed. In the case of an accessory (one who assisted in the mechanics or planning) to a crime or conspiracy, advocates would argue that this person might never have been violent and does not pose a future threat of violence to society.

There have been several, largely anecdotal, studies of the rate of recidivism among individuals paroled after serving lengthy sentences. The re-arrest rates were found to be extremely low. This is thought to be due to several factors. First, the decades spent in prison are likely to be an extremely effective deterrent to re-offending. Second, inmates may have learned marketable skills while incarcerated to transfer to the workplace outside prison. Third, individuals may have outgrown criminal or gang affiliations from their youths and matured to the point that a life of crime is no longer appealing. Fourth, these individuals may simply be too old or too infirm to be efficient criminals. One approach to effective sentencing would be the creation of a formula that determines the ideal mix of incarceration, education, and training in order to sharply reduce recidivism without costing the state and federal governments excessive amounts of money to build and staff prisons to house "lifers."

FURTHER RESOURCES

Books

Gainsborough, Jenny, and Marc Mauer. *Diminishing Returns: Crime and Incarceration in the 1990s.* Washington, D.C.: The Sentencing Project , 2000.

King, Ryan S., and Marc Mauer. *Aging Behind Bars: Three Strikes Seven Years Later.* Washington, D.C.: The Sentencing Project, 2001.

Mauer, Marc, Ryan S. King, and Malcolm C. Young. *The Meaning of "Life": Long Prison Sentences in Context.* Washington, D.C.: The Sentencing Project, 2004.

Web sites

U.S. Department of Justice. Bureau of Justice Statistics. "Criminal Sentencing Statistics." <http://www.ojp.usdoj.gov/bjs/sent.htm> (accessed February 8, 2006).

U.S. Department of Justice. Bureau of Justice Statistics. "Reentry Trends in the United States." <http://www.ojp.usdoj.gov/bjs/reentry/reentry.htm> (accessed February 8, 2006).

The Price of Low Expectations

Newspaper article

By: William Raspberry

Date: October 17, 2005

Source: William Raspberry. "The Price of Low Expectations." The *Washington Post*. (October 17, 2005): A15.

About the Author: William Raspberry is a Pulitzer-Award-winning journalist who has been writing for the *Washington Post* for more than four decades. His work has been highly acclaimed, and he has received numerous awards and honorary doctorates. His weekly column for the *Washington Post* focuses on social and political commentary. In addition to writing for the *Post*, Raspberry also teaches at Duke University.

INTRODUCTION

The per capita rate of incarceration in the United States has risen dramatically since the *tough on crime*, *war on drugs*, and *three strikes* legislation of recent decades. Not only have the incarceration rates skyrocketed, so have the apparent recidivism rates; due, in large part, to the increasing strictness of parole and probation regulations. The United States now has surpassed Russia as the country with the greatest overall percentage of prisoners, with a rate of more than 720 per 100,000. At the start of the twenty-first century, the American population was just over 295 million, with more than two million people behind bars.

According to the Bureau of Justice Statistics, at the end of 2004 there were roughly 2,136,000 people incarcerated in local, state, or federal correctional facilities. There were nearly five million more individuals on parole or probation at the same time.

There are significant racial disparities in the incarceration rates: there are roughly seven times as many African-American males as Caucasian males in the jail or prison systems in the United States, although they represent less than thirteen percent of the overall population. There are also significantly more males of color than white males, both in terms of actual numbers and by percentage of the general population, on Death Row, despite their general population statistics. Overall, about half of the entire jail or prison population is African-American. According to figures published by the Human Rights Watch, African Americans are eighty-eight times more likely to be directly involved in the correctional system than Caucasians.

On average, about one third of the African-American male population of the United States has been personally impacted by the correctional system, either because they are in local, state, or federal jail or prison, because they are on parole or probation, or because they are awaiting criminal trial or post-conviction sentencing. Not only are African-American males far more likely to be convicted of a crime, they are more likely to be stopped, questioned, detained, or arrested than their Caucasian peers, particularly if they are below the age of thirty-five.

▮ PRIMARY SOURCE

In one recent year, just under half of all young black men in the District of Columbia were in prison, on parole or probation, awaiting trial or sentencing, or being sought on a warrant. In Baltimore, one in five black men aged 20 to 30 was in custody. Numbers like these no longer surprise.

This may: "High levels of incarceration concentrated in impoverished communities have a destabilizing effect on community life, so that the most basic underpinnings of informal social control are damaged. This, in turn, reproduces the very dynamics that sustain crime." The quote, from Todd Clear, a professor of criminal justice at the City University of New York, was called to my attention by Eric Lotke, who has expanded on Clear's work.

It sums up what I was trying to say in a recent column about elephants and delinquency.

Several readers wondered if I was advocating the unleashing on hapless inner-city communities of killers, rapists, drug fiends and sex abusers as a way of providing role models for young men. (Teenage male elephants in a South African game park stopped their delinquent behavior after several adult bulls were introduced into the herd.) Wouldn't the herd (and wouldn't America's inner cities) be worse off with the introduction of adult males of certifiable bad behavior?

It's a good question, and I offer three responses.

The first is that most of the crimes that account for the post-1980 swelling of America's inmate population were nonviolent offenses: drug offenses overwhelmingly, but also petty theft, larceny, shoplifting, etc.—exacerbated by mandatory sentencing and three-strikes legislation. It's reasonable to ask whether rehabilitation efforts and non-prison punishment might be a saner way to deal with these crimes that are virtually denuding many communities of their male populations. No one is advocating the release of gangbangers, street thugs and killers.

The second response is that the men we are talking about, while they may not be paragons, are not necessarily dangers to their communities. Analogies might include members of the Mafia, who, in some cases, made their immediate communities more stable, and men like Saddam Hussein, Anastasio Somoza or Jean-Bertrand Aristide, whose removal (for whatever well-intended reasons) left their societies significantly less stable. Sometimes even good intentions can blow up in our face.

And here's the third: We are not inherently good or bad, law-abiding or criminal, but are nudged by forces both within and outside us into becoming what we become.

Some combination of forces has convinced dismaying numbers of black men that they are largely unnecessary. The society isolates them as dangerous, or potentially so; employers assume they are unreliable, without fundamental skills and unlikely to learn on the job; their neighbors fear (or admire) them as ruthless; and even the mothers of their children may not consider them fit material for husbands.

These forces include changing community values and changing attitudes toward marriage and childrearing, of course, but they also include an incarceration rate that makes spending time behind bars predictable and, as a result, removes its deterrent power. The decline in marriage strips families of their adult men; the senseless increase in incarceration strips *communities* of theirs.

Thus, fatherlessness and incarceration feed each other in a deadly symbiosis. Black leaders haven't been able to see and resist it because of their near-exclusive focus on racism as the cause of everything that goes wrong. Whites haven't seen it because of their over-weening fear of black crime. And so the downward pull of dismal expectations continues.

A few individuals are able to rise above the low expectations of others, but most of us tend to become what those around expect us to be. And if irresponsible behavior is what they expect, that's what we tend to give them. And so men who might have gone a different way in response to signals that their families and communities valued and depended on them react instead to signals that tell them they are users and takers and, at best, sperm donors.

I keep on my office wall a framed quotation from Goethe: "If you treat an individual as he is, he will stay as he is, but if you treat him as if he were what he ought to be and could be, he will become what he ought to be and could be."

Not always, of course, but maybe often enough.

SIGNIFICANCE

The racial disparities in the American penal system have far-reaching effects; people with criminal records, particularly those with felony convictions (especially violent or drug-related conviction histories) and prison histories, have a very difficult time obtaining secure jobs, particularly those with pay scales at or above the median. Because so many more African-Americans than Caucasians have criminal histories, there is a disproportionately large percentage of the population that is disenfranchised, or is unlikely to obtain gainful employment that will offer remuneration above the poverty level. As a result, a significant number of formerly incarcerated individuals (of all races) will return to the pursuit of criminal activities, particularly those involving drug sales and trafficking, as a means of making sufficient income.

In studying overall rates, there have been oft-quoted statistics that crime, especially crime that is of a violent nature, more often occurs with African-American perpetrators and victims. Demographic research indicates that crime is most likely to occur within the most impoverished and least educated segments of the populace. In the United States, there are a disproportionate number of African-Americans and other cultural minorities living within those circumstances.

Demographic data indicates that the majority of those incarcerated in the state penitentiary system have minimal educations, most have not completed high school or earned a G.E.D., and many did not finish the first six grades of school. Nearly half were unemployed (in the conventional sense) at the time of arrest, a significant number had never held any sort of regular job, or been required to adhere to a regular daily routine. Among state prisoners, there are a disproportionate number of individuals who report having experienced learning disabilities, attention difficulties, childhood diagnoses of conduct disorders or behavioral problems, and backgrounds of abuse, neglect, or out-of-home placements. These are concerns associated with extreme poverty and lack of family support, rather than with any particular culture, ethnicity, or race.

According to data published by the United States Commission on Civil Rights, about one in fifteen youthful Caucasian males have been involved with the American penal system in some fashion—whether incarcerated, awaiting sentencing, under adjudication, or on parole or probation. The rate climbs to one in ten for young Hispanic males, and further rises to one in three for African-American male youth (young adults). This same group (United States Commission on Civil Rights) states that nearly eight in ten male African-Americans will be arrested at some point in their lives. Civil Rights groups assert that the large disparity between African-American and Caucasian incarceration percentages is due, in part, to social perceptions. There is believed to be an ingrained stereotype that African-Americans, particularly males, are more aggressive, threatening, and prone to criminal violence than their Caucasian counterparts. Prison and judicial system research reports indicate that, on average, African-American males receive more serious convictions and harsher sentences than do Caucasians who commit the same crimes. African-American males are far more likely to receive the death sentence than Caucasian males. Regardless of the race of the perpetrator, those who commit capital offenses are far more likely to receive the death penalty if the victim was Caucasian.

Perhaps the most telling statistics, from the perspective of racial bias, occur in the realm of youthful offenders: young black males are more than twice as likely to bypass the juvenile justice system and be sent to prison on a first offense as their Caucasian peers. Among all of the youthful offenders who are arrested and criminally charged (non drug-related crimes), African-American males are more than six times as likely to receive a prison sentence and be incarcerated in an adult correctional facility than are Caucasian males. For very young first offenders, African-Americans are nearly ten times more likely than Caucasian males to be remanded to juvenile detention facilities. For drug-related, non-violent charges, very young African-American males are nearly fifty times more likely than Caucasian youths to be remanded to juvenile detention facilities. Not only are the expectations exceedingly low for African-Americans (particularly young males), the penalties for criminal activity may be overwhelmingly high.

FURTHER RESOURCES

Books

The System in Black and White: Exploring the Connections Between Race, Crime, and Justice, edited by Michael W. Markowitz and Delores D. Jones-Brown. Westport, Conn.: Praeger Publishers, 2000.

Weich, Ronald, and Carlos Angulo. *Justice on Trial: Racial Disparities in the American Criminal Justice System*. Washington, D.C.: Leadership Conference on Civil Rights, 2000.

Web sites

The Black Commentator. "Mass Incarceration is an Abomination." <http://www.blackcommentator.com/147/147_cover_incarceration.html> (accessed March 5, 2006).

Bureau of Justice Statistics. "Prison Statistics: Summary Findings." <http://www.ojp.usdoj.gov/bjs/prisons.htm> (accessed March 5, 2006).

Human Rights Watch. "Racism, Racial Discrimination, Xenophobia and All Forms of Discrimination." <http://www.hri.ca/racism/Submitted/Author/humanrightswatch.shtml> (accessed March 5, 2006).

U.S. Commission on Civil Rights. "Highlights." <http://www.usccr.gov/index.html> (accessed March 5, 2006).

The Washington Post Writer's Group. "William Raspberry." <http://www.postwritersgroup.com/raspberry.htm> (accessed March 5, 2006).

McMartin Preschooler: "I Lied"

Newspaper article

By: Kyle Zirpolo and Debbie Nathan

Date: October 30, 2005

Source: Zirpolo, Kyle, and Debbie Nathan. "McMartin Preschooler: 'I Lied.' *Los Angeles Times* (October 30, 2005).

About the Author: Kyle Zirpolo is a California grocery store manager. As a child, he was involved in the McMartin Preschool child molestation case. He testified at the grand jury hearing that brought the initial indictments against most of the center's staff, but was not a witness at any of the trial proceedings. Now a parent himself, Zirpolo has admitted he made false accusations and offered fabricated testimony as a child.

INTRODUCTION

The McMartin Preschool case is unique in American history. The investigation and trial lasted for nearly seven years, the longest on record; it cost more than $15 million taxpayer dollars; and when it was all over, no convictions were handed down, although Raymond Buckey had served five years in prison, and his mother Peggy had been incarcerated for nearly three. It was also among the earliest multivictim–multioffender (MVMO) cases.

Ultimately, hundreds of children were involved in questioning, examinations (both physical and psychological), and in trial testimony. It launched what appeared to be a chain reaction of MVMO and child sexual abuse cases involving preschools and day care centers across the country over the next decade. Among the many startling revelations of the McMartin Preschool trial and cases like it was that children's memories can be strongly and easily influenced.

The psychological examiners in the original case were from a behavioral health firm called the Children's Institute International (CII). To coerce the subjects into giving desired responses, they asked leading questions, telling those being interrogated that other children from the preschool had already revealed abuses. "Correct" answers were then rewarded in various ways. Ultimately, more than 350 children were deemed to have been abused. A physician examined

Peggy McMartin Buckey and Raymond Buckey confer during their 1990 trial. Their lawyer Dean Gits, sits between them. AP IMAGES

150 of them and concluded that about 120 had been victimized, despite the lack of any physical evidence.

The accusations were eventually leveled at more than 100 teachers and staff at a church and eight other preschools and day care centers in the Manhattan Beach, California, area. Seven adults—the McMartin Preschool owners, four teachers, and Raymond Buckey—were charged with more than 200 counts of child abuse involving forty or more children. In 1986 the district attorney dropped charges against all the adults involved except Peggy McMartin Buckey and her son Raymond. Evidence was presented for more than three years in their criminal trials. By early 1990 Peggy Buckey had been acquitted of all charges; Raymond was acquitted on all but thirteen counts, retried on some of them, and ultimately acquitted as well.

In the end, nine preschools and day care centers went out of business, and the lives and professional reputations of those accused or prosecuted were enormously affected. Legal costs were devastating, and even worse for those who went to trial. Peggy McMartin Buckey and Raymond Buckey spent years in prison before being acquitted, and will suffer repercussions of their incarceration for the rest of their lives.

After the McMartin case, there was a barrage of MVMO cases against preschool and day care centers across the United States, all with similarly sensational accusations. Those wrongly accused with molestation or child sexual abuse suffered professional and financial losses—since it is extremely difficult to obtain employment in a child care or service-related field subsequent after such an accusation, regardless of its veracity, since acquittal is not always synonymous with exoneration.

PRIMARY SOURCE

"McMartin Pre-Schooler: 'I Lied'"

A long-delayed apology from one of the accusers in the notorious McMartin Preschool molestation case.

My mother divorced my father when I was 2 and she met my stepfather, who was a police officer in Manhattan Beach. They had five children after me. In addition, my stepfather has three older children. In the combined family, I'm the only one of the nine children he didn't father. I always remember wanting him to love me. I was always trying excessively hard to please him. I would do anything for him.

My stepbrothers and stepsisters and a half-brother and half-sister went to McMartin. So did I. I only remember being happy there. I never had any bad feeling about the school—no bad auras or vibes or anything. Even to this day, talking about it or seeing pictures or artwork that I did at McMartin never brings any bad feelings. All my memories are positive.

The thing I remember about the case was how it took over the whole city and consumed our whole family. My parents would ask questions: "Did the teachers ever do things to you?" They talked about Ray Buckey, whom I had never met. I don't even have any recollection of him attending the school when I was going there.

The first time I went to CII [Children's Institute International, now known as Children's Institute, Inc., a respected century-old L.A. County child welfare organization where approximately 400 former McMartin children were interviewed and given genital exams, and where many were diagnosed as abuse victims], we drove there, our whole family. I remember waiting . . . for hours while my brothers and sisters were being interviewed. I don't remember how many days or if it was just one day, but my memory tells me it was weeks, it seemed so long. It was an ordeal. I remember thinking to myself, "I'm not going to get out of here unless I tell them what they want to hear."

We were examined by a doctor. I took my clothes off and lay down on the table. They checked my butt, my penis. There was a room with a lot of toys and stuffed animals and dolls. The dolls were pasty white and had hair where the private parts were. They wanted us to take off their clothes. It was just really weird.

I remember them asking extremely uncomfortable questions about whether Ray touched me and about all the teachers and what they did—and I remember telling them nothing happened to me. I remember them almost giggling and laughing, saying, "Oh, we know these things happened to you. Why don't you just go ahead and tell us? Use these dolls if you're scared.

Anytime I would give them an answer that they didn't like, they would ask again and encourage me to give them the answer they were looking for. It was really obvious what they wanted. I know the types of language they used on me: things like I was smart, or I could help the other kids who were scared.

I felt uncomfortable and a little ashamed that I was being dishonest. But at the same time, being the type of person I was, whatever my parents wanted me to do, I would do. And I thought they wanted me to help protect my little brother and sister who went to McMartin.

Later my parents asked if the teachers took pictures and played games with us. Games like "Naked Movie Star." I remember my mom asking me. She would ask if they sang the song, and I didn't know what she was talking about, so she would sing something like, "Who you are, you're a naked movie star." I'm pretty sure that's the first time I ever heard that: from my mom. After she asked me a hundred times, I probably said yeah, I did play that game.

The lawyers had all my stories written down and knew exactly what I had said before. So I knew I would have to say those exact things again and not have anything be different, otherwise they would know I was lying. I put a lot of pressure on myself. At night in bed, I would think hard about things I had said in the past and try to repeat only the things I knew I'd said before.

I'm not saying nothing happened to anyone else at the McMartin Pre-School. I can't say that—I can only speak for myself. Maybe some things did happen. Maybe some kids made up stories about things that didn't really happen, and eventually started believing they were telling the truth. Maybe some got scared that the teachers would get their families because they were lying. But I never forgot I was lying.

But the lying really bothered me. One particular night stands out in my mind. I was maybe 10 years old and I tried to tell my mom that nothing had happened. I lay on the bed crying hysterically—I wanted to get it off my chest, to tell her the truth. My mother kept asking me to please tell her what was the matter. I said she would never believe me. She persisted: "I promise I'll believe you! I love you so much! Tell me what's bothering you!" This went on for a long time: I told her she wouldn't believe me, and she kept assuring me she would. I remember finally telling her, "Nothing happened! Nothing ever happened to me at that school."

She didn't believe me.

SIGNIFICANCE

False accusations damage the accused, the accuser, and anyone who encourages the accusations. During the height of the MVMO cases in the 1980s and early 1990s, those gathering data for the cases asked children leading and targeted questions, such as: We already know that you were forced to play the horsey game, because all of the other children have told us. Tell me what room you were in when she made you take off your clothes and play it. It was also quite common to ask the same or substantially similar questions repeatedly until the desired responses were given.

At that time it was believed that children were uncomfortable disclosing abuse by trusted adults, and that they would try to hide or deny its occurrence. Children were thought unlikely to lie under oath, and that memories were fairly concrete—that is, they were unlikely to change over time and weren't particularly affected by suggestion.

Although research supports the desire of children to tell the truth, even more indicates that memories can be implanted, or created; that they will take cues from the words and emotions of trusted adults; that they have trouble distinguishing the boundary between reality and fantasy; and have only a limited understanding of the absolute nature of truth. Cornell University Psychology Professor Steven Ceci, in his work on the suggestibility of children in the realm of false allegations of sexual abuse, has concluded that children can not only be influenced to incorporate false memories, but are likely to broaden and deepen them over time, adding improbable details as they reinforce the created "memory."

Another prevalent belief among the investigators at that time, explicitly stated in court and public records, was that they fully believed that the abuse had, in fact, occurred. Several said that the children could only begin to heal if they detailed the explicit and graphic nature of the abuse perpetrated upon them and did their part to ensure that those who had allegedly committed these acts would be punished and never again allowed work with children.

Truthful testimony is difficult for young children who are questioned in a directed or coercive manner. They may testify to a memory that has been "given" to them by directed and repeated questioning, then reinforced by praise and rewards over time. This makes them compelling, if not accurate, witnesses. One of the most critical elements in the MVMO abuse allegation cases is the manner in which the information was initially elicited: In virtually every instance, an adult suspected abuse and questioned the child, who initially denied any sexual abuse. Far more credible is the situation in which a child comes to a trusted adult and spontaneously details abuse or mistreatment without being led in any way. It has now become standard practice to audio- and videotape interviews with alleged abuse victims, to ascertain that they have not been led or coerced.

The effect of false accusations is both enormous and long-lasting. Many wrongfully accused defendants have been made to stand trial, erroneously convicted or imprisoned, lost visitation or custody of their children (particularly in acrimonious divorce and child custody battles), been financially devastated by legal costs; lost jobs or livelihoods as a result of allegations or convictions—even though they have been exonerated or had their records expunged.

It is quite likely that the young accusers from the MVMO cases during the last two decades of the twentieth century will live not knowing if they were actually victims of heinous child sexual abuse, believe that they were irrevocably harmed, or bear the burden of knowing that they falsely accused trusted adults of behavior that did not occur. When it comes to false accusations, everyone involved suffers.

FURTHER RESOURCES

Books

Bjorklund, David J. *False-Memory Creation in Children and Adults: Theory, Research, and Implications.* Mahwah, New Jersey: Lawrence Erlbaum Associates, 2000.

Tong, Dean. *Elusive Innocence: A Survival Guide for the Falsely Accused.* Lafayette, Louisiana: Huntington House Publishers, 2001.

Baker, Robert A., ed. *Child Sexual Abuse and False Memory Syndrome.* Amherst, New York: Prometheus Books, 1998.

Campbell, Terence W. *Smoke and Mirrors: The Devastating Effect of False Sexual Abuse Claims.* New York, New York: Insight Books, 1998.

Web sites

PBS Online. Frontline. " Innocence Lost: The Plea. Other Well-Known Cases Involving Child Abuse in Day Care Settings." <http://www.pbs.org/wgbh/pages/frontline/shows/innocence/etc/other.html#3> (accessed February 9, 2006).

CIA Holds Terror Suspects in Secret Prisons

Newspaper article

By: Dana Priest

Date: November 2, 2005

Source: Priest, Dana. "CIA Holds Terror Suspects in Secret Prisons." *Washington Post* (November 2, 2005), A01.

About the Author: Dana Priest reports on national security for the *Washington Post*. She previously served as an investigative reporter, writing about the military, and as the correspondent to the Pentagon. She is the author of the book, *The Mission: Waging War and Keeping Peace with America's Military*, published by W.W. Norton and Company in 2003.

INTRODUCTION

The United States government's war on terrorism began following the attacks of September 11, 2001, on the World Trade Center in New York, and on the Pentagon in Virginia. As part of the government's efforts to put an end to this global threat, the CIA implemented a number of classified programs to uncover information regarding potential future terrorist acts, including holding individuals perceived to be a threat within a network of secret prisons around the world. These prisoners were hidden away and interrogated without the knowledge of the public or of the majority of government officials, including the United States Congress, which is in charge of monitoring the CIA's covert activities. The existence of these hidden prisons came to light only when it was revealed that interrogations of the prisoners held in some U.S. prison facilities abroad included mistreatment and torture, and that the conditions in the prisons themselves were far below those considered to be humane.

▮ PRIMARY SOURCE

The CIA has been hiding and interrogating some of its most important al Qaeda captives at a Soviet-era compound in Eastern Europe, according to U.S. and foreign officials familiar with the arrangement.

The secret facility is part of a covert prison system set up by the CIA nearly four years ago that at various times has included sites in eight countries, including Thai-

land, Afghanistan and several democracies in Eastern Europe, as well as a small center at the Guantanamo Bay prison in Cuba, according to current and former intelligence officials and diplomats from three continents.

The hidden global internment network is a central element in the CIA's unconventional war on terrorism. It depends on the cooperation of foreign intelligence services, and on keeping even basic information about the system secret from the public, foreign officials and nearly all members of Congress charged with overseeing the CIA's covert actions.

The existence and locations of the facilities—referred to as "black sites" in classified White House, CIA, Justice Department and congressional documents—are known to only a handful of officials in the United States and, usually, only to the president and a few top intelligence officers in each host country....

But the revelations of widespread prisoner abuse in Afghanistan and Iraq by the U.S. military—which operates under published rules and transparent oversight of Congress—have increased concern among lawmakers, foreign governments and human rights groups about the opaque CIA system. Those concerns escalated last month, when Vice President Cheney and CIA Director Porter J. Goss asked Congress to exempt CIA employees from legislation already endorsed by 90 senators that would bar cruel and degrading treatment of any prisoner in U.S. custody.

Although the CIA will not acknowledge details of its system, intelligence officials defend the agency's approach, arguing that the successful defense of the country requires that the agency be empowered to hold and interrogate suspected terrorists for as long as necessary and without restrictions imposed by the U.S. legal system or even by the military tribunals established for prisoners held at Guantanamo Bay....

The secret detention system was conceived in the chaotic and anxious first months after the Sept. 11, 2001, attacks, when the working assumption was that a second strike was imminent....

It is illegal for the government to hold prisoners in such isolation in secret prisons in the United States, which is why the CIA placed them overseas, according to several former and current intelligence officials and other U.S. government officials. Legal experts and intelligence officials said that the CIA's internment practices also would be considered illegal under the laws of several host countries, where detainees have rights to have a lawyer or to mount a defense against allegations of wrongdoing.

Host countries have signed the U.N. Convention Against Torture and Other Cruel, Inhuman or Degrading

Treatment or Punishment, as has the United States. Yet CIA interrogators in the overseas sites are permitted to use the CIA's approved "Enhanced Interrogation Techniques," some of which are prohibited by the U.N. convention and by U.S. military law. They include tactics such as "waterboarding," in which a prisoner is made to believe he or she is drowning.

Some detainees apprehended by the CIA and transferred to foreign intelligence agencies have alleged after their release that they were tortured, although it is unclear whether CIA personnel played a role in the alleged abuse. Given the secrecy surrounding CIA detentions, such accusations have heightened concerns among foreign governments and human rights groups about CIA detention and interrogation practices....

DEALS WITH 2 COUNTRIES

Among the first steps was to figure out where the CIA could secretly hold the captives. One early idea was to keep them on ships in international waters, but that was discarded for security and logistics reasons....

The CIA program's original scope was to hide and interrogate the two dozen or so al Qaeda leaders believed to be directly responsible for the Sept. 11 attacks, or who posed an imminent threat, or had knowledge of the larger al Qaeda network. But as the volumes of leads pouring into the CTC from abroad increased, and the capacity of its paramilitary group to seize suspects grew, the CIA began apprehending more people whose intelligence value and links to terrorism were less certain, according to four current and former officials.

Several former and current intelligence officials, as well as several other U.S. government officials with knowledge of the program, express frustration that the White House and the leaders of the intelligence community have not made it a priority to decide whether the secret internment program should continue in its current form, or be replaced by some other approach....

SIGNIFICANCE

The abuse of prisoners held in Iraq, Afghanistan, and Guantanamo Bay, raised the question of what type of actions the U.S. government was prepared to implement and/or condone in the name of uncovering information regarding terrorist activity. Even as the conditions at Guantanamo and Abu Ghraib were publicized, the U.S. government refused to discuss their special "black sites," the top secret prisons that have been established in a number of foreign countries with the cooperation of those nations' senior leaders. The CIA's initial goal was to interrogate approximately two

A Romanian military staff member stands in a doorway on the Mihail Kogalniceanu airbase, 2005. The Soviet-era facility has become a key focus of a European investigation into allegations that the CIA operated secret prisons where suspected terrorists were interrogated. AP IMAGES

dozen Al Qaeda leaders that were suspected of direct involvement with the September 11 attacks, but the numbers grew as the CIA continued to detain individuals suspected of having even the smallest connection to terrorist factions. Because these prison facilities were kept hidden, personnel were at liberty to use whatever methods they deemed appropriate, and were not held accountable for their actions. Individuals were held for months at a time on no more than the vaguest suspicion of terrorist activities, without access to legal counsel or even to basic human comforts. After their release, some claimed to have been tortured, and it was unclear whether United States personnel were at fault.

Congress, foreign governments, and various human rights organizations around the world have been forced to question the actions of the CIA—the body ultimately responsible for establishing these secret prison camps—as a result of the treatment of the prisoners. The CIA's response, however, was that the war on terrorism gave them the right to implement special tactics when dealing with potential terrorists. These tactics included holding prisoners for indefinite periods of time, despite lack of definitive evidence against them, and ignoring certain strictures set down for the treatment of prisoners, both during war time and in peace. Yet, imprisoning suspects in this manner would be illegal in the United States, which is why the CIA went to the effort of establishing prisons abroad. Both the White House and the CIA encouraged Congress to assist them in maintaining their silence regarding their techniques in the war on terrorism, citing national security as their reason for refusing to divulge further information. They even went so far as to request that CIA employees not be held to the guidelines regarding the decent treatment of prisoners.

The governments of most civilized nations, in accordance with United Nations Convention Against Torture, have an agreed upon set of rules that govern the manner in which prisoners of war must be treated, regardless of any crimes committed by those prisoners. These rules ensure that prisoners are held in humane conditions and that they are not tortured as part of any questioning they might undergo. Pain is not considered an acceptable tool in gaining information or a confession from a prisoner of war. The premise is that, even during a war, people cannot be allowed to use any means at their disposal to achieve their goals, because if they do, they risk becoming as lawless as the evils against which they are fighting. It is not just a question of the legality of the system, but the morality of it. Do extreme instances of violence, such as terrorist attacks that kill innocent civilians, excuse the use of radical methods in order to obtain information about similar potential events? Or does use of extreme force against possible enemy threats simply reduce everyone concerned to the same level of behavior? Should an alleged terrorist be stripped of his human rights based on his own actions?

Regardless of the legitimacy of the CIA's actions in keeping these foreign prisons a secret, investigations into U.S. personnel and their behavior in Guantanamo Bay and Abu Ghraib uncovered inhumane conditions and treatment of prisoners. As a result, U.S. government officials have been forced to reassess the efficacy and morality of this particular aspect of the war on terrorism.

FURTHER RESOURCES

Periodicals

Harding, Luke. "After Abu Ghraib." *The Guardian* (September 20, 2004).

Hersh, Seymour M. "The Gray Zone: How a Secret Pentagon Program Came to Abu Ghraib." *The New Yorker* (May 24, 2004).

Web sites

PBS. "Washington Week." <http://www.pbs.org/weta/washingtonweek/aroundthetable/priest.html> (accessed January 14, 2006).

Heavy Hand of the Secret Police Impeding Reform in Arab World

Newspaper article

By: Neil MacFarquhar

Date: November 14, 2005

Source: Neil MacFarquhar. "Heavy Hand of the Secret Police Impeding Reform in Arab World." The *New York Times* (November 14, 2005): A-1. <http://www.nytimes.com/2005/11/14/international/middleeast/14jordan.html?> (accessed March 10, 2006).

About the Author: Neil MacFarquhar is a veteran foreign correspondent currently writing for the *New York Times* and has operated as a correspondent in the Middle East for more than twelve years, including five years as the Cairo bureau chief. He studied at Stanford University and is fluent in Arabic and French. During the prelude to the Gulf War, MacFarquhar occupied a hotel in Dhahran, Saudi Arabia for seven months, and wrote the book *The Sand Café* about the experience.

INTRODUCTION

In 1916, the French and British entered into a secret agreement to divide the Ottoman Empire into French and British-administered areas. The understanding partitioned Turkey, Syria, Lebanon, Iraq, and Palestine into mandates ruled by the European powers. A year later, in 1917, the League of Nations agreed to the Balfour Declaration, which called for the creation of a Jewish state in the British-mandated region of Palestine. These two agreements put into motion the creation of the modern Arab world. France controlled mandates over Syria and Lebanon and

Egyptian activists shout during a 2005 demonstration in Cairo calling for the release of detained banned Muslim Brotherhood members, who were among hundreds detained in a crackdown by Egypt's secret police on the opposition movement during protests earlier in the year. Arabic slogans read "We are coming with our dreams." AP IMAGES

Great Britain administered mandates over Palestine, Iraq, and Transjordan (today known as Jordan). Britain placed into power the sons of the Sharif in Mecca in an effort to pacify the Arabs over the Jewish question. Many ethnic groups, such as the Kurds, sought the creation of their own nation-states. However, European interests did not allow for this and as a result led to several ethnically blended countries. At the close of World War II, France and Britain began to withdraw their influence over the Arab states. As a result, countries such as Syria, Lebanon, and Iraq would encounter ethnically motivated security issues in the decades that followed.

In the development of independent nation-states, many Arab countries chose to create a *mukhabarat* (meaning "intelligence") department as a branch of their government. In Egypt, the Mukhabarat al-Aama or Al-Mukhabarat al-Ammah operate to gather gen-

eral intelligence and security services. In Jordan, the Dairat al Mukhabarat functions as the intelligence branch of the government. In Syria, Idarat al-Mukhabarat al-Amma operates as the intelligence and security service.

Although many Arab states operate as republics, basic freedoms such as speech and assembly are not afforded to citizens and the utilization of respective mukhabarat services are often a result of the ethnic turmoil within the states and neighboring states. Lebanon, for example, has operated under the influence of Syria for decades following a bloody struggle between Christians and Muslims. As a result, the Syrian Idarat al-Mukhabarat al-Amma has operated within Lebanon. A report by Human Rights Watch explains the "disappearance" of Lebanese men at the hands of the security service. Plain-clothed Syrian operatives seize individuals without providing detainees or their families with an official or written explanation or detention order.

In Iraq, before the U.S.-led coalition invasion, the mukhabarat functioned as the strongest element of the state security system. Operating under the Ministry of Internal Affairs, the agency was tasked with overseeing the police networks and state institutions. The organization consisted of both internal security and external security. However, after the 1990 Gulf War, much of the agency's focus surrounded anti-regime activities.

Egypt's Nasser established the security service. Under Nasser, this service used intrusive tactics to deter public meetings perceived as unfriendly to the government. Under Anwar Sadat, however, the agencies loosened their tactics. However, this led to the surprise assassination of Sadat and unrest during the late 1980s led by radical Islamists. The size of the intelligence force is unknown. However, the group is known to monitor opposition politicians, political activists, foreign diplomats, subversives, and journalists.

PRIMARY SOURCE

HEAVY HAND OF THE SECRET POLICE IMPEDING REFORM IN ARAB WORLD

At a cultural festival last year, Sameer al-Qudah recited a poem of his depicting Arab rulers as a notch below pirates and highwaymen on the scale of honorable professions. Within days, Jordan's intelligence police summoned him.

Mr. Qudah, sentenced to a year in jail for a similar offense in 1996, was apprehensive but not surprised. The secret police, or mukhabarat in Arabic, is one of the most powerful and ubiquitous forces in the Arab world. Jordan's network had surreptitiously videotaped his reading.

"We are hungry for freedoms like the right to express ourselves," said Mr. Qudah, 35, whose day job is supervising construction projects as a civil engineer. "But our country lives under the fist of the mukhabarat."

In Jordan and across the region, those seeking democratic reform say the central role of each country's secret police force, with its stealthy, octopuslike reach, is one of the biggest impediments. In the decades since World War II, as military leaders and monarchs smothered democratic life, the security agencies have become a law unto themselves.

Last week's terror attacks in Amman accentuate one reason that even some Jordanians who consider themselves reformers justify the secret police's blanket presence—the fear that violence can spill across the border.

But others argue that the mukhabarat would be more effective if it narrowed its scope to its original mandate of ensuring security.

"The department has become so big that its ability to concentrate is diluted," said Labib Kamhawi, a businessman active in human rights. "The fact that the intelligence is involved in almost everything on the political and economic level, as well as security, might have loosened its grip on security."

In Jordan, one of the region's most liberal countries, the intelligence agencies vet the appointment of every university professor, ambassador and important editor. The mukhabarat eavesdrops with the help of evidently thousands of Jordanians on its payroll, similar to the informant networks in the Soviet bloc.

The secret police chiefs live above the law. The last head of the Jordanian mukhabarat routinely overruled the smoking ban on Royal Jordanian Airways, lighting up as he pleased. No one dared challenge him.

The State Department's annual human rights report, unusually critical of a staunch ally, particularly one that offers widespread cooperation on terrorism issues, said the lack of accountability within the mukhabarat and the police resulted "in a climate of impunity" and underscored "significant restrictions on freedom of speech, press, assembly and association." It said the agents "sometimes abuse detainees physically and verbally" and "allegedly also use torture."

Although the Bush administration has cited the need for democratic change in the Middle East as a reason for going to war in Iraq, the threat of instability on Jordan's border may actually be restricting democratic freedoms there.

Even with the bombings in Amman as the latest reminder of the threats to Jordan's security, many activists deem progress impossible unless the influence of the mukhabarat is curbed.

"The issue of security has become a nightmare," Mr. Kamhawi said, contending that Jordan had failed to find the balance between democracy and security. "If you give a speech against the policy of the government, this is a threat to security. If you demonstrate against this or that, it is a threat to security. It hits on all aspects of life and it is a severe hindrance to any change."

Getting a senior mukhabarat officer to speak to a journalist is extremely rare. The Jordanian mukhabarat made the head of its domestic affairs branch available for this article on condition that he not be identified, but what he said offered meager insight into the agency's inner workings.

"There is no freedom like that in Jordan," he said with enthusiasm in Arabic. "You are a free man in a free country."

However, Mahmoud A. al-Kharabsheh, a maverick member of Parliament who joined the mukhabarat in 1974 and retired as its head in 1991, spoke candidly. The mukhabarat, he said, runs Jordan's politics.

"Some Parliament members allow the mukhabarat to intervene in how they vote because they depend on them for help in getting re-elected," he said. "They enter into 90 percent of the political decisions in this country."

Keeping Watch

Omnipresent secret police exist in every Arab country. Indeed, mukhabarat (pronounced moo-kah-bah-RAHT) is among the first Arabic words expatriates learn, particularly reporters.

This reporter's experience in Egypt is telling:

Once in late 2001, I was loitering outside the Cairo headquarters of the secret police, an unfamiliar building, and was detained. My Egyptian assistant and I were ushered into the office of a polite major, whose walls were hung with roughly 10 diplomas from the F.B.I., including one for interrogation.

"Is this an interrogation?" I asked.

"No, it's just tea," the major responded, grinning.

After a brief, friendly conversation about my impressions of Egypt, we were released.

But in the years since, whenever I was involved in any reporting in Egypt that state security considered dubious, the major would call to inquire.

In Jordan, interviews over three weeks recently with dozens of people—including members of Parliament, former ministers, journalists, professional association leaders and businessmen—turned up tales of frequent encounters with the secret police.

Muhammad Atiyeh, 51, described two encounters, the first after he undertook the seemingly innocuous task of trying to set up an organization of single parents. The group was denied a license, he said, then the Ministry of the Interior's security arm rejected him as president for seven months.

The organization "had nothing to do with politics, and yet they interfered," said Mr. Atiyeh, who thinks Jordanian citizens should have a right to know what their secret police files contain. "I have never done anything against the society or the government or the regime, so I am still waiting for someone to explain why."

In another incident, Mr. Atiyeh and a few friends, in a puckish mood on a winter weekend in 2004, decided to decorate a stretch of exterior wall at his house with graffiti.

One man wrote a line from the Constitution stating that that personal freedom is protected. Another wrote, "Love is immeasurable." A third scrawled, "Life comes first." Mr. Atiyeh himself wrote an Arab proverb about the absence of choice.

Three days later, the phone rang. The secret police summoned him and ultimately ordered him to paint over the graffiti because it might be "misinterpreted."

In a recent poll by the Center for Strategic Studies at the University of Jordan, more than 80 percent of the respondents said they feared criticizing the government publicly. More than three quarters said they feared taking part in any political activity.

Jordan has never been a police state on the gory scale of neighbors like Iraq, and it is not surprising to find Jordanians who feel they can speak openly about political issues. But for most Jordanians, the mukhabarat remains a source of fear. Some Jordanians avoid uttering the word, whispering "the friends" instead.

Maj. Gen. Rouhi Hikmet Rasheed, a 33-year army veteran and former top military dentist, ran for Parliament in 2003 on a platform calling for a constitutional monarchy. His campaign drew the attention of the head of the mukhabarat, Maj. Gen. Saad Kheir, who warned him to stop, Dr. Rasheed said.

"He told me that if I meant we should have a monarch like Britain's, this is not in the best interests of the country," Dr. Rasheed, 62, now a Parliament member, recalled. He was shocked by what came next: "He said, 'You are a son of the regime, we trust you, but if your sons want to work in Jordan in the future, it might affect them.'"

General Kheir declined a written request for an interview, and the senior mukhabarat official interviewed for this article said he was unaware of such a call.

Poetry and Politics

Mr. Qudah, the poet, said the secret police summoned him for the first time in high school. His offense was helping to lead a 1988 protest against the death of Khalil al-Wazir, a Palestinian guerrilla leader assassinated by Israeli commandos in Tunis.

But he notes that there are far worse places in the region than Jordan. "It's not that we are better than the countries around us," he said. "We are just less bad."

Mr. Qudah was born in 1970 in Ajloun, about 30 miles north of the capital, into a sprawling east Jordanian tribal clan. The oldest of nine children, he remembers his first poem was an ode to the snow falling on the local reservoir that fed the surrounding orchards of apples, figs and olives.

Mr. Qudah's political education started in grade school, when he was particularly engaged by the history lessons surrounding the 1916 Sykes-Picot agreement, the British-French pact that divided the Arab world into separate countries and laid the groundwork for a Jewish homeland.

He said he eventually absorbed every history book in the school library, and grew up yearning for a pan-Arab state. Unlike many native Jordanians, Mr. Qudah takes no issue with Palestinian refugees settling here permanently.

Expressing topical ideas through poetry is an Arab tradition. Criticism of Jordan's stagnant political situation always brings an enthusiastic crowd response, Mr. Qudah notes. "It is like music, you are making a speech but in a musical way."

It also brings another kind of attention. As an undergraduate, he said, the mukhabarat questioned him 20 times after poetry recitals critical of the government.

Still, he notes, "you cannot form a political party by reciting poetry," something he would like to do to push for bigger, specific demands, like appointing the prime minister from among elected members of Parliament, rather than by the king.

Political parties were banned here for decades. Most are legal again, but are either religious or promote failed ideologies like Baathism, a vision of a secular Arab renaissance hijacked by the likes of Saddam Hussein and Hafez al-Assad.

The personal costs of any serious organizing effort hobbles reformers, Mr. Qudah and others said.

"If you work in the daylight you might be imprisoned for a year or two, but you can still come back and work," Mr. Qudah said about overt political organizing. "But to work in the daylight you have to be very persuasive, serious, honest, and you can't quit as soon as the government offers temptations, so you compromise."

Today, the drab headquarters of six major professional associations are the hub of Jordan's unofficial opposition, a role the government has sought to curb by writing a draft law that bans their political activity. The proposed law was heavily criticized by Human Rights Watch as a step backward for democratic change. For the moment, the building is still a host of endless political seminars. On a recent night, the minister of political development showed up to discuss reform. Participants mocked his ministry as an absurd example of the top-down attempts to change the system that are doomed for lack of public participation.

Still, Mr. Qudah says he wants to change the reality that most Arabs have no say in how their countries are run. Nor can such reforms be held hostage by the likely deranged types who carry out terrorist attacks like those here last week, he believes. Good security is a separate issue.

"Why does this part of the world lack any kind of democratic practices?" he asked. "To respect your own intelligence means you cannot accept the way things are, you cannot live with the official lie that all is well in the Arab world."

SIGNIFICANCE

As democracy begins to flourish in the Middle East, Western powers have begun to place pressure on Arab states to loosen the oppressive tactics used by security services on citizens. In May 2005, King Abdullah II removed Saad Kheir from his position as director-general of the General Intelligence Department (GID). Kheir held the position for over four years and Abdullah replaced him with career intelligence officer Lieutenant General Samih Asfoura, a U.S.-trained counterintelligence specialist. Sahmoud Kharabshed, an independent member of the Jordanian Parliament, stated after the change in leadership, "Security must not dictate politics…the GID has expanded their jurisdiction to politics beyond their security roles. They have interfered in appointments and the decisions of governments." The move was seen as a shift in government policies that would encourage privatizations and foreign investment.

Following the assassination of former Prime Minister Rafiq Hariri, several of Lebanon's security chiefs resigned. The demise of these leaders, generally operating under Syrian influence, were seen as a weakening of Syrian control over the country and a victory for the pro-democracy movement in Lebanon.

FURTHER RESOURCES

Periodicals

Blanche, Ed. "Arab Intelligence Services in the Crosshairs." *Middle East* (June 2005).

Web sites

BBC. "The Sykes-Picot Agreement." <http://news.bbc.co.uk/1/hi/in_depth/middle_east/2001/israel_and_the_palestinians/key_documents/1681362.stm> (accessed March 10, 2006).

Federation of American Scientists (FAS). "Egypt: Intelligence Agencies." <http://www.fas.org/irp/world/egypt/index.html> (accessed March 10, 2006).

GlobalSecurity.org. "Iraqi Intelligence Services." <http://www.globalsecurity.org/intell/world/iraq/mukhabarat.htm> (accessed March 10, 2006).

Human Rights Watch. "The Methodology of Enforced Disappearances in Lebanon." <http://www.hrw.org/reports/1997/syria/Syria-04.htm> (accessed March 10, 2006).

Recent Firearms Research

Internet article

By: David Hemenway

Date: December 19, 2005

Source: http://www.hsph.harvard.edu/hicrc/Firearms.htm

About the Author: Dr. David Hemenway is the director of the Harvard Injury Control Research Center upon whose website the review below was published. His research in the area of injury prevention has covered motor vehicle injury, falls, fractures, suicide and child abuse. He is currently looking at gun injuries and related issues, such as firearm storage practices, the costs and benefits of gun ownership and the relationship between the number of guns and gun-related homicide, suicide and accidental death.

INTRODUCTION

Guns—or firearms—can be used legitimately and safely in sport, assuming the owner knows how to look after and use the weapon. But illegal or careless use of guns is the leading cause of homicide and suicide in the U.S. and a significant cause of accidental death too, claiming around eighty lives each day. Many more suffer lasting pain and disability from gunshot wounds. Gunfights seen in the movies and on TV

Two men examine a display of handguns at the 124th national convention of the National Rifle Association (NRA) in 1995. © MARK PETERSON/CORBIS

rarely reflect the reality of the damage such powerful weapons can inflict upon the human body.

The nature and severity of a gunshot wound depends upon the type of gun and bullet used, how far away it was fired from and where it enters the body. A bullet is a high speed projectile and when it lands in the body it gives up its kinetic energy. A penetrating gunshot wound is one which enters the body but does not leave it—so there is no exit wound and the bullet is found in the body, possibly at some distance from the place where it entered. A perforating wound enters the body, travels through it and then exits, leaving an exit wound. During its path through the body, the bullet may ricochet—or bounce off—bone like the skull or ribs, which may deflect it from entering the brain or heart.

The damage caused by a gunshot wound occurs because it creates a temporary cavity along its path which then collapses, creating a resultant shock wave which passes through the surrounding tissue. The damage caused depends upon which organ or tissues are affected but, in general, a slow bullet will cause an area of damage that is about three times its diameter. For a high speed bullet, which has greater kinetic energy, the damage extends to ten or more times its diameter. Should the bullet hit the brain, heart or spinal cord, then death may be more or less spontaneous because of the sudden loss of vital functions. If it hits elsewhere then death, if it occurs, will be by exsanguination (bleeding to death) or by infection of the wound inflicted, which is common in war situations. The extract below looks at some of the risk factors contributing to the high rate of gunshot wounds in the USA, which could form the basis of policy for reducing the high death and disability toll from gun violence.

▮ PRIMARY SOURCE

GUN PREVALENCE AND DEATH

Guns and homicide (literature review).

We performed a review of the academic literature on the effects of gun availability on homicide rates.

Major Findings: A broad array of evidence indicates that gun availability is a risk factor for homicide, both in the Untied States and across high income countries. Case-control studies, ecological time-series and cross-sectional studies indicate that in homes, cities, states and regions in the US, where there are more guns, both men and women are at higher risk for homicide, particularly firearm homicides.

Publication: Hepburn, Lisa; Hemenway, David. "Firearm Availability and Homicide: A Review of the Literature." *Aggression and Violent Behavior: A Review Journal.* 2004; 9:417-440.

Gun availability and suicide in the Northeast

We analyzed data on suicide and suicide attempts for states in the Northeast.

Major Findings: Even after controlling for rates of attempted suicide, states with more guns had higher rates of suicide. Case fatality rates ranged from over ninety percent for firearms to under five percent for drug overdoses, cutting and piercing (the most common methods of attempted suicide). Hospital workers rarely see the type of suicide (firearm suicide) that is most likely to end in death.

Publication: Miller, Matthew; Hemenway, David; Azrael, Deborah. "Firearms and Suicide in the Northeast" *Journal of Trauma.* in press.

Publication: Miller, Matthew; Azrael, Deborah; Hemenway, David. "The Epidemiology of Case Fatality Rates for Suicide in the Northeast." *Annals of Emergency Medicine.* 2004; 723-30.

Gun availability and suicide in the US

Using survey data on rates of household gun ownership levels across states and years, in a cross-sectional analysis we used data for 1999–2001 for all states, and in a time-series analysis, we used national data for 1981–2001.

Major Findings: States with higher levels of household gun ownership had higher rates of firearm suicide and overall suicide. This relationship held for both genders and all age groups. It remained true after accounting for poverty, urbanization and unemployment. There was no association between gun prevalence and non-firearm suicide. Longitudinally, at the same time that fewer households contained guns, the firearm suicide and overall suicide rate fell. There was no evidence of method substitution.

Gun versus non-gun suicide by children

We analyzed data from the Arizona Childhood Fatality Review Team comparing youth gun suicide with suicide by other means.

Major Findings: Children who use a firearm to commit suicide had fewer identifiable risk factors for suicide, such as expressing suicidal thoughts. Gun suicides appear more impulsive and spontaneous than suicide by other means.

Publication: Azrael, Deborah; Hemenway, David; Miler, Matthew; Barber, Catherine; Schackner, Robert. "Youth Suicide: Insights from five Years of Arizona Child

Review Team Data." *Suicide and Life Threatening Behavior.* 2004; 34:36-43.

Firearm storage and unintentional firearm death across U.S. states

We analyzed data from the 2002 Behavioral Risk Factor Surveillance System which asked questions about guns and gun storage in the home, combined with information on deaths from the National Center for Health Statistics.

Major Findings: Both Firearm prevalence and questionable storage practices (I.e. storing firearms loaded and unlocked) were associated with higher rates of unintentional firearm deaths.

Submission: Miller, Matthews; Azrael, Deborah; Hemenway, David; Vriniotis, Mary. "Firearm Storage Practices and Rates of Unintentional Firearm Deaths in the United States." *Accident Analysis and prevention.* 2005; 37: 661-667.

Murder followed by suicide in Kentucky.

We analyzed data from the Kentucky Firearms Injury Statistics Program for 1998–2000.

Major findings: While less than seven percent of all firearm homicides were followed by a firearm suicide, in two-thirds of the cases in which a woman was shot in an intimate partner-related homicide, the male perpetrator then killed himself with the firearm. Few of these female victims had contact with the Department of Community-based Services.

Publication: Walsh, Sabrina; Hemenway, David. "Intimate partner Violence: Homicides followed by Suicides in Kentucky." *Journal of the Kentucky medical Association.* 2005 Jan;103(1):10-3.

II GUN THREATS AND SELF-DEFENSE GUN USE

Guns threats against, self-defense gun use by adolescents

We analyzed data from a telephone survey of 5,800 California adolescents aged twelve to seventeen, which asked questions about gun threats against, and self-defense gun use by these young people.

Major Findings: These young people were far more likely to be threatened with a gun than to use a gun in self-defense, and most of the reported self-defense gun uses were hostile interactions between armed adolescents. Males, smokers, binge drinkers, those who threatened others and whose parents were less likely to know their whereabouts were more likely both to be threatened with a gun and to use a gun in self-defense.

Publication: Hemenway, David; Miller, Matthew. "Gun Threats Against and Self-Defense Gun Use by California Adolescents." *Archives of pediatrics and Adolescent Medicine.* 2004; 158:395-400.

Batterers' use of guns

We conducted a survey and analyzed data collected from over eight thousand males enrolled in a certified batterer intervention program in Massachusetts, 1999–2003.

Major Findings: Recent gun owners were eight times more likely to have threatened their partners with a gun than non-gun owners. Four main types of gun threat against partners were (a) threatening to shoot then, (b) threatening to shoot a pet or person the victim cares about, (c) cleaning, holding or loading a gun during an argument, and (d) shooting a gun during an argument.

Submission: Rothman, Emily; Hermenway, David; Miller, Matthews; Azrael, Deborah. "Batterers' Use of Guns to Threaten Intimate Partners" *Journal of the American Medical Women's Association.* 2005, 60:62-68.

III GUN OWNERSHIP, STORAGE, CARRYING AND USE

Unsupervised firearm handling by adolescents

We analyzed data from a telephone survey of over 5,800 California adolescents conducted in 2000-01.

Major Findings: One-third of adolescents reported handling a firearm, 5% without adult supervision or knowledge. Smoking, drinking and parents not knowing the child's whereabouts in the afternoon were associated with unsupervised gun handling. These events usually occur away from home, with friends. Half involve shooting the gun.

Publication: Miller, Matthew; Hemenway, David. "Unsupervised Firearm Handling by California Adolescents." *Injury Prevention.* 2004; 10:163-68.

Concealed carrying by adolescents

We analyzed data from over 1,800 youth in Chicago.

Major findings: Aspects of the neighborhood (social disorder, safety, collective efficacy) were important predictors of illegal gun carrying by youth.

Publication: Molnar, Beth; Miller, Matthew; Azrael, Deborah; Buka Steven. Neighborhood predictors of concealed firearm carrying among children and adolescents: results from the project on human development in Chicago neighborhoods. *Archives of Pediatric Adolescent Medicine.* 2004; 158:657-64.

IV SOCIAL EFFECTS AND POLICY

Public health approach

This chapter summarizes the public health problems caused by firearms, and the public health approach to reducing firearm injuries.

Publication: Hemenway, David. "A Public Health Approach to Firearms Policy" in Mechanic, D. Policy Challenges in Modern Health Care. New Brunswick, NJ: Rutgers University Press, 2005.

Effect on homicide of gun carrying laws

We analyzed the effect on homicide of changes in state-level gun carrying laws using pooled cross-sectional time-series data for fifty states from 1979–1998.

Major Findings: There was no statistically significant association between changes in concealed carry laws and state homicide rates. The finding was consistent across a variety of models.

Publication: Hepburn, Lisa; Miller, Matthew; Azrael, Deborah; Hemenway, David. "The Effect of Nondiscretionary Concealed Weapon Carrying Laws on Homicide." *Journal of Trauma*. 2004; 56:676-681.

Effect of child access prevention laws on unintentional child firearms fatalities

We analyzed the effect on unintentional firearm fatalities to children of child access prevention (CAP) laws, which allow a firearm owner to be charged with a crime if a child gains access to an unsecured firearm, using pooled cross-sectional time series data for fifty states from 1979–2000.

Major findings: States that enacted CAP laws—with felony rather than misdemeanor penalties—experienced great subsequent declines in the rate of unintentional firearms deaths for children from birth to fourteen compared to states not enacting CAP laws.

Submission: Hepburn, Lisa; Azrael, Deborah; Miller, Matthew; Hemenway, David. The effect of child access prevention laws on unintentional child firearm fatalities, 1979–2000.

V SURVEILLANCE AND DATA QUALITY

Measures of firearm prevalence

Various proxy measures for the prevalence of firearm ownership were compared with surveys-based estimates.

Major Findings: One proxy, the percentage of suicides with a firearm, performed consistently better than other measures in cross-sectional comparisons.

Publication: Azrael D, Cook PJ, Miller M. State and local prevalence of firearms ownership: Measurement, structure and trends. *Journal of Quantitative Criminology*. 2004; 20:43-62. See also National Bureau of Economic Research Working Paper #8570.

SIGNIFICANCE

Gunshot wounds are not only an issue in the U.S. Around the world, 300,000 people a year die from gunshot wounds and a million more suffer disabling injuries. The ensuing cost to the health services is significant. In the U.S., the medical cost per injury is said to be 17,000 dollars and in Canada, gunshot wounds cost the nation five billion dollars a year. There are indirect public health effects of guns too—they play a role in conflict in many countries, leading to migration of the population, disruption of their infrastructure and the spread of infection. Sexual violence at gunpoint poses an increased risk of HIV/AIDS and other sexually transmitted infections.

Gun violence, then, can be seen as a public health problem. As with many other public health problems, there are various approaches to control. One way is the so-called zero tolerance approach which has been tried with smoking, drugs and HIV infection. If guns were banned, the argument goes, there would be no gun violence, just as sexual abstinence could eliminate the spread of HIV. However, many people believe they have the right to own a gun—either for sport or to use in self-defense. Another way might be to try to control the circulation of guns used deliberately to harm people by requiring owners to register their weapons. This is perhaps similar to trying to control the sale of tobacco and restrict its use. Many studies, such as the ones described in the extract above, have shown that gun availability is indeed a risk factor for homicide. This would seem to present a good argument for restricting the sale of guns, in the interests of the population at large. The way in which this might be done, however, is open for debate. There is also a case for more training for gun owners so that weapons do not pose a risk of accident, nor do they find their way into the wrong hands. It is also important to consider the reduction of gun violence in the context of reducing all kinds of violence, whether against others or against oneself. If gun use is restricted, people may turn to other means of suicide, showing that what is also needed is a strategy to tackle depression and other mental health problems.

FURTHER RESOURCES

Books

James, Stuart H., and Jon J. Nordby. *Forensic Science*. Boca Raton, FL, CRC Press, 2003

Lyle, Douglas. *Forensics for Dummies*, Hoboken, N.J., Wiley, 2004

Web sites

International Action Network on Small Arms. "The Public Health Approach to Preventing Gun Violence." <http://www.iansa.org/issues/public_health.htm> (accessed March 27, 2006)

Sources Consulted

BOOKS AND WEBSITES

AAA Foundation for Traffic Safety. "Controlling Road Rage: A Literature Review and Pilot Study." <http://www.aaafoundation.org/resources/index.cfm?button=roadrage> (accessed on January 31, 2006).

Agency for Toxic Substances and Disease Registry (ATSDR). "Agency for Toxic Substances and Disease Registry (ATSDR)." <http://www.atsdr.cdc.gov> (accessed on April 22, 2006).

Alan Guttmacher Institute. "Lessons From Before Roe: Will Past Be Prologue?" <http://www.agi-usa.org/pubs/ib_5-03.html> (accessed on January 8, 2006).

American Academy of Child and Adolescent Psychiatry. "Child Sexual Abuse No. 9." <http://www.aacap.org/publications/factsfam/sexabuse.htm> (accessed on March 2, 2006).

American Association for the Advancement of Science (AAAS). "American Association for the Advancement of Science (AAAS)." <http://www.aaas.org> (accessed on April 22, 2006).

American Bar Association. "FAQs and Web Resources on the Impeachment Process." <http://www.abanet.org/publiced/impeach2.html> (accessed on January 31, 2006).

American Civil Liberties Union. "Racial Profiling Old and New." <http://www.aclu.org/racialjustice/racialprofiling/index.html> (accessed on January 12, 2006).

American Kurdish Information Network. "Torture and Prisons in Turkey." <http://kurdistan.org/Prisons/watson.html> (accessed on February 15, 2006).

American Psychiatric Association. *Diagnostic and Statistical Manual of Mental Disorders*. 4th ed. Washington, D.C.: American Psychiatric Association, 1994.

American Psychological Association. "Study With Twins Finds Differences In Certain Attitudes Partly Due To Genetic Factors." <http://www.trinity.edu/~mkearl/death-5.html> (accessed on February 10, 2006).

American Rhetoric. "American Rhetoric." <http://www.americanrhetoric.com/> (accessed on April 30, 2006).

American Sociological Association. "Labor and Labor Movements." <http://www.bgsu.edu/departments/soc/prof/mason/ASA/> (accessed on April 30, 2006).

Americanwest.com. "The Pleasant Valley War." <http://www.americanwest.com/vispages/msmith1.htm> (accessed on February 17, 2006).

Amnesty International. "The Death Penalty." <http://web.amnesty.org/pages/deathpenalty-index-eng> (accessed on February 27, 2006).

Anbinder, Tyler. *Five Points: The 19th Century New York City Neighborhood That Invented Tap Dance, Stole Elections, and Became the World's Most Notorious Slum*. New York: Plume Books, 2002.

Animal Legal Defense Fund. "Zero tolerance for cruelty!" <http://cats.about.com/gi/dynamic/offsite.htm> (accessed on March 04, 2006).

Annual Review of Public Health. "Annual Review of Public Health." <http://arjournals.annualreviews.org/loi/publhealth> (accessed on April 22, 2006).

Arasse, Daniel. *The Guillotine and The Terror*. London: Allen Lane/Penguin Press, 1989.

Arendt, Hannah. *Eichmann in Jerusalem: A Report on the Banality of Evil*. New edition. New York: Penguin, 1994.

Assumption College. "Revues and other Vanities: The Commodification of Fantasy in the 1920s." <http://www.assumption.edu/ahc/Vanities/default.html> (accessed on March 8, 2006).

Atran, Scott. "Genesis and Future of Suicide Terrorism." <http://www.interdisciplines.org/terrorism/papers/1/6> (accessed on February 5, 2006).

Australian Bureau of Statistics. "Aboriginal and Torres Strait Islander Peoples: Contact with the Law." <http://www.abs.gov.au/ausstats/> (accessed on March 2, 2006).

Australian Government: Department of Foreign Affairs and Trade. "Ancient Heritage, Modern Society." <http://www.dfat.gov.au/aib/history.html> (accessed on March 2, 2006).

Australian Human Rights and Equal Opportunity Commission. "Aboriginal and Torres Strait Islander Social Justice." <http://www.hreoc.gov.au/social_justice/croc/sub3.htm> (accessed on March 2, 2006).

Baker, Robert A., ed. Child Sexual Abuse and False Memory Syndrome. Amherst, New York: Prometheus Books, 1998.

Ball, Howard. Murder in Mississippi: United States v. Price and the Struggle for Civil Rights. Lawrence, Kansas: University Press of Kansas, 2004.

Barndollar, Lue Diver. What Really Happened on October 5, 1892: An Attempt at an Accurate Account of the Dalton Gang and Coffeyville. Coffeyville, Kansas: Coffeyville Historical Society, 2001.

Bartley, Paula. Emmeline Pankhurst. New York: Routledge, 2002.

Bass, Ellen, and Laura Davis. The Courage to Heal: A Guide for Women Survivors of Child Sexual Abuse. New York: Collins Books, 1994.

Baumslag, Naomi. Murderous Medicine: Nazi Doctors, Human Experimentation, and Typhus. Westport, Conn.: Praeger, 2005.

Belenko, Steven R., ed. Drugs and Drug Policy in America: A Documentary History. Westport, Conn.: Greenwood Press, 2000.

Berger, K.T. Zen Driving. New York: Ballantine Books, 1988.

Berger, Raoul. Impeachment: The Constitutional Problems. Cambridge: Harvard University Press, 1973.

Betts, Raymond F. A History of Popular Culture: More of Everything, Faster, and Brighter. New York: Routledge, 2004.

Bjorklund, David J. False-Memory Creation in Children and Adults: Theory, Research, and Implications. Mahwah, N.J.: Lawrence Erlbaum Associates, 2000.

Blairworks. "SocioWeb." <http://www.socioweb.com/> (accessed on April 30, 2006).

Bosnian Institute. "Report on the Events in Srebrenica." <http://www.bosnia.org.uk/news/> (accessed on January 31, 2006).

Brain Fingerprinting Laboratories. "A New Paradigm." <http://www.brainwavescience.com> (accessed on January 13, 2006).

Braithwaite, J. Crime, Shame and Reintegration. Cambridge, Mass.: Cambridge University Press, 1992.

Brandon, Craig. The Electric Chair: An Unnatural American History. Jefferson, N.C.: McFarland & Company, 1999.

British Broadcasting Corporation (BBC). "A Brief History of Lying." <http://news.bbc.co.uk/1/hi/uk/1740746.stm> (accessed on January 13, 2006).

British Broadcasting Corporation (BBC). "Charges Facing Saddam." <http://news.bbc.co.uk/2/hi/middle_east/3320293.stm> (accessed on January 10, 2005).

British Broadcasting Corporation (BBC). "Crime Case Closed: Infamous Criminals—David Berkowitz, Son of Sam." <http://www.bbc.co.uk/crime/caseclosed/berkowitz1.shtml> (accessed on February 4, 2006).

British Broadcasting Corporation (BBC). "Rwanda Genocide: Ten Years On." <http://news.bbc.co.uk/1/hi/in_depth/africa/2004/rwanda/default.stm> (accessed on January 8, 2006).

British Library. "British Library Images Online." <http://www.imagesonline.bl.uk/britishlibrary/> (accessed on April 22, 2006).

British Monarchy. "Victoria." <http://www.royal.gov.uk/output/Page118.asp> (accessed on February 9, 2006).

Bryan, Geoffrey. Off With His Head!. London: Hutchinson, 1934.

Bumgarner, Jeffrey B. Profiling and Criminal Justice in America: A Reference Handbook. Santa Barbara, Calif: ABC-CLIO, 2004.

Bureau of Justice Statistics. "Prison Statistics: Summary Findings." <http://www.ojp.usdoj.gov/bjs/prisons.htm> (accessed on March 5, 2006).

Burns, Michael. France and the Dreyfus Affair: A Brief Documentary History. Bedford: St. Martin, 1998.

California State University, Fresno. "Landmark Cases." <http://smith.soehd.csufresno.edu/landmark.html> (accessed on January 19, 2005).

Campbell, Terence W. Smoke and Mirrors: The Devastating Effect of False Sexual Abuse Claims. New York, New York: Insight Books, 1998.

Card Watch. "Card Watch Raises Awareness of All Types of Plastic Card Fraud." <http://www.cardwatch.org.uk/> (accessed on March 27, 2006).

Carlson, Peter M. and Judith Simon Garrett. Prison and Jail Administration: Practice and Theory. Gaithersburg, Md: Aspen Publishers, 1999.

Casarjian, Robin. Houses of Healing: A Prisoner's Guide to Inner Power and Freedom. Boston, Massachusetts: The Lionheart Foundation, 1995.

Casebook. "Jack the Ripper." <http://www.casebook.org> (accessed on February 17, 2006).

Cassels, Lavender. The Archduke and the Assassin: Sarajevo, June 28th 1914. New York: Stein and Day, 1985.

Catholic League. "Sexual Abuse in Social Context: Catholic Clergy and Other Professionals." <http://www.catholicleague.org/research/abuse_in_social_context.htm> (accessed on March 2, 2006).

Catholic World News. "CBS News Distorts 1962 Vatican Document." <http://www.cwnews.com/news/viewstory.cfm?recnum=24023> (accessed on March 10, 2006).

CBS News. "Instruction on the Manner of Proceeding in Cases of Solicitation." <http://www.cbsnews.com/htdocs/pdf/Criminales.pdf> (accessed on March 10, 2006).

CBS News. "Taint of Church Sex Scandal Lingers." <http://www.cbsnews.com/stories/2002/04/19/national/main506674.shtml> (accessed on March 10, 2006).

CBS News. "1,000 Boston Church Abuse Victims." <http://www.cbsnews.com/stories/2003/07/21/national/main564121.shtml> (accessed on March 12, 2006).

Centers for Disease Control and Prevention. "Centers for Disease Control and Prevention." <http://www.cdc.gov> (accessed on April 22, 2006).

Centre for Digital Library Research. "BUBL LINK Social Sciences." <http://bubl.ac.uk/link/linkbrowse.cfm?menuid=2822> (accessed on April 30, 2006).

Cesarani, David. *Eichmann: His Life and Crimes.* New York: Vintage Books, 2005.

CharlesLindbergh.com. "Charles A. Lindbergh Jr. Kidnapping, March 1, 1932." <http://www.charleslindbergh.com/kidnap/index.asp> (accessed on February 25, 2006).

Chicago Historical Society. "History Files: Chicago Black Sox." <http://www.chicagohs.org/history/blacksox.html> (accessed on March 12, 2006).

Child Labor Coalition. "Youth Peddling Crews: Sweatshops of the Streets." <http://www.stopchildlabor.org/teensandstudents/doortodoor.htm> (accessed on March 05, 2006).

Children, Family, and Youth Consortium. "University of Minnesota." <http://www.cyfc.umn.edu/> (accessed on April 30, 2006).

China Daily. "US Nationals Arrested for DVD Piracy." <http://www2.chinadaily.com.cn/english/doc/2004-07/30/content_353431.htm> (accessed on February 14, 2006).

Christensen, Loren W. *Gangbangers: Understanding the Deadly Minds of America's Street Gangs.* Boulder, Colo.: Paladin Press, 1999.

Christian Science Monitor. "Columbine Seeks Closure—Out of Court." <http://www.csmonitor.com/2001/1129/p2s1-usju.html> (accessed on February 2, 2006).

Christian Science Monitor. "Graves Found that Confirm Bosnia Massacre." <http://www.pulitzer.org/year/1996/international-reporting/works/ROHDE-NOV16.html> (accessed on March 23, 2006).

Chronic Disease Prevention Branch. "Chronic Disease Prevention Branch." <http://www.cdc.gov/nccdphp> (accessed on April 22, 2006).

Chronicle of Philanthropy: Philanthropy Careers. "Advocacy Groups Discover the Power of Blogs to Spread Their Messages." <http://philanthropy.com/jobs/2004/08/19/20040819-32353.htm> (accessed on March 13, 2006).

City College of New York Libraries. Reference and Research. "Government Views of the Rosenberg Spy Case." <http://www.ccny.cuny.edu/library/Divisions/Government/rosenbergs.html> (accessed on January 14, 2006).

Civil Code. "Information Sheet 80: Piracy." <http://www.napoleon-series.org/research/government/c_code.html> (accessed on March 8, 2006).

Connecticut's Heritage Gateway. "An Orderly and Descent Government." <http://www.ctheritage.org/aodg/index.html> (accessed on February 1, 2006).

Corbett, James. *Everton: The School of Science.* London: Macmillan, 2003.

core-online.org. "Freedom Summer." <http://www.core-online.org/history/freedom_summer.htm> (accessed on March 7, 2006).

Cornell University. "Making of America." <http://cdl.library.cornell.edu/moa/> (accessed on April 30, 2006).

Crime Culture. "Film Noir." <http://www.crimeculture.com/Contents/Film%20Noir.html> (accessed on February 26, 2006).

Crime Library. "The Polygraph." <http://www.crimelibrary.com/forensics/polygraph/> (accessed on February 11, 2006).

Crime Library. "Young Killers—The Death of James Bulger." <http://www.crimelibrary.com/classics3/bulger/> (accessed on January 22, 2006).

Crime Library. "Little Bohemia." <http://www.crimelibrary.com/gangsters_outlaws/outlaws/dillinger/1.html> (accessed on February 25, 2006).

CTV.ca. "Looters Take Advantage of Katrina Devastation." <http://www.ctv.ca/servlet/ArticleNews/story/CTVNews/20050830_hurricane_katrina_050830/> (accessed on March 7, 2006).

Cummings, John. *Goombata: The Rise and Fall of John Gotti and his Gang.* New York: Little, Brown, 1990.

Cyber-Rights & Cyber-Liberties. "Regulation of Child Pornography on the Internet." <http://www.cyber-rights.org/reports/child.htm> (accessed on January 14, 2006).

Dallek, Robert. *John F. Kennedy: An Unfinished Life.* London: Penguin, 2004.

Davis, Jeanie Lerche. "Getting a Grip on Roadway Anger." <http://www.webmd.com/content/article/35/1728_56860> (accessed on January 31, 2006).

De Groot, Gerard J. *A Noble Cause?: America and the Vietnam War.* New York: Pearson Education, 2000.

Death Penalty Information Center. "Methods of Execution." <http://www.deathpenaltyinfo.org/article.php?scid=8&did=245> (accessed on February 26, 2006).

DeathPenaltyInfo.org. "Death Penalty Information." <http://www.deathpenaltyinfo.org> (accessed on February 27, 2006).

DeBenedetti, Charles. *An American Ordeal: The Antiwar Movement of the Vietnam Era*. Syracuse, NY: Syracuse University Press, 1997.

Dedera, Don. *A Little War of Our Own: The Pleasant Valley Feud Revisited*. Flagstaff, Ariz.: Northland Press, 1988.

Dedijier, Vladimir. *The Road to Sarajevo*. New York: Simon and Schuster, 1966.

Demir, Jenna Shearer. "The Trafficking of Women for Sexual Exploitation." *United Nations High Commission for Refugees*. United Nations, 2003.

Department of Justice. "United States Attorneys Manual." <http://www.usdoj.gov/usao/eousa> (accessed on February 27, 2006).

Department of Justice, Federal Bureau of Investigation. *The School Shooter: A Threat Assessment Perspective*. Quantico, Virginia: National Center for the Analysis of Violent Crime, 2000.

DeVillers, David. *The John Brown Slavery Revolt Trial: A Headline Court Case*. Berkeley Heights, N.J.: Enslow Publishers, 2000.

Digilogical. "Social Sciences Virtual Library." <http://www.dialogical.net/socialsciences/index.html> (accessed on April 30, 2006).

Direct Selling Education Foundation. "Is that traveling sales job for you?" <http://www.dsef.org/information2175/information_show.htm?doc_id=29943> (accessed on March 05, 2006).

Directory for Child Welfare. "Child Welfare Research Institute." <http://www.childwelfare.com/> (accessed on April 30, 2006).

Doctors Without Borders. "Doctors Without Borders." <http://www.doctorswithoutborders.org/> (accessed on April 30, 2006).

Dostoevsky, Fyodor Mikhailovich. *The Brothers Karamazov*. New York: Bantam Classics, 1984.

Dostoevsky, Fyodor Mikhailovich. *The Idiot*. New York: Oxford University Press, 1998.

Douglas, Lyle. *Forensics for Dummies*. Hoboken, N.J.: Wiley, 2004.

Drivers.com. "Behavior: Road Rage." <http://www.drivers.com/article/167/> (accessed on January 31, 2006).

Drug War Chronicle. "Raising awareness of the consequences of drug prohibition." <http://stopthedrugwar.org/index.shtml> (accessed on March 28, 2006).

Dunning, Eric, John Williams, and Patrick Murphy. *Football on Trial: Spectator Violence and Development in the Football World*. London: Routledge, 1990.

Economist.com. "Crime in the United States." <http://www.economist.com/background/displayBackground.cfm?story_id=1270755> (accessed on February 2, 2006).

Economist.com. "Prison and Beyond: A Stigma That Never Fades." <http://www.economist.com/world/na/displayStory.cfm?story_id=1270755> (accessed on February 2, 2006).

Elikann, Peter T. *The Tough-On-Crime Myth: Real Solutions to Cut Crime*. New York: Insight Books, 1996.

Eysenck, Hans J. *Crime and Personality*. Boston, Massachusetts: Houghton Mifflin Company, 1964.

Famous Trials in American History. "Tennessee vs. John Scopes: The 'Monkey Trial', 1925." <http://www.law.umkc.edu/faculty/projects/ftrials/scopes/scopes.htm> (accessed on November 1, 2005).

Federal Bureau of Investigation. "Federal Bureau of Investigation." <http://www.fbi.gov/> (accessed on March 28, 2006).

Federal Bureau of Investigation. "Internet Fraud." <http://www.fbi.gov/majcases/fraud/internetschemes.htm> (accessed on March 28, 2006).

Federal Reserve Bank of San Francisco. "Plastic Fraud." <http://www.frbsf.org/publications/consumer/plastic.html> (accessed on March 27, 2006).

Federation of American Scientists. "Federation of American Scientists, ProMED Initiative." <http://www.fas.org/promed> (accessed on April 22, 2006).

Federation of American Scientists. "Egypt: Intelligence Agencies." <http://www.fas.org/irp/world/egypt/index.html> (accessed on March 10, 2006).

FedStats. "FedStats." <http://www.fedstats.gov> (accessed on April 22, 2006).

Fighting Piracy News Desk. "Fight Against Piracy." <http://www.dvd-intelligence.com/news_desk/piracy_newsdesk.htm> (accessed on February 14, 2006).

Filmsite.org. "Film Noir." <http://www.filmsite.org/filmnoir.html> (accessed on February 26, 2006).

Findlaw/West. "Findlaw." <http://public.findlaw.com/library/> (accessed on April 30, 2006).

Finkelman, Paul, ed. *His Soul Goes Marching On: Responses to John Brown and the Harpers Ferry Raid*. Charlottesville, Va.: University Press of Virginia, 1995.

Florida Department of Corrections. "National Profile of the Female Offender." <http://www.dc.state.fl.us/pub/Females/status102001/national.html> (accessed on February 26, 2006).

Florida Department of Law Enforcement. "Firearm Involved Violent Crimes." <http://www.fdle.state.fl.us/FSAC/Crime_Trends/violent/Reg_FA_2004.ppt> (accessed February 28, 2006).

Food and Drug Administration. "Food and Drug Administration." <http://www.fda.gov> (accessed on April 22, 2006).

Fordham University. "Internet Modern History Sourcebook." <http://www.fordham.edu/halsall/mod/modsbook.html> (accessed on April 30, 2006).

Frontline (PBS). "The Triumph of Evil." <http://www.pbs.org/wgbh/pages/frontline/shows/evil/> (accessed on January 8, 2006).

Gacono, Carl B., ed. The Clinical and Forensic Assessment of Psychopathy: A Practitioner's Guide. Mahwah, N.J.: Lawrence Erlbaum Associates, 2000.

Gainsborough, Jenny, and Marc Mauer. Diminishing Returns: Crime and Incarceration in the 1990s. Washington, D.C.: The Sentencing Project, 2000.

GAO (Government Account Office). "Site Map." <http://www.gao.gov/sitemap.html> (accessed on April 22, 2006).

Gerhardt, Michael J. The Federal Impeachment Process: A Constitutional and Historical Analysis. Chicago: University of Chicago Press, 2000.

Giannangelo, Stephen J. The Psychopathology of Serial Murder: A Theory of Violence. Westport, Conn.: Praeger Publishers, 1996.

Giuliani, Rudolph W., and Kevin Kurson. Leadership. New York: Miramax Books, 2004.

Glassner, Barry. The Culture of Fear: Why Americans are Afraid of the Wrong Things. New York, New York: Basic Books, 1999.

Glenny, Misha. The Balkans: Nationalism, War and the Great Powers 1804–1999. London: Granta, 2000.

Global Policy Forum. "International Criminal Tribunal for Rwanda." <http://www.globalpolicy.org/intljustice/rwandaindx.htm> (accessed on January 8, 2006).

Global Security.org. "Hanbali Islam." <http://www.globalsecurity.org/military/intro/islam-hanbali.htm> (accessed on January 6, 2005).

Global Security.org. "Iraqi Intelligence Services." <http://www.globalsecurity.org/intell/world/iraq/mukhabarat.htm> (accessed on March 10, 2006).

Goldfarb, Ronald. Perfect Villains, Imperfect Heroes: Robert F. Kennedy's War Against Organised Crime. Sterling, Va.: Capital Books, 2002.

Goldrick-Jones, Amanda. Men Who Believe in Feminism. Westport, Connecticut: Praeger, 2002.

Goldstein, Arnold P. The Psychology of Group Aggression. New York: John Wiley & Sons, 2002.

Graphix Communications. "The Alfred Dreyfus Affair." <http://www.dreyfuscase.com/index.html> (accessed on February 26, 2006).

Guardian Unlimited. "Special Report: Hurricane Katrina." <http://www.guardian.co.uk/katrina/0,16441,1560620,00.html> (accessed on March 5, 2006).

Guardian Unlimited. "Special Report: Michael Jackson Trial." <http://www.guardian.co.uk/jackson/0,15819,1428022,00.html> (accessed on February 22, 2006).

Gunaratna, Rohan. Inside Al Qaeda: Global Network of Terror. New York: Berkley Trade, 2003.

Hallwas, John E. The Bootlegger: A Story of Small-Town America. Chicago: University of Illinois Press, 1998.

Hanchett, Leland J., Jr. Arizona's Graham-Tewksbury Feud. Cave Creek, Ariz.: Pine Rim Publishing, 1994.

Harris Interactive. "More Than Two-Thirds of Americans Continue to Support the Death Penalty." <http://www.harrisinteractive.com/harris_poll/index.asp?PID=431> (accessed on February 10, 2006).

Harris, David. Profiles in Injustice: Why Racial Profiling Cannot Work. New York: W.W. Norton, 2003.

Haynes, J.E., and H. Klehr. Venona: Decoding Soviet Espionage in America. Yale University Nota Bene, 1999.

Hearst, Patty, with Alvin Moscow. Every Secret Thing. London: Methuen, 1982.

Helen Prejean, CSJ. "Helen Prejean." <http://www.prejean.org> (accessed on March 12, 2006).

Herbert Shapiro. White Violence and Black Response: From Reconstruction to Montgomery. Amherst, Mass.: University of Massachusetts Press, 1988.

Hernandez, Arturo. Peace in the Streets: Breaking the Cycle of Gang Violence. Washington, D.C.: Child Welfare League of America, 1998.

Hersh, Seymour. The Dark Side of Camelot. London: Harper Collins, 1998.

Heumann, Milton. Good Cop, Bad Cop: Racial Profiling and Competing Views of Justice. New York: P. Lang, 2003.

Hirsh, James S. Hurricane: the Miraculous Journey of Rubin Carter. New York: Houghton Mifflin, 2000.

History of the Death Penalty in Illinois. "30 Years of the Death Penalty." <http://www.truthinjustice.org/dphistory-IL.htm> (accessed on February 27, 2006).

HIV Criminal Law and Policy Project. "HIV-specific Criminal Transmission Laws." <http://www.hivcriminallaw.org/laws/hivspec.cfm> (accessed on March 28, 2006).

Hoffman, David. The Oligarchs: Wealth and Power in Modern Russia. New York: Public Affairs, 2004.

Holbert, Steve, and Lisa Rose. The Color of Guilt & Innocence: Racial Profiling and Police Practices in America. San Ramon, Calif.: Page Marque Press, 2004.

Hood, Roger. The Death Penalty: A Worldwide Perspective. Oxford, U.K.: Oxford University Press, 2004.

Hosking, Geoffrey. Russia and the Russians. London: Allen Lane, 2000.

Hugo, Victor. Les Miserables. Seattle, Wash.: Signet, 1987.

Human Kindness Foundation. "Prison-Ashram Project." <http://www.humankindness.org/project.html> (accessed on March 11, 2006).

Human Rights Center. University of California, Berkeley. "Hidden Slaves: Forced Labor in the United States." <http://www.hrcberkeley.org/download/hiddenslaves_report.pdf> (accessed on January 10, 2006).

Human Rights Watch. "Human Rights Watch." <http://www.hrw.org/> (accessed on April 30, 2006).

Human Rights Watch. "Promises Broken: An Assessment of Children's Rights on the 10th Anniversary of the Convention on the Rights of the Child." <http://www.hrw.org/campaigns/crp/promises/labor.html> (accessed on March 5, 2006).

Human Rights Watch. "Saudi Arabia." <http://www.hrw.org/worldreport99/mideast/saudi.html> (accessed on January 6, 2005).

Humane Society of the United States. "Legislation and Laws." <http://www.hsus.org/legislation_laws/> (accessed on March 04, 2006).

HumanTrafficking.com. "Human Traffic." <http://www.humantrafficking.com> (accessed on March 5, 2005).

Husak, Douglas N. Legalize This! The Case for Decriminalizing Drugs. New York: Verso, 2002.

Innocence Project. "Innocence Project." <http://www.innocenceproject.org> (accessed on February 26, 2006).

Institute for Intergovernmental Research. "National Youth Gang Center (NYGC)." <http://www.iir.com/nygc> (accessed on March 5, 2006).

International Action Network on Small Arms. "The Public Health Approach to Preventing Gun Violence." <http://www.iansa.org/issues/public_health.htm> (accessed on March 28, 2006).

International Commission on Missing Persons. "Missing Persons." <http://www.ic-mp.org/> (accessed on March 23, 2006).

International Justice Project. "Daryl Renard Atkins." <http://www.internationaljusticeproject.org/retardationDatkins.cfm> (accessed on January 14, 2006).

International Labor Organization. "Campaign Against Trafficking in Persons." <http://www.ilo.org/public/english/protection/migrant/projects/traffick/index.htm> (accessed on January 10, 2006).

International Maritime Organization. "Piracy and Armed Robbery against Ships." <http://www.imo.org/Safety/> (accessed on March 8, 2006).

Interpol. "Trafficking in Human Beings." <http://www.interpol.int/Public/THB/default.asp> (accessed on March 5, 2005).

Irey, Elmer L. The Tax Dodgers: The Inside Story of the T-Men's War with America's Political and Underworld Hoodlums. New York: Greenberg, 1948.

Jackson, Andrew R.W., and Julie M.Jackson. Forensic Science. Harlow, England:Pearson, 2004.

James, Stuart H., and Jon J. Nordy, eds. Forensic Science: An Introduction to Scientific and Investigative Techniques. Boca Raton, Fla.: CRC Press, 2003.

Jenness, Valerie, and Kendal Broad. Hate Crimes: New Social Movements and the Politics of Violence. New York: Aldine De Gruyter, 1997.

Johnson, Robert. Death Work: A Study of the Modern Execution Process. Pacific Grove, Calif.: Brooks Cole, 1990.

Joyce, C. Patrick. Sarajevo Shots: A Study in the Immediate Origins of the First World War. New York: Revisionist Press, 1978.

Judah, Tim. The Serbs: History, Myth and the Destruction of Yugoslavia. New Haven, CT: Yale University Press, 2000.

Justice Policy Institute. "New national report shows that drug-free zone laws fail to protect youth from drug sales, worsen racial disparity in prisons: Growing movement to change ineffective laws finds support among lawmakers and law enforcement officials." <http://www.justicepolicy.org/article.php?id=571> (accessed on March 28, 2006).

Juvenile Forensic Evaluation Resource Center. "Female Juvenile Delinquency: Risk Factors and Promising Interventions." <http://www.ilppp.virginia.edu/Juvenile_Forensic_Fact_Sheets/FemJuv.html> (accessed on January 12, 2006).

Juvenile Justice. "Contemporary Theories Explaining Deviancy." <http://husky1.stmarys.ca/~evanderveen/wvdv/Juvenile_justice/contemporary_theories_deviancy.htm> (accessed on January 12, 2006).

Kempado, K., Sanghera, J., and B. Pattanaik, eds. Trafficking and Prostitution Reconsidered: New Perspectives on Migration, Sex Work, and Human Rights. Boulder, Colo.: Paradigm Publishers, 2005.

Kids Against Drugs—Campaign for Drug-Free Families. "Home Page and Statement of Purpose." <http://www.kidsagainstdrugs.com/> (accessed on March 28, 2006).

King, Ryan S., and Marc Mauer. Aging Behind Bars: Three Strikes Seven Years Later. Washington, D.C.: The Sentencing Project, 2001.

Kipnis, Aaron. Angry Young Men: How Parents, Teachers and Counselors Can Help "Bad Boys" Become Good Men. San Francisco, CA: Jossey-Bass, 1999.

Kistler, John. People Promoting and People Opposing Animal Rights: In Their Own Words. Westport, Connecticut: Greenwood Press, 2002.

Klein, Joe. The Natural: The Misunderstood Presidency of Bill Clinton. London: Coronet, 2002.

Klein, Malcolm W. The American Street Gang: Its Nature, Prevalence, and Control. New York: Oxford University Press, 1997.

Knight Ayton Management. "Justin Webb." <http://www. knightayton.co.uk/frameset.html?http://www.knightayton.co.uk/justin_webb.html> (accessed on March 7, 2006).

Knupfer, Anne Meis. *Reform and Resistance: Gender, Delinquency, and America's First Juvenile Court*. New York: Routledge, 2001.

Kobler, John. *Capone: The Life and World of Al Capone*. New York: Putnam's, 1971.

Krane, Dale, and Stephen D. Shaffer. *Mississippi Government & Politics: Modernizers Versus Traditionalists*. Lincoln, Nebraska: University of Nebraska Press, 1992.

Kupers, Terry. *Prison Madness: The Mental Health Crisis Behind Bars and What We Must Do About It*. San Francisco, California: Jossey-Bass, 1999.

KY-3 News—Springfield, MO. "Sex predator stings spur new legislation." <http://www.ky3.com/news/2293456.html> (accessed on March 28, 2006).

Kyvig, David, ed. *Unintended Consequences of Constitutional Amendments*. Athens Ga.: University of Georgia Press, 2000.

La-Legal.com. "How the Code Napoleon makes Louisiana law different." <http://www.la-legal.com/history_louisiana_law.htm> (accessed March 8, 2006).

Lamay, Craig L., and Everette E. Dennis, eds. *The Culture of Crime*. New Brunswick, NJ: Transaction, 1995.

Lanier, Mark M., and Stuart Henry. *Essential Criminology*. Boulder, Colorado: Westview Press, 1998.

Larson, Edward. *Trial and Error: The American Controversy Over Creation and Evolution*. New York, Oxford University Press, 2003.

Lavelle, Patrick. *Shadow of the Ripper: The Secret Story of the Man who Helped the Ripper to Kill and Kill Again*. London: John Blake Publishing, 2003.

Legal Information Institute, Cornell University. "Atkins v. Virginia." <http://supct.law.cornell.edu/supct/html/00-8452.ZS.html> (accessed on January 14, 2006).

Legal Information Institute, Cornell University. "Code of Federal Regulations." <http://www4.law.cornell.edu/cfr/> (accessed on April 22, 2006).

LegalDay. "Operation Ore." <http://www.legalday.co.uk/current/ore.htm> (accessed on January 14, 2006).

Leuchter, Fred A. *Modular Electrocution System Manual: State of Tennessee*. Boston, Mass.: Fred A. Leuchter Associates, 1989.

Levy, Peter B. *The Civil Rights Movement*. Westport, Connecticut: Greenwood Press, 1998.

Library of Congress. "Library of Congress Online Catalog." <http://catalog.loc.gov/cgi-bin/Pwebrecon.cgi?DB=local&PAGE=First> (accessed on April 22, 2006).

Library of Congress. "Thomas." <http://thomas.loc.gov/> (accessed on April 30, 2006).

Library of Congress. "A Century of Lawmaking." <http://rs6.loc.gov/ammem/amlaw/lawhome.html> (accessed on April 30, 2006).

Library of Congress. "American Memory." <http://memory.loc.gov/ammem/index.html> (accessed on April 30, 2006).

Lipschultz, Jeremy Harris. *Free Expression in the Age of the Internet: Social and Legal Boundaries*. Boulder, Colorado: Westview Press, 2000.

Lively, Donald E. *Foreshadows of the Law: Supreme Court Dissents and Constitutional Development*. Westport, Connecticut: Praeger, 1992.

London Walks. "Jack the Ripper Information." <http://www.london-walks.co.uk/28/index.shtml> (accessed on February 17, 2006).

Louisiana State University. "Federal Government Agencies Directory." <http://www.lib.lsu.edu/gov/fedgov.html> (accessed on April 30, 2006).

Lozoff, Bo. *We're All Doing Time: A Guide to Getting Free*. Durham, NC: Human Kindness Foundation, 1985.

Lozoff, Bo. *It's a Meaningful Life, It Just Takes Practice*. New York, New York: Penguin Compass, 2000.

Lyle, Douglas P. *Forensics for Dummies*. Hoboken, NJ: Wiley, 2004.

Lytton, Timothy D., ed. *Suing the Gun Industry: A Battle at the Crossroads of Gun Control and Mass Torts*. Ann Arbor, MI: University of Michigan Press, 2005.

Markowitz, Michael W. and Delores D. Jones-Brown, eds. *The System in Black and White: Exploring the Connections Between Race, Crime, and Justice*. Westport, Conn.: Praeger Publishers, 2000.

Mass, Peter. *The Valachi Papers*. New York: Harper Collins, 1968.

Massachusetts Bar Association. "Lawyer's Journal: Fingerprint Identification and its Aura of Infallibility." <http://www.massbar.org/publications/lawyersjournal/article/> (accessed on March 28, 2006).

Matera, Dary. *John Dillinger: The Life and Death of America's First Celebrity Criminal*. New York: Carroll and Graf, 2005.

Mauer, Marc, Ryan S. King, and Malcolm C. Young. *The Meaning of "Life": Long Prison Sentences in Context*. Washington, D.C.: The Sentencing Project, 2004.

McLean, Christopher, Maggie Carey, and Cheryl White, eds. *Men s Ways of Being*. Boulder, Colorado: Westview Press, 1996.

MegaLaw.com. "Death Penalty/Capital Punishment Law." <http://www.megalaw.com/top/deathpenalty.php> (accessed on February 26, 2006).

Men Against Sexual Assault at the University of Rochester. "About Men Against Sexual Assault." <http://sa.rochester.edu/masa/about.php> (accessed on March 13, 2006).

Men Against Sexual Assault at the University of Rochester. "Sexual Assault Statistics." <http://sa.rochester.edu/masa/stats.phpl> (accessed on March 5, 2006).

Men Can Stop Rape. "Making Our Communities Stronger." <http://www.mencanstoprape.org/index.htm> (accessed on March 13, 2006).

Mental Health Matters. "Stockholm Syndrome." <http://www.mental—health—matters.com/articles/article.php?artID=469> (accessed on March 5, 2006).

Miles, Anthony. *Devil's Island: Colony of the Damned.* Berkeley, CA: Ten Speed Press, 1988.

Missingkids.com. "Prostitution of Children and Child Sex Tourism." <http://www.missingkids.com/en_US/publications/NC73.> (accessed on February 28, 2006).

Moffitt, Arnol, John Malouf, and Craig Thompson. *Drug Precipice: Illicit Drugs, Organised Crime, Fallacies of Legalisation, Worsening Problems, Solutions.* Sydney, New South Wales: University of New South Wales Press, 1998.

Moghalu, Kingsley. *Rwanda's Genocide: The Policies of Global Injustice.* New York: Palgrave Macmillan, 2005.

Morbidity and Mortality Weekly Report. "Morbidity and Mortality Weekly Report." <http://www.cdc.gov/mmwr> (accessed on April 22, 2006).

Morrison, Blake. *As If.* London: Granta Books, 1998.

Morse, Christopher J. *New York Criminal Procedure.* Durham, N.C.: Carolina Academic Press, 2004.

National Academies. "Health & Medicine at the National Academies." <http://www.nationalacademies.org/health/> (accessed on April 22, 2006).

National Academies. "The National Academies: Advisers to the Nation on Science, Engineering, and Medicine." <http://www.nationalacademies.org/> (accessed on April 22, 2006).

National Academy of Sciences. "National Academy of Sciences." <http://www.nas.edu> (accessed on April 22, 2006).

National Archives and Records Administration. "National Archives and Records Administration." <http://www.archives.gov/index.html> (accessed on April 30, 2006).

National Center for Biotechnology Information. "PubMed." <http://www.ncbi.nlm.nih.gov/entrez/query.fcgi?DB=pubmed> (accessed on April 22, 2006).

National Center for Missing and Exploited Children. "Missing and Exploited Children." <http://www.missingkids.com> (accessed on February 2, 2006).

National Center for Policy Analysis. "Ballistic Imaging: Not Ready for Prime Time." <http://www.ncpa.org/pub/bg/bg160> (accessed on January 8, 2006).

National Center for Post-Traumatic Stress Syndrome. "Child Sexual Abuse." <http://www.ncptsd.va.gov/facts/specific/fs_child_sexual_abuse.html> (accessed on March 2, 2006).

National Commission Against Drunk Driving (NCADD). "Sanctioning and Supervising Impaired Drivers." <http://www.ncadd.com/sanction_iis.cfm> (accessed on February 8, 2006).

National Council of La Raza. "National Council of La Raza." <http://www.nclr.org/> (accessed on April 30, 2006).

National Data Archive on Child Abuse and Neglect. "Cornell Univeristy." <http://www.ndacan.cornell.edu/> (accessed on April 30, 2006).

National Gang Crime Research Center. "Gang Profiles." <http://www.ngcrc.com/profile/profile.html> (accessed on March 5, 2006).

National Institute on Alcohol Abuse and Alcoholism. "NIAAA - National Institute on Alcohol Abuse and Alcoholism." <http://www.niaaa.nih.gov> (accessed on April 22, 2006).

National Institute on Drug Abuse. "Drug Abuse." <http://www.nida.nih.gov> (accessed on January 8, 2006).

National Institutes of Health. "National Institutes of Health." <http://www.nih.gov> (accessed on April 22, 2006).

National Library of Medicine. "Environmental Health and Toxicology." <http://sis.nlm.nih.gov/enviro.html> (accessed on April 22, 2006).

National Library of Medicine. "History of Medicine." <http://www.nlm.nih.gov/hmd/index.html> (accessed on April 22, 2006).

National Library of Medicine. "NLM-National Library of Medicine." <http://www.nlm.nih.gov/> (accessed on April 22, 2006).

National Organization for Men Against Sexism. "A Brief History of NOMAS." <http://www.nomas.org/briefhistory.html> (accessed on March 13, 2006).

National Public Radio. "One Mother's Story." <http://www.npr.org/programs/morning/features/2002/feb/postpartum/020218.postpartum.html> (accessed on January 18, 2006).

National Review Online. "The Mafia, Misunderstood: Hollywood Fails to Capture the Complexity of the Real Thing." <http://www.nationalreview.com/hibbs/hibbs200409290835.asp> (accessed on February 28, 2006).

National Toxicology Program. "National Toxicology Program." <http://ntp-server.niehs.nih.gov> (accessed on April 22, 2006).

Nelson, Marilyn, and Philippe Lardy. *A Wreath for Emmett Till.* New York: Houghton Mifflin Company, 2005.

Netanyahu, Benjamin. *Fighting Terrorism: How Democracies Can Defeat Domestic and International Terrorists.* New York: Farrar, Straus and Giroux, 2001.

New Hampshire Society of Certified Public Accountants. "Computer Forensics: Electronic Trail of Evidence." <http://www.nhscpa.org/May2002News/forensics.htm> (accessed on March 23, 2006).

New Jersey Law Network. "New Jersey Law." <http://www.njlawnet.com/megan.html> (accessed on March 05, 2006).

New South Wales Government's Archives and Records Management Authority. "Welcome to State Records NSW." <http://www.records.nsw.gov.au/staterecords/welcome_to_state_records_nsw_1556.asp> (accessed on March 2, 2006).

New York City. "Biography of Rudolph Giuliani." <http://www.nyc.gov/html/records/rwg/html/bio.html> (accessed on January 12, 2006).

New York City. "Freeing the Economy from Organized Crime and Restoring Open, Competitive Markets." <http://www.nyc.gov/html/rwg/html/97/orgcrime.html> (accessed on January 12, 2006).

New York State Department of Correctional Services. "Department of Correctional Services." <http://www.docs.state.ny.us/> (accessed on February 10, 2006).

News Channel 11—Lubbock, Texas. "Internet Watchdog Group Helps Lubbock Authorities Nab Sexual Predator." <http://www.kcbd.com/Global/story/> (accessed on March 28, 2006).

Nicholls, Andy. *Scally: The Story of a Category C Football Hooligan.* Ramsbottom, UK: Milo Books, 2002.

North Carolina Wesleyan College. "Scientific Lie Detection." <http://faculty.ncwc.edu/mstevens/425/lecture21.htm> (accessed on February 11, 2006).

NOVA Online. "Read Venona Intercepts." <http://www.pbs.org/wgbh/nova/venona/intercepts.html> (accessed on January 8, 2006).

Nussbaum, Martha C., and Cass R. Sunstein. *Animal Rights: Current Debates and New Directions.* New York, New York: Oxford University Press, 2004.

ON LINE opinion: Australia's e-journal of social and political debate. "How maximum-security jails make the baddest of men even worse." <http://www.onlineopinion.com.au/view.asp?article=842> (accessed on January 8, 2006).

Opie, Robert Frederick. *Guillotine: The Timbers of Justice.* Stroud, U.K.: Sutton Publishing, 2003.

Pape, Robert A. *Dying to Win: The Strategic Logic of Suicide Terrorism.* New York: Random House, 2005.

Paradise, Paul R. *Trademark Counterfeiting, Product Piracy, and the Billion Dollar Threat to the U.S. Economy.* Westport, Conn.: Quorum Books, 1999.

Parent Watch Inc.: A Clearinghouse for Information on Traveling Sales Crews. "Missing Persons." <http://www.parentwatch.org/missing/missing.html> (accessed on March 05, 2006).

Park Dietz and Associates. "Areas of Expertise." <http://www.parkdietzassociates.com/index3.htm> (accessed on February 17, 2006).

Pegram, Thomas R. *Battling Demon Rum: The Struggle for a Dry America, 1800–1933.* Chicago: Ivan R. Dee, 1998.

Perry, Robert J., Dona Wilpolt, and Charles A. King. *Getting Free Behind the Walls: Comprehensive Addictions Treatment.* Santa Fe, N. Mex.: New Mexico Corrections Department, 2000.

Pharma-Lexicon International. "MediLexicon." <http://www.medilexicon.com/> (accessed on April 22, 2006).

Pileggi, Nicholas. *Wise Guys.* New York: Simon and Schuster, 1985.

Posner, Gerald. *Case Closed.* New York: Random House, 1993.

Powers, Ron. *Mark Twain: A Life.* New York: Free Press, 2005.

Preece, Harold. *The Dalton Gang: End of an Outlaw Era.* New York: Hastings House, 1963.

Prevent Abuse Now.com. "Sexual Abuse." <http://www.prevent-abuse-now.com/> (accessed on March 4, 2006).

Prison Policy Initiative. "Incarceration Is Not an Equal Opportunity Punishment." <http://www.prisonpolicy.org/articles/notequal.shtml> (accessed on February 2, 2006).

Prison Policy Initiative. "The Prison Index." <http://www.prisonpolicy.org/articles/prisonindex_highincarceration.pdf> (accessed on February 2, 2006).

Pro-death Penalty.com. "Who Speaks for the Victims of Those We Execute?" <http://www.prodeathpenalty.com/> (accessed on January 14, 2006).

Pro-Death Penalty.Org. "Standing United for the Death Penalty." <http://www.prodeathpenalty.org/> (accessed on March 7, 2006).

Project Gutenberg. "Online Book Catalog-Overview." <http://www.gutenberg.org/catalog/> (accessed on April 22, 2006).

Protection Project. "Hearing before the Senate Committee on the Judiciary, Subcommittee on the Constitution, Civil Rights and Property Rights. Examining U.S. Efforts to Combat Human Trafficking and Slavery." <http://www.protectionproject.org/re3.htm> (accessed on February 22, 2006).

Public Broadcasting System (PBS). "American Experience: The Murder of Emmett Till." <http://www.pbs.org/wgbh/amex/till> (accessed on March 5, 2006).

Public Broadcasting System (PBS). "Washington Week." <http://www.pbs.org/weta/washingtonweek/aroundthetable/priest.html> (accessed on January 14, 2006).

Public Broadcasting System (PBS). "Innocence Lost: The Plea. Other Well-Known Cases Involving Child Abuse in Day Care Settings." <http://www.pbs.org/wgbh/pages/frontline/shows/innocence/etc/other.html#3> (accessed on February 9, 2006).

Publiclibraries.com. "National Libraries of the World." <http://www.publiclibraries.com/world.htm> (accessed on April 22, 2006).

Quayle, Ethel & Max Taylor. *Child Pornography: An Internet Crime*. New York, New York: Brunner-Routledge, 2003.

Raab, Selwyn. *Five Families: The Rise, Decline, and Resurgence of America's Most Powerful Mafia Empires*. New York: Thomas Dunne Books, 2005.

Radosh, R., and J. Milton. *The Rosenberg File*. 2nd ed. Holt, Rinehart, and Winston, 1997.

Raeburn, Antonia. *The Militant Suffragettes*. London: Joseph, 1973.

Ranalli, Ralph. *Deadly Alliance: The FBI's Secret Partnership With the Mob*. New York: Harper Collins, 2001.

Recording Industry Association of America (RIAA). "Anti-Piracy." <http://www.riaa.com/issues/piracy/default.asp> (accessed on February 14, 2006).

Redfield, Peter. *Space in the Tropics: From Convicts to Rockets in French Guiana*. Berkeley: University of California Press, 2000.

Reppetto, Thomas. *American Mafia: A History of Its Rise to Power*. New York: Henry Holt, 2004.

Rhodes, Lorna. *Total Confinement: Madness and Reason in the Maximum Security Prison*. Berkeley, California: University of California Press, 2004.

Robert Gordon University. "An introduction to Social Policy." <http://www2.rgu.ac.uk/publicpolicy/socialpolicy.htm> (accessed on April 30, 2006).

Roberts, S. *The Brother: The Untold Story of the Rosenberg Case*. Random House, 2001.

Rogers, Mary Elizabeth, ed. *The Impossible H. L. Mencken*. New York: Doubleday, 1991.

Ross, Jeffrey Ian and Steven Ian Richards. *Behind Bars: Surviving Prison*. New York: Alpha, 2002.

Royal Canadian Mounted Police (RCMP Gazette). "Just the Facts." <http://www.gazette.rcmp-grc.gc.ca/article-en.html/> (accessed on January 14, 2006).

Royal Canadian Mounted Police (RCMP). "Media Coverage of Organized Crime: Impact on Public Opinion?" <http://www.rcmp-grc.gc.ca/ccaps/media_e.htm> (accessed on November 2, 2005).

Royal Naval Museum. "Information Sheet 80: Piracy." <http://www.royalnavalmuseum.org/info_sheets_piracy.htm> (accessed on March 8, 2006).

Royal Society, (UK). "Science issues." <http://www.royalsoc.ac.uk/landing.asp?id=6> (accessed on April 22, 2006).

Russo, Gus. *The Outfit: The Role of Chicago's Underworld in the Shaping of Modern America*. London: Bloomsbury, 2003.

Sacco, Joe, and Christopher Hitchens. *Safe Area Gorazde: The War in Eastern Bosnia 1992–1995*. London: Random House, 1997.

Safe Youth.org. "Youth Gangs." <http://www.safeyouth.org/scripts/teens/gangs.asp> (accessed on February 7, 2006).

Salon.com. "The Mystery of O.J. Simpson." <http://www.salon.com/media/1998/02/03media.html> (accessed on March 20, 2006).

Samenow, Stanton E. *Inside the Criminal Mind*. New York, New York: Crown Business, 1984.

San Francisco Chronicle. "Editorial: Doors Closing for Lifers—Again." <http://sfgate.com/cgi-bin/article.cgi?f=/c/a/2005/10/17/EDGDKF8ODH1.DTL> (accessed on January 31, 2006).

Sanders, William B. *Gangbangs and Drive-Bys: Grounded Culture and Juvenile Gang Violence*. New York: Aldine De Gruyter, 1994.

Schaffer Library of Drug Policy. "End the War." <http://www.druglibrary.org/Schaffer/debate/mcn/mcn3.htm> (accessed on March 28, 2006).

Schaffer Library of Drug Policy. "The Consumers Union Report—Licit and Illicit Drugs." <http://www.druglibrary.org/SCHAFFER/library/studies/cu/cumenu.htm> (accessed on March 28, 2006).

Schlesinger, Louis B. *Sexual Murder—Catathymic and Compulsive Homicides*. Boca Raton, Fla.: CRC Press, 2004.

Schoenberg, Robert J. *Mr. Capone*. New York: William Morrow, 1992.

Shambhala Sun Online. "A Nation Behind Bars." <http://www.shambhalasun.com/Archives/Columnists/> (accessed on March 11, 2006).

Short, Jr., James F. *Poverty, Ethnicity, and Violent Crime*. Boulder, Colorado: Westview Press, 1997.

Silicon Valley Regional Computer Forensics Laboratory. "Silicon Valley Regional Computer Forensics Laboratory." <http://www.svrcfl.org/> (accessed on March 23, 2006).

Silver, Alain and Elizabeth Ward, eds. *Film Noir: An Encyclopedic Reference to the American Style*. Woodstock, N.Y.: Overlook Press, 1993.

Simon Wiesenthal Center. "Simon Wiesenthal Center." <http://www.wiesenthal.com> (accessed on April 30, 2006).

Sinclair, Andrew. *Prohibition: The Era of Excess*. New York: Harper & Row, 1962.

Sister Helen Prejean. "Personal blog." <http://sisterhelen.typepad.com> (accessed on March 12, 2006).

Smolla, Rodney A., ed. *A Year in the Life of the Supreme Court*. Durham, North Carolina: Duke University Press, 1995.

Soering, Jens. *An Expensive Way to Make Bad People Worse: An Essay on Prison Reform from an Insider's Perspective.* New York: Lantern Books, 2004.

SOSIG. "Social Science Information Gateway." <http://www.sosig.ac.uk/> (accessed on April 30, 2006).

Southern Poverty Law Center. "Intelligence Report: Recognizing and Responding to Hate Crimes." <http://www.splcenter.org/intel/law.jsp> (accessed on March 10, 2006).

Spencer, Suzy. *Breaking Point.* New York: St. Martin's, 2002.

Stanford University. "Stanford Prevention Research Center." <http://prevention.stanford.edu> (accessed on April 22, 2006).

Sterling, Theodore F. *The Enron Scandal.* New York: Nova Science Publishing, 2002.

Substance Abuse & Mental Health Services Administration (SAMHSA). "Substance Abuse & Mental Health Services Administration (SAMHSA)." <http://www.samhsa.gov/index.aspx> (accessed on April 22, 2006).

Sugden, Philip. *The Complete History of Jack the Ripper.* New York: Carroll and Graf, 1994.

Supreme Court of the United States. "The Court and Constitutional Interpretation." <http://www.supremecourtus.gov/about/constitutional.pdf> (accessed on March 28, 2006).

Sutherland, E. H. *Social Attitudes: Mental Deficiency and Crime.* New York: Henry Holt, 1931.

Sutherland, John, and Diane Canwell. *Crime.* London: Flame Tree, 2003.

Szasz, Thomas. *Our Right to Drugs: The Case for a Free Market.* Westport, Connecticut: Praeger, 1992.

Taylor, William Banks. *Down on Parchman Farm: The Great Prison in the Mississippi Delta.* Columbus, Ohio: Ohio State University Press, 1999.

The Future of Children. "Future of Children." <http://www.futureofchildren.org/> (accessed on April 30, 2006).

The Vincentian Center for Church and Society. "Legal Arguments Against the Death Penalty." <http://www.vincenter.org/95/gregory.html> (accessed on February 27, 2006).

Thompson, Hunter S. *Hells Angels.* New York: Ballantine Books, 1966.

Thompson, Julius E. *The Black Press in Mississippi.* Gainesville, Fla.: University Press of Florida, 1993.

Till-Mobley, Mamie, and Christopher Benson. *Death of Innocence: The Story of the Hate Crime that Changed America.* New York: Random House, 2003.

Toland, John. *The Dillinger Days.* New York: Random House, 1971.

Toledo, Gregory. *The Hanging of Old Brown: A Story of Slaves, Statesmen, and Redemption.* Westport, Conn.: Praeger, 2002.

Tong, Dean. *Elusive Innocence: A Survival Guide for the Falsely Accused.* Lafayatte, Louisiana: Huntington House Publishers, 2001.

Tonry, Michael, ed. *The Handbook of Crime and Punishment.* New York: Oxford University Press, 2000.

Tonry, Michael, ed. *Crime and Justice: A Review of Research.* Chicago: University of Chicago Press, 1997.

Treherne, John. *The Strange Life of Bonnie and Clyde.* Lanham, Md.: Cooper Square Press, 2000.

Trinity College. "The Saloons of Hartford's East Side 1870–1910." <http://www.trincoll.edu/depts/tcn/Research_Reports/60.htm> (accessed on February 1, 2006).

Trinity University. "Moral Debates of Our Times." <http://www.trinity.edu/~mkearl/death-5.html> (accessed on February 10, 2006).

Truth in Justice. "FBI Informant System Called a Failure." <http://www.truthinjustice.org/corrupt-FBI.htm> (accessed on February 13, 2006).

U.N. Office of the High Commissioner for Human Rights. "Convention on the Rights of the Child." <http://www.unhchr.ch/html/menu3/b/k2crc.htm> (accessed on January 9, 2006).

United Kingdom (U.K.) Home Office. "Internet Crime." <http://www.homeoffice.gov.uk/crime-victims/reducing-crime/internet-crime/> (accessed on January 14, 2006).

United Nations. "International Criminal Tribunal for Rwanda." <http://65.18.216.88/default.htm> (accessed on January 8, 2006).

United Nations. "United Nations Office of the High Commissioner for Human Rights." <http://www.ohchr.org/english/> (accessed on April 30, 2006).

United States Census Bureau. "Census Bureau." <http://www.census.gov/> (accessed on April 30, 2006).

United States Citizenship and Immigration Services. "United States Citizenship and Immigration Services." <www.uscis.gov> (accessed on April 30, 2006).

United States Commission on Civil Rights. "Highlights." <http://www.usccr.gov/index.html> (accessed on March 5, 2006).

United States Department of Justice. "Child Pornography." <http://www.usdoj.gov/criminal/ceos/childporn.html> (accessed on March 20, 2006).

United States Department of Justice Drug Enforcement Administration. "Speaking Out Against Drug Legalization." <http://www.dea.gov/demand/speakout/speaking_out-may03.pdf> (accessed on January 8, 2006).

United States Department of Justice. Bureau of Justice Statistics. "American Indians and Crime." <http://www.ojp.usdoj.gov/bjs/abstract/aic.htm> (accessed on March 2, 2006).

United States Department of Justice. Bureau of Justice Statistics. "Criminal Offender Statistics." <http://www.ojp.usdoj.gov/bjs/crimoff.htm> (accessed on February 2, 2006).

United States Department of Justice. Bureau of Justice Statistics. "Criminal Sentencing Statistics." <http://www.ojp.usdoj.gov/bjs/sent.htm> (accessed on February 8, 2006).

United States Department of Justice. Bureau of Justice Statistics. "Reentry Trends in the United States." <http://www.ojp.usdoj.gov/bjs/reentry/reentry.htm> (accessed on February 8, 2006).

United States Department of Justice. Office of Justice Programs. "Amber Alert." <http://www.amberalert.gov> (accessed on February 2, 2006).

United States Department of Justice. Office of the Inspector General. *Federal Bureau of Investigation Compliance with Attorney General's Investigative Guidelines.* Washington, D.C.: Government Printing Office, 2005.

United States Department of State. International Information Programs. "Trade Official Urges China To Punish IPR Violators Forcefully." <http://usinfo.state.gov/ei/Archive/2005/Apr/15-94765.html> (accessed on February 14, 2006).

United States Dept. of Commerce and Labor, Bureau of the Census. "Paupers in Almshouses 1904." <http://www.poorhousestory.com/LegalSummaryCover.htm> (accessed on February 1, 2006).

United States Holocaust Memorial Museum. "Online Exhibitions: War Crimes Trials." <http://www.ushmm.org/wlc/article/> (accessed on February 27, 2006).

United States House of Representatives. "Committee on the Judiciary." <http://judiciary.house.gov/> (accessed on February 22, 2006).

United States House of Representatives. "The United States House of Representatives." <http://www.house.gov/> (accessed on April 30, 2006).

United States Office of Public Health and Science. "Office of Public Health and Science." <http://phs.os.dhhs.gov/ophs> (accessed on April 22, 2006).

United States Public Interest Research Group. "PIRG Consumer Fact Sheet." <http://www.pirg.org/consumer/banks/debit/debitcards1.htm> (accessed on March 27, 2006).

United States Senate. "The United States Senate." <http://www.senate.gov/> (accessed on April 30, 2006).

United States State Department. "Trafficking in Person's Report, June 2005." <http://www.state.gov/documents/organization/47255.pdf> (accessed on January 10, 2006).

United States Treasury Bureau of Engraving and Printing. "Anti-Counterfeiting Security Features." <http://www.moneyfactory.gov/section.cfm/7/35> (accessed on January 14, 2006).

United States Treasury Bureau of Engraving and Printing. "The New Color of Money. Safer. Smarter. More Secure." <http://www.moneyfactory.gov/newmoney> (accessed on March 6, 2006).

University of Alaska Anchorage. Justice Center. "Death Penalty Statistics." <http://justice.uaa.alaska.edu/death/stats.html> (accessed on February 10, 2006).

University of Arkansas. "No Immunity Request by Local Attorney Could Land Her Tough Sanctions, Maybe Jail." <http://law.uark.edu/library/finals/brill/web/the-client/marksway2.htm> (accessed on February 27, 2006).

University of California San Francisco. Center for AIDS Prevention Studies—AIDS Research Institute. "Is There a Role for Criminal Law in HIV Prevention?" <http://www.caps.ucsf.edu/publications/criminalization.html> (accessed on March 2, 2006).

University of Iowa Hospitals and Clinics. "Sadism." <http://www.uihealthcare.com/topics/mentalemotionalhealth/ment3168.html> (accessed on February 17, 2006).

University of Missouri—Kansas City School of Law. "Famous American Trials: The O.J. Simpson Trial, 1995." <http://www.law.umkc.edu/faculty/projects/ftrials/Simpson/simpson.htm> (accessed on March 20, 2006).

University of Missouri—Kansas City School of Law. "Famous Trials: The Rosenberg Trial." <http://www.law.umkc.edu/faculty/projects/ftrials/rosenb/ROSENB.HTM; (accessed January 28, 2006).> (accessed on March 5, 2005).

University of Pennsylvania. "The Commercial Sexual Exploitation of Children In the U.S., Canada and Mexico." <http://caster.ssw.upenn.edu/~restes/CSEC_Files/Exec_Sum_020220.pdf> (accessed on February 28, 2006).

University of Southern California. Annenberg Online Journalism Review. "Net Changes Game of Political Advocacy for Groups on the Right and Left." <http://www.ojr.org/ojr/glaser/1073429305.php> (accessed on March 13, 2006).

University of Washington School of Law. "The Hurricane." <http://lib.law.washington.edu/ref/hurricane.htm> (accessed on January 11, 2006).

Van Every, Edward. *Sins of New York: As "Exposed" by the Police Gazette.* New York: Frederick A. Stokes, 1930.

Victorian Web. "The Cornhill, Great Expectations, and the Convict System in Nineteenth-Century England." <http://www.victorianweb.org/authors/dickens/ge/convicts.html> (accessed on February 13, 2006).

Vila, Bryan, and Cynthia Morris. *Capital Punishment in the United States: A Documentary History.* Westport, Conn.: Greenwood, 1997.

Wakefield, Dan. *Revolt in the South.* New York: Grove Press, 1960.

Walker, Samuel. *Taming the System: The Control of Discretion in Criminal Justice, 1950–1990.* New York: Oxford University Press, 1993.

Washington Post. "FBI Agents Often Break Informant Rules." <http://www.washingtonpost.com/wp-dyn/content/article/2005/09/12/AR2005091201825.html> (accessed on February 11, 2006).

WashingtonTimes.com. "Psyching out crime excuses." <http://www.washingtontimes.com/commentary/> (accessed on March 07, 2006).

Weich, Ronald, and Carlos Angulo. *Justice on Trial: Racial Disparities in the American Criminal Justice System.* Washington, D.C.: Leadership Conference on Civil Rights, 2000.

Weintraub, Stanley. *Victoria: An Intimate Biography.* New York, Dutton, 1996.

Welch, Michael. *Punishment in America: Social Control and the Ironies of Imprisonment.* Thousand Oaks, Calif.: Sage, 1999.

Wells, Ida B. *On Lynchings.* New York: Humanity Press, 2002.

White House Office of Communications. "The White House." <http://www.whitehouse.gov/news/> (accessed on April 30, 2006).

Whitman, James O. *Harsh Justice: Criminal Punishment and the Widening Divide Between America and Europe.* New York: Oxford University Press, 2003.

Williams, John, Eric Dunning, and Patrick Murphy. *Hooligans Abroad.* 2nd ed. London: Routledge, 1985.

Wilson, Colin. *The Mammoth Book of Crime.* London: Robinson, 1998.

Worcester Telegram & Gazette News. "Cyber-sleuths target sexual predators." <http://www.telegram.com/apps/pbcs.dll/> (accessed on March 28, 2006).

World Health Organization. "World Health Organization." <http://www.who.int/en> (accessed on April 22, 2006).

Yale University Law School. "Avalon Project." <http://www.yale.edu/lawweb/avalon/avalon.htm> (accessed on April 30, 2006).

Yale-New Haven Teachers Institute. "The Negro Holocaust: Lynching and Race Riots in the United States, 1880–1950." <http://www.yale.edu/ynhti/curriculum/units/1979/2/79.02.04.x.html#b> (accessed on March 10, 2006).

Young, Cathy. *Ceasefire!: Why Women and Men Must Join Forces to Achieve Equality.* New York: Free Press, 1999.

Zimring, Franklin E. *The Contradictions of American Capital Punishment.* New York: Oxford University Press, 2003.

Zimring, Franklin, Gordon Hawkins, and Sam Kamin. *Punishment and Democracy: Three Strikes and You're Out in California.* New York: Oxford University Press, 2001.

Index

Boldface indicates a primary source.
Italics indicates an illustration on the page.